# Key to map pages

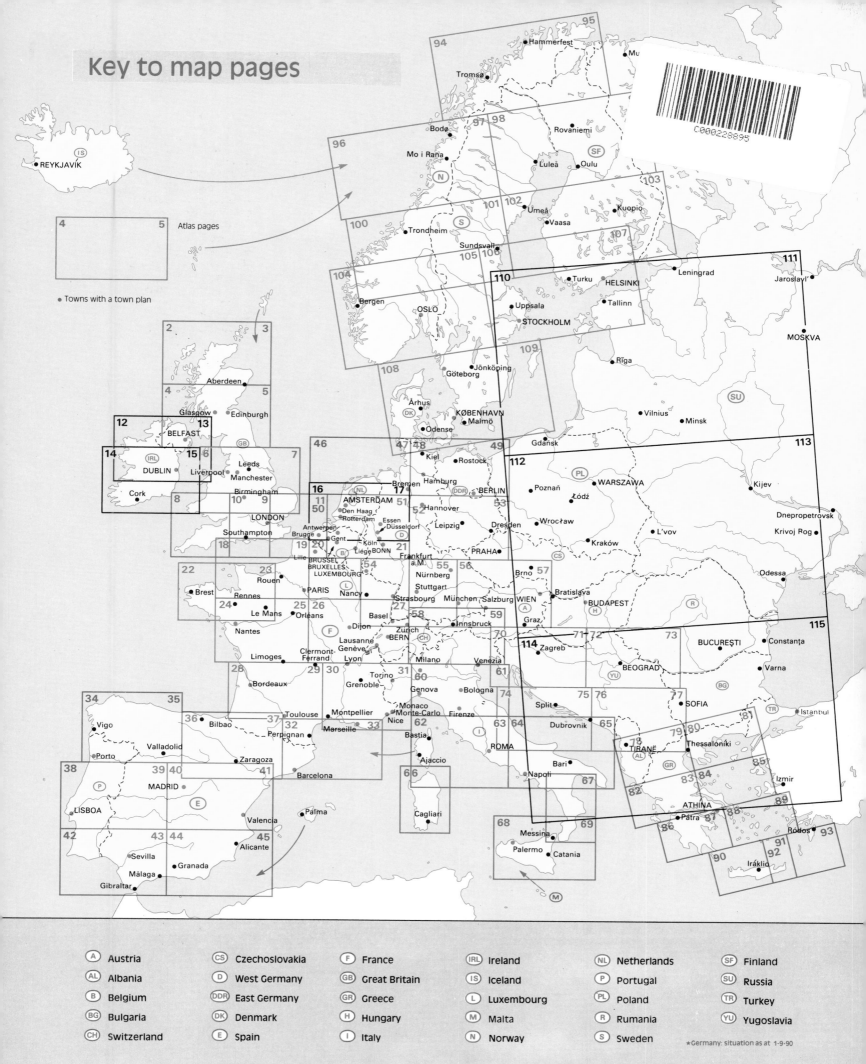

REYKJAVÍK

| 4 | 5 |

Atlas pages

• Towns with a town plan

(A) Austria
(AL) Albania
(B) Belgium
(BG) Bulgaria
(CH) Switzerland

(CS) Czechoslovakia
(D) West Germany
(DDR) East Germany
(DK) Denmark
(E) Spain

(F) France
(GB) Great Britain
(GR) Greece
(H) Hungary
(I) Italy

(IRL) Ireland
(IS) Iceland
(L) Luxembourg
(M) Malta
(N) Norway

(NL) Netherlands
(P) Portugal
(PL) Poland
(R) Rumania
(S) Sweden

(SF) Finland
(SU) Russia
(TR) Turkey
(YU) Yugoslavia

*Germany: situation as at 1-9-90

# MICHELIN®
## Road Atlas of
# Europe

First published 1988 by
The Hamlyn Publishing Group Limited
a division of the Octopus Publishing Group
Michelin House, 81 Fulham Road, London SW3 6RB

Second edition 1991
First impression 1991

All maps © Michelin et Cie Propriétaires-Éditeurs 1991

Creation, graphic arrangement, text pages XII-XVI and Index
© The Hamlyn Publishing Group Limited 1991

Mapping of Great Britain on pages 2-11
based upon Ordnance Survey mapping with the permission of
the Controller of Her Majesty's Stationery Office, Crown copyright
reserved.

Mapping of Northern Ireland on pages 12-13
based upon Ordnance Survey mapping with the permission of
the Controller of Her Majesty's Stationery Office, Crown copyright
reserved. Permit No 223.

Mapping of the Republic of Ireland on pages 12-15
based on Ordnance Survey by permission of the Government of
the Republic of Ireland. Permit No 4990.

In spite of the care taken in the production of this
book, it is possible that a defective copy may have
escaped our attention. If this is so, please return it to
your bookseller, who will exchange it for you, or contact
The Hamlyn Publishing Group Limited.

The representation in this atlas of a road is no evidence
of the existence of a right of way.

ISBN    Hardback  0 600 57163 7
ISBN    Softback  0 600 57259 5
ISBN    Deluxe edition  0 600 57226 9

Printed and bound in Germany

# MICHELIN®

# Road Atlas of
# Europe

**MICHELIN®**
Touring Services

PAUL HAMLYN

# Michelin

**MICHELIN** tyres and road maps have a reputation unsurpassed throughout Europe for quality and technical excellence in their respective fields.

It is appropriate that, at a time when the twelve member states of the European Economic Community are preparing for a single European market in 1993, Michelin should provide a new Road Atlas of Europe, compiled from their authoritative cartography, designed to meet the needs of the professional driver and holidaymaker alike.

There are over a hundred pages of mapping in this Atlas, showing the road network from North Cape to Gibraltar and from the Atlantic to the Black Sea. A full range of symbols show road categories and widths, towns and cities and places of interest as well as numerous other details, in keeping with Michelin's reputation for accuracy, legibility and up-to-date information.

Seventy town plans are included to help the driver negotiate built-up areas and the 'Driving in Europe' section provides details of national motoring regulations which are useful to know when crossing national frontiers. The comprehensive index locates about 30 000 towns and features.

The map showing 'Climates in Europe' will assist travellers in deciding which is the best season to visit a particular country.

The indispensable road mapping can be used in conjunction with other Michelin publications which provide complementary information on accommodation and sightseeing. The Red Guides, in particular the 'Europe' volume which contains a selection of hotels and restaurants in major European cities, and the Green Guides to the various countries of Europe are ideal companions for this Atlas.

Michelin are always happy to receive suggestions and comments from readers of their publications; taking these into account when preparing new editions can only improve their service to the public.

Thank you in advance and have a good journey!

**MICHELIN** maps and guides complement one another: use them together!

# Contents

**Inside front cover**
Key to symbols

IV   Michelin
VI   **Route Planning**
X    **Distances in Europe**
XII  **Driving in Europe**

1    **Key to symbols**
2    **Western Europe** at a scale of 1: 1 000 000
78   **Greece** at a scale of 1: 700 000
94   **Scandinavia** at a scale of 1: 1 500 000
110  **Eastern Europe** at a scale of 1: 3 000 000

116  **Index of place names**

**Inside back cover**
Climates in Europe

## Plans of cities and principal towns

| | | | |
|---|---|---|---|
| 118 ● Amsterdam | 137 ● Dublin | 155 ● Lausanne | 174 ● Oslo |
| 120 ● Antwerpen | 137 ● Düsseldorf | 156 ● Liège | 69 ● Palermo |
| 86 ● Athína | 138 ● Edinburgh | 157 ● Lille | 176 ● Paris |
| 122 ● Barcelona | 139 ● Essen | 158 ● Lisboa | 180 ● Porto |
| 123 ● Basel | 140 ● Firenze | 159 ● Liverpool | 62 ● Roma |
| 124 ● Belfast | 141 ● Frankfurt a. M. | 160 ● London | 184 ● Rotterdam |
| 125 ● Berlin | 143 ● Genève | 163 ● Luxembourg | 188 ● Salzburg |
| 126 ● Bern | 143 ● Genova | 162 ● Lyon | 190 ● Sevilla |
| 127 ● Birmingham | 142 ● Gent | 164 ● Madrid | 192 ● Stockholm |
| 126 ● Bologna | 144 ● Glasgow | 165 ● Manchester | 193 ● Strasbourg |
| 128 ● Bonn | 145 ● Göteborg | 33 ● Marseille | 194 ● Stuttgart |
| 129 ● Bordeaux | 146 ● Den Haag | 166 ● Milano | 196 ● Torino |
| 46 ● Bremen | 46 ● Hamburg | 167 ● Monaco | 197 ● Toulouse |
| 130 ● Brugge | 147 ● Hannover | 168 ● München | 199 ● Valencia |
| 131 ● Bruxelles-Brussel | 107 ● Helsinki | 170 ● Nantes | 200 ● Venezia |
| | 149 ● Istanbul | 65 ● Napoli | 203 ● Wien |
| 130 ● Budapest | 152 ● København | 171 ● Nice | 205 ● Zürich |
| 136 ● Dijon | 153 ● Köln | 172 ● Nürnberg | |

# Route planning

*Jan Mayen*

Ísafjörður

Akureyri

**REYKJAVÍK**  (IS)

Seyðisfjörður

*Vatnajökull*
2119 △

CERCLE   POLAIRE   ARCTIQUE

SEA

NORVÈGE

NORWEGIAN   DE

MER

*Hitra*

Kristiansund

Ålesund

2470 △
*Jotunheimen*

*Føroyar*

O C E A N

A T L A N T I Q U E

*Shetland*

**Bergen**  (N)

Skien

*Orkney*

Stavanger

Thurso

*Hebrides*

*Skye*

Inverness
*Loch Ness*

1344 △
*Ben Nevis*

Aberdeen

Skagerrak

Dundee

A T L A N T I C

O C É A N

**Glasgow**

**Edinburgh**

NORTH   SEA

(DK)

Londonderry

Stranraer

Carlisle

Newcastle

MER   DU   NORD

**Belfast**

Esbjerg

Galway

(IRL)

*Man*

*IRISH SEA*

York

**DUBLIN**

**Leeds**

**Liverpool**

Limerick

*Shannon*

**Manchester**

Sheffield

Groningen

Cork

*St. George's Channel*

(GB)

Nottingham

*Ijsselmeer*

(NL)

**Bremen**

**Birmingham**

Coventry

Norwich

**Hannove**

Cardiff

Cambridge

**AMSTERDAM**

Oxford

**Den Haag**

Southampton

**LONDON**

*Thames*

**Rotterdam**

*Waal*

Essen   Dortmund

Plymouth

Portsmouth

Dover

Brugge

**Düsseldorf**

Kassel

*Land's End*

*ENGLISH CHANNEL*

*LA MANCHE*

Calais

Gent

**Antwerpen**

(B)

Aachen

**Köln**

(D)

**Lille**

**BRUSSEL**
**BRUXELLES**   Liège

**BONN**

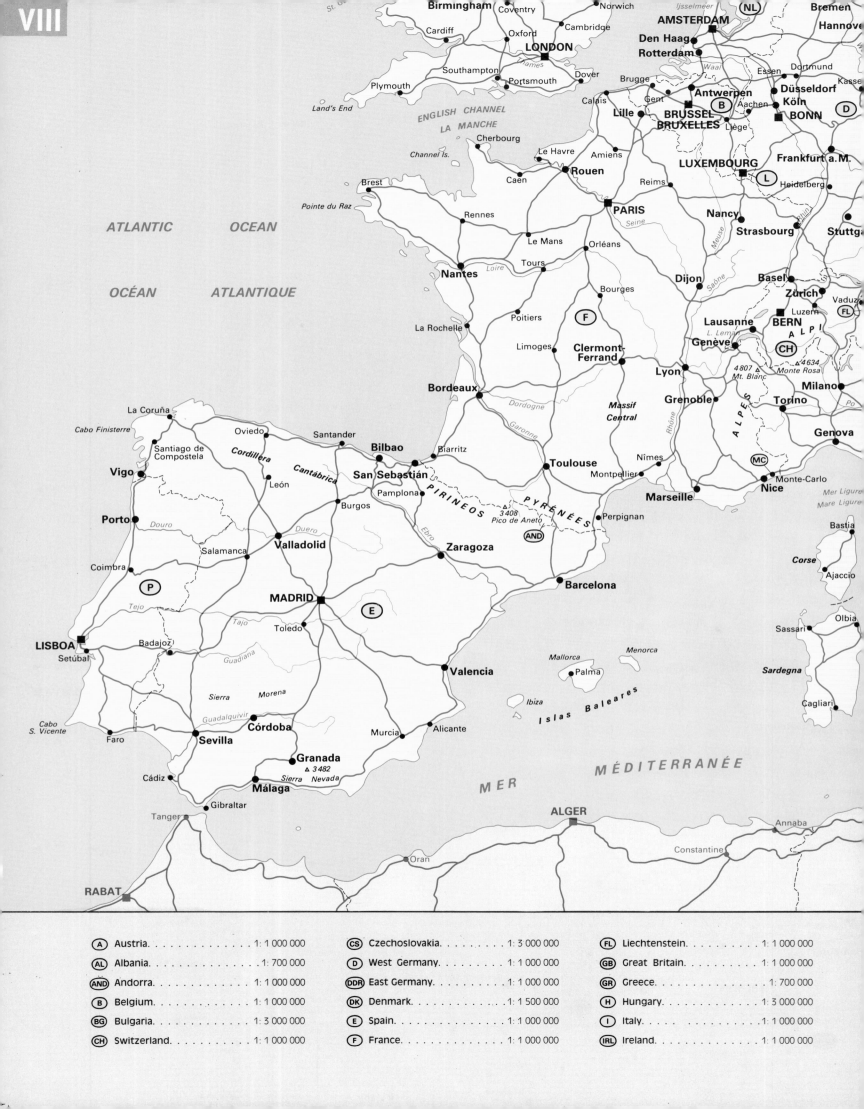

Birmingham Coventry Norwich IJsselmeer (NL) Bremen Hannover
Cardiff Oxford Cambridge AMSTERDAM
LONDON Den Haag
Rotterdam
Southampton Dover Brugge Essen Dortmund Kasse
Plymouth Portsmouth Calais Gent Antwerpen Aachen Düsseldorf Köln
Land's End ENGLISH CHANNEL Lille BRUSSEL Liège (B) BONN (D)
LA MANCHE Cherbourg BRUXELLES
Channel Is. Le Havre Amiens LUXEMBOURG Frankfurt a. M.
Pointe du Raz Caen Rouen Reims (L) Heidelberg
Brest
ATLANTIC OCEAN PARIS Nancy
Rennes Seine Strasbourg Stuttga
Le Mans Orléans
OCÉAN ATLANTIQUE Tours Dijon Saône Basel Zürich
Nantes Loire Bourges Vaduz (FL)
(F) Lausanne BERN ALPI
La Rochelle Poitiers L. Léman Luzern
Limoges Clermont- Genève (CH)
Ferrand Lyon 4807 △ △4634 Monte Rosa
Bordeaux Mt. Blanc Milano
Dordogne Grenoble Torino
Garonne Massif Rhône ALPES Po
Central Nîmes Genova
La Coruña Toulouse
Cabo Finisterre Oviedo Santander Bilbao Biarritz Montpellier (MC)
Santiago de Cordillera San Sebastián PIRINEOS PYRÉNÉES Marseille Monte-Carlo
Compostela Cantábrica Pamplona Nice Mer Ligure
Vigo León 3408 AND Perpignan Mare Ligure
△ Bastia
Burgos Pico de Aneto
Porto Valladolid Corse
Douro Duero Zaragoza Ajaccio
Salamanca Duero
Coimbra Barcelona
(P) MADRID Olbia
Tejo (E) Sassari
LISBOA Toledo Mallorca Menorca
Setúbal Badajoz Tajo
Guadiana Valencia Palma Sardegna
Sierra Morena Ibiza Islas Baleares Cagliari
Guadalquivir
Cabo Córdoba Murcia Alicante
S. Vicente Faro Sevilla
Granada MÉDITERRANÉE
△ 3482
Cádiz Sierra Nevada MER
Málaga
Gibraltar ALGER Annaba
Tanger
Oran Constantine
RABAT

(A) Austria. . . . . . . . . . . . . 1: 1 000 000
(AL) Albania. . . . . . . . . . . . 1: 700 000
(AND) Andorra. . . . . . . . . . . 1: 1 000 000
(B) Belgium. . . . . . . . . . . . 1: 1 000 000
(BG) Bulgaria. . . . . . . . . . . 1: 3 000 000
(CH) Switzerland. . . . . . . . . 1: 1 000 000

(CS) Czechoslovakia. . . . . . . . 1: 3 000 000
(D) West Germany. . . . . . . . . 1: 1 000 000
(DDR) East Germany. . . . . . . . 1: 1 000 000
(DK) Denmark. . . . . . . . . . . 1: 1 500 000
(E) Spain. . . . . . . . . . . . . 1: 1 000 000
(F) France. . . . . . . . . . . . 1: 1 000 000

(FL) Liechtenstein. . . . . . . . 1: 1 000 000
(GB) Great Britain. . . . . . . . 1: 1 000 000
(GR) Greece. . . . . . . . . . . . 1: 700 000
(H) Hungary. . . . . . . . . . . . 1: 3 000 000
(I) Italy. . . . . . . . . . . . . 1: 1 000 000
(IRL) Ireland. . . . . . . . . . . 1: 1 000 000

| | | | | | |
|---|---|---|---|---|---|
| (IS) | Iceland. . . . . . . . . . . . | 1: 2 400 000 | (P) | Portugal. . . . . . . . . . . | 1: 1 000 000 |
| (L) | Luxembourg. . . . . . . . . | 1: 1 000 000 | (PL) | Poland. . . . . . . . . . . . | 1: 3 000 000 |
| (M) | Malta. . . . . . . . . . . . | 1: 1 000 000 | (R) | Rumania. . . . . . . . . . | 1: 3 000 000 |
| (MC) | Monaco. . . . . . . . . . . | 1: 1 000 000 | (RSM) | San Marino. . . . . . . . | 1: 1 000 000 |
| (N) | Norway. . . . . . . . . . . | 1: 1 500 000 | (S) | Sweden. . . . . . . . . . . | 1: 1 500 000 |
| (NL) | Netherlands. . . . . . . . | 1: 1 000 000 | (SF) | Finland. . . . . . . . . . . | 1: 1 500 000 |

| | | | |
|---|---|---|---|
| (SU) | Russia. . . . . . . . . . . . | 1: 3 000 000 |
| (TR) | Turkey. . . . . . . . . . . . | 1: 3 000 000 |
| (V) | Vatican City. . . . . . . . | 1: 140 000 |
| (YU) | Yugoslavia. . . . . . . . . | 1: 1 000 000 |

* Germany: situation as at 1-9-90

| | Amsterdam | Athína | Barcelona | Bari | Basel | Belfast | Beograd | Bergen | Berlin | Bilbao | Birmingham | Bordeaux | Brest | Brussel/Bruxelles | Bucuresti | Budapest | Clermont-Ferrand | Dublin | Dubrovnik | Edinburgh | Firenze | Frankfurt a. M. | Genève | Göteborg | Hamburg | Hannover | Helsinki | Istambul | Kijev | København | Köln | Leningrad | Lille | Lisboa |
|---|---|---|---|---|---|---|---|---|---|---|---|---|---|---|---|---|---|---|---|---|---|---|---|---|---|---|---|---|---|---|---|---|---|---|
| Athína | 2836 | | | | | | | | | | | | | | | | | | | | | | | | | | | | | | | | | |
| Barcelona | 1547 | 3090 | | | | | | | | | | | | | | | | | | | | | | | | | | | | | | | | |
| Bari | 1971 | 2621 | 1792 | | | | | | | | | | | | | | | | | | | | | | | | | | | | | | | |
| Basel | 745 | 2466 | 1029 | 1226 | | | | | | | | | | | | | | | | | | | | | | | | | | | | | | |
| Belfast | 1341 | 3874 | 2046 | 2690 | 1508 | | | | | | | | | | | | | | | | | | | | | | | | | | | | | |
| Beograd | 1718 | 1118 | 1972 | 1503 | 1348 | 2756 | | | | | | | | | | | | | | | | | | | | | | | | | | | | |
| Bergen | 1817 | 4017 | 3178 | 3244 | 2187 | 3112 | 2899 | | | | | | | | | | | | | | | | | | | | | | | | | | | |
| Berlin | 669 | 2584 | 1853 | 1811 | 862 | 1906 | 1466 | 1463 | | | | | | | | | | | | | | | | | | | | | | | | | | |
| Bilbao | 1424 | 3422 | 607 | 2124 | 1174 | 1755 | 2304 | 3196 | 1990 | | | | | | | | | | | | | | | | | | | | | | | | | |
| Birmingham | 782 | 3316 | 1487 | 2131 | 950 | 535 | 2198 | 2554 | 1348 | 1196 | | | | | | | | | | | | | | | | | | | | | | | | |
| Bordeaux | 1081 | 3240 | 633 | 1942 | 831 | 1412 | 2122 | 2853 | 1647 | 334 | 853 | | | | | | | | | | | | | | | | | | | | | | | |
| Brest | 1098 | 3501 | 1242 | 2278 | 1096 | 1244 | 2383 | 2870 | 1664 | 965 | 686 | 627 | | | | | | | | | | | | | | | | | | | | | | |
| Brussel/Bruxelles | 204 | 2792 | 1365 | 1777 | 551 | 1150 | 1674 | 1969 | 781 | 1229 | 591 | 886 | 903 | | | | | | | | | | | | | | | | | | | | | |
| Bucuresti | 2221 | 1238 | 2611 | 2142 | 1987 | 3259 | 639 | 3200 | 1711 | 2943 | 2701 | 2761 | 2886 | 2177 | | | | | | | | | | | | | | | | | | | | |
| Budapest | 1393 | 1510 | 1952 | 1482 | 1073 | 2431 | 392 | 2372 | 883 | 2283 | 1873 | 2041 | 2058 | 1349 | 828 | | | | | | | | | | | | | | | | | | | |
| Clermont-Ferrand | 902 | 2752 | 648 | 1485 | 477 | 1337 | 1634 | 2636 | 1311 | 706 | 779 | 365 | 808 | 706 | 2273 | 1614 | | | | | | | | | | | | | | | | | | |
| Dublin | 1053 | 3586 | 1758 | 2402 | 1220 | 165 | 2468 | 2824 | 1618 | 1467 | 247 | 1124 | 956 | 862 | 2971 | 2143 | 1049 | | | | | | | | | | | | | | | | | |
| Dubrovnik | 2024 | 1265 | 2049 | 1580 | 1425 | 2892 | 525 | 3204 | 1771 | 2381 | 2333 | 2199 | 2480 | 1970 | 1164 | 787 | 1711 | 2604 | | | | | | | | | | | | | | | | |
| Edinburgh | 1289 | 3823 | 1994 | 2638 | 1457 | 251 | 2705 | 3061 | 1855 | 1703 | 484 | 1360 | 1193 | 1098 | 3208 | 2380 | 1286 | 416 | 2840 | | | | | | | | | | | | | | | |
| Firenze | 1391 | 2115 | 1075 | 720 | 646 | 2098 | 997 | 2664 | 1231 | 1407 | 1539 | 1225 | 1686 | 1197 | 1636 | 976 | 883 | 1810 | 1074 | 2046 | | | | | | | | | | | | | | |
| Frankfurt a. M. | 446 | 2396 | 1318 | 1553 | 327 | 1549 | 1278 | 1864 | 566 | 1502 | 991 | 1159 | 1176 | 402 | 1781 | 953 | 776 | 1261 | 1583 | 1498 | 973 | | | | | | | | | | | | | |
| Genève | 885 | 2446 | 770 | 1203 | 259 | 1492 | 1328 | 2446 | 1121 | 1102 | 934 | 682 | 1081 | 703 | 1967 | 1307 | 310 | 1204 | 1405 | 1441 | 611 | 586 | | | | | | | | | | | | |
| Göteborg | 1005 | 3205 | 2366 | 2432 | 1375 | 2300 | 2087 | 812 | 651 | 2384 | 1742 | 2041 | 2058 | 1157 | 2388 | 1560 | 1824 | 2012 | 2392 | 2249 | 1852 | 1052 | 1634 | | | | | | | | | | | |
| Hamburg | 441 | 2780 | 1802 | 2007 | 811 | 1736 | 1662 | 1384 | 289 | 1820 | 1178 | 1477 | 1494 | 593 | 2026 | 1198 | 1260 | 1448 | 1967 | 1685 | 1427 | 488 | 1070 | 572 | | | | | | | | | | |
| Hannover | 386 | 2637 | 1659 | 1864 | 668 | 1623 | 1519 | 1527 | 288 | 1707 | 1065 | 1364 | 1381 | 498 | 2022 | 1194 | 1117 | 1335 | 1824 | 1572 | 1284 | 345 | 927 | 715 | 151 | | | | | | | | | |
| Helsinki | 1204 | 2540 | 2388 | 2346 | 1397 | 2441 | 1422 | 1186 | 505 | 2525 | 1883 | 2182 | 2199 | 1316 | 1858 | 1030 | 1846 | 2153 | 1893 | 2390 | 1766 | 1101 | 1656 | 662 | 776 | 823 | | | | | | | | |
| Istambul | 2665 | 1171 | 2919 | 2450 | 2295 | 3703 | 947 | 3846 | 2413 | 3251 | 3145 | 3069 | 3330 | 2621 | 692 | 1339 | 2581 | 3415 | 1326 | 3652 | 1944 | 2225 | 2275 | 3034 | 2609 | 2466 | 2369 | | | | | | | |
| Kijev | 2017 | 2311 | 3114 | 2644 | 2187 | 3254 | 1336 | 2844 | 1383 | 3338 | 2696 | 2995 | 3012 | 2129 | 1073 | 1162 | 2636 | 2966 | 1861 | 3203 | 2138 | 1914 | 2339 | 2032 | 1670 | 1636 | 1146 | 489 | | | | | | |
| København | 738 | 2938 | 2099 | 2165 | 1108 | 2033 | 1820 | 1079 | 384 | 2117 | 1475 | 1774 | 1791 | 890 | 2121 | 1293 | 1557 | 1745 | 2125 | 1982 | 1585 | 785 | 1367 | 267 | 305 | 448 | 795 | 2767 | 1765 | | | | | |
| Köln | 264 | 2579 | 1342 | 1714 | 488 | 1361 | 1461 | 1802 | 575 | 1440 | 803 | 1097 | 1114 | 211 | 1964 | 1136 | 802 | 1073 | 1766 | 1310 | 1134 | 189 | 747 | 990 | 426 | 292 | 1110 | 2408 | 1923 | 723 | | | | |
| Leningrad | 1637 | 2973 | 2821 | 2779 | 1830 | 2874 | 1855 | 1619 | 938 | 2958 | 2316 | 2615 | 2632 | 1749 | 2625 | 1463 | 2279 | 2586 | 2326 | 2823 | 2199 | 1534 | 2089 | 1095 | 1209 | 1256 | 433 | 2041 | 1552 | 1228 | 1543 | | | |
| Lille | 283 | 2910 | 1308 | 1836 | 610 | 1046 | 1792 | 2055 | 849 | 1139 | 487 | 799 | 716 | 116 | 2295 | 1467 | 645 | 758 | 2088 | 994 | 1256 | 520 | 669 | 1243 | 679 | 566 | 1384 | 2739 | 2197 | 976 | 329 | 1817 | | |
| Lisboa | 2322 | 4320 | 1285 | 3022 | 2072 | 2653 | 3202 | 4094 | 2888 | 907 | 2094 | 1232 | 1863 | 2127 | 3841 | 3181 | 1604 | 2365 | 3279 | 2601 | 2305 | 2400 | 2000 | 3282 | 2718 | 2605 | 3423 | 4149 | 4236 | 3015 | 2338 | 3856 | 2037 | |
| Liverpool | 971 | 3504 | 1676 | 2320 | 1138 | 416 | 2386 | 2742 | 1536 | 1385 | 165 | 1042 | 874 | 780 | 2889 | 2061 | 967 | 167 | 2522 | 365 | 1728 | 1179 | 1122 | 1930 | 1366 | 1253 | 2071 | 3333 | 2884 | 1663 | 991 | 2504 | 676 | 2283 |
| London | 719 | 3252 | 1424 | 2068 | 886 | 722 | 2134 | 2490 | 1284 | 1133 | 196 | 790 | 622 | 528 | 2637 | 1809 | 715 | 434 | 2270 | 612 | 1476 | 927 | 870 | 1678 | 1114 | 1001 | 1819 | 3081 | 2632 | 1411 | 739 | 2252 | 424 | 2031 |
| Luxembourg | 391 | 2637 | 1148 | 1560 | 334 | 1338 | 1519 | 1994 | 767 | 1290 | 779 | 947 | 964 | 218 | 1993 | 1165 | 608 | 1050 | 1758 | 1286 | 980 | 248 | 486 | 1182 | 618 | 484 | 1302 | 2466 | 2115 | 915 | 193 | 1735 | 334 | 2188 |
| Lyon | 917 | 2559 | 630 | 1292 | 400 | 1415 | 1441 | 2548 | 1223 | 962 | 857 | 538 | 1018 | 735 | 2080 | 1421 | 172 | 1127 | 1518 | 1364 | 690 | 688 | 151 | 1736 | 1172 | 1029 | 1758 | 2388 | 2548 | 1469 | 711 | 2191 | 682 | 1860 |
| Madrid | 1812 | 3760 | 686 | 2462 | 1562 | 2143 | 2642 | 3584 | 2378 | 397 | 1584 | 722 | 1353 | 1617 | 3281 | 2622 | 1094 | 1855 | 2719 | 2091 | 1745 | 1890 | 1440 | 2772 | 2208 | 2095 | 2913 | 3589 | 3726 | 2505 | 1828 | 3346 | 1527 | 658 |
| Málaga | 2360 | 4086 | 1012 | 2788 | 2025 | 2691 | 2968 | 4132 | 2849 | 945 | 2132 | 1270 | 1901 | 2165 | 3607 | 2948 | 1644 | 2403 | 3045 | 2639 | 2071 | 2314 | 1766 | 3320 | 2756 | 2643 | 3384 | 3915 | 4110 | 3053 | 2376 | 3817 | 2075 | 634 |
| Marseille | 1228 | 2621 | 493 | 1323 | 710 | 1727 | 1503 | 2859 | 1534 | 825 | 1168 | 648 | 1218 | 1046 | 2142 | 1483 | 417 | 1439 | 1580 | 1675 | 606 | 999 | 452 | 2047 | 1483 | 1340 | 2069 | 2450 | 2645 | 1780 | 1023 | 2502 | 992 | 1723 |
| Milano | 1088 | 2128 | 973 | 878 | 343 | 1810 | 1010 | 2493 | 1040 | 1305 | 1251 | 1123 | 1398 | 894 | 1649 | 989 | 629 | 1522 | 1087 | 1758 | 298 | 670 | 323 | 1681 | 1117 | 974 | 1575 | 1957 | 2151 | 1414 | 831 | 2008 | 953 | 2203 |
| Moskva | 2463 | 3169 | 3630 | 3306 | 2639 | 3700 | 2194 | 2313 | 1829 | 3784 | 3142 | 3441 | 3458 | 2575 | 1931 | 1918 | 3088 | 3412 | 2705 | 3649 | 2800 | 2360 | 2898 | 1789 | 2116 | 2082 | 1127 | 1347 | 858 | 2211 | 2369 | 694 | 2643 | 4682 |
| München | 837 | 2063 | 1370 | 1224 | 399 | 1794 | 945 | 2018 | 585 | 1615 | 1236 | 1272 | 1421 | 769 | 1506 | 678 | 918 | 1506 | 1184 | 1743 | 644 | 397 | 599 | 1206 | 781 | 638 | 1120 | 1892 | 1744 | 939 | 580 | 1553 | 887 | 2513 |
| Nantes | 887 | 3290 | 945 | 1923 | 847 | 1168 | 2172 | 2659 | 1453 | 669 | 609 | 325 | 302 | 692 | 2675 | 1847 | 465 | 880 | 2125 | 1116 | 1331 | 965 | 726 | 1847 | 1283 | 1170 | 1988 | 3119 | 2801 | 1580 | 903 | 2421 | 604 | 1567 |
| Napoli | 1878 | 2602 | 1562 | 261 | 1133 | 2585 | 1484 | 3151 | 1718 | 1894 | 2026 | 1712 | 2173 | 1684 | 2123 | 1463 | 1370 | 2297 | 1561 | 2533 | 490 | 1460 | 1098 | 2339 | 1914 | 1771 | 2253 | 2431 | 2625 | 2072 | 1621 | 2686 | 1743 | 2792 |
| Nice | 1387 | 2434 | 656 | 1136 | 658 | 1886 | 1316 | 2808 | 1355 | 988 | 1327 | 808 | 1377 | 1205 | 1955 | 1295 | 577 | 1598 | 1393 | 1834 | 419 | 985 | 478 | 1996 | 1432 | 1289 | 1890 | 2263 | 2457 | 1729 | 1146 | 2323 | 1152 | 1886 |
| Nürnberg | 666 | 2171 | 1427 | 1391 | 436 | 1715 | 1053 | 1867 | 434 | 1668 | 1157 | 1325 | 1342 | 622 | 1556 | 728 | 885 | 1427 | 1351 | 1664 | 811 | 226 | 695 | 1055 | 610 | 467 | 969 | 2000 | 1759 | 788 | 409 | 1402 | 740 | 2566 |
| Oslo | 1321 | 3521 | 2682 | 2748 | 1691 | 2616 | 2403 | 496 | 967 | 2700 | 2058 | 2357 | 2374 | 1473 | 2704 | 1876 | 2140 | 2328 | 2708 | 2565 | 2168 | 1368 | 1950 | 316 | 888 | 1031 | 690 | 3350 | 2348 | 583 | 1306 | 1123 | 1559 | 3598 |
| Palermo | 2599 | 3322 | 2283 | 691 | 1853 | 3305 | 2204 | 3872 | 2439 | 2614 | 2747 | 2432 | 2893 | 2404 | 2843 | 2184 | 2091 | 3017 | 2281 | 3254 | 1210 | 2180 | 1818 | 3060 | 2635 | 2492 | 2974 | 3151 | 3346 | 2793 | 2341 | 3407 | 2464 | 3512 |
| Paris | 504 | 2912 | 1091 | 1735 | 553 | 965 | 1794 | 2275 | 1069 | 922 | 407 | 579 | 597 | 308 | 2297 | 1469 | 426 | 677 | 1937 | 914 | 1143 | 587 | 538 | 1463 | 899 | 786 | 1604 | 2741 | 2417 | 1196 | 520 | 2037 | 221 | 1820 |
| Porto | 2143 | 4141 | 1167 | 2843 | 1893 | 2474 | 3023 | 3915 | 2709 | 728 | 1915 | 1053 | 1684 | 1948 | 3662 | 3002 | 1425 | 2186 | 3100 | 2422 | 2126 | 2221 | 1821 | 3103 | 2539 | 2426 | 3244 | 3970 | 4057 | 2836 | 2159 | 3677 | 1858 | 314 |
| Praha | 950 | 2154 | 1711 | 1596 | 720 | 1999 | 1036 | 1839 | 350 | 1952 | 1441 | 1609 | 1626 | 906 | 1361 | 533 | 1169 | 1711 | 1261 | 1948 | 1016 | 510 | 979 | 1027 | 665 | 603 | 859 | 1983 | 1389 | 760 | 693 | 1292 | 1024 | 2850 |
| Roma | 1665 | 2389 | 1349 | 449 | 920 | 2372 | 1271 | 2938 | 1505 | 1681 | 1813 | 1499 | 1960 | 1471 | 1910 | 1250 | 1157 | 2084 | 1348 | 2320 | 277 | 1247 | 885 | 2126 | 1701 | 1558 | 2040 | 2218 | 2412 | 1859 | 1408 | 2473 | 1530 | 2579 |
| Rovaniemi | 2483 | 4683 | 3844 | 3910 | 2853 | 3778 | 3565 | 2824 | 2129 | 3862 | 3220 | 3519 | 3536 | 2635 | 3866 | 3038 | 3302 | 3490 | 3870 | 3727 | 3330 | 2530 | 3112 | 1528 | 2050 | 2193 | 837 | 4512 | 2557 | 1745 | 3288 | 1005 | 2721 | 4760 |
| Salzburg | 980 | 1932 | 1539 | 1172 | 536 | 1952 | 814 | 2161 | 728 | 1772 | 1393 | 1429 | 1578 | 927 | 1363 | 535 | 1076 | 1664 | 1052 | 1900 | 660 | 540 | 736 | 1349 | 924 | 781 | 1263 | 1761 | 1601 | 1082 | 723 | 1696 | 1045 | 2670 |
| Sevilla | 2295 | 4117 | 1043 | 2819 | 2056 | 2626 | 2999 | 4067 | 2880 | 880 | 2067 | 1205 | 1836 | 2100 | 3638 | 2979 | 1577 | 2338 | 3076 | 2574 | 2102 | 2345 | 1797 | 3255 | 2691 | 2578 | 3415 | 3946 | 4141 | 2988 | 2311 | 3848 | 2010 | 417 |
| Sofia | 2104 | 818 | 2358 | 1889 | 1734 | 3142 | 386 | 3285 | 1852 | 2690 | 2584 | 2508 | 2769 | 2060 | 420 | 778 | 2020 | 2854 | 765 | 3091 | 1383 | 1664 | 1714 | 2473 | 2048 | 1905 | 1808 | 561 | 1493 | 2206 | 1847 | 2241 | 2178 | 3588 |
| Stockholm | 1368 | 3568 | 2729 | 2795 | 1738 | 2663 | 2450 | 1021 | 1014 | 2747 | 2105 | 2404 | 2421 | 1520 | 2751 | 1923 | 2187 | 2375 | 2755 | 2612 | 2215 | 1415 | 1997 | 497 | 935 | 1078 | 165 | 3397 | 2395 | 630 | 1353 | 598 | 1606 | 3645 |
| Strasbourg | 634 | 2438 | 1110 | 1371 | 145 | 1450 | 1320 | 2076 | 751 | 1264 | 892 | 918 | 1080 | 439 | 1881 | 1053 | 563 | 1162 | 1559 | 1399 | 791 | 216 | 404 | 1264 | 700 | 557 | 1286 | 2267 | 2076 | 997 | 377 | 1719 | 549 | 2162 |
| Stuttgart | 622 | 2302 | 1258 | 1404 | 267 | 1592 | 1184 | 2046 | 631 | 1413 | 1034 | 1070 | 1219 | 558 | 1745 | 917 | 716 | 1304 | 1423 | 1541 | 824 | 204 | 526 | 1234 | 670 | 527 | 1166 | 2131 | 1956 | 967 | 365 | 1599 | 676 | 2311 |
| Thessaloníki | 2350 | 511 | 2604 | 2135 | 1980 | 3388 | 632 | 3531 | 2098 | 2936 | 2830 | 2754 | 3015 | 2306 | 727 | 1024 | 2266 | 3100 | 779 | 3337 | 1629 | 1910 | 1960 | 2719 | 2294 | 2151 | 2054 | 660 | 1800 | 2452 | 2093 | 2487 | 2424 | 3834 |
| Torino | 1154 | 2263 | 779 | 997 | 409 | 1699 | 1145 | 2596 | 1157 | 1110 | 1140 | 864 | 1287 | 905 | 1784 | 1124 | 492 | 1411 | 1222 | 1647 | 395 | 736 | 252 | 1784 | 1220 | 1077 | 1692 | 2092 | 2286 | 1517 | 897 | 2125 | 961 | 2008 |
| Toulouse | 1199 | 2994 | 388 | 1696 | 933 | 1611 | 1876 | 3082 | 1757 | 447 | 1053 | 244 | 870 | 1003 | 2515 | 1856 | 384 | 1323 | 1953 | 1560 | 979 | 1222 | 675 | 2270 | 1706 | 1563 | 2292 | 2823 | 3018 | 2003 | 1246 | 2725 | 923 | 1345 |
| Tromsø | 3041 | 5241 | 4402 | 4468 | 3411 | 4336 | 4123 | 1893 | 2687 | 4420 | 3778 | 4077 | 4094 | 3193 | 4424 | 3596 | 3860 | 4048 | 4428 | 4285 | 3888 | 3088 | 3670 | 2570 | 2608 | 2751 | 1367 | 5070 | 3087 | 2303 | 3026 | 1535 | 3279 | 5318 |
| Trondheim | 1865 | 4065 | 3226 | 3292 | 2235 | 3160 | 2947 | 717 | 1511 | 3244 | 2602 | 2901 | 2918 | 2017 | 3248 | 2420 | 2684 | 2872 | 3252 | 3109 | 2712 | 1912 | 2494 | 1394 | 1432 | 1575 | 949 | 3894 | 2892 | 1127 | 1850 | 1382 | 2103 | 4142 |
| Valencia | 1892 | 3435 | 361 | 2137 | 1374 | 2391 | 2317 | 3523 | 2198 | 606 | 1832 | 771 | 1402 | 1710 | 2956 | 2297 | 993 | 2103 | 2394 | 2339 | 1420 | 1663 | 1115 | 2711 | 2147 | 2004 | 2733 | 3264 | 3459 | 2444 | 1687 | 3166 | 1653 | 924 |
| Venezia | 1283 | 1878 | 1229 | 760 | 605 | 2072 | 760 | 2512 | 1079 | 1561 | 1513 | 1379 | 1660 | 1156 | 1399 | 739 | 891 | 1784 | 837 | 2020 | 254 | 891 | 585 | 1700 | 1275 | 1132 | 1614 | 1707 | 1901 | 1433 | 1026 | 2047 | 1215 | 2459 |
| Warszawa | 1223 | 2188 | 2390 | 2066 | 1399 | 2460 | 1070 | 2050 | 589 | 2544 | 1902 | 2201 | 2218 | 1335 | 1506 | 678 | 1848 | 2172 | 1465 | 2409 | 1560 | 1120 | 1658 | 1238 | 876 | 842 | 352 | 2017 | 794 | 971 | 1129 | 785 | 1403 | 3442 |
| Wien | 1150 | 1862 | 1833 | 1341 | 830 | 2188 | 744 | 2131 | 642 | 2141 | 1630 | 1798 | 1815 | 1106 | 1071 | 243 | 1370 | 1900 | 969 | 2137 | 835 | 710 | 1030 | 1319 | 957 | 951 | 924 | 1691 | 1309 | 1052 | 893 | 1357 | 1224 | 3039 |
| Zagreb | 1337 | 1499 | 1591 | 1122 | 967 | 2375 | 381 | 2518 | 1085 | 1923 | 1817 | 1741 | 2002 | 1293 | 1020 | 350 | 1253 | 2087 | 618 | 2324 | 616 | 897 | 947 | 1706 | 1281 | 1138 | 1287 | 1328 | 1512 | 1439 | 1080 | 1720 | 1411 | 2821 |
| Zürich | 831 | 2416 | 1058 | 1176 | 86 | 1594 | 1298 | 2267 | 852 | 1260 | 1036 | 917 | 1182 | 637 | 1816 | 988 | 597 | 1306 | 1375 | 1543 | 596 | 412 | 287 | 1455 | 891 | 748 | 1387 | 2245 | 2054 | 1188 | 573 | 1820 | 696 | 2158 |

# Distances in Europe

Distances are calculated from centres and along the best roads from a motoring point of view - not necessarily the shortest

Example: **Luxembourg – Warszawa** 1321 km

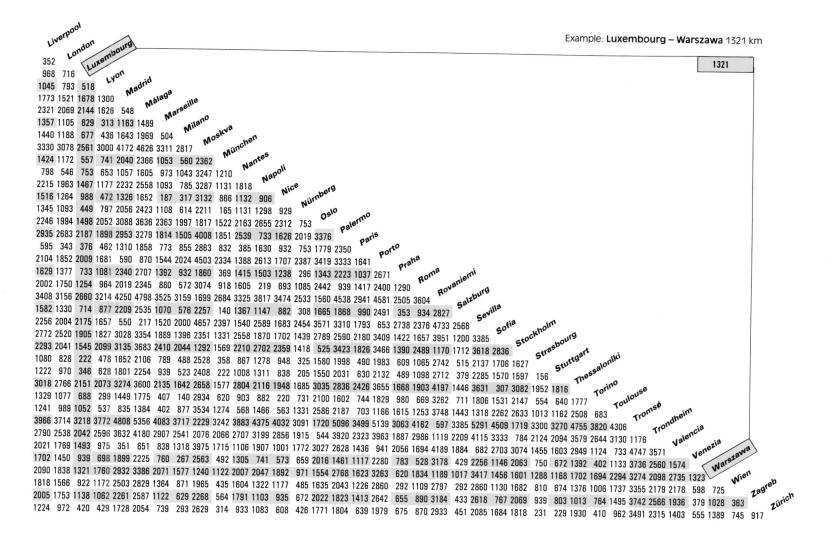

| | | | | | | | | | | | | | | | | | | | | | | | | | | | | | | | | | | | | | |
|---|---|---|---|---|---|---|---|---|---|---|---|---|---|---|---|---|---|---|---|---|---|---|---|---|---|---|---|---|---|---|---|---|---|---|---|---|---|
| *Liverpool* | | | | | | | | | | | | | | | | | | | | | | | | | | | | | | | | | | | | | |
| 352 | *London* | | | | | | | | | | | | | | | | | | | | | | | | | | | | | | | | | | | | |
| 968 | 716 | *Luxembourg* | | | | | | | | | | | | | | | | | | | | | | | | | | | | | | | | 1321 | | | |
| 1045 | 793 | 518 | *Lyon* | | | | | | | | | | | | | | | | | | | | | | | | | | | | | | | | | | |
| 1773 | 1521 | 1678 | 1300 | *Madrid* | | | | | | | | | | | | | | | | | | | | | | | | | | | | | | | | | |
| 2321 | 2069 | 2144 | 1626 | 548 | *Málaga* | | | | | | | | | | | | | | | | | | | | | | | | | | | | | | | | |
| 1357 | 1105 | 829 | 313 | 1163 | 1489 | *Marseille* | | | | | | | | | | | | | | | | | | | | | | | | | | | | | | | |
| 1440 | 1188 | 677 | 436 | 1643 | 1969 | 504 | *Milano* | | | | | | | | | | | | | | | | | | | | | | | | | | | | | | |
| 3330 | 3078 | 2561 | 3000 | 4172 | 4626 | 3311 | 2817 | *Moskva* | | | | | | | | | | | | | | | | | | | | | | | | | | | | | |
| 1424 | 1172 | 557 | 741 | 2040 | 2366 | 1053 | 560 | 2362 | *München* | | | | | | | | | | | | | | | | | | | | | | | | | | | | |
| 798 | 546 | 753 | 653 | 1057 | 1605 | 973 | 1043 | 3247 | 1210 | *Nantes* | | | | | | | | | | | | | | | | | | | | | | | | | | | |
| 2215 | 1963 | 1467 | 1177 | 2232 | 2558 | 1093 | 785 | 3287 | 1131 | 1818 | *Napoli* | | | | | | | | | | | | | | | | | | | | | | | | | | |
| 1516 | 1264 | 988 | 472 | 1326 | 1652 | 187 | 317 | 3132 | 866 | 1132 | 906 | *Nice* | | | | | | | | | | | | | | | | | | | | | | | | | |
| 1345 | 1093 | 449 | 797 | 2056 | 2423 | 1108 | 614 | 2211 | 165 | 1131 | 1298 | 929 | *Nürnberg* | | | | | | | | | | | | | | | | | | | | | | | | |
| 2246 | 1994 | 1498 | 2052 | 3088 | 3636 | 2363 | 1997 | 1817 | 1522 | 2163 | 2655 | 2312 | 753 | *Oslo* | | | | | | | | | | | | | | | | | | | | | | | |
| 2935 | 2683 | 2187 | 1898 | 2953 | 3279 | 1814 | 1505 | 4008 | 1851 | 2539 | 733 | 1626 | 2019 | 3376 | *Palermo* | | | | | | | | | | | | | | | | | | | | | | |
| 595 | 343 | 376 | 462 | 1310 | 1858 | 773 | 855 | 2863 | 832 | 385 | 1630 | 932 | 753 | 1779 | 2350 | *Paris* | | | | | | | | | | | | | | | | | | | | | |
| 2104 | 1852 | 2009 | 1681 | 590 | 870 | 1544 | 2024 | 4503 | 2334 | 1388 | 2613 | 1707 | 2387 | 3419 | 3333 | 1641 | *Porto* | | | | | | | | | | | | | | | | | | | | |
| 1629 | 1377 | 733 | 1081 | 2340 | 2707 | 1392 | 932 | 1860 | 369 | 1415 | 1503 | 1238 | 296 | 1343 | 2223 | 1037 | 2671 | *Praha* | | | | | | | | | | | | | | | | | | | |
| 2002 | 1750 | 1254 | 964 | 2019 | 2345 | 880 | 572 | 3074 | 918 | 1605 | 219 | 693 | 1085 | 2442 | 939 | 1417 | 2400 | 1290 | *Roma* | | | | | | | | | | | | | | | | | | |
| 3408 | 3156 | 2660 | 3214 | 4250 | 4798 | 3525 | 3159 | 1699 | 2684 | 3325 | 3817 | 3474 | 2533 | 1560 | 4538 | 2941 | 4581 | 2505 | 3604 | *Rovaniemi* | | | | | | | | | | | | | | | | |
| 1582 | 1330 | 714 | 877 | 2209 | 2535 | 1070 | 576 | 2257 | 140 | 1367 | 1147 | 882 | 308 | 1665 | 1868 | 990 | 2491 | 353 | 934 | 2827 | *Salzburg* | | | | | | | | | | | | | | | |
| 2256 | 2004 | 2175 | 1657 | 550 | 217 | 1520 | 2000 | 4657 | 2397 | 1540 | 2589 | 1683 | 2454 | 3571 | 3310 | 1793 | 653 | 2738 | 2376 | 4733 | 2566 | *Sevilla* | | | | | | | | | | | | | | |
| 2772 | 2520 | 1905 | 1827 | 3028 | 3354 | 1889 | 1396 | 2351 | 1331 | 2558 | 1870 | 1702 | 1439 | 2789 | 2590 | 2180 | 3409 | 1422 | 1657 | 3951 | 1200 | 3385 | *Sofia* | | | | | | | | | | | | | |
| 2293 | 2041 | 1545 | 2099 | 3135 | 3683 | 2410 | 2044 | 1292 | 1569 | 2210 | 2702 | 2359 | 1418 | 525 | 3423 | 1826 | 3466 | 1390 | 2489 | 1170 | 1712 | 3618 | 2836 | *Stockholm* | | | | | | | | | | | | |
| 1080 | 828 | 222 | 478 | 1652 | 2106 | 789 | 488 | 2528 | 358 | 867 | 1278 | 948 | 325 | 1580 | 1998 | 490 | 1983 | 609 | 1065 | 2742 | 515 | 2137 | 1706 | 1627 | *Strasbourg* | | | | | | | | | | | |
| 1222 | 970 | 346 | 628 | 1801 | 2254 | 939 | 523 | 2408 | 222 | 1008 | 1311 | 838 | 205 | 1550 | 2031 | 630 | 2132 | 489 | 1098 | 2712 | 379 | 2285 | 1570 | 1597 | 156 | *Stuttgart* | | | | | | | | | | | |
| 3018 | 2766 | 2151 | 2073 | 3274 | 3600 | 2135 | 1642 | 2658 | 1577 | 2804 | 2116 | 1948 | 1685 | 3035 | 2836 | 2426 | 3655 | 1668 | 1903 | 4197 | 1446 | 3631 | 307 | 3082 | 1952 | 1816 | *Thessaloníki* | | | | | | | | | | |
| 1329 | 1077 | 688 | 299 | 1449 | 1775 | 407 | 140 | 2934 | 620 | 903 | 882 | 220 | 731 | 2100 | 1602 | 744 | 1829 | 980 | 669 | 3262 | 711 | 1806 | 1531 | 2147 | 554 | 640 | 1777 | *Torino* | | | | | | | | | |
| 1241 | 989 | 1052 | 537 | 835 | 1384 | 402 | 877 | 3534 | 1274 | 568 | 1466 | 563 | 1331 | 2586 | 2187 | 703 | 1166 | 1615 | 1253 | 3748 | 1443 | 1318 | 2262 | 2633 | 1013 | 1162 | 2508 | 683 | *Toulouse* | | | | | | | | |
| 3966 | 3714 | 3218 | 3772 | 4808 | 5356 | 4083 | 3717 | 2229 | 3242 | 3883 | 4375 | 4032 | 3091 | 1720 | 5096 | 3499 | 5139 | 3063 | 4162 | 597 | 3385 | 5291 | 4509 | 1719 | 3300 | 3270 | 4755 | 3820 | 4306 | *Tromsø* | | | | | | | |
| 2790 | 2538 | 2042 | 2596 | 3632 | 4180 | 2907 | 2541 | 2076 | 2066 | 2707 | 3199 | 2856 | 1915 | 544 | 3920 | 2323 | 3963 | 1887 | 2986 | 1119 | 2209 | 4115 | 3333 | 784 | 2124 | 2094 | 3579 | 2644 | 3130 | 1176 | *Trondheim* | | | | | | |
| 2021 | 1769 | 1493 | 975 | 351 | 651 | 838 | 1318 | 3975 | 1715 | 1106 | 1907 | 1001 | 1772 | 3027 | 2628 | 1436 | 941 | 2056 | 1694 | 4189 | 1884 | 682 | 2703 | 3074 | 1455 | 1603 | 2949 | 1124 | 733 | 4747 | 3571 | *Valencia* | | | | | |
| 1702 | 1450 | 939 | 698 | 1899 | 2225 | 760 | 267 | 2563 | 492 | 1305 | 741 | 573 | 659 | 2016 | 1461 | 1117 | 2280 | 783 | 528 | 3178 | 429 | 2256 | 1146 | 2063 | 750 | 672 | 1392 | 402 | 1133 | 3736 | 2560 | 1574 | *Venezia* | | | | |
| 2090 | 1838 | 1321 | 1760 | 2932 | 3386 | 2071 | 1577 | 1240 | 1122 | 2007 | 2047 | 1892 | 971 | 1554 | 2768 | 1623 | 3263 | 620 | 1834 | 1189 | 1017 | 3417 | 1456 | 1601 | 1288 | 1168 | 1702 | 1694 | 2294 | 3274 | 2098 | 2735 | 1323 | *Warszawa* | | | |
| 1818 | 1566 | 922 | 1172 | 2503 | 2829 | 1364 | 871 | 1965 | 435 | 1604 | 1322 | 1177 | 485 | 1635 | 2043 | 1226 | 2860 | 292 | 1109 | 2797 | 292 | 2860 | 1130 | 1682 | 810 | 674 | 1376 | 1006 | 1737 | 3355 | 2179 | 2178 | 598 | 725 | *Wien* | | |
| 2005 | 1753 | 1138 | 1062 | 2261 | 2587 | 1122 | 629 | 2268 | 564 | 1791 | 1103 | 935 | 672 | 2022 | 1823 | 1413 | 2642 | 655 | 890 | 3184 | 433 | 2618 | 767 | 2069 | 939 | 803 | 1013 | 764 | 1495 | 3742 | 2566 | 1936 | 379 | 1028 | 363 | *Zagreb* | |
| 1224 | 972 | 420 | 429 | 1728 | 2054 | 739 | 293 | 2629 | 314 | 933 | 1083 | 608 | 426 | 1771 | 1804 | 639 | 1979 | 675 | 870 | 2933 | 451 | 2085 | 1684 | 1818 | 231 | 229 | 1930 | 410 | 962 | 3491 | 2315 | 1403 | 555 | 1389 | 745 | 917 | *Zürich* |

# Driving in Europe

## Introduction

The information panels which follow give the principal motoring regulations for all the countries included in this atlas; an explanation of the symbols is given below, together with some additional notes.

🔧 The name, address and telephone number of the national motoring organisation or organisations; the initials FIA and AIT indicate membership of the international touring associations, the Fédération Internationale de l'Automobile and the Alliance Internationale de Tourisme

🔿 Speed restrictions in kilometres per hour applying to:

🏛 motorways

🅰 dual carriageways

🅰 single carriageways

🏭 urban areas

Where restrictions for 'trailers' or 'towing' are given, it may be assumed that these apply to both trailers and caravans

🍷 The maximum permitted level of alcohol in the bloodstream. This should not be taken as an acceptable level; it is NEVER sensible to drink and drive

🎗 Whether the wearing of seat belts is compulsory

👶 Restrictions applying to children

△ Whether a warning triangle must be carried

🔲 Whether a first aid kit must be carried

💡 Whether a spare bulb kit must be carried

⬭ Whether crash helmets are compulsory for motorcyclists

🏛 Whether tolls are payable on motorways and/or other parts of the road network

⛽ Whether petrol concessions or restrictions apply

🔿 The minimum age for drivers

📖 Documentation required; note that while insurance for driving at home usually provides the legally required minimum third party cover abroad, it will not provide cover against damage, fire, theft or personal accident; for this reason, an International Motoring Certificate (Green Card) is recommended for all countries and essential where 'Green Card required' is given

★ In this section are given any other regulations not falling into the categories above

## Andorra

🔧 **Automobil Club d'Andorra**, FIA, Babet Camp 4, Andorra-la-Vella    Tel: 20-8-90

| 🏛 | 🅰 | 🅰 | 🏭 |
|---|---|---|---|
| 🔿 | 70 | 70 | 40 km/h |

🍷 0.08%

🎗 Compulsory if fitted for driver and front seat passengers

👶 Children under 10 years of age not allowed in front seats

△ Recommended (compulsory if vehicle exceeds 3000 kg)

🔲 Recommended

💡 Compulsory

⬭ Compulsory for motorcyclists and passengers

🏛

⛽

🔿 18

📖 Valid driving licence; Vehicle registration document or Vehicle on hire certificate; Green Card recommended; National vehicle identification plate

## Austria

🔧 **Österreicher Automobil-, Motorrad- und Touring Club (ÖAMTC)**, FIA & AIT, Schubertring 1-3, 1010 Wien 1    Tel: (01) 711997

| 🏛 | 🅰 | 🅰 | 🏭 |
|---|---|---|---|
| 🔿 100-130 | | 100 | 50 km/h |
| 100 | | 80 | 50 km/h |
| | | | if towing trailer over 14.5 cwt |
| 100 | 100 | 100 | 50 km/h |
| | | | if towing trailer under 14.5 cwt |

🍷 0.08%

🎗 Compulsory if fitted for driver and front and rear seat passengers

👶 Children under 12 years of age not allowed in front seats

△ Compulsory

🔲 Compulsory

💡 Compulsory

⬭ Compulsory for motorcyclists and passengers

🏛 Tolls payable on motorways for Brenner (A13), Tauern (part of the A10), and a section of the A9 north of Graz, as well as on certain roads (especially trans-alpine routes) and tunnels

⛽

🔿 18

📖 Valid driving licence; Vehicle registration document or Vehicle on hire certificate; Green Card compulsory; National vehicle identification plate

★ Towing is forbidden on certain alpine routes

## Belgium

🔧 **Royal Automobile Club de Belgique (RACB)**, FIA, 53 rue d'Arlon, 1040 Bruxelles Tel: (02) 2300810

**Touring Club Royal de Belgique (TCB)**, AIT, 44 rue de la Loi, 1040 Bruxelles Tel: (02) 2332211

**Vlaamse Automobilistenbond (VTB-VAB)**, Sint-Jacobs Markt 45, 2000 Antwerpen Tel: (03) 2203211

| 🏛 | 🅰 | 🅰 | 🏭 |
|---|---|---|---|
| 🔿 120 | 90 | 90 | 60 km/h |

🍷 0.08%

🎗 Compulsory if fitted for driver and front and rear seat passengers

👶 Children under 12 years of age not allowed in front seats

△ Compulsory

🔲 Recommended

💡

⬭ Compulsory for motorcyclists

🏛

⛽

🔿 18

📖 Valid driving licence; Vehicle registration document or Vehicle on hire certificate; Green Card recommended; National vehicle identification plate

## Bulgaria

🔧 **Union of Bulgarian Motorists (SBA)**, FIA & AIT, 6 Sveta Sofia St., Sofia C Tel: (02) 87 88 01/87 88 02

| 🏛 | 🅰 | 🅰 | 🏭 |
|---|---|---|---|
| 🔿 100 | 80 | 80 | 60 km/h |

🍷 0.0%

🎗 Compulsory if fitted for driver and front seat passengers

👶 Children under 10 years of age not allowed in front seats

△ Compulsory

🔲 Compulsory

💡 Compulsory

⬭ Compulsory for motorcyclists

🏛

⛽ Foreign motorists must buy fuel with coupons available in unlimited quantities at border posts and within Bulgaria

🔿 18

📖 Valid driving licence or International Driving Permit; Vehicle registration document or Vehicle on hire certificate; Green Card required; National vehicle identification plate

## Czechoslovakia

🔧 **Ústřední Automotoklub ČSSR**, FIA & AIT, Na Strži 4, 14000 Praha 4    Tel: (02) 43 20 41

|  | 🚗 | ⚠ | Ⓐ | 🏔 |
|---|---|---|---|---|
| 🚗 | 110 | 90 | 90 | 60 km/h |

🍷 0.0%  any alcohol found in the bloodstream may result in prosecution

🔧 Compulsory if fitted for driver and front seat passengers

👶 Children under 12 years of age not allowed in front seats

△ Compulsory

🔲 Compulsory

💡

⭕ Crash helmets and goggles compulsory for drivers of motorcycles over 50cc; crash helmets only for passengers

🚧

⛽ Petrol coupons can be purchased at frontier posts, Tuzex shops and banks; also from Czech Tourist Bureau Cedok (London) Ltd

⊖ 18

🖥 Valid driving licence; Vehicle registration document or Vehicle on hire certificate; Green Card, valid for Czechoslovakia, required; National vehicle identification plate

## Denmark

🔧 **Forenede Danske Motorejere (FDM)**, AIT, Firstovvej 32, 2800 Lyngby Tel: (45) 93 08 00

|  | 🚗 | ⚠ | Ⓐ | 🏔 |
|---|---|---|---|---|
| 🚗 | 100 | 80 | 80 | 50 km/h |
|  | 70 | 70 | 70 | 50 km/h if towing |

🍷 0.08%

🔧 Compulsory if fitted for driver and front seat passengers over 15 years

👶

△ Compulsory

🔲 Recommended

💡

⭕ Compulsory for motorcyclists and passengers

🚧

⛽

⊖ 17

🖥 Valid driving licence; Vehicle registration document or Vehicle on hire certificate; Green Card recommended; National vehicle identification plate

## Finland

🔧 **Autoliitto (Automobile and Touring Club of Finland) (ATCF)**, FIA & AIT, Kansakoulukatu 10, 00101 Helsinki 10   Tel: (90) 6940022

|  | 🚗 | ⚠ | Ⓐ | 🏔 |
|---|---|---|---|---|
| 🚗 | 120 |  | 80-100 | 50 km/h |
|  | 80 |  | 80 | 50 km/h towing if trailer has brakes |
|  | 60 |  | 60 | 50 km/h towing if trailer unbraked |

🍷 0.05%

🔧 Compulsory if fitted for driver and front and rear seat passengers

👶

△ Compulsory

🔲 Recommended

💡 Recommended

⭕ Compulsory for motorcyclists and passengers

🚧

⛽

⊖ 18

🖥 Valid driving licence; Vehicle registration document or Vehicle on hire certificate; Green Card recommended; National vehicle identification plate

★ Compulsory use of headlights at all times outside built-up areas

## France

🔧 **Automobile Club de France**, FIA, 6-8 Place de la Concorde, 75008 Paris   Tel: (01) 42 65 08 26
**Association Française des Automobiles-Clubs (AFA)**, FIA & AIT, 9 rue Anatole de la Forge, 75017 Paris   Tel: (01) 42 27 82 00

|  | 🚗 | ⚠ | Ⓐ | 🏔 |
|---|---|---|---|---|
| 🚗 | 110-130 | 110 | 90 | 60 km/h |
|  | 100-110 | 100 | 80 | 60 km/h if wet |

🍷 0.08% or 0.40 mg per litre of air exhaled

🔧 Compulsory if fitted for driver and front and rear seat passengers

👶 Children under 10 years of age not allowed in front seats

△ Compulsory unless hazard warning lights are fitted; triangle and lights compulsory for cars pulling caravans or trailers and for vehicles greater than 3.5 tons

🔲 Recommended

💡 Recommended

⭕ Compulsory for motorcyclists and passengers

🚧 Tolls payable on most motorways although short urban sections of motorway around Paris and some other major cities are free; tolls also payable on some major bridges and in some tunnels

⛽

⊖ 18

🖥 Valid driving licence; Vehicle registration document or Vehicle on hire certificate; Green Card recommended; National vehicle identification plate

## FDR (West Germany)

🔧 **Allgemeiner Deutscher Automobil-Club (ADAC)**, FIA & AIT, Am Westpark 8, 8000 München 70   Tel: (089) 76760
**Automobil-Club von Deutschland (AvD)**, FIA, Lyonerstraße 16, 6000 Frankfurt am Main 71 Tel: (069) 66060

|  | 🚗 | ⚠ | Ⓐ | 🏔 |
|---|---|---|---|---|
| 🚗 | 130* | 130* | 100 | 50 km/h |
|  | 80 | 80 | 80 | 50 km/h if towing |

*recommended

🍷 0.08%

🔧 Compulsory if fitted for driver and front and rear seat passengers

👶 Children under 12 years of age not allowed in front seats

△ Compulsory

🔲 Compulsory

💡

⭕ Compulsory for motorcyclists and passengers

🚧

⛽

⊖ 18

🖥 Valid driving licence; Vehicle registration document or Vehicle on hire certificate; Green Card recommended; National vehicle identification plate

Germany: situation as at 1 September 1990

## DDR (East Germany)

🔧 **Allgemeiner Deutscher Motorsport-Verband der DDR**, FIA, 60 Charlottenstraße, 108 Berlin (Ost)   Tel: (02) 2071931/2071932

|  | 🚗 | ⚠ | Ⓐ | 🏔 |
|---|---|---|---|---|
| 🚗 | 100 | 80 | 80 | 50 km/h |
|  | 80 | 80 | 80 | 50 km/h if towing |

🍷 0.0%  any alcohol found in the bloodstream may result in prosecution

🔧 Compulsory if fitted for driver and front seat passengers

👶 Children under 7 years of age not allowed in front seats

△ Compulsory

🔲 Compulsory

💡 Compulsory

⭕ Compulsory for motorcyclists; smoking not allowed whilst driving

🚧

⛽

⊖ 18

🖥 Valid driving licence; Vehicle registration document or Vehicle on hire certificate; Green Card recommended; National vehicle identification plate

Germany: situation as at 1 September 1990

## Great Britain

🔧 **Automobile Association (AA)**, FIA & AIT, Fanum House, Basingstoke, Hampshire RG21 2EA Tel: (0256) 20123

**Royal Automobile Club (RAC)**, FIA & AIT, Lansdowne Road, Croydon CR9 2JA Tel: (081) 686 2525

| 🏛 | 🛦 | 🅰 | 🛏 |
|---|---|---|---|
| 🅰 112 | 112 | 96 | 48 km/h |
| 96 | 96 | 80 | 48 km/h if towing |

🍷 0.08%

🔖 Compulsory if fitted for driver and front seat passengers; compulsory if fitted in back seats for children under 14

🫑 Children under 1 year of age travelling in front seat must be strapped in or placed in a child's safety seat

△

🔲 Recommended

🔦

⭕ Compulsory for motorcyclists and passengers

🏛 Tolls payable on certain major bridges and tunnels

🛢

⊖ 17

🖥 Valid driving licence; Vehicle registration document or Vehicle on hire certificate; Green Card recommended; National vehicle identification plate

★ Drive on the left!

## Greece

🔧 **The Automobile and Touring Club of Greece (ELPA)**, FIA & AIT, 2-4 Messogion, 115 27 Athína   Tel: (01) 779 1615
**Hellenic Touring Club**, AIT, 12 Politehniou, 104 33 Athína   Tel: (01) 524 0854

| 🏛 | 🛦 | 🅰 | 🛏 |
|---|---|---|---|
| 🅰 100 | 80 | 80 | 50 km/h |

🍷 0.05%

🔖 Compulsory if fitted for driver and front seat passengers

🫑 Children under 10 years of age not allowed in front seats

△ Compulsory

🔲 Compulsory

🔦

⭕ Compulsory for motorcyclists and passengers

🏛 Tolls payable on most 'national' roads

🛢

⊖ 17

🖥 Valid driving licence; Vehicle registration document or Vehicle on hire certificate; Green Card required; National vehicle identification plate

★ Fire extinguisher compulsory

## Hungary

🔧 **Magyar Autóklub (MAK)**, FIA & AIT, Rómer Floris utca 4a, Budapest 11   Tel: (01) 152 040

| 🏛 | 🛦 | 🅰 | 🛏 |
|---|---|---|---|
| 🅰 120 | 100 | 100 | 50-60 km/h |
| 80 | 70 | 70 | 50 km/h if towing |

🍷 0.0%   if the alcohol test changes colour, the driver is taken to a hospital for a blood test and his driving licence confiscated

🔖 Compulsory if fitted for driver and front seat passengers

🫑 Children under 6 years of age not allowed in front seats

△ Compulsory

🔲 Recommended

🔦 Compulsory

⭕ Compulsory for motorcyclists and passengers

🏛

🛢 Petrol can only be purchased with coupons obtainable at the border, at IBUSZ offices or in hotels; unused coupons not refundable

⊖ 18

🖥 Valid driving licence; Vehicle registration document or Vehicle on hire certificate; Green Card strongly recommended; National vehicle identification plate

## Iceland

🔧 **Felag Islenskra Bifreidaeigenda (FIB)**, FIA & AIT, Borgatun 33, 105 Reykjavik Tel: (01) 29999

| 🏛 | 🛦 | 🅰 | 🛏 |
|---|---|---|---|
| 🅰 | 70 | 70 | 50 km/h |

🍷 0.05%

🔖 Compulsory for driver and front seat passengers; rear seat belts recommended

🫑 Children in rear seats must be strapped in or placed in a child's safety seat

△ Recommended

🔲 Recommended

🔦 Recommended

⭕ Compulsory for motorcyclists and passengers

🏛

🛢

⊖ 17

🖥 Driver's passport; Valid driving licence; Vehicle registration document or Vehicle on hire certificate; Green Card, valid for Iceland, required; Temporary importation permit; National vehicle identification plate

★ Vehicle mud flaps compulsory; headlights compulsory at all times; vehicles with deisel engines are subject to a special charge on entry to Iceland

## Ireland

🔧 **Automobile Association (AA)**, FIA & AIT, 23 Suffolk Street, Dublin 2   Tel: (01) 779481
**Royal Automobile Club (RAC)**, FIA & AIT, 34 Dawson Street, Dublin 2   Tel: (01) 775141

| 🏛 | 🛦 | 🅰 | 🛏 |
|---|---|---|---|
| 🅰 88 | 88 | 64-88 | 48 km/h |
| 56 | 56 | 56 | 48 km/h if towing |

🍷 0.10%

🔖 Compulsory if fitted for driver and front seat passengers

🫑 Children under 12 years of age not allowed in front seats unless strapped in or placed in a child's safety seat

△ Recommended

🔲 Recommended

🔦 Recommended

⭕ Compulsory for motorcyclists and passengers

🏛 Toll payable on two bridges over River Liffey in Dublin

🛢

⊖ 17

🖥 Valid driving licence; Vehicle registration document or Vehicle on hire certificate; Green Card recommended; National vehicle identification plate

★ Drive on the left!

## Italy

🔧 **Automobile Club d'Italia (ACI)**, FIA & AIT, Via Marsala 8, 00185 Roma   Tel: (06) 49981
**Touring Club Italiano (TCI)**, AIT, Corso Italia 10, 20122 Milano   Tel: (02) 85261

| 🏛 | 🛦 | 🅰 | 🛏 |
|---|---|---|---|
| 🅰 110*-130 | 110*-130 | 90 | 50 km/h |
| 110*-130 | 110*-130 | 90 | 50 km/h if towing |

\* for vehicles up to 1100 cc

🍷 Severe penalties for drinking and driving

🔖 Compulsory in front (and in back if installed)

🫑 Children under 12 not allowed in front unless seat is fitted with child restraint system

△ Compulsory

🔲 Recommended

🔦 Compulsory

⭕ Compulsory for motorcyclists and passengers

🏛 Tolls payable on most motorways

🛢 Coupons at a discount available at RAC, AA, and Port Offices and frontier Automobile Clubs to personal callers; must be paid for in foreign currency

⊖ 18

🖥 Valid driving licence (translation in Italian recommended); Vehicle registration document or Vehicle on hire certificate; Green Card recommended; Temporary importation document; National vehicle identification plate

## Luxembourg

🔧 **Automobile Club du Grand Duché de Luxembourg (ACL)**, FIA & AIT,
13 route de Longwy, 8007 Bertrange
Tel: (012) 45 00 45

| 🚗 | 🚐 | 🅰 | 🚚 |
|---|---|---|---|
| 🔄 90 | 75 | 75 | 60 km/h |

🍷 0.08%

🎗 Compulsory if fitted for driver and front seat passengers

⬛ Children under 10 years of age not allowed in front seats

△ Compulsory

➕ Recommended

💡

⭕ Compulsory

🚗

🔋

🔄 18

🖥 Valid driving licence; Vehicle registration document or Vehicle on hire certificate; Green Card recommended; National vehicle identification plate

## Netherlands

🔧 **Koninklijke Nederlandsche Automobiel Club (KNAC)**, FIA, Westvlietweg 118,
Leidschendam   Tel: (070) 399 74 51
**Koninklijke Nederlandsche Toeristenbond (ANWB)**, AIT, Wassenaarseweg 220, Den Haag
Tel: (070) 314 71 47

| 🚗 | 🚐 | 🅰 | 🚚 |
|---|---|---|---|
| 🔄 100-120 | 80 | 80 | 50 km/h |
| 80 | 80 | 80 | 50 km/h if towing |

🍷 0.05%

🎗 Compulsory if fitted for driver and front seat passengers

⬛ Children under 12 years of age not allowed in front seats unless child is under 4 years of age and using a child's safety seat

△ Compulsory

➕ Recommended

💡

⭕ Compulsory for motorcyclists and passengers

🚗 Tolls payable on: Zeeland Brug, Kiltunnel (from Dordrecht – Hoekse Waard) and Prins Willem Alexander Brug

🔋

🔄 18

🖥 Valid driving licence; Vehicle registration document or Vehicle on hire certificate; Green Card recommended; National vehicle identification plate

## Norway

🔧 **Kongelig Norsk Automobilklub (KNA)**, FIA, Drammensveien 20c, 0255 Oslo 2
Tel: (02) 56 19 00
**Norges Automobil-Forbund (NAF)**, AIT, Storgata 2, 0155 Oslo 1   Tel: (02) 34 15 00

| 🚗 | 🚐 | 🅰 | 🚚 |
|---|---|---|---|
| 🔄 80-90 | 80-90 | 80-90 | 50 km/h |
| 80 | 80 | 80 | 50 km/h if towing trailer with braking system |
| 60 | 60 | 60 | 50 km/h if towing trailer without braking system |

🍷 0.05%

🎗 Compulsory if fitted for driver and front and rear seat passengers

⬛ Children are allowed in front if seat is fitted with child restraint system and seat and belt can be adapted to their size

△ Compulsory

➕ Recommended

💡 Recommended

⭕ Compulsory for motorcyclists and passengers

🚗 Tolls payable on most new major roads

🔋

🔄 18 or 20 depending on the type of vehicle

🖥 Valid driving licence; Vehicle registration document or Vehicle on hire certificate; Green Card recommended; National vehicle identification plate

★ Dipped headlights compulsory at all times

## Poland

🔧 **Polski Zwiazek Motorowy (PZM)**, FIA & AIT, Kazimierzowska 66, 02-518 Warszawa
Tel: (022) 499361/499212
**Auto Assistance**, Krucza 6-14, 00-537 Warszawa   Tel: (022) 293541/210467

| 🚗 | 🚐 | 🅰 | 🚚 |
|---|---|---|---|
| 🔄 110 | 100 | 90 | 50 km/h |
| 70 | 70 | 70 | 50 km/h if towing |

🍷 0.0%

🎗 Compulsory, outside built-up areas, if fitted for driver and front seat passenger

⬛ Children under 10 years of age not allowed in front seats

△ Compulsory

➕ Recommended

💡 Recommended

⭕ Compulsory for motorcyclists and passengers

🚗

🔋

🔄 18

🖥 Valid driving licence; International Driving Permit after 3 months; Vehicle registration document or Vehicle on hire certificate; Green Card, valid for Poland, required; National vehicle identification plate

## Portugal

🔧 **Automóvel Club de Portugal (ACP)**, FIA & AIT, Rua Rosa Araújo 24, 1200 Lisboa
Tel: (01) 736121

| 🚗 | 🚐 | 🅰 | 🚚 |
|---|---|---|---|
| 🔄 120 | 90 | 90 | 60 km/h |
| 100 | 70 | 70 | 50 km/h if towing |

🍷 0.05%

🎗 Compulsory if fitted for driver and front seat passengers outside built-up areas

⬛ Children under 12 years of age not allowed in front seat

△ Compulsory

➕ Recommended

💡 Compulsory

⭕ Compulsory for motorcyclists

🚗 Tolls payable on some motorways and bridges

🔋

🔄 17

🖥 Valid driving licence; Vehicle registration document or Vehicle on hire certificate; Green Card required; National vehicle identification plate

★ Vehicle mud flaps are compulsory

## Romania

🔧 In the event of breakdown or accident contact **National Tourist Office Carpaţi-Bucureşti**, Bd Magheru 7, Bucureşti   Tel: (400) 145160
**Automobile-Club roumain**, FIA & AIT
Strada Nikos Beloianis 27   Tel: (400) 155510

| 🚗 | 🚐 | 🅰 | 🚚 |
|---|---|---|---|
| 🔄 70-90* | 60-90* | 60-90* | 60 km/h |

*according to cylinder capacity

🍷 0.0%   any alcohol found in the bloodstream may result in immediate imprisonment

🎗 Compulsory if fitted

⬛ Children under 12 years of age not allowed in front seats

△ Compulsory

➕ Compulsory

💡 Recommended

⭕ Compulsory for motorcyclists and passengers

🚗 Tolls payable on some major routes

🔋 Coupons obtainable with convertible currency only at frontier posts, tourist offices, the Automobile Club and some hotels; for use at PECO filling stations

🔄 18

🖥 Valid driving licence; Vehicle registration document or Vehicle on hire certificate; Green Card, valid for Romania, required; National vehicle identification plate

## Spain

🔧 **Real Automóvil Club de España (RACE)**, FIA & AIT, José Abascal 10, 28003 Madrid
Tel: (91) 447 3200

| 🏛 | 🛣 | 🅰 | 🚚 |
|---|---|---|---|
| 🎧 120 | 120 | 100 | 60 km/h |
| 80 | 80 | 80 | 60 km/h if towing |

these limits are increased by 20 km/h for overtaking

🍷 0.08%
🔖 Compulsory if fitted for driver and front seat passengers outside built-up areas
● Children under 10 years of age not advised in front seats
△ Two are compulsory for vehicles with 9 or more seats; recommended for other vehicles
🔲 Recommended
🕯 Compulsory
⭕ Compulsory for motorcycles but not for mopeds
🏛 Tolls payable on most motorways and Cadí tunnel
🛢
🔂 18
📖 International Driving Permit required if 'pink' EEC licence not held; Vehicle registration document or Vehicle on hire certificate; Green Card required; Bail Bond strongly recommended; National vehicle identification plate

## Sweden

🔧 **Motormännens Riksförbund (M)**, AIT, Sturegatan 32, Stockholm   Tel: (08) 7 82 38 00

| 🏛 | 🛣 | 🅰 | 🚚 |
|---|---|---|---|
| 🎧 110 | 70-110 | 70-110 | 50 km/h |
| 90* | 70-90* | 70-90* | 50 km/h |
| 70 | 70 | 70 | 50 km/h if towing with braking device |
| 40 | 40 | 40 | 40 km/h if towing with no braking device |

*limit imposed 21 June - 19 August

🍷 0.02%
🔖 Compulsory if fitted for driver and front and rear seat passengers
●
△ Compulsory
🔲 Recommended
🕯 Compulsory
⭕ Compulsory for motorcyclists and passengers
🏛
🛢
🔂 18
📖 Valid driving licence; Vehicle registration document or Vehicle on hire certificate; Green Card required; National vehicle identification plate
★ Dipped headlights compulsory at all times

## Switzerland

🔧 **Automobile Club de Suisse (ACS)**, FIA, Wasserwerkgasse 39, 3000 Bern 13
Tel: (031) 22 47 22

**Touring Club Suisse (TCS)**, AIT, 9 rue Pierre-Fatio, 1211 Genève 3   Tel: (022) 737 12 12

| 🏛 | 🛣 | 🅰 | 🚚 |
|---|---|---|---|
| 🎧 120 | 80 | 80 | 50 km/h |
| 80 | 80 | 80 | 50 km/h if towing – up to 20 cwt trailer |
| 60 | 60 | 60 | 50 km/h if towing – over 20 cwt trailer |

🍷 0.08%
🔖 Compulsory if fitted for driver and front seat passengers
● Children under 12 years of age not allowed in front seats
△ Compulsory
🔲 Compulsory
🕯
⭕ Compulsory for motorcyclists and passengers
🏛 Vignette compulsory: obtainable from frontier posts, post offices or garages; separate vignette required for trailer or caravan
🛢
🔂 18
📖 Valid driving licence; Vehicle registration document or Vehicle on hire certificate; Green Card required; National vehicle identification plate

## Turkey

🔧 **Turkiye Turing ve Otomobil Kurumu (TTOK)**, FIA & AIT, Halaskargasi Cad. 364, 80222 Sisli, Istanbul   Tel: (01) 1314631/6

| 🏛 | 🛣 | 🅰 | 🚚 |
|---|---|---|---|
| 🎧 | 90 | 90 | 50 km/h |
| | 70 | 70 | 40 km/h if towing |

🍷 0.05%
🔖 Compulsory if fitted for driver and front seat passengers
● Children under 12 years of age not allowed in front seats
△ Two must be carried – one to place in front of the vehicle, one behind
🔲 Compulsory
🕯
⭕ Compulsory for motorcyclists
🏛 Tolls payable on some roads
🛢
🔂 18
📖 Passport; valid driving licence; International Driving Permit advised, compulsory if driving Turkish vehicle (obtainable at frontier with 2 photos and 54 000 Turkish Lire); Vehicle registration document or Vehicle on hire certificate; Green Card required – must cover European and Asian regions; National vehicle identification plate
★ Fire extinguisher, chock and towrope compulsory

## USSR

🔧 In the event of breakdown or accident contact officer of State Automobile Inspection (Militia) or nearest office of Intourist (obliged to give tourists assistance)

| 🏛 | 🛣 | 🅰 | 🚚 |
|---|---|---|---|
| 🎧 90 | 90 | 90 | 60 km/h |

🍷 0.0%
🔖 Compulsory if fitted for driver and front seat passengers
● Children under 12 years of age not allowed in front seats
△ Compulsory
🔲 Compulsory
🕯 Recommended
⭕ Compulsory
🏛 Road tax payable on entry to USSR though some foreign cars exempt
🛢 Petrol coupons recommended; obtainable at border posts
🔂 18
📖 Valid driving licence meeting requirements of International Convention on Road Traffic; Vehicle registration document or Vehicle on hire certificate; Car insurance obtainable on entry to USSR at Ingosstrakh offices or at Intourist offices; Itinerary card, service coupons and motor routes map issued by Intourist; Customs obligation to take the car out of the country on departure; National vehicle identification plate
★ Fire extinguisher compulsory

## Yugoslavia

🔧 **Auto-Moto Savez Jugoslavija (AMSJ)**, FIA & AIT, Ruzveltova 18, 11001 Beograd
Tel: (011) 401699

| 🏛 | 🛣 | 🅰 | 🚚 |
|---|---|---|---|
| 🎧 120 | 100 | 80 | 60 km/h |
| 80 | 80 | 80 | 60 km/h if towing |

🍷 0.05%
🔖 Compulsory if fitted for driver and front and rear seat passengers
● Children under 12 years of age not allowed in front seats
△ Compulsory – two are necessary if towing trailer or caravan
🔲 Compulsory
🕯 Compulsory
⭕ Compulsory for motorcyclists and passengers
🏛 Tolls payable on several major roads, Tito Bridge, Krk Island Bridge and Ucka Tunnel
🛢 Concessionary petrol coupons available at frontier posts for purchase with convertible currency; unused coupons refundable at place of purchase
🔂 18
📖 Valid driving licence; Vehicle registration document or Vehicle on hire certificate; Green Card required; National vehicle identification plate

## Signos convencionales

Para más información ver el interior de la cubierta anterior

Importancia de los itinerarios

Autopista con calzadas separadas
con calzada única
Autovía con calzadas separadas
Número de acceso
Accesos: completo – medio acceso
parcial – sin precisión
Carretera de comunicación internacional o nacional asfaltada:
calzadas separadas
4 carriles – 3 carriles
2 carriles anchos – 2 carriles
Carretera de comunicación interregional asfaltada:
calzadas separadas
2 carriles o más – 2 carriles estrechos
Sin asfaltar: transitable, con macadán
Otra carretera asfaltada – sin asfaltar
Carretera en construcción
10-1991  Fecha prevista de entrada en servicio

Distancias en kilómetros (totales o parciales)

12  en autopista:
tramo de peaje

5  12  7
5  7  tramo libre

12  en carretera

5  7
14  10  GB e IRL: en millas
24  en kilómetros
39

Transporte

Línea férrea – Tren-coche
B  Barcaza – Barcaza (DK, N, S, SF)
Enlace marítimo: permanente – de temporada
Aeropuerto

## Segni convenzionali

Vedere la legenda completa all'interno della copertina

Importanza degli itinerari

Autostrada a carreggiate separate
a carreggiata unica
Doppia carreggiata di tipo autostradale
Numero dello svincolo
Svincoli: completo – semi-svincolo
parziale – non precisato
Strada di comunicazione internazionale o nazionale rivestita:
a carreggiate separate
a 4 corsie – a 3 corsie
a 2 corsie larghe – a 2 corsie
Strada di comunicazione interregionale rivestita:
a carreggiate separate
a 2 corsie e più – a 2 corsie strette
Non rivestita: carrozzabile, in macadam
Altre strade con rivestimento – senza rivestimento
Strada in costruzione
10-1991  Apertura prevista

Distanze in chilometri (totali e parziali)

12  su autostrada:
tratto a pedaggio

5  12  7
5  7  tratto esente da pedaggio

12  su strada

5  7
14  10  GB e IRL: in miglia
24  in chilometri
39

Trasporti

Ferrovia – trasporto automobili per ferrovia
B  Su chiatta – su chiatta (DK, N, S, SF)
Collegamento via-traghetto: tutto l'anno – stagionale
Aeroporto

## Zeichenerklärung

Vollständige Zeichenerklärung siehe Umschlaginnenseite

Verkehrsbedeutung der Straßen

Autobahn mit getrennten Fahrbahnen
mit nur einer Fahrbahn
Schnellstraße mit getrennten Fahrbahnen
Nummer der Anschlußstelle
Anschlußstellen: Autobahnein- und/oder
-ausfahrt – ohne Angabe
Internationale bzw. nationale Hauptverkehrsstraße mit Belag:
getrennte Fahrbahnen
4 Fahrspuren – 3 Fahrspuren
2 breite Fahrspuren – 2 Fahrspuren
Überregionale Verbindungsstraße mit Belag:
getrennte Fahrbahnen
2 u. mehr Fahrspuren – 2 schmale Fahrspuren
Ohne Belag: befahrbar, mit Makadam
Sonstige Straßen: mit Belag, ohne Belag
Straße im Bau
10-1991  Voraussichtliches Datum der Verkehrsfreigabe

Entfernungsangaben in Kilometern (Gesamt- und Teilentfernungen)

12  auf der Autobahn:
gebührenpflichtiger Abschnitt

5  12  7
5  7  gebührenfreier Abschnitt

12  auf anderen Straßen

5  7
14  10  in GB und IRL: in Meilen
24  in Kilometern
39

Transport

Bahnlinie – Autoreisezug
B  Fähre – Fähre (DK, N, S, SF)
Schiffsverbindung: ganzjährig – während der Saison
Flughafen

## Verklaring der tekens

Zie voor de volledige verklaring der tekens de binnenzijde van het omslag

Belang van het wegennet

Autosnelweg met gescheiden rijbanen
met één rijbaan
Dubbele rijbaan van het type autosnelweg
Nummer knooppunt/aansluiting
Knooppunten/aansluitingen : volledig – half
gedeeltelijk – niet nader aangegeven
Internationale of nationale verharde verbindingsweg:
gescheiden rijbanen
4 rijstroken – 3 rijstroken
2 brede rijstroken – 2 rijstroken
Regionale verharde verbindingsweg:
gescheiden rijbanen
2 of meer rijstroken – 2 smalle rijstroken
Onverhard: berijdbaar, macadamweg
Andere weg: verhard – onverhard
Weg in aanleg
10-1991  Vermoedelijke datum ingebruikneming

Afstanden in kilometers (totaal en gedeeltelijk)

12  op de autosnelweg:
gedeelte met tol

5  12  7
5  7  tolvrij gedeelte

12  op de weg

5  7
14  10  GB en IRL: in mijlen
24  in kilometers
39

Vervoer

Spoorweg – Autotrein
B  Veerpont – Veerpont (DK, N, S, SF)
Scheepvaartverbinding : permanent – alleen in het seizoen
Luchthaven

## Légende

Voir la légende complète à l'intérieur de la couverture

Importance des itinéraires

Autoroute à chaussées séparées
à une seule chaussée
Double chaussée de type autoroutier
Numéro d'échangeur
Échangeurs: complet – demi-échangeur
partiel – sans precision
Route de liaison internationale ou nationale revêtue:
chaussées séparées
4 voies – 3 voies
2 voies larges – 2 voies
Route de liaison interrégionale revêtue:
chaussées séparées
2 voies et plus – 2 voies étroites
Non revêtue: carrossable, en macadam
Autre route revêtue – non revêtue
Route en construction
10-1991  Date de mise en service prévue

Distances en kilomètres (totalisées et partielles)

12  sur autoroute:
section à péage

5  12  7
5  7  section libre

12  sur route

5  7
14  10  GB et IRL: en miles
24  en kilomètres
39

Transport

Voie ferrée – Train-auto
B  Bac – Bac (DK, N, S, SF)
Liaison maritime: permanente – saisonnière
Aéroport

## Key to symbols

A full key to symbols appears inside the front cover

Road classification

Motorway: dual carriageway
single carriageway
Dual carriageway with motorway characteristics
Interchange number
Interchange: complete – half
limited – unspecified
International and national surfaced road network:
dual carriageway
four lanes – three lanes
two wide lanes – two lanes
Interregional surfaced road network:
dual carriageway
two lanes or more – two narrow lanes
Unsurfaced: suitable for vehicles, macadam
Other surfaced road – unsurfaced
Road under construction
10-1991  Scheduled opening date

Distances in kilometres (total and intermediate)

12  on motorway:
toll section

5  12  7
5  7  free section

12  on other roads

5  7
14  10  GB and IRL: in miles
24  in kilometres
39

Transportation

Railway – Motorail
B  Ferry – Ferry (DK, N, S, SF)
Car ferry: all the year – seasonal
Airport

A     B     C

1

2

3

4

Cape Wrath

*Whiten Head*

Durness

Butt of Lewis
Port of Ness

Kinlochbervie   A 838

16   A 857

20

Scourie   908 △ *Foinaven*   927 △   Tongue

31

LEWIS   Barvas

A 884   Laxford Bridge   *Ben Hope*

A 858   A 857   12

Carloway   292 △

34

*Eddrachillis Bay*   Kylestrome   Altnaharra   Ben K...

*THE MINCH*   A 894   39   961 △

Stornoway   Portnaguran

Garynahine   A 859   *Tiumpan Head*

*Broad Bay*   A 866   40   Ben K...

574 △   12   *Eye Peninsula*

A 837   34   Inchnadamph

Lochinver   998 △   A 838

36   *Rubha Còigeach*   *Ben More Assynt*

A 859   849 △   Ledmore

Hushinish   Clisham   572 △

B 887   1799 △

*Kebock Head*   *Coigach*   18   A 837   La...

*West Loch Tarbert*   Tarbert   743 △   27 A 83...

**W E S T E R N**   *Loch Broom*

Toe Head   24   Harris   A 837   31   Bonar Bridge

A 859   Leverburgh

*Rubha Réidh*   Laide   *Gruinard Bay*   *Ullapool*

Rodel   **I S L E S**

Renish Point   Dundonnell   29   15   *Bonar Bridge*

North Uist   1062 △   1084 △   *Eas...*

Tigharry   A 865   *Sound of Harris*   Gairloch   A 832   *Beinn Dearg*

25   A 865   Lochmaddy   12

A 867   *Waternish Point*   Staffin   *Sgurr Mòr* △   19   Ben Wyvis

13 △ 347   A 855   20   980   57   92   1046 △

Balivanich   A 865   *Loch Snizort*   Uig   A 822   *Loch Fannich*   *Wester*   *Ross*   Garve   Dingwall

Benbecula   Dunvegan Head   34   *Rona*   Liathach   Kinlochewe   15

Creagorry   *The Storr*   16   719 △   Torridon   1054 △   A 896   9   Achnasheen   A 832   Contin

A 850   22   *Sound of Raasay*   *Loch Torridon*   Shieldaig   19   A 890   Muir of Ord

Dunvegan   A 856   A 855   Portree   *Glen Carron*   A 831

South Uist   22   Bracadale   *Raasay*   896 △   A 896   24   1083 △   A 833

A 865   620 △   *Idrigill Point*   21   *Inner Sound*   Lochcarron   Cannich   A 831

A 863   9   444 △   Stromeferry   A 890   Drumnadrochit

*SEA OF*   *Loch Bracadale*   Sligachan   Sconser   *Scalpay*   Kyle of Lochalsh   A 890   *H I G H*   *A*   *Glen More*

Daliburgh   *THE HEBRIDES*   **SKYE**   17   A 850   Broadford   A 850   Dornie   △ *Carn Eige*   29

Lochboisdale   *The Cuillins*   A 881   14   Kyleakin   *Eilean Donan Castle*   1183 △

993 △   Kylerhea   B   Shiel Bridge   Foyers

*Sound of Barra*   Elgol   Isleornsay   Glenelg   *A' Chràlaig*   Invermoriston   33   White Bridge

17   32   1120 △   A 887   69   7

Barra   A 888   *Canna*   A 851   50   43   *Monadhliat*

383 △   Bayhirivagh   Ardvasar   *Sound of Sleat*   80   16   Fort Augustus   942 △

Castlebay   *Rhum*   812 △   *Mallaig*   *Loch Quoich*   13   Invergarry   *Carn Ban* △

*Sound of Rhum*   △ *Sgurr na Ciche*   *Glen*   15   Newtonm...

Mingulay   *Eigg*   1040 △   *Albyn*   25   Laggan   A 86

19   *Loch Morar*   *Loch Arkaig*   *Loch Lochy*   40   *Creag Meagaidh*

Barra Head   76   Arisaig   46   Glenfinnan   *Caledonian Canal*   1130 △   *Loch Laggan*   Dalwhinnie

*Muck*   A 830   882 △   27   Spean Bridge   A 86   30

A 861   *Loch Shiel*   10

33   888 △   Fort William   *Ben Alder*   1148 △   *Loch Ericht*   Pa...

Kilchoan   528 △   Salen   1344 △   *Ben Nevis*   1148 △   *Schieha...*

*Coll*   Arinagour   B 8007   Strontian   A 861   13   Inchree   **S**   **O**   **M**

Corran   9   Onich   *Blackwater Resr.*

*Tiree*   Tobermory   Ballachulish   *Glen Coe*   33   Kinloch Rannoch

Dervaig   B 8073   19   A 884   Kentallen   1141 △   *Bidean*   *nam Bian*   A 82   *Loch Rannoch*

Scarinish   A 848   *Linnhe*   Portnacroish

*Flannan I.*

**H E B R I D E S**

4

A     B     C

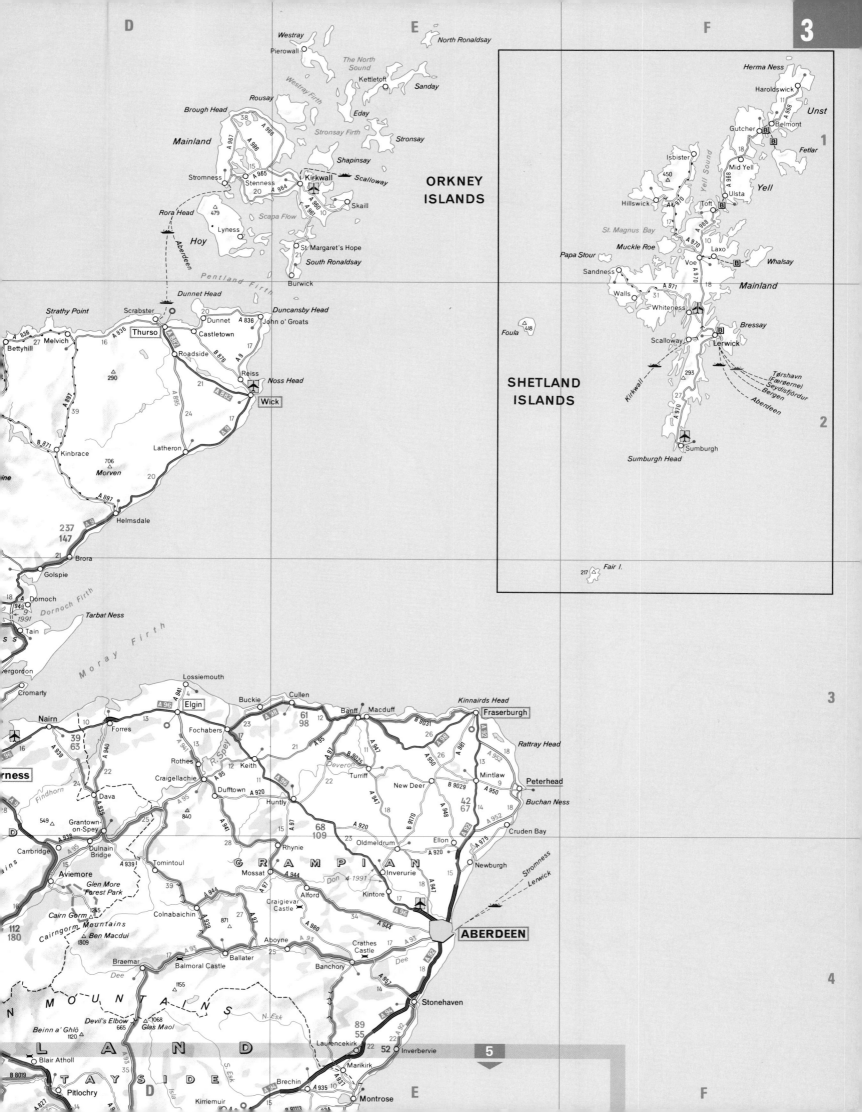

MAYO
SLIGO
ROSCOMMON
LEITR
LON
IRELAND
GALWAY
WEST
CLARE
TIPPERARY
LIMERICK
KERRY
CORK
WATE
Inishkea
Bangor
Blacksod Bay
Achill Island
Keel
Ballycroy
Nephin Beg Range
Crossmolina
Ballina / Béal an Átha
Inishcrone
L. Conn
The Ox Mountains
Strandhill
Sligo / Sligeach
Manorhamilton
Ballysadare
Ballymote
Tobercurry
Charlestown
Swinford
Foxford
Nephin
Pontoon
Mulrany
Corraun
Newport
Castlebar / Caisleán an Bharraigh
Clare Island
Clew Bay
Westport / Cathair na Mart
Louisburgh
Croagh Patrick
Inishturk
Inishbofin
Inishshark
Rinvyle Pt.
Mweelrea Mts.
Killary Harbour
Partry Mountains
Letterfrack
Leenane
The Twelve Pins
Maumturk Mts.
Clifden / An Clochán
Connemara
Slyne Head
Roundstone
Maam Cross
Gortmore
Carna
Kilkieran Bay
Lettermullan
Gorumna Island
Oughterard
Lough Mask
Lough Corrib
Ballinrobe
Kilmaing
Clonbur
Cong
Headford
Ballintober
Claremorris
Kiltamagh
Connaught
Ballyhaunis
Tuam / Tuaim
Dunmore
Glennamaddy
Ballymoe
Castlerea
Frenchpark
Ballaghaderreen
Boyle / Mainistir na Búille
Gorteen
L. Gara
Elphin
Tulsk
Strokestown
Carrick-on-Shannon / Cora Droma Rúisc
Mohill
Dowra
Drumkeeran
Lough Allen
Drumshanbo
Keadew
L. Key
L. Arrow
L. Gill
Lanesborough
Roscommon / Ros Comáin
Longford
Mount Bellew
Ballyforan
Lough Ree
Athlone / Baile Átha Luain
Ballinasloe / Béal Átha na Sluaighe
Athenry
Galway / Gaillimh
Oranmore
Spiddle
Barna
Galway Bay
Aran Islands
Inishmore
Kilronan
Inishmaan
Inisheer
Black Head
Craughwell
Loughrea
Ardrahan
Kinvarra
Ballyvaughan
Lisdoonvarna
Kilfenora
Cliffs of Moher
Lahinch
Ennistimon
Corrofin
Gort
Portumna
Clonfert
Clonmacnoise
Ferbane
Banagher
Cloghan
Kilcormac
Birr
Kinnitty
Slieve Bloom
Borrisokane
Lough Derg
Milltown Malbay
Spanish Point
Ennis / Inis
Tulla
Scarriff
Knappogue Castle
Broadford
Kilmurry
Killaloe
Creegh
Kilkee
Kilrush
Killimer
Labasheeda
Killadysert
Shannon
Newmarket on Fergus
Bunratty Castle
Loop Head
Kilbaha
Mouth of the Shannon
River Shannon
Tarbert
Ballybunnion
Askeaton
Adare
Rathkeale
LIMERICK / LUIMNEACH
Newport
Nenagh / An tAonach
Moneygall
Roscrea
Dolla
Templemore
Thurles / Durlas
Holycross Abbey
Milestone
Urlingford
Listowel
Ballyduff
Kerry Head
Ballyheige
Tralee Bay
Tralee / Trá Lí
Abbeyfeale
Newcastle West
Croom
Hospital
Tipperary / Tiobraid Árann
Cashel / Caiseal
Killenaule
Fethard
Kilmallock
Dromcolliher
Rath Luirc (Charleville)
Galty Mountains
Caher
Clonmel / Cluain Meala
Slievenamon
Brandon Head
Brandon Mountain
Sybil Head
Clogher Head
Dingle
Anascaul
Slieve Mish Mts.
Castlemaine
Great Blasket I.
Slea Head
Dingle Bay
Castleisland
Killorglin
Glenbeigh
L. Caragh
Killarney / Cill Airne
Newmarket
Boherboy
Kanturk
Buttevant
Kildorrery
Mitchelstown
Clogheen
Knockmealdown Mts.
Comeragh Mts.
Doulus Head
Knight's Town
Valencia Island
Cahersiveen
Ring of Kerry
Iveragh
Carrantuohill
Macgillycuddy's Reeks
Muckross House
L. Leane
Mangerton Mountain
Rathmore
Millstreet
Mallow / Mala
Fermoy
Lismore
Cappoquin
Dungarvan / Dún Garbhán
Dungarvan Harb.
Helvick Head
St. Finan's Bay
Bolus Head
Skellig
Waterville
L. Currane
Sneem
Kilgarvan
Kenmare
Derrynasaggart Mts.
Macroom
Coachford
Blarney
CORK / CORCAIGH
Midleton
Tallow
R. Blackwater
Youghal / Eochaill
Youghal Bay
Ardmore
Kenmare River
Lauragh
Beara
Caha Mts.
Glengarriff
Pass of Keimaneigh
Castletownbere
Dursey Island
Bere I.
Bantry / Beanntraí
Bantry Bay
Dunmanway
Bandon
Ringaskiddy
Cobh / An Cóbh
Crosshaven
Ballycotton
Kinsale
Sheep's Head
Dunmanus Bay
Skull
Rosscarbery
Clonakilty
Timoleague
Skibbereen
Roaringwater Bay
Mizen Head
Galley Head
Toe Head
Old Head of Kinsale
Roscoff
le Havre

A B C

18

1

Guernsey

St. Peter Po

2

Cork Plymouth
Batz

Ploumanach
Trégastel · Perros-Guirec
I. de Bréhat
pnte de l'Arcouest

Roscoff
St Pol-
de-Léon
Pleumeur-Bodou
Trébeurden
Primel-Trégastel
Plougasnou
Locquirec
Pleubian
Tréguier
Lézardrieux
Paimpol
Brignogan
Plouescat
Carantec
St Michel-
en-Gl
Lannion
la Roche
Derrien
Pontrieux
St Quay-
Portrieux
Cap Fréhel

l'Aber-Wrac'h
Lesneven
Plouvien
Taulé
Plestin
Plouaret
Bégard
Lanvollon
Plouha
Étables
Binic
Sables-d'Or
Erquy
St Ca
Ploudalmézeau
le Folgoët
Plouzévédé
Plabennec
Landivisiau
Morlaix
Plouigneau
Belle-Isle-
en-Terre
Guingamp
Châtelaudren
Plouagat
le Val-André
Matignon

Lampaul
St Renan
Guipavas
Thégonnec
Guimiliau
Plougonven
D787
Bourbriac
St Brieuc
Plédran
Lamballe
Jugon
le
Molène
BREST
Landerneau
Sizun
Brennilis
Huelgoat
Callac
Quintin
Ploeuc
Moncontour
Collinée
Broons
Plancoët
le Conquet
Plougastel-
Daoulas
Daoulas
Rumengol
le Faou
Monts
d'A
CÔTES
St Nicolas-du-Pélem
Corlay
Uzel
Plouguenast
pnte de St Mathieu
Camaret
Landévennec
Pleyben
Châteauneuf-
du-Faou
Maël-Carhaix
Rostrenen
Gouarec
Mûr-de-
Bretagne
Merdrignac
pnte de Penhir
Crozon
Menez-Hom
Carhaix-
Plouguer
Montagnes
Gourin
Loudéac
la Chèze
la Trinité-
Porhoët
Morgat
Châteaulin
Noires
Guémené
Cléguérec
N164
Cap de la Chèvre
Douarnenez
Tréboul
Locronan
Briec
le Faouët
Pontivy
Rohan
Josselin
I. de Sein
Pont-Croix
Odet
Scaër
Kernascléden
Bubry
Ploërmel
pnte du Raz
Audierne
Quimper
Rosporden
Bannalec
Arzano
Plouay
Locminé
Elven
Malestroit
Plonéour-
Lanvern
Fouesnant
Quimperlé
Riec
Plouay
Baud
St Jean-
Brévelay
Pont-l'Abbé
Bénodet
Beg-Meil
Concarneau
Pont-
Aven
Port-Scorff
Hennebont
Plûvigner
Gr Champ
St Guénolé
Loctudy
Port-Manech
Moëlan
Larmor
Ste Anne-d'A
Questembert
Guilvinec
pnte de Penmarch
le Pouldu
Lorient
Auray
Vannes
Rochefort-
en-T.
Iles de Glénan
Port-Louis
Étel
Locmariaquer
Muzillac
Groix
Belz
Carnac
la Trinité
Port-Navalo
Sarzeau
Damgan
Pénestin
I. de Groix
St Pierre
St Gildas-
de-Rhuys
Quiberon
Houat
Piriac
Sauzon
le Palais
Hœdic
la Turballe
Guérande
le Croisic
la Baule
Belle-Ile
Batz
le Pouliguen
Pornichet
St NAZAIRE
pnte de St Gildas

24

3

4

A B C

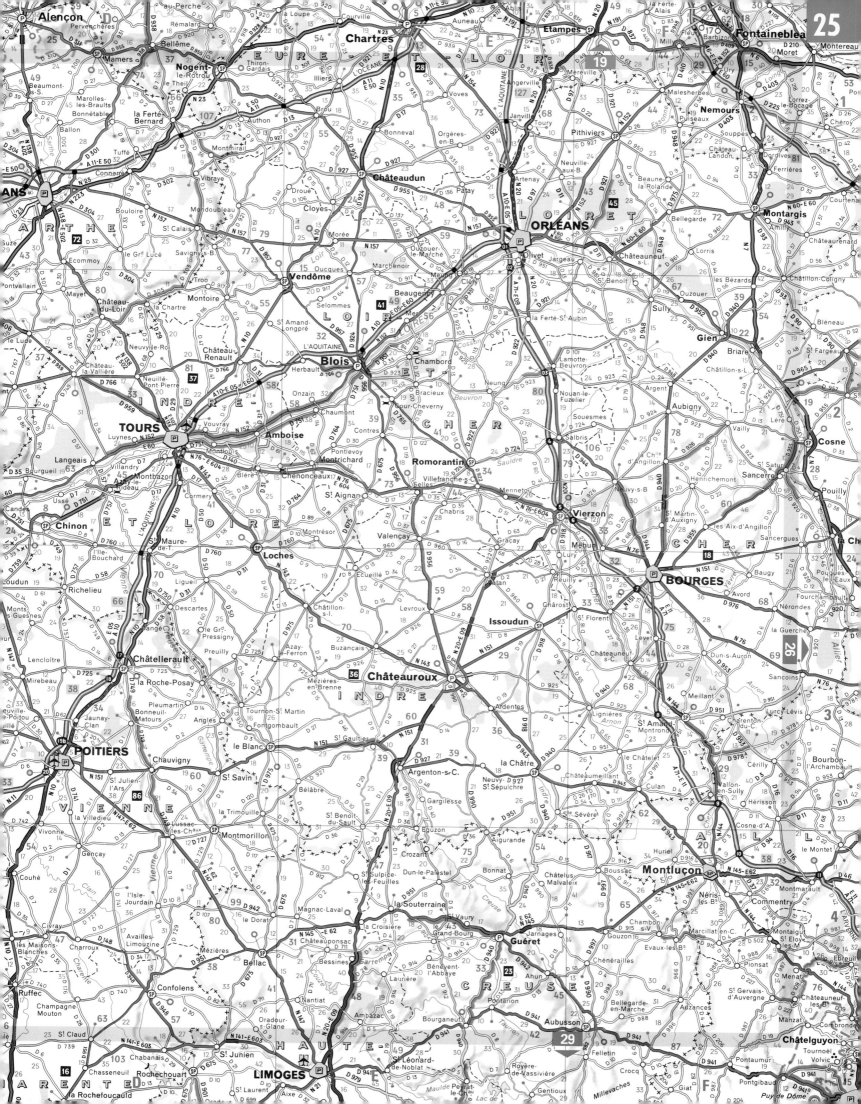

Moret — Montereau — Bray — Marigny-le-Châtel — Marcilly-le-Hayer — Piney — Doulaincourt — Liffol-le-Grd

**TROYES** — **B** — Estissac — **20** — Lusigny — Vendeuvre — Bar-s-Aube — Colombey-2-Églises — Bologne — Andelot — St Blin

Sens — Villeneuve-l'Archevêque — Aix-en-Othe — Bouilly — Bar-s-Seine — Les Riceys — Essoyes — Mussy — **Chaumont** — Clefmont

Souppes — Château-Landon — Courtenay — St Julien-du-S. — Joigny — Migennes — St Florentin — Chaource — Chablis — Tonnerre — Tanlay — Châtillon-s-S. — Châteauvillain — Arc-en-Barrois — Nogent — Montigny-le-Roi — Neuilly-l'Évêque

Montargis — Châtillon-Coligny — Charny — Aillant — **Auxerre** — Chablis — Tonnerre — Ancy-le-Franc — **Langres** — Auberive — Longeau

Briare — St Fargeau — Toucy — Bléneau — Coulanges-la-V. — Vermenton — Nitry — Noyers — Montbard — Venarey-les-Laumes — Aignay-le-Duc — Grancey-le-Chau — Selongey — Fontaine-Française

Cosne — St Amand-en-Puisaye — Clamecy — **Vézelay** — **Avallon** — Guillon — Semur-en-Auxois — Alise-St-Reine — St Seine-l'Abb — Is-s-Tille — Gemeaux — Mirebeau

Sancerre — Donzy — Varzy — Brinon — Corbigny — Lormes — Quarré-les-Tombes — Saulieu — Précy-s/s-Thil — Vitteaux — Sombernon — **DIJON** — Genlis — Auxonne

La Charité — Prémery — Montsauche — Les Settons — Liernais — Arnay-le-Duc — Bligny — Gevrey-Chambertin — Nuits-St-Georges — St Jean-de-Losne — **Dole**

Baugy — Pougues-les-Eaux — Guérigny — St Saulge — Château-Chinon — Lucenay-l'Évêque — **Beaune** — Seurre — Chaussin

**Nevers** — Châtillon-en-Bazois — Moulins-Englibert — St Léger — Épinac — Nolay — Meursault — la Rochepot — Verdun — Pierre-de-Bresse

Fourchambault — St Bénin-d'Azy — Imphy — la Machine — St Honoré — Mont Beuvray — **Autun** — Couches — Chagny — **Chalon-s-S.** — Louhans

Decize — Fours — Luzy — Mesvres — **le Creusot** — Montcenis — Montchanin — Buxy — St Germain-du-Plain — Bletterans

St Pierre-le-Moûtier — Dornes — Toulon — Issy-l'Évêque — **Montceau-les-Mines** — Blanzy — **71** — Mont-St-Vincent — St Gengoux-National — Sennecey-le-Gr — Lons-le-Saunier

Bourbon-l'Archambault — Chevagnes — Bourbon-Lancy — Gueugnon — Palinges — Cormatin — **Tournus** — Beaufort

Souvigny — Dompierre — **Moulins** — Digoin — **Paray-le-Monial** — Charolles — St Bonnet-de-Joux — Cluny — Cuisery — St Amour

Neuilly-le-Réal — Varennes-s-A. — Jaligny — le Donjon — Anzy-le-Duc — la Clayette — Matour — **Mâcon** — Pont-de-Veyle — Montrevel — St Julien

Montmarault — St Pourçain — Lapalisse — Marcigny — Semur-en-B. — la Chap-de-Guinchay — Bâgé-le-Châtel — Treffort

Commentry — Chantelle — St Germain-des-Fossés — la Pacaudière — Charlieu — Chauffailles — Belleville — **Bourg-en-Bresse**

**VICHY** — Cusset — Gannat — Bellerive — Ambierle — Belmont — Cours — Villefranche-s-Saône — St Trivier-s-M. — Villars-les-Dombes

Châtelguyon — Riom — Thiers — St Germain-Laval — **Roanne** — Thizy — Lamure — Tarare — l'Arbresle — **LYON**

**CLERMONT-FERRAND** — Royat — Billom — Noirétable — Boën — Feurs — St Symphorien-de-Lay — St Foy-l'Argentière

CÔTE-D'OR — YONNE — NIÈVRE — SAÔNE-ET-LOIRE — ALLIER — LOIRE — RHÔNE — AIN — HAUTE-MARNE

A    B    C

Major places:

Saintes · Cognac · Angoulême · Royan · Périgueux · Bergerac · BORDEAUX · Libourne · Arcachon · Agen · Marmande · Villeneuve-sur-Lot · Mont-de-Marsan · Dax · Bayonne · BIARRITZ · Hendaye · St-Jean-de-Luz · PAU · Tarbes · Auch · Condom · Brantôme

Regions/waters: GIRONDE · LANDES · LOT-ET-GARONNE · GERS · DORDOGNE · CHARENTE · CHARENTE-MARITIME · PYRÉNÉES · GARONNE · Dordogne · Charente

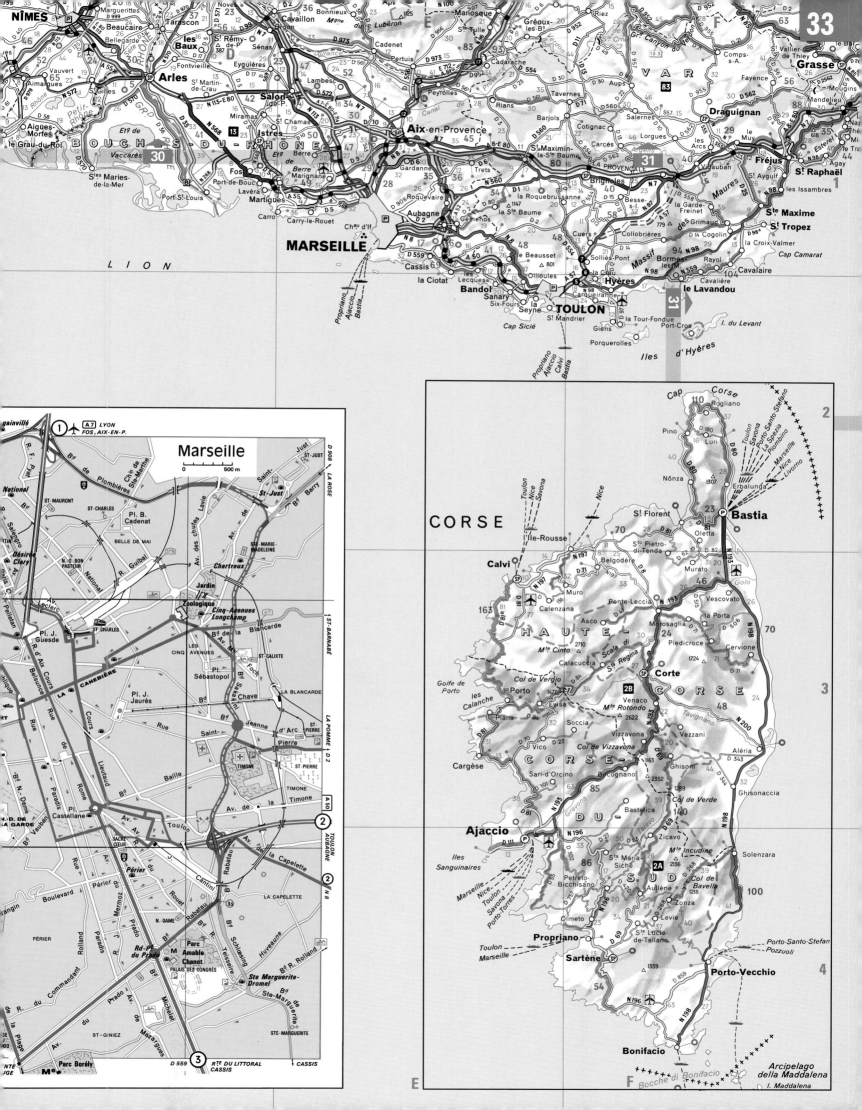

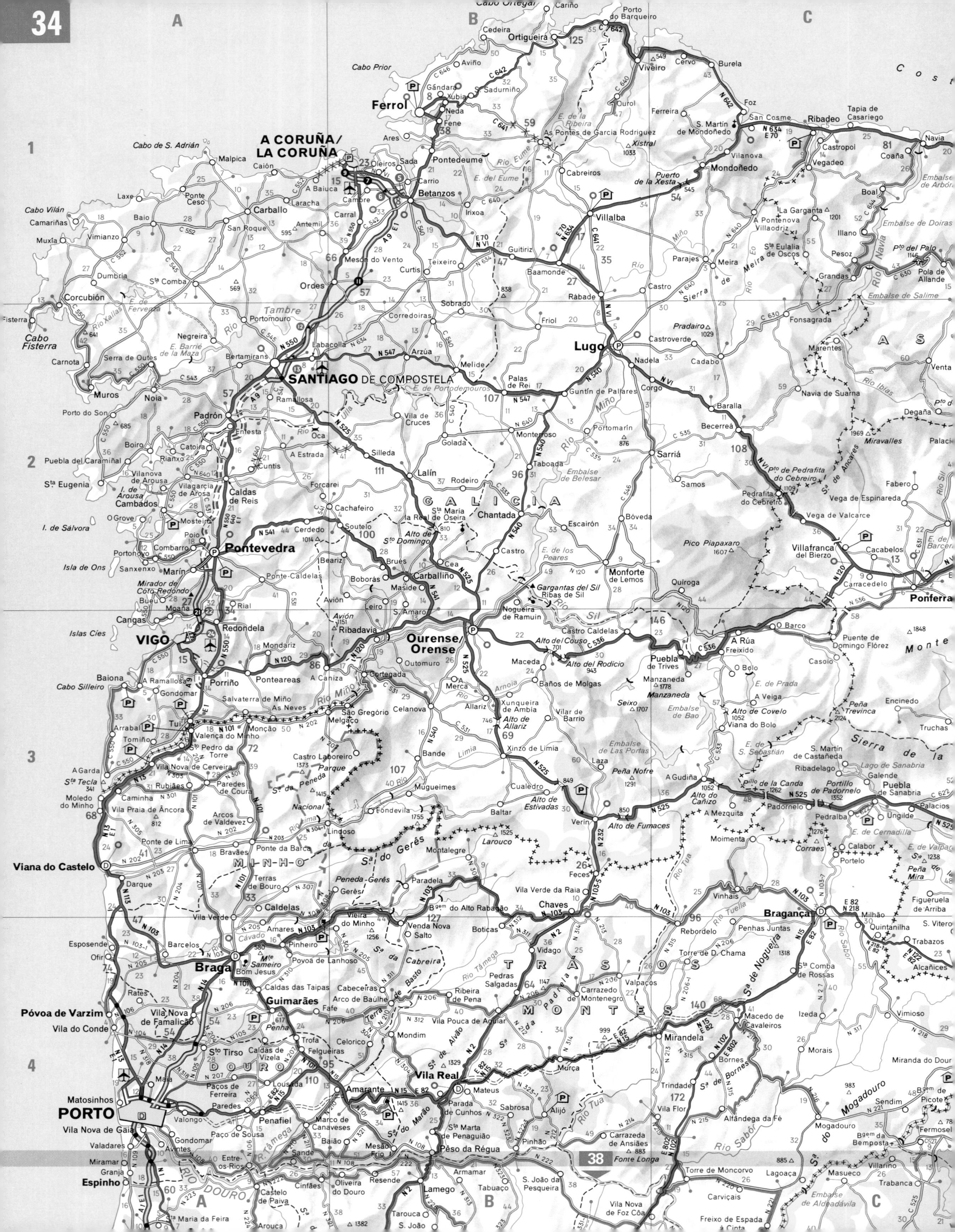
A
B
C
1
2
3
4
Cabo Ortegal
Cariño
Porto do Barqueiro
Cedeira
Ortigueira
Viveiro
Cervo
Burela
Cabo Prior
Aviño
Gándara
Xubia
S. Sadurniño
Ferrol
Neda
Fene
Ourol
Ferreira
Foz
San Cosme
Ribadeo
Tapia de Casariego
S. Martín de Mondoñedo
A CORUÑA/ LA CORUÑA
Cabo de S. Adrián
Malpica
Caión
Ares
Pontedeume
Sada
Oleiros
As Pontes de Garcia Rodriguez
Xistral
Vilanova
Mondoñedo
Castropol
Vegadeo
Navia
Coaña
Embalse de Arbón
Cabo Vilán
Camariñas
Laxe
Ponte Ceso
Laracha
A Baiuca
Cambre
Carrio
Betanzos
Irixoa
Cabreiros
Puerto de la Xesta
Boal
Embalse de Doiras
Baio
Carballo
Carral
Villalba
A Pontenova
Villaodriz
La Garganta
Illano
Muxía
Vimianzo
San Roque
Antemil
Mesón do Vento
Guitiriz
Teixeiro
Curtis
Baamonde
Parajes
Meira
Sta Eulalia de Oscos
Pesoz
Pto del Palo
Pola de Allande
Dumbría
Sta Comba
Ordes
Grandas
Embalse de Salime
Corcubión
Fisterra
Cabo Fisterra
E. de Fervenza
Río Xallas
Tambre
Portomouro
Sobrado
Corredoiras
Rábade
Castro
Friol
Sierra de Meira
Pradairo
Fonsagrada
Carnota
Negreira
E. Barrié de la Maza
Bertamirans
Labacolla
Arzúa
Melide
Lugo
Castroverde
Nadela
Cadabo
Marentes
Serra de Outes
SANTIAGO DE COMPOSTELA
E. de Portodemouros
Palas de Rei
Guntín de Pallares
Corgo
Navia de Suarna
Venta
Muros
Noia
Ramallosa
Baralla
Río Ibias
Porto do Son
Padrón
Vila de Cruces
Monterroso
Portomarín
Becerreá
Degaña
Enfesta
Oca
Golada
Rio Miño
Miravalles
Palacio
Boiro
Catoira
A Estrada
Silleda
Sarriá
Puebla del Caramiñal
Rianxo
Cuntis
Taboada
Pto de Pedrafita do Cebreiro
Sa de Ancares
Vilanova de Arousa
Vilagarcía de Arosa
Lalín
Rodeiro
Embalse de Belesar
Samos
Fabero
Sta Eugenia
I. de Arousa
Cambados
Caldas de Reis
Forcarei
Pedrafita do Cebreiro
Vega de Espinareda
O Grove
Mosteiro
Cachafeiro
GALICIA
Sta Maria la Real de Oseira
Chantada
Bóveda
Vega de Valcarce
I. de Sálvora
Poio
Cerdedo
Soutelo
Alto de Sto Domingo
Escairón
Pico Piapaxaro
Combarro
Pontevedra
Portonovo
Sanxenxo
Beariz
Brués
Cea
Castro
E. de los Peares
Monforte de Lemos
Villafranca del Bierzo
Cacabelos
Isla de Ons
Marín
Ponte-Caldelas
Boborás
Carballiño
Gargantas del Sil
Ribas de Sil
Quiroga
Carracedelo
Mirador de Coto Redondo
Maside
Ponferrada
Bueu
Moaña
Rial
Avión
Leiro
S. Amaro
Nogueira de Ramuin
Cangas
Redondela
Ribadavia
Castro Caldelas
O Barco
Islas Cíes
VIGO
Mondariz
Ourense/ Orense
Alto del Couso
A Rúa
Puente de Domingo Flórez
Monte
Outomuro
Maceda
Alto del Rodicio
Puebla de Trives
Freixido
Casoio
Baiona
A Ramallosa
Porriño
Ponteareas
A Cañiza
Cortegada
Manzaneda
O Bolo
Cabo Silleiro
Gondomar
A Merca
Baños de Molgas
E. de Prada
A Veiga
Salvaterra de Miño
As Neves
Allariz
Xunqueira de Ambía
Vilar de Barrio
Seixo
Embalse de Bao
Alto de Covelo
Peña Trevinca
Encinedo
Arrabal
Tui
São Gregório
Melgaço
Celanova
Alto de Allariz
Viana do Bolo
Tomiño
Valença do Minho
Monção
Truchas
Sto Pedro da Torre
Castro Laboreiro
Bande
Xinzo de Limia
Embalse de Las Portas
E. de S. Sebastián
S. Martín de Castañeda
Sierra de la
A Garda
Vila Nova de Cerveira
Parque Nacional
Limia
Laza
Peña Nofre
Ribadelago
Lago de Sanabria
Sta Tecla
Rubiães
Paredes de Coura
Sa da Peneda
Mugueimes
Cualedro
A Gudiña
Pto de la Canda
Portillo de Padornelo
Galende
Puebla de Sanabria
Moledo do Minho
Caminha
Vila Praia de Âncora
Arcos de Valdevez
Fondevila
Alto de Estivadas
Baltar
Alto del Cañizo
Padornelo
Pedralba
Ungilde
Palacios
Verín
Alto de Fumaces
A Mezquita
E. de Cernadilla
Lindoso
Larouco
Moimenta
Corraes
Calabor
Ponte de Lima
Bravães
Ponte da Barca
Montalegre
Sa do Gerês
Portelo
E. de Valpaço
Peña Mira
Viana do Castelo
MINHO
Feces
Darque
Terras de Bouro
Peneda-Gerês
Paradela
Gerês
Vila Verde da Raia
Vinhais
Figueruela de Arriba
Caldelas
Bgem do Alto Rabagão
Chaves
Bragança
Milhão
Vila Verde
Vieira do Minho
Venda Nova
Rebordelo
Quintanilha
S. Vitero
Esposende
Amares
Salto
Boticas
Penhas Juntas
Trabazos
Ofir
Barcelos
Pinheiro
Sa da Cabreira
Vidago
Torre de D. Chama
Braga
Mte Sameiro
Bom Jesus
Póvoa de Lanhoso
TRÁS-OS-MONTES
Sa de Nogueira
Alcañices
Rates
Caldas das Taipas
Cabeceiras de Basto
Pedras Salgadas
Carrazedo de Montenegro
Valpaços
Sta Comba de Rossas
Póvoa de Varzim
Vila Nova de Famalicão
Guimarães
Arco de Baúlhe
Ribeira de Pena
Fafe
Vila do Conde
Penha
Vila Pouca de Aguiar
Mondim
Macedo de Cavaleiros
Izeda
Vimioso
Mirandela
Sto Tirso
Trofa
Caldas de Vizela
Felgueiras
Celorico
Sa de Alvão
Morais
DOURO
Maia
Paços de Ferreira
Lousada
Amarante
Vila Real
Murça
Bornes
Sa de Bornes
Miranda do Douro
Matosinhos
PORTO
Valongo
Paredes
Penafiel
Mateus
Trindade
Sendim
Bgem de Picote
Vila Nova de Gaia
Gondomar
Paço de Sousa
Marco de Canaveses
Sa do Marão
Parada de Cunhos
Sabrosa
Alijó
Vila Flor
Alfândega da Fé
Mogadouro
Sa do Mogadouro
Valadares
Avintes
Baião
Sta Marta de Penaguião
Pinhão
Carrazeda de Ansiães
Bgem da Bemposta
Fermoselle
Miramar
Granja
Espinho
Entre-os-Rios
Sande
Mesão Frio
Pêso da Régua
Fonte Longa
38
R. Tâmega
Rio Sabor
Villarino
Cinfães
Oliveira do Douro
Resende
Armamar
Lamego
S. João da Pesqueira
Torre de Moncorvo
Lagoaça
Masueco
Trabanca
Castelo de Paiva
Tabuaço
Carviçais
Vila Nova de Foz Côa
Embalse de Aldeadávila
Sta Maria da Feira
Arouca
Tarouca
S. João
Freixo de Espada à Cinta
Rio Douro

## Major cities and places

**SANTANDER** C. de Ajo
**BILBAO**
**Baracaldo**
**BIARRITZ**
St Jean-de-Luz
Hendaye
**DONOSTIA-S. SEBASTIÁN**
**VITORIA-GASTEIZ**
**PAMPLONA**
**BURGOS**
**Logroño**
**Soria**
**Tudela**
**Calatayud**
**Tarazona**

### Regions
GOLFO DE VIZ(CAYA)
Costa Vasca
PAÍS VASCO
EUSKADI
LA RIOJA
NAVARRA
Sierra de la Demanda
Peñas de Cervera
GUADARRAMA

### Selected place names

Torrelavega, Vargas, Puente Viesgo, Corvera de Toranzo, Ontaneda, Alceda, Villacarriedo, Solares, Liérganes, Arredondo, Ramales de la Victoria, Colindres, Ampuero, El Puente, Laredo, Castro Urdiales, Algorta, Portugalete, Santurtzi, Las Arenas, Plentzia, Bakio, Bermeo, Cabo Machichaco, Mungia, Gernika-Lumo, Lekeitio, Ondárroa, Zumaia, Deba, Markina, Alzola, Eibar, Elgóibar, Zestoa, Azkoitia, Azpeitia, Lasarte, Hernani, Andoain, Villabona, Tolosa, Ordizia, Beasain, Zarautz, Pasaia-Pasajes, Irun, Behobia, Oyarzun, Hondarribia, Fuenterrabia, Vera de Bidasoa, Ainhoa, Espelette, Cambo-les-Bains, Ustaritz, Anglet, Bayonne, Capbreton, Tarnos, St Pée, Biriatou

Arenadillo, Arnedo, El Villar de Arnedo, Calahorra, Alfaro, Castejón, Arguedas, Valtierra, Corella, Cintruénigo, Fitero, Cervera del Río Alhama, Ágreda, Tarazona, Borja, Magallón, Gallur, Luceni, Cortes, Mallén

Aranda de Duero, Peñaranda de Duero, Langa de Duero, El Burgo de Osma, San Esteban de Gormaz, Berlanga de Duero, Almazán, Medinaceli, Sigüenza, Atienza, Ayllón, Riaza, Sepúlveda, Boceguillas, Cantalejo, Pedraza de la Sierra, Prádena, Buitrago del Lozoya

Briviesca, Monasterio de Rodilla, Belorado, Sto Domingo de la Calzada, Nájera, Navarrete, Fuenmayor, Cenicero, Haro, Laguardia, Oyón, Los Arcos, Viana, Estella, Puente la Reina, Tafalla, Olite, Falces, Peralta, Marcilla, Caparroso

Miranda de Ebro, Zambrana, Labastida, Pancorbo, Oña, Frías, Trespaderne, Medina de Pomar, Villarcayo, Espinosa de los Monteros, Cilleruelo de Bezana, Soncillo

Covarrubias, Lerma, Salas de los Infantes, Barbadillo del Mercado, Canales de la Sierra, Neila, Vinuesa, Navaleno, S. Leonardo de Yagüe, Abejar, Calatañazor, Numancia, Garray

A    B    C

34

42

**Espinho**
**Aveiro**
**Viseu**
**Guarda**
**COIMBRA**
**Figueira da Foz**
**Covilhã**
**Leiria**
**Batalha**
**Nazaré**
**Fátima**
**Tomar**
**Castelo Branco**
**Santarém**
**Portalegre**
**Torres Vedras**
**Sintra**
**Estoril**
**LISBOA**
**Setúbal**
**Évora**
**Elvas**

RIO DOURO
RIO TEJO
RIO TEJO
RIO SADO
RIO GUADIANA

PORTUGAL

SERRA DA ESTRELA

BEIRA LITORAL
BEIRA ALTA
BEIRA BAIXA

Peso da Régua · Armamar · S. João da Pesqueira · Penedono
Lamego · Tabuaço · Moimenta da Beira · Sernancelhe
Tarouca · S. João de Tarouca · Castro Daire · Vila Nova de Paiva
Aguiar da Beira · Trancoso · Vila Franca das Naves
Celorico da Beira · Fornos de Algodres · Penalva do Castelo
Mangualde · Nelas · Seia · Manteigas · Valhelhas · Gouveia
Tondela · Canas de Senhorim · Carregal do Sal · Oliveira do Hospital
S. Romão · Loriga · Penhas da Saúde · Belmonte · Caria
Covilhã · Tortosendo · Fundão · Paul · Silvares · Alpedrinha
S. Vicente da Beira · Vale de Prazeres · Sarzedas · Alcains
Escalos de Cima · Idanha a Nova · Rosmaninhal · Malpica

Espinho · Ovar · Estarreja · Aveiro · Ílhavo · Vagos · Águeda
Oliveira do Bairro · Anadia · Mealhada · Luso · Buçaco
Cantanhede · Mira · Coimbra · Condeixa-a-Nova · Soure · Penela
Lousã · Góis · Arganil · Miranda do Corvo · Pombal
Figueira da Foz · Montemor-o-Velho · Pedrógão Grande · Sertã
Oleiros · Proença-a-Nova · Vila de Rei · Mação · Abrantes
Gavião · Nisa · Alpalhão · Castelo de Vide · Marvão · Valencia de Alcántara

Leiria · Marinha Grande · S. Pedro de Moel · Batalha · Nazaré
Alcobaça · Caldas da Rainha · Óbidos · Peniche · Bombarral
Fátima · Ourém · Tomar · Torres Novas · Entroncamento
Golegã · Chamusca · Almeirim · Santarém · Cartaxo · Rio Maior
Torres Vedras · Mafra · Ericeira · Sintra · Cascais · Estoril
Lisboa · Amadora · Loures · Alverca · Vila Franca de Xira
Setúbal · Almada · Barreiro · Montijo · Palmela · Sesimbra
Évora · Estremoz · Borba · Vila Viçosa · Elvas · Campo Maior
Portalegre · Crato · Flor da Rosa · Alter do Chão · Monforte
Arronches · Fronteira · Sousel · Redondo · Vendas Novas
Montemor-o-Novo · Arraiolos · Ponte de Sor · Avis · Coruche

Cabo Mondego · Cabo Carvoeiro · Cabo da Roca · Cabo Raso · Cabo Espichel
Praia de Mira · Praia de Tocha · Praia da Vieira · S. Martinho do Porto
Ilha Berlenga · Ilha da Baleal · Foz do Arelho · Peniche
Costa da Caparica · Península de Tróia · Comporta · Alcácer do Sal

A    B    C

1

2

Sesimbra
Península de Tróia
Comporta
Casa Branca
Melides
Costa de Sto André
Cidade Nova de Sto André
Santiago do Cacém
Sines
Cabo de Sines
Abela
Ermidas-Aldeia
Alvalade
S. Domingos
Tanganheira
Bgem de Campilhas
Cercal
Vila Nova de Milfontes
Sta Luzia
S. Martinho das Amoreiras
Garvão
Odemira
S. Teotónio
Sta Clara-a-Velha
Sabóia
Bgem de Sta Clara
Odeceixe
Aljezur
Monchique
Serra de Monchique
Alfambra
Bordeira
Porto de Lagos
Silves
S. Marcos da Serra
S. Bartolomeu de Messines
Vila do Bispo
Lagos
Alvor
Portimão
Praia da Rocha
Sagres
Carvoeiro
Armação de Pêra
Albufeira
Lagoa
Alcantarilha
Ferreiras
Paderne
Boliqueime
Quarteira
Almancil

Alcácer do Sal
Alcáçovas
S. Cristóvão
Bgem de Pego do Altar
Aguiar
S. Manços
Montoito
Monsaraz
Reguengos de Monsaraz
São Marcos do Campo
Mourão
Cheles
Alconchel
Torrão
Viana do Alentejo
Portel
Sta Margarida do Sádão
Odivelas
Bgem de Odivelas
Alvito
Bgem do Alvito
Vidigueira
Alqueva
Bgem de Alqueva
Cuba
Azinheira dos Barros
Beringel
S. Matias
Pedrógão
Moura
Ferreira do Alentejo
Beja
Brinches
Pias
Safara
Ervidel
Baleizão
Serpa
Aljustrel
Albernoa
Vale de Açor
Rib.ª de Terges
Aldeia Nova de S. Bento
Vila Verde de Ficalho
Rosal de la Frontera
Aroche
Castro Verde
Ourique
Alcaria Ruiva
Mina de S. Domingos
Mértola
S. João dos Caldeireiros
Almodôvar
Santana da Serra
Ameixial
Martim Longo
Alcoutim
Sanlúcar de Guadiana
Cachopo
Odeleite
Peralva
Barranco Velho
Alcaria do Cume
Loulé
S. Brás de Alportel
Sta Catarina
Cacela
Castro Marim
Vila Real de Sto António
Tavira
Estói
Moncarapacho
Albergaria
Fuseta
Faro
Olhão
Cabo de Sta Maria

Salvaterra de los Barros
Higuera de Vargas
Valle de Matamoros
Jerez de los Caballeros
Oliva de la Frontera
Zahinos
Rio Ardila
S. Cristóbal
Barcarrota
Villanueva del Fresno
Granja
Amareleja
Barrancos
Encinasola
Sobral da Adiça
Aroche
Cortegana
Almonaster la Real
Galaroza
Aracena
Cabezo Gordo
Sta Bárbara
S. Telmo
El Cerro de Andévalo
Paymogo
Cabezas Rubias
Puebla de Guzmán
Tharsis
Calañas
Zalamea la Real
Minas de Riotinto
Embalse del Chanza
El Almendro
Alosno
Villanueva de los Castillejos
Villablanca
Ayamonte
Isla Cristina
La Antillas
Huelva
El Rompido
Cartaya
Lepe
Punta Umbría
S. Juan del Puerto
Moguer
Palos de la Frontera
La Rábida
Rociana del Condado
Gibraleón
Beas
Trigueros
Niebla
Bonares
Mazagón

GOLFO DE CÁDIZ

Torre de la Higuera

---

3

ILHA DE PORTO SANTO
Porto Santo

ARQUIPÉLAGO DA MADEIRA

Porto Moniz
Santana
Pico Ruivo
Funchal
Desertas

ILHA DA MADEIRA   1/2 750 000

---

4

1/2 750 000

OCEANO ATLÂNTICO

ISLAS CANARIAS

LANZAROTE
Haria
Teguise
Parque Nacional de Timanfaya
Arrecife
Playa Blanca
Corralejo

FUERTEVENTURA
La Oliva
Puerto del Rosario
Betancuria
Pájara
Tuineje
Gran Tarajal
Punta de Jandía

Cádiz

Barlovento
Los Sauces
Puntagorda
Parque Nacional de la Caldera de Taburiente
Los Llanos de Aridane
Sta Cruz de la Palma
Fuencaliente
LA PALMA

TENERIFE
La Laguna
Puerto de la Cruz
Icod de los Vinos
La Orotava
Güímar
Sta Cruz de Tenerife
Teide
Parque Nacional del Teide
Guía de Isora
Granadilla de Abona
Los Cristianos

Vallehermoso
Hermigua
Garajonay (Parque Nacional)
S. Sebastián
GOMERA

Gáldar
Arucas
S. Nicolás de Tolentino
Cruz de Tejeda
LAS PALMAS DE GRAN CANARIA
Telde
Maspalomas
GRAN CANARIA

HIERRO
Valverde
Frontera
Puerto de la Estaca

Cap Juby
Tarfaya

AFRIQUE

A    B    C

A    B    C

1

2

3

4

**Hamburg**

0        3 km

**Bremen**

0    2 km

LANGENHORN
SCHNELSEN
FUHLSBÜTTEL
NIENDORF
EIDELSTEDT
HAMBURG NORDWEST
LURUP
TIERPARK HAGENBECK
STELLINGEN
EPPENDORF
WINTERHUDE BARMBEK
STADTPARK
OHLSDORF
BRAMFELD
WELLINGSBÜTTEL
ALSTERDORF
BAHRENFELD
ALTONA
OTTENSEN
OTHMARSCHEN
FLOTTBEK
BLANKENESE
WANDSBEK
HAMM
HORNER RAMPE
HÄFEN
ELBBRÜCKE
BILLBROOK
FINKENWERDER
HAMBURG WALTERSHOF
KÖHLBRANDBRÜCKE
WILHELMSBURG
ALTENWERDER
KIRCHDORF
SPADENLAND
MOORFLEET
HARBURG
HARBURGER BERGE
HAMBURG HEIMFELD
NEULAND
HAMBURG STILLHORN
HAMBURG HARBURG

INDUSTRIEHAFEN
GRÖPELINGEN
HAFEN
WOLTMERSHAUSEN
HUCHTING
NEUSTADT
FINDORFF
SCHWACHHAUSEN
BÜRGER PARK
HORN-LEHE
HUCKELRIEDE
HABENHAUSEN
HEMELINGEN

NOORDZEE
NOORDZEE
WADDENEILANDEN
Terschelling
West-Terschelling
Oost-Vlieland
Vlielana
Oosterend
Hollum
Leeuwar
Harlingen
De Koog
Texel
Den Burg
Den Helder
Den Oever
Afsluitdijk
IJsselmeer
Workum
Staveren
Sloten
NOORD-NEDER
HOLLAND
Schagen
Medemblik
Bergen
Bergen aan Zee
Egmond aan Zee
Alkmaar
Hoorn
Enkhuizen
Urk
Markermeer
Beverwijk
Purmerend
Edam
Volendam
Lelystad Haven

50

# DEUTSCHLAND

**Major cities:**
Aschaffenburg · Bamberg · Weiden · Würzburg · Erlangen · Fürth · NÜRNBERG · Amberg · Heilbronn · Ansbach · Ingolstadt · Ludwigsburg · STUTTGART · Schwäbisch Gmünd · Heidenheim · AUGSBURG · MÜNCHEN · Esslingen · Göppingen · Böblingen · Tübingen · Reutlingen · Ulm · Neu-Ulm · Dachau · Memmingen · Landsberg · Kempten · Ravensburg · Friedrichshafen · Konstanz · Lindau · Bregenz · St. Gallen · Dornbirn · Garmisch · Partenkirchen · INNSBRUCK · Seefeld

**Regions:** WÜRTTEMBERG · BAYERN · TIROL

**Water/geography:** Main · Donau · Bodensee · Altmühl · Lech · Iller · Wörnitz · Romantische Straße · Deutsche Alpenstraße · Fränkische Rezat · Ammersee · Staffelsee · Forggensee

**Other places:**
Lohr · Karlstadt · Werneck · Gerolzhofen · Ebrach · Wiesentheid · Schlüsselfeld · Pommersfelden · Forchheim · Gräfenberg · Auerbach · Eschenbach · Kirchenthumbach · Pegnitz · Ebermannstadt · Gössweinstein · Behringersmühle · Kitzingen · Iphofen · Volkach · Höchstadt · Herzogenaurach · Lauf · Hersbruck · Hirschau · Sulzbach-Rosenberg · Wertheim · Freudenberg · Miltenberg · Amorbach · Tauberbischofsheim · Ochsenfurt · Marktbreit · Neustadt an der Aisch · Emskirchen · Langenzenn · Zirndorf · Schwabach · Roth · Feucht · Altdorf · Neumarkt · Velburg · Burglengenfeld · Walldürn · Buchen · Bad Mergentheim · Weikersheim · Niederstetten · Creglingen · Rothenburg ob der Tauber · Uffenheim · Bad Windsheim · Markt Erlbach · Heilsbronn · Windsbach · Abenberg · Hilpoltstein · Berching · Greding · Dietfurt · Beilngries · Riedenburg · Kelheim · Osterburken · Adelsheim · Krautheim · Dörzbach · Schrozberg · Blaufelden · Leutershausen · Herrieden · Feuchtwangen · Gunzenhausen · Pleinfeld · Weißenburg · Ellingen · Treuchtlingen · Pappenheim · Eichstätt · Lenting · Mosbach · Künzelsau · Langenburg · Gerabronn · Crailsheim · Dinkelsbühl · Wassertrüdingen · Oettingen · Wemding · Monheim · Harburg · Donauwörth · Neuburg · Karlshuld · Reichertshofen · Pfaffenhofen · Freising · Moosburg · Neckarsulm · Öhringen · Gaildorf · Schwäbisch Hall · Ellwangen · Bopfingen · Nördlingen · Wallerstein · Kaisheim · Rain · Pöttmes · Aichach · Allershausen · Heilbronn · Weinsberg · Sulzbach · Murrhardt · Backnang · Welzheim · Aalen · Wasseralfingen · Oberkochen · Neresheim · Dillingen · Höchstädt · Wertingen · Meitingen · Gersthofen · Dasing · Friedberg · Odelzhausen · Sulzemoos · Marbach · Winnenden · Waiblingen · Schorndorf · Lorch · Heubach · Steinheim · Giengen · Lauingen · Gundelfingen · Günzburg · Burgau · Zusmarshausen · Göggingen · Mering · Maisach · Fürstenfeldbruck · Germering · Karlsfeld · Sindelfingen · Herrenberg · Nürtingen · Neuffen · Metzingen · Kirchheim u. Teck · Weilheim · Wiesensteig · Merklingen · Laichingen · Blaubeuren · Geislingen · Gerstetten · Herbrechtingen · Niederstotzingen · Langenau · Leipheim · Burgau · Gilching · Gauting · Starnberg · Herrsching · Wolfratshausen · Holzkirchen · Geretsried · Rottenburg · Münsingen · Ehingen · Vöhringen · Illertissen · Weißenhorn · Buchloe · Inning · Utting · Dießen · Rott · Wessobrunn · Weilheim · Tutzing · Feldafing · Bad Wiessee · Bad Tölz · Tuttlingen · Meßkirch · Pfullendorf · Ostrach · Bad Waldsee · Bad Wurzach · Leutkirch · Wolfegg · Marktoberdorf · Kaufbeuren · Obergünzburg · Schongau · Peißenberg · Penzberg · Gmund · Sigmaringen · Riedlingen · Biberach a.d. Riß · Bad Buchau · Ochsenhausen · Berkheim · Heimertingen · Steinheim · Bad Wörishofen · Türkheim · Mindelheim · Thannhausen · Krumbach · Schwabmünchen · Königsbrunn · Bobingen · Babenhausen · Schwendi · Laupheim · Dietenheim · Altenstadt · Weingarten · Ravensburg · Wangen · Isny · Kißlegg · Wolfegg · Dietmannsried · Sonthofen · Hindelang · Oberstdorf · Immenstadt · Pfronten · Füssen · Reutte · Oberammergau · Linderhof · Ettal · Walchensee · Kochel · Lenggries · Mittenwald · Scharnitz · Zugspitze · Telfs · Imst

NÜRNBERG

REGENSBURG

Amberg

Weiden

MÜNCHEN

AUGSBURG

Landshut

Straubing

Deggendorf

Passau

Ingolstadt

Rosenheim

SALZBURG

INNSBRUCK

Garmisch Partenkirchen

Kitzbühel

Bad Reichenhall

Berchtesgaden

Bad Ischl

Gmunden

Zell am See

Badgastein

Domažlice

Klatovy

Strakonice

Prachatice

Bayerisch Eisenstein

Železná Ruda

**BRNO**
**WIEN**
**BRATISLAVA**
**LINZ**
**GRAZ**

České Budějovice · Jihlava · Třebíč · Znojmo · Brno · Vyškov · Blansko · Tišnov · Kuřim · Velká Bíteš · Velké Meziříčí · Náměšť · Rosice · Ivančice · Židlochovice · Moravský Krumlov · Moravské Budějovice · Jevišovice · Hrušovany · Drnholec · Mikulov · Břeclav · Hodonín · Holíč · Kúty

Tábor · Pelhřimov · Pacov · Mladá Vožice · Sezimovo-Ústí · Kamenice · Třešť · Telč · Dačice · Jemnice · Slavonice · Nová Bystřice · Jindřichův Hradec · Soběslav · Veselí · Třeboň · Hluboká · Bernartice · Milevsko

Gmünd · České Velenice · Neunagelberg · Schrems · Waidhofen · Heidenreichstein · Litschau · Gramatten · Dobersberg · Drosendorf · Raabs · Gr.-Siegharts · Retz · Hardegg · Geras · Pulkau · Haté · Kleinhaugsdorf · Laa an der Thaya · Jetzelsdorf · Hevlín · Hrádek · Šatov · Drasenhofen · Poysdorf · Hohenau · Wilfersdorf · Zistersdorf · Bernhardsthal · Poštorná

Freistadt · Unterweißenbach · Königswiesen · Arbesbach · Groß Gerungs · Zwettl · Rastenfeld · Gföhl · Langenlois · Krems · Stein · Dürnstein · Spitz · Weißenkirchen · Horn · Eggenburg · Maissau · Ziersdorf · Göllersdorf · Hollabrunn · Ernstbrunn · Stockerau · Korneuburg · Wolkersdorf · Gänserndorf · Angern · Marchegg · Stupava · Malacky · Dürnkrut

Linz · Urfahr · Gallneukirchen · Pregarten · Mauthausen · Enns · Asten · Perg · Grein · Mönchdorf · Laimbach · Pöggstall · Maria Taferl · Melk · Pöchlarn · St. Pölten · Herzogenburg · Traismauer · Tulln · Klosterneuburg · Judenau · St. Christophen · Neulengbach · Pressbaum · Purkersdorf · Mödling · Schwechat · Fischamend Markt · Bruck · Hainburg · Bad Deutsch-Altenburg · Berg · Kittsee · Hegyeshalom · Nickelsdorf · Neusiedl

Steyr · St. Florian · Neuhofen an der Krems · Haag · Aschbach Markt · St. Peter in der Au · Amstetten · Euratsfeld · Wieselburg · Purgstall · Scheibbs · Gresten · Waidhofen · Gaming · Lunz · Göstling · Mariazell · Annaberg · St. Aegyd · Türnitz · Lilienfeld · Traisen · Hainfeld · Kirchberg a.d. Pielach · Wilhelmsburg · Obergrafendorf · Mank · St. Leonhard · Ybbs · Persenbeug

Baden · Mödling · Alland · Mayerling · Bad Vöslau · Pottenstein · Berndorf · Wöllersdorf · Pernitz · Gutenstein · Puchberg · Neunkirchen · Ternitz · Wiener Neustadt · Ebenfurth · Leobersdorf · Sollenau · Traiskirchen · Ebreichsdorf · Mannersdorf · Purbach · Eisenstadt · Rust · Mörbisch · Mattersburg · Klingenbach · Sopron · Pamhagen · Frauenkirchen · Podersdorf

Liezen · Admont · Rottenmann · Trieben · Hohentauern · Donnersbachwald · Oberwölz · St. Michael · Knittelfeld · Zeltweg · Fohnsdorf · Judenburg · Weißkirchen · Scheifling · Neumarkt · Murau · St. Lambrecht · Seckau · Gaal · Kapfenberg · Bruck an der Mur · Leoben · Trofaiach · Vordernberg · Eisenerz · Hieflau · Wildalpen · Mürzzuschlag · Mürzsteg · Krieglach · Langenwang · Kindberg · Semmering · Aspang · Kirchschlag · Friedberg · Pinkafeld · Oberwart · Hartberg · Pöllau · Weiz · Gleisdorf · Graz · Voitsberg · Köflach · Gratkorn · Frohnleiten

Leoben · Donawitz · St. Michael · Kalsdorf · Wildon · Leibnitz · Deutschlandsberg · Wolfsberg · Bad St. Leonhard · Twimberg · Packsattel · Stainz · Feldbach · Fehring · Bad Gleichenberg · Bad Radkersburg · Mureck · Fürstenfeld · Güssing · Moschendorf · Heiligenkreuz · Jennersdorf · Szentgotthárd · Körmend · Szombathely · Kőszeg · Bük · Rechnitz · Lockenhaus · Oberpullendorf · Deutschkreutz · Nagycenk · Fertőszentmiklós · Lövő · Sopron

NIEDERÖSTERREICH · STEIERMARK · BURGENLAND

**60**

Castiglioncello
Maritt.
Solvay
Cecina
S 68
Riparbella
9
35 Val d'Elsa
Monteri
72
S 68
Pomarance
Larderello
Radico
VIA AURELIA
Cecina
Canneto
Metall
1060
Marina di Castagneto-Donoratico
Sassetta
Suvereto
Monterotondo Maritt.
Massa Maritt.
6-1991
S. Vincenzo
Campiglia Maritt.
Venturina
Montioni
S 398
S 1
S 197
Ribolla
Gorgona Bas.
Porto Torres
Palermo

I. di Gorgona

1

I. di Capraia

Piombino
Follonica
Punta Ala
Grosseto

Cap Corse
110 Rogliano
Pino
Luri
D 80
Nònza
1307
St Florent
Toulon
Savona
Porto-Santo-Stefano
La Spezia
Piombino
Marseille
Nice
Livorno
Erbalunga
23 P Bastia
Oletta

Arcipelago

Livorno
Bastia

Portoferraio
Marciana Marina
Cavo
Rio Marina

Castiglione della Pescaia
Marina di Grosseto

CORSE
l'Ile-Rousse
Calvi
N 197
70
D 81
Sto Pietro-di-Tenda
Belgodère
Murato
Murato
N 193
D 515
Vescovato
la Porta
N 198
70
Marina di Campo
Isola d'Elba

Toscano

2

163
D 81
HAUTE-
Asco
Mte Cinto 2710
Calacuccia
Col de Vergio
Porto 1472
les Calanche
Evisa
Piana
D8
Vico
Soccia
Cargèse
Sari-d'Orcino
Scala di
Ste Regina
CORSE
Morosaglia
Piedicroce
Cervione
1724
Corte
SP
2B
Venaco
Mte Rotondo 2622
Vizzavona
Col de Vizzavona
N 193
Vezzani
Tavignano
48
N 200
24
Aléria
D 343
Ghisoni
2352
1289
Ghisonaccia

I. di Gorgona

I. Pianosa

I. di Montecristo

I. d. Giglio
Giglio P

3

CORSE
DU-
Gravona
85
Bocognano
Bastelica
140
Col de Verde
D 69
Zicavo
Mte Incudine 2136
Ajaccio
Iles Sanguinaires
N 196
86
Petreto-Bicchisano
Sta Maria Siché
2A
SUD
Aullène
Col de Bavella 1218
Zonza
100
Solenzara
N 198
Olmeto
Levie
Marseille
Nice
Toulon
Savona
Porto-Torres
Propriano
Toulon
Marseille
Sartène
SP
1339
Sta Lucie-de-Tallano
D 859
Porto-Vecchio
Porto-Santo-Stefano
Pozzuoli

Roma
0        3 km

4

54
N 196
LA
63
N 198

Bonifacio
Bocche di Bonifacio

Arcipelago della Maddalena
I. Maddalena

66

66

Sta Teresa Gallura
S 133
18
La Maddalena
I. Caprera
Palau
Arzachena
Baja Sardinia
Porto Cervo
Costa Smeralda

Isola Asinara
I. Falcone
Stintino
Golfo dell'
Asinara
Porto Torres
Platamona Lido
Sorso
Castelsardo
Sedini
Nulvi
Martis
Trinità d'Agultu e V.
S. Antonio
Aggius
Calangianus
Tempio Pausania
Mte Limbara 1362
Monti
S 127
Luogosanto
S 125
61
Olbia
S 125
Loiri
Telti
Padru
Mte Nieddu
57
121
Toulon
Ajaccio
Genova
Livorno
Arzachena
Porto Rotondo
Golfo Aranci
Civitavecchia
Genova
Livorno
Arbatax
I. Tavolara
Lago del
A                    B

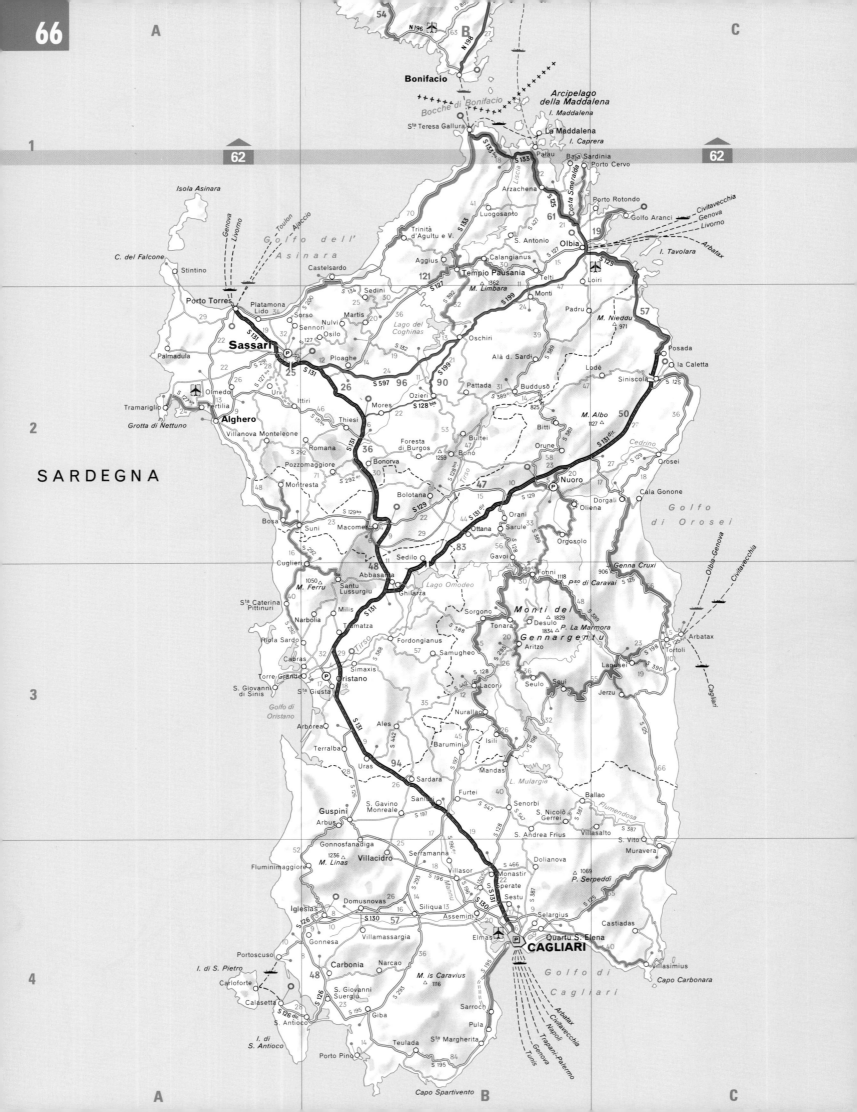

A     B     C

**SICILIA**

*I s o l e*

I. di Ustica

I. Filicudi

I. Alicudi

*M A R E   T I R R E N O*

Cagliari
Genova
Livorno
Napoli

Tunis
Ustica

Capo Gallo
Sferracavallo   Mondello
M. Pellegrino

Punta Raisi   30   A 29   Capaci
S. Vito lo Capo   Torre d. Impiso   Cinisi   S 113   Carini
**PALERMO**
S. Stefano
di Camastra
153

606
Solunto
Cefalù
27

S. 113   Monreale
**Bagheria**
Casteldaccia
Mistretta
26

*Golfo di Castellammare*
63
Misilmeri
Altavilla
Termini
Imerese
S 113
A 20
Collesano
Castelbuono
48

46   S 186
Piana
d. Albanesi
S 121
Trabia
A 19
Pto. Carbonara
△1979
C. del Contrasto
1107
Femm

Castellammare
d. Golfo
22
**Partinico**
30
Marineo
Caccamo
Buonfornello
Montemaggiore
Belsito
S 120
Petralia
Gangi
S 120

Trapani   Erice
S 187   34
Alcamo
16
S. Cipirello
58
Villafrati
S 285
Caltavuturo
M
S 645
Nicosia

I. di
Levanzo
Paceco   Fulgatore
Segesta
S 119
R.ca Busambra
△1613
Roccapalumba
50
Alia
126
66
Leonforte
S 117

**Isole Egadi**
42   A 29   50
Calatafimi
24
Corleone
Lercara
Friddi
Resuttano
56
S 117

I. Maréttimo   I. Favignana
Birgi
50
41   A 29
Salemi
S 119
57
Prizzi
S 188
126
S 121
S.ta Caterina
Villarmosa
**Enna**
Valg
Car

38   S 115
Ninfa
Partanna
S.ta Margherita
di Belice
Chiusa Sclafani
Alessandria
d. Rocca
Mussomeli
**Caltanissetta**
35
Aido

**Marsala**
S 188
Sambuca
di Sicilia
Castelfermini
S. Cataldo
Pietraperzia
**Piazza Arme**

**Castelvetrano**
22   A 29   24
Menfi
Caltabellotta
S. Biagio Platani
Montedoro
Serradifalco
Barrafranca

Mazara d. Vallo
Campobello
di Mazara
Selinunte   Marinella
93
Ribera
Aragona
58
Delia
Sommatino
Mazzarino
S 117

**Sciacca**
Raffadali
S 640
**Canicatti**
Riesi
S 190

**Agrigento**
Favara
Naro
Campobello
di Licata
Ravanusa
81
Nis

Porto Empedocle
Palma
di Montechiaro
72
Butera

*M A R E*
Licata
34
**Gela**

**A**

Trapani

Pantelleria   Tracino
836

*I. di Pantelleria*

I. di Linosa

*I s o l e
P e l a g i e*

Porto Empedocle
I. di Lampedusa
Lampedusa

**B**

*Gozo*
Victoria   Nadur
Mgarr   *Comino*
Mellieha
Siracusa
Mosta   Sliema
Rabat   **Valletta**
Dingli   Vittoriosa
249   Zejtun
**MALTA**   Zurrieq   Birzebugga
*Filfola*

A     B     C

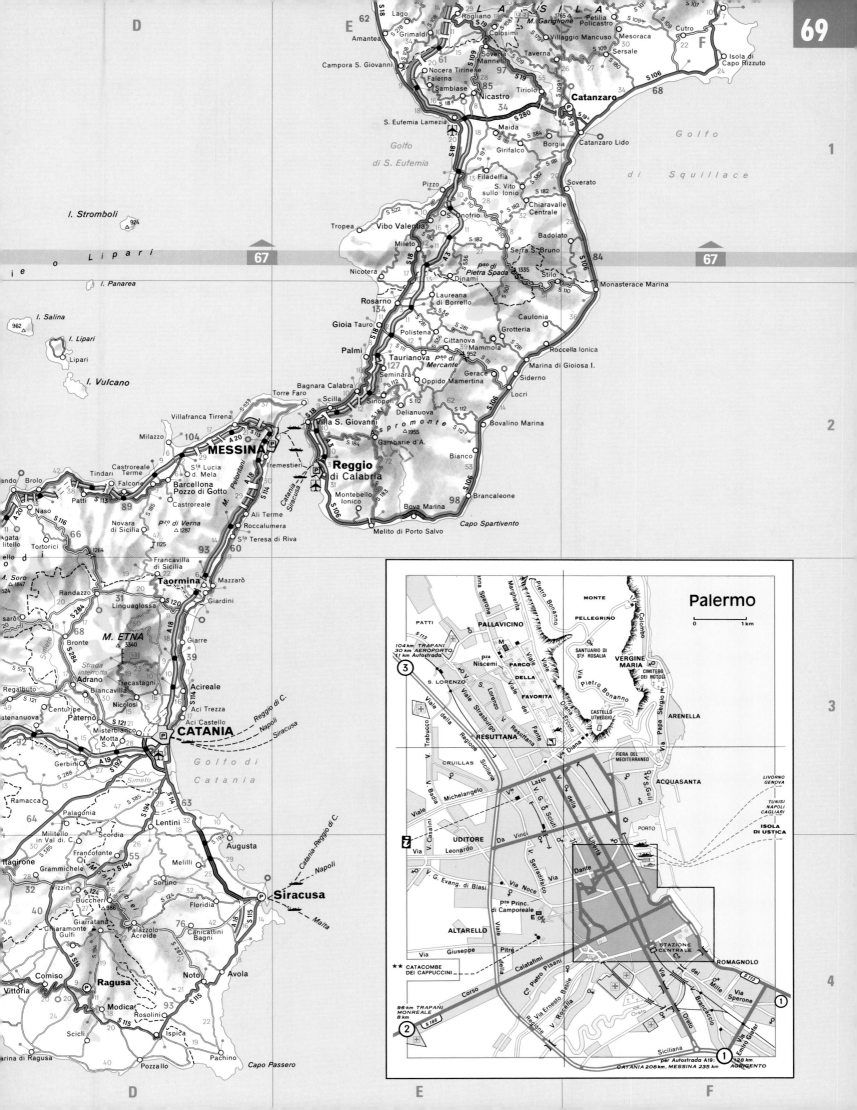

## Map labels (main map — Calabria / Sicily)

D · E · 62 · F

**Calabria region:**
Lago · Rogliano · M. Ganghione · Petilia Policastro · S107
Amantea · Grimaldi · Colosimi · Villaggio Mancuso · Mesoraca · Cutro
Campora S. Giovanni · Nocera Tirinese · Soveria Mannelli · Taverna · S109 · Sersale · Isola di Capo Rizzuto
Falerna · Sambiase · Tiriolo · **Catanzaro**
Nicastro · S280 · S19
S. Eufemia Lamezia · Maida
*Golfo di S. Eufemia* · Girifalco · Borgia · Catanzaro Lido · *Golfo di Squillace*
Pizzo · Filadelfia · S. Vito sullo Ionio · Soverato
Tropea · Vibo Valentia · S. Onofrio · Chiaravalle Centrale
Mileto · Badolato
Nicotera · P.zo di Pietra Spada · Serra S. Bruno · Stilo · Monasterace Marina
Dinami · S110
Rosarno · Laureana di Borrello · Caulonia
Gioia Tauro · Polistena · Grotteria
Palmi · Cittanova · Mammola · Roccella Ionica
Taurianova · P.zo di Mercante · Gerace · Marina di Gioiosa I.
Seminara · Oppido Mamertina · Siderno
Bagnara Calabra · Delianuova · Locri
Torre Faro · Scilla · Sinopoli
Villa S. Giovanni · Aspromonte
Gambarie d'A.
**Reggio di Calabria** · Bianco
Montebello Ionico · Brancaleone
Bova Marina · *Capo Spartivento*
Melito di Porto Salvo

**Sicily region:**
I. Stromboli · I. Panarea · Lipari · I. Salina · I. Lipari · Lipari · I. Vulcano
Brolo · Milazzo · Villafranca Tirrena · **MESSINA**
Patti · Tindari · Castroreale Terme · Falcone · Barcellona Pozzo di Gotto · S.ta Lucia d. Mela · Castroreale
Naso · Novara di Sicilia · P.zo di Verna · Tremestieri
Tortorici · Francavilla di Sicilia · Alì Terme · Roccalumera · S.ta Teresa di Riva
M. Soro · Randazzo · **Taormina** · Mazzarò · Giardini
Linguaglossa · S120
Bronte · **M. ETNA** · Giarre
Adrano · Trecastagni · Acireale
Biancavilla · Nicolosi · Aci Trezza · Aci Castello
Regalbuto · Paternò · Misterbianco · **CATANIA** · Reggio di C. / Napoli / Siracusa
Centuripe · Motta S.A. · Gerbini · *Golfo di Catania*
Ramacca · Palagonia · Augusta
Militello in Val di C. · Lentini · Melilli
Grammichele · Scordia · Sortino
Vizzini · Buccheri · Floridia · **Siracusa** · Catania-Reggio di C. / Napoli
Giarratana · Palazzolo Acreide · Canicattini Bagni · Malta
Chiaramonte Gulfi · Noto · Avola
Comiso · **Ragusa** · S115
Vittoria · Modica · Rosolini
Scicli · Ispica · Pachino
Marina di Ragusa · Pozzallo · *Capo Passero*

## Palermo (inset map)

**Palermo** · 0 — 1 km
PATTI · PALLAVICINO · MONTE PELLEGRINO · VERGINE MARIA
104 km TRAPANI / 30 km AEROPORTO / 11 km Autostrada
S. Lorenzo · Niscemi · PARCO DELLA FAVORITA · SANTUARIO DI S.TA ROSALIA · CASTELLO UTVEGGIO · CIMITERO DEI ROTOLI · ARENELLA
RESUTTANA
CRUILLAS · FIERA DEL MEDITERRANEO · ACQUASANTA · LIVORNO / GENOVA
Michelangelo · TUNISI / NAPOLI / CAGLIARI
UDITORE · PORTO · ISOLA DI USTICA
ALTARELLO
★★ CATACOMBE DEI CAPPUCCINI
STAZIONE CENTRALE · ROMAGNOLO
96 km TRAPANI / MONREALE 8 km
Via Sperone · S113
2 · 1
Siciliana · per Autostrada A19: CATANIA 208 km, MESSINA 235 km · AGRIGENTO 128 km

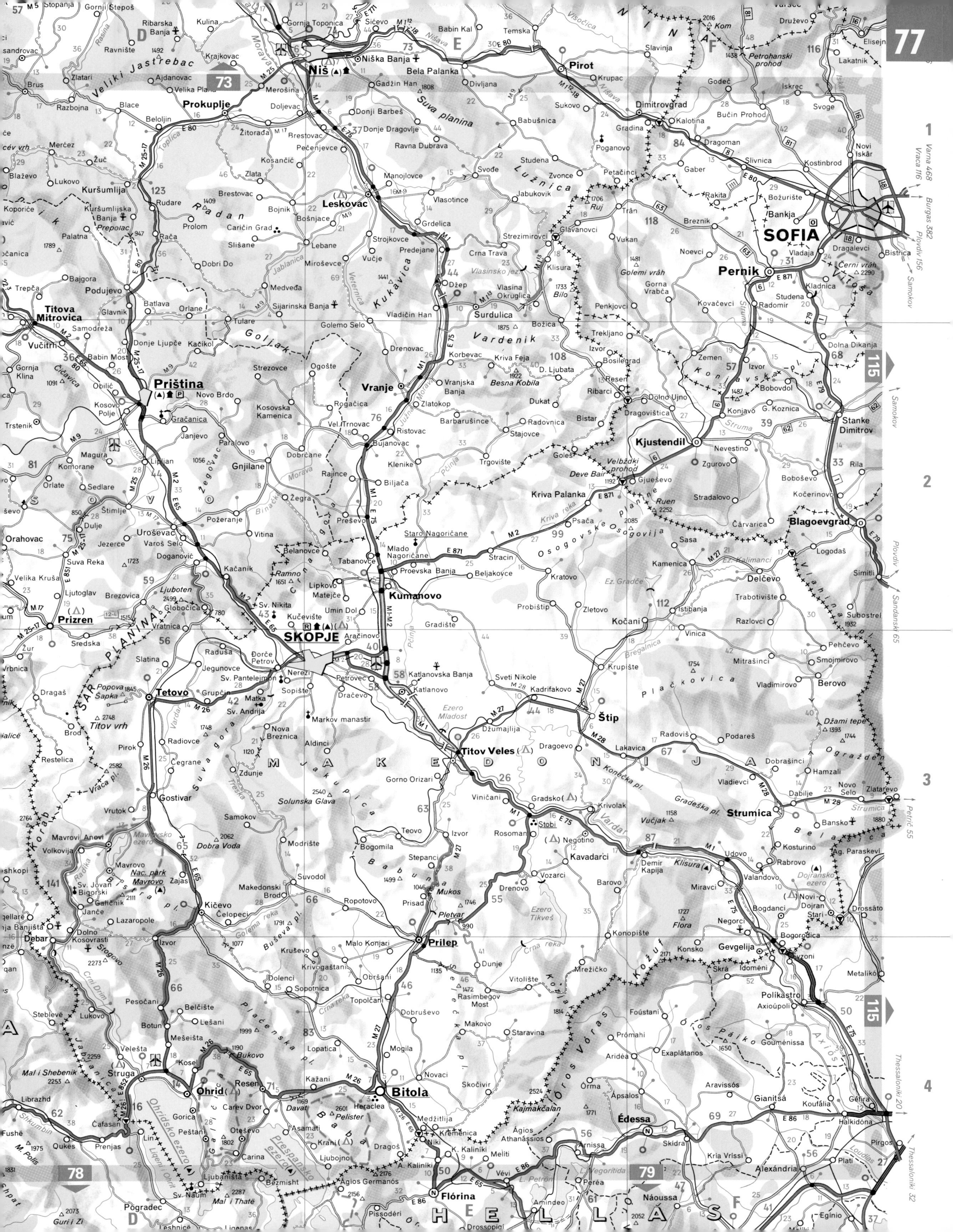

SOFIA
Pernik
Pirot
Dimitrovgrad
Kjustendil
Blagoevgrad
Niš
Niška Banja
Bela Palanka
Leskovac
Prokuplje
Titova Mitrovica
Priština
Vranje
Kriva Palanka
Kumanovo
SKOPJE
Tetovo
Gostivar
Prizren
Debar
Ohrid
Struga
Bitola
Štip
Strumica
Delčevo
Berovo
Titov Veles
Prilep
Kavadarci
Gevgelija
Kočani
Probištip
Radoviš
Flórina
Édessa
Náoussa
Polikástro
Goménissa
Aridéa
Halkidóna

MAKEDONIJA
HELLAS

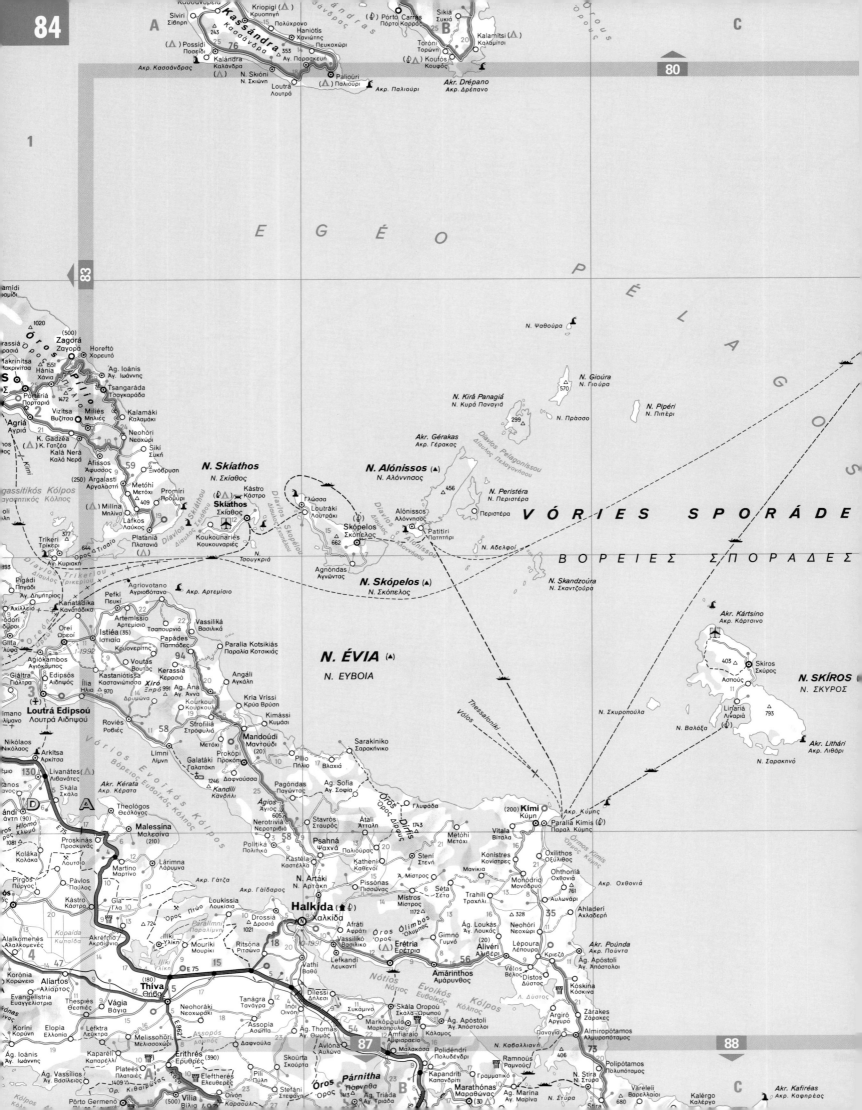

### N. LÍMNOS (▲)
Ν. ΛΗΜΝΟΣ

Mirina
Μύρινα

Akr. Moúrdzeflos
Ακρ. Μούρτζεφλος

Katálako
Κατάλακκο

Atsiki
Ατσική

Panagia
Παναγία

Ifestia
Ηφαιστία

Kondopoúli
Κοντοπούλι

Dáfni
Δάφνη

Kondiás
Κοντιάς

Livadohóri
Λιβαδοχώρι

Moúdros
Μούδρος

Kaminia
Καμίνια

Polióhni
Πολιόχνη

Fissini
Φίσινη

Skandáli
Σκανδάλι

Akr. Ag. Irinis
Ακρ. Αγ. Ειρήνης

Akr. Kalamáki
Ακρ. Καλαμάκι

Áy. Evstrátios

N. Ág. Efstrátios
Ν. Άγ. Εύστράτιος

Akr. Tripití
Ακρ. Τρυπιτή

Thessaloniki

Kumkale
Intepe
Truva
Kumkale
Yiğitler
Bozcaada
Geyikli
Ezíne
Bayramiç
Firanlı
Ayvacık
Gülpınar
Behramkale
Baba Br.

### N. LÉSVOS (▲)
Ν. ΛΕΣΒΟΣ

Míthimna
Μήθυμνα

Akr. Mólivos
Ακρ. Μόλυβος

Sikaminiá
Συκαμινιά

Pétra
Πέτρα

Mandamádos
Μανταμάδος

Skoutáros
Σκουτάρος

Stipsi
Στύψη

Fília
Φίλια

Ándissa
Άντισσα

Skalahóri
Σκαλοχώρι

Ag. Paraskeví
Αγ. Παρασκευή

Kaloní
Καλλονή

Mistegná
Thermí
Θερμή

Sigri
Σίγρι

Batoússa

Parákila
Παράκοιλα

Pámfila
Πάμφυλα

Eressós
Ερεσός

Ágra

Lámbou Mili
Λάμπου Μύλοι

Mória

Skála Eressoú
Σκάλα Έρεσού

Messótopos
Μεσότοπος

Vassiliká
Βασιλικά

Keramiá
Κεραμία

Mitilíni
Μυτιλήνη

Skála
Σκάλα

Agiássos
Αγιάσος

Neápoli

Polihnitos
Πολιχνίτος

Ambelikó
Αμπελικό

Papádos
Παππάδος

Loutrá
Λουτρά

Vrissa
Βρίσα

Skópelos
Σκόπελος

Pérama
Πέραμα

Krátigos
Κράτηγος

Vaterá
Βατερά

Paleohóri
Παλαιοχώρι

Akr. Ag. Fokás
Ακρ. Αγ. Φωκάς

Plomári
Πλωμάρι

Akr. Agriliá
Ακρ. Αγριλιά

### N. Psará
Ν. Ψαρά

Agiásmata
Αγιάσματα

Kambiá
Καμπιά

Akr. Vamvakás
Ακρ. Βαμβακάς

N. Inoússes
Ν. Οινούσσες

Karaburun

Melaniós
Μελανιός

Kéramos
Κέραμος

Pelinéo
Πελιναίο

Mármaro
Μάρμαρο

Küçükbahçe

Psará
Ψαρά

N. Andipsara
Ν. Αντίψαρα

Volissós
Βολισσός

Kardámila
Καρδάμυλα

Inoússes
Οινούσσες

N. Passás
Ν. Πασάς

Mordoğan

### N. HÍOS (▲)
Ν. ΧΙΟΣ

Skála Volissoú
Σκάλα Βολισσού

Pityoús
Πιτυούς

Langáda
Λαγκάδα

Sidiroúnta
Σιδηρούντα

Marathóvounos
Μαραθόβουνος

Anávatos
Ανάβατος

Vrondádos
Βροντάδος

Kara Adası

Néa Moní
Νέα Μονή

Híos
Χίος

Lithío
Λιθίο

Halkió
Χαλκειό

Karfás
Καρφάς

Koca Dağ

Tholopotámi
Θολοποτάμι

Kalimassiá
Καλλιμασιά

Çeşme

Véssa
Βέσσα

Passá-Limáni
Πασά-Λιμάνι

Armólia
Αρμόλια

Nénita
Νένητα

Şifne

Mestá
Μεστά

Pirgí
Πυργί

Kalamoti
Καλαμωτή

Alaçatı

Emboriós
Εμπορειός

Kómi
Κώμη

Akr. Mástiho
Ακρ. Μάστιχο

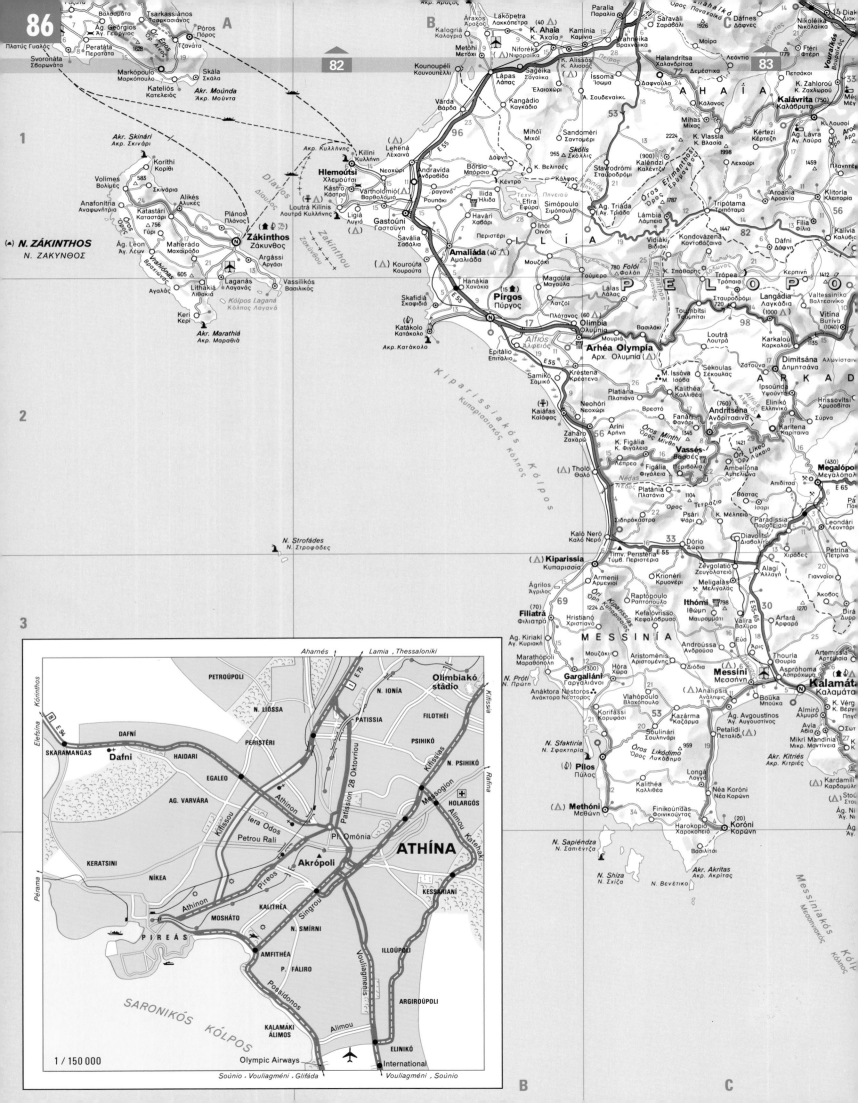

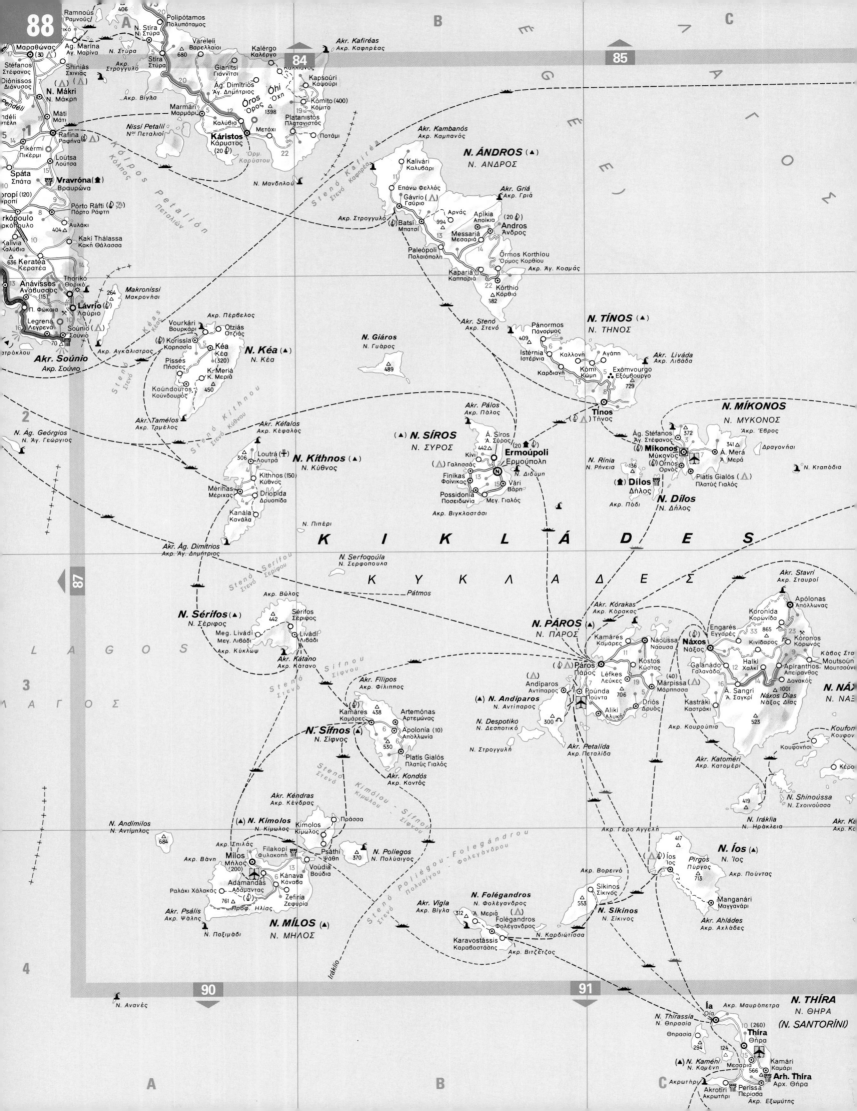

A · 406
Ramnoús
Ραμνούς
N. Stira
N. Στύρα
Polipótamos
Πολυπόταμος

Marathónas
Μαραθώνας (30)
Ag. Marina
Αγ. Μαρίνα
Stira
Στύρα
Varélei
Βαρελαίοι
Kalérgo
Καλέργο
Akr. Kafiréas
Ακρ. Καφηρέας

Stéfanos
Στέφανος
Shiniás
Σχινιάς
680
Gianítsi
Γιανίτσι
Ag. Dimitrios
Αγ. Δημήτριος
Kyklhaioi
Κυκλιαίοι

Diónissos
Διόνυσος
N. Mákri
N. Μάκρη
Óros
Όρος
Óhi
Όχη
Kapsóuri
Καψούρι

Máti
Μάτι
Marmári
Μαρμάρι
Όros Όρος 1398
Kómito (400)
Κόμιτο

Rafína
Ραφήνα
Kalýdia
Καλύδια
Metóhi
Μετόχι
Platanistós
Πλατανιστός

Pikérmi
Πικέρμι
Nissi Petalií
Νησί Πεταλιοί
Káristos
Κάριστος (20)
Akr. Vígla
Ακρ. Βίγλα
Potámi
Ποτάμι

Loútsa
Λούτσα
Όρμ. Καρύστου

Spáta
Σπάτα
Vravróna
Βραυρώνα

Pórto Ráfti
Πόρτο Ράφτη
Akr. Kambanós
Ακρ. Καμπανός

Avláki
Αυλάκι
N. ÁNDROS
N. ΑΝΔΡΟΣ

Kaki Thálassa
Κακή Θάλασσα
Kalivári
Καλυβάρι

Keratéa
Κερατέα 636
Epáno Fellós
Επάνω Φελλός
Akr. Griá
Ακρ. Γριά

Gávrio
Γαύριο
Arnás
Αρνάς
Apíkia
Αποίκια (20)

Anávissos
Ανάβυσσος (15)
264
Makroníssi
Μακρόνησι
Batsi
Μπατσί 994
Messariá
Μεσαριά
Andros
Άνδρος

Lávrio
Λαύριο
Paleópoli
Παλαιόπολη
Όrmos Korthíou
Όρμος Κορθίου

Legrená
Λεγρενά
Soúnio
Σούνιο
Kaparia
Καππαριά
Akr. Ag. Kosmás
Ακρ. Αγ. Κοσμάς

Akr. Soúnio
Ακρ. Σούνιο
Vourkári
Βουρκάρι
Otziás
Οτζιάς
Akr. Pérdelos
Ακρ. Πέρδελος
Kórthio
Κόρθιο 582
N. TÍNOS
N. ΤΗΝΟΣ

Korissía
Κορησσία
Kéa
Κέα (320)
N. KÉA
N. ΚΕΑ
N. Giáros
N. Γιάρος
Pánormos
Πάνορμος 409

Pissés
Πίσσες
K. Meriá
Κ. Μεριά
489
Istérnia
Ιστέρνια
Kallóni
Καλλόνη
Agápi
Αγάπη
Akr. Liváda
Ακρ. Λιβάδα

Koúndouros
Κούνδουρος 450
Akr. Támelos
Ακρ. Τάμελος
Akr. Kéfalos
Ακρ. Κέφαλος
Kardianí
Καρδιανή
Kómi
Κώμη
Exómvourgo
Εξώμβουργο 729

Akr. Pálos
Ακρ. Πάλος
Tinos
Τήνος
N. MÍKONOS
N. ΜΥΚΟΝΟΣ

N. Ág. Geórgios
N. Αγ. Γεώργιος
N. SÍROS
N. ΣΥΡΟΣ
Á. Síros
Ά. Σύρος 442
Ág. Stéfanos
Αγ. Στέφανος 372
Akr. Évros
Ακρ. Έβρος

Loutrá
Λουτρά 306
N. KÍTHNOS
N. ΚΥΘΝΟΣ
Kíni
Κίνι
Ermoúpoli
Ερμούπολη
341
Míkonos
Μύκονος
Á. Merá
Ά. Μερά

Kíthnos
Κύθνος (150)
Galissás
Γαλησσάς
Finikas
Φοίνικας
Á. Didimi
Ά. Δίδυμη
N. Rínia
N. Ρήνεια
Ornós
Ορνός
136
Dragonási
Δραγονήσι

Mérihas
Μέριχας
Droiopida
Δρυοπίδα
Possidonia
Ποσειδωνία
Vári
Βάρη
Dílos
Δήλος
Platís Gialós
Πλατύς Γιαλός
N. Ktapodia
N. Κταπόδια

Kanála
Κανάλα
Mégú. Gialós
Μεγ. Γιαλός
N. Dílos
N. Δήλος

Akr. Ag. Dimítrios
Ακρ. Αγ. Δημήτριος
Akr. Vigklostási
Ακρ. Βιγκλοστάσι
Akr. Pódi
Ακρ. Πόδι

N. Serfopoúla
N. Σερφοπούλα
K I K L Á D E S

N. Serfopoúla
N. Σερφοπούλα
K Y K Λ Á Δ E Σ

Pátmos
Πάτμος

Akr. Vólos
Ακρ. Βόλος

N. SÉRIFOS
N. ΣΕΡΙΦΟΣ
Sérifos
Σέριφος 442
Akr. Stavrí
Ακρ. Σταυροί

Meg. Livádi
Μεγ. Λιβάδι
Livádi
Λιβάδι
Akr. Kórakas
Ακρ. Κόρακας
Apólonas
Απόλλωνας

Koronída
Κορωνίδα
865
Kóronos
Κόρονος

Akr. Kýklow
Ακρ. Κύκλωψ
Akr. Kátano
Ακρ. Κάτανο
N. PÁROS
N. ΠΑΡΟΣ
Náxos
Νάξος

Kamáres
Καμάρες
Naoússa
Νάουσσα
Engarés
Εγγαρές
Kinídaros
Κινίδαρος

Akr. Fílipos
Ακρ. Φίλιππος
Kostos
Κώστος
Apíranthos
Απείρανθος
Moutsoún
Μουτσούνα

L A G O S
L A G O S
Paros
Πάρος
Léfkes
Λεύκες (40)
Galanádo
Γαλανάδο
Halki
Χαλκί
N. NÁX
N. ΝΑΞ

Kamáres
Καμάρες 438
Artemónas
Αρτεμώνας
Andiparos
Αντίπαρος
Roúnda
Ρούντα
Mársissa
Μάρπισσα 706
Á. Sangrí
Ά. Σαγκρί
Kastráki
Καστράκι

N. Sifnos
N. ΣΙΦΝΟΣ
Apolonía (10)
Απολλωνία 530
N. Andíparos
N. Αντίπαρος
Driós
Δρυός
Náxos Dias
Νάξος Διας 523

Platis Gialós
Πλατύς Γιαλός
Aliki
Αλυκή
Koufon
Κουφον

Akr. Kondós
Ακρ. Κοντός
N. Despotikó
N. Δεσποτικό 300
Akr. Petalída
Ακρ. Πεταλίδα
Kastráki
Καστράκι
Koufonísi
Κουφονήσι

Akr. Kéndras
Ακρ. Κένδρας
N. Stroggilí
N. Στρογγυλή
Akr. Katoméri
Ακρ. Κατομέρι
N. Kéro
N. Κέρο

N. Andímilos
N. Αντίμηλος
Kímolos
Κίμωλος
419
N. Shinoússa
N. Σχινούσσα

N. KÍMOLOS
N. ΚΙΜΩΛΟΣ
Prássa
Πράσσα
N. Iráklia
N. Ηράκλεια
Akr. Ke

684
Kímolos
Κίμωλος
Akr. Géro Aggelí
Ακρ. Γέρο Αγγελή
N. Iráklia
N. Ηράκλεια

Akr. Spiliés
Ακρ. Σπηλιές
Psáthi
Ψάθη 417

Akr. Vánu
Ακρ. Βάνυ
Milos
Μήλος (200)
Filakopí
Φυλακωπή 13
N. Pollegos
N. Πολύαιγος 370
N. Ios
N. Ιος
N. ÍOS
N. ΙΟΣ

Adámandas
Αδάμαντας
Voúdia
Βούδια
Pirgos
Πύργος 713

Ralaki Hálakas
Ραλάκι Χάλακας
Kánava
Κάναβα 761
Ios
Ίος

Akr. Psális
Ακρ. Ψάλης
Zefiria
Ζεφυρία
Akr. Borinó
Ακρ. Βορεινό
Sikinos
Σίκινος
Manganári
Μαγγανάρι

N. MÍLOS
N. ΜΗΛΟΣ
Akr. Vígla
Ακρ. Βίγλα
N. Folégandros
N. Φολέγανδρος
N. Sikinos
N. Σίκινος

N. Paximádi
N. Παξιμάδι
312
Á. Meriá
Ά. Μεριά
Folegandros
Φολέγανδρος 553
Akr. Ahládes
Ακρ. Αχλάδες

N. Ananés
N. Ανάνες
Karavostássis
Καραβοστάσης
N. Kardiótissa
N. Καρδιώτισσα
Akr. Vitzétzos
Ακρ. Βιτζέτζος

Ia
Ία
Akr. Mavrópetra
Ακρ. Μαυρόπετρα
N. THÍRA
N. ΘΗΡΑ

N. Thirassía
N. Θηρασία
Thíra
Θήρα (260)
(N. SANTORÍNI)

Thirasía
Θηρασία 294
124
Kamári
Καμάρι

N. Kaméni
N. Καμένη 566
Arh. Thíra
Αρχ. Θήρα

Akrotíri
Ακρωτήρι
Perissa
Περίσσα
Akr. Exomýtis
Ακρ. Εξωμύτης

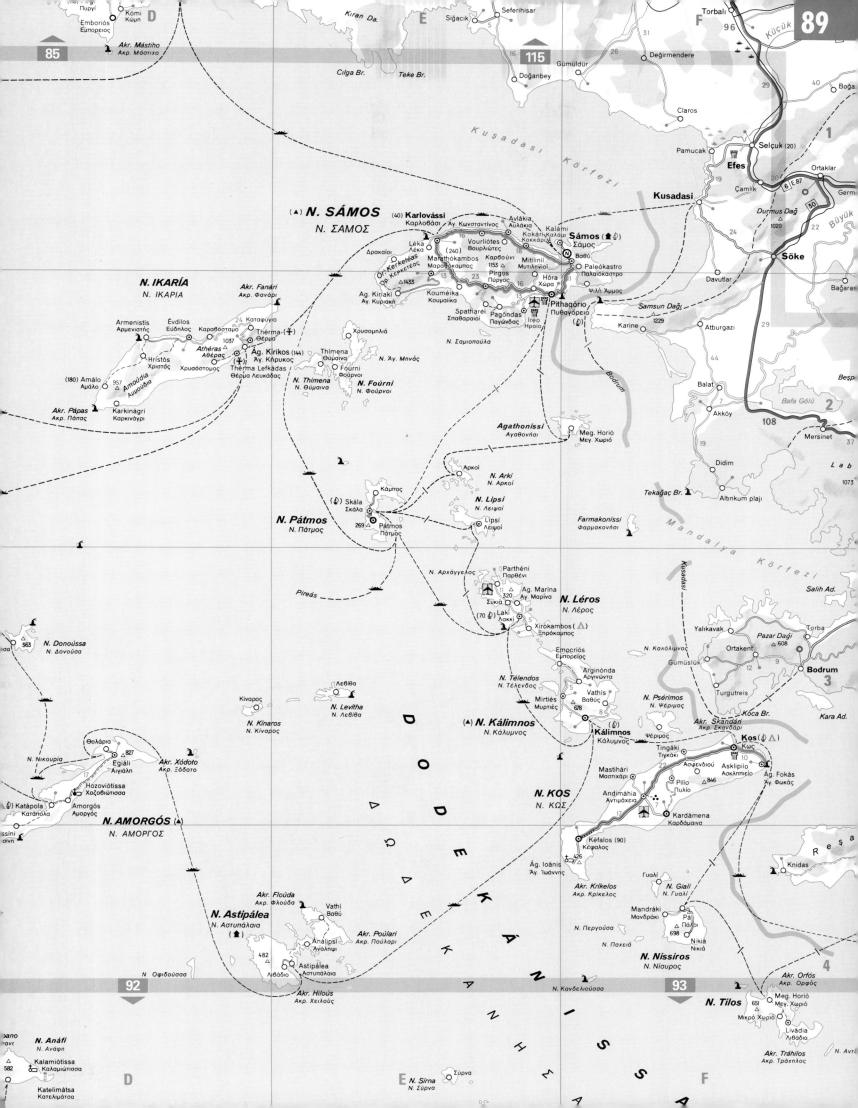

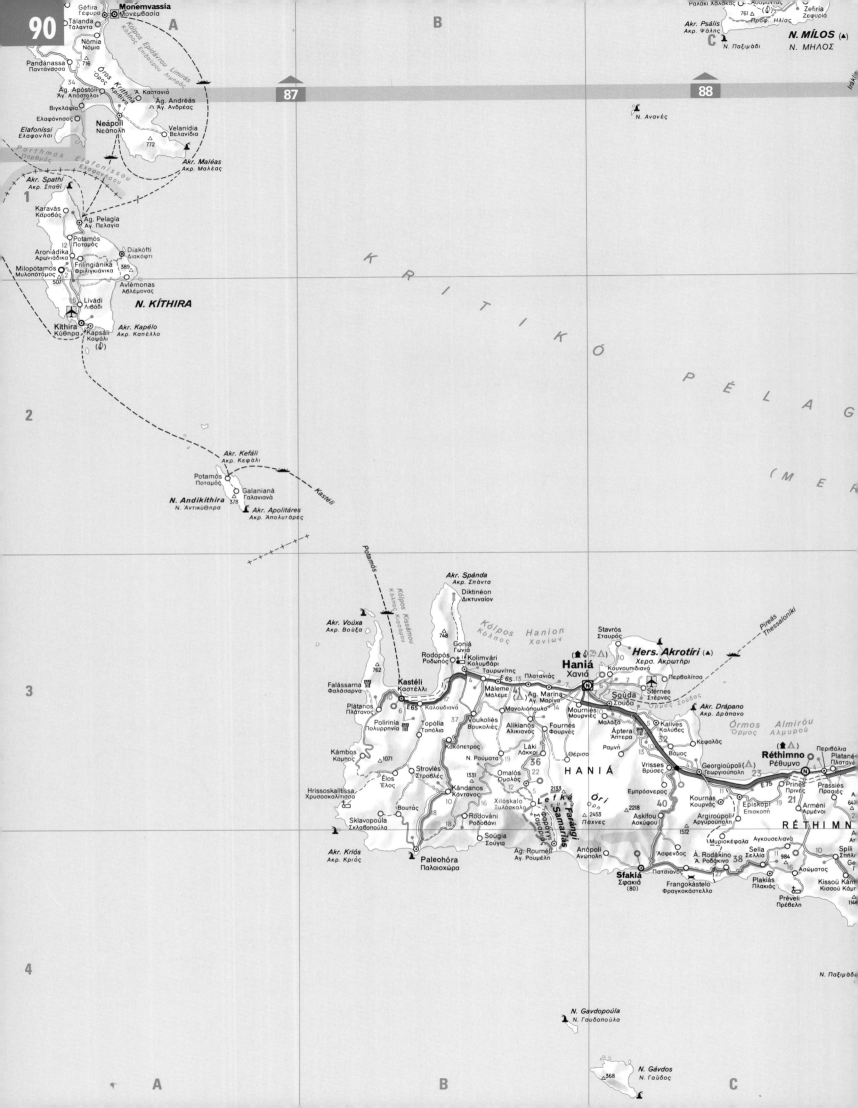

A B C

**Monemvassía**
Μονεμβασία

Gefíra
Γέφυρα

Tálanda
Τάλαντα

Nómia
Νόμια

Pandánassa
Παντάνασσα

716

34

Ág. Apóstoli
Άγ. Απόστολι

Ά. Kastaniá
Ά. Καστανιά

Ág. Andréas
Άγ. Ανδρέας

Vigklafía
Βιγκλάφια

Elafónissos
Ελαφόνσος

**Neápoli**
Νεάπολη

Velanídia
Βελανίδια

*Elafoníssi*
Ελαφόνηαι

Diakófti
Διακόφτι

772

*Akr. Maléas*
Ακρ. Μαλέας

N. MÍLOS (▲)
N. ΜΗΛΟΣ

*Akr. Psális*
Ακρ. Ψάλις

N. Παξιμάδι

N. Ananés
N. Ανανές

*Akr. Spathí*
Ακρ. Σπαθί

Karavás
Καραβάς

Ag. Pelagia
Αγ. Πελαγία

Potamós
Ποταμός

12

Aroniádika
Αρωνιάδικα

Frilingiánika
Φριλιγγιάνικα

Diakófti
Διακόφτι

Milopótamos
Μυλοπόταμος

389

2

507

Avlémonas
Αβλέμονας

6

Livádi
Λιβάδι

**N. KÍTHIRA**

**Kíthira**
Κύθηρα

Kapsáli
Καψάλι

*Akr. Kapélo*
Ακρ. Καπέλλο

*Akr. Kefáli*
Ακρ. Κεφάλι

Potamós
Ποταμός

Galanianá
Γαλανιανά

378

**N. Andikíthira**
N. Άντικύθηρα

*Akr. Apolitáres*
Ακρ. Απολυτάρες

*Kastéli*

K R I T I K Ó   P É L A G   (M E R

*Potamós*

*Akr. Spánda*
Ακρ. Σπάντα

Diktinéon
Δικτυναίον

748

*Akr. Voúxa*
Ακρ. Βούξα

*Kólpos Kissámou*
Κόλπος Κισσάμου

*Kólpos Haníon*
Κόλπος Χανίων

Stavrós
Σταυρός

**Hers. Akrotíri** (▲)
Χερσ. Ακρωτήρι

*Pireás Thessaloníki*

762

Rodopós
Ροδωπός

Goniá
Γωνιά

Kolimvári
Κολυμβάρι

Plataniás
Πλατανιάς

**Haniá**
Χανιά

Kounoupidianá
Κουνουπιδιανά

Perdolítsa
Περδολίτσα

E65   13

Fragokástelo
Φραγκοκάστελλο

7

*Falássarna*
Φαλάσαρνα

**Kastéli**
Καστέλλι

17

Máleme
Μάλεμε

Ag. Marína
Αγ. Μαρίνα

**Soúda**
Σούδα

Stérnes
Στέρνες

*Akr. Drápano*
Ακρ. Δράπανο

*Órmos Soúdas*
Όρμος Σούδας

*Órmos Almiroú*
Όρμος Αλμυρού

10

Plátanos
Πλάτανος

E65

Kaloudianá
Καλουδιανά

Manoliópoulo
Μανολιόπουλο

14

Mourniés
Μουρνιές

Maláxa
Μαλάξα

Kalíves
Καλύβες

5

37

Polirinía
Πολυρρηνία

Topólia
Τοπόλια

Voukoliés
Βουκολιές

Alikianós
Αλικιανός

Fournés
Φουρνές

Áptera
Άπτερα

13

Vámos
Βάμος

**Réthimno**
Ρέθυμνο

Perivólia
Περιβόλια

Platané
Πλατανέ

*Kámbos*
Κάμπος

1071

Kakópetros
Κακόπετρος

N. Roúmata
N. Ρούματα

Láki
Λάκκοι

19

Theriso
Θέρισα

Ramní
Ραμνή

Kefalás
Κεφαλάς

4

Georgioúpoli (△)
Γεωργιούπολη

23

Prassiés
Πρασσιές

Prinés
Πρινές

21

Strovlés
Στρωβλές

1331

Ómalos
Ομαλός

36

22

Vrisses
Βρύσες

E75

Armeni
Αρμένι

*Hrissoskalítissa*
Χρυσοσκαλίτισσα

Élos
Έλος

12

Kándanos
Κάντανος

2133

*Lefká Óri*
Λευκά Όρι

Emprósneros
Εμπρόσνερος

Kournás
Κουρνάς

Episkopí
Επισκοπή

19

**RÉTHIMN**

2218

**HANIÁ**

*Soúgia*
Σούγια

5

8

Ródováni
Ροδοβάνι

Xilóskalo
Ξυλόσκαλο

2453

*Farángi Samariás*
Φαράγγι Σαμαριάς

Páchnes
Πάχνες

Askífou
Ασκίφου

1512

40

Argiroúpoli
Αργυρούπολη

Myriokéfala
Μυριοκέφαλα

Sklavopoúla
Σκλαβοπούλα

10

16

18

Áspendos
Άσφενδος

Á. Rodákino
Ά. Ροδάκινο

38

Sélia
Σελλία

11

984

Spíli
Σπήλι

*Akr. Kriós*
Ακρ. Κριός

**Paleohóra**
Παλαιοχώρα

Ag. Roumél
Αγ. Ρουμέλη

Anópoli
Ανώπολη

16

Asómatos
Ασώματος

Patsianós
Πατσιανός

27

Plakiás
Πλακιάς

Kissoú Kám
Κισσού Κάμ

**Sfakiá**
Σφακιά
(80)

Frangokástelo
Φραγκοκάστελλο

Préveli
Πρέβελη

1146

N. Gavdopoúla
N. Γαυδοπούλα

N. Gávdos
N. Γαύδος

368

A B C

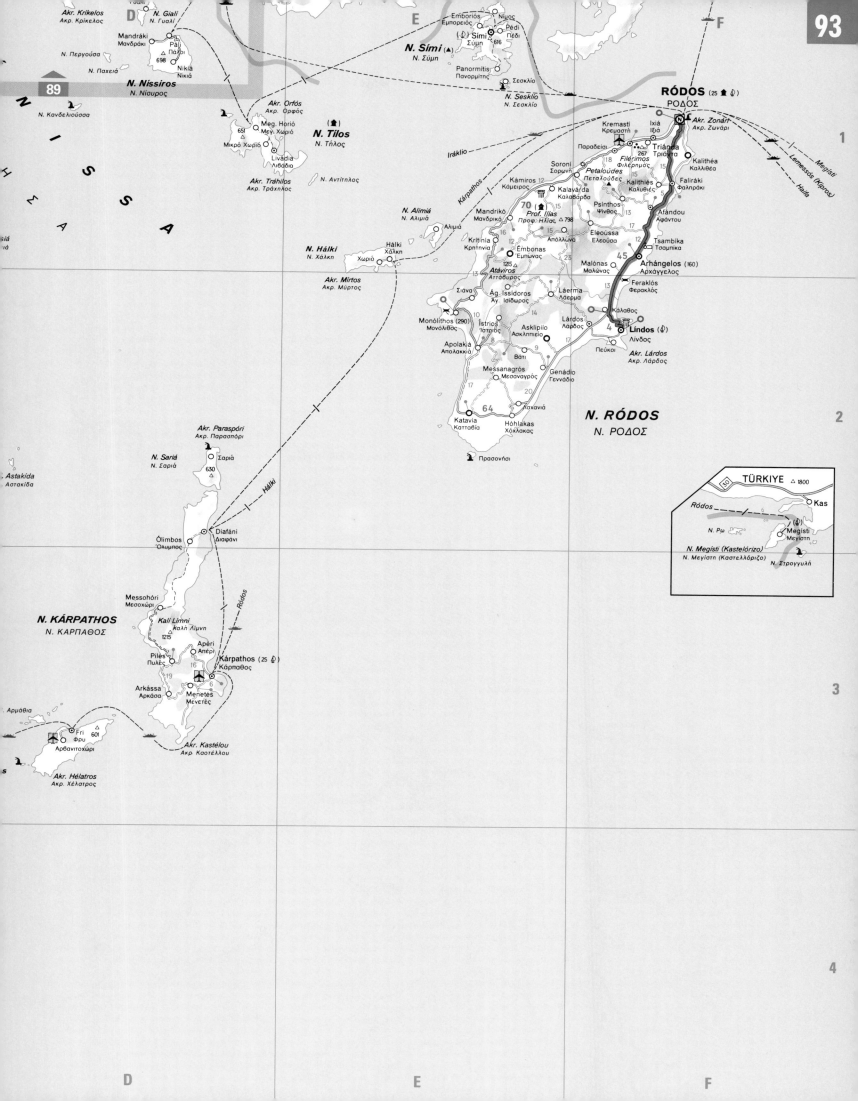

A            B            C

66°33

Cercle polaire arctique
Norðurheimskautsbaugur    Grímsey

Hornbjarg

**1**

Bolungarvík
(△) **Ísafjörður**
Norðurfjörður
Þingeyri
*Gláma*
Patreksfjörður
Brjánslækur
*Flatey*

*Drangajökull*
925

122

Siglufjörður
Ólafsfjörður
Dalvík   *Hrísey*
Árskógssandur

85 Raufarhöfn
29
Kópasker 78
867    Þórshöfn
*Bakkaflói*
38   36
Húsavík
*Dettifoss*
70
Vopnafjörður

*Breiðafjörður*
Stykkishólmur
Grundarfjörður
Ólafsvík
*Snæfellsnes*
1448

Blönduós
**Sauðárkrókur** 115
Varmahlíð (△)
Laugar
Búðardalur
425

**Akureyri** (△) 🛧
*Mývatn*
📷 (△)
274
107

Egilsstaðir 🛧
🛧 **Seyðisfjörður**
(△)
Neskaupsta
Eskifjörður

**2**

Borgarnes
Reykholt   Húsafell (△)
*Langjökull*
Hveravellir
*Hofsjökull*
△1765
Nýidalur

*Askja*
Dreki
190
*Skjálfandafljót*
123
135

241
166

**Akranes**
📷 (△) **REYKJAVÍK**
Garður
Sandgerði
**Keflavík** 🛧
Grindavík

Þingvellir
△914 (△)
365
*Þingvallavatn*
Hveragerði
Selfoss
Þorlákshöfn
Hella (△)
Hvolsvöllur

*Geysir*
Laugarvatn (△)
*Gullfoss*
*Hvítá*
*Hekla*
△1491
Landmannalaugar

**VATNAJÖKULL**
(△) Skaftafell
△2119
461
*Skeiðarársandur*
130

🛧 **Höfn**

**3**

*Mýrdals-*
*jökull*
Þórsmörk
135   249
*Skógafoss*
📷
Vík
Vestmannaeyjar

ATLANTSHAF
ATLANTSHAF

1 / 2 400 000
0       50 km

**FØROYAR**
**FÆRØERNE**
( **DK** )

*Seyðisfjörður*
*NORÐOYAR*
Viðareiði
Gjógv
882
Eiði
Tjørnuvík
*Kunoy* *Viðoy*
Oyndarfjørður
Svínoy
790 △
*Streymoy*
*Borðoy*
Klaksvík
Hvalvík
Vestmanna
Leirvík
Mykines
722 *Vágar*
20
58
*Eysturoy*
Sørvágur
Toftir

**Tórshavn** ( △ ▲ )

Kirkjubøur
Skopun
*Sandoy*
△479
Sandur
Skálavík

Lerwick-Bergen-Hanstholm-Esbjerg

*Suðuroyarfjørður*
Hvalba
616 △ 10
Tvøroyri
Fámjin
*Suðuroy*
Vágur
Sumba

*Hurtigrute*

(△) Sør-Flatanger

N O R S K E   H A V E T

100

Osen
Roan

**4**

0       30 km

Harsvik

A            B            C

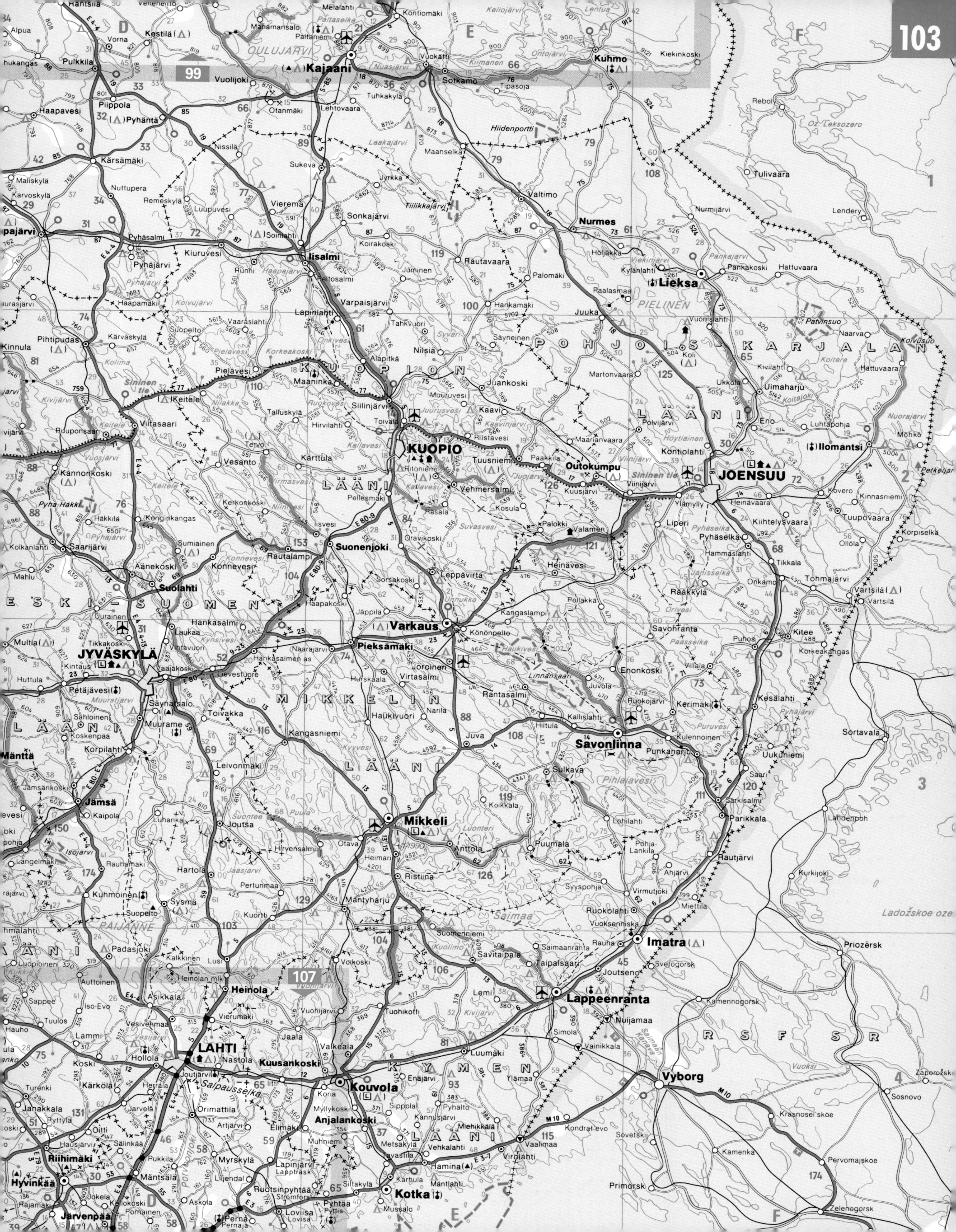

99

107

**Kajaani**
**Kuhmo**
**Iisalmi**
**Nurmes**
**Lieksa**
POHJOIS-KARJALAN LÄÄNI
PIELINEN
**KUOPIO**
**Outokumpu**
**JOENSUU**
**Ilomantsi**
KUOPION LÄÄNI
**Suonenjoki**
**Varkaus**
**Pieksämäki**
**Savonlinna**
ESKI-SUOMEN LÄÄNI
**Suolahti**
**JYVÄSKYLÄ**
**Jämsä**
**Mänttä**
MIKKELIN LÄÄNI
**Mikkeli**
**Imatra**
**Lappeenranta**
PÄIJÄNNE
SAIMAA
**Heinola**
**Lahti**
**Kouvola**
**Kuusankoski**
**Anjalankoski**
**Vyborg**
KYMEN LÄÄNI
**Kotka**
**Hamina**
**Riihimäki**
**Hyvinkää**
**Järvenpää**
S F S R
Ladožskoe oze

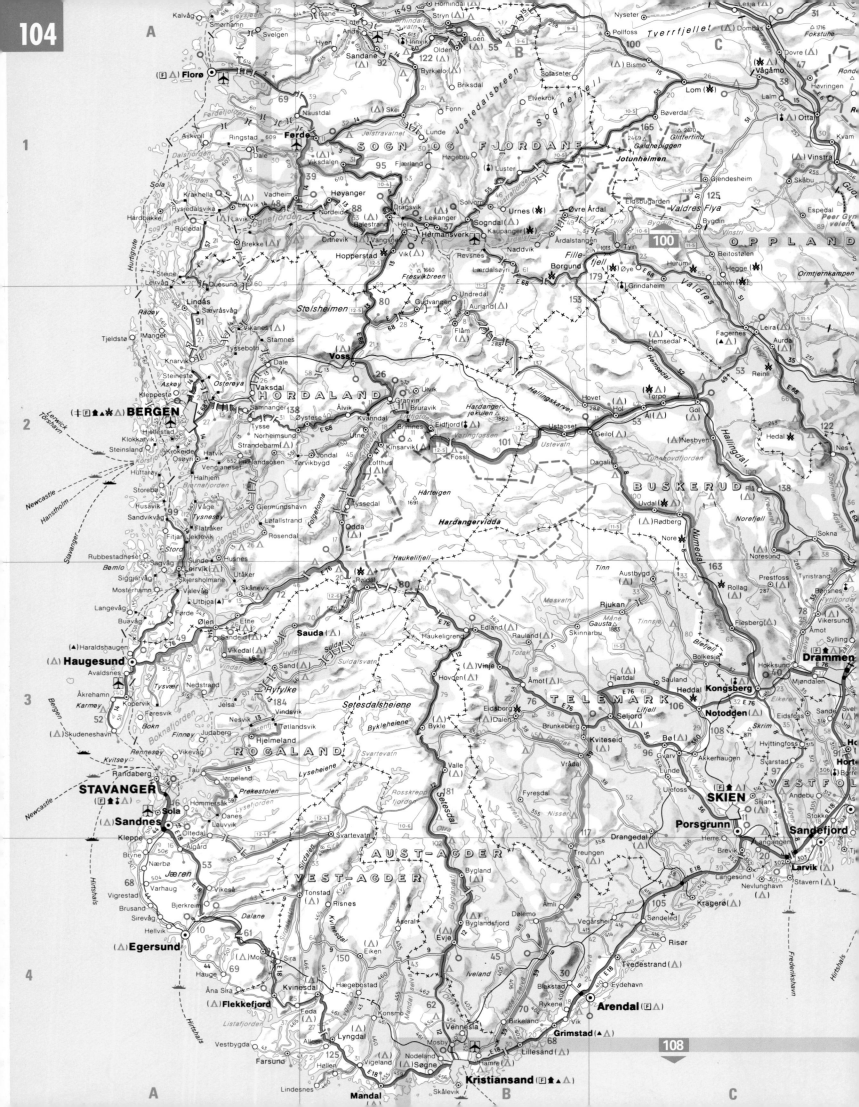

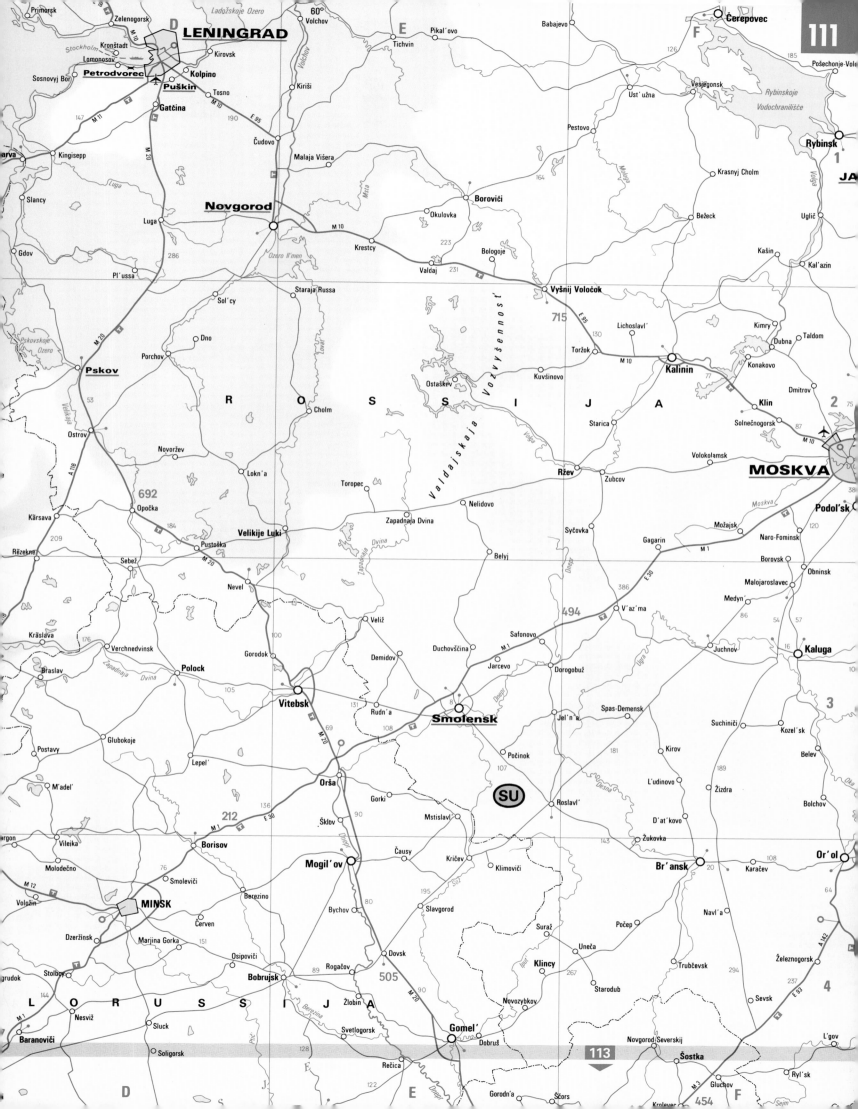

# Index Register Índice Indice

**(F)** Lorsqu'un nom figure plusieurs fois dans l'index, une précision est ajoutée entre parenthèses pour permettre de l'identifier plus facilement: pays, région ou ville la plus proche, élément géographique d'après les abréviations ci-dessous.

**(GB)** Where there are two or more identical place names, the name of the distinguishing country or region or nearest large town is given in brackets; geographical features are indicated by the abbreviations below.

**(D)** Tritt ein Name mehrfach im Register auf, wird er durch eine in Klammern gesetzte nähere Bestimmung genauer definiert. Sie finden folgende Zusätze: Land, Region oder nächstgelegene Stadt, geographische Gegebenheiten, ggf. abgekürzt

**(NL)** Bij namen die meermalen in het register voorkomen, staat tussen haakjes een aanduiding ter verklaring: het land, de streek, de dichtstbijgelegen stad of een geografisch gegeven (zie de afkortingen hieronder).

**(E)** Para poder localizar más fácilmente un nombre que figura varias veces en el índice, se añade entre paréntesis el país, la región o ciudad más cercana, o un elemento geográfico, con las abreviaturas siguientes.

**(I)** Quando un nome figura più volte nell'indice, una precisazione viene aggiunta tra parentesi per permettere d'identificarlo più facilmente: nazione, regione o città la più vicina, elemento geografico come da abbreviazioni qui di seguito.

| | | | | | |
|---|---|---|---|---|---|
| Ákr | Ákra, Akrotírion | Liq | Liquen | Pk | Park |
| B | Bay, Baie, Bucht, Bahía, Baía, Bukt(en), Bugt, Bukhta | Meg | Méga, Megál, -a, -i, -o | Pl | Planina |
| | | Mikr. | Mikr-í, -ón | Pque | Parque |
| Bgem | Barragem | Mgne(s) | Montagne(s) | Prov | Province |
| C | Cape, Cap, Cabo, Capo | M, Mte(s) | Maj, Maj'e, Monte(s) | Pso | Passo |
| Co | County | Mt(s), *Mt(s)* | Mount(s), Mountain(s), Mont(s) | Pt(e) | Point(e) |
| Ch | Chaîne | | | Rib | Ribeirão |
| Chan | Channel | Mti | Monti, Muntii | R, *R* | River, Rivière, Rio, Ria, Rijeka |
| Dépt | Département | Nac | Nacional(e) | Reg | Region, Région |
| Emb | Embalse | Nat | National | Res | Reservoir, Reservoire |
| Ez | Ezero | Naz | Nazionale | Sa | Sierra, Serra |
| G | Gulf, Golfe, Golfo | N | Nissi, Nissos | Sd | Sound, Sund |
| Gges | Gorges | Ni | Nissiá, Nissi | St | Saint, Sankt, Sint |
| I(s), *I(s)* | Isle(s), Island(s), Ile(s), Ilha(s), Isla(s), Isola(e) | Os | Ostrov(a) | Ste(s) | Sainte(s) |
| | | Ot | Otok(i), Otoci | Teh L | Tehnití Límni |
| Jez | Jezero, Jezioro | Oz | Ozero(a) | V | Valley, Vale, Vallée, Val, Valle, Vall |
| K | Kanal, Kanaal | P | Pass | | |
| L, *L* | Lake, Loch, Lough, Llyn, Lac, Laguna, Lago, Límni | Pal | Paleós, á, ó | | |
| | | Pen | Peninsula, Penisola | | |

## A

| | | | |
|---|---|---|---|
| | | Abanilla | 45 D2 |
| | | Abano Terme | 61 D1 |
| Aachen | 51 D3 | Abbadia San | |
| Aalen | 55 E2 | Salvatore | 63 D1 |
| Aalsmeer | 16 C2 | Abbasanta | 66 B3 |
| Aalst | 50 B3 | Abbazia di | |
| Aalten | 17 D3 | Casamari | 63 F3 |
| Aalter | 50 B3 | Abbazia di | |
| Äänekoski | 103 D2 | Fossanova | 63 F3 |
| Aapajärvi | 95 F4 | Abbazia di | |
| Aarau | 27 F2 | Montecassino | 64 A3 |
| Aarberg | 27 E2 | Abbazia San Clemente | |
| Aarburg | 27 F2 | a Casauria | 64 A2 |
| Aare | 58 A3 | Abbeville | 19 E2 |
| Aargau | 27 F2 | Abbeyfeale | 14 B3 |
| Aarlen | 21 D2 | Abbeyleix | 12 C4 |
| Aarschot | 50 C3 | Abbey Town- | 5 D4 |
| Aavasaksa | 98 C2 | Abbiategrasso | 60 A1 |
| Abades | 40 A1 | Abborrträsk | 98 B3 |
| Abadiño | 36 B1 | Abbots Bromley | 6 C3 |
| A Baiuca | 34 A1 | Abbotsbury | 9 D3 |

| | | | |
|---|---|---|---|
| Abcoude | 16 C2 | Aberhonddu | 8 C1 |
| Abejar | 36 B3 | Aberlady | 5 D2 |
| Abejuela | 41 E3 | Aberpennar | 8 C2 |
| Abela | 42 A1 | Aberporth | 8 B1 |
| Abelvær | 97 D4 | Abersoch | 6 A3 |
| Abenberg | 55 E2 | Abertawe | 8 C2 |
| Abenójar | 39 F4 | Aberteifi | 8 B1 |
| Åbenrå | 108 A4 | Abertillery | 9 D2 |
| Abensberg | 55 E2 | Aber-Wrac'h, l' | 22 A2 |
| Aberaeron | 8 C1 | Aberystwyth | 8 C1 |
| Aberdar | 8 C2 | Abetone | 60 C3 |
| Aberdare | 8 C2 | Abiego | 37 E3 |
| Aberdaron | 6 A3 | Abingdon | 9 E2 |
| Aberdaugleddau | 8 B2 | Abington | 5 D3 |
| Aberdeen | 3 E4 | Abisko | 94 B3 |
| Aberdovey | 6 A3 | Abisko (Nat park) | 94 B3 |
| Aberfeldy | 4 C1 | Abla | 44 B3 |
| Aberfoyle | 4 C2 | Ablis | 19 E4 |
| Abergavenny | 9 D2 | Åbo | 107 D2 |
| Abergele | 6 B2 | Abondance | 27 E3 |
| Abergwaun | 8 B1 | Abony | 112 B4 |

| | | | |
|---|---|---|---|
| Aboyne | 3 E4 | | |
| Abrantes | 38 B3 | | |
| Abreschviller | 21 E4 | | |
| Abrets, les | 30 C1 | | |
| Abriès | 31 E2 | | |
| Abruzzo | 63 F2 | | |
| Abruzzo, Parco | | | |
| Nazionale d' | 64 A2 | | |
| Abstadt-Tailfingen | 55 D3 | | |
| Abtenau | 59 E1 | | |
| Åby | 105 F4 | | |
| Åbybro | 108 B2 | | |
| A Caniza | 34 A3 | | |
| Acceglio | 31 E2 | | |
| Accettura | 65 D4 | | |
| Acciaroli | 67 D1 | | |
| Accous | 37 D1 | | |
| Accrington | 6 C2 | | |
| Acebo | 39 D2 | | |
| Acedo | 36 B2 | | |
| Acehuche | 39 D3 | | |

| | | | |
|---|---|---|---|
| Acerno | 64 B4 | Aflenz Kurort | 57 E3 |
| Acerra | 64 B4 | Afráti | 84 B4 |
| Aceuchal | 39 D4 | Afsluitdijk | 16 C1 |
| Ache | 59 E1 | A Garda | 34 A3 |
| Achenkirch | 59 D1 | Agathoníssi | 89 E2 |
| Achenpaß | 56 A4 | Agay | 31 E4 |
| Achensee | 59 D1 | Agazzano | 60 B2 |
| Achern | 54 C3 | Agde | 30 A4 |
| Acheux | 19 E2 | Agdenes | 100 C1 |
| Achill I | 12 A2 | Agen | 28 C3 |
| Achim | 17 F1 | Åger | 37 F3 |
| Achnacroish | 4 B1 | Ager | 56 C3 |
| Achnasheen | 2 C3 | Ageranós | 87 D4 |
| A'Chràlaig | 2 C4 | Agerbæk | 108 A3 |
| Aci Castello | 69 D3 | Agger | 17 E4 |
| Acipayam | 115 F4 | Aggius | 66 B1 |
| Acireale | 69 D3 | Aggsbach-Dorf | 57 E2 |
| Aci Trezza | 69 D3 | Aggsbach-Markt | 57 E2 |
| Acle | 7 F3 | Agiá | 83 F1 |
| A Coruña | 34 B1 | Agiá, Akr | 83 F4 |
| Acqualagna | 61 E4 | Agía Ána (Évia) | 84 A3 |
| Acquapendente | 63 D1 | Agía Ána (Viotía) | 83 F4 |
| Acquasanta Terme | 63 F1 | Agía Efimía | 82 B4 |
| Acquasparta | 63 E1 | Agía Efthimía | 83 E4 |
| Acquaviva delle | | Agía Ekateríni, Akr | 82 A1 |
| Fonti | 65 D3 | Agía Fotiá | 91 F4 |
| Acqui-Terme | 60 A2 | Agía Galíni | 91 D4 |
| Acri | 67 E2 | Agía Kiriakí | |
| Ada | 72 C1 | (Makedonía) | 78 C3 |
| Adaja, R | 39 F2 | Agía Kiriakí | |
| Adak | 98 A3 | (Pelopónissos) | 86 B3 |
| Ådalsel | 104 C2 | Agía Kiriakí | |
| Adamandás | 88 A4 | (Sámos) | 89 E2 |
| Adamclisi | 115 E1 | Agía Lávra | 86 C1 |
| Adamello | 58 C3 | Agía Marína | |
| Adamello Brenta, | | (Égina) | 87 F2 |
| Parco Naturale | 58 C3 | Agía Marína (Kríti) | 90 B3 |
| Adamello, Mont' | 58 C3 | Agía Marína (Léros) | 89 E3 |
| Adamuz | 43 F2 | Agía Marína | |
| Adanero | 39 F1 | (Stereá Eláda) | 83 E3 |
| Adapazarı | 115 F3 | Agía Marína | |
| Adare | 14 B3 | (Stereá Eláda) | 88 A1 |
| Adaševci | 72 B3 | Agía Paraskeví | |
| Adda | 60 B2 | (Lésvos) | 85 F2 |
| Adelboden | 27 E3 | Agía Paraskeví | |
| Adelfia | 65 D3 | (Makedonía) | 80 C2 |
| Adelsheim | 55 D1 | Agía Paraskiés | 91 E4 |
| Ademuz | 41 D3 | Agía Pelagía | |
| Adenau | 51 E4 | (Kíthira) | 90 A1 |
| Ådendro | 79 F3 | Agía Pelagía (Kríti) | 91 D3 |
| Adéres, Óros | 87 E2 | Agía Rouméli | 90 B4 |
| Adica, Sa da | 42 C1 | Agiásma | 80 C2 |
| Adige | 61 D1 | Agiásmata | 85 E4 |
| Adjud | 113 E4 | Agía Sofía (Évia) | 84 B3 |
| Admont | 57 D3 | Agía Sofía | |
| Adolfström | 97 F3 | (Pelopónissos) | 87 D2 |
| Adorf | 53 D3 | Agía Sotíra | 87 E1 |
| Adour | 28 B4 | Agiássos | 85 F2 |
| Adra | 44 B4 | Agía Triáda (Kríti) | 91 D4 |
| Adradas | 36 B4 | Agía Triáda | |
| Adrall | 32 A3 | (Makedonía) | 79 F3 |
| Adrano | 69 D3 | Agía Triáda | |
| Adria | 61 D2 | (Pelopónissos) | 86 C1 |
| Adriatic Sea | 114 A3 | Agía Triáda (Stereá | |
| Adzaneta | 41 E3 | Eláda) | 87 F1 |
| Aegean Sea | 115 E4 | Agía Varvára | 91 D4 |
| Aenona | 74 C1 | Agiófilo | 83 D1 |
| Aerinó | 83 F2 | Agiókambos (Évia) | 83 F3 |
| Ærø | 108 B4 | Agiókambos | |
| Ærøskøbing | 108 B4 | (Thessalía) | 83 F1 |
| A Estrada | 34 A2 | Agionóri | 87 E2 |
| Aetópetra | 82 B1 | Ágio Óros | 80 C4 |
| Aetós (Kefaloniá) | 82 B4 | Agiopigí | 83 D2 |
| Aetós (Makedonía) | 79 D3 | Ágios | 84 A3 |
| Aetós (Stereá | | Ágios Anárgiri | |
| Eláda) | 82 C3 | (Pelopónissos) | 87 D3 |
| Aetsä | 107 D2 | Ágios Andónios | |
| Afándou | 93 F1 | (Thessalía) | 83 E2 |
| Áfarnes | 100 B2 | Ágios Andónios | 80 A3 |
| Aféa | 87 F2 | Ágios Andréas | |
| Affi | 60 C1 | (Arkadía) | 87 D2 |
| Afiónas | 82 A1 | Ágios Andréas | |
| Áfissos | 83 F2 | (Lakonía) | 87 E4 |
| Áfitos | 80 B4 | Ágios Apóstoli | |
| Afjord | 100 C1 | (Évia) | 84 B4 |
| Åfjorden | 104 A1 | Ágios Apóstoli | |
| Aflenzer Seeberg | 57 E3 | (Pelopónissos) | 87 E4 |

Ágios Apóstoli (Stereá Eláda) 84 B4
Ágios Athanássios (Dráma) 80 C2
Ágios Athanássios (Péla) 79 D2
Ágios Avgoustínos 86 C3
Ágios Déka 91 D4
Ágios Dimítrios, Akr 88 A3
Ágios Dimítrios (Évia) 88 A1
Ágios Dimítrios (Lakonía) 87 D3
Ágios Dimítrios (Makedonía) 79 E4
Ágios Dimítrios (Messinía) 87 D4
Ágios Dimítrios (Stereá Eláda) 83 D3
Ágios Dionissios 79 E4
Ágios Efstrátios, N 85 D2
Ágios Fokás 89 F3
Ágios Fokás, Akr 85 F3
Ágios Geórgios (Évia) 83 F3
Ágios Geórgios, N 87 F2
Ágios Geórgios (Lassíthi) 91 E4
Ágios Geórgios (Stereá Eláda) 83 D3
Ágios Geórgios (Zákinthos) 86 A1
Ágios Georgíou, Órmos 87 E3
Ágios Germanós 79 D2
Ágios Górdis 82 A1
Ágios Harálambos 81 E2
Ágios Ioánis, Akr 91 F3
Ágios Ioánis (Dodekánissa) 89 F4
Ágios Ioánis (Pelopónissos) 87 E2
Ágios Ioánis (Stereá Eláda) 83 F4
Ágios Ioánis (Thessalía) 83 F3
Ágios Ioánis (Thessalía) 83 F2
Ágios Irínis, Akr 85 D1
Ágios Issídoros 93 E2
Ágios Kírikos 89 D2
Ágios Konstandínos (Stereá Eláda) 83 F3
Ágios Konstandínos (Thessalía) 83 E2
Ágios Kosmás (Grevená) 79 D4
Ágios Kosmás (Kavála) 80 C2
Ágios Léon 86 A1
Ágios Loukás 84 B4
Ágios Mámas 80 A4
Ágios Márkos 80 A2
Ágios Mathéos 82 A2
Ágios Míronas 91 D4
Ágios Nikítas 82 B3
Ágios Nikólaos (Etolía-Akarnanía) 82 B3
Ágios Nikólaos (Fokída) 83 E4
Ágios Nikólaos (Fthiótida) 83 F3
Ágios Nikólaos (Hers.Methánon) 87 E2
Ágios Nikólaos (Ípiros) 82 B1
Ágios Nikólaos (Kríti) 91 E4
Ágios Nikólaos (Lakonía) 87 D3
Ágios Nikólaos (Makedonía) 80 B4
Ágios Nikólaos (Messinía) 86 C3
Ágios Pandeleímonos 79 D3
Ágios Pángalos, Akr 83 E4
Ágios Paraskeví (Ípiros) 78 C4
Ágios Paraskeví (Makedonía) 79 F2
Ágios Pávlos 80 A3
Ágios Pétros 87 D2
Ágios Pnévma 80 B2
Ágios Pródromos 80 A3
Ágios Sóstis 83 E3
Ágios Stéfanos (Kikládes) 88 C2
Ágios Stéfanos (Stereá Eláda) 87 F1
Ágios Theódori (Makedonía) 79 D4
Ágios Theódori (Pelopónissos) 87 E1
Ágios Theódori (Thessalía) 83 F3
Ágios Thomás (Kríti) 91 D4
Ágios Thomás (Stereá Eláda) 84 B4
Ágios Vassílios (Makedonía) 80 A3
Ágios Vassílios (Stereá Eláda) 84 A4
Ágios Vissários 83 E2
Agíou Órous, Kólpos 80 C4
Agira 68 C3
Agly 32 B2
Ágnanda 82 C2
Agnanderó 83 D2
Agnandi 83 F3
Agnóndas 84 B3
Agnone 64 B2
Agnoúnda 87 E2
Agon-Coutainville 18 B3
Agorá 80 C2
Agordo 59 D3
Agost 45 E1
Agout 29 D4
Agrafiótis 83 D2
Agramunt 37 F3
Agrate Br. 60 A1
Agreda 36 C3
Agreliá 83 D1
Agri 65 D4
Agriá 83 F2
Agrigento 68 B4
Agriliá 82 C4
Agriliá, Akr 85 F3
Ágrilos 86 B3
Agrínio 82 C3
Agriovótano 83 F3
Agropoli 64 B4
Agskaret 97 E2
Aguadulce (Almería) 44 B4
Aguadulce (Sevilla) 43 E3
Aguas Vivas, R 37 D4
Aguaviva 41 E2
A Gudiña 34 C3
Agudo 39 F4
Agueda 38 B1
Agueda, R 39 D2
Aguiar 42 B1
Aguiar da Beira 38 C1
Aguilafuente 40 A1
Aguilar 43 F2
Aguilar de Campóo 35 F2
Aguilar del Alfambra 41 E2
Aguilar, Emb de 35 F2
Águilas 44 C3
Ahaía 86 C1
Aharnés 87 F1
Ahaus 17 E3
Åheim 100 A3
Ahelóos 82 C4
Ahendriás 91 E4
Ahérondas 82 B2
Ahigal 39 D2
Ahílio (Kérkira) 82 A1
Ahílio (Thessalía) 83 E2
Ahinós 80 B2
Ahjärvi 103 F3
Ahladerí 84 B4
Ahládes, Akr 88 C4
Ahladohóri 80 B1
Ahlainen 102 B3
Ahlbeck 49 E2
Ahlen 17 E3
Ahlhorn 17 F1
Ahrensbök 48 B2
Ahrensburg 48 B2
Ahrweiler 51 E4
Ähtäri 102 C2
Ähtärinjärvi 102 C2
Ähtävänjoki 102 C2
Ahtopol 115 E2
Ahun 25 E4
Åhus 109 D3
Ahvenanmaa 106 C3
Ahvenselkä 99 E1
Aichach 55 F3
Aidenbach 56 B2
Aidone 68 C3
Aigen 56 C2
Aigle 27 E3
Aigle, Bge de l' 29 E1
Aigle, l' 19 D4
Aignan 28 C4
Aignay-le-Duc 26 C2
Aigoual, Mt 29 F3
Aigre 24 C4
Aigrefeuille-d'Aunis 24 B4
Aigrefeuille-sur-Maine 24 B3
Aiguablava 32 C3
Aiguebelette 30 C1
Aiguebelle 31 D1
Aigueperse 26 A4
Aigues 30 C3
Aigues-Mortes 30 B4
Aigües Tortes, Parque Nac de 37 F2
Aiguilles 31 E2
Aiguillon 28 C3
Aiguillon, l' 24 B4
Aigurande 25 E4
Ailefroide 31 D2
Aillant 26 A1
Ailly-le-Haut-locher 19 E2
Ailly-sur-Noye 19 F2
Ailsa Craig 4 B3
Aimargues 30 B4
Aime 31 D1
Ain 27 D3
Ain (Dépt) 26 C4
Ainhoa 28 A4
Ainsa 37 E2
Ainsdale 6 B2
Ainzón 36 C3
Airaines 19 E2
Airasca 31 E2
Airdrie 4 C2
Aire *R* 7 D2
Aire 19 F1
Aire, I del 45 F2
Aire, Sa de 38 B3
Aire-sur-l'Adour 28 B4
Airisto 107 D3
Airolo 58 A3
Airvault 24 C3
Aisne 20 A3
Aisne (Dépt) 20 A2
Aitana 45 E1
Aiterhofen 56 B2
Aitrach 55 E3
Aitzgorri 36 B1
Aiud 112 C4
Aix-d'Angillon, les 26 A2
Aixe 29 D1
Aix-en-Othe 26 B1
Aix-en-Provence 30 C4
Aix, I d' 24 B4
Aix-les-Bains 27 D4
Aizenay 24 B3
Ajaccio 33 E4
Ajaureforsen 97 F3
Ajdanovac 77 D1
Ajdovščina 70 A2
Ajka 112 A4
Ajo 35 F1
Ajo, C de 36 A1
Ajos 99 D3
Ajtos 115 E2
Akarnaniká, Óri 82 C3
Äkäsjokisuu 95 D4
Äkäskero 95 D4
Äkäslompolo 95 D4
Akçakoca 115 F3
Aken 53 D1
Åkersberga 106 B3
Akershus 105 D3
Åkers styckebruk 106 B4
Akhisar 115 F4
Åkirkeby 109 D4
Akkajaure 94 B4
Akkerhaugen 104 C3
Akku 95 E3
Akranes 96 A2
Akráta 87 D1
Ákrathos, Akr 80 C4
Akréfnio 83 F4
Åkrehamn 104 A3
Akrestrømmen 100 C3
Akrítas 79 D2
Akrítas, Akr 86 C4
Akrogiáli 80 B3
Akropótamos 80 B3
Akrotíri 91 E1
Akrovoúni 80 C2
Aktí Apólona 87 F2
Akujärvi 95 F3
Akureyri 96 B1
Ål 104 C2
Ala 60 C1
Ala di Stura 31 E1
Alà dei Sardi 66 B2
Alaejos 35 E4
Alagí 86 C3
Alagna Valsesia 27 F4
Alagnon 29 F2
Alagón 37 D3
Alagón, R 39 D2
Alagonía 86 C3
Alahärmä 102 C2
Ala-Honkajoki 102 B3
Alaior 45 F2
Alajärvi 102 C2
Alakylä 99 D1
Alalkomenés 83 F4
Alameda 43 F3
Alamillo 43 F1
Alanäs 101 F1
Aland 48 C3
Åland 106 C3
Alandroal 38 C4
Alange 39 D4
Alange, Emb de 39 D4
Alanis 43 E2
Alapitkä 103 E2
Alaraz 39 E1
Alarcón 40 C3
Alarcón, Emb de 40 C3
Alar del Rey 35 F3
Alaşehir 115 F4
Alassio 31 F3
Alastaro 107 D2
Alatoz 41 D4
Alatri 63 F3
Alavieska 102 C1
Ala-Vuokki 99 F4
Alavus 102 C2
Alba 31 F2
Alba Adriatica 64 A1
Albacete 40 C4
Albacken 101 F2
Alba de Tormes 39 E1
Albæk 108 B1
Albaida 45 E1
Albaida, Pto de 45 E1
Alba Iulia 114 C1
Albaladejo 44 B1
Albalate de Cinca 37 E3
Albalate del Arzobispo 37 D4
Albalate de las Nogueras 40 C2
Alban 29 E3
Albánchez 44 C3
Albano di Lucania 65 D4
Albano Laziale 63 E3
Albarca 37 F4
Albarella, I 61 D1
Albares 35 D2
Albarracín 41 D2
Albarracín, Sa de 41 D2
Albatana 45 D1
Albatera 45 D2
Albena 115 E2
Albenga 31 F3
Albens 27 D4
Alberche, R 39 F2
Alberga 105 F4
Albergaria-a-Velha 38 B1
Alberique 41 E4
Albernoa 42 B1
Alberobello 65 E3
Albersdorf 48 A2
Albert 19 F2
Albert Kanaal 50 C3
Albertville 27 D4
Albestroff 21 E3
Albi 29 E3
Albiano 31 F1
Albinia 63 D2
Albino 58 B4
Albisola Marina 60 A3
Albocácer 41 F2
Albolodúy 44 B3
Albolote 44 A3
Albo, M 66 C2
Alborea 41 D4
Ålborg 108 B2
Ålborg Bugt 108 B2
Albox 44 C3
Albstadt-Ebingen 55 D3
Albufeira 42 A3
Albujón 45 D2
Albulapass 58 B3
Albuñol 44 A4
Alburno, Mte 64 C4
Alburquerque 38 C3
Alby (F) 27 D4
Alby (S) 101 E3
Alcácer do Sál 42 A1
Alcáçovas 42 B1
Alcadozo 44 C1
Alcafozes 38 C2
Alcains 38 C2
Alcalá de Chivert 41 F2
Alcalá de Guadaira 43 D3
Alcalá de Henares 40 B2
Alcalá de la Selva 41 E2
Alcalá del Júcar 41 D4
Alcalá de los Gazules 43 D4
Alcalá del Río 43 D2
Alcalá la Real 44 A3
Alcamo 68 B3
Alcampel 37 E3
Alcanadre, R 37 E3
Alcanar 41 F2
Alcanede 38 A3
Alcanena 38 B3
Alcanhões 38 B3
Alcañices 34 C4
Alcañiz 37 E4
Alcántara 39 D3
Alcántara, Emb de 39 D3
Alcantarilha 42 A2
Alcantarilla 45 D2
Alcaracejos 43 E1
Alcaraz 44 B1
Alcaraz, Sa de 44 C1
Alcaria do Cume 42 B2
Alcaria Ruiva 42 B2
Alcarrache, R 42 C1
Alcarràs 37 E4
Alcaudete 43 F3
Alcaudete de la Jara 39 F3
Alcázar de San Juan 40 B4
Alceda 35 F2
Alcester 9 E1
Alcoba 39 F4
Alcobaça 38 A3
Alcoba de los Montes 39 F4
Alcobendas 40 B2
Alcoceber 41 F3
Alcochete 38 A4
Alcolea 43 F2
Alcolea de Cinca 37 E3
Alcolea del Pinar 36 B4
Alcolea del Río 43 E2
Alconchel 42 C1
Alcora 41 E3
Alcorisa 41 E2
Alcorlo, Emb de 40 B1
Alcoutim 42 B2
Alcover 37 F4
Alcoy 45 E1
Alcubierre 37 D3
Alcubierre, Sa de 37 D3
Alcubilla de Avellaneda 36 A3
Alcublas 41 E3
Alcudia 45 F2
Alcudia de Crespins 41 E4
Alcudia de Guadix 44 B3
Alcuéscar 39 D4
Aldeacentenera 39 E3
Aldeadávila, Emb de 34 C4
Aldea del Cano 39 D3
Aldea del Fresno 40 A2
Aldea del Rey 44 A1
Aldeanueva de Ebro 36 C3
Aldeanueva de la Vera 39 E2
Aldeanueva del Camino 39 E2
Aldeburgh 11 E1
Aldeia da Ponte 39 D2
Aldeia Nova de São Bento 42 C1
Alderney 18 A2
Aldershot 9 F3
Aldinci 77 E3
Aldocer 40 C2
Aledo 44 C2
Aleksandrija 113 F2
Aleksandrovac (Srbija) 73 D3
Aleksandrovac (Srbija) 77 D1
Aleksa Šantić 72 B1
Aleksinac 73 E4
Alençon 23 F3
Alenquer 38 A3
Alentejo 42 B1
Alepohóri (Pelopónissos) 87 D2
Alepohóri (Stereá Eláda) 87 E1
Aléria 33 F3
Alès 30 B3
Ales 66 B3
Aleşd 112 C4
Alessandria 60 A2
Alessandria d. Rocca 68 B3
Ålestrup 108 A2
Ålesund 100 A2
Aletschhorn 27 F3
Alexandria (GB) 4 C2
Alexándria (GR) 79 F3
Alexandria (RO) 115 D2
Alexandroúpoli 81 E2
Alf 51 E4
Alfajarín 37 D3
Alfambra (E) 41 D2
Alfambra (P) 42 A2
Alfambra, R 41 E2
Alfândega da Fé 34 C4
Alfaro 36 C3
Alfarrás 37 E3
Alfaz del Pi 45 E1
Alfedena 64 A2
Alfeizerão 38 A3
Alfeld (Bayern) 55 F1
Alfeld (Niedersachsen) 52 B1
Alfiós 86 B2
Alfonsine 61 D2
Alfonso XIII, Emb de 44 C2
Alford (Grampian) 3 E4
Alford (Lincs) 7 E3
Alfreton 7 D3
Alfta 101 F4
Algaida 45 F3
Algar 43 D4
Ålgård 104 A4
Algar de Palancia 41 E3
Algarinejo 43 F3
Algarrobo 43 F4
Algarve 42 B2
Algatocín 43 E4
Algeciras 43 D4
Algemesí 41 E4
Alghero 66 A2
Alginet 41 E4
Algodonales 43 E3
Algodor, R 40 A3
Algora 40 C1
Algorta 36 B1
Algoz 42 A2
Alhama de Almería 44 B3
Alhama de Aragón 36 C4
Alhama de Granada 43 F3
Alhama de Murcia 45 D2
Alhambra 40 B4
Alhamilla, Sa 44 B3
Alhaurín el Grande 43 E4
Alhóndiga 40 B2
Alia (E) 39 E3
Alia (I) 68 C3
Aliaga 41 E2
Aliaguilla 41 D3
Aliákmona, L 79 E4
Aliákmonas 79 D4
Aliartos 83 F4
Alibunar 73 D2
Alicante 45 E2
Alicudi, I 68 C2
Alicún de Ortega 44 B2
Alife 64 B3
Alijó 34 B4
Alikés 86 A1
Alikianós 90 B3
Alikí (Kikládes) 88 C3
Alikí (Thássos) 81 D3
Alimiá, N 93 E1
Alingsås 108 C1
Alinyà 32 A3
Aliseda 39 D3
Alise-Ste-Reine 26 B2
Aliste, R 35 D4
Alistráti 80 B2
Ali Terme 69 D2
Alivéri 84 B4
Aljezur 42 A2
Aljibe 43 D4
Aljucén 39 D4
Aljustrel 42 B1
Alkionídon, Kólpos 87 E1
Alkmaar 16 C2
Allaire 22 C4
Allaman, M 76 C4
Allanche 29 E2
Alland 57 E3
Allariz 34 B3
Alleen 104 B4
Alleghe 59 D3
Allègre 29 F2
Allen, L 12 C2
Allensbach 55 D4
Allentsteig 57 E2
Allepuz 41 E2
Aller 48 A4
Allersberg 55 F1
Allershausen 55 F3
Alleuze 29 F2
Allevard 31 D1
Allier (Dépt) 26 A3
Allier *R* 26 A3
Allinge-Sandvig 109 D4
Allo 36 C2
Alloa 5 D2
Allonnes 23 F4
Allos 31 D3
Allos, Col d' 31 D3
Alloza 41 E1
Allstedt 52 C2
Almacelles 37 E3
Almáchar 43 F3
Almada 38 A4
Almadén 39 F4
Almadén de la Plata 43 D2
Almadenejos 43 F1
Almagro 40 A4
Almajano 36 B3
Almansa 45 D1
Almansil 42 B3
Almanza 35 E2
Almanzora, R 44 B3
Almanzor, Pico 39 E2
Almaraz 39 E3
Almargen 43 E3
Almarza 36 B3
Almazán 36 B4
Almazora 41 E3
Almedinilla 43 F3
Almeida (E) 35 D4
Almeida (P) 39 D1
Almeirim 38 B3
Almelo 17 D2
Almenar 37 E3
Almenara 41 E3
Almenaras 44 B1
Almenara, Sa de la 44 C3
Almenar de Soria 36 B3
Almendra, Emb de 35 D4
Almendral 38 C4

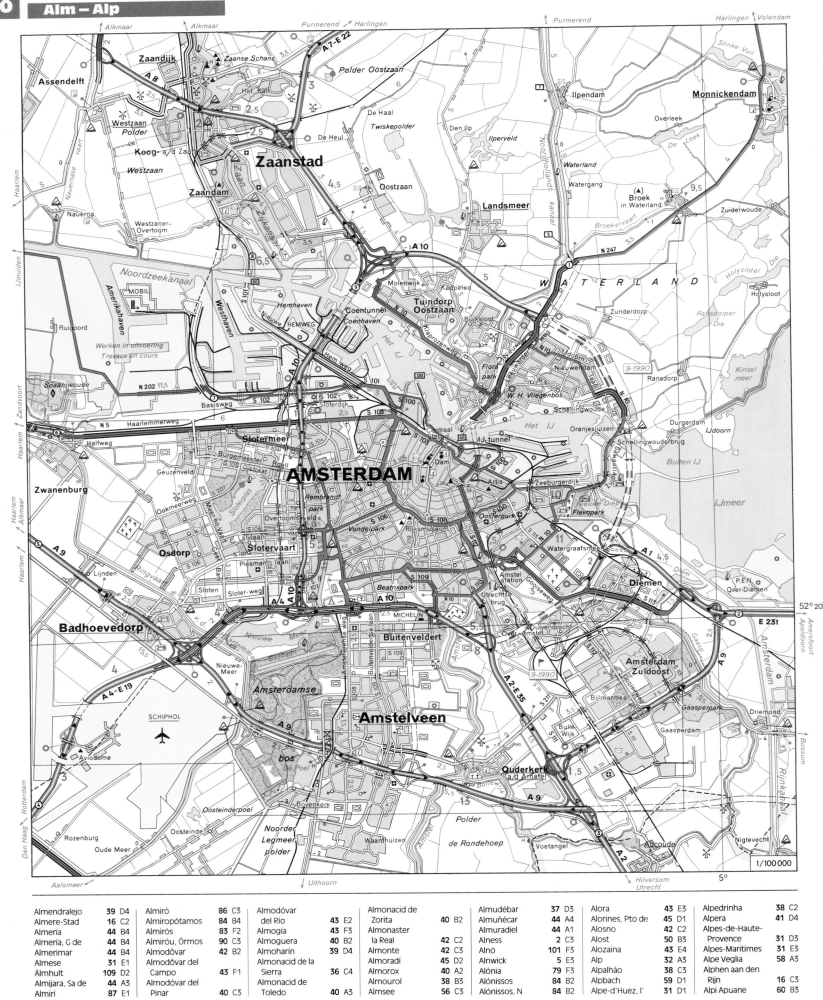

| | | | | | | | | | | | |
|---|---|---|---|---|---|---|---|---|---|---|---|
| Almendralejo | 39 D4 | Almiró | 86 C3 | Almodóvar del Río | 43 E2 | Almonacid de Zorita | 40 B2 | Almudébar | 37 D3 | Alora | 43 E3 | Alpedrinha | 38 C2 |
| Almere-Stad | 16 C2 | Almiropótamos | 84 B4 | Almogía | 43 F3 | Almonaster la Real | 42 C2 | Almuñécar | 44 A4 | Alorines, Pto de | 45 D1 | Alpera | 41 D4 |
| Almeria | 44 B4 | Almirós | 83 F2 | Almoguera | 40 B2 | Almonte | 42 C3 | Almuradiel | 44 A1 | Alosno | 42 C2 | Alpes-de-Haute- |
| Almería, G de | 44 B4 | Almiróu, Órmos | 90 C3 | Almoharín | 39 D4 | Almoradí | 45 D2 | Alness | 2 C3 | Alost | 50 B3 | Provence | 31 D3 |
| Almerimar | 44 B4 | Almodóvar | 42 B2 | Almonacid de la | | Almorox | 40 A2 | Alnö | 101 F3 | Alozaina | 43 E4 | Alpes-Maritimes | 31 E3 |
| Almese | 31 E1 | Almodóvar del | | Sierra | 36 C4 | Almourol | 38 B3 | Alnwick | 5 E3 | Alp | 32 A3 | Alpe Veglia | 58 A3 |
| Almhult | 109 D2 | Campo | 43 F1 | Almonacid de | | Almsee | 56 C3 | Alónia | 79 F3 | Alpalhão | 38 C3 | Alphen aan den |
| Almijara, Sa de | 44 A3 | Almodóvar del | | Toledo | 40 A3 | | | Alónissos | 84 B2 | Alpbach | 59 D1 | Rijn | 16 C3 |
| Almiri | 87 E1 | Pinar | 40 C3 | | | | | Alónissos, N | 84 B2 | Alpe-d'Huez, l' | 31 D1 | Alpi Apuane | 60 B3 |

Alpiarça 38 B3
Alpignano 31 E1
Alpi Orobie 58 B3
Alpirsbach 54 C3
Alpua 99 D4
Alqueva 42 B1
Alqueva, Bgem de 42 B1
Alquézar 37 E3
Als 108 B2
Als (Reg) 108 B4
Alsasua 36 B2
Alsdorf 17 D4
Alsen 101 E2
Alsfeld 52 A3
Alstahaug 97 D3
Alston 5 E4
Alta 95 D2
Altaelva 95 D2
Altafjorden 95 D2
Altamura 65 D3
Alta, Sa 41 D2
Altastenberg 17 F4
Altaussee 56 C3
Altavilla 68 B3
Altdöbern 53 E1
Altdorf (CH) 58 A2
Altdorf (D) 55 F1
Altea 45 E1
Altedo 61 D2
Altena 17 E4
Altenahr 51 E4
Altenau 52 B2
Altenberg 53 E3
Altenberge 17 E3
Altenburg 53 D3
Altenholz 48 A1
Altenhundem 17 F4
Altenkirchen (D) 51 E3
Altenkirchen (DDR) 49 D1
Altenmarkt (D) 56 B3
Altenmarkt (Salzburg) 59 F1
Altenmarkt (Steiermark) 57 D3
Altenstadt 55 E3
Altensteig 54 C3
Altentreptow 49 D2
Altenwalde 47 F2
Alte Oder 49 E3
Alter do Chão 38 C3
Altglashütten 54 C4
Altheim 56 C3
Althofen 70 B1
Altkirch 27 E1
Altlandsberg 49 E4
Altlengbach 57 E2
Altmühl 55 F2
Altmühlsee 55 E2
Altmünster 56 C3
Altnaharra 2 C2
Alto Campó 35 F2
Alto Cruz 36 C4
Alto de Allariz 34 B3
Alto de Barazar 36 B1
Alto de Covelo 34 C3
Alto de Estividas 34 B3
Alto de Fumaces 34 B3
Alto del Couso 34 B3
Alto del Portalé 37 E4
Alto del Rodicio 34 B3
Alto de Santo Domingo 34 B2
Alto do Cañizo 34 C3
Alto Laza 37 D2
Altomira 40 B2
Alton 9 F3
Altopascio 60 C3
Alto Rabagão, Bgem do 34 B3
Altorricon 37 E3
Altotero 36 A2
Altötting 56 B3
Altrincham 6 C2
Alt Ruppin 49 D3
Altshausen 55 D4
Altstätten 58 B2
Altura 41 E3
Altweilnau 51 F4
Alustante 41 D2
Alva 4 C2
Alvaiázere 38 B2
Alvalade 42 A1
Alvão, Sa de 34 B4
Alva, R 38 B2
Alvdal 100 C3
Älvdalen 101 E4
Alvelos, Sa de 38 B2
Alverca do Ribatejo 38 A4
Alvesta 109 D2
Alvignac 29 D2
Ålvik 104 B2
Alvito 42 B1
Alvito, Bgem do 42 B1
Älvkarleby 106 B2
Alvor 42 A2
Älvros 101 E3
Älvsborgs Län 108 C1
Älvsbyn 98 B3
Alyth 5 D1
Alytus 110 C4
Alz 56 B3
Alzenau 52 A4
Alzey 54 C1
Alzira 41 E4
Alzola 36 B1
Alzon 29 F3
Alzonne 32 B1
Amadora 38 A4
Åmål 105 E4
Amalfi 64 B4
Amaliáda 86 B1
Amaliápoli 83 F2
Amálo 89 D2
Amance 27 D1
Amancey 27 D2
Amandola 61 F4
Amantea 67 E3
Amárandos (Ípiros) 78 C4
Amárandos (Thessalía) 83 D2
Amarante 34 B4
Amareleja 42 C1
Amares 34 A4
Amárinthos 84 B4
Amatrice 63 F1
Amay 50 C4
Amaya 35 F3
Ambarès-et-Lagrave 28 B2
Ambasaguas 35 E2
Ambazac 25 E4
Ambelákia (Thessalía) 83 E1
Ambelákia (Thráki) 81 F1
Ambelía 83 E2
Ambelikó 85 F3
Ambelióna 86 C2
Ambelónas 83 E1
Amberg 55 F1
Ambérieu-en-Bugey 26 C4
Ambert 29 F1
Ambès 28 B2
Ambierle 26 B4
Amble 5 E3
Ambleside 5 D4
Amblève 51 D4
Amboise 25 D2
Ambra 61 D4
Ambrières-les-Vallées 18 C4
Ameixial 42 B2
Ameland 16 C1
Amelia 63 E2
Amélie-les-Bains-Palalda 32 B3
Amelinghausen 48 B3
Amer 32 B3
A Merca 34 B3
Amerongen 16 C3
Amersfoort 16 C3
Amersham 9 F2
Amesbury 9 E3
A Mezquita 34 C3
Amfiaraío 84 B4
Amfíklia 83 E3
Amfilohía 82 C3
Amfípoli 80 B2
Ámfissa 83 E4
Amiata, Mont' 63 D1
Amiens 19 F2
Amigdaleónas 80 C2
Amigdaliá 83 E4
Amíndeo 79 D3
Åmli 104 B4
Amlwch 6 A2
Ammanford 8 C2
Ämmänsaari 99 E3
Ammarfjället 97 F3
Ammarnäs 97 F3
Ammel 56 A4
Ammersattel 55 F4
Ammersee 56 A3
Amohóri 79 D3
Amolianí 80 B4
Amorbach 55 D1
Amorebieta 36 B1
Amorgós 89 D3
Amorgós, N 89 D3
Amório 81 F1
Åmot (Buskerud) 104 C3
Åmot (S) 105 F2
Åmot (Telemark) 104 B3
Åmotfors 105 D3
Amótopos 82 C2
Amou 28 B4
Amoudára 91 D3
Amoudára 91 E4
Amoúdia 89 D2
Ampezzo 59 E3
Ampfing 56 B3
Amphion 27 D3
Amplepuis 26 B4
Amposta 41 F2
Ampthill 9 F2
Ampudia 35 E4
Ampuero 36 A1
Amriswil 58 B1
Amrum 47 F1
Amsele 98 B4
Amstelveen 16 C2
Amsterdam 16 C2
Amstetten 57 D3
Amungen 101 E4
Amurrio 36 B1
Amusco 35 F3
Amvrakía, L 82 C3
Amvrakikós Kólpos 82 C3
Anadia 38 B1
Anáfi 91 E1
Anáfi, N 91 F1
Anafonítria 86 A1
Anagni 63 F3
Anáktora Néstoros 86 B3
Análipsi 83 F4
Análipsi 92 C1
Análipsis 86 C3
Ananjev 113 E3
Anaráhi 79 D3
Anárgiri 79 D3
Anarjohka 95 E2
Anascaul 14 A3
Ånaset 102 B1
Åna Sira 104 A4
Anatolí (Ípiros) 82 C1
Anatolí (Kríti) 91 E4
Anatolí (Thessalía) 83 F1
Anatolikí Rodópi 81 D2
Anatolikó 79 D3
Änättijärvi 99 F4
Anávatos 85 E4
Anávissos 87 F2
Anávra (Karditsa) 83 E2
Anávra (Magnissía) 83 E3
An Cabhán 13 D3
Ancares, Sa de 34 C2
Ancenis 23 D4
Ancerville 20 C4
Anchuras 39 F3
An Clochán 12 A3
An Cóbh 14 C4
Ancona 61 F3
Ancy-le-Franc 26 B1
Anda 100 A3
Andalo 58 C3
Åndalsnes 100 B2
Andalucía 43 E2
Andarax, R 44 B3
Andartikó 79 D2
Andebu 104 C3
Andelot 26 C1
Andelys, les 19 E3
Andenes 94 A3
Andenne 50 C4
Anderlues 50 B4
Andermatt 58 A3
Andernach 51 E4
Andernos 28 A2
Anderstorp 109 D2
Andfjorden 94 B3
Andígonos 79 D3
Andikíra 83 E4
Andikíras, Kólpos 83 E4
Andikíthira, N 90 A2
Andimáhia 89 F3
Andímilos, N 88 A4
Andinítsa 83 E3
Andíparos 88 B3
Andíparos, N 88 B3
Andípaxi, N 82 B2
Andípsara, N 85 E4
Andírio 83 D4
Ándissa 85 E2
Andoain 36 C1
Andorno Micca 31 F1
Andorra 41 E1
Andorra la Vella 32 A2
Andosilla 36 C2
Andover 9 E3
Andøya 94 A3
Andratx 45 E3
Andravída 86 B1
Andretta 64 C3
Andrézieux-Bouthéon 30 B1
Andria 65 D3
Andrijevica 76 C2
Andrítsena 86 C2
Andros 88 B1
Ándros, N 88 B1
Androússa 86 C3
Andselv 94 B3
Andújar 43 F2
Anduze 30 B3
Aneby 109 D1
Ånes 100 B2
Anet 19 E4
Aneto, Pico de 37 E2
Angáli 84 A3
Ånge (Jämtlands Län) 101 E2
Ånge (Västernorrlands Län) 101 E3
Angeja 38 B1
Ängelholm 108 C3
Angeli 95 E3
Angelohóri 79 E3
Angelókastro (Pelopónissos) 87 E2
Angelókastro (Stereá Eláda) 82 C4
Anger 57 E4
Angera 58 A4
Ångermanälven 101 F2
Angermünde 49 E3
Angern 57 F2
Angers 23 E4
Angerville 25 E1
Ängesån 98 C2
Anghiari 61 D4
Angístis, Stathmós 80 B2
Angístri 87 E2
Angístri, N 87 E2
Angístro 80 B1
Angítis 80 B2
Angles 25 D3
Anglès (E) 32 B3
Anglès (F) 32 B1
Anglesey, I of 6 A2
Anglesola 37 F3
Anglet 28 A4
Anglure 20 B4
Angoulême 28 C1
Angri 64 B4
Angsö 106 C3
Angües 37 E3
Anguiano 36 B2
Anguillara Veneta 61 D1
Angvik 100 B2
Anholt 108 C2
Aniane 30 A4
Aniche 20 A1
Aniene 63 F2
Ánixi 79 D4
Anizy-le-Château 20 A3
Anjalankoski 107 F2
Anjum 47 D3
Ankaran 70 A3
Ankarsrum 109 E1
Anklam 49 E2
Ankogel 59 E2
An Longfort 12 C3
An Muileann gCearr 13 D3
Ånn 101 D2
Ånn L 101 D2
Annaberg 57 E3
Annaberg-Buchholz 53 E3
Annaburg 53 E1
Annan 5 D3
Annan, R 5 D3
Anndalsvågen 97 D3
Annecy 27 D4
Annemasse 27 D4
Annevoie-Rouillon 50 C4
Annonay 30 B1
Annone Veneto 59 E4
Annot 31 D3
Annweiler 54 C2
Áno Drossiní 81 E2
Anógia 87 D3
Anógia 91 D3
Áno Hóra 83 D4
Anoia, R 32 A4
Áno Kalendíni 82 C2
Áno Kaliníki 79 D2
Áno Kómi 79 E4
Áno Lefkími 82 A2
Áno Melás 79 D3
Áno Merá 88 C2
Anópoli 90 C4
Áno Polidéndri 83 F1
Áno Poróia 80 A2
Áno Rodákino 90 C4
Áno Sangrí 88 C3
Áno Síros 88 B2
Añover de Tajo 40 A3
Áno Viános 91 E4
Áno Vrondoú 80 B2
Áno Zervohóri 79 E3
Ansbach 55 E1
Anse 26 C4
Ansedonia 63 D2
Ansião 38 B2
Ansnes 100 C1
Ansó 37 D2
Anstruther 5 D2
An tAonach 12 C4
Antas 44 C3
Antegnate 60 B1
Antemil 34 A1
Antequera 43 F3
Anterselva 59 D2
Ánthia 81 E2
Anthíli 83 E3
Anthís 80 B2
Antholz 59 D2
Anthótopos 83 E2
Antibes 31 E4
Antifer, Cap d' 19 D3
An tInbhear Mór 15 E3
Antnäs 98 C3
Antraigues 30 B2
Antrain 18 B4
Antrim 13 E2
Antrim (Co) 13 E2
Antrim Coast 13 E1
Antrim Mts 13 E1
Antrodoco 63 F2
Anttola 103 E3
Antwerpen 50 B3
Antwerpen (Prov) 50 C3
An Uaimh 13 D3
Anvers 50 B3
Anzano di Puglia 64 C3
Anzio 63 E3
Anzola d'Ossola 58 A4
Anzy-le-Duc 26 B4
Aoiz 36 C2
Aóos 78 C4
Aosta 27 E4
Aoste 27 E4
Apatin 72 B2
Apatovac 71 D2
Apecchio 61 E4
Apeldoorn 17 D2
Apen 47 E3
Apéri 93 D3
Aphrodisias 115 F4
Apidiá 87 D3
Apíkia 88 B1
Apíranthos 88 C3
Apolakiá 93 E2
Apolda 52 C3
Apolitáres, Akr 90 A2
Apólonas 88 C3
Apolonia (Kiklädes) 88 B3
Apolonía (Makedonía) 80 B3
A Pontenova Villaodriz 34 C1
Apóstoli 90 C4
Äppelbo 105 E2
Appenweier 54 C3
Appenzell 58 B2
Appiano 59 D3
Appingedam 47 D3
Appleby 5 D4
Aprica 58 C3
Apricena 64 C2
Aprilia 63 E3
Ápsalos 79 E2
Apt 30 C3
Áptera 90 C3
Aquileia 59 F3
Aquitaine, L' 25 E2
Arabba 59 D3
Aracena 42 C2
Aracena, Emb de 43 D2
Aracena, Sa de 42 C2
Aračinovo 77 E3
Arad 112 C4
Årådalsfjorden 104 B1
Arada, Sa de 38 B1
Aragón 37 D3
Aragona 68 B4
Aragón, R 36 C2
Arahnéo, Óros 87 E2
Aráhova (Etolía-Akarnanía) 83 D3
Aráhova (Viotía) 83 E4
Arákinthos, Óros 83 D4
A Ramallosa 34 A3
Aramits 37 D1
Aranda de Duero 36 A3
Aranđelovac 73 D3
Aran I 12 C1
Aran Is 12 A4
Aranjuez 40 B3
Arantzazu 36 B1
Aran, Vall d' 37 F2
Araquil, R 36 C2
Ara, R 37 E2
Aras de Alpuente 41 D3
Arasluokta 97 F1
Árahthos 82 C2
Áratos 81 E2
Aravaca 40 A2
Aravis, Col des 27 D4
Aravissós 79 E2
Áraxos 86 B1
Áraxos, Akr 86 B1
Arazede 38 B2
Arba, R 36 C3
Arbatax 66 C3
Arbeca 37 F4
Arbesbach 57 D2
Arboga 105 F3
Arbois 27 D3
Arbon 58 B1
Arbón, Emb de 34 C1
Arborea 66 B3
Arborio 31 F1
Arbrå 101 F4
Arbroath 5 E1
Arbresle, l' 26 B4
Arbúcies 32 B4
Arbus 66 B3
Arc 31 D1
Arcachon 28 A2
Arce 64 A3
Arcen 17 D3
Arc-en-Barrois 26 C1
Arceniega 36 A1
Arcevia 61 E4
Archena 45 D2
Arches 27 D1
Archiac 28 B1
Archidona 43 F3
Arcidosso 63 D1
Arcipelago Toscano 62 B1
Arcis 20 B4
Arciz 113 E4
Arco 58 C4
Arco de Baúlhe 34 B4
Arcos 35 F3
Arcos de Jalón 36 B4
Arcos de la Frontera 43 D3
Arcos de Valdevez 34 A3
Arcouest, Pte de l' 22 C2
Arcs, les (Savoie) 31 D1
Arcs, les (Var) 31 D4
Arcusa 37 E2
Arda 115 E3
Ardales 43 E3
Årdalstangen 104 B1
Ardánio 81 F2
Ardara 12 C1
Árdas 81 F1
Ardbeg 4 B2
Ardèche (Dépt) 30 B2
Ardèche R 30 B2
Ardèche, Gges de l' 30 B3
Ardee 13 D3
Ardennes (Dépt) 20 B3
Ardennes, Canal des 20 C3
Ardentes 25 E3
Ardentinny 4 C2
Ardes 29 F1
Ardez 58 B2
Ardglass 13 E2
Ardila, R 42 C1
Ardila, Rib de 42 C1
Ardisa 37 D3
Ardlussa 4 B2
Ardmore 14 C4
Ardrahan 12 B4
Ardres 19 E1
Ardrishaig 4 B2
Ardrossan 4 C2
Ards Pen 13 E2
Arduaine 4 B1
Ardvasar 2 B4
Åre 101 D2
Arenas de Cabrales 35 E2
Arenas de Iguña 35 F2
Arenas de San Juan 40 B4
Arenas de San Pedro 39 F2
Arendal 104 C4
Arendonk 50 C3
Arendsee 48 C3
Arenos, Emb de 41 E3
Arenys de Mar 32 B4
Arenzano 60 A3
Areópoli 87 D4
Arès 28 A2
Ares (Galicia) 34 B1
Ares (Valencia) 41 E2
Ares, Col des 37 F2
Ares, Pto de 32 B3
Åreskutan 101 D2
Aréthoussa 80 B3
Aretí 80 A3
Arévalo 39 F1
Arez 38 C3
Arezzo 61 D4
Arfará 86 C3
Argalastí 83 F2
Argamasilla de Alba 40 B4
Argamasilla de Calatrava 44 A1
Arganda 40 B2
Arganil 38 B2
Arga, R 36 C2
Argássi 86 A2
Argelès 32 B2
Argelès-Gazost 37 E1
Argens 31 D4
Argent 25 F2
Argenta 61 D2
Argentan 19 D4
Argentario, Mte 63 D2
Argentat 29 D2
Argente 41 D2
Argentera 31 E3
Argentière 27 E4
Argentière-la-Bessée, l' 31 D2
Argentona 32 B4
Argenton-Château 24 C3
Argenton-sur-Creuse 25 E3
Argentré-du-Plessis 23 E3
Arginónda 89 F3
Argirádes 82 A2

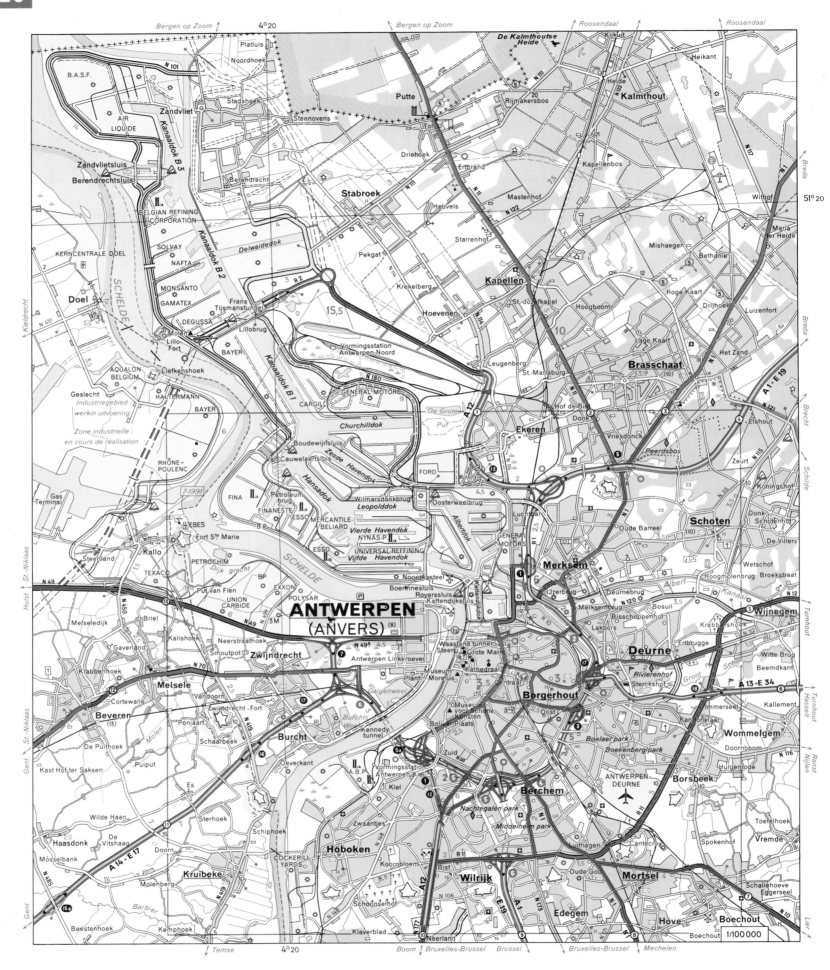

| Name | Map | Grid |
|------|-----|------|
| Argiró | 84 | B4 |
| Argiropoúlio | 83 | E1 |
| Argiroúpoli | 90 | C3 |
| Argithéa | 83 | D2 |
| Argolída | 87 | E2 |
| Argolikós Kólpos | 87 | E2 |
| Árgos | 87 | D2 |
| Árgos Orestikó | 79 | D3 |
| Argos, R | 44 | C2 |
| Argostóli | 82 | B4 |
| Arguedas | 36 | C3 |
| Argueil | 19 | E3 |
| Arguellite | 44 | B1 |
| Arguis | 37 | D2 |
| Argyll | 4 | B1 |
| Argyll Forest Park | 4 | C2 |
| Arhánes | 91 | D4 |
| Arhángelos (Makedonía) | 79 | E2 |
| Arhángelos (Ródos) | 93 | F1 |
| Arhéa Epídavros | 87 | E2 |
| Arhéa Kleonés | 87 | D1 |
| Arhéa Kórinthos | 87 | E1 |
| Arhéa Neméa | 87 | D1 |
| Arhéa Olympía | 86 | C2 |
| Arhéa Thíra | 91 | E1 |
| Århus | 108 | B3 |
| Arianá | 81 | E2 |
| Ariano Irpino | 64 | B3 |
| Ariano nel Polesine | 61 | D2 |
| Aridéa | 79 | E2 |
| Ariège (Dépt) | 32 | A2 |
| Ariège R | 32 | A2 |
| Arija | 35 | F2 |
| Arild | 108 | C3 |
| Arilje | 72 | C4 |
| Arinagour | 2 | B4 |
| Aríni | 86 | C2 |
| Ariño | 37 | D4 |
| Arinthod | 27 | D3 |
| Arisaig | 2 | B4 |
| Arisaig, Sd of | 2 | B4 |
| Arísti | 78 | C4 |
| Aristoménis | 86 | C3 |
| Arisvi | 81 | E2 |
| Aritzo | 66 | B3 |
| Arive | 36 | C2 |
| Ariza | 36 | B4 |
| Árjäng | 105 | D3 |
| Arjeplog | 98 | A3 |
| Arjona | 44 | A2 |
| Arkádi | 91 | D3 |
| Arkadía | 86 | C2 |
| Arkaig, L | 2 | C4 |
| Arkalohóri | 91 | E4 |
| Arkássa | 93 | D3 |
| Arkessíni | 89 | D3 |
| Arkí, N | 89 | E2 |
| Arkítsa | 83 | F3 |
| Arklow | 15 | E3 |
| Arkona, Kap | 49 | D1 |
| Arkoúdi, N | 82 | B4 |
| Arlaban, Pto de | 36 | B1 |
| Arlanc | 29 | F1 |
| Arlanda | 106 | B3 |
| Arlanza, R | 36 | A3 |
| Arlanzón | 36 | A2 |
| Arlanzón, R | 35 | F3 |
| Arlbergpaß | 58 | B2 |
| Arlberg-Straßentunnel | 58 | B2 |
| Arlempdes | 30 | A2 |
| Arles (Bouches-du-Rhône) | 30 | B4 |
| Arles (Pyrénées-Orientales) | 32 | B3 |
| Arlesheim | 27 | E2 |
| Arlon | 21 | D2 |
| Arlsleben | 52 | C2 |
| Armação de Pêra | 42 | A3 |
| Armadale | 5 | D2 |
| Arma di Taggia | 31 | F3 |
| Armagh | 13 | D2 |
| Armagh (Co) | 13 | D2 |
| Armamar | 34 | B4 |
| Arméni | 90 | C3 |
| Armenií | 86 | C3 |
| Armenistís | 89 | D2 |
| Armentières | 19 | F1 |
| Armilla | 44 | A3 |
| Armólia | 85 | E4 |
| Armunia | 35 | D3 |
| Árna | 87 | D3 |
| Arnac-Pompadour | 29 | D1 |
| Arnay-le-Duc | 26 | B2 |
| Arnéa | 80 | B3 |
| Arneburg | 48 | C4 |
| Arnedillo | 36 | B3 |
| Arnedo | 36 | C3 |
| Árnes | 41 | F2 |
| Árnes | 105 | D3 |
| Arnhem | 17 | D3 |
| Arni | 60 | B3 |
| Árnissa | 79 | E2 |
| Arno | 60 | C4 |
| Arnoldstein | 59 | F2 |
| Arnon | 25 | F3 |
| Arnøy | 94 | C2 |
| Arnsberg | 17 | F3 |
| Arnstadt | 52 | C3 |
| Arnstein | 52 | B4 |
| Aroania, Óri | 86 | C1 |
| Aroche | 42 | C2 |
| Aroche Mt | 42 | C1 |
| Arogí | 81 | D2 |
| Arolsen | 52 | A2 |
| Arona | 58 | A4 |
| Aroniádika | 90 | A1 |
| Aronkylä | 102 | B3 |
| Áros | 104 | C3 |
| Arosa | 58 | B2 |
| Arouca | 38 | B1 |
| Arousa, I de | 34 | A2 |
| Arøysund | 104 | C3 |
| Arpajon | 19 | F4 |
| Arpela | 99 | D3 |
| Arquata del Tronto | 63 | F1 |
| Arques (Pas-de-Calais) | 19 | F1 |
| Arques (Seine-Maritime) | 19 | E2 |
| Arquillos | 44 | A2 |
| Arrabal | 34 | A3 |
| Arrábida, Sa da | 38 | A4 |
| Arracourt | 21 | D4 |
| Arraiolos | 38 | B4 |
| Arran | 4 | B2 |
| Arras | 19 | F2 |
| Arrasate-Mondragon | 36 | B1 |
| Arreau | 37 | E2 |
| Arrecife | 42 | C4 |
| Arredondo | 36 | A1 |
| Arrée, Mts d' | 22 | B2 |
| Arrens | 37 | E2 |
| Arrifana | 38 | C1 |
| Arrigorriaga | 36 | B1 |
| Arriondas | 35 | E1 |
| Arrochar | 4 | C2 |
| Arromanches | 18 | C3 |
| Arronches | 38 | C4 |
| Arroux | 26 | B3 |
| Arrow, L | 12 | C2 |
| Arroyo de la Luz | 39 | D3 |
| Arroyo del Ojanco | 44 | B1 |
| Arroyo de San Serván | 39 | D4 |
| Arroyomolinos de León | 43 | D1 |
| Arroyomolinos de Montánchez | 39 | D4 |
| Arruda dos Vinhos | 38 | A3 |
| Árs | 108 | A2 |
| Ars (Charente-Maritime) | 24 | B4 |
| Ars (Moselle) | 21 | D3 |
| Arsiè | 59 | D3 |
| Arsiero | 59 | D4 |
| Árs Kógssanður | 96 | B1 |
| Arsunda | 106 | B2 |
| Arsy | 19 | F3 |
| Artà | 45 | F2 |
| Árta | 82 | C2 |
| Árta (Nomos) | 82 | C2 |
| Arta Terme | 59 | E3 |
| Arteaga, G de | 36 | B1 |
| Artemissía | 86 | C3 |
| Artemíssio (Évia) | 83 | F3 |
| Artemíssio (Pelopónissos) | 87 | D2 |
| Artemónas | 88 | B3 |
| Artena | 63 | F3 |
| Artenay | 25 | E1 |
| Artern | 52 | C2 |
| Artesa de Segre | 37 | F3 |
| Artessianó | 83 | D2 |
| Artfjället | 97 | E3 |
| Arth (CH) | 58 | A2 |
| Arth (D) | 56 | B2 |
| Arthurstown | 15 | D4 |
| Arties | 37 | F2 |
| Artjärvi | 107 | F2 |
| Artotína | 83 | D3 |
| Artruix, C de | 45 | F2 |
| A Rúa | 34 | C3 |
| Arucas | 42 | B4 |
| Arudy | 37 | D1 |
| Arundel | 9 | F3 |
| Arve | 27 | E4 |
| Árvi | 91 | E4 |
| Arvidsjaur | 98 | A3 |
| Árvik | 100 | A2 |
| Arvika | 105 | E3 |
| Årviksand | 94 | C2 |
| Arzachena | 66 | B1 |
| Arzacq-Arraziguet | 28 | B4 |
| Arzano | 22 | B3 |
| Aržano | 75 | E1 |
| Arzberg | 53 | D4 |
| Arzignano | 60 | C1 |
| Árzos | 81 | F1 |
| Arzúa | 34 | B2 |
| As | 50 | C3 |
| Aš | 53 | D4 |
| Åsa | 108 | C2 |
| Asamati | 77 | D4 |
| Åsarna | 101 | E2 |
| Åsarp | 109 | D1 |
| Ascain | 28 | A4 |
| Ascha | 56 | B2 |
| Aschach | 56 | C2 |
| Aschaffenburg | 52 | A4 |
| Aschau | 56 | B3 |
| Aschbach Markt | 57 | D3 |
| Ascheberg (Nordrhein-Westfalen) | 17 | E3 |
| Ascheberg (Schleswig-Holstein) | 48 | B2 |
| Aschendorf | 17 | E1 |
| Aschersleben | 52 | C2 |
| Asciano | 61 | D4 |
| Ascione, Colle d' | 67 | F3 |
| Asco | 33 | F3 |
| Ascó | 37 | E4 |
| Ascoli Piceno | 63 | F1 |
| Ascoli Satriano | 64 | C3 |
| Ascona | 58 | A3 |
| Åse | 94 | A3 |
| Åseda | 109 | E2 |
| Åsele | 101 | F1 |
| Åsen | 101 | D1 |
| Asenovgrad | 115 | D3 |
| Åseral | 104 | B4 |
| Asfáka | 82 | B1 |
| Asfeld | 20 | B3 |
| Åsgårdstrand | 104 | C3 |
| Ashbourne (GB) | 6 | C3 |
| Ashbourne (IRL) | 13 | D3 |
| Ashburton | 8 | C4 |
| Ashby de la Zouch | 6 | C3 |
| Ashford | 11 | D3 |
| Ashington | 5 | E1 |
| Ashton-under-Lyne | 6 | C2 |
| Asiago | 59 | D4 |
| Asikkala | 107 | F2 |
| Asin | 37 | D3 |
| Asinara, G dell' | 66 | B1 |
| Asinara, I | 66 | A1 |
| Ask | 105 | D3 |
| Askainen | 107 | D2 |
| Askeaton | 14 | B3 |
| Askersund | 105 | F4 |
| Askifou | 90 | C3 |
| Askim | 105 | D3 |
| Áskio, Óros | 79 | D3 |
| Askja | 96 | C2 |
| Asklipiío (Dodekánissa) | 89 | F3 |
| Asklipiío (Ródos) | 93 | E2 |
| Askola | 107 | F2 |
| Askós | 80 | A3 |
| Askøy | 104 | A2 |
| Askvoll | 104 | A1 |
| Asmunti | 99 | D3 |
| Asnæs | 108 | B3 |
| Asnen | 109 | D2 |
| As Neves | 34 | A3 |
| Asola | 60 | B1 |
| Asolo | 59 | D4 |
| Aspang | 57 | F3 |
| Aspatria | 5 | D4 |
| Aspe | 45 | D2 |
| Aspe, Gave d' | 37 | D1 |
| Asperg | 55 | D2 |
| Aspet | 37 | F2 |
| Aspin, Col d' | 37 | E2 |
| As Ponte de Garcia Rodriguez | 34 | B1 |
| Áspra Spítia | 83 | E4 |
| Aspres | 30 | C2 |
| Áspro | 79 | E3 |
| Aspróhoma | 86 | C3 |
| Asprókavos, Akr | 82 | A2 |
| Aspromonte | 67 | E4 |
| Asprópirgos | 87 | F1 |
| Asproválta | 80 | B3 |
| Asse | 50 | B3 |
| Assemini | 66 | B4 |
| Assen | 17 | D1 |
| Assens | 108 | B3 |
| Assergi | 63 | F2 |
| Assíni | 87 | E2 |
| Assisi | 63 | E1 |
| Aßmannshausen | 51 | F4 |
| Assomáton | 91 | D3 |
| Assopía | 84 | A4 |
| Assopós (Korinthía) | 87 | D1 |
| Assopós (Lakonía) | 87 | E4 |
| Assopós R | 87 | E1 |
| Ássos (Ípiros) | 82 | B2 |
| Ássos (Kefaloniá) | 82 | B4 |
| Astaffort | 28 | C3 |
| Astafjorden | 94 | B3 |
| Astakída, N | 93 | D2 |
| Astakós | 82 | C4 |
| Asten | 57 | D3 |
| Asti | 31 | F2 |
| Astipálea | 92 | C1 |
| Astipálea, N | 92 | C1 |
| Astorga | 35 | D3 |
| Åstorp | 108 | C3 |
| Ástros | 87 | D2 |
| Astudillo | 35 | F3 |
| Asturias | 34 | C2 |
| Asvestádes | 81 | F1 |
| Asvestohóri | 82 | B1 |
| Asvestópetra | 79 | D3 |
| Atalaia | 38 | A3 |
| Atalándi | 83 | F3 |
| Atalaya de la Calzada | 44 | A1 |
| Atalayassa | 45 | D4 |
| Átali | 84 | B3 |
| Ataquines | 39 | F1 |
| Atarfe | 44 | A3 |
| Atáviros | 93 | E2 |
| Ateca | 36 | C4 |
| Atella | 64 | C3 |
| Atessa | 64 | B2 |
| Ath | 50 | B4 |
| Athamánon, Óri | 82 | C2 |
| Athánio | 82 | B3 |
| Athboy | 13 | D3 |
| Athenry | 12 | B3 |
| Athéras | 89 | D2 |
| Athéras, Akr | 82 | B4 |
| Atherstone | 9 | E1 |
| Athína | 87 | F1 |
| Áthira | 79 | F2 |
| Athlone | 12 | C3 |
| Áthos | 80 | C4 |
| Athy | 13 | D4 |
| Atienza | 36 | B4 |
| Atiki-Piréas | 87 | F1 |
| Atina | 64 | A3 |
| Átokos, N | 82 | C4 |
| Atouguia da Baleia | 38 | A3 |
| Åtran | 108 | C2 |
| Åtran R | 108 | C2 |
| Atri | 64 | A1 |
| Atsiki | 85 | D1 |
| Attendorn | 17 | F4 |
| Attersee | 56 | C3 |
| Attersee L | 56 | C3 |
| Attigliano | 63 | E2 |
| Attigny | 20 | B3 |
| Attleborough | 11 | D1 |
| Attnang | 56 | C3 |
| Åtvidaberg | 109 | E1 |
| Au | 55 | F2 |
| Aub | 55 | E1 |
| Aubagne | 30 | C4 |
| Aubange | 21 | D2 |
| Aube | 20 | B4 |
| Aube (Dépt) | 20 | B4 |
| Aubenas | 30 | B2 |
| Aubenton | 20 | B2 |
| Auberive | 26 | C1 |
| Aubeterre | 28 | C1 |
| Aubigny (Cher) | 25 | F2 |
| Aubigny (Pas-de-Calais) | 19 | F2 |
| Aubin | 29 | E3 |
| Aubisque, Col d' | 37 | E1 |
| Aubonne | 27 | D3 |
| Aubrac | 29 | F2 |
| Aubrac, Mts d' | 29 | F2 |
| Aubusson | 25 | F4 |
| Auch | 28 | C4 |
| Auchencairn | 4 | C3 |
| Auchterarder | 5 | D1 |
| Auchtermuchty | 5 | D1 |
| Aude (Dépt) | 32 | B2 |
| Aude R | 32 | B1 |
| Audenge | 28 | A2 |
| Audeux | 27 | D2 |
| Audierne | 22 | A3 |
| Audincourt | 27 | E2 |
| Audlem | 6 | C3 |
| Audruicq | 19 | F1 |
| Audun-le-Roman | 21 | D3 |
| Audun-le-Tiche | 21 | D3 |
| Aue R | 48 | A4 |
| Aue | 53 | D3 |
| Auer | 59 | D3 |
| Auerbach (D) | 55 | F1 |
| Auerbach (DDR) | 53 | D3 |
| Auffach | 59 | D1 |
| Aughnacloy | 13 | D2 |
| Aughrim | 13 | D4 |
| Augsburg | 55 | F3 |
| Augusta | 69 | D4 |
| Augustenborg | 108 | B4 |
| Augustów | 110 | C4 |
| Augustusburg | 53 | E3 |
| Aukan | 100 | B2 |
| Aukra | 100 | B2 |
| Aulanko | 107 | E2 |
| Auletta | 64 | C4 |
| Aulla | 60 | B3 |
| Aullène | 33 | F4 |
| Aulnay | 24 | C4 |
| Aulne | 22 | B3 |
| Aulnoye-Aymeries | 20 | B2 |
| Aulus-les-Bains | 37 | F2 |
| Auma | 53 | D3 |
| Aumale | 19 | E2 |
| Aumetz | 21 | D3 |
| Aumont-Aubrac | 29 | F2 |
| Aunay-sur-Odon | 18 | C3 |
| Auneau | 19 | E4 |
| Auneuil | 19 | E3 |
| Auning | 108 | B2 |
| Aups | 31 | D4 |
| Aura | 107 | D2 |
| Aurajoki | 107 | D2 |
| Auray | 22 | C4 |
| Aurdal | 104 | C2 |
| Aure | 100 | B2 |
| Aurich | 47 | E3 |
| Aurignac | 37 | F1 |
| Aurillac | 29 | E2 |
| Aurland | 104 | B2 |
| Auron | 31 | E3 |
| Auron R | 25 | F3 |
| Auronzo di Cadore | 59 | E2 |
| Auros | 28 | B3 |
| Aursjøen | 100 | B3 |
| Aursuden | 101 | D2 |
| Ausonia | 64 | A3 |
| Außernbrünst | 56 | C2 |
| Ausso Corno | 59 | F3 |
| Aust-Agder | 104 | B4 |
| Austbygd | 104 | C3 |
| Austvågøy | 94 | A3 |
| Auterive | 37 | F1 |
| Authie | 19 | F2 |
| Autol | 36 | C3 |
| Autrans | 30 | C1 |
| Autrey | 26 | C2 |
| Auttoinen | 107 | E1 |
| Autun | 26 | B3 |
| Auvézère | 28 | C2 |
| Auvillar | 28 | C3 |
| Auxerre | 26 | B2 |
| Auxi-le-Château | 19 | E2 |
| Auxonne | 26 | C2 |
| Availles-Limouzine | 25 | D4 |
| Avala | 73 | D3 |
| Avaldsnes | 104 | A3 |
| Avallon | 26 | B2 |
| Avaloirs, Mt des | 23 | E3 |
| Ávas | 81 | E2 |
| Avaviken | 98 | A3 |
| Ávdira | 81 | D2 |
| Avebury | 9 | E2 |
| A Veiga | 34 | C3 |
| Aveiras de Cima | 38 | A3 |
| Aveiro | 38 | B1 |
| Aveiro, R de | 38 | B1 |
| Aven Armand | 29 | F3 |
| Aven d'Orgnac | 30 | B3 |
| Averøya | 100 | B2 |
| Aversa | 64 | B4 |
| Avesnes | 20 | B2 |
| Avesnes-le-Comte | 19 | F2 |
| Avesta | 105 | F3 |
| Avetrana | 65 | E4 |
| Aveyron | 29 | D3 |
| Aveyron (Dépt) | 29 | E3 |
| Avezzano | 63 | F2 |
| Avgerinós | 79 | D4 |
| Avgó | 82 | C2 |
| Avia | 86 | C3 |
| Aviano | 59 | E3 |
| Aviémonas | 90 | A2 |
| Aviemore | 3 | D4 |
| Aviés | 79 | E4 |
| Avigliana | 31 | E1 |
| Avigliano | 64 | C4 |
| Avignon | 30 | B3 |
| Ávila | 39 | F2 |
| Ávila, Sa de | 39 | F2 |
| Avilés | 35 | D1 |
| Aviño | 34 | B1 |
| Avintes | 34 | A4 |
| Avión | 34 | B2 |
| Avioth | 20 | C3 |
| Avis | 38 | B4 |
| Avisio | 59 | D3 |
| Avize | 20 | B3 |
| Avlákia | 89 | E1 |
| Avlí | 80 | C2 |
| Avliótes | 82 | A1 |
| Avlóna | 84 | B4 |
| Avlum | 108 | A2 |
| Avola | 69 | D4 |
| Avon (Co) | 9 | D2 |
| Avon R (Hants) | 9 | E1 |
| Avon R (Warw) | 9 | E3 |
| Avonmouth | 9 | D2 |
| Avord | 25 | F3 |
| Avoriaz | 27 | E4 |
| Avranches | 18 | B4 |
| Avre | 19 | D4 |
| Avtovac | 76 | A2 |
| Awe, L | 4 | B1 |
| Axams | 59 | D2 |
| Axat | 32 | B2 |
| Axiohóri | 79 | F2 |
| Axiós | 79 | F3 |
| Axioúpoli | 79 | F2 |
| Ax-les-Thermes | 32 | A2 |
| Axminster | 9 | D3 |
| Axós | 91 | D3 |
| Ay | 20 | B3 |
| Ayamonte | 42 | B2 |
| Aydin | 115 | F4 |
| Ayedo | 36 | B3 |
| Ayerbe | 37 | D3 |
| Aylesbury | 9 | F2 |
| Ayllón | 36 | A4 |
| Ayllón, Sa de | 36 | A4 |
| Aylsham | 7 | F3 |
| Ayna | 44 | C1 |
| Ayora | 41 | D4 |
| Ayr | 4 | C3 |
| Ayre, Pt of | 6 | A1 |
| Ayvacık | 115 | E4 |
| Ayvalik | 115 | E4 |
| Aywaille | 51 | D4 |
| Azáceta, Pto de | 36 | B2 |
| Azaila | 37 | D4 |
| Azambuja | 38 | A3 |
| Azanja | 73 | D3 |
| Azaruja | 38 | B4 |
| Azay-le-Ferron | 25 | E3 |
| Azay-le-Rideau | 25 | D2 |
| Azinheira dos Barros | 42 | A1 |
| Azkoitia | 36 | B1 |
| Aznalcázar | 43 | D3 |
| Aznalcóllar | 43 | D2 |
| Azpeitia | 36 | B1 |
| Azuaga | 43 | E1 |
| Azuara | 37 | D4 |
| Azuer, R | 40 | A4 |
| Azuqueca de Henares | 40 | B2 |
| Azután, Emb de | 39 | F3 |
| Azzano Decimo | 59 | E3 |

## B

| | | | |
|---|---|---|---|
| Baad | 58 B2 | Bačko Petrovo | |
| Baal | 17 D4 | Selo | 72 C1 |
| Baamonde | 34 B1 | Bačkovo | 115 D3 |
| Baarle-Nassau | 16 C4 | Bacoli | 64 A4 |
| Baarn | 16 C2 | Bacqueville | 19 D2 |
| Baba | 77 E4 | Baczyna | 49 F3 |
| Babadag | 113 E4 | Bad Aibling | 56 B3 |
| Babajevo | 111 E1 | Badajoz | 38 C4 |
| Babelsberg | 49 D4 | Badalona | 32 B4 |
| Babenhausen | | Bad Aussee | 56 C3 |
| (Bayern) | 55 E3 | Bad Bentheim | 17 E2 |
| Babenhausen | | Bad Bergzabern | 54 C2 |
| (Hessen) | 52 A4 | Bad Berka | 52 C3 |
| Babina Greda | 71 F3 | Bad Berleburg | 17 F4 |
| Babin Kal | 73 F4 | Bad Berneck | 53 D3 |
| Babin Most | 77 D2 | Bad Bertrich | 51 E4 |
| Babino Polje | 75 D3 | Bad Bevensen | 48 B3 |
| Babin Potok | 70 C4 | Bad Bibra | 52 C2 |
| Babljak | 76 B2 | Bad Blankenburg | 52 C3 |
| Babuna | 77 E3 | Bad Brambach | 53 D4 |
| Babušnica | 77 E1 | Bad Bramstedt | 48 A2 |
| Bač | 72 B2 | Bad Brückenau | 52 B4 |
| Bački Breg | 72 B1 | Bad Buchau | 55 D3 |
| Bacău | 113 D4 | Bad Camberg | 51 F4 |
| Baccarat | 21 E4 | Bad Deutsch | |
| Bæccegæhal'di | 94 C2 | Altenburg | 57 F2 |
| Baceno | 58 A3 | Bad Doberan | 48 C2 |
| Bacharach | 51 E4 | Bad Driburg | 52 A2 |
| Bächistock | 58 A2 | Bad Düben | 53 D2 |
| Bachmač | 113 F1 | Bad Dürkheim | 54 C1 |
| Bačina | 73 E4 | Bad Dürrenberg | 53 D2 |
| Bačka Palanka | 72 B2 | Bad Durrheim | 54 C3 |
| Bäckaskog | 109 D3 | Bad Elster | 53 D4 |
| Bačka Topola | 72 B1 | Bad Ems | 51 E4 |
| Backe | 101 F1 | Baden (A) | 57 F3 |
| Bäckebo | 109 E2 | Baden (CH) | 27 F2 |
| Bäckefors | 105 E3 | Baden-Baden | 54 C2 |
| Bački Breg | 71 F1 | Bad Endorf | 56 B3 |
| Bački Brestovac | 72 B2 | Badenweiler | 54 C4 |
| Bački Monoštor | 72 B2 | Baden- | |
| Bački Petrovac | 72 B2 | Württemberg | 55 D3 |
| Backnang | 55 D2 | Baderna | 70 A3 |
| Bačko Gradište | 72 C2 | Bad Essen | 17 F2 |
| Bačko Novo Selo | 72 B2 | Bad | |
| | | Frankenhausen | 52 C2 |
| | | Bad Freienwalde | 49 E3 |
| Bad Friedrichshall | 55 D2 | Bad Münder | 52 A1 |
| Bad Gandersheim | 52 B1 | Bad Münster am | |
| Badgastein | 59 E2 | Stein-Ebernburg | 54 B1 |
| Bad Gleichenberg | 57 F4 | Bad Münstereifel | 51 E4 |
| Bad Godesberg | 51 E3 | Bad Muskau | 53 F1 |
| Bad Goisern | 56 C3 | Bad Nauheim | 52 A4 |
| Bad Gottleuba | 53 E3 | Bad Nenndorf | 52 A1 |
| Bad Griesbach | 56 C2 | Bad Neuenahr- | |
| Bad Grund | 52 B2 | Ahrweiler | 51 E4 |
| Bad Hall | 57 D3 | Bad Neustadt | 52 B4 |
| Bad Harzburg | 52 B1 | Bad Oeynhausen | 17 F2 |
| Bad Herrenalb | 54 C2 | Badolato | 67 F3 |
| Bad Hersfeld | 52 B3 | Badolatosa | 43 F3 |
| Bad Hofgastein | 56 C4 | Badonviller | 21 E4 |
| Bad Homburg | 51 F4 | Bad Orb | 52 A4 |
| Bad Honnef | 51 E3 | Badovinci | 72 B3 |
| Bad Honnigen | 51 E4 | Bad Peterstal- | |
| Badia Polesine | 61 D2 | Griesbach | 54 C3 |
| Badia Tedalda | 61 D3 | Bad Pyrmont | 52 A1 |
| Bad Iburg | 17 F2 | Bad Radkersburg | 70 C1 |
| Badija | 75 E2 | Bad Ragaz | 58 B2 |
| Bad Ischl | 56 C3 | Bad Rappenau | 55 D2 |
| Bad Karlshafen | 52 A2 | Bad Reichenhall | 56 B3 |
| Bad Kissingen | 52 B4 | Bad Rippoldsau- | |
| Bad Kleinen | 48 C2 | Schapbach | 54 C3 |
| Bad | | Bad Rothenfelde | 17 F2 |
| Kleinkirchheim | 59 F2 | Bad Saarow- | |
| Bad König | 55 D1 | Pieskow | 49 E4 |
| Bad Königshofen | 52 B4 | | |
| Bad Kösen | 52 C2 | | |
| Bad Kreuznach | 54 B1 | | |
| Bad Krozingen | 54 C4 | | |
| Bad Laasphe | 17 F4 | | |
| Bad Langensalza | 52 B3 | | |
| Bad Lauchstädt | 53 D2 | | |
| Bad Lausick | 53 D2 | | |
| Bad Lauterberg | 52 B2 | | |
| Bad Leonfelden | 57 D2 | | |
| Bad Liebenstein | 52 B3 | | |
| Bad Liebenwerda | 53 E2 | | |
| Bad Liebenzell | 54 C2 | | |
| Bad Lippspringe | 17 F3 | | |
| Badljevina | 71 D2 | | |
| Bad Meinberg | 52 A2 | | |
| Bad Mergentheim | 55 D1 | | |
| Bad Mitterndorf | 56 C4 | | |
| Bad Sachsa | 52 B2 | Bad Urach | 55 D3 |
| Bad Säckingen | 54 C4 | Bad Vibel | 52 A4 |
| Bad St Leonhard | 57 D4 | Bad Vöslau | 57 F3 |
| Bad Salzdetfurth | 52 B1 | Bad Waldsee | 55 D4 |
| Bad Salzschlirf | 52 B3 | Bad Wiessee | 56 B3 |
| Bad Salzuflen | 17 F2 | Bad Wildungen | 52 A3 |
| Bad Salzungen | 52 B3 | Bad Wilsnack | 48 C3 |
| Bad Schallerbach | 56 C3 | Bad Wimpfen | 55 D2 |
| Bad Schandau | 53 F2 | Bad Windsheim | 55 E1 |
| Bad | | Bad Wörishofen | 55 E3 |
| Schmiedeberg | 53 D1 | Bad Wurzach | 55 E4 |
| Bad Schönborn | 54 C2 | Bad Zwischenahn | 47 E3 |
| Bad | | Bae Colwyn | 6 B2 |
| Schussenried | 55 D3 | Baena | 43 F2 |
| Bad Schwalbach | 51 F4 | Baeza | 44 A2 |
| Bad Schwartau | 48 B2 | Bagà | 32 A3 |
| Bad Segeberg | 48 B2 | Bâge-le-Châtel | 26 C4 |
| Bad Soden | 51 F4 | Bagenalstown | 15 D3 |
| Bad Soden- | | Bagenkop | 108 B4 |
| Salmünster | 52 A4 | Bagheria | 68 B3 |
| Bad Sooden- | | Bagnacavallo | 61 D2 |
| Allendorf | 52 B2 | Bagnara Calabra | 67 E4 |
| Bad Sulza | 52 C2 | Bagnères-de- | |
| Bad Sülze | 49 D2 | Bigorre | 37 E1 |
| Bad | | Bagnères-de- | |
| Tatzmannsdorf | 57 F4 | Luchon | 37 E2 |
| Bad Tennstedt | 52 C2 | Bagni del Masino | 58 B3 |
| Bad Tölz | 56 A4 | Bagni di Lucca | 60 C3 |
| Badules | 36 C4 | Bagno a Ripoli | 61 D3 |
| | | Bagno di | |
| | | Romagna | 61 D3 |
| | | Bagnoles-de- | |
| | | l'Orne | 18 C4 |
| | | Bagnoli del Trigno | 64 B2 |
| | | Bagnolo Mella | 60 B1 |
| | | Bagnols-les-Bains | 29 F3 |
| | | Bagnols-sur-Cèze | 30 B3 |
| | | Bagnoregio | 63 E1 |
| | | Bagolino | 58 C4 |
| | | Bagrationovsk | 110 B4 |
| | | Bagrdan | 73 E4 |
| | | Baia Mare | 112 C3 |
| | | Baiano | 64 B4 |
| | | Baião | 34 B4 |
| | | Baiersbronn | 54 C3 |
| | | Baignes-Ste- | |
| | | Radegonde | 28 B1 |
| | | Baigneux-les-Juifs | 26 C2 |
| | | Baile Átha Cliath | 13 E4 |
| | | Baile Átha Luain | 12 C3 |
| | | Băile Herculane | 114 C1 |
| | | Bailén | 44 A2 |
| | | Băile Tuşnad | 113 D4 |
| | | Bailieborough | 13 D3 |
| | | Bailleul | 19 F1 |
| | | Bain-de-Bretagne | 23 D3 |
| | | Bains-les-Bains | 27 D1 |
| | | Baio | 34 A1 |

### Barcelona

Baiono 34 A3
Bais 23 E3
Baise 28 C3
Baise-Darré 37 E1
Baja 114 B1
Baja Sardinia 66 B1
Bajgora 77 D1
Bajina Bašta 72 C4
Bajmok 72 B1
Bajram Curri 76 C2
Bajša 72 B1
Bajzë 76 B3
Bakar 70 B3
Bakarac 70 B3
Bakewell 6 C3
Bakio 36 B1
Bakkaflói 96 C1
Bakony 112 A4
Bakvattnet 101 E1
Bala 6 B3
Balaguer 37 F3
Balanegra 44 B4
Balaruc 30 A4
Balassagyarmat 112 A4
Balaton 112 A4
Balatonfüred 112 B4
Balatonkeresztúr 112 A4
Balazote 40 C4
Balbigny 26 B4
Balbriggan 13 E3
Balčik 115 E2
Balderschwang 55 E4
Baldock 9 F2
Baldo, Mte 58 C4
Bale 70 A4
Baleal 38 A3
Baleizão 42 B1
Balerma 44 B4
Balestrand 100 A3
Bali 91 D3
Balikesir 115 E4
Balinge 106 B3
Balingen 55 D3
Balivanich 2 A3
Ballachulish 2 C4
Ballaghaderreen 12 C3
Ballangen 94 B3
Ballantrae 4 B3
Ballao 66 B3
Ballater 3 D4
Ballaugh 6 A1
Ballenstedt 52 C2
Balleroy 18 C3
Ballerup 108 C3
Ballina 12 B2
Ballinamore 12 C3
Ballinasloe 12 C3
Ballingarry 14 C3
Ballinrobe 12 B3
Ballintober 12 B3
Ballobar 37 E4
Ballon 23 F3
Ballon d'Alsace 27 E1
Ballstad 97 E1
Ballybay 13 D2
Ballybofey 12 C1
Ballybunnion 14 A4
Ballycastle (IRL) 12 B2
Ballycastle (N Ire) 13 E1
Ballyclare 13 E2
Ballyconnell 12 C2
Ballycotton 14 C4
Ballycroy 12 B2
Ballyduff 14 B3
Ballyforan 12 C3
Ballygawley 13 D2
Ballyhaunis 12 B3
Ballyheige 14 A3
Ballyjamesduff 13 D3
Ballymahon 12 C3
Ballymena 13 E2
Ballymoe 12 C3
Ballymoney 13 E1
Ballymore 12 C3
Ballymote 12 C2
Ballynahinch 13 E2
Ballysadare 12 C2
Ballyshannon 12 C2
Ballyvaughan 12 B4
Balmaseda 36 A1
Balme 31 E1
Balmoral Castle 3 D4
Balneario de
  Panticosa 37 E2

Balsareny 32 A3
Balsfjorden 94 B2
Balsicas 45 D2
Balsorano 63 F2
Bålsta 106 B3
Balsthal 27 E2
Balta 113 E3
Baltanás 35 F4
Baltar 34 B3
Baltic Sea 110 B3
Baltijsk 110 B4
Baltinglass 13 D4
Baltrum 47 E3
Bambalió 82 C3
Bamberg 52 C4
Bambíni 82 C3
Bamburgh 5 E3
Bampton 8 C3
Banagher 12 C4
Banat 114 C1
Banatska Palanka 73 D2
Banatska Topola 72 C1
Banatski Brestovac 73 D3
Banatski Dvor 72 C2
Banatski Karlovac 73 D2
Banatsko
  Aranđelovo 72 C1
Banatsko
  Karađorđevo 72 C2
Banatsko Novo
  Selo 73 D2
Banbridge 13 E2
Banbury 9 E1
Banchory 3 E4
Bande 34 B3
Bandak 104 B2
Bandırma 115 E3
Bandol 30 C4
Bandon 14 B4
Bandon R 14 B4
Bañeres 45 E1
Banff 3 E3
Bangor (IRL) 12 B2
Bangor (N Ire) 13 E2
Bangor (Wales) 6 A2
Bangsund 97 D4
Banie 49 E3
Banja (Srbija) 73 D3
Banja (Srbija) 76 B1
Banja Koviljača 72 B3
Banja Luka 71 E3
Banjani 72 C3
Banja Vrućica 71 F3
Banjska 76 C1
Bankeryd 109 D1
Bann (N Ire) 13 D1
Bann (Wexford) 15 D3
Bannalec 22 B3
Banon 30 C3
Bañon 41 D2
Baños de Cerrato 35 F4
Baños de la Encina 44 A2
Baños de la
  Fuensanta 44 C2
Baños de Molgas 34 B3
Baños de
  Montemayor 39 E2
Baños de
  Fuensanta 35 E1
Banova Jaruga 71 D2
Banovići 71 F4
Banque de
  Fraiture 51 D4
Banque Michel 51 D4
Bansin 49 E2
Banská-Bystrica 112 B3
Banská-Štiavnica 112 B3
Bansko 77 F3
Bantry 14 B4
Bantry B 14 A4
Banyalbufar 45 E2
Bañuela 43 F1
Banyoles 32 B3
Banyuls 32 C3
Bao, Emb de 34 C3
Bapaume 19 F2
Bar (SU) 113 D3
Bar (YU) 76 B3
Baracaldo 36 B1
Baraći 71 E4
Baradla 112 B3
Barahona 36 B4
Barajas 40 B2
Barajas de Melo 40 B3

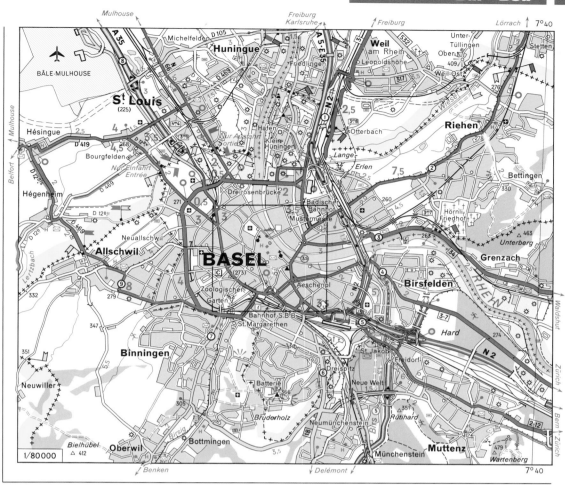

Barajevo 73 D3
Baralla 34 C2
Barane 76 C2
Baranoviči 111 D4
Baraqueville 29 E3
Barasona, Emb de 37 E3
Barbadillo del
  Mercado 36 A3
Barban 70 A3
Barbarano
  Vicentino 61 D1
Barbarušince 77 E2
Barbastro 37 E3
Barbat 70 B4
Barbate de Franco 43 D4
Barbate, Emb de 43 D4
Barbazan 37 F2
Barberino di
  Mugello 60 C3
Barbezieux 28 B1
Barbizon 19 F4
Barbotan 28 B3
Barby 52 C1
Barca de Alva 39 D1
Barca, Emb de la 35 D1
Barcarrota 42 C1
Barcellona Pozzo
  di Gotto 69 D2
Barcelona 32 B4
Barcelonnette 31 D2
Barcelos 34 A4
Barcena, Emb de 34 C2
Barchfeld 52 B3
Barcis 59 E3
Barcones 36 B4
Barcs 114 A1
Bardal 101 D1
Bardejov 112 B3
Bardi 60 B2
Bardineto 31 F3
Bardolino 60 C1
Bardonecchia 31 D1
Bardu 94 B3
Bardufoss 94 B3
Bare 76 B1
Barèges 37 E2
Barentin 19 D3

Barenton 18 C4
Bares, Estaca de 34 B 1
Barfleur 18 B2
Barfleur, Pte de 18 B2
Bargas 40 A3
Bargoed 9 D2
Bargteheide 48 B2
Bari 65 D3
Barić Draga 70 C4
Barisciano 63 F2
Barjac 30 B3
Barjols 31 D4
Barlby 7 D2
Bar, le 31 E3
Bar-le-Duc 20 C4
Barletta 65 D3
Barlinek 49 F3
Barlovento 42 A4
Barmouth 6 A3
Barmstedt 48 A2
Barna 12 B3
Barnard Castle 5 E4
Barneveld 16 C3
Barneville 18 B3
Barnsley 7 D2
Barnstaple 8 C3
Barnstorf 17 F1
Barntrup 52 A1
Barovo 77 E3
Barquiero 38 B2
Barr 21 E4
Barra 2 A4
Barracas 41 E3
Barrachina 41 D2
Barraco 39 F2
Barrafranca 68 C4
Barra Head 2 A4
Barrancos 42 C1
Barranco Velho 42 A2
Barranda 44 C2
Barra, Sd of 2 A4
Barrax 40 C4
Barrea 64 A2
Barre-des-
  Cévennes 29 F3
Barreiro 38 A4

Barrême 31 D3
Barrhead 4 C2
Barrhill 4 C1
Barri 9 D2
Barrow 13 D4
Barrow-in-Furness 6 B1
Barrow, R 15 D3
Barruecopardo 39 D1
Barruelo de
  Santullán 35 F2
Barry 9 D2
Barsinghausen 52 A1
Bar-sur-Aube 26 B1
Bar-sur-Seine 26 B1
Barth 49 D1
Barthe-de-Neste,
  la 37 E1
Barton-upon-
  Humber 7 D2
Barumini 66 B3
Baruth 53 E1
Barvas 2 B2
Barycz 112 A2
Barzio 58 B4
Bašaid 72 C1
Bàscara 32 B3
Baschi 63 E1
Basconcillos del
  Tozo 35 F2
Basel 27 E2
Baselga di Pinè 59 D3
Bas-en-Basset 30 B1
Basento 65 D4
Basildon 11 D2
Basilicata 65 D4
Basingstoke 9 E3
Baška 70 B3
Baška Voda 75 E2
Baške Oštarije 70 C4
Baslow 6 C3
Basovizza 59 F4
Bas-Rhin 21 E4
Bassano del
  Grappa 59 D4
Bassée, la 19 F1
Bassella 37 F3

Bassens 28 B2
Bassum 17 F1
Båstad 108 C3
Bastasi 71 D4
Bastelica 33 F3
Bas'tevarri 95 D3
Bastia 33 F2
Bastide-de-Sérou,
  la 37 F2
Bastogne 20 C2
Bastunäsfjället 97 E4
Basturäsk 98 B4
Batajnica 72 C3
Batak 115 D3
Batalha 38 B3
Batea 41 F1
Bath 9 D2
Bathgate 5 D2
Bâtie-Neuve, la 31 D2
Batina 72 B1
Batlava 77 D1
Batočina 73 D3
Båtsfjord 95 F1
Batsí 88 B1
Battaglia Terme 61 D1
Battenberg 17 F4
Battice 51 D3
Battipaglia 64 B4
Battle 11 D3
Baud 22 C3
Baugé 23 E4
Baugy 26 A2
Baule, la 24 A2
Baume, Cirque de 27 D3
Baume-les-
  Dames 27 D2
Baumholder 54 B1
Bauska 110 C3
Bautzen 53 F2
Baux, les 30 B3
Bavanište 73 D2
Bavay 20 B1
Bavella, Col de 33 F4

Båven 106 B4
Baveno 58 A4
Bawtry 7 D2
Bayard, Col 31 D2
Bayerisch
  Eisenstein 56 C1
Bayerischer Wald 56 B2
Bayern 55 F2
Bayeux 18 C3
Bayhirivagh 2 A4
Bayındır 115 F4
Bayon 21 D4
Bayonne 28 A4
Bayreuth 52 C4
Bayrischzell 56 B4
Baza 44 B3
Bazas 28 B3
Baza, Sa de 44 B3
Bazoches-sur-
  Hoëne 19 D4
Bazzano 60 C2
Beachy Head 10 C3
Beaconsfield 9 F2
Béal an Átha 12 B2
Béal Átha na
  Sluaighe 12 C3
Beaminster 9 D3
Beanntraí 14 B4
Beara 14 A4
Beariz 34 B2
Beas 42 C2
Beasain 36 C1
Beas de Segura 44 B2
Beattock 5 D3
Beaucaire 30 B3
Beaufort (Jura) 26 C3
Beaufort (Savoie) 27 E4
Beaufort-en-
  Vallée 23 E4
Beaugency 25 E2
Beaujeu 26 C4
Beaulieu (Alpes-
  Maritime) 31 E3
Beaulieu (Corrèze) 29 D2
Beaulieu (GB) 9 E3
Beaumaris 6 A2
Beaumesnil 19 D3

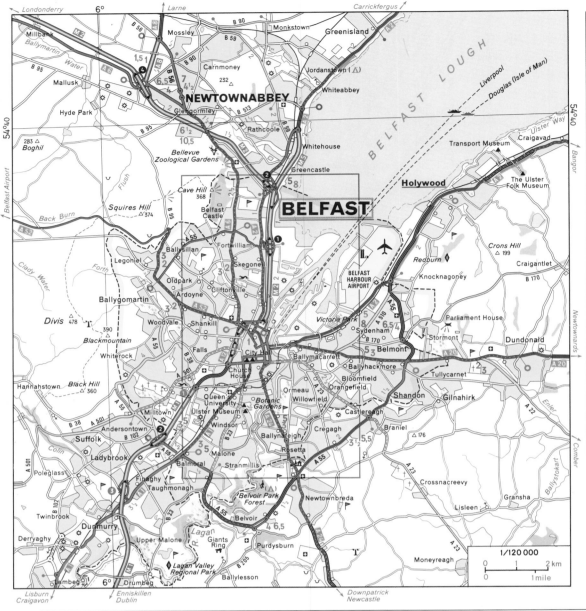

| | | |
|---|---|---|
| Bellinzona | 58 | A3 |
| Bell-lloc d'Urgell | 37 | F3 |
| Bello | 41 | D1 |
| Bellpuig | 37 | F4 |
| Belluno | 59 | E3 |
| Bellver | 45 | E3 |
| Bellver de Cerdanya | 32 | A3 |
| Bélmez | 43 | E1 |
| Belmont (F) | 26 | B4 |
| Belmont (GB) | 3 | F1 |
| Belmonte (Asturias) | 35 | D1 |
| Belmonte (Castilla-la-Mancha) | 40 | C3 |
| Belmonte (P) | 38 | C2 |
| Belmont-sur-Rance | 32 | B1 |
| Belmullet | 12 | A2 |
| Belo Brdo | 76 | C1 |
| Belogradčik | 114 | C1 |
| Belo jez | 72 | C2 |
| Beloljin | 77 | D1 |
| Belœil | 50 | B4 |
| Belo Polje | 76 | C2 |
| Belopolje | 113 | F1 |
| Belorado | 36 | A2 |
| Belorussija | 111 | D4 |
| Belpech | 32 | A2 |
| Belper | 6 | C3 |
| Belsay | 5 | E3 |
| Belsh | 76 | C4 |
| Beltinci | 70 | C1 |
| Belturbet | 13 | D2 |
| Belušić | 73 | E4 |
| Belvedere Marittimo | 67 | E2 |
| Belver | 37 | E3 |
| Belvès | 28 | C2 |
| Belvis de la Jara | 39 | F3 |
| Belyj | 111 | E2 |
| Belz | 22 | C4 |
| Belzig | 53 | D1 |
| Bembézar, Emb de | 43 | E2 |
| Bembézar, R | 43 | E2 |
| Bembibre | 35 | D2 |
| Bemposta | 38 | B3 |
| Bemposta, Bgem da | 34 | C4 |
| Benabarre | 37 | E3 |
| Benaguacil | 41 | E3 |
| Benahadux | 44 | B3 |
| Ben Alder | 2 | C4 |
| Benalmádena | 43 | F4 |
| Benalúa de las Villas | 44 | A3 |
| Benamargosa | 43 | F3 |
| Benamaurel | 44 | B2 |
| Benameji | 43 | F3 |
| Benamocarra | 43 | F3 |
| Benaoján | 43 | E4 |
| Ben Armine | 3 | D2 |
| Benasal | 41 | E2 |
| Benasque | 37 | E2 |
| Benavente (E) | 35 | D3 |
| Benavente (P) | 38 | A4 |
| Benavides | 35 | D3 |
| Benbecula | 2 | A3 |
| Ben Chonzie | 4 | C1 |
| Ben Cruachan | 4 | B1 |
| Bendery | 113 | E4 |
| Bendorf | 51 | E4 |
| Benediktbeuern | 56 | A4 |
| Benešov (Severočeský) | 53 | F3 |
| Benešov (Středočeský) | 53 | F4 |
| Bénévent-l'Abbaye | 25 | E4 |
| Benevento | 64 | B3 |
| Benfeld | 21 | E4 |
| Benfleet | 11 | D2 |
| Bengtsfors | 105 | D4 |
| Ben Hope | 2 | C2 |
| Beničanci | 71 | E2 |
| Benicarló | 41 | F2 |
| Benicasim | 41 | F3 |
| Benidorm | 45 | E1 |
| Benifaió | 41 | E4 |
| Beninar, Emb de | 44 | B3 |
| Benissa | 45 | E1 |
| Benítses | 82 | A1 |
| Ben Klibreck | 2 | C2 |

| | | |
|---|---|---|
| Benkovac | 74 | C1 |
| Ben Lawers | 4 | C1 |
| Ben Lomond | 4 | C1 |
| Ben Macdui | 3 | D4 |
| Ben More (Grampian) | 4 | C1 |
| Ben More (Mull) | 4 | B1 |
| Ben More Assynt | 2 | C2 |
| Benneckenstein | 52 | B2 |
| Ben Nevis | 2 | C4 |
| Bénodet | 22 | B3 |
| Benquerencia de la Serena | 43 | E1 |
| Bensberg | 17 | E4 |
| Bensersiel | 47 | E3 |
| Bensheim | 54 | C1 |
| Bentley | 7 | D2 |
| Ben Vorlich | 4 | C1 |
| Ben Wyvis | 2 | C3 |
| Bény-Bocage, le | 18 | C3 |
| Beočin | 72 | C2 |
| Beograd | 73 | D3 |
| Bérarde, la | 31 | D2 |
| Berat | 114 | C4 |
| Berbegal | 37 | E3 |
| Berberana | 36 | B1 |
| Berbería, C de | 45 | D4 |
| Berceto | 60 | B3 |
| Berching | 55 | F2 |
| Berchtesgaden | 56 | C4 |
| Berck-sur-Mer | 19 | E1 |
| Berdičev | 113 | E2 |
| Beregovo | 112 | C3 |
| Bereguardo | 60 | A2 |
| Bere I | 14 | A4 |
| Berek | 71 | D2 |
| Bere Regis | 9 | D3 |
| Beret | 37 | F2 |
| Berettyóújfalu | 112 | C4 |
| Berezina | 111 | E4 |
| Berezino | 111 | D4 |
| Berg (A) | 57 | F2 |
| Berg (Nordland) | 97 | D3 |
| Berg (S) | 101 | E2 |
| Berg (Troms) | 94 | B2 |
| Berga (DDR) | 52 | C2 |
| Berga (E) | 32 | A3 |
| Bergama | 115 | E4 |
| Bergamo | 60 | B1 |
| Bergara | 36 | B1 |
| Bergby | 106 | B2 |
| Bergedorf | 48 | B3 |
| Bergen (B) | 50 | B4 |
| Bergen (DDR) | 49 | D1 |
| Bergen (N) | 104 | A2 |
| Bergen (Niedersachsen) | 48 | A4 |
| Bergen (Niedersachsen) | 48 | B3 |
| Bergen (NL) | 16 | C2 |
| Bergen aan Zee | 16 | C2 |
| Bergen op Zoom | 16 | B4 |
| Bergerac | 28 | C2 |
| Berggießhübel | 53 | F2 |
| Berghamn fjärden | 107 | D3 |
| Bergheim | 17 | D4 |
| Bergisch Gladbach | 17 | E4 |
| Bergnäset | 98 | C3 |
| Bergneustadt | 17 | E4 |
| Bergö | 102 | B2 |
| Berg-Rudolphstein | 53 | D3 |
| Bergsjö | 101 | F3 |
| Bergsviken | 98 | B3 |
| Bergues | 19 | F1 |
| Bergum | 47 | D3 |
| Bergün | 58 | B3 |
| Beringel | 42 | B1 |
| Beringen | 50 | C3 |
| Berja | 44 | B4 |
| Berka | 52 | B3 |
| Berkåk | 100 | C2 |
| Berkel | 17 | D2 |
| Berkhamsted | 9 | F2 |
| Berkheim | 55 | E3 |
| Berkhof | 48 | A4 |
| Berkovica | 114 | C1 |
| Berkovići | 75 | F2 |
| Berkshire | 9 | E2 |
| Berlaimont | 20 | A2 |
| Berlanga | 43 | D1 |
| Berlanga de Duero | 36 | B3 |
| Berlebeck | 17 | F3 |
| Berlenga, I | 38 | A3 |

| | | | | | | | | | | | | |
|---|---|---|---|---|---|---|---|---|---|---|---|---|
| Beaumetz-lès-Loges | 19 | F2 | Bečej | 72 | C2 | Begejski kanal | 72 | C2 | Bélâbre | 25 | E3 | Belgorod-Dnestrovskij | 113 | F4 |
| Beaumont (B) | 50 | B4 | Becerreá | 34 | C2 | Beg-Meil | 22 | B3 | Bela Crkva (Srbija) | 72 | C3 | Belianes | 37 | F4 |
| Beaumont (Dordogne) | 28 | C2 | Bec-Helloin, le | 19 | D3 | Begna | 104 | C2 | Bela Crkva (Vojvodina) | 73 | D2 | Belice | 68 | B3 |
| Beaumont (Manche) | 18 | B2 | Bécherel | 23 | D3 | Begov Han | 71 | F4 | Belaja Cerkov' | 113 | E2 | Beli Drim | 76 | C2 |
| Beaumont (Val d'Oise) | 19 | F3 | Bechet | 115 | D2 | Bégude-de-Mazenc, la | 30 | C2 | Belalcázar | 43 | E1 | Beli Manastir | 71 | F2 |
| Beaumont-de-Lomagne | 28 | C3 | Bechhofen | 55 | E2 | Begues | 32 | A4 | Belanovce | 77 | E2 | Belin-Béliet | 28 | B3 |
| Beaumont-le-Roger | 19 | D3 | Bečići | 76 | B3 | Begur | 32 | C3 | Belanovica | 73 | D3 | Beli Potok | 73 | F4 |
| Beaumont-sur-Sarthe | 23 | F3 | Becilla de Valderaduey | 35 | E3 | Behalúa de Guadix | 44 | B3 | Bela Palanka | 77 | E1 | Belišće | 71 | F2 |
| Beaune | 26 | C2 | Beckenried | 58 | A2 | Behobia | 28 | A4 | Belasica | 77 | F3 | Beli Timok | 73 | F4 |
| Beaune-la-Rolande | 25 | F1 | Beckington | 9 | D3 | Behringersmühle | 52 | C4 | Belcaire | 32 | A2 | Beljakovce | 77 | E2 |
| Beaupréau | 24 | C2 | Beckum | 17 | F3 | Beiarn | 97 | E2 | Belchen | 54 | C4 | Beljanica | 73 | E3 |
| Beauraing | 50 | C4 | Bečov | 53 | E4 | Beilen | 17 | D1 | Belchite | 37 | D4 | Beljina | 73 | D3 |
| Beaurepaire | 30 | C1 | Bedale | 6 | C1 | Beilngries | 55 | F2 | Belčište | 77 | D4 | Bellac | 25 | D4 |
| Beaurepaire-en-Bresse | 26 | C3 | Bédarieux | 30 | A4 | Beinn a'Ghlò | 3 | D4 | Belcoo | 12 | C2 | Bellagio | 58 | B4 |
| Beausset, le | 31 | D4 | Beddgelert | 6 | A3 | Beinn an Oir | 4 | B2 | Bel'cy | 113 | E3 | Bellano | 58 | B4 |
| Beauvais | 19 | E3 | Bedekesa | 47 | F3 | Beinn Bheigeir | 4 | B2 | Belec | 70 | C2 | Bellaria | 61 | E3 |
| Beauvoir (Deux-Sèvres) | 24 | C4 | Bedford | 9 | F1 | Beinn Dearg | 2 | C3 | Belecke | 17 | F3 | Bellcaire d'Urgell | 37 | F3 |
| Beauvoir (Vendée) | 24 | A3 | Bedfordshire | 9 | F1 | Beira Alta | 38 | B1 | Belegiš | 72 | C2 | Belledonne, Chaîne de | 31 | D1 |
| Bebington | 6 | B2 | Bedlington | 5 | E3 | Beira Baixa | 38 | C2 | Belej | 70 | B4 | Bellegarde (Ain) | 27 | D4 |
| Bebra | 52 | B3 | Bedmar | 44 | A2 | Beira Litoral | 38 | B1 | Beleña, Emb de | 40 | B1 | Bellegarde (Gard) | 30 | B3 |
| Beccles | 11 | E1 | Bednja | 70 | C1 | Beisfjord | 94 | B3 | Belesar, Emb de | 34 | B2 | Bellegarde (Loiret) | 25 | F1 |
| Becedas | 39 | E2 | Bedonia | 60 | B3 | Beith | 4 | C2 | Belev | 111 | F3 | Bellegarde-en-Marche | 25 | E4 |
| Beceite | 41 | F2 | Bedum | 47 | D3 | Beitostølen | 104 | C1 | Bele Vode | 76 | C1 | Belle-Ile | 22 | B4 |
| | | | Bedwas | 9 | D2 | Beitstadfjorden | 101 | D1 | Belfast | 13 | E2 | Belle-Isle-en-Terre | 22 | B2 |
| | | | Bedworth | 9 | E1 | Beius | 112 | C4 | Belfast L | 13 | E2 | Bellême | 23 | F3 |
| | | | Beeford | 7 | E2 | Beja | 42 | B1 | Belford | 5 | E3 | Bellencombre | 19 | E2 |
| | | | Beelitz | 49 | D4 | Béjar | 39 | E2 | Belfort | 27 | E2 | Bellerive | 26 | A4 |
| | | | Beerfelden | 55 | D1 | Béjar, Pto de | 39 | E2 | Belforte all'Isauro | 61 | E3 | Belleville | 26 | C4 |
| | | | Beeskow | 49 | E4 | Békés | 112 | C4 | Belgern | 53 | E2 | Belley | 27 | D4 |
| | | | Beetzendorf | 48 | B4 | Békéscsaba | 112 | C4 | België | 16 | B3 | | | |
| | | | Bégard | 22 | C2 | Bel | 41 | F2 | Belgique | 50 | B3 | | | |
| | | | Begejci | 72 | C2 | Bělá | 56 | B1 | Belgodère | 33 | F2 | | | |

## Berlin

Berlevåg 95 F1
Berlin (Ost) 49 E4
Berlin (West) 49 D4
Bermejales, Emb 43 F3
Bermeja, Sa 43 F3
Bermeo 36 B1
Bermillo 35 D4
Bern 27 E2
Bernalda 65 D4
Bernardsthal 57 F1
Bernartice 57 D1
Bernau (Baden-Württemberg) 54 C4
Bernau (Bayern) 56 B3
Bernau (DDR) 49 E4
Bernaville 19 F2
Bernay 19 D3
Bernburg 52 C1
Berndorf 57 E3
Berne 47 F3
Bernesga, R 35 D2
Bernina, Piz 58 B3
Bernina, Pso del 58 B3
Bernkastel-Kues 54 B1
Bernsdorf 53 F2
Bernstein 57 F3
Beroun 53 F4
Berounka 53 F4
Berovo 77 F3
Ber'oza 112 C1
Ber'ozovka 113 F3
Berra 61 D2
Berre 30 C4
Berre, Etang de 30 C4
Beršad' 113 E3
Bersenbrück 17 E2
Bertamirans 34 A2
Bertinoro 61 D3
Bertrix 20 C2
Berwang 58 C1
Berwick-upon-Tweed 5 E2
Berwyn 6 B3
Berzocana 39 E3
Berzosa 39 D1
Besalú 32 B3
Besançon 27 D2
Besande 35 E2
Besaya, R 35 F2
Besbre 26 B3
Besigheim 55 D2
Beška 72 C2
Besna Kobila 77 E2
Besse 29 E1
Bessèges 30 C3
Besse-sur-Issole 31 D4
Bessines 25 E4
Betancuria 42 C4
Betanzos 34 B1
Betelu 36 C1
Bétera 41 E3
Beteta 40 C2
Bétharram, Grottes de 37 E1
Bethesda 6 A2
Béthune 19 F1
Béthune R 19 E2
Bettna 106 A4
Bettola 60 B2
Bettolle 61 D4
Bettyhill 3 D2
Betws-y-Coed 6 A3
Betz 19 F3
Betzdorf 51 F3
Beuil 31 E3
Beura 58 A4
Beuron 55 D3
Beuvray, Mont 26 B3
Beuvron 25 E2
Beuzeville 19 D3
Bevagna 63 E4
Beveren-Waas 50 B3
Beverley 7 D2
Beverstedt 47 F3
Beverungen 52 A2
Beverwijk 16 C2
Bewdley 9 D1
Bex 27 E3
Bexhill 11 D3
Beynac 29 D2
Beynat 29 D2
Bežanija 72 C3
Bézards, les 26 A1
Bezas 41 D2

Bezdan 72 B1
Bezdrep 57 D1
Bežeck 111 F1
Béziers 30 A4
Bezmisht 77 D4
Béznar 44 A3
Biała Podlaska 112 C1
Białowieska 112 C1
Białystok 112 C1
Biancavilla 69 D3
Bianco 67 E4
Bianco, M 27 E4
Biandrate 31 F1
Biar 45 D1
Biarritz 28 A4
Biasca 58 A3
Bibbiena 61 D4
Biberach 54 C3
Biberach an der Riß 55 E3
Bibinje 74 C1
Bibione 59 F4
Bibury 9 E2
Bicaj 76 C3
Bicaz 113 D4
Bicester 9 E2
Bichl 56 A4
Bidache 28 A4
Bidasoa, R 36 C1
Bidart 28 A4
Biddenden 11 D3

Bidean nam Bian 4 C1
Bideford 8 C3
Biebelried 55 E1
Biedenkopf 17 F4
Biel 27 E2
Bielefeld 17 F2
Bielerhöhe 58 B2
Biella 31 F1
Bielsa 37 E2
Bielsa, Tunnel de 37 E2
Bielsko-Biała 112 B3
Bielsk Podlaski 112 C1
Bienne R 27 D3
Bienne 27 E2
Bientina 60 C4
Bienvenida 43 D1
Bierné 23 E4
Bierre 26 B2
Biesbosch 16 C3
Biescas 37 D2
Biese 48 C4
Biesenthal 49 E3
Bietigheim-Bissingen 55 D2
Biferno 64 B2
Biga 115 E3
Biggar 5 D2
Biggleswade 9 F1
Bignasco 58 A3
Bihać 70 C3

Bihorului, M 112 C4
Bijele Poljane 76 B2
Bijeljani 75 F2
Bijeljina 72 B3
Bijelo Brdo 71 F2
Bijelolasica 70 B3
Bijelo Polje 76 B2
Bilbao 36 B1
Bileća 76 A2
Bilecik 115 F3
Bilećko jez 76 A2
Biłgoraj 112 C2
Bilina 53 E3
Biljača 77 E2
Biljanovac 76 C1
Bilje 71 F2
Billericay 11 D2
Billingham 5 E4
Billingshurst 10 C3
Billom 29 F1
Billund 108 A3
Bilo 77 E1
Bilogora 71 D2
Bilto 94 C2
Bilzen 50 C3
Binaced 37 E3
Binača Morava 77 D2
Binasco 58 A3
Binche 50 B4

Binéfar 37 E3
Bingen 51 F4
Bingham 7 D3
Bingley 6 C2
Bingsjö 101 E4
Binic 22 C2
Binz 49 D1
Bioča 76 C2
Bioče 76 B2
Biograd 74 C1
Biogradsko, nac park 76 B2
Biokovo 75 E2
Biot, le 27 E4
Birchington 11 D2
Birgi 68 A3
Birkebeiner veien 104 C1
Birkeland 104 B4
Birkenfeld 54 B1
Birkenhead 6 B2
Birkenwerder 49 D4
Birkerød 108 C3
Birkfeld 57 E4
Birlad 113 E4
Birmingham 9 E1
Birnau 55 D4
Birr 12 C4
Biržai 110 C3

Birzebugga 68 B4
Bisaccia 64 C3
Biscarrosse 28 A3
Biscarrosse-Plage 28 A3
Bisceglie 65 D3
Bischofsgrün 53 D4
Bischofsheim 52 B4
Bischofshofen 59 E1
Bischofswerda 53 F2
Bischofswiesen 56 C4
Bischofszell 58 A1
Bischwiller 21 E2
Bisenti 63 F1
Biševo 75 D2
Bishop Auckland 5 E4
Bishop's Castle 9 D1
Bishop's Stortford 10 C2
Bisignano 67 E2
Bisko 75 D1
Bismark 48 C4
Bismo 100 B3
Bispgården 101 F2
Bispingen 48 A3
Bistar 77 E2
Bistra pl 77 D3
Bistrica (Crna Gora) 76 B2
Bistrica (Srbija) 76 B1
Bistrica ob S. 70 C2
Bistričak 71 E4
Bistrița 113 D4

Bistrița R 113 D4
Bitburg 54 A1
Bitche 21 E3
Bitetto 65 D3
Bitola 77 E4
Bitonto 65 D3
Bitterfeld 53 D2
Bitti 66 B2
Bizákos 82 C3
Bizau 58 B2
Bizovac 71 F2
Bjala 115 D2
Bjärkøy 94 B3
Bjästa 102 A2
Bjelašnica 75 F1
Bjelašnica 76 A2
Bjelovar 71 D2
Bjerkreim 104 A4
Bjerkvik 94 B3
Bjerringbro 108 B2
Bjørkelangen 105 D3
Bjørketorp 109 E3
Björkfjället 97 F3
Björkliden 94 B3
Björklinge 106 B3
Björköby 102 B2
Björksele 98 A4
Bjørli 100 B3
Björna 102 A2

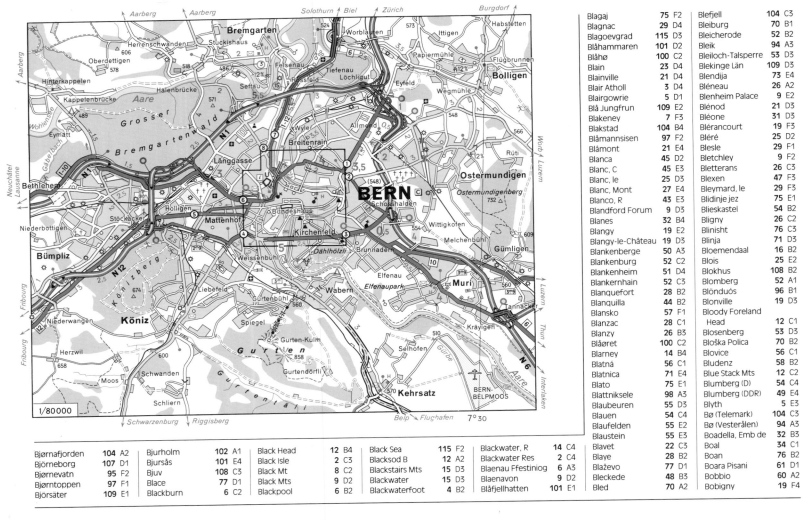

| | | | | | | |
|---|---|---|---|---|---|---|
| Blagaj | 75 F2 | | Blefjell | 104 C3 | | |
| Blagnac | 29 D4 | | Bleiburg | 70 B1 | | |
| Blagoevgrad | 115 D3 | | Bleicherode | 52 B2 | | |
| Blåhammaren | 101 D2 | | Bleik | 94 A3 | | |
| Blåhø | 100 C2 | | Bleiloch-Talsperre | 53 D3 | | |
| Blain | 23 D4 | | Blekinge Län | 109 D3 | | |
| Blainville | 21 D4 | | Blendija | 73 E4 | | |
| Blair Atholl | 3 D4 | | Bléneau | 26 A2 | | |
| Blairgowrie | 5 D1 | | Blenheim Palace | 9 E2 | | |
| Blå Jungfrun | 109 E2 | | Blénod | 21 D3 | | |
| Blakeney | 7 F3 | | Bléone | 31 D3 | | |
| Blakstad | 104 B4 | | Blérancourt | 19 F3 | | |
| Blåmannsisen | 97 F2 | | Bléré | 25 D2 | | |
| Blåmont | 21 E4 | | Blesle | 29 F1 | | |
| Blanca | 45 D2 | | Bletchley | 9 F2 | | |
| Blanc, C | 45 E3 | | Bletterans | 26 C3 | | |
| Blanc, le | 25 D3 | | Blexen | 47 F3 | | |
| Blanc, Mont | 27 E4 | | Bleymard, le | 29 F3 | | |
| Blanco, R | 43 E3 | | Blidinje jez | 75 E1 | | |
| Blandford Forum | 9 D3 | | Blieskastel | 54 B2 | | |
| Blanes | 32 B4 | | Bligny | 26 C2 | | |
| Blangy | 19 E2 | | Blinisht | 76 C3 | | |
| Blangy-le-Château | 19 D3 | | Blinja | 71 D3 | | |
| Blankenberge | 50 A3 | | Bloemendaal | 16 B2 | | |
| Blankenburg | 52 C2 | | Blois | 25 E2 | | |
| Blankenheim | 51 D4 | | Blokhus | 108 B2 | | |
| Blankernhain | 52 C3 | | Blomberg | 52 A1 | | |
| Blanquefort | 28 B2 | | Blönduós | 96 B1 | | |
| Blanquilla | 44 B2 | | Blonville | 19 D3 | | |
| Blansko | 57 F1 | | Bloody Foreland | | | |
| Blanzac | 28 C1 | |   Head | 12 C1 | | |
| Blanzy | 26 B3 | | Blosenberg | 53 D3 | | |
| Blåøret | 100 C2 | | Bloška Polica | 70 B2 | | |
| Blarney | 14 B4 | | Blovice | 56 C1 | | |
| Blatná | 56 C1 | | Bludenz | 58 B2 | | |
| Blatnica | 71 E4 | | Blue Stack Mts | 12 C2 | | |
| Blato | 75 E1 | | Blumberg (D) | 54 C4 | | |
| Blattniksele | 98 A3 | | Blumberg (DDR) | 49 E4 | | |
| Blaubeuren | 55 D3 | | Blyth | 5 E3 | | |
| Blauen | 54 C4 | | Bø (Telemark) | 104 C3 | | |
| Blaufelden | 55 E2 | | Bø (Vesterålen) | 94 A3 | | |
| Blaustein | 55 E3 | | Boadella, Emb de | 32 B3 | | |
| Blavet | 22 C3 | | Boal | 34 C1 | | |
| Blaye | 28 B2 | | Boan | 76 B2 | | |
| Blaževo | 77 D1 | | Boara Pisani | 61 D1 | | |
| Bleckede | 48 B3 | | Bobbio | 60 A2 | | |
| Bled | 70 A2 | | Bobigny | 19 F4 | | |

| | | | | | | | | | | | |
|---|---|---|---|---|---|---|---|---|---|---|---|
| Bjørnafjorden | 104 A2 | Bjurholm | 102 A1 | Black Head | 12 B4 | Black Sea | 115 F2 | Blackwater, R | 14 C4 | | |
| Bjørneborg | 107 D1 | Bjursås | 101 E4 | Black Isle | 2 C3 | Blacksod B | 12 A2 | Blackwater Res | 2 C4 | | |
| Bjørnevatn | 95 F2 | Bjuv | 108 C3 | Black Mt | 8 C2 | Blackstairs Mts | 15 D3 | Blaenau Ffestiniog | 6 A3 | | |
| Bjørntoppen | 97 F1 | Blace | 77 D1 | Black Mts | 9 D2 | Blackwater | 15 D3 | Blaenavon | 9 D2 | | |
| Björsäter | 109 E1 | Blackburn | 6 C2 | Blackpool | 6 B2 | Blackwaterfoot | 4 B2 | Blåfjellhatten | 101 E1 | Bled | 70 A2 |

## Bologna

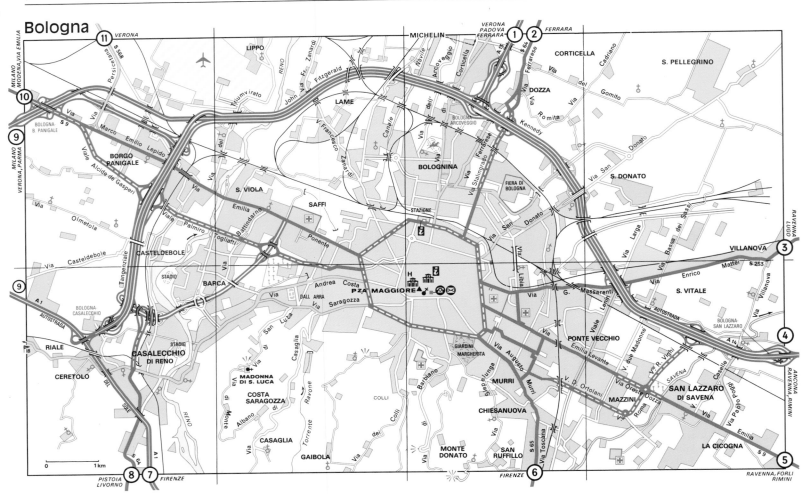

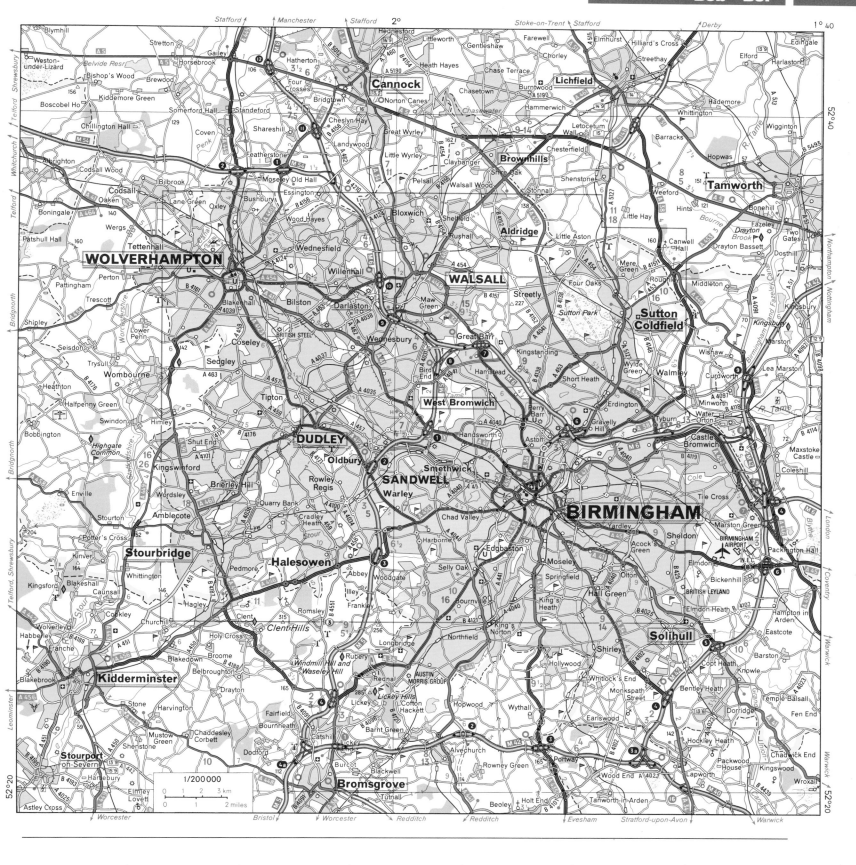

| | | | | | | | | | | |
|---|---|---|---|---|---|---|---|---|---|---|
| Bobingen | 55 F3 | Bocche di | | Boda | 101 E4 | Bodman- | | Bogdaniec | 49 F3 | Bogomila | 77 E3 | Böhlen | 53 D2 |
| Böblingen | 55 D2 | Bonifacio | 33 F4 | Böda | 109 F2 | Radolfzell | 55 D4 | Bogë | 76 C2 | Bogomolje | 75 E2 | Böhme | 48 A4 |
| Boblitz | 53 E1 | Bocco, Pso del | 60 B3 | Bodafors | 109 D2 | Bodmin | 8 B4 | Bogen (D) | 56 B2 | Bogorodika | 77 F4 | Böhmenkirch | 55 E2 |
| Boborás | 34 B2 | Boceguillas | 36 A4 | Boddani | 72 B2 | Bodø | 97 E1 | Bogen (N) | 94 B3 | Bogovina | 73 E4 | Böhmer Wald | 56 B1 |
| Bobova | 72 C4 | Bocholt | 17 D3 | Bode | 52 C1 | Boecillo | 35 E4 | Bogense | 108 B3 | Bogøy | 97 E1 | Bohmte | 17 F2 |
| Bóbr | 53 F1 | Bochov | 53 E4 | Bodegraven | 16 C3 | Boëge | 27 D4 | Bogetići | 76 B2 | Boguslav | 113 E2 | Böhönye | 114 A1 |
| Bobrinec | 113 F3 | Bochum | 17 E3 | Boden | 98 B3 | Boen | 26 B4 | Boglárlelle | 112 B4 | Bogutovac | 73 D4 | Boiano | 64 B3 |
| Bobrovica | 113 E2 | Bockel | 48 A3 | Bodenmais | 56 B1 | Boeza | 35 D2 | Bognanco | 27 F4 | Bohain-en- | | Boiro | 34 A2 |
| Bobrujsk | 111 E4 | Bockenem | 52 B1 | Bodensee | 58 B1 | Boffalora | 60 A1 | Bognes | 94 A4 | Verman-dois | 20 A2 | Bois-d'Amont | 27 D3 |
| Bočac | 71 E4 | Böckstein | 59 E2 | Bodenteich | 48 B4 | Bogarra | 44 C1 | Bognor Regis | 9 F3 | Boherboy | 14 B3 | Boitzenburg | 49 E3 |
| Bocairent | 45 E1 | Bockum-Hövel | 17 E3 | Bodenwerder | 52 A1 | Bogatić | 72 C3 | Bogodol | 75 F1 | Bohinjska Bistrica | 70 A2 | Bóixols | 37 F3 |
| Bocca Trabaria | 61 E4 | Bocognano | 33 F3 | Bodenwöhr | 56 B1 | Bogdanci | 77 F3 | Bogojevo | 72 B2 | Bohinjsko jez | 70 A2 | Boizenburg | 48 B3 |

Bonn

| | | | | | | | | | | | |
|---|---|---|---|---|---|---|---|---|---|---|---|
| Bojana | 76 B3 | Bollullos de la | | Boñar | 35 E2 | Bonorva | 66 B2 | Borello | 61 D3 | Borgo Tufico | 61 E4 | Bornos | 43 D3 |
| Bøjden | 108 B4 | Mitación | 43 D2 | Bonar Bridge | 2 C3 | Bønsnes | 104 C3 | Borensberg | 105 F4 | Borgo Val di Taro | 60 B3 | Bornos, Emb de | 43 D3 |
| Bojnik | 77 D1 | Bollullos par del | | Bonares | 42 C2 | Boo | 106 B4 | Boréon, le | 31 E3 | Borgo Valsugana | 59 D3 | Boroughbridge | 7 D1 |
| Boka Kotorska | 76 A3 | Condado | 42 C2 | Bonassola | 60 B3 | Boom | 50 B3 | Borga | 107 F2 | Borgsjö | 101 F3 | Borovec | 115 D3 |
| Bøkfjorden | 95 F2 | Bolmen | 109 D2 | Bondeno | 60 C2 | Boos | 19 E3 | Borgafjäll | 97 E3 | Borgund | 104 B1 | Boroviči | 111 E1 |
| Bokn | 104 A3 | Bolnåos de | | Bondone, Mte | 58 C3 | Bootle | 6 B2 | Borga-fjällen | 97 E4 | Borgvattnet | 101 F2 | Borovnica | 70 B2 |
| Boknafjorden | 104 A3 | Calatrava | 40 A4 | Bonefro | 64 B2 | Bopfingen | 55 E2 | Borgarnes | 96 A2 | Boriĉje | 76 B2 | Borovo | 72 B2 |
| Bol | 75 E2 | Bologna | 60 C2 | Bologne | 26 C1 | Boppard | 51 E4 | Børgefjell | 97 E3 | Borisov | 111 D4 | Borovsk | 111 F1 |
| Bøla | 101 D1 | Bologne | 26 C1 | Bonete | 45 D1 | Bor (CS) | 53 E4 | Børgefjellet | 97 E3 | Borispol' | 113 E2 | Borre | 104 C3 |
| Bolbec | 19 D3 | Bologoje | 111 E1 | Bonette, Col de la | 31 D3 | Bor (YU) | 73 E3 | Borger | 17 D1 | Borja (E) | 36 C3 | Borriol | 41 E3 |
| Bolchov | 111 F3 | Bolos | 40 B4 | Boraĉko jez | 75 F1 | Börger | 17 E1 | Borja (YU) | 71 E4 | Borris | 15 D3 |
| Bolera, Emb de la | 44 B2 | Bolotana | 66 B2 | Borås | 108 C1 | Borba | 38 C4 | Borghetto | 63 E3 | Borken | 17 E3 | Borrisokane | 12 C4 |
| Bolesławiec | 112 A2 | Bolsena | 63 D1 | Borbollón, Emb de | 39 D2 | Borghetto S.S. | 31 F3 | Borkenes | 94 A3 | Borşa | 113 D3 |
| Boleszkowice | 49 E3 | Bolsena, L di | 63 D2 | Bonn | 51 E3 | Borbona | 63 F1 | Borgholm | 109 E2 | Børkop | 108 B3 | Børselv | 95 E1 |
| Bolgrad | 113 E4 | Bolsward | 16 C1 | Bonnåsjøen | 97 F1 | Borča | 72 C3 | Borgholzhausen | 17 F2 | Borkum | 47 D3 | Børselva | 95 E2 |
| Boliden | 98 B4 | Boltaña | 37 E2 | Bonnat | 25 E4 | Borci | 75 F1 | Borghorst | 17 E2 | Borlänge | 105 F2 | Børselvfjellet | 95 E2 |
| Boliqueime | 42 B2 | Boltenhagen | 48 B2 | Bonndorf | 54 C4 | Bordeaux | 28 B2 | Borgia | 67 F3 | Bormes-les- | | Bórsio | 86 B1 |
| Boljanići | 76 B1 | Bolton | 6 C2 | Bonnétable | 23 F3 | Bordeira | 42 A2 | Borgomanero | 58 A4 | Mimosas | 31 D4 | Bort-les-Orgues | 29 E1 |
| Boljevac | 73 E4 | Bolungarvík | 96 A1 | Bonneuil-Matours | 25 D3 | Bordères-Louron | 37 E2 | Borgone | 31 E1 | Bormida | 60 A2 | Börtnan | 101 E2 |
| Boljevci | 72 C3 | Bolus Head | 14 A4 | Bonneval (Eure- | | Border Forest | | Borgonovo Val | | Bormio | 58 C3 | Borzna | 113 F1 |
| Boljkovci | 73 D4 | Bolzano | 59 D3 | et-Loir) | 25 E1 | Park, The | 5 D3 | Tidone | 60 B2 | Born | 48 C1 | Borzonasca | 60 A3 |
| Boljuni | 75 F2 | Bombarral | 38 A3 | Bonneval (Savoie) | 31 E1 | Borders Region | 5 D3 | Borgorose | 63 F2 | Borna | 53 D2 | Bosa | 66 A2 |
| Bolkesjø | 104 C3 | Bomenzien | 48 C3 | Bonneville | 27 D4 | Bordesholm | 48 A2 | Borgo San | | Bornes | 34 C4 | Bosanci | 70 C3 |
| Bollebygd | 108 C1 | Bom Jesus | 34 A4 | Bonneville, la | 19 E4 | Bordighera | 31 E3 | Dalmazzo | 31 E2 | Bornes, Sa de | 34 C4 | Bosanska Dubica | 71 D3 |
| Bollène | 30 B3 | Bømlo | 104 A3 | Bonnières | 19 E3 | Bordøy | 96 A3 | Borgo San | | Bornholm | 109 D4 | Bosanska Gradiška | 71 E3 |
| Bollnäs | 101 F4 | Bonaigua, Pto de | | Bonnieux | 30 C3 | Bore | 60 B2 | Lorenzo | 61 D3 | Bornhöved | 48 B2 | Bosanska |
| Bollstabruk | 101 F2 | la | 37 F2 | Bono | 66 B2 | Bore | 60 B2 | Borgosesia | 58 A4 | Börnicke | 49 D4 | Kostajnica | 71 D3 |

# Bordeaux

| | | | |
|---|---|---|---|
| Bosanska Krupa | 71 D3 | Bourne, Gges de la | 30 C2 |
| Bosanska Rača | 72 B3 | Bournemouth | 9 E3 |
| Bosanski Brod | 71 E3 | Bourniá, Akr | 87 E3 |
| Bosanski Kobaš | 71 E3 | Bousquet-d'Orb, | |
| Bosanski Novi | 71 D3 | le | 30 A4 |
| Bosanski Petrovac | 71 D4 | Boussac | 25 F4 |
| Bosanski Šamac | 71 F3 | Boussens | 37 F1 |
| Bosansko Grahovo | 71 D4 | Boutonne | 24 C4 |
| Bosansko Petrovo | | Bouxwiller | 21 E3 |
| Selo | 71 F3 | Bouzonville | 21 D3 |
| Bosco | 61 E4 | Bovalino Marina | 67 F4 |
| Bosco | | Bova Marina | 67 E4 |
| Chiesanuova | 59 D4 | Bovan | 73 E4 |
| Bosilegrad | 77 E2 | Bovec | 70 A2 |
| Bosiljevo | 70 C3 | Bóveda | 34 B2 |
| Bosjökloster | 109 D3 | Bøverdal | 100 B3 |
| Boskoop | 16 C3 | Boves | 19 F2 |
| Bosna | 71 F4 | Boves | 31 E3 |
| Bosna i | | Bovey Tracy | 8 C3 |
| Hercegovina | 71 E4 | Bovolone | 60 C1 |
| Bošnjace | 77 E1 | Bowes | 5 E4 |
| Bošnjaci | 72 B3 | Bowness | 6 B1 |
| Bossòst | 37 F2 | Bowness-on- | |
| Bostan | 75 E2 | Solway | 5 D3 |
| Boštanj | 70 B2 | Boxholm | 109 E1 |
| Boston | 7 E3 | Boxmeer | 17 D3 |
| Bosut | 72 B2 | Boxtel | 16 C3 |
| Botev | 115 D2 | Boyle | 12 C2 |
| Botevgrad | 115 D2 | Boyne | 13 D3 |
| Bothel | 5 D4 | Božaj | 76 B3 |
| Boticas | 34 B4 | Božava | 74 C1 |
| Botley | 9 E3 | Bozdoğan | 115 F4 |
| Botngård | 100 C | Bozel | 31 D1 |
| Botnie, G de | 102 A3 | Bozen | 59 D3 |
| Botoš | 72 C2 | Božica | 77 E2 |
| Botoşani | 113 D3 | Boži Dar | 53 E3 |
| Botrange | 51 D4 | Bozouls | 29 E3 |
| Botsmark | 102 A1 | Bozüyük | 115 F3 |
| Botte Donato, Mte | 67 F2 | Bozzolo | 60 C2 |
| Bottenhavet | 102 A3 | Bra | 31 F2 |
| Bottniska Viken | | Brabant | 50 B3 |
| Pohjanlahti | 102 A3 | Brač | 75 E2 |
| Bottrop | 17 E3 | Bracadale | 2 B3 |
| Botun | 77 D4 | Bracadale, L | 2 B3 |
| Bouaye | 24 B2 | Bracciano | 63 E2 |
| Boucau | 28 A4 | Bracciano, L di | 63 E2 |
| Bouchain | 20 A2 | Bracco, Pso del | 60 B3 |
| Bouches-du- | | Bračevci | 71 D2 |
| Rhône | 30 B4 | Bracieux | 25 E2 |
| Boudry | 27 E2 | Bräcke | 101 E2 |
| Bouillon | 20 C2 | Brackenheim | 55 D2 |
| Bouilly | 26 B1 | Brackley | 9 E2 |
| Boúka | 86 C3 | Bracknell | 9 F2 |
| Boulay-Moselle | 21 D3 | Brackwede | 17 F3 |
| Boulogne (Haute- | | Brad | 112 C4 |
| Garonne) | 37 F1 | Bradano | 65 D4 |
| Boulogne (Pas-de- | | Bradashesh | 76 C4 |
| Calais) | 19 E1 | Bradford | 6 C2 |
| Boulogne R | 24 B3 | Bradford-on-Avon | 9 D2 |
| Bouloire | 23 F3 | Bradina | 75 F1 |
| Boulou, le | 32 B2 | Brading | 9 E3 |
| Boumort | 37 F3 | Bradwell-on-Sea | 11 D2 |
| Bourbon-Lancy | 26 B3 | Braemar | 3 D4 |
| Bourbon- | | Braga | 34 A4 |
| l'Archambault | 26 A3 | Bragança | 34 C3 |
| Bourbonne-les- | | Braguia, Pto de | 35 F2 |
| Bains | 27 D1 | Braies, L di | 59 D2 |
| Bourboule, la | 29 E1 | Brăila | 113 E4 |
| Bourbourg | 19 E1 | Braine | 20 A3 |
| Bourbriac | 22 C2 | Braine-le-Comte | 50 B4 |
| Bourdeaux | 30 C2 | Braintree | 11 D2 |
| Bourdeilles | 28 C1 | Brake | 47 F3 |
| Bourg | 28 B2 | Brakel | 52 A2 |
| Bourg-Achard | 19 D3 | Bräkne-Hoby | 109 D3 |
| Bourganeuf | 25 E4 | Brallo di Pregola | 60 A2 |
| Bourg-Argental | 30 B1 | Brálos | 83 E3 |
| Bourg-de-Péage | 30 C2 | Bramming | 108 A3 |
| Bourg-de-Visa | 28 C3 | Brampton | 5 D3 |
| Bourg-d'Oisans, le | 31 D2 | Bramsche | 17 E2 |
| Bourg-en-Bresse | 26 C4 | Brancaleone | 67 E4 |
| Bourges | 25 F3 | Brancion | 26 C3 |
| Bourget, le | 30 C1 | Brand | 58 B2 |
| Bourg-Lastic | 29 E1 | Brandbu | 105 D2 |
| Bourg-Madame | 32 A3 | Brande | 108 A3 |
| Bourgneuf -en- | | Brandenburg | 49 D4 |
| Retz | 24 B3 | Brand-Erbisdorf | 53 E3 |
| Bourgogne | 26 C2 | Brander, Pass of | 4 B1 |
| Bourgoin-Jallieu | 30 C1 | Brandis | 53 D2 |
| Bourg-St-Andéol | 30 B3 | Brändö | 107 D2 |
| Bourg-St-Maurice | 31 D1 | Brandon | 11 D1 |
| Bourgtheroulde | 19 D3 | Brandon Head | 14 A3 |
| Bourgueil | 25 D2 | Brandon Mt | 14 A3 |
| Bourmont | 26 C1 | Brandýs Stará | |
| Bourne | 7 D3 | Boleslav | 53 F3 |

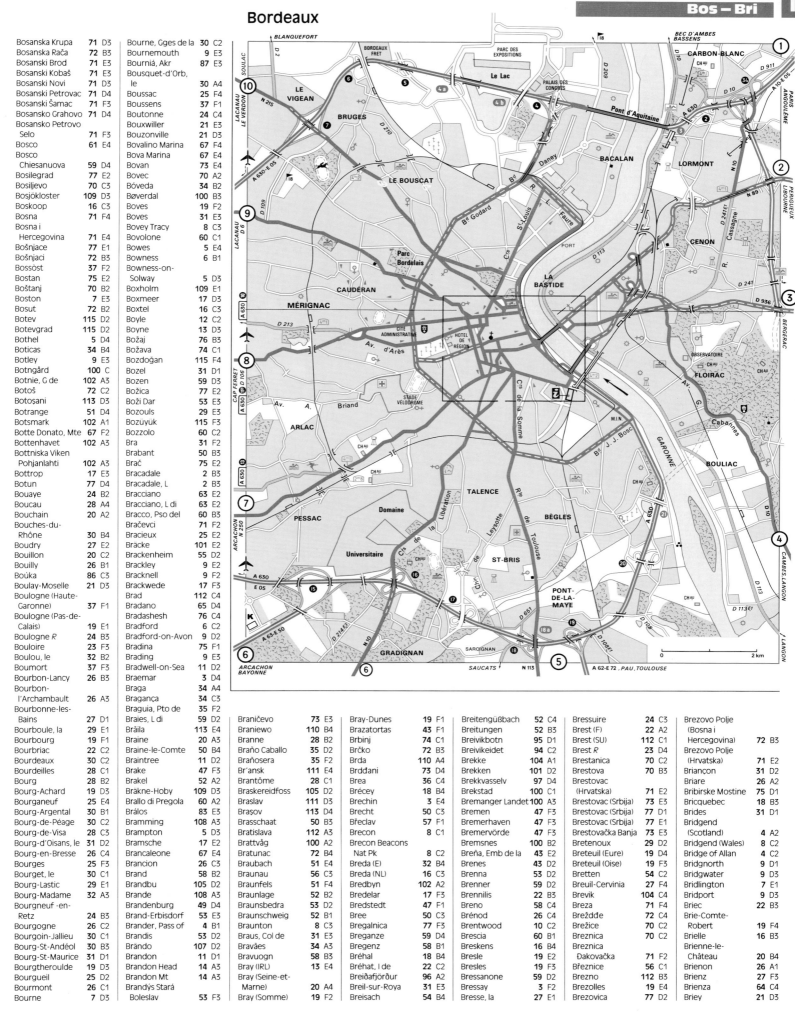

| | | | | | | | | |
|---|---|---|---|---|---|---|---|---|
| Braničevo | 73 E3 | Bray-Dunes | 19 F1 | Breitengüßbach | 52 C4 | Bressuire | 24 C3 | Brezovo Polje |
| Braniewo | 110 B4 | Brazatortas | 43 F1 | Breitungen | 52 B3 | Brest (F) | 22 A2 | (Bosna i |
| Branne | 28 B2 | Brbinj | 74 C1 | Breivikbotn | 95 D1 | Brest (SU) | 112 C1 | Hercegovina) | 72 B3 |
| Braño Caballo | 35 D2 | Brčko | 72 B3 | Breivikeidet | 94 C2 | Brest R | 23 D4 | Brezovo Polje |
| Brañosera | 35 F2 | Brda | 110 A4 | Brekke | 104 A1 | Brestanica | 70 C2 | (Hrvatska) | 71 E2 |
| Br'ansk | 111 E4 | Brdđani | 73 D4 | Brekken | 101 D2 | Brestova | 70 B3 | Briançon | 31 D2 |
| Brantôme | 28 C1 | Brea | 36 C4 | Brekkvasselv | 97 D4 | Brestovac | | Briare | 26 A2 |
| Braskereidfoss | 105 D2 | Brécey | 18 B4 | Brekstad | 100 C1 | (Hrvatska) | 71 E2 | Bribirske Mostine | 75 D1 |
| Braslaw | 111 D3 | Brechin | 3 E4 | Bremanger Landet | 100 A3 | Brestovac (Srbija) | 73 E3 | Bricquebec | 18 B3 |
| Braşov | 113 D4 | Brecht | 50 C3 | Bremen | 47 F3 | Brestovac (Srbija) | 77 D1 | Brides | 31 D1 |
| Brasschaat | 50 B3 | Břeclav | 57 F1 | Bremerhaven | 47 F3 | Brestovac (Srbija) | 77 E1 | Bridgend | |
| Bratislava | 112 A3 | Brecon | 8 C1 | Bremervörde | 47 F3 | Brestovačka Banja | 73 E3 | (Scotland) | 4 A2 |
| Brattvåg | 100 A2 | Brecon Beacons | | Bremsnes | 100 B2 | Bretenoux | 29 D2 | Bridgend (Wales) | 8 C2 |
| Bratunac | 72 B4 | Nat Pk | 8 C2 | Breña, Emb de la | 43 E2 | Breteuil (Eure) | 19 D4 | Bridge of Allan | 4 C1 |
| Braubach | 51 E4 | Breda (E) | 32 B4 | Brenes | 43 D2 | Breteuil (Oise) | 19 F3 | Bridgnorth | 9 D1 |
| Braunau | 56 C3 | Breda (NL) | 16 C3 | Brenna | 53 D2 | Bretten | 54 C2 | Bridgwater | 8 C3 |
| Braunfels | 51 F4 | Bredbyn | 102 A2 | Brenner | 59 D2 | Breuil-Cervinia | 27 F4 | Bridlington | 7 E1 |
| Braunlage | 52 B2 | Bredelar | 17 F3 | Brennilis | 22 B3 | Brevik | 104 C4 | Bridport | 9 D3 |
| Braunsbedra | 53 D2 | Bredstedt | 47 F1 | Breno | 58 C4 | Breza | 71 F4 | Briec | 22 B3 |
| Braunschweig | 52 B1 | Bree | 50 C3 | Brénod | 26 C4 | Brežđde | 72 C4 | Brie-Comte- |
| Braunton | 8 C3 | Bregalnica | 77 F3 | Brentwood | 10 C2 | Brežice | 70 C2 | Robert | 19 F4 |
| Braus, Col de | 31 E3 | Breganze | 59 D4 | Brescia | 60 B1 | Breznica | 70 C2 | Brielle | 16 B3 |
| Bravães | 34 A3 | Bregenz | 58 B1 | Breskens | 16 B4 | Breznica | | Brienne-le- |
| Bravuogn | 58 B3 | Bréhal | 18 B4 | Bresle | 19 E2 | Đakovačka | 71 F2 | Château | 20 B4 |
| Bray (IRL) | 13 E4 | Bréhat, I de | 22 C2 | Bresles | 19 F3 | Březnice | 56 C1 | Brienon | 26 A1 |
| Bray (Seine-et- | | Breiðafjörður | 96 A2 | Bressanone | 59 D2 | Brezno | 112 B3 | Brienz | 27 F3 |
| Marne) | 20 A4 | Breil-sur-Roya | 31 E3 | Bressay | 3 F2 | Brezolles | 19 E4 | Brienza | 64 C4 |
| Bray (Somme) | 19 F2 | Breisach | 54 B4 | Bresse, la | 27 E1 | Brezovica | 77 D2 | Briey | 21 D3 |

| | | |
|---|---|---|
| Brig | 27 | F3 |
| Brigg | 7 | D2 |
| Brighouse | 6 | C2 |
| Brightlingsea | 11 | D2 |
| Brighton | 10 | C3 |
| Brignogan | 22 | A2 |
| Brignoles | 31 | D4 |
| Brihuega | 40 | B2 |
| Briksdal | 100 | A3 |
| Brilon | 17 | F3 |
| Brimnes | 104 | B2 |
| Brinches | 42 | A1 |
| Brindisi | 65 | F3 |
| Brinon | 26 | A2 |
| Brioni | 70 | A4 |
| Brionne | 19 | D3 |
| Brioude | 29 | F1 |
| Brioux | 24 | C4 |
| Briouze | 18 | C4 |
| Brisighella | 61 | D3 |
| Brissac-Quincé | 24 | C2 |
| Brissago | 58 | A3 |
| Bristol | 9 | D2 |
| Bristol Chan | 8 | C2 |
| Brive-la-Gaillarde | 29 | D2 |
| Briviesca | 36 | A2 |
| Brixen | 59 | D2 |
| Brixham | 8 | C4 |
| Brixlegg | 59 | D1 |
| Brjánslækur | 96 | A1 |
| Brka | 72 | B3 |
| Brna | 75 | E2 |
| Brnaze | 75 | D1 |
| Brno | 57 | F1 |
| Bro (Gotlands Län) | 109 | F4 |
| Bro (Stockholms Län) | 106 | B3 |
| Broad B | 2 | B2 |
| Broadford (GB) | 2 | B3 |
| Broadford (IRL) | 12 | B4 |
| Broad Haven | 12 | B2 |
| Broad Law | 5 | D3 |
| Broadstairs | 11 | D3 |
| Broadway | 9 | E1 |
| Broager | 108 | A4 |
| Broby | 109 | D3 |
| Brocken | 52 | B2 |
| Brod (Bosna i Hercegovina) | 76 | A1 |
| Brod (Makedonija) | 77 | D3 |
| Brodarevo | 76 | B1 |
| Brodica | 73 | E3 |
| Brodick | 4 | B2 |
| Brod na Kupi | 70 | B3 |
| Brodnica | 112 | B1 |
| Brody (PL) | 53 | F1 |
| Brody (SU) | 113 | D2 |
| Broglie | 19 | D3 |
| Brohl-Lützing | 51 | E4 |
| Brolo | 69 | D2 |
| Bromarv | 107 | D3 |
| Brombachsee | 55 | E2 |
| Brome | 48 | B4 |
| Bromölla | 109 | D3 |
| Bromsgrove | 9 | E1 |
| Bromyard | 9 | D1 |
| Bronchales | 41 | D2 |
| Brønderslev | 108 | B2 |
| Broni | 60 | A2 |
| Brønnøysund | 97 | D3 |
| Brøns | 108 | A3 |
| Bronte | 69 | D3 |
| Bronzani Majdan | 71 | D3 |
| Broom, L | 2 | C2 |
| Broons | 22 | C3 |
| Brora | 3 | D3 |
| Brösarp | 109 | D3 |
| Brossac | 28 | B1 |
| Brøstadbotn | 94 | B3 |
| Brotas | 38 | B4 |
| Broto | 37 | E2 |
| Brotton | 5 | F4 |
| Brøttum | 105 | D2 |
| Brou (Ain) | 26 | C4 |
| Brou (Eure-et-Loir) | 25 | E1 |
| Brouage | 24 | B4 |
| Brough | 5 | E4 |
| Brough Head | 3 | D1 |
| Broughshane | 13 | E1 |
| Broughton-in-Furness | 6 | B1 |
| Brouis, Col de | 31 | E3 |
| Brovst | 108 | B2 |
| Brownhills | 9 | E1 |
| Brozas | 39 | D3 |
| Bruay-en-Artois | 19 | F1 |
| Bruay-sur-l'Escaut | 20 | A1 |
| Bruchsal | 54 | C2 |
| Brück | 53 | D1 |
| Bruck (D) | 56 | B1 |
| Bruck (Niederösterreich) | 57 | F2 |
| Bruck (Salzburg) | 59 | E1 |
| Bruck an der Mur | 57 | E4 |
| Brückl | 70 | B1 |
| Bruckmühl | 56 | B3 |
| Brüel | 48 | C2 |
| Brués | 34 | B2 |
| Bruges | 50 | A3 |
| Brugg | 27 | F2 |
| Brügge | 17 | E4 |
| Brugge | 50 | A3 |
| Brühl | 17 | E4 |
| Brújula, Pto de la | 36 | A2 |
| Bruksvallarna | 101 | D2 |
| Brûlon | 23 | E3 |
| Brumath | 21 | E4 |
| Brummen | 17 | D3 |
| Brumunddal | 105 | D2 |
| Bruneck | 59 | D2 |
| Brunete | 40 | A2 |
| Brunflo | 101 | E2 |
| Brunico | 59 | D2 |
| Brünigpass | 27 | F3 |
| Bruniquel | 29 | D3 |
| Brunkeberg | 104 | B3 |
| Brunnen | 58 | A2 |
| Brunsbüttel | 47 | F2 |
| Brunssum | 17 | D4 |
| Bruntál | 112 | A3 |
| Bruravik | 104 | B2 |
| Brus | 77 | D1 |
| Brusand | 104 | A4 |
| Brušane | 70 | C4 |
| Brusasco | 31 | F1 |
| Brusnik | 73 | F3 |
| Brussel | 50 | B3 |
| Brusson | 27 | F4 |
| Brüssow | 49 | E2 |
| Bruton | 9 | D3 |
| Bruvno | 70 | C4 |
| Bruxelles | 50 | B3 |
| Bruyères | 27 | D1 |
| Brvenik | 76 | C1 |
| Bryne | 104 | A4 |
| Brynmawr | 9 | D2 |
| Brzan | 73 | D3 |
| Brza Palanka | 73 | F3 |
| Brzeće | 77 | D1 |
| Brzeg | 112 | A2 |
| Buarcos | 38 | B2 |
| Buavåg | 104 | A3 |
| Bubry | 22 | C3 |
| Bučač | 113 | D3 |
| Buçaco | 38 | B2 |
| Buccheri | 69 | D4 |
| Bucchianico | 64 | A2 |
| Bucelas | 38 | A4 |
| Buchan Ness | 3 | E3 |
| Büchen | 48 | B3 |
| Buchen | 55 | D1 |
| Buchenwald | 52 | C3 |
| Buchholz | 48 | A3 |
| Buchloe | 55 | E3 |
| Buchs | 58 | B2 |
| Buchy | 19 | E3 |
| Bucine | 61 | D4 |
| Bučje | 73 | F4 |
| Bückeburg | 52 | A1 |
| Buckfastleigh | 8 | C4 |
| Buckhaven | 5 | D2 |
| Buckie | 3 | D3 |
| Buckingham | 9 | F2 |
| Buckinghamshire | 9 | F2 |
| Buckovička Banja | 73 | D3 |
| Buckow | 49 | E4 |
| Bückwitz | 49 | D3 |
| Bučovice | 57 | F1 |
| Bucovina | 113 | D3 |
| Bucureşti | 115 | D1 |
| Bud | 100 | B2 |
| Budapest | 112 | B4 |
| Búðardalur | 96 | A2 |
| Buddon Ness | 5 | D1 |
| Buddusò | 66 | B2 |
| Bude | 8 | B3 |
| Büdelsdorf | 48 | A2 |
| Budimlić Japra | 71 | D3 |
| Büdingen | 52 | A4 |
| Budinščina | 70 | C2 |
| Budleigh Salterton | 8 | C3 |
| Budrio | 61 | D2 |
| Budva | 76 | B3 |
| Budyně nad Ohře | 53 | F3 |
| Buenache de Alarcón | 40 | C3 |
| Buen Amor | 39 | E1 |
| Buenavista de Valdavia | 35 | E3 |
| Buendia | 40 | C2 |
| Buendia, Emb de | 40 | C2 |
| Buet, Mt | 27 | E4 |
| Bueu | 34 | A2 |
| Bug | 112 | C1 |
| Bugeat | 29 | D1 |
| Bugojno | 71 | E4 |
| Bugøynes | 95 | F2 |
| Bugue, le | 28 | C2 |
| Bühl | 54 | C3 |
| Builth Wells | 9 | D1 |
| Buin, Piz | 58 | B2 |
| Buis-les-Baronnies | 30 | C3 |
| Buitrago del Lozoya | 40 | B1 |

## Brugge

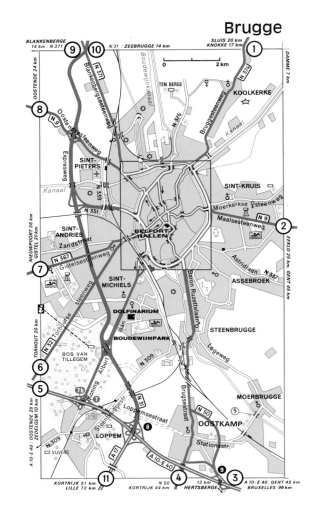

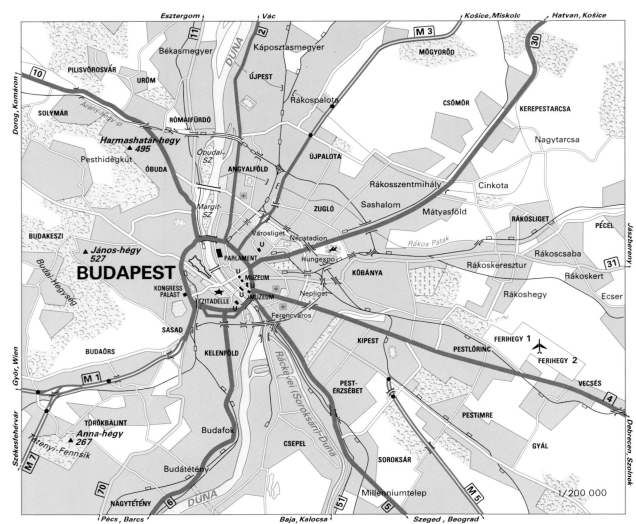

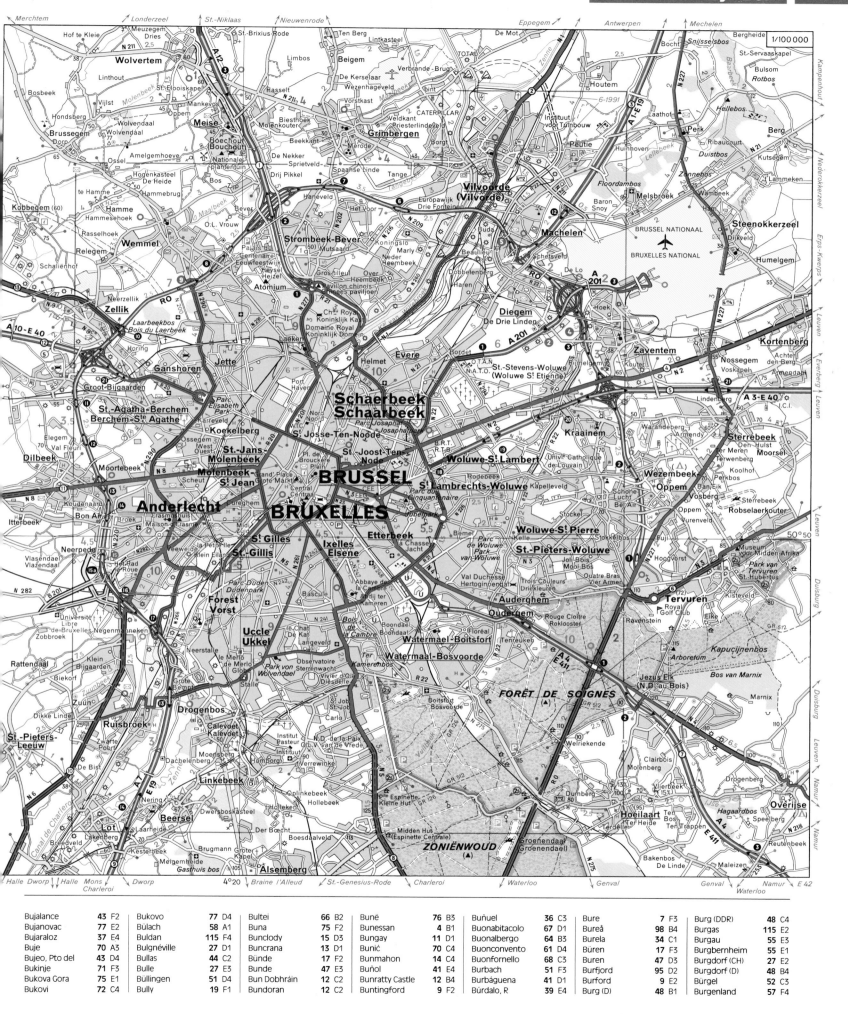

| | | | | | | | | | | | | |
|---|---|---|---|---|---|---|---|---|---|---|---|
| Bujalance | 43 F2 | Bukovo | 77 D4 | Bultei | 66 B2 | Bunë | 76 B3 | Buñuel | 36 C3 | Bure | 7 F3 | Burg (DDR) | 48 C4 |
| Bujanovac | 77 E2 | Bülach | 58 A1 | Buna | 75 F2 | Bunessan | 4 B1 | Buonabitacolo | 67 D1 | Bureå | 98 B4 | Burgas | 115 E2 |
| Bujaraloz | 37 E4 | Buldan | 115 F4 | Bunclody | 15 D3 | Bungay | 11 D1 | Buonalbergo | 64 B3 | Burela | 34 C1 | Burgau | 55 E3 |
| Buje | 70 A3 | Bulgnéville | 27 D1 | Buncrana | 13 D1 | Bunić | 70 C4 | Buonconvento | 61 D4 | Büren | 17 F3 | Burgbernheim | 55 E1 |
| Bujeo, Pto del | 43 D4 | Bullas | 44 C2 | Bünde | 17 F2 | Bunmahon | 14 C4 | Buonfornello | 68 C3 | Buren | 47 D3 | Burgdorf (CH) | 27 E2 |
| Bukinje | 71 F3 | Bulle | 27 E3 | Bunde | 47 E3 | Buñol | 41 E4 | Burbach | 51 F1 | Burfjord | 95 D1 | Burgdorf (D) | 48 B4 |
| Bukova Gora | 75 E1 | Büllingen | 51 D4 | Bun Dobhráin | 12 C2 | Bunratty Castle | 12 B4 | Burbáguena | 41 D1 | Burford | 9 E2 | Bürgel | 52 C3 |
| Bukovi | 72 C4 | Bully | 19 F1 | Bundoran | 12 C2 | Buntingford | 9 F2 | Búrdalo, R | 39 E4 | Burg (D) | 48 B1 | Burgenland | 57 F4 |

Burgess Hill 10 C3
Burggrub 52 C4
Burghasungen 52 A2
Burghausen 56 B3
Burgjoß 52 B4
Burgkunstadt 52 C4
Burglengenfeld 55 F1
Burgohondo 39 F2
Burgos 35 F3
Burgsinn 52 B4
Burgstädt 53 E3
Burg Stargard 49 D2
Burgsvik 109 F4
Burgsviken 109 F4
Burguete 36 C1
Burgui 37 D2
Burguillo, Emb de 39 F2
Burguillos del Cerro 43 D1
Burhaniye 115 E4
Burhave 47 F3
Burie 28 B1
Burjassot 41 E4
Burk 53 F2
Burkau 53 F2
Burnham 9 D3
Burnham-on-Crouch 11 D2
Burnley 6 C2
Burntisland 5 D2
Buronzo 31 F1
Burrel 76 C3
Burriana 41 E3
Burrow Head 4 C4
Burry Port 8 C2
Bursa 115 F3
Burscheid 17 E4
Bürstadt 54 C1
Burton-upon-Trent 6 C3
Burträsk 98 B4
Burwick 3 E1
Bury 6 C2
Buryn' 113 F1
Bury St Edmunds 11 D1
Busalla 60 A3
Busambra, Rca 68 B3
Busca 31 E2
Buševa pl 77 D3
Buševec 70 C2
Bushat 76 C3
Bushmills 13 E1
Buskerud 104 C2
Buško Blato 75 E1
Busko-Zdrój 112 B2
Busovača 71 F4
Bussang 27 E1
Busseto 60 B2
Bussière-Badil 28 C1
Bussolengo 60 C1
Bussum 16 C2
Busto Arsizio 60 A1
Busto de Bureba 36 A2
Büsum 47 F2
Bute 4 B2
Butera 68 C4
Buthrotum 114 C4
Buttermere 5 D4
Buttevant 14 B3
Butt of Lewis 2 B2
Buttstädt 52 C2
Butzbach 51 F4
Bützow 48 C2
Buxtehude 48 A3
Buxton 6 C3
Buxy 26 C3
Buzançais 25 E3
Buzancy 20 C3
Buzău 113 E4
Buzău *R* 113 E4
Buzet 70 A3
Bužim 70 C3
Bychov 111 E4
Bydgoszcz 112 A1
Bygdeå 102 B1
Bygdin 100 B3
Bygdin *L* 100 B3
Bygdsiljum 102 B1
Bygland 104 B4
Byglandsfjord 104 B4
Byglandsfjord *L* 104 B4
Bykle 104 B3
Bykleheiene 104 B3
Bylderup-Bov 108 A4
Byrkjelo 100 A3
Byske 98 B4
Byskeälven 98 B3
Bytom 112 B2
Bytów 110 A4
Byxelkrok 109 E2

# C

Cabañaquinta 35 D2
Cabañas 44 B2
Cabanes 41 F3
Cabannes, les 32 A2
Čabar 70 B3
Cabeceiras 34 B4
Cabeço de Vide 38 C3
Cabella Ligure 60 A2
Cabeza del Buey 39 E4
Cabezas Rubias 42 C2
Cabezo Gordo 42 C2
Cabezón 35 E4
Cabezón de la Sal 35 F2
Cabezuela del Valle 39 E2
Cabo de Gata 44 C4
Cabourg 18 C3
Cabra 43 F2
Cabra del Santo Cristo 44 A2
Cabras 66 A3
Cabre, Col de 30 C2
Cabreira, Sa da 34 B4
Cabreiros 34 B1
Cabrejas, Pto de 40 C3
Cabrejas, Sa de 36 A3
Cabréra 36 C4
Cabrera, I de 45 F3
Cabrera, Sa de la 34 C3
Cabrerets 29 D3
Cabriel, R 41 D3
Cabril, Bgem do 38 B2
Cabrillas 39 E1
Cabrito, Pto del 43 D4
Cabuérniga 35 F2
Čabulja 75 E1
Cacabelos 34 C2
Čačak 73 D4
Caccamo 68 B3
Cacela 42 B3
Cáceres 39 D3
Cachafeiro 34 A2
Cachopo 42 B2
Čačinci 71 E2
Cadabo 34 C2
Cadalso de los Vidrios 40 A2
Cadaqués 32 C3
Cadarache 30 C3
Cadaval 38 A3
Čađavica 71 E4
Čadca 112 B3
Cadelbosco di Sopra 60 C2
Cadenabbia 58 B4
Cadena, Pto de la 45 D2
Cadenberge 47 F2
Cadenet 30 C3
Cader Idris 6 A3
Cádiar 44 A3
Cadillac 28 B2
Cadipietra 59 D2
Cadi, Serra del 32 A3
Cádiz 43 D4
Cádiz, B de 43 D4
Cádiz, G de 42 C3
Cadouin 28 C2
Čadyr-Lunga 113 E4
Caen 18 C3
Caerdydd 9 D2
Caerfyrddin 8 C2
Caergybi 6 A2
Caernarfon 6 A3
Caernarfon B 6 A3
Caerphilly 9 D2
Caersws 9 D1
Cafasan 77 D4
Cagli 61 E4
Cagliari 66 B4
Cagliari, G di 66 B4
Čaglin 71 E2
Cagnano Varano 64 C2
Cagnes 31 E3
Caha Mts 14 A4
Caher 14 C3
Cahersiveen 14 A4
Cahore Pt 15 E3
Cahors 29 D3
Caia, Bgem do 38 C4
Caianello 64 A3
Caión 34 A1
Cairn Gorm 3 D4
Cairngorm Mts 3 D4
Cairnryan 4 B3
Cairo Montenotte 31 F2
Caiseal 14 C3
Caisleán an Bharraigh 12 B3
Caistor 7 D2
Caivano 64 B4
Cajarc 29 D3
Čajetina 72 C4
Čajniče 76 B1
Čakor 76 C2
Čakovec 70 C1
Čakovice 53 F3
Çal 115 F4
Calabor 34 C3
Calabria 67 E2
Calaceite 41 F1
Calacuccia 33 F3
Cala d'Or 45 F3
Cala, Emb de la 43 D2
Calaf 37 F3
Calafat 114 C2
Calafell 37 F4
Calafort Ros Láir 15 D4
Cala Gonone 66 C2
Calahonda 44 A4
Calahorra 36 C2
Calais 19 E1
Calamocha 41 D1
Calañas 42 C2
Calanche, les 33 E3
Calanda 41 E1
Calanda, Emb de 41 E2
Calangianus 66 B1
Cala'n Porter 45 F2
Calar Alto 44 B3
Călărași 115 E1
Cala Ratjada 45 F2
Calasetta 66 A4
Calasparra 44 C2
Calatafimi 68 B3
Calatañazor 36 B3
Calatayud 36 C4
Calatorao 36 C4
Calau 53 E1
Calazzo 64 B3
Calbe 52 C1
Calcena 36 C3
Caldaro 59 D3
Caldarola 61 F4
Caldas da Rainha 38 A3
Caldas das Taipas 34 A4
Caldas de Reis 34 A2
Caldas de Vizela 34 A4
Caldeirão, Sa do 42 B2
Caldelas 34 A3
Caldera de Taburiente, Pque Nac de la 42 A4
Calderina 40 A4
Caldes de Boí 37 F2
Caldes de Malavella 32 B3
Caldes de Montbui 32 A4
Caldirola 60 A2
Caledonian Canal 2 C4
Calella (Palamós) 32 C3
Calella (Pinedo de Mar) 32 B4
Calenzana 33 F3
Calera de León 43 D1
Calera y Chozas 39 F3
Caleruega 36 A3
Caletta, la 66 C2
Cálig 41 F2
Călimănești 115 D1
Călimani, M 113 D4
Calitri 64 C3
Calizzano 31 F3
Callac 22 B3
Callan 15 D3
Callander 4 C1
Calla, Pso della 61 D3
Callington 8 C4
Callosa de Ensarria 45 E1
Callosa de Segura 45 D2
Calmazzo 61 E3
Calmbach 54 C2
Calne 9 E2
Calolziocorte 58 B4
Calonge 32 B3
Calpe 45 E1
Caltabellotta 68 B3
Caltagirone 69 D4
Caltanissetta 68 C3
Caltavuturo 68 C3
Caluso 31 E1
Calvados 18 C3
Calvi 33 E3
Calvitero 39 E2
Calvörde 48 C4
Calw 54 C2
Calzada de Calatrava 44 A1
Calzada de Valdunciel 39 E1
Cam 9 F1
Camacho, Pto 44 A3
Camaiore 60 C3
Camaldoli 61 D3
Camaleño 35 E2
Camarasa 37 F3
Camarasa, Emb de 37 F3
Camarat, Cap 31 D4
Camarena 40 A2
Camarès 32 B1
Camaret 22 A3
Camarillas 41 E2
Camarillas, Emb de 44 C1
Camariñas 34 A1
Camarzana 35 D3
Camas 43 D2
Cambados 34 A2
Cambas 38 C2
Camberley 9 F2
Cambil 44 A2
Cambo-les-Bains 28 A4
Camborne 8 B4
Cambrai 20 A2
Cambre 34 B1
Cambremer 19 D3
Cambrian Mts 8 C1
Cambridge 10 C1
Cambridgeshire 10 C1
Cambrils de Mar 37 F4
Camburg 52 C3
Camelford 8 B3
Camerino 61 E4
Camigliatello Silano 67 E2
Caminha 34 A3
Caminomorisco 39 D2
Caminreal 41 D2
Camogli 60 A3
Campagna 64 C4
Campagne-lès-Hesdin 19 E2
Campan 37 E1
Campana 67 F2
Campanario 39 E4
Campania 64 B4
Campaspero 35 F4
Campbeltown 4 B3
Campello 45 E1
Campi Bisenzio 60 C3
Campiglia Marittima 62 C1
Campilhas, Bgem de 42 A1
Campillo de Altobuey 41 D3
Campillo de Aragón 36 C4
Campillo de Arenas 44 A2
Campillo de Llerena 43 D1
Campillos 43 E3
Campione 58 A4
Campi Salentina 65 F4
Campitello M 64 B3
Campli 63 F1
Campo 37 E2
Campobasso 64 B3
Campobello di Licata 68 C4
Campobello di Mazara 68 A3
Campo Carlo Magno 58 C3
Campo de Beisteros 38 B1
Campo de Caso 35 E2
Campo de Criptana 40 B4
Campo di Fiori 58 A4
Campo di Giove 64 A2
Campodonico 61 E4
Campoformido 59 F3
Campogalliano 60 C2
Campo Imperatore 63 F1
Campo Ligure 60 A3
Campo Maior 38 C4
Campomanes 35 D2
Campomarino 64 B2
Campora San Giovanni 67 E3
Camporredondo, Emb de 35 E2
Camporrobles 41 D3
Campos 45 F3
Camposampiero 59 D4
Campos, Canal de 35 E4
Campotosto, L di 63 F1
Campo Tures 59 D2
Camprodon 32 B3
Camucia 61 D4
Camuñas 40 B3
Cañada de Benatanduz 41 E2
Cañadas, Pto 43 D1
Çanakkale 115 E3
Çanakkale Boğazı 115 E3
Canal du Nord 19 F2
Canal du Rhône au Rhin 27 E2
Canales de la Sierra 36 A3
Canals 41 E4
Canal San Bovo 59 D3
Cañamero 39 E3
Canarias, Is 42 B4
Canas de Senhorim 38 C1
Cañaveral 39 D3
Cañaveral de León 43 D2
Cañaveras 40 C2
Canazei 59 D3
Cancale 18 B4
Cancárix 45 D1
Canche 19 E1
Cancon 28 C2
Candanchu 37 D2
Candas 35 D1
Candasnos 37 E4
Candé 23 E4
Candeeiros, Sa dos 38 A3
Candela 64 C3
Candelaria, Sa 39 E2
Candelario 39 E2
Candelaro 64 C2
Candeleda 39 F2
Candes 25 D2
Canelles, Emb de 37 F3
Canelli 31 F2
Canero 35 D1
Canet de Mar 32 B4
Cañete 41 D3
Cañete de las Torres 43 F2
Cañete la Real 43 E3
Canet-Plage 32 B2
Canfranc-Estación 37 D2
Cangas 34 A3
Cangas de Narcea 34 C2
Cangas de Onís 35 E1
Canha 38 B4
Canicatti 68 C4
Canicattini Bagni 69 D4
Canigou, Pic du 32 B2
Cañigral 41 D3
Caniles 44 B3
Canin, M 59 F3
Canino 63 D2
Canis 18 B3
Cañizál 39 E1
Canjáyar 44 B3
Canna 2 B4
Cannero Riviera 58 A4
Cannes 31 E4
Canneto 60 C4
Cannich 2 C3
Cannobio 58 A4
Cannock 9 E1
Canonbie 5 D3
Canosa di Puglia 64 C3
Canourgue, la 29 F3
Cansano 64 A2
Cansiglio 59 E3
Cantabria 35 F2
Cantal (Dépt) 29 E2
Cantal, Mts du 29 E2
Cantalapiedra 39 F1
Cantalejo 40 A1
Cantalpino 39 E1
Cantanhede 38 B2
Cantavieja 41 E2
Čantavir 72 B1
Canterbury 11 D3
Cantillana 43 D2
Cantoira 31 E1
Cantoral 35 E2
Cantoria 44 C3
Cantù 60 A1
Canvey I 11 D2
Cany-Barville 19 D2
Caorle 59 E4
Caorso 60 B2
Capaccio 64 C4
Capaci 68 B3
Capalbio 63 D2
Capannelle, Pso delle 63 F1
Caparde 72 B4
Caparroso 36 C2
Capbreton 28 A4
Cap Corse 33 F2
Cap-d'Agde, le 30 A4
Cap d'Antibes 31 E4
Capdenac-Gare 29 E2
Capel Curig 6 A3
Capelle, la 20 B2
Capendu 32 B2
Capestang 30 A4
Capestrano 64 A2
Capileira 44 A3
Capistrello 63 F2
Čapljina 75 F2
Capmany 32 B3
Cappelle sul Tavo 64 A1
Cappoquin 14 C4
Capracotta 64 A2
Capraia, I di 62 B1
Caprera, I 66 B1
Capri 64 B4
Capriati a Volturno 64 A3
Capri, I di 64 B4
Captieux 28 B3
Capua 64 B3
Capurso 65 D3
Capvern 37 E1
Caracal 115 D2
Caracuel 40 A4
Caragh, L 14 A4
Caraman 29 D4
Caramanico Terme 64 A2
Caramulo 38 B1
Caramulo, Sa do 38 B1
Caransebeș 114 C1
Carantec 22 B2
Caravaca de la Cruz 44 C2
Caravai, Pso di 66 B3
Caravius, M. is 66 B4
Carbajales de Alba 35 D4
Carballiño 34 B2
Carballo 34 A1
Carbayo 35 D2
Carbonara, C 66 C4
Carbonara, Pzo 68 C3
Carbon-Blanc 28 B2
Carboneras 44 C3
Carboneras de Guadazaón 41 D3
Carbonero el Mayor 40 A1
Carbonia 66 B4
Carbonin 59 E2
Carbonne 37 F1
Carcaboso 39 D2
Carcabuey 43 F3
Carcaixent 41 E4
Carcans 28 A2
Carcans-Plage 28 A2
Carcare 31 F2
Carcassonne 32 B1
Carcastillo 36 C2
Carcès 31 D4
Carche 45 D1
Čardak 71 F4
Çardak 115 F4
Cardedeu 32 B4
Cardeña 43 F1
Cardener, R 32 A4
Cardenete 41 D3
Cardiff 9 D2
Cardigan 8 B1
Cardigan B 8 B1
Cardona 32 A3
Carei 112 C3
Carentan 18 B3
Cares, R 35 E2
Carevdar 71 D2
Carev Dvor 77 D4
Cargèse 33 E3
Carhaix-Plouguer 22 B3
Caria 38 C2
Cariati 67 F2
Caričin Grad 77 D1
Carignan 20 C2
Carignano 31 E2
Carina 77 D4
Cariñena 36 C4

| Name | Map | Grid |
|---|---|---|
| Carini | 68 | B3 |
| Cariño | 34 | B1 |
| Carinola | 64 | A3 |
| Carisio | 31 | F1 |
| Carlet | 41 | E4 |
| Carling | 21 | D3 |
| Carlingford | 13 | E3 |
| Carlingford L | 13 | E3 |
| Carlisle | 5 | D3 |
| Carlit, Pic | 32 | A2 |
| Carloforte | 66 | A4 |
| Carlow | 13 | D4 |
| Carlow (Co) | 13 | D4 |
| Carloway | 2 | B2 |
| Carluke | 4 | C2 |
| Carmagnola | 31 | E2 |
| Carmarthen | 8 | C2 |
| Carmarthen B | 8 | B2 |
| Carmaux | 29 | E3 |
| Carmona | 43 | E2 |
| Carna | 12 | A3 |
| Carnac | 22 | C4 |
| Carnaio, Pso del | 61 | D3 |
| Carn Ban | 2 | C4 |
| Carndonagh | 13 | D1 |
| Carnedd Llewelyn | 6 | A3 |
| Carn Eige | 2 | C3 |
| Carneros, Pto de los | 39 | F4 |
| Carnew | 15 | D3 |
| Carnforth | 6 | B1 |
| Carnia | 59 | F3 |
| Carnia (Reg) | 59 | F3 |
| Carnlough | 13 | E1 |
| Carnon | 30 | B4 |
| Carnota | 34 | A2 |
| Carnoustie | 5 | D1 |
| Carnsore Pt | 15 | D4 |
| Carnwath | 5 | D2 |
| Caroch | 41 | E1 |
| Carolles | 18 | B4 |
| Carovigno | 65 | E3 |
| Carpaneto Piacentino | 60 | B2 |
| Carpatii Meridionali | 114 | C1 |
| Carpenedolo | 60 | B1 |
| Carpentras | 30 | C3 |
| Carpi | 60 | C2 |
| Carpignano Sesia | 58 | A4 |
| Carpineti | 60 | C3 |
| Carpineto Romano | 63 | F3 |
| Carpinone | 64 | A3 |
| Carquefou | 24 | B2 |
| Carqueiranne | 31 | D4 |
| Carracedelo | 34 | C2 |
| Carradale | 4 | B2 |
| Carraig na Siúire | 14 | C3 |
| Carral | 34 | B1 |
| Carrantuohill | 14 | A4 |
| Carranza | 36 | A1 |
| Carrara | 60 | B3 |
| Carrascal | 41 | E2 |
| Carrascosa del Campo | 40 | C3 |
| Carrascoy | 45 | D2 |
| Carrasqueta, Pto de la | 45 | E1 |
| Carrazeda de Ansiães | 34 | B4 |
| Carrazedo de Montenegro | 34 | B4 |
| Carrbridge | 3 | D4 |
| Carregado | 38 | A3 |
| Carregal do Sal | 38 | B2 |
| Carreña de Cabrales | 35 | E1 |
| Carrickfergus | 13 | E2 |
| Carrickmacross | 13 | D3 |
| Carrick-on-Shannon | 12 | C3 |
| Carrick-on-Suir | 14 | C3 |
| Carrigart | 12 | C1 |
| Carrio | 34 | B1 |
| Carrión de Calatrava | 40 | A4 |
| Carrión de los Condes | 35 | E3 |
| Carrión, R | 35 | E3 |
| Carrizo de la Ribera | 35 | D2 |
| Carro | 30 | C4 |
| Carrouges | 18 | C4 |
| Carrù | 31 | F2 |
| Carry-le-Rouet | 30 | C4 |
| Carsoli | 63 | F2 |
| Cartagena | 45 | D3 |
| Cártama | 43 | F4 |
| Cartaxo | 38 | A3 |
| Cartaya | 42 | C2 |
| Carter Bar | 5 | D3 |
| Carteret | 18 | B3 |
| Carvajal | 43 | F4 |
| Carvoeira | 42 | A3 |
| Carvoeiro, C | 38 | A3 |
| Carviçais | 39 | D1 |
| Carvin | 19 | F1 |
| Casabermeja | 43 | F3 |
| Casa Branca (Alentejo) | 42 | A1 |
| Casa Branca (Ribatejo) | 38 | B4 |
| Casacalenda | 64 | B2 |
| Casalarreina | 36 | B2 |
| Casalbordino | 64 | B2 |
| Casalbuttano | 60 | B1 |
| Casal di Principe | 64 | A4 |
| Casalecchio di Reno | 60 | C2 |
| Casale Monferrato | 31 | F1 |
| Casale sul Sile | 59 | E4 |
| Casalmaggiore | 60 | B2 |
| Casalpusterlengo | 60 | B2 |
| Casamassima | 65 | D3 |
| Casamicciola Terme | 64 | A4 |
| Casa Nuevas | 44 | C2 |
| Casarabonela | 43 | E3 |
| Casarano | 65 | F4 |
| Casar de Cáceres | 39 | D3 |
| Casares | 43 | E4 |
| Casares de las Hurdes | 39 | D2 |
| Casariche | 43 | E3 |
| Casarsa | 59 | E3 |
| Casas de Don Pedro | 39 | E4 |
| Casas de Fernando Alonso | 40 | C4 |
| Casas de Juan Núñez | 41 | D4 |
| Casas del Puerto | 45 | D1 |
| Casas de Luján | 40 | B3 |
| Casas de Miravete | 39 | E3 |
| Casas Ibáñez | 41 | D4 |
| Casasimarro | 40 | C4 |
| Casatejada | 39 | E3 |
| Casavieja | 39 | F2 |
| Cascais | 38 | A4 |
| Cascante | 36 | C3 |
| Cascia | 63 | E1 |
| Casciana Terme | 60 | C4 |
| Cascina | 60 | C4 |
| Casei Gerola | 60 | A2 |
| Caselle in Pittari | 67 | D1 |
| Caselle Torinese | 31 | E1 |
| Caserio del Puente | 35 | D3 |
| Caserta | 64 | B3 |
| Casetas | 37 | D3 |
| Cas-gwent | 9 | D2 |
| Cashel | 14 | C3 |
| Casicas del Río Segura | 44 | B2 |
| Casillas | 39 | D2 |
| Casina | 60 | C2 |
| Casinos | 41 | E3 |
| Casnewydd | 9 | D2 |
| Casoio | 34 | C3 |
| Casola in Lunigiana | 60 | B3 |
| Casoli | 64 | A2 |
| Casoria | 64 | B4 |
| Caspe | 37 | E4 |
| Cassà de la Selva | 32 | B3 |
| Cassagnes-Begonhès | 29 | E3 |
| Cassano allo Ionio | 67 | E2 |
| Cassano delle Murge | 65 | D3 |
| Cassel | 19 | F1 |
| Cassino | 64 | A3 |
| Cassis | 30 | C4 |
| Castalla | 45 | D1 |
| Castanet-Tolosan | 29 | D4 |
| Castanheira de Pêra | 38 | B2 |
| Castaños, Pto de los | 39 | D3 |
| Castasegna | 58 | B3 |
| Casteggio | 60 | A2 |
| Castejón | 36 | C3 |
| Castejón de Monègros | 37 | E4 |
| Castejón de Sos | 37 | E2 |
| Castejón de Valdejasa | 37 | D3 |
| Castelbuono | 68 | C3 |
| Casteldaccia | 68 | B3 |
| Casteldelfino | 31 | E2 |
| Castel del Monte (Abruzzo) | 63 | F2 |
| Castel del Monte (Puglia) | 65 | D3 |
| Castel del Rio | 61 | D3 |
| Castel di Sangro | 64 | A2 |
| Castelfidardo | 61 | F4 |
| Castelfiorentino | 60 | C4 |
| Castelfranco Emilia | 60 | C2 |
| Castelfranco in Miscano | 64 | B3 |
| Castelfranco Veneto | 59 | D4 |
| Castel Gandolfo | 63 | E3 |
| Casteljaloux | 28 | B3 |
| Castellabate | 67 | D1 |
| Castellammare di Stabbia | 64 | B4 |
| Castellammare d. Golfo | 48 | B3 |
| Castellammare, G di | 68 | B3 |
| Castellamonte | 31 | E1 |
| Castellana Grotte | 65 | E3 |
| Castellane | 31 | D3 |
| Castellaneta | 65 | E4 |
| Castellar de la Muela | 41 | D2 |
| Castellar del Vallès | 32 | A4 |
| Castellar de Santiago | 44 | B1 |
| Castellar de Santisteban | 44 | B2 |
| Castell' Arquato | 60 | B2 |
| Castelldans | 37 | F4 |
| Castelldefels | 32 | A4 |
| Castell de Ferro | 44 | A4 |
| Castelleone | 60 | B1 |
| Castellfollit de la Roca | 32 | B3 |
| Castellina in Chianti | 61 | D4 |
| Castelló de la Plana | 41 | F3 |
| Castello del Lago | 64 | B3 |
| Castelló d'Empúries | 32 | B3 |
| Castellolí | 32 | A4 |
| Castellón de la Plana | 41 | F3 |
| Castellón de Rugat | 45 | E1 |
| Castellote | 41 | E2 |
| Castello Tesino | 59 | D3 |
| Castellterçol | 32 | A4 |
| Castelluccio | 63 | F1 |
| Castel Madama | 63 | F2 |
| Castelmassa | 60 | C2 |
| Castelmauro | 64 | B2 |
| Castelmoron | 28 | C3 |
| Castelnaudary | 32 | A1 |
| Castelnau-de-Médoc | 28 | B2 |
| Castelnau-de-Montmiral | 29 | D3 |
| Castelnau-Magnoac | 37 | E1 |
| Castelnau-Montratier | 29 | D3 |
| Castelnau-Rivière-Basse | 28 | B4 |
| Castelnovo ne' Monti | 60 | B3 |
| Castelnuovo Berardenga | 61 | D4 |
| Castelnuovo Bocca d'Adda | 60 | B2 |
| Castelnuovo della Daunia | 64 | B3 |
| Castelnuovo di Garfagnana | 60 | C3 |
| Castelnuovo di Porto | 63 | E2 |
| Castelnuovo Scrivia | 60 | A2 |
| Castelo Branco | 38 | C2 |
| Castelo de Bode, Bgem do | 38 | B3 |
| Castelo de Paiva | 34 | A4 |
| Castelo de Vide | 38 | C3 |
| Castelraimondo | 61 | E4 |
| Castelrotto | 59 | D3 |
| Castel San Giovanni | 60 | A2 |
| Castel San Lorenzo | 64 | C4 |
| Castel San Pietro Terme | 61 | D3 |
| Castelsardo | 66 | B1 |
| Castelsarrasin | 29 | D3 |
| Castelserás | 41 | E1 |
| Casteltermini | 68 | B3 |
| Castelvecchio Subequo | 63 | F2 |
| Castelvetrano | 68 | A3 |
| Castel Volturno | 64 | A4 |
| Castets | 28 | A3 |
| Castiadas | 66 | C4 |
| Castiglioncello | 60 | C4 |
| Castiglione d'Adda | 60 | B2 |
| Castiglione dei Pepoli | 60 | C3 |
| Castiglione del Lago | 61 | D4 |
| Castiglione della Pescaia | 62 | C1 |
| Castiglione delle Stiviere | 60 | C1 |
| Castiglione in Teverina | 63 | E1 |
| Castiglione Messer Marino | 64 | B2 |
| Castiglione Olona | 60 | A1 |
| Castiglion Fiorentino | 61 | D4 |
| Castilblanco | 39 | F4 |
| Castilblanco de los Arroyos | 43 | D2 |
| Castilla, Canal de | 35 | E4 |
| Castilla-La Mancha | 40 | A4 |
| Castilla-León | 35 | F4 |
| Castilla, Mar de | 40 | C2 |
| Castilleja del Campo | 43 | D2 |
| Castilléjar | 44 | B2 |
| Castillejo | 39 | E1 |
| Castillejo de Martin Viejo | 39 | D1 |
| Castillo de Loarre | 37 | D3 |
| Castillo de Locubín | 43 | F2 |
| Castillon, Bge de | 31 | D3 |
| Castillon-en-Couserans | 37 | F2 |
| Castillon-la-Bataille | 28 | B2 |
| Castillonnès | 28 | C2 |
| Castillo, Pto del | 44 | A3 |
| Castillo y Elejabeitia | 36 | B1 |
| Castilruiz | 36 | C3 |
| Castions di Strada | 59 | F3 |
| Castlebar | 12 | B3 |
| Castlebay | 2 | A4 |
| Castlebellingham | 13 | D3 |
| Castleblayney | 13 | D3 |
| Castlecomer | 13 | D4 |
| Castledawson | 13 | D2 |
| Castlederg | 13 | D2 |
| Castledermot | 13 | D4 |
| Castle Douglas | 4 | C3 |
| Castleford | 7 | D2 |
| Castleisland | 14 | B3 |
| Castlemaine | 14 | A3 |
| Castlepollard | 13 | D3 |
| Castlerea | 12 | C3 |
| Castlerock | 13 | D1 |
| Castleton | 6 | C2 |
| Castletownbere | 14 | A4 |
| Castletown (I of Man) | 6 | A1 |
| Castletown (Scotland) | 3 | D2 |
| Castlewellan | 13 | E2 |
| Castocalbón | 35 | D3 |
| Castrejón | 39 | F1 |
| Castrejón, Emb de | 40 | A3 |
| Castres | 32 | B1 |
| Castries | 30 | B4 |
| Castril | 44 | B2 |
| Castrillo de la Reina | 36 | A3 |
| Castrillo de Villavega | 35 | F3 |
| Castro | 34 | B2 |
| Castro Caldelas | 34 | B3 |
| Castrocaro Terme | 61 | D3 |
| Castrocontrigo | 35 | D3 |
| Castro Daire | 38 | C1 |
| Castro del Rio | 43 | F2 |
| Castroreale | 69 | D2 |
| Castrogeriz | 35 | F3 |
| Castroreale Terme | 69 | D2 |
| Castro Marim | 42 | B2 |
| Castromonte | 35 | E4 |
| Castronuevo | 35 | D4 |
| Castronuño | 35 | E4 |
| Castropol | 34 | C1 |
| Castrop-Rauxel | 17 | E3 |
| Castrotierra | 35 | E3 |
| Castro Urdiales | 36 | A1 |
| Castroverde | 34 | C2 |
| Castro Verde | 42 | B2 |
| Castroverde de Campos | 35 | E3 |
| Castrovillari | 67 | E2 |
| Castuera | 39 | E4 |
| Cataluña | 32 | A3 |
| Catalunya | 37 | F3 |
| Catania | 69 | D3 |
| Catania, G di | 69 | D3 |
| Catanzaro | 67 | F3 |
| Catanzaro Lido | 67 | F3 |
| Catarroja | 41 | E4 |
| Cateau, le | 20 | A2 |
| Catelet, le | 20 | A2 |
| Catenanuova | 69 | D3 |
| Catež | 70 | C2 |
| Cathair na Mart | 12 | B3 |
| Čatići | 71 | F4 |
| Catignano | 64 | A2 |
| Catoira | 34 | A2 |
| Catoute | 35 | D2 |
| Catral | 45 | D2 |
| Catria, Mte | 61 | E4 |
| Cattenom | 21 | D3 |
| Cattolica | 61 | E3 |
| Catus | 29 | D2 |
| Caudebec | 19 | D3 |
| Caudete | 45 | D1 |
| Caudiel | 41 | E3 |
| Caudry | 20 | A2 |
| Caulnes | 23 | D3 |
| Caulonia | 67 | F4 |
| Caumont-l'Eventé | 18 | C3 |
| Caunes | 32 | B1 |
| Caussade | 29 | D3 |
| Čausy | 111 | E4 |
| Cauterets | 37 | E2 |
| Cava de' Tirreni | 64 | B4 |
| Cávado, R | 34 | A4 |
| Cavaglià | 31 | F1 |
| Cavaillon | 30 | C3 |
| Cavalaire | 31 | D4 |
| Cavalerie, la | 29 | F3 |
| Cavalese | 59 | D3 |
| Cavalière | 31 | D4 |
| Cavan | 13 | D3 |
| Cavan (Co) | 13 | D3 |
| Cavarzere | 61 | D1 |
| Cavazzo | 59 | E3 |
| Čavdarhisar | 115 | F4 |
| Cavero, Pto de | 36 | C4 |
| Cavezzo | 60 | C2 |
| Cavo | 62 | C1 |
| Cavo, Mte | 63 | E3 |
| Cavour | 31 | E2 |
| Cayeux | 19 | E2 |
| Caylar, le | 29 | F3 |
| Caylus | 29 | D3 |
| Cayolle, Col de la | 31 | E3 |
| Cayres | 29 | F2 |
| Cazalla de la Sierra | 43 | D2 |
| Cazals | 29 | D2 |
| Cazaubon | 28 | B3 |
| Cazaux | 28 | A2 |
| Cazères | 37 | F1 |
| Cazin | 70 | C3 |
| Čazma | 71 | D2 |
| Cazorla | 44 | B2 |
| Cazorla, Sa de | 44 | B2 |
| Cea | 34 | B2 |
| Ceanannus Mor | 13 | D3 |
| Cea, R | 35 | E3 |
| Ceatharlach | 13 | D4 |
| Cebolla | 39 | F3 |
| Cebollera | 36 | B3 |
| Cebreros | 40 | A2 |
| Ceccano | 63 | F3 |
| Cece | 112 | B4 |
| Cechy | 53 | F4 |
| Cecina | 60 | C4 |
| Cecina R | 60 | C4 |
| Cecita, L di | 67 | F2 |
| Ceclavin | 39 | D3 |
| Cedeira | 34 | B1 |
| Cedillo, Bgem de | 38 | C3 |
| Cedrillas | 41 | E2 |
| Cedrino | 66 | C2 |
| Cedynia | 49 | E3 |
| Cefalù | 68 | C3 |
| Cega, R | 40 | A1 |
| Cegléd | 112 | B4 |
| Ceglie Messapico | 65 | E3 |
| Čegrane | 77 | D3 |
| Cehegín | 44 | C2 |
| Čehotina | 76 | A1 |
| Ceira, R | 38 | C2 |
| Čejč | 57 | F1 |
| Celákovice | 53 | F3 |
| Celano | 63 | F2 |
| Celanova | 34 | B3 |
| Celavevo | 72 | B2 |
| Čelebić | 75 | D1 |
| Čelebići | 76 | B1 |
| Celemín, Emb de | 43 | D4 |
| Čelić | 72 | B3 |
| Čelinac Donji | 71 | E3 |
| Celje | 70 | B2 |
| Cella | 41 | D2 |
| Celle | 48 | B4 |
| Celle Ligure | 60 | A3 |
| Celles | 24 | C4 |
| Čelopeci | 77 | D3 |
| Celorico | 34 | B4 |
| Celorico da Beira | 38 | C1 |
| Čemerna pl | 73 | D4 |
| Čemernica | 71 | E4 |
| Čemerno | 76 | A2 |
| Cenajo, Emb del | 44 | C1 |
| Cencenighe | 59 | D3 |
| Cenicero | 36 | B2 |
| Čenta | 72 | C2 |
| Centelles | 32 | B4 |
| Cento | 60 | C2 |
| Cento Croci, Pso | 60 | B3 |
| Central Region | 4 | C1 |
| Centre, Canal du | 26 | B3 |
| Centuripe | 69 | D3 |
| Cepagatti | 64 | A2 |
| Čepin | 71 | F2 |
| Ceppo | 63 | F1 |
| Ceprano | 63 | F3 |
| Cer | 72 | C3 |
| Čeralije | 71 | E2 |
| Cerbère | 32 | C3 |
| Cercal (Alentejo) | 42 | A1 |
| Cercal (Estremadura) | 38 | A3 |
| Cercedilla | 40 | A2 |
| Čevo | 76 | B2 |
| Cerchiara di Calabria | 67 | E2 |
| Cerchov | 56 | B1 |
| Cerdedo | 34 | A2 |
| Cerdeira | 39 | D2 |
| Cère | 29 | E2 |
| Cerea | 60 | C1 |
| Cereda, Pso di | 59 | D3 |
| Ceres | 31 | E1 |
| Ceresole Reale | 31 | E1 |
| Céret | 32 | B3 |
| Cerezo de Abajo | 36 | A4 |
| Cerezo de Riotirón | 36 | A3 |
| Cerignola | 64 | C3 |
| Cérilly | 26 | A3 |
| Cerisiers | 26 | A1 |
| Cerisy-la-Salle | 18 | B3 |
| Cerizay | 24 | C3 |
| Čerkassy | 113 | F2 |
| Cerknica | 70 | B2 |
| Cerkniško jez | 70 | B2 |
| Cerkno | 70 | A2 |
| Cerler | 37 | E2 |
| Černá | 56 | C2 |
| Cerna | 71 | F2 |
| Cernache de Bonjardim | 38 | B2 |
| Čern'achovsk | 110 | B4 |
| Cernadilla, Emb de | 34 | C3 |
| Cernavodă | 115 | E1 |
| Cernay | 27 | E1 |
| Černigov | 113 | E1 |
| Cernik | 71 | E3 |
| Cernobbio | 58 | B4 |
| Černobyl' | 113 | E1 |
| Cernomorskoje | 113 | F4 |
| Černovcy | 113 | D3 |
| Cerreto, Pso del | 60 | B3 |
| Cerreto Sannita | 64 | B3 |
| Cerrigydrudion | 6 | B3 |
| Cèrrik | 76 | C4 |
| Certaldo | 60 | C4 |
| Certosa di Pavia | 60 | A2 |
| Cervales | 39 | E3 |
| Cervaro | 64 | C3 |
| Cervati, Mte | 67 | D1 |
| Cervatos de la Cueza | 35 | E3 |
| Cervera | 37 | F3 |
| Cervera de la Cañada | 36 | C4 |
| Cervera del Rio Alhama | 36 | C3 |
| Cervera de Pisuerga | 35 | F2 |
| Cerveteri | 63 | E2 |
| Cervia | 61 | E3 |
| Cervialto, Mte | 64 | C4 |
| Cervignano del Friuli | 59 | F3 |
| Cervinara | 64 | B3 |
| Cervino | 27 | E4 |
| Cervione | 33 | F3 |
| Cervo | 34 | C1 |
| Červonograd | 112 | C2 |
| Cesana Torinese | 31 | D2 |
| Cesarica | 70 | C4 |
| Cesarò | 69 | D3 |
| Cesena | 61 | D3 |
| Cesenatico | 61 | E3 |
| Cēsis | 110 | C2 |
| Česka Kamenice | 53 | F2 |
| Česká Lípa | 53 | F3 |
| České Budějovice | 57 | D1 |
| České Velenice | 57 | D2 |
| Český Krumlov | 57 | D2 |
| Česma | 71 | D2 |
| Çeşme | 115 | E4 |
| Cespedosa | 39 | E2 |
| Cetina (E) | 36 | C4 |
| Cetina R (YU) | 75 | D1 |
| Cetinje | 76 | B3 |
| Cetraro | 67 | E2 |
| Ceutí | 45 | D2 |
| Ceva | 31 | F2 |
| Cevedale, Mte | 58 | C3 |
| Cévennes, Parc Nat des | 29 | F3 |
| Cevico de la Torre | 35 | F4 |
| Çevo | 76 | B2 |
| Ceyrat | 29 | F1 |
| Ceyzériat | 26 | C4 |
| Cèze | 30 | B3 |
| Chabanais | 25 | D4 |
| Chabeuil | 30 | C2 |
| Chablis | 26 | B1 |
| Chabris | 25 | E2 |
| Chagny | 26 | C3 |
| Chailland | 23 | E3 |
| Chaillé | 24 | B3 |
| Chaise-Dieu, la | 29 | F1 |
| Chalabre | 32 | A2 |
| Chalais | 28 | C1 |
| Chalamont | 26 | C4 |
| Chalampé | 27 | E1 |
| Chalindrey | 26 | C1 |
| Challans | 24 | B3 |
| Challes | 31 | D1 |
| Chalonnes | 24 | C2 |
| Châlons-sur-Marne | 20 | B3 |
| Chalon-sur-Saône | 26 | C3 |

| Name | Page | Grid |
|---|---|---|
| Châlus | 28 | C1 |
| Cham | 56 | B1 |
| Chambéry | 31 | D1 |
| Chambley | 21 | D3 |
| Chambly | 19 | F3 |
| Chambon, Bge du | 31 | D2 |
| Chambon-Feugerol-les, le | 30 | B1 |
| Chambon-sur-Lac | 29 | E1 |
| Chambon-sur-Lignon, le | 30 | B2 |
| Chambon-sur-Voueize | 25 | F4 |
| Chambord | 25 | E2 |
| Chambre, la | 31 | D1 |
| Chamonix | 27 | E4 |
| Champagnac-de-Belair | 28 | C1 |
| Champagne-Mouton | 25 | D4 |
| Champagnole | 27 | D3 |
| Champdeniers | 24 | C3 |
| Champeaux | 23 | D3 |
| Champéry | 27 | E4 |
| Champex | 27 | E4 |
| Champlitte | 26 | C2 |
| Champlon, Bre.de | 50 | C4 |
| Champoluc | 27 | F4 |
| Champorcher | 31 | E1 |
| Champs-sur-Tarentaine | 29 | E1 |
| Champtoceaux | 24 | B2 |
| Chamrousse | 31 | D1 |
| Chamusca | 38 | B3 |
| Chanac | 29 | F3 |
| Chanas | 30 | B1 |
| Chança, R | 42 | C2 |
| Chantada | 34 | B2 |
| Chantelle | 26 | A4 |
| Chantemerle | 31 | D2 |
| Chantilly | 19 | F3 |
| Chantonnay | 24 | B3 |
| Chanza, Emb del | 42 | B2 |
| Chaource | 26 | B1 |
| Chapel-en-le-Frith | 6 | C2 |
| Chapelle-d'Angillon, la | 25 | F2 |
| Chapelle-de-Guinchay, la | 26 | C4 |
| Chapelle-en-Valgaudemar, la | 31 | D2 |
| Chapelle-en-Vercors, la | 30 | C2 |
| Chapineria | 40 | A2 |
| Charbonnières | 26 | C4 |
| Charco Redondo, Emb de | 43 | D4 |
| Chard | 9 | D3 |
| Charente | 28 | B1 |
| Charente (Dépt) | 28 | C1 |
| Charente-Maritime | 24 | B4 |
| Charenton-du-Cher | 25 | F3 |
| Charité, la | 26 | A2 |
| Charleroi | 50 | B4 |
| Charlestown | 12 | B3 |
| Charleville | 14 | B3 |
| Charleville-Mézières | 20 | C2 |
| ·Charlieu | 26 | B4 |
| Charlottenberg | 105 | D3 |
| Charly | 20 | A3 |
| Charmes | 21 | D4 |
| Charny (Meuse) | 20 | C3 |
| Charny (Yonne) | 26 | A1 |
| Charolles | 26 | B3 |
| Chârost | 25 | E3 |
| Charquemont | 27 | E2 |
| Charroux | 25 | D4 |
| Chartre, la | 23 | F4 |
| Chartres | 19 | E4 |
| Châs | 38 | B1 |
| Chasseneuil | 28 | C1 |
| Chasseral la Neuveville | 27 | E2 |
| Chasseron, le | 27 | D3 |
| Châtaigneraie, la | 24 | C3 |
| Château-Arnoux | 31 | D3 |
| Châteaubourg | 23 | D3 |
| Châteaubriant | 23 | D4 |
| Château-Chinon | 26 | B2 |
| Château-de-Bonaguil | 29 | D2 |
| Château de Ventadour | 29 | E1 |
| Château d'Oex | 27 | E3 |
| Château-du-Loir | 23 | F4 |
| Châteaudun | 25 | E1 |
| Châteaugiron | 23 | D3 |
| Château-Gontier | 23 | E4 |
| Château-Landon | 25 | F1 |
| Château-la-Vallière | 25 | D2 |
| Château, le | 24 | B4 |
| Châteaulin | 22 | B3 |
| Châteaumeillant | 25 | F3 |
| Châteauneuf (Charente) | 28 | B1 |
| Châteauneuf (Ille-et-Vilaine) | 18 | B4 |
| Châteauneuf-de-Randon | 29 | F2 |
| Châteauneuf-du-Faou | 22 | B3 |
| Châteauneuf-du-Pape | 30 | B3 |
| Châteauneuf-en-Thymerais | 19 | E4 |
| Châteauneuf-la-Forêt | 29 | D1 |
| Châteauneuf-les-Bains | 26 | A4 |
| Châteauneuf-sur-Cher | 25 | F3 |
| Châteauneuf-sur-Loire | 25 | F1 |
| Châteauneuf-sur-Sarthe | 23 | E4 |
| Châteauponsac | 25 | E4 |
| Château-Porcien | 20 | B3 |
| Château-Queyras | 31 | D2 |
| Château-Regnault | 20 | C2 |
| Châteaurenard (Loiret) | 25 | F1 |
| Châteaurenard (Vaucluse) | 30 | B3 |
| Château-Renault | 25 | D2 |
| Châteauroux | 25 | E3 |
| Château-Salins | 21 | D4 |
| Château-Thierry | 20 | A3 |
| Châteauvillain | 26 | C1 |
| Châtel | 27 | E3 |
| Châtelaillon-Plage | 24 | B4 |
| Châtelard, le | 27 | D4 |
| Châtelaudren | 22 | C2 |
| Châteldon | 26 | A4 |
| Châtelet | 50 | C4 |
| Châtelet, le (Cher) | 25 | F3 |
| Châtelet, le (Seine-et-Marne) | 19 | F4 |
| Châtelguyon | 26 | A4 |
| Châtellerault | 25 | D3 |
| Châtel-Montagne | 26 | B4 |
| Châtel-St-Denis | 27 | E3 |
| Châtel-sur-Moselle | 21 | D4 |
| Châtelus-Malvaleix | 25 | E4 |
| Châtenois | 27 | D1 |
| Chatham | 11 | D2 |
| Châtillon | 27 | F4 |
| Châtillon-Coligny | 26 | A1 |
| Châtillon-en-Bazois | 26 | B2 |
| Châtillon-en-Diois | 30 | C2 |
| Châtillon-sur-Chalaronne | 26 | C4 |
| Châtillon-sur-Indre | 25 | E3 |
| Châtillon-sur-Loire | 26 | A2 |
| Châtillon-sur-Marne | 20 | B3 |
| Châtillon-sur-Seine | 26 | B1 |
| Châtre, la | 25 | E3 |
| Chatsworth House | 6 | C3 |
| Chatteris | 9 | F1 |
| Chaudes-Aigues | 29 | F2 |
| Chauffailles | 26 | B4 |
| Chaufour | 19 | E4 |
| Chaulnes | 19 | F2 |
| Chaumergy | 26 | C3 |
| Chaumont-en-Vexin | 19 | E3 |
| Chaumont (Haute-Marne) | 26 | C1 |
| Chaumont (Loir-et-Cher) | 25 | E2 |
| Chauny | 20 | A2 |
| Chausey, I | 18 | B4 |
| Chaussin | 26 | C3 |
| Chauvigny | 25 | D3 |
| Chaux-de-Fonds, la | 27 | E2 |
| Chaves | 34 | B3 |
| Chazelles | 30 | B1 |
| Cheb | 53 | D4 |
| Cheddar Gorge | 9 | D3 |
| Chef-Boutonne | 24 | C4 |
| Cheles | 42 | C1 |
| Chelm | 112 | C2 |
| Chełmno | 112 | A1 |
| Chelmsford | 11 | D2 |
| Cheltenham | 9 | E2 |
| Chelva | 41 | D3 |
| Chemillé | 24 | C2 |
| Chemin | 26 | C3 |
| Chénérailles | 25 | F4 |
| Chenonceaux | 25 | E2 |
| Chepstow | 9 | D2 |
| Cher | 25 | F3 |
| Cher (Dépt) | 25 | F2 |
| Chera | 41 | D3 |
| Cherbourg | 18 | B2 |
| Chéroy | 26 | A1 |
| Cherson | 113 | F3 |
| Chert | 41 | F2 |
| Cheshire | 6 | C2 |
| Cheshunt | 9 | F2 |
| Chesne, le | 20 | C3 |
| Cheste | 41 | E4 |
| Chester | 6 | B3 |
| Chesterfield | 7 | D3 |
| Chester-le-Street | 5 | E4 |
| Chevagnes | 26 | A3 |
| Chevillon | 20 | C4 |
| Cheviot Hills, The | 5 | E3 |
| Cheviot, The | 5 | E3 |
| Chèvre, Cap de la | 22 | A3 |
| Chevreuse | 19 | E4 |
| Cheylard, le | 30 | B2 |
| Chèze, la | 22 | C3 |
| Chiampo | 59 | D4 |
| Chianciano Terme | 63 | D1 |
| Chianti | 61 | D4 |
| Chiaramonte Gulfi | 69 | D4 |
| Chiaravalle | 61 | F3 |
| Chiaravalle Centrale | 67 | F3 |
| Chiari | 60 | B1 |
| Chiasso | 58 | A4 |
| Chiavari | 60 | A3 |
| Chiavenna | 58 | B3 |
| Chichester | 9 | F3 |
| Chiclana de la Frontera | 43 | D4 |
| Chieming | 56 | B3 |
| Chiemsee | 56 | B3 |
| Chieri | 31 | E1 |
| Chiers | 20 | C3 |
| Chiesa in Valmalenco | 58 | B3 |
| Chiesina Uzz. | 60 | C3 |
| Chieti | 64 | A2 |
| Chiltern Hills | 9 | F2 |
| Chimay | 50 | B4 |
| Chimorra | 43 | E1 |
| Chinchilla de Monte Aragón | 41 | D4 |
| Chinchón | 40 | B2 |
| Chinon | 25 | D2 |
| Chioggia | 61 | D1 |
| Chioula, Col de | 32 | A2 |
| Chipiona | 42 | C3 |
| Chippenham | 9 | E2 |
| Chipping Campden | 9 | E1 |
| Chipping Norton | 9 | E2 |
| Chipping Sodbury | 9 | D2 |
| Chirivel | 44 | C2 |
| Chisineu-Criş | 112 | C4 |
| Chisone | 31 | E2 |
| Chiusa | 59 | D2 |
| Chiusa di Pesio | 31 | E2 |
| Chiusa Sclafani | 68 | B3 |
| Chiusatorte | 59 | F3 |
| Chiusi | 63 | D1 |
| Chiva | 41 | E4 |
| Chivasso | 31 | F1 |
| Chlum u Třeboně | 57 | D1 |
| Chmel'nickij | 113 | D2 |
| Chmel'nik | 113 | E2 |
| Chociwel | 49 | F2 |
| Chodov | 53 | E4 |
| Chojna | 49 | E3 |
| Chojnice | 110 | A4 |
| Chojniki | 113 | E1 |
| Cholet | 24 | C3 |
| Chollerford | 5 | D4 |
| Cholm | 111 | E2 |
| Chomutov | 53 | E3 |
| Chorges | 31 | D2 |
| Chorley | 6 | C2 |
| Chorol | 113 | F2 |
| Choszczno | 49 | F3 |
| Chotin | 113 | D3 |
| Chouto | 38 | B3 |
| Chrastava | 53 | F2 |
| Christchurch | 9 | E3 |
| Christiansfeld | 108 | A3 |
| Christiansø | 109 | D4 |
| Chur | 58 | B2 |
| Church Stretton | 9 | D1 |
| Chust | 112 | C3 |
| Ciamarella | 31 | E1 |
| Cians, Gorges du | 31 | E3 |
| Ćićarija | 70 | A3 |
| Čičavica | 77 | D2 |
| Cicciano | 64 | B4 |
| Čićevac | 73 | E4 |
| Čićevo | 76 | A2 |
| Cidacos, R | 36 | B3 |
| Cidade Nova de Santo André | 42 | A1 |
| Cidones | 36 | B3 |
| Ciechanów | 112 | B1 |
| Ciechocinek | 112 | B1 |
| Ciempozuelos | 40 | B2 |
| Cíes, Is | 34 | A3 |
| Cieszyn | 112 | B3 |
| Cieza | 45 | D2 |
| Cifuentes | 40 | C2 |
| Cigliano | 31 | F1 |
| Cigüela R | 40 | B3 |
| Cijara, Emb de | 39 | F4 |
| Cijevna | 76 | B3 |
| Cilavegna | 60 | A1 |
| Čilipi | 76 | A3 |
| Cill Airne | 14 | B4 |
| Cillas | 36 | C4 |
| Cill Chainnigh | 15 | D3 |
| Cilleros | 39 | D2 |
| Cilleruelo de Bezana | 35 | F2 |
| Cill Mhantáin | 13 | E4 |
| Cima Brenta | 58 | C3 |
| Cimadolmo | 59 | E4 |
| Cima d'Asta | 59 | D3 |
| Cima Presanella | 58 | C3 |
| Čimišlija | 113 | E4 |
| Cimone, Mte | 60 | C3 |
| Cîmpeni | 112 | C4 |
| Cîmpina | 115 | D1 |
| Cîmpulung | 115 | D1 |
| Cîmpulung Moldovenesc | 113 | D3 |
| Cinca, R | 37 | E3 |
| Cincar | 75 | E1 |
| Cinctorres | 41 | E2 |
| Ciney | 50 | C4 |
| Cinfães | 34 | A4 |
| Cingoli | 61 | F4 |
| Cinigiano | 63 | D1 |
| Cinisi | 68 | B3 |
| Cinovec | 53 | E3 |
| Cinque Terre | 60 | B3 |
| Cintegabelle | 32 | A1 |
| Cinto, M | 33 | F3 |
| Cintruénigo | 36 | C3 |
| Ciórraga | 36 | B1 |
| Ciotat, la | 30 | C4 |
| Čiovo | 75 | D2 |
| Cirencester | 9 | E2 |
| Cirey | 21 | E4 |
| Ciria | 36 | C3 |
| Ciriè | 31 | E1 |
| Cirò | 67 | F2 |
| Cirò Marina | 67 | F2 |
| Čirpan | 115 | D2 |
| Cisa, Pso della | 60 | B3 |
| Cisneros | 35 | E3 |
| Čista | 74 | C1 |
| Cista Provo | 75 | E1 |
| Cisterna di Latina | 63 | F3 |
| Cisternino | 65 | E3 |
| Cistierna | 35 | E2 |
| Čitluk (Mostar) | 75 | F2 |
| Čitluk (Posušje) | 75 | E1 |
| Cittadella | 59 | D4 |
| Città del Pieve | 63 | D1 |
| Città di Castello | 61 | E4 |
| Cittaducale | 63 | F2 |
| Cittanova | 67 | E4 |
| Cittareale | 63 | F1 |
| Città Sant' Angelo | 64 | A1 |
| Ciudad Encantada | 40 | C3 |
| Ciudad Real | 40 | A4 |
| Ciudad Rodrigo | 39 | D1 |
| Ciutadella de Menorca | 45 | F1 |
| Cividale del Friuli | 59 | F3 |
| Civita Castellana | 63 | E2 |
| Civitanova Marche | 61 | F4 |
| Civitavecchia | 63 | D2 |
| Civitella del Tronto | 63 | F1 |
| Civitella Roveto | 63 | F2 |
| Civray | 25 | D4 |
| Čivril | 115 | F4 |
| Clacton-on-Sea | 11 | D2 |
| Clain | 25 | D4 |
| Clairvaux-les-Lacs | 27 | D3 |
| Clamecy | 26 | A2 |
| Claonaig | 4 | B2 |
| Clapham | 6 | C1 |
| Clara | 12 | C4 |
| Clare | 11 | D1 |
| Clare | 12 | B3 |
| Clare (Co) | 12 | B4 |
| Clare I | 12 | A3 |
| Claremorris | 12 | B3 |
| Claudy | 13 | D1 |
| Clausthal-Zellerfeld | 52 | B2 |
| Claut | 59 | E3 |
| Claviere | 31 | D2 |
| Clavin, Pto de | 39 | D3 |
| Claye-Souilly | 19 | F4 |
| Clayette, la | 26 | B4 |
| Clear I | 14 | A4 |
| Clécy | 18 | C4 |
| Clefmont | 26 | C1 |
| Cléguérec | 22 | C3 |
| Clelles | 30 | C2 |
| Clères | 19 | E3 |
| Clermont | 19 | F3 |
| Clermont-en-Argonne | 20 | C3 |
| Clermont-Ferrand | 29 | F1 |
| Clermont-l'Hérault | 30 | A4 |
| Clervaux | 21 | D2 |
| Cléry | 25 | E2 |
| Cles | 58 | C3 |
| Clevedon | 9 | D2 |
| Cleveland Hills | 7 | D1 |
| Cleveleys | 6 | B2 |
| Clew B | 12 | B3 |
| Clifden | 12 | A3 |
| Clisham | 2 | B2 |
| Clisson | 24 | B2 |
| Clitheroe | 6 | C2 |
| Cloghan | 12 | C4 |
| Clogheen | 14 | C3 |
| Clogherhead | 13 | E3 |
| Clogher Head | 14 | A3 |
| Clogh Mills | 13 | E1 |
| Clonakilty | 14 | B4 |
| Clonbur | 12 | B3 |
| Clondalkin | 13 | D4 |
| Clones | 13 | D2 |
| Clonfert | 12 | C4 |
| Clonmacnoise | 12 | C4 |
| Clonmel | 14 | C3 |
| Cloppenburg | 17 | E1 |
| Clovelly | 8 | B3 |
| Cloyes | 25 | E1 |
| Cluain Meala | 14 | C3 |
| Cluj-Napoca | 112 | C4 |
| Clun | 9 | D1 |
| Cluny | 26 | C3 |
| Clusaz, la | 27 | D4 |
| Cluse de Pontarlier | 27 | D3 |
| Cluses | 27 | E4 |
| Clusone | 58 | B4 |
| Clwyd | 6 | B3 |
| Clyde | 4 | C2 |
| Clydebank | 4 | C2 |
| Clyde, Firth of | 4 | B2 |
| Coachford | 14 | B4 |
| Coalisland | 13 | D2 |
| Coalville | 9 | E1 |
| Coaña | 34 | C1 |
| Côa, R | 39 | D2 |
| Coatbridge | 4 | C2 |
| Cobeña | 40 | B2 |
| Cobh | 14 | C4 |
| Coburg | 52 | C4 |
| Coca | 40 | A1 |
| Coca, Pso di | 58 | B3 |
| Cocentaina | 45 | E1 |
| Cochem | 51 | E4 |
| Cockburnspath | 5 | E2 |
| Cockermouth | 5 | D4 |
| Codevigo | 61 | D1 |
| Codigoro | 61 | D2 |
| Codogno | 60 | B2 |
| Codos | 36 | C4 |
| Codroipo | 59 | E3 |
| Coesfeld | 17 | E3 |
| Coevorden | 17 | D2 |
| Cofrentes | 41 | D4 |
| Coghinas, L del | 66 | B2 |
| Cognac | 28 | B1 |
| Cogne | 31 | E1 |
| Cogolin | 31 | D4 |
| Cogolludo | 40 | B1 |
| Coigach | 2 | C2 |
| Coimbra | 38 | B2 |
| Coín | 43 | E4 |
| Coina | 38 | A4 |
| Čoka | 72 | C1 |
| Col | 70 | A2 |
| Colares | 38 | A4 |
| Colbe | 17 | F4 |
| Colchester | 11 | D2 |
| Coldbackie | 2 | C2 |
| Colditz | 53 | D2 |
| Coldstream | 5 | E2 |
| Coleford | 9 | D2 |
| Coleraine | 13 | D1 |
| Colfiorito | 63 | E1 |
| Colico | 58 | B3 |
| Coligny | 26 | C3 |
| Colindres | 36 | A1 |
| Colintraive | 4 | B2 |
| Coll | 2 | A4 |
| Collado Bajo | 41 | D2 |
| Coll de Nargó | 37 | F3 |
| Collecchio | 60 | B2 |
| Colle di Val d'Elsa | 60 | C4 |
| Colleferro | 63 | F3 |
| Colle Isarco | 59 | D2 |
| Colle Salvetti | 60 | C4 |
| Colle Sannita | 64 | B3 |
| Collesano | 68 | C3 |
| Colli a Volturno | 64 | A3 |
| Collina, Pso della | 60 | C3 |
| Collinée | 22 | C3 |
| Colline Metallifere | 60 | C4 |
| Collio | 58 | C4 |
| Collioure | 32 | B2 |
| Collobrières | 31 | D4 |
| Collodi | 60 | C3 |
| Collonges | 27 | D4 |
| Collonges-la-Rouge | 29 | D2 |
| Colmar | 27 | E1 |
| Colmars | 31 | D3 |
| Colmenar | 43 | F3 |
| Colmenar de Oreja | 40 | B3 |
| Colmenar Viejo | 40 | A2 |
| Colnabaichin | 3 | D4 |
| Colne | 6 | C2 |
| Colobraro | 65 | D4 |
| Cologna Veneta | 60 | C1 |
| Cologne | 28 | C4 |
| Colombey-les-Belles | 21 | D4 |
| Colombey-les-Deux-Eglises | 26 | C1 |
| Colombière, Col de la | 27 | D4 |
| Colombres | 35 | F1 |
| Colomera | 44 | A3 |
| Colonsay | 4 | A2 |
| Colorno | 60 | B2 |
| Colosimi | 67 | F3 |
| Columbretes, I | 41 | F3 |
| Colunga | 35 | E1 |
| Colwyn Bay | 6 | B3 |
| Comacchio | 61 | D2 |
| Comăneşti | 113 | D4 |
| Coma-ruga | 37 | F4 |
| Combarro | 34 | A2 |
| Combeaufontaine | 27 | D1 |
| Combe Laval | 30 | C2 |
| Combe Martin | 8 | C3 |
| Comber | 13 | E2 |
| Combloux | 27 | E4 |
| Combourg | 18 | B4 |
| Combronde | 26 | A4 |
| Comeglians | 59 | E2 |
| Comeragh Mts | 14 | C3 |
| Comillas | 35 | F1 |
| Comines | 19 | F1 |
| Comino | 68 | B4 |
| Comiso | 69 | D4 |
| Commentry | 26 | A4 |
| Commercy | 20 | C4 |
| Como | 58 | B3 |
| Como, L di | 58 | B3 |
| Cómpeta | 43 | F3 |
| Compiègne | 19 | F3 |
| Comporta | 38 | A4 |
| Comps-sur-Artuby | 31 | D3 |
| Comunanza | 63 | F1 |
| Concarneau | 22 | B3 |
| Conches | 19 | D4 |
| Concordia sulla Secchia | 60 | C2 |
| Condat | 29 | E1 |
| Condé | 20 | A1 |
| Conde, Emb del | 43 | E3 |
| Condé-en-Brie | 20 | A3 |
| Condeixa-a-Nova | 38 | B2 |
| Condé-sur-Noireau | 18 | C4 |
| Condom | 28 | C3 |
| Condrieu | 30 | B1 |
| Conegliano | 59 | E3 |
| Conejeros, Pto de los | 38 | C4 |
| Conflans | 21 | D3 |
| Confolens | 25 | D4 |
| Cong | 12 | B3 |
| Congleton | 6 | C3 |
| Congost de Tresponts | 32 | A3 |
| Congosto de Valdavia | 35 | E2 |
| Congresbury | 9 | D2 |
| Conil de la Frontera | 43 | D4 |
| Conisbrough | 7 | D2 |
| Coniston | 5 | D4 |
| Conlie | 23 | F3 |
| Conliège | 26 | C3 |
| Connaught | 12 | B3 |
| Connel | 4 | B1 |
| Connemara | 12 | A3 |
| Connerré | 23 | F3 |
| Conn, L | 12 | B2 |
| Čonoplja | 72 | B1 |
| Conques | 29 | E2 |
| Conquet, le | 22 | A2 |
| Conquista | 43 | F1 |
| Conselice | 61 | D2 |
| Conselve | 61 | D1 |
| Consett | 5 | E4 |
| Constância | 38 | B3 |
| Constanţa | 115 | E1 |
| Constantina | 43 | E2 |
| Consuegra | 40 | A3 |
| Consuma | 61 | D3 |
| Contamines, les | 27 | E4 |
| Contarina | 61 | D2 |
| Conthey | 27 | E3 |
| Contigliano | 63 | E2 |
| Contin | 2 | C3 |
| Contrasto, C del | 68 | C3 |
| Contraviesa, Sa de la | 44 | B4 |
| Contreras, Emb de | 41 | D3 |
| Contres | 25 | E2 |
| Contrexéville | 27 | D1 |
| Contursi | 64 | C4 |
| Conty | 19 | F2 |
| Convento de Calatrava | 44 | A1 |
| Conversano | 65 | E3 |
| Conwy | 6 | A2 |
| Cookstown | 13 | D2 |
| Cootehill | 13 | D3 |
| Čop | 112 | C3 |
| Cope | 45 | D3 |

Cope, C 45 D3
Copertino 65 F4
Copparo 61 D2
Corabia 115 D2
Cora Droma Rúisc 12 C3
Corato 65 D3
Coray 22 B3
Corbeil-Essonnes 19 F4
Corbie 19 F2
Corbigny 26 B2
Corbola 61 D2
Corbones, R 43 E2
Corbridge 5 E3
Corby 9 F1
Corcaigh 14 B4
Corcieux 27 E1
Córcoles, R 40 C4
Corconte 35 F2
Corcubión 34 A1
Cordes 29 D3
Córdoba 43 F2
Cordobilla de Lácara 39 D4
Cordobilla, Emb de 43 F3
Corduente 40 C2
Corella 36 C3
Coreses 35 D4
Corfe Castle 9 E3
Corgo 34 B2
Cori 63 F3
Coria 39 D2
Coria del Río 43 D3
Corias 34 C2
Corigliano Calabro 67 F2
Corinaldo 61 E3
Coripe 43 E3
Cork 14 B4
Cork (Co) 14 B4
Corlay 22 C3
Corleone 68 B3
Corleto Perticara 65 D4
Çorlu 115 E3
Cormatin 26 C3
Cormeilles 19 D3
Cormery 25 D2
Cormons 59 F3
Cornago 36 C3
Cornellana 35 D1
Corniche des Cévennes 29 F3
Corniglio 60 B3
Cornimont 27 E1
Cornuda 59 D4
Cornus 29 F3
Cornwall 8 B4
Corps 31 D2
Corraes 34 C3
Corral de Almaguer 40 B3
Corral de Cantos 39 F3
Corralejo 42 C4
Corrales 35 D4
Corran 2 C4
Corraun 12 B2
Corredoiras 34 B2
Correggio 60 C2
Corrèze 29 D1
Corrèze (Dépt) 29 D1
Corrèze *R* 29 D2
Corrib, L 12 B3
Corridonia 61 F4
Corrofin 12 B4
Corse 33 E2
Corse-du-Sud 33 F3
Corsham 9 D2
Čortanovci 72 C2
Corte 33 F3
Corte de Peleas 39 D4
Cortegada 34 B3
Cortegana 42 C2
Cortemaggiore 60 B2
Cortemilia 31 F2
Corteolona 60 A2
Cortes de Aragón 41 E1
Cortes de Baza 44 B2
Cortes de la Frontera 43 E4
Cortijos Nuevos 44 B2
Cortina d'Ampezzo 59 E3
Čortkov 113 D3
Cortona 61 D4
Coruche 38 B4
Corvara in Badia 59 D3
Corvera 45 D2
Corvera Toranzo 35 F2
Corwen 6 B3
Cosenza 67 E2
Cosham 9 E3
Cosne 26 A2
Cosne-d'Allier 26 A3
Cossato 31 F1
Cossé-le-Vivien 23 E3
Cosson 25 E2
Cossonay 27 D3
Costa Blanca 45 E2
Costa Brava 32 C3
Costa da Caparica 38 A4
Costa del Sol 44 A4
Costa de Santo André 42 A1
Costalunga, Pso di 59 D3
Costa Smeralda 66 B1
Costa Vasca 36 B1
Costa Verde 35 D1
Costigliole d'Asti 31 F2
Coswig (Dresden) 53 E2
Coswig (Halle) 53 D1
Côte-d'Or (Dépt) 26 C2
Côtes-du-Nord 22 C3
Côte-St-André, la 30 C1
Cotignac 31 D4
Cottbus 53 F1
Coubet, Collado de 32 B3
Coubre, Pointe de la 28 A1
Couches 26 B3
Couço 38 B4
Coucy-le-Château-Auffrique 20 A3
Couesnon 23 D3
Couhé 25 D4
Couilly 19 F4
Couiza 32 B2
Coulanges 26 A2
Coulanges-la-Vineuse 26 A2
Coulommiers 19 F4
Coulon 24 C4
Coulonges 24 C3
Coupar Angus 5 D1
Couptrain 18 C4
Courchevel 31 D1
Cour-Cheverny 25 E2
Courçon 24 C4
Courmayeur 27 E4
Couronne, la 28 C1
Courpière 29 F1
Cours 26 B4
Coursan 32 B1
Coursegoules 31 E3
Courseulles 18 C3
Courson-les-Carrières 26 A2
Courtenay 26 A1
Courthézon 30 C3
Courtine, la 29 E1
Courtomer 19 D4
Courtown 15 E3
Courtrai 50 A3
Courville 19 E4
Cousin 26 B2
Coussey 20 C4
Coutances 18 B3
Coutras 28 B2
Couvertoirade, la 29 F3
Couvin 50 C4
Couze 25 E4
Cova da Iria 38 B3
Covadonga 35 E1
Covadonga, Pque Nac de la Sa de 35 E2
Covarrubias 36 A3
Coventry 9 E1
Covilhã 38 C2
Cowbridge 8 C2
Cowdenbeath 5 D2
Cowes 9 E3
Cowfold 10 C3
Cozes 28 B1
Craco 65 D4
Craigavon 13 E2
Craigellachie 3 D3
Craighouse 4 B2
Craigievar Castle 3 E4
Craignure 4 B1
Crail 5 D2
Crailsheim 55 E2
Craiova 115 D2
Cranborne 9 E3
Crans 27 E3
Craon 23 E3
Craonne 20 B3
Craponne 29 F1
Crathes Castle 3 E4
Crati 67 E2
Crato 38 C3
Craughwell 12 B4
Crau, la 31 D4
Craven Arms 9 D1
Crawinkel 52 C3
Crawley 10 C3
Creag Meagaidh 2 C4
Creagorry 2 A3
Crécy 20 A2
Crécy-en-Ponthieu 19 E2
Crécy-la-Chapelle 19 F4
Crediton 8 C3
Creegh 12 B4
Creeslough 12 C1
Creglingen 55 E1
Creil 19 F3
Crema 60 B1
Crémieu 26 C4
Cremona 60 B2
Créon 28 B2
Crepaja 73 D2
Crépy-en-Valois 19 F3
Cres 70 B4
Cres *I* 70 B4
Crescentino 31 F1
Crespino 61 D2
Crest 30 C2
Cresta 58 B3
Cresta del Gallo 45 D2
Créteil 19 F4
Crêtes, Route des 27 E1
Creully 18 C3
Creuse 25 E4
Creuse (Dépt) 25 E4
Creusot, le 26 B3
Creußen 53 D4
Creutzwald 21 D3
Creuzburg 52 B3
Crevacuore 58 A4
Crevalcore 60 C2
Crèvecœur-le-Grand 19 E3
Crevillente 45 D2
Crewe 6 C3
Crewkerne 9 D3
Crianlarich 4 C1
Criccieth 6 A3
Crickhowell 9 D2
Cricklade 9 E2
Crieff 4 C1
Criel 19 E2
Crikvenica 70 B3
Crimmitschau 53 D3
Crinan 4 B2
Criquetot-l'Esneval 19 D3
Crissolo 31 E2
Crişu Alb 112 C4
Crişu Negru 112 C4
Crişu Repede 112 C4
Crivitz 48 C2
Crkvice 76 A2
Crmljan 76 C2
Črmošnjice 70 B2
Črna 70 B1
Crna Bara (Srbija) 72 B3
Crna Bara (Vojvodina) 72 C1
Crnac (Hrvatska) 71 E2
Crnac (Srbija) 76 C1
Crna Gora 76 B2
Crna gora 77 E2
Crna reka 77 E4
Crna Trava 77 E1
Crnča 72 B4
Crni Drim 77 D4
Crni Guber 72 C4
Crni Lug (Bosna i Hercegovina) 75 D1
Crni Lug (Hrvatska) 70 B3
Crni Timok 73 E4
Crni vrh *Mt* (Bosna i Hercegovina) 71 D4
Črni vrh *Mt* (Slovenija) 70 B1
Crni vrh *Mt* (Srbija) 76 B1
Črni vrh (Slovenija) 70 A2
Crnivec 70 B2
Crnjelovo Donje 72 B3
Črnkovci 71 F2
Crno jez 76 B2
Črnomelj 70 B3
Croagh Patrick 12 B3
Croce dello Scrivano, Pso 64 C4
Croce Domini, Pso di 58 C4
Crocello, Pso di 64 C4
Crocq 25 F4
Croisic, le 24 A2
Croisière, la 25 E4
Croix de Fer, Col de la 31 D1
Croix Haute, Col de la 30 C2
Croix-Valmer, la 31 D4
Crolly 12 C1
Cromarty 3 D3
Cromer 7 F3
Crook 5 E4
Croom 14 B3
Cross Fell 5 D4
Cross Hands 8 C2
Crosshaven 14 C4
Crossmaglen 13 D3
Crossmolina 12 B2
Crotone 67 F3
Crotoy, le 19 E2
Crowborough 10 C3
Crowland 9 F1
Crowle 7 D2
Croyde 8 C3
Croydon 9 F2
Crozant 25 E4
Crozon 22 A3
Cruden Bay 3 E3
Crudgington 6 C3
Crumlin 13 E2
Cruseilles 27 D4
Crussol 30 B2
Cruz 40 B3
Cruzamento de Pegões 38 A4
Cruz da Légua 38 A3
Cruz de Tejeda 42 B4
Crven Grm 75 E2
Crvenka 72 B2
Crymmych 8 B1
Csongrád 112 B4
Csorna 112 A4
Cuacos 39 E2
Cualedro 34 B3
Cuba 42 B1
Cubel 36 C4
Cucalón, Sa de 41 D1
Cuckfield 10 C3
Cudillero 35 D1
Čudovo 111 D1
Čudskoje Ozero 110 C1
Cuéllar 35 F4
Cuenca 40 C3
Cuenca, Serr de 40 C3
Cuerda 41 D3
Cuerda del Pozo, Emb de la 36 B3
Cuers 31 D4
Cuerva 40 A3
Cueva de la Pileta 43 E4
Cueva de la Vieja 41 D4
Cueva de Nerja 44 A4
Cueva Foradada, Emb de 41 E1
Cueva, Sa do 35 E1
Cuevas de Altamira 35 F1
Cuevas de Artà 45 F3
Cuevas de Canalobre 45 E1
Cuevas del Aguila 39 F2
Cuevas del Amanzora 44 C3
Cuevas del Becerro 43 E3
Cuevas del Campo 44 B2
Cuevas del Drac 45 F3
Cuevas del Valle 39 F2
Cuevas de San Clemente 35 F3
Cuevas de San Marcos 43 F3
Cuevas de Valporquero 35 D2
Cuevas de Vinromá 41 F2
Cuglieri 66 A3
Cuijk 17 D3
Cuillin Sd 2 B4
Cuillins, The 2 B3
Cuiseaux 26 C3
Cuisery 26 C3
Culan 25 F3
Culdaff 13 D1
Culebra, Sa de la 34 C3
Culemborg 16 C3
Cúllar Baza 44 B2
Cullen 3 E3
Cullera 41 E4
Cullompton 8 C3
Culoz 27 D4
Culross 5 D2
Cumbernauld 4 C2
Cumbre Alta 39 F3
Cumbres Mayores 42 C1
Cumbria 5 D4
Cumbrian Mts 5 D4
Cumiana 31 E2
Čumić 73 D3
Cumnock 4 C3
Cunault 24 C2
Cuneo 31 E2
Cunlhat 29 F1
Čunski 70 B4
Cuorgné 31 E1
Cupar 5 D1
Cupello 64 B2
Cupramontana 61 E4
Cuprija 73 E4
Cure 26 B2
Cure, la 27 D3
Curia 38 B1
Currane, L 14 A4
Curtea de Argeş 115 D1
Curtis 34 B1
Čurug 72 C2
C'urupinsk 113 F3
Cusano Mutri 64 B3
Cushendall 13 E1
Cushendun 13 E1
Cusna, Mte 60 C3
Cusset 26 A4
Cutro 67 F3
Cuxhaven 47 F2
Cvikov 53 F3
Čvrsnica 75 E1
Čvrstec 71 D2
Cwmbrân 9 D2
Cybinka 49 F4
Cysoing 20 A1
Czarnków 112 A1
Czersk 110 A4
Częstochowa 112 B2
Człuchów 112 A1


# D


Dabar 70 C3
Dąbie 49 E2
Dabie, Jez 49 E2
Dabilje 77 F3
Dabo 21 E4
Dachau 55 F3
Dachsteingruppe 59 F1
Dačice 57 E1
Dadiá 81 F2
Dáfnes 86 C1
Dáfni (Límnos) 85 D1
Dáfni (Makedonía) 80 C4
Dáfni (Pelopónissos) 86 C1
Dáfni (Stereá Eláda) 83 D4
Dafní (Stereá Eláda) 87 F1
Dáfnio 87 D3
Dafnónas (Stereá Eláda) 83 D3
Dafnónas (Thráki) 80 C2
Dafnotí 82 C2
Dafnoúdi, Akr 82 B4
Dagali 104 C2
Dagebüll 47 F1
Dagenham 10 C2
Dahlen 53 E2
Dahlenburg 48 B3
Dahme (D) 48 B2
Dahme (DDR) 53 E1
Dahme *R* 53 E1
Dahn 54 B2
Daimiel 40 A4
Daimuz 41 E4
Dajt, Mal i 76 C4
Đakovica 76 C2
Đakovo 71 F2
Đala 72 C1
Dalälven 106 A3
Dalane 104 A4
Dalbeattie 4 C3
Dalbosjön 105 E4
Dalby 109 D3
Dale (Hordaland) 104 A2
Dale (Sogn og Fjordane) 104 A1
Dalen 104 B3
Dalhem 109 F4
Dalias 44 B4
Daliburgh 2 A3
Dalj 72 B2
Dalkeith 5 D2
Dalkey 13 E4
Dalmally 4 C1
Dalmellington 4 C3
Dalmine 60 B1
Dalry 4 C2
Dalsbruk 107 D3
Dalsfjorden 104 A1
Dalsjöfors 109 D1
Dals Långed 105 D4
Dalton 6 B1
Daluis, Gorges de 31 E3
Dalvik 96 B1
Dalwhinnie 2 C4
Damaskiniá 79 D3
Damássi 83 E1
Damazan 28 C3
Damelevières 21 D4
Damgan 22 C4
Damianó 79 F2
Dammartin-en-Goële 19 F3
Damme 17 F2
Damnjane 76 C2
Dampierre 27 D2
Dampierre-sur-Salon 27 D2
Damville 19 E4
Damvillers 20 C3
Dangé 25 D3
Danilovgrad 76 B2
Dannemarie 27 E2
Dannenberg 48 B3
Dão, R 38 C1
Daoulas 22 B3
Darda 71 F2
Dardesheim 52 C1
Darfo Boario Terme 58 C4
Dargilan, Grotte de 29 F3
Dargun 49 D2
Darlington 5 E4
Darłowo 110 A4
Darmstadt 54 C1
Darney 27 D1
Daroca 36 C4
Darque 34 A3
Darß 48 C1
Dartford 10 C2
Dartmoor Nat Pk 8 C3
Dartmouth 8 C4
Daruvar 71 E2
Darwen 6 C2
Dasburg 51 D4
Dasing 55 F3
Dassel 52 B2
Dassohóri 81 D2
Dassow 48 B2
D'at'kovo 111 F3
Datteln 17 E3
Daugava 110 C3
Daugavpils 110 C3
Daun 51 E4
Dava 3 D3
Davat 77 D4
Daventry 9 E1
Davia 87 D2
Davidovac 73 F2
Dávlia 83 F4
Davor 71 E3
Davos 58 B2
Dawlish 8 C3
Dax 28 A4
Deàdnu 95 E2
Deal 11 D3
Deauville 19 D3
Deba 36 B1
Debar 77 D3
Debarska Banja Banjišta 77 D3
Debeli Lug 73 E3
Debeli vrh 70 B2
Debeljača 72 C2
Dębica 112 B2
De Bilt 16 C3
Dęblin 112 C2
Dębno 49 F3
Debrc 72 C3
Debrecen 112 C4
Dečani 76 C2
Decazeville 29 E2
Děčín 53 F3
Decize 26 A3
Dedemsvaart 17 D2
Dee (Scotland) 3 D4
Dee (Wales/Eng) 6 B3
Degaña 34 C2
Degebe, R 38 B4

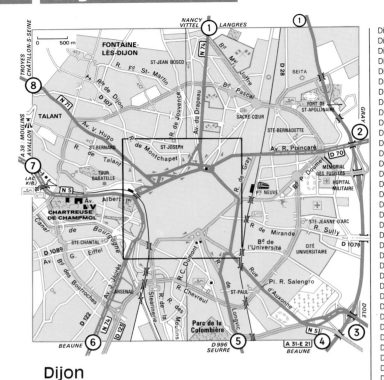

## Dijon

Dídima 87 E2
Dídimo, Óros 87 E2
Didimótiho 81 F1
Die 30 C2
Dieburg 52 A4
Diedorf 52 B2
Diego Alvaro 39 E2
Diekirch 21 D2
Diemel 52 A2
Diemelstadt 52 A2
Diepholz 17 F2
Dieppe 19 E2
Dierdorf 51 E4
Dieren 17 D3
Diesdorf 48 B4
Dießen 56 A3
Diest 50 C3
Dietenheim 55 E3
Dietfurt 55 F2
Dietikon 27 F2
Dietmannsried 55 E4
Dieulefit 30 C2
Dieulouard 21 D4
Dieuze 21 D4
Diez 51 F4
Diezma 44 A3
Differdange 21 D3
Digerkampen 100 B3
Digermulen 94 A4
Dignano 59 E3
Digne-les-Bains 31 D3
Digoin 26 B3
Dijle 50 C3
Dijon 26 C2
Dikanäs 97 F3
Dikea 81 F1
Dikela 81 E2
Diksmuide 50 A3
Diktéo Ándro 91 E4
Diktinéon 90 B3
Dikti, Óros 91 E4
Dilessi 84 B4
Dilináta 82 B4
Dilj 71 E2
Dillenburg 51 F3
Dillingen (Bayern) 55 E2
Dillingen (Saarland) 54 A2
Dilofos 81 F1
Dílos 88 C2
Dílos, N 88 C2
Dímena 87 E2
Dimitra 83 E1
Dimitrítsi 80 B2
Dimitrovgrad (BG) 115 D3
Dimitrovgrad (YU) 77 F1
Dimitsána 86 C2
Dinami 67 E4
Dinan 18 B4
Dinant 50 C4
Dinar 115 F4
Dinara Mt 75 D1
Dinara (Reg) 75 D1
Dinard 18 B4
Dinbych 6 B3
Dinbych-y-pysgod 8 B2
Dingelstädt 52 B2
Dingle 14 A3
Dingle 105 D4
Dingle (Reg) 14 A3
Dingle B 14 A3
Dingli 68 B4
Dinglingen 54 C3
Dingolfing 56 B2
Dingwall 2 C3
Dinjiška 70 C4
Dinkelsbühl 55 E2
Dinklage 17 F2
Dinslaken 17 D3
Dio 79 F4
Diónissos 87 F1
Dióriga Korínthou 87 E1
Dipótama 80 C1
Dippoldiswalde 53 E2
Diráhio 86 C3
Dirfís, Óros 84 B3
Disentis 58 A3
Disgrazia, Mte 58 B3
Dispílio 79 D3
Diss 11 D1
Dissen 17 F2
Dístomo 83 E4
Dístos 84 B4
Ditiki Rodópi 80 C1

Dittaino 69 D3
Ditzingen 55 D2
Divača 70 A3
Divaráta 82 B4
Divčibare 72 C4
Dives 18 C3
Dives R 18 C3
Divič 72 B4
Divjakë 76 C4
Divljana 77 E1
Divonne 27 D3
Divor, Bgem do 38 B4
Divor, Rib de 38 B4
Divoúnia, Ni 92 C2
Dívri 83 E3
Divuša 71 D3
Djupini 96 A3
Djupvik 94 C2
Djurås 105 E2
Djursland 108 B2
Dmitrov 111 F2
Dnepr 111 E3
Dneprodzeržinsk-oje
Dneprodzeržinskoje Vodochranilišče 113 F2
Dneprovskij Liman 113 F3
Dnestr 112 C3
Dnestrovskij Liman 113 F4
Dno 111 D2
Dobanovci 72 C3
Dobbiaco 59 E2
Dobel 54 C2
Dobele 110 C3
Döbeln 53 E2
Doberlug-Kirchhain 53 E1
Döbern 53 F1
Dobersberg 57 E1
Dobieszczyn 49 E2
Doboj 71 F3
Dobošnica 71 F3
Dobra (PL) 49 F2
Dobra (YU) 73 E3
Dobra R 70 C3
Dobra Voda 73 D4
Dobra Voda Mt 77 D3
Dobrašinci 77 F3
Dobratsch 59 F2
Dobrčane 77 D2
Dobri Do 77 D1
Dobrinj 70 B3
Dobříš 53 F4
Dobrljin 71 D3
Dobrna 70 B1
Dobromani 75 F2
Dobro Polje 76 A1
Dobrovnik 70 C1
Dobrun 72 C4
Dobruš 111 E4
Dobruševo 77 E4
Dobrzany 49 F2
Dobšiná 112 B3
Docksta 102 A2
Doc Penfro 8 B2
Dodekánissa 89 E3
Dodóni 82 C1
Doesburg 17 D3
Doetinchem 17 D3
Doganović 77 D2
Dogliani 31 F2
Doiráni 79 F2
Doiránis, L 79 F2
Doiras, Emb de 34 C1
Dojransko Ez 77 F3
Dokanj 72 B3
Dokka 104 C2
Dokkum 47 D3
Dokós, N 87 E3
Doksy 53 F3
Dolac 76 C2
Dol-de-Bretagne 18 B4
Dole 26 C2
Dôle, la 27 D3
Dølemo 104 B4
Dolenci 77 D4
Dolenja Vas 70 B2
Dolenjske Toplice 70 B2
Dolga Vas 71 D1
Dolgellau 6 A3
Doliana 78 C4
Dolianá 83 D1
Dolianova 66 B4

Dolíhi 79 E4
Dolina 112 C3
Doljani 71 D4
Doljevac 77 D1
Dolla 12 C4
Döllach 59 E2
Dollar 5 D2
Dolle 48 C4
Dolo 61 D1
Dolomiti 59 D3
Dolores 45 D2
Dolovo 73 D2
Dol Poustevna 53 F2
Domaševo 75 F2
Domažlice 56 B1
Dombås 100 B3
Dombasle 21 D4
Dombóvár 114 B1
Domburg 16 B3
Domène 30 C1
Doméniko 83 E1
Domèvre-en-Haye 21 D4
Domfront 18 C4
Dömitz 48 C3
Domme 29 D2
Dommitzsch 53 D2
Domnista 83 D3
Domodossola 58 A4
Domokós 83 E2
Dompaire 27 D1
Dompierre 26 B3
Domrémy 20 C4
Domusnovas 66 B4
Domžale 70 B2
Don (England) 7 D2
Don (Scotland) 3 E4
Donaghadee 13 E2
Doña María Ocaña 44 B3
Doña Mencía 43 F2
Doñana, Parque Nac de 43 D3
Donau 56 C2
Donaueschingen 54 C4
Donauwörth 55 E2
Donawitz 57 E4
Don Benito 39 E4
Doncaster 7 D2
Donegal 12 C1
Donegal B 12 C2
Donegal (Co) 12 C1
Dongen 16 C3
Donges 23 D4
Donington 7 E3
Donja Bebrina 71 F3
Donja Brela 75 E4
Donja Brezna 76 B2
Donja Bukovica 76 B2
Donja Kamenica 72 C3
Donja Šatornja 73 D3
Donje Crniljevo 72 C3
Donje Dragovlje 77 E1
Donje Ljupče 77 D2
Donji Andrijevci 71 F3
Donji Barbeš 77 E1
Donji Kanzanci 75 D1
Donji Lapac 71 D4
Donji Malovan 75 E1
Donji Miholjac 71 E2
Donji Milanovac 73 E3
Donji Ruzani 75 D1
Donji Seget 75 D2
Donji Vakuf 71 E4
Donji Vijačani 71 E3
Donji Zemunik 74 C1
Dönna 97 D3
Donnemarie-Dontilly 20 A4
Donnersbachwald 57 D4
Dønnes 97 D2
Donon 21 E4
Donon, Col du 21 E4
Donostia-San Sebastián 36 C1
Donoússa, N 89 D3
Donzère 30 B2
Donzy 26 A2
Doorn 16 C3
Doornik 50 A4
Dora Baltéa 27 E4
Dora Riparia 31 E1

Dorat, le 25 D4
Đorče Petrov 77 D3
Dorchester 9 D3
Dordives 25 F1
Dordogne 29 E1
Dordogne (Dépt) 28 C2
Dordogne R 28 B2
Dordrecht 16 C3
Dore 29 F1
Dório 86 C3
Dorkáda 80 A2
Dorking 10 C3
Dormagen 17 E4
Dormans 20 A3
Dornbirn 58 B2
Dornburg 52 C3
Dorndorf 52 B3
Dornes 26 A3
Dornie 2 B3
Dornoch 3 D3
Dornoch Firth 3 D3
Dornstetten 54 C3
Dornum 47 E3
Dorog 112 B4
Dorogobuž 111 E3
Dorohoi 113 D3
Dorotea 101 F1
Dörpstedt 48 A1
Dorset 9 D3
Dorsten 17 E3
Dortan 27 D3
Dortmund 17 E3
Dortmund-Ems-Kanal 17 E2
Dorum 47 F3
Dörzbach 55 D1
Dosbarrios 40 B3
Dos Hermanas 43 D3
Dosse 49 D3
Douai 19 F2
Douarnenez 22 A3
Doubs 26 C3
Doubs (Dépt) 27 D2
Doucier 27 D3
Doudeville 19 D2
Doué 24 C2
Douglas (I of Man) 6 A1
Douglas (Scotland) 4 C2
Doukáto, Akr 82 B3
Doulaincourt 20 C4
Doulevant-le-Château 20 C4
Doullens 19 F2
Doulus Head 14 A4
Doune 4 C2
Doupov 53 E3
Dourdan 19 E3
Dourgne 32 A1
Douro 34 A4
Douro, R 34 A4
Douvaine 27 D3
Douve 18 B3
Douvres 18 C3
Dover 11 D3
Dover, Str of 11 D3
Dovre 100 C3
Dovrefjell 100 C3
Dovsk 111 E4
Down 13 E2
Downham Market 10 C1
Downpatrick 13 E2
Dowra 12 C2
Doxarás 83 E2
Doxáto 80 C2
Dozulé 19 D3
Drac 30 C2
Dračevo 77 E3
Drachten 17 D1
Drag 94 A4
Dragalovci 71 E3
Dragaš 77 D3
Drăgănani 115 D1
Dragaši 76 B1
Draginac 72 C3
Draginje 72 C3
Dragocvet 73 D4
Dragoevo 77 E3
Dragoman 114 C2
Dragonera, I 45 E3
Dragoni 64 B3

Degerfjärden 102 A2
Degerfors 105 E4
Degerndorf 56 B4
Deggendorf 56 B2
Dego 31 F2
Degracias 38 B2
De Haan 50 A3
Dehesa de Montejo 35 F2
Deià 45 E2
Deidesheim 54 C1
Deinze 50 B3
Deiva Marina 60 B3
Dej 112 C4
Deje 105 E3
Dejë, Mal 76 C3
De Koog 16 C1
Delčevo 77 F2
Delden 17 D2
Deleitosa 39 E3
Delémont 27 E2
Deléria 83 E1
Delet Teili 106 C3
Delfi 83 E4
Delft 16 B3
Delfzijl 47 D3
Delia 68 C4
Delianuova 67 E4
Deliblato 73 D2
Deliblatska Peščara 73 D2
Deliceto 64 C3
Delimeđe 76 C1
Delitzsch 53 D2
Delle 27 E2
Dellen, N 101 F3
Dellen, S 101 F3
Delme 21 D3
Delmenhorst 47 F3
Delnice 70 B3
Delsbo 101 F3
Delta Dunării 113 E4
Delvin 13 D3
Delvináki 82 B1
Demanda, Sa de la 36 B2
Demer 50 C3
Demidov 111 E3
Demirci 115 F4
Demir Kapija 77 F3
Demmin 49 D2
Demoiselles, Grotte des 29 F3
Demonía 87 E4
Denain 20 A1
Denbigh 6 B3
Den Burg 16 C1
Dendermonde 50 B3

Dendre 50 B4
Dendrohóri 79 D3
Denekamp 17 E2
Den Haag 16 B3
Den Helder 16 C1
Denia 45 E1
Denizli 115 F4
Denkendorf 55 F2
Dennington 11 D1
Denny 4 C2
Den Oever 16 C1
Dent de Vaulion 27 D3
De Panne 50 A3
Đeravica 76 C2
Derby 6 C3
Derbyshire 6 C3
Der Chantecoq, L du 20 C4
Đerdap, H.E. 73 F2
Đerdap, Klisura 73 E3
Derekoy 115 E2
Derenburg 52 C1
Derg, L (Clare) 12 C4
Derg, L (Donegal) 12 C2
Der Grabow 49 D1
Dermatás, Akr 83 F1
Dermbach 52 B3
Derneburg 52 B1
Derravaragh, L 13 D3
Derrynasaggart Mts 14 B4
Derryveagh Mts 12 C1
Deruta 63 E1
Dervaig 4 B1
Derval 23 D4
Dervéni 87 D1
Derventa 71 E3
Dervíziana 82 B2
Diabléret 87 D1
Diablerets, les 27 E3
Diablerets, les Mt 27 E3
Diafáni 93 D2
Diakófti 90 A1
Diakoftó 86 C1
Diamante 67 E2
Día, N 91 E3
Diano Marina 31 F3
Diápora Nissiá 87 E1
Diávlos Alonníssou 84 B2
Diávlos Oreón 83 F3
Diávlos Pelagoníssou 84 B2
Diávlos Skiáthou 84 A2
Diávlos Skopélou 84 A2
Diávlos Trikeríou 83 F3
Diávlos Zákinthou 86 A1
Diavolítsi 86 C3
Diávolo, Pso del 64 A2
Diavolórema 81 E2
Dibbersen 48 A3
Dicmo 75 D1
Dicomano 61 D3

Deskáti 83 D1
Desna 111 F3
Despotikó, N 88 B3
Despotovac 73 E3
Despotovo 72 B2
Dessau 53 D1
Destriana 35 D3
Desulo 66 B3
Desvres 19 E1
Deta 114 C1
Đetinja 72 C4
Detmold 52 A1
Dettelbach 55 E1
Dettifoss 96 C1
Deurne 17 D3
Deutsche Alpenstraße 55 E4
Deutsche Bucht 47 E2
Deutschkreutz 57 F3
Deutschlandsberg 70 B1
Deutsch-Wagram 57 F2
Deux-Alpes, les 31 D2
Deux-Sèvres 24 C3
Deva 114 C1
Deve Bair 77 E2
Deventer 17 D2
Deveron 3 E3
Devetak 72 B4
Devil's Bridge 8 C1
Devil's Elbow 3 D4
Devizes 9 E2
Devnja 115 E2
Dewsbury 6 C2
Deza 36 C4
Desborough 9 F1
Descartes 25 D3
Desenzano 60 B1
Desertas 42 A3
Desfiladero de Despeñaperros 44 A1
Desfiladero de la Hermida 35 F2
Desfiladero de los Beyos 35 E2
Desfiladero del Teverga 35 D2
Desfina 83 E4
Desimirovac 73 D4
Desio 60 A1

# DUBLIN / BAILE ÁTHA CLIATH

Howth / Binn Éadair

Dún Laoghaire

Scale 1/120 000

| | | | | | | | | | |
|---|---|---|---|---|---|---|---|---|---|
| Dragør | 108 C3 | Drenthe | 17 D1 | Drøbak | 105 D3 | | | | |
| Dragoš | 77 E4 | Drépano | | Drobeta-Turnu | | | | | |
| Dragotiná | 82 A2 | (Makedonía) | 79 E3 | Severin | 114 C1 | | | | |
| Dragović | 71 E2 | Drépano | | Drochtersen | 48 A2 | | | | |
| Dragovića Polje | 76 B2 | (Pelopónissos) | 87 E2 | Drogheda | 13 D3 | | | | |
| Dragozetići | 70 B3 | Drépano, Akr | | Drogobyč | 112 C3 | | | | |
| Dragsfjärd | 107 D3 | (Anáfi) | 91 E1 | Droichead Átha | 13 D3 | | | | |
| Dragsvik | 100 A3 | Drépano, Akr | | Droichead Nua | 13 D4 | | | | |
| Draguignan | 31 D4 | (Makedonía) | 80 B4 | Droitwich | 9 E1 | | | | |
| Dráma | 80 C2 | Dresden | 53 E2 | Drokija | 113 E3 | | | | |
| Dráma (Nomos) | 80 C2 | Dreux | 19 E4 | Dromcolliher | 14 B3 | | | | |
| Drammen | 104 C3 | Drežnik-Grad | 70 C3 | Drôme (Dépt) | 30 C2 | | | | |
| Drammen selva | 104 C3 | Driebergen | 16 C3 | Drôme R | 30 C2 | | | | |
| Drangajökull | 96 A1 | Driebes | 40 B2 | Dromore (Down) | 13 E2 | | | | |
| Drangedal | 104 C3 | Driméa | 83 E3 | Dromore (Tyrone) | 13 D2 | | | | |
| Dranske | 49 D1 | Drimós | 79 F3 | Dronero | 31 E2 | | | | |
| Drápano, Akr | 90 C3 | Drin | 76 C3 | Dronfield | 7 D2 | | | | |
| Drasenhofen | 57 F1 | Drina | 76 A1 | Drongaráti | 82 B4 | | | | |
| Drau | 59 F2 | Drini i Zi | 77 D3 | Dronne | 28 C1 | | | | |
| Dráva | 71 E2 | Drinit, Gjiri i | 76 B3 | Dronninglund | 108 B2 | | | | |
| Dravograd | 70 B1 | Drinjača | 72 B4 | Dronten | 16 C2 | | | | |
| Drawno | 49 F2 | Drinjača R | 72 B4 | Drosendorf Stadt | 57 E1 | | | | |
| Drawsko | | Drinovci | 75 E2 | Drossáto | 79 F2 | | | | |
| Pomorskie | 112 A1 | Driopída | 88 A2 | Drosseró | 79 E2 | | | | |
| Draženov | 56 B1 | Driós | 88 C3 | Drossiá | 84 A4 | | | | |
| Draževac | 72 C3 | Drisht | 76 C3 | Drossohóri | 83 E4 | | | | |
| Drebkau | 53 F1 | Driva | 100 B2 | Drossopigí (Árta) | 82 C3 | | | | |
| Dreki | 96 C2 | Drlače | 72 C4 | Drossopigí | | | | | |
| Drenewydd | 9 D1 | Drnholec | 57 F1 | (Ioánina) | 78 C4 | | | | |
| Drenovac | 77 E2 | Drniš | 75 D1 | Drossopigí | | | | | |
| Drenovci | 72 B3 | Drnje | 71 D1 | (Makedonía) | 79 D3 | | | | |
| Drenovo | 77 E3 | Drnovo | 70 C2 | Drottningholm | 106 B4 | | | | |

# Düsseldorf

| | | | | | | | | | | | | | | |
|---|---|---|---|---|---|---|---|---|---|---|---|---|---|---|
| Droué | 25 E1 | Dubovac | 73 D2 | Dugo Selo | 70 C2 | Duncansby Head | 3 E2 | Dunnamanagh | 13 D1 | Durham | 5 E4 | Dvor | 71 D3 |
| Drulingen | 21 E3 | Dubovsko | 71 D4 | Duingt | 27 D4 | Dundalk | 13 D3 | Dún na nGall | 12 C2 | Durham (Co) | 5 E4 | Dyfed | 8 C1 |
| Drumkeeran | 12 C2 | Dubrava (Hrvatska) | 71 D2 | Duino | 59 F3 | Dundalk B | 13 E3 | Dunnet | 3 D2 | Durlach | 54 C2 | Dyje | 57 E1 |
| Drummore | 4 B4 | Dubrava (Pelješac) | 75 F2 | Duisburg | 17 D3 | Dun Dealgan | 13 D3 | Dunnet Head | 3 D2 | Durlas | 14 C3 | Dyrnes | 100 B1 |
| Drumnadrochit | 2 C3 | Dubrava Stara | 71 E3 | Dukagjin | 76 C2 | Dundee | 5 D1 | Dunoon | 4 C2 | Durmanec | 70 C2 | Dyrøya | 94 B3 |
| Drumochter, Pass | | Dubrave | 71 F3 | Dukat | 77 E2 | Dundonnell | 2 C3 | Duns | 5 E2 | Durmitor | 76 B2 | Džami tepe | 77 F3 |
| of | 2 C4 | Dubrave Donje | 72 B3 | Duleek | 13 D3 | Dundrum B | 13 E2 | Dunshaughlin | 13 D3 | Durness | 2 C2 | Džaniċi | 75 F1 |
| Drumshanbo | 12 C2 | Dubravica | 73 D3 | Dulje | 77 D2 | Dunfanaghy | 12 C1 | Dunstable | 9 F2 | Dürnkrut | 57 F2 | Džep | 77 E1 |
| Drusenheim | 21 F4 | Dubrovnik | 76 A2 | Dülken | 17 D4 | Dunfermline | 5 D2 | Dunster | 8 C3 | Dürnstein | 57 E2 | Dzermiádo | 91 E4 |
| Druskininkai | 110 C4 | Ducey | 18 B4 | Dülmen | 17 E3 | Dungannon | 13 D2 | Dun-sur-Auron | 25 F3 | Durrës | 76 C4 | Dzeržinsk | 111 D4 |
| Druten | 16 C3 | Ducherow | 49 E2 | Dulnain Bridge | 3 D4 | Dún Garbhán | 14 C4 | Dunvegan | 2 B3 | Durrësit, Gjiri i | 76 C4 | Dzierżoniów | 112 A2 |
| Drvenik (Hrvatska) | 75 D2 | Duchkov | 53 E3 | Dulovo | 115 E2 | Dungarvan | 14 C4 | Dunvegan Head | 2 B3 | Durrow | 12 C4 | Dziwnów | 49 E1 |
| Drvenik (Hrvatska) | 75 E1 | Duchovščina | 111 E3 | Dumbarton | 4 C2 | Dungarvan | | Duolbbadasgai'sa | 95 E1 | Dursey I | 14 A4 | Džumajlija | 77 E3 |
| Dryburgh | 5 D3 | Duclair | 19 D3 | Dumbria | 34 A1 | Harbour | 14 C4 | Đurakovac | 76 C2 | Dursley | 9 D2 | Dżwirzyno | 49 F1 |
| Drymen | 4 C2 | Dudelange | 21 D3 | Dumfries | 4 C3 | Dungeness | 11 D3 | Durance | 30 C3 | Durtal | 23 E4 | |
| Duben | 53 E1 | Duderstadt | 52 B2 | Dumfries and | | Dungiven | 13 D1 | Durango | 36 B1 | Duruelo de la | | |
| Dubí | 53 E3 | Dudley | 9 E1 | Galloway | 4 C3 | Dunglow | 12 C1 | Duran, Pso | 59 D3 | Sierra | 36 B3 | |
| Dubica | 71 D3 | Dudweiler | 54 B2 | Dun | 20 C3 | Dunje | 77 E4 | Duras | 28 C2 | Dusina | 75 F1 | |
| Dublin | 13 E4 | Dueñas | 35 E4 | Dunaföldvár | 112 B4 | Dunkeld | 5 D1 | Duratón, R | 40 A1 | Düsseldorf | 17 E4 | |
| Dublin (Co) | 13 D4 | Duero, R | 35 D4 | Dunajevcy | 113 D3 | Dunkerque | 19 F1 | Durban-Corbières | 32 B2 | Duved | 101 D2 | |
| Dubna | 111 F2 | Duesund | 104 A1 | Dunărea | 113 E4 | Dún Laoghaire | 13 E4 | Durbuy | 50 C4 | Duvno | 75 E1 | |
| Dubňany | 57 F1 | Dufftown | 3 D3 | Dunaújváros | 112 B4 | Dun-le-Palestel | 25 E4 | Dúrcal | 44 A3 | Duži (Bosna i | | |
| Dubno | 113 D2 | Duga Poljana | 76 C2 | Dunav | 72 B2 | Dunmanus B | 14 A4 | Đurđevac | 71 D2 | Hercegovina) | 75 F2 | |
| Dubona | 73 D3 | Duga Resa | 70 C3 | Dunav | 114 D2 | Dunmanway | 14 B4 | Đurđevića Tara | 76 B1 | Duži (Bosna i | | |
| Dubossary | 113 E3 | Dugi Otok | 74 C1 | Dunbar | 5 E2 | Dunmore | 12 B3 | Durdevik | 72 B4 | Hercegovina) | 76 A2 | |
| Duboštica | 71 F4 | Dugi Rat | 75 D2 | Dunblane | 4 C2 | Dunmore East | 15 D4 | Düren | 51 D3 | Dverberg | 94 A3 | |

# E

| | | | | | | | | | | | | | | |
|---|---|---|---|---|---|---|---|---|---|---|---|---|---|---|
| | | East Linton | 5 D2 | Ebersbach | 53 F2 | Echarmeaux, les | 26 B4 | Ecouché | 18 C4 | Egie | 87 D4 | Eisfeld | 52 C3 |
| | | East Retford | 7 D2 | Ebersberg | 56 B3 | Echarri-Aranaz | 36 C2 | Ecrins, les | 31 D2 | Egilsstaðir | 96 C2 | Eišiškés | 110 C4 |
| Eaglescliffe | 5 E4 | East Sussex | 10 C3 | Eberstein | 70 B1 | Echegárate, Pto | | Ecrins, Massif des | 31 D2 | Égina | 87 E2 | Eisleben | 52 C2 |
| Eaní | 79 D4 | Eaux-Bonnes | 37 D2 | Eberswalde | 49 E3 | de | 36 B1 | Ecrins, Parc Nat | | Égina, N | 87 F2 | Eislingen | 55 D2 |
| Earith | 10 C1 | Eauze | 28 B3 | Ebmath | 53 D3 | Echelles, les | 30 C1 | des | 31 D2 | Eginio | 79 F3 | Eisriesenwelt- | |
| Earlston | 5 D2 | Ebbw Vale | 9 D2 | Eboli | 64 C4 | Echt | 17 D4 | Ecueillé | 25 E3 | Égio | 83 E4 | Höhle | 59 E1 |
| Earn | 5 D1 | Ebeleben | 52 C2 | Ebrach | 52 C4 | Echte | 52 B2 | Ed | 105 D4 | Égira | 87 D1 | Eitorf | 51 E3 |
| Easingwold | 7 D1 | Ebeltoft | 108 B3 | Ebreichsdorf | 57 F3 | Echternach | 21 D2 | Eda glasbruk | 105 D3 | Egletons | 29 D1 | Eivissa | 45 D4 |
| Easky | 12 B2 | Eben | 59 F1 | Ebreuil | 26 A4 | Écija | 43 E2 | Edam | 16 C2 | Eglinton | 13 D1 | Ejea de los | |
| Eastbourne | 10 C3 | Ebenfurth | 57 F3 | Ebro, Emb del | 35 F2 | Ečka | 72 C2 | Edane | 105 E3 | Egloffstein | 55 F1 | Caballeros | 37 D3 |
| East Dereham | 7 F3 | Ebensee | 56 C3 | Ebro, R | 37 D4 | Eckartsberga | 52 C2 | Eday | 3 E1 | Egmond aan Zee | 16 C2 | Ejulve | 41 E2 |
| Easter Ross | 2 C3 | Eberbach | 55 D1 | Ebstorf | 48 B3 | Eckernförde | 48 A1 | Eddrachillis B | 2 C2 | Egósthena | 87 E1 | Ekára | 83 E2 |
| East Grinstead | 10 C3 | Ebermannstadt | 52 C4 | Eccleshall | 6 C3 | Eckerö | 106 C3 | Ede | 16 C3 | Egremont | 5 D4 | Ekenäs | 107 E3 |
| East Kilbride | 4 C2 | Ebern | 52 C4 | Eceabat | 115 E3 | Ecommoy | 23 F4 | Edelény | 112 B3 | Egtved | 108 A3 | Ekshärad | 105 E3 |
| Eastleigh | 9 E3 | Eberndorf | 70 B1 | Echallens | 27 D3 | Ecos | 19 E3 | Edelweißspitze | 59 E2 | Egués | 36 C2 | Eksjö | 109 D1 |
| | | | | | | | | Eden | 5 D4 | Eguzon | 25 E3 | Elafohóri | 81 F1 |
| | | | | | | | | Edenderry | 13 D4 | Ehinádes Nissiá | 82 C4 | Elafoníssi | 87 E4 |
| | | | | | | | | Edenkoben | 54 C2 | Ehingen | 55 D3 | Élafos | 82 B2 |
| | | | | | | | | Eder | 52 A3 | Ehinos | 81 D2 | El Algar | 45 D2 |
| | | | | | | | | Eder-Stausee | 52 A3 | Ehra-Lessien | 48 B4 | El Almendro | 42 C2 |
| | | | | | | | | Édessa | 79 E3 | Ehrang-Pfalzel | 54 A1 | El Aquián | 44 B4 |
| | | | | | | | | Edewecht | 47 E3 | Ehrenberg | 52 B3 | El Arahal | 43 E3 |
| | | | | | | | | Edgeworthstown | 12 C3 | Ehrenhausen | 70 C1 | El Arenal | 45 E3 |
| | | | | | | | | Edinburgh | 5 D2 | Ehrwald | 58 C1 | El Atazar, Emb de | 40 B1 |
| | | | | | | | | Edipsós | 83 F3 | Eibar | 36 B1 | Eláti (Makedonía) | 79 E4 |
| | | | | | | | | Edirne | 115 E3 | Eibenstock | 53 D3 | Eláti (Thessalía) | 83 D2 |
| | | | | | | | | Edland | 104 B3 | Eibiswald | 70 B1 | Eláti Mt | 82 B3 |
| | | | | | | | | Edolo | 58 C3 | Eichstätt | 55 F2 | Elátia | 83 F3 |
| | | | | | | | | Edremit | 115 E4 | Eide | 100 B2 | Elatohóri | 79 E3 |
| | | | | | | | | Edsåsdalen | 101 D2 | Eider | 48 A2 | Elatoú | 83 D4 |
| | | | | | | | | Edsbro | 106 B3 | Eidfjord | 104 B2 | Elatóvrissi | 83 D3 |
| | | | | | | | | Edsbyn | 101 E4 | Eidfjorden | 104 B2 | Elba, Isola d' | 62 C2 |
| | | | | | | | | Edsele | 101 F2 | Eiði | 96 A3 | El Barco de Ávila | 39 E2 |
| | | | | | | | | Eeklo | 50 B3 | Eidkjosen | 94 B2 | Elbasan | 76 C4 |
| | | | | | | | | Eelde | 47 D3 | Eidsborg | 104 B3 | Elbe | 48 B3 |
| | | | | | | | | Eemshaven | 47 D3 | Eidsbugarden | 100 B3 | Elbe-Lübeck-Kanal | 48 B2 |
| | | | | | | | | Eferding | 56 C2 | Eidsdal | 100 B2 | El Berrón | 35 D1 |
| | | | | | | | | Efes | 115 E4 | Eidsfjorden | 94 A3 | Elbe-Seitenkanal | 48 B4 |
| | | | | | | | | Efira | 86 B1 | Eidsfoss | 104 C3 | Elbeuf | 19 D3 |
| | | | | | | | | Efkarpía | | Eidsvåg | 100 B2 | Elbigenalp | 58 C2 |
| | | | | | | | | (Makedonía) | 79 F2 | Eidsvoll | 105 D2 | Elbingerode | 52 C2 |
| | | | | | | | | Efkarpía | | Eigg | 2 B4 | Elbląg | 110 B4 |
| | | | | | | | | (Makedonía) | 80 B2 | Eikelandsosen | 104 A2 | El Bodón | 39 D2 |
| | | | | | | | | Eforie | 115 E1 | Eiken | 104 B4 | El Bonillo | 40 C4 |
| | | | | | | | | Efxinoúpoli | 83 F2 | Eikeren | 104 C3 | El Bosque | 43 E3 |
| | | | | | | | | Egadi, Is | 68 A3 | Eikesdal | 100 B2 | Elburg | 17 D2 |
| | | | | | | | | Ega, R | 36 C2 | Eilean Donan | | El Burgo | 43 E3 |
| | | | | | | | | Egeln | 52 C1 | Castle | 2 B3 | El Burgo de Osma | 36 A3 |
| | | | | | | | | Egéo Pélagos | 84 A1 | Eilenburg | 53 D2 | El Burgo Ranero | 35 E3 |
| | | | | | | | | Eger | 112 B3 | Eilsleben | 52 C1 | El Cabaco | 39 E2 |
| | | | | | | | | Egersund | 104 A4 | Einbeck | 52 B2 | El Caló | 45 D4 |
| | | | | | | | | Egeskov | 108 B4 | Eindhoven | 16 C3 | El Campo de | |
| | | | | | | | | Egestorf | 48 A3 | Einsiedeln | 58 A2 | Peñaranda | 39 F1 |
| | | | | | | | | Egg | 58 B1 | Eisenach | 52 B3 | El Carpio | 43 F2 |
| | | | | | | | | Eggenburg | 57 E2 | Eisenberg | 53 D3 | El Carpio de Tajo | 39 F3 |
| | | | | | | | | Eggenfelden | 56 B2 | Eisenerz | 57 D3 | El Casar de | |
| | | | | | | | | Eggesin | 49 E2 | Eisenerzer Alpen | 57 D3 | Talamanca | 40 B2 |
| | | | | | | | | Eggum | 94 A3 | Eisenhüttenstadt | 49 F4 | El Castillo de las | |
| | | | | | | | | Eghezée | 50 C4 | Eisenkappel | 70 A1 | Guardas | 43 D2 |
| | | | | | | | | Egiáli | 89 D3 | Eisenstadt | 57 F3 | | |

| Name | Pg | Grid |
|---|---|---|
| El Centenillo | 44 | A1 |
| El Cerro de Andévalo | 42 | C2 |
| Elche | 45 | D2 |
| Elche de la Sierra | 44 | C1 |
| El Coronil | 43 | D3 |
| El Cubillo | 41 | D3 |
| El Cubo de Don Sancho | 39 | D1 |
| El Cubo de Tierra del Vino | 39 | E1 |
| El Cuervo | 43 | D3 |
| Elda | 45 | D1 |
| Elde | 48 | C3 |
| Eldena | 48 | C3 |
| Elefsína | 87 | F1 |
| Eleftherés (Makedonía) | 80 | C2 |
| Eleftherés (Stereá Eláda) | 87 | E1 |
| Eleftherés (Thessalía) | 83 | E1 |
| Eléfthero | 78 | C4 |
| Eleftherohóri | 79 | D4 |
| Eleftheroúpoli | 80 | C2 |
| El Ejido | 44 | B4 |
| Elemir | 72 | C2 |
| Elena | 115 | D2 |
| Eleófito | 82 | C3 |
| Eleohóri | 80 | C3 |
| Eleohória | 80 | A3 |
| Eleónas | 83 | E4 |
| Eleoússa | 93 | F1 |
| El Escorial | 40 | A2 |
| El Espinar | 40 | A2 |
| El Figueró | 32 | B4 |
| El Formigal | 37 | D2 |
| Elgå | 100 | D3 |
| Elgin | 3 | D3 |
| Elgóibar | 36 | B1 |
| Elgol | 2 | B4 |
| El Grado | 37 | E3 |
| El Grado, Emb de | 37 | E3 |
| El Grao | 41 | E4 |
| El Grau | 41 | F3 |
| Elhovo | 115 | D2 |
| El Hoyo de Pinares | 40 | A2 |
| Eliá | 87 | D4 |
| Elie | 5 | D2 |
| Elikónas, Óros | 83 | F4 |
| Elimäki | 107 | F2 |
| Eliniko | 86 | C2 |
| Elinohóri | 81 | F1 |
| Elizondo | 36 | C1 |
| Elk | 110 | C4 |
| Ellesmere | 6 | B3 |
| Ellesmere Port | 6 | B2 |
| Ellingen | 55 | E2 |
| Ellon | 3 | E4 |
| Ellös | 108 | C1 |
| Ellrich | 52 | B2 |
| Ellwangen | 55 | E2 |
| El Madroño | 42 | C2 |
| El Maestrazgo | 41 | E2 |
| Elmas | 66 | B4 |
| El Masnou | 32 | B4 |
| El Molar | 40 | B2 |
| El Molinillo | 40 | A3 |
| El Moral | 44 | C2 |
| Elmshorn | 48 | A2 |
| Elne | 32 | B2 |
| Elnesvågen | 100 | B2 |
| Elóna | 87 | D3 |
| Elopía | 83 | F4 |
| Elorn | 22 | B2 |
| Élos (Kriti) | 90 | B3 |
| Élos (Pelopónnisos) | 87 | D4 |
| Eloúnda | 91 | E3 |
| Eloyes | 27 | D1 |
| El Pardo | 40 | A2 |
| El Paular | 40 | A1 |
| El Pedernoso | 40 | B3 |
| El Pedroso | 43 | D2 |
| El Perelló (Catalunya) | 41 | F2 |
| El Perelló (Valencia) | 41 | E4 |
| Elphin | 12 | C3 |
| El Picazo | 40 | C4 |
| El Pinell de Brai | 41 | F1 |
| El Pobo de Dueñas | 41 | D2 |
| El Pont d'Armentera | 37 | F4 |
| El Portal | 43 | D4 |
| El Port de la Selva | 32 | C3 |
| El Port de Llança | 32 | B3 |
| El Prat de Llobregat | 32 | A4 |
| El Puente | 36 | A1 |
| El Puente del Arzobispo | 39 | F3 |
| El Puerto de Sagunto | 41 | E3 |
| El Puerto de Santa Maria | 43 | D4 |
| El Real de la Jara | 43 | D2 |
| El Real de San Vicente | 39 | F2 |
| El Remolcador Pto | 41 | E3 |
| El Robledo | 39 | F4 |
| El Rocío | 42 | C3 |
| El Romeral | 40 | B3 |
| El Rompido | 42 | C3 |
| El Ronquillo | 43 | D2 |
| El Royo | 36 | B3 |
| El Rubio | 43 | E3 |
| Elsa | 60 | C4 |
| El Saler | 41 | E4 |
| El Salobral | 40 | C4 |
| El Saucejo | 43 | E3 |
| Elsdorf | 17 | D4 |
| Elserdorf | 55 | F2 |
| El Serrat | 32 | A2 |
| Elsfleth | 47 | F3 |
| Elsterberg | 53 | D3 |
| Elsterwerda | 53 | E2 |
| El Tiemblo | 40 | A2 |
| Eltisley | 9 | F1 |
| Eltmann | 52 | C4 |
| El Toboso | 40 | B3 |
| El Torcal | 43 | F3 |
| Eltz | 51 | E4 |
| El Vado, Emb de | 40 | B1 |
| Elvanfoot | 4 | C3 |
| Elvas | 38 | C4 |
| Elvekrok | 100 | B3 |
| El Vellón, Emb de | 40 | A2 |
| El Vendrell | 37 | F4 |
| El Vicario, Emb de | 40 | A4 |
| El Villar de Arnedo | 36 | C2 |
| El Viso | 43 | E1 |
| El Viso del Alcor | 43 | D2 |
| Elx | 45 | D2 |
| Ely | 10 | C1 |
| Elygsfors | 109 | E2 |
| Elzach | 54 | C3 |
| Elze | 52 | B1 |
| Emån | 109 | E2 |
| Embessós | 82 | C3 |
| Embid | 41 | D1 |
| Embid de Ariza | 36 | C4 |
| Émbonas | 93 | E1 |
| Emboriós (Híos) | 89 | D1 |
| Emboriós (Sími) | 93 | E1 |
| Embrun | 31 | D2 |
| Emden | 47 | E3 |
| Emet | 115 | F4 |
| Emilia-Romagna | 60 | C3 |
| Emlichheim | 17 | E2 |
| Emmaboda | 109 | E2 |
| Emmeloord | 16 | C2 |
| Emmen | 17 | E1 |
| Emmendingen | 54 | C3 |
| Emmerich | 17 | D3 |
| Emocriós | 89 | F3 |
| Em. Papás | 80 | B2 |
| Empoli | 60 | C4 |
| Empúries | 32 | C3 |
| Ems | 17 | E1 |
| Emsdetten | 17 | E2 |
| Ems-Jade-Kanal | 47 | E3 |
| Emskirchen | 55 | E1 |
| Enafors | 101 | D2 |
| Enäjärvi | 103 | E4 |
| Enånger | 101 | F4 |
| Encamp | 32 | A2 |
| Encausse | 37 | E1 |
| Encinas de Abajo | 39 | E1 |
| Encinasola | 42 | C1 |
| Encinedo | 34 | C3 |
| Endelave | 108 | B3 |
| Endrinal | 39 | E2 |
| Enego | 59 | D3 |
| Enfesta | 34 | A2 |
| Eng | 59 | D1 |
| Engadin | 58 | B3 |
| Engarés | 88 | C3 |
| Engelberg | 27 | F3 |
| Engelhartszell | 56 | C2 |
| Engeløya | 97 | E1 |
| Engelsdorf | 53 | D2 |
| Engelskirchen | 17 | E4 |
| Engen | 58 | A1 |
| Enger | 17 | F2 |
| Engerdal | 101 | D3 |
| Enghien | 50 | B3 |
| England | 9 | F1 |
| English Channel | 10 | A4 |
| Engstingen | 55 | D3 |
| Enguera | 41 | E4 |
| Enguidanos | 41 | D3 |
| Enhammarsfjärden | 101 | F4 |
| Enipéas | 83 | E2 |
| Enkhuizen | 16 | C2 |
| Enköping | 106 | B3 |
| Enna | 68 | C3 |
| Enneberg | 59 | D2 |
| Ennell, L | 12 | C3 |
| Ennepetal | 17 | E4 |
| Ennezat | 26 | A4 |
| Ennis | 12 | B4 |
| Enniscorthy | 15 | D3 |
| Enniskerry | 13 | D4 |
| Enniskillen | 13 | D2 |
| Ennistimon | 12 | B4 |
| Enns | 57 | D3 |
| Enns R | 57 | D3 |
| Eno | 103 | F2 |
| Enol, L | 35 | E2 |
| Enonkoski | 103 | F3 |
| Enontekiö | 95 | D3 |
| Énos, Óros | 86 | A1 |
| Enschede | 17 | E2 |
| Ensisheim | 27 | E1 |
| Entlebuch | 27 | F2 |
| Entraygues-sur-Truyère | 29 | E2 |
| Entredichos | 40 | C3 |
| Entre-os-Rios | 34 | A4 |
| Entrepeñas, Emb de | 40 | C2 |
| Entrevaux | 31 | E3 |
| Entrèves | 27 | E4 |
| Entroncamento | 38 | B3 |
| Envalira, Pto de | 32 | A2 |
| Envermeu | 19 | E2 |
| Enviken | 101 | E1 |
| Enz | 54 | C2 |
| Enza | 60 | B2 |
| Eochaill | 14 | C4 |
| Eolie o Lipari, Is | 69 | D2 |
| Eo, R | 34 | C1 |
| Epanomí | 79 | F3 |
| Epe | 17 | D2 |
| Epernay | 20 | B3 |
| Epernon | 19 | E4 |
| Epidávrou, Kólpos | 87 | E3 |
| Epidávrou Limirás, Kólpos | 87 | E4 |
| Épila | 36 | C3 |
| Epinac | 26 | B3 |
| Epinal | 27 | D1 |
| Epine, l' | 20 | B3 |
| Episkopí (Kríti) | 90 | C3 |
| Episkopí (Kríti) | 91 | E3 |
| Episkopí (Makedonía) | 79 | E3 |
| Episkopí (Pelopónnisos) | 87 | E3 |
| Epitálio | 86 | B2 |
| Eppan | 59 | D3 |
| Epping | 10 | C2 |
| Eppingen | 55 | D2 |
| Epsom | 10 | C3 |
| Eptahóri | 78 | C4 |
| Eptálofos | 83 | E3 |
| Epte | 19 | E3 |
| Epworth | 7 | D2 |
| Eraclea | 59 | E4 |
| Eraclea-Mare | 59 | E4 |
| Eräjärvi | 103 | D3 |
| Erásmio, N. | 81 | D2 |
| Eratiní | 83 | E4 |
| Eratinó | 80 | C2 |
| Erátira | 79 | D3 |
| Erba | 58 | B4 |
| Erbach | 55 | D1 |
| Erbalunga | 33 | F2 |
| Erbendorf | 53 | D4 |
| Ercina, L de la | 35 | E2 |
| Ercolano | 64 | B4 |
| Érd | 112 | B4 |
| Erdek | 115 | E3 |
| Erdevik | 72 | B2 |
| Erding | 56 | A3 |
| Erdre | 23 | D4 |
| Erdut | 72 | B2 |
| Eresma, R | 40 | A1 |
| Eressós | 85 | E2 |
| Erétria | 84 | B4 |
| Erezée | 50 | C4 |
| Erfde | 48 | A2 |
| Erft | 17 | D4 |
| Erftstadt | 51 | E3 |
| Erfurt | 52 | C3 |
| Erges, R | 39 | D2 |
| Ergoldsbach | 56 | B2 |
| Eriboll, L | 2 | C2 |
| Ericeira | 38 | A3 |
| Erice | 68 | A3 |
| Ericht, L | 2 | C4 |
| Erikoússa, N | 78 | A4 |
| Eriksberg | 106 | A4 |
| Eriksmåle | 109 | E2 |
| Erillas | 43 | E1 |
| Erimanthos | 86 | C2 |
| Erímanthos, Óros | 86 | C1 |
| Eripol, Pto del | 37 | E3 |
| Erithrés | 87 | E1 |
| Erkelenz | 17 | D4 |
| Erkner | 49 | E4 |
| Erla | 37 | D3 |
| Erlangen | 55 | F1 |
| Erlsbach | 59 | E2 |
| Ermenonville | 19 | F3 |
| Ermidas-Aldeia | 42 | A1 |
| Ermióni | 87 | E2 |
| Ermoúpoli | 88 | B2 |
| Ermsleben | 52 | C2 |
| Erndtebrück | 17 | F4 |
| Erne | 13 | D1 |
| Ernée | 23 | E3 |
| Erne, R | 12 | C2 |
| Ernestinovo | 71 | F2 |
| Ernstbrunn | 57 | F2 |
| Erquy | 22 | C2 |
| Errazu | 36 | C1 |
| Errigal Mt | 12 | C1 |
| Erris Head | 12 | A2 |
| Erskine Bridge | 4 | C2 |
| Erstein | 21 | E4 |
| Ervenik | 75 | D1 |
| Ervidel | 42 | B1 |
| Ervy | 26 | B1 |
| Erwitte | 17 | F3 |
| Erzberg | 57 | D3 |
| Erzen | 76 | C4 |
| Erzgebirge | 53 | E3 |
| Esbjerg | 108 | A3 |
| Esblada | 37 | F4 |
| Esbo | 107 | E3 |
| Escabas, R | 40 | C2 |
| Escairón | 34 | B2 |
| Escalada | 35 | F2 |
| Escalante | 36 | A1 |
| Escaldes, les | 32 | A2 |
| Escalona | 40 | A2 |
| Escalonilla | 40 | A3 |
| Escalos de Cima | 38 | C2 |
| Escandón, Pto de | 41 | D2 |
| Escároz | 37 | D2 |
| Escárène, l' | 31 | E3 |
| Escatrón | 37 | D4 |
| Escaut (B) | 50 | B3 |
| Escaut (F) | 20 | A2 |
| Esch (D) | 51 | F4 |
| Esch (L) | 21 | D2 |
| Eschede | 48 | B4 |
| Eschenbach | 53 | D4 |
| Eschershausen | 52 | B1 |
| Eschwege | 52 | B2 |
| Eschweiler | 51 | D3 |
| Escombreras | 45 | D3 |
| Escorihuela | 41 | E2 |
| Escudo, Pto del | 35 | F2 |
| Escúllar | 44 | B3 |
| Escurial | 39 | E4 |
| Esens | 47 | E3 |
| Esera, R | 37 | E2 |
| Esgueva | 35 | F4 |
| Esguevillas de Esgueva | 35 | F4 |
| Esher | 9 | F2 |
| Esino | 61 | E4 |
| Esk | 5 | D3 |
| Eskifjörður | 96 | C2 |
| Eskilstuna | 106 | A4 |
| Eskisehir | 115 | F3 |
| Eskoriatza | 36 | B1 |
| Esla, R | 35 | D4 |
| Eslarn | 56 | B1 |
| Eslohe | 17 | F4 |
| Eslöv | 109 | D3 |
| Espa | 105 | D2 |
| Espadañedo | 34 | C3 |
| Espadán, Sa de | 41 | E3 |
| Espalion | 29 | E3 |
| Esparreguera | 32 | A4 |
| Espedal | 100 | C3 |
| Espejo | 43 | F2 |
| Espelette | 28 | A4 |
| Espelkamp | 17 | F2 |
| Espenschied | 51 | F4 |
| Espera | 43 | D3 |
| Esperó, Pta | 45 | F2 |
| Espichel, C | 38 | A4 |
| Espiel | 43 | E1 |
| Espigüete | 35 | E2 |
| Espinama | 35 | E2 |
| Espinho | 34 | A4 |
| Espinilla | 35 | F2 |
| Espinosa de Cerrato | 35 | F4 |
| Espinosa de los Monteros | 36 | A1 |
| Espoo | 107 | E3 |
| Esporles | 45 | E3 |
| Esposende | 34 | A4 |
| Espot | 37 | F2 |
| Espuña, Sa de | 44 | C3 |
| Esquedas | 37 | D3 |
| Esquivias | 40 | A2 |
| Esse | 102 | C1 |
| Essen (Niedersachsen) | 17 | E2 |
| Essen (Nordrhein-Westfalen) | 17 | E3 |
| Essenbach | 56 | B2 |
| Essex | 11 | D2 |
| Essími | 81 | E2 |
| Esslingen | 55 | D2 |
| Essonne | 25 | F1 |
| Essoyes | 26 | B1 |
| Est, Canal de l' | 27 | D1 |
| Estaca, Pto de la | 42 | A4 |
| Estacas de Trueba, Pto de las | 35 | F2 |
| Estadilla | 37 | E3 |
| Estagel | 32 | B2 |
| Estaires | 19 | F1 |
| Estarreja | 38 | B1 |
| Estats, Pic d' | 37 | F2 |
| Estavayer | 27 | E3 |
| Este | 61 | D1 |
| Estella | 36 | C2 |
| Estepa | 43 | E3 |
| Estepona | 43 | E4 |
| Esteras de Medina | 36 | B4 |
| Esterel | 31 | E4 |
| Esternay | 20 | A4 |
| Esterri d'Àneu | 37 | F2 |
| Estissac | 26 | B1 |
| Estói | 42 | B3 |
| Estonija | 110 | C2 |
| Estoril | 38 | A4 |
| Estrela, Sa da | 38 | C2 |
| Estrella | 44 | A1 |
| Estremadura | 38 | A3 |
| Estremoz | 38 | C4 |
| Estret de Collegats | 37 | F3 |
| Estrées-St-Denis | 19 | F3 |
| Esztergom | 112 | B4 |
| Etables | 22 | C2 |

Essen

| | | |
|---|---|---|
| Etain | 20 | C3 |
| Etampes | 19 | F4 |
| Etaples | 19 | E1 |
| Etel | 22 | B4 |
| Etelhem | 109 | F4 |
| Etive, L | 4 | B1 |
| Etna, M | 69 | D3 |
| Etne | 104 | A3 |
| Etolía-Akarnanía | 82 | C3 |
| Etolikó | 82 | C4 |
| Etrépagny | 19 | E3 |
| Etretat | 19 | D2 |
| Ettelbruck | 21 | D2 |
| Etten | 16 | C3 |
| Ettenheim | 54 | C3 |
| Ettington | 9 | E1 |
| Ettlingen | 54 | C2 |
| Eugénie-les-Bains | 28 | B4 |
| Eume, Emb del | 34 | B1 |
| Eume, R | 34 | B1 |
| Eupen | 51 | D4 |
| Eura | 107 | D2 |
| Eurajoki | 107 | D2 |
| Euratsfeld | 57 | D3 |
| Eure | 19 | E4 |
| Eure (Dépt) | 19 | E3 |
| Eure-et-Loir | 25 | E1 |
| Europabrücke | 59 | D2 |
| Europoort | 16 | B3 |
| Euskadi | 36 | B2 |
| Euskirchen | 51 | E3 |
| Eußenhausen | 52 | B3 |
| Eutin | 48 | B2 |
| Evangelismós | 83 | E1 |
| Evangelistria | 83 | F4 |
| Evaux-les-Bains | 25 | F4 |
| Evendorf | 48 | B3 |
| Evenes | 94 | B3 |
| Evenskjær | 94 | B3 |
| Evergem | 50 | B3 |
| Everöd | 109 | D3 |
| Evertsberg | 101 | E4 |
| Evesham | 9 | E1 |
| Evian | 27 | D3 |
| Évia, N | 84 | B3 |
| Evijärvi | 102 | C2 |
| Évinos | 83 | D3 |
| Evisa | 33 | F3 |
| Evje | 104 | B4 |
| Évdilos | 89 | D2 |
| Évialo | 81 | D2 |
| Evolène | 27 | E4 |
| Évora | 38 | B4 |
| Évoramonte | 38 | B4 |
| Evran | 18 | B4 |
| Evrecy | 18 | C3 |
| Evreux | 19 | E3 |
| Evritanía | 83 | D2 |
| Evron | 23 | E3 |
| Evropós | 79 | F2 |
| Évros | 81 | F2 |
| Évros R | 81 | F2 |
| Evrostína | 87 | D1 |
| Evrótas | 87 | D3 |
| Evry | 19 | F4 |
| Évzoni | 79 | F2 |
| Exaplátanos | 79 | E2 |
| Éxarhos | 83 | F4 |
| Excideuil | 29 | D1 |
| Exe | 8 | C3 |
| Exeter | 8 | C3 |
| Exmes | 19 | D4 |
| Exmoor Nat Pk | 8 | C3 |
| Exmouth | 8 | C3 |
| Exohí (Ípiros) | 78 | C4 |
| Exohí (Makedonía) | 79 | E3 |
| Exohí (Makedonía) | 80 | B1 |
| Exómvourgo | 88 | C2 |
| Exter | 17 | C2 |
| Extremadura | 39 | E4 |
| Eydehavn | 104 | C4 |
| Eye | 9 | F1 |
| Eyemouth | 5 | E2 |
| Eye Pen | 2 | B2 |
| Eygues | 30 | C2 |
| Eyguières | 30 | C4 |
| Eygurande | 29 | E1 |
| Eyjafjörður | 96 | B1 |
| Eymet | 28 | C2 |
| Eymoutiers | 29 | D1 |
| Eyre | 28 | B3 |
| Eyrieux | 30 | B2 |
| Eysturoy | 96 | A3 |
| Eyzies, les | 29 | D2 |
| Ezcaray | 36 | B2 |
| Eze | 31 | E3 |
| Ezine | 115 | E4 |

# F

| | | |
|---|---|---|
| Faak | 59 | F2 |
| Fabara | 37 | E4 |
| Fåberg | 105 | D2 |
| Fabero | 34 | C2 |
| Fåborg | 108 | B4 |
| Fabriano | 61 | E4 |
| Fábricas de Ríopar | 44 | C1 |
| Fabro | 63 | D1 |
| Facinas | 43 | D4 |
| Facture | 28 | A2 |
| Faenza | 61 | D3 |
| Færøerne | 96 | A3 |
| Faeto | 64 | B3 |
| Fafe | 34 | A4 |
| Fågåras | 113 | D4 |
| Fågårasului, M | 113 | D4 |
| Fågelfors | 109 | E2 |
| Fagernes (Oppland) | 104 | C2 |
| Fagernes (Troms) | 94 | C2 |
| Fagersta | 105 | F3 |
| Fairford | 9 | E2 |
| Fair Head | 13 | E1 |
| Fair I | 3 | F3 |
| Fakenham | 7 | E3 |
| Fakovići | 72 | C4 |
| Fakse | 108 | C4 |
| Fakse Ladeplads | 108 | C4 |
| Falaise | 18 | C4 |
| Falakró, Óros | 80 | C1 |
| Falássarna | 90 | B3 |
| Falcade | 59 | D3 |
| Falces | 36 | C2 |
| Falconara Marittima | 61 | F3 |
| Falcone | 69 | D2 |
| Falcone, C del | 66 | A1 |
| Falerna | 67 | E3 |
| Faliráki | 93 | F1 |
| Falkefjellet | 95 | F1 |
| Falkenberg (D) | 53 | E2 |
| Falkenberg (S) | 108 | C2 |
| Falkensee | 49 | D4 |
| Falkenstein | 53 | D3 |
| Falkirk | 4 | C2 |
| Falkland | 5 | D2 |
| Falkonéra, N | 87 | F3 |
| Falköping | 109 | D1 |
| Fallersleben | 48 | B4 |
| Fällfors | 98 | B3 |
| Fallingbostel | 48 | A4 |
| Falmouth | 8 | B4 |
| Falset | 37 | F4 |
| Falster | 108 | C4 |
| Falterona Mte | 61 | D3 |
| Fålticeni | 113 | D3 |
| Falun | 105 | F2 |
| Falzarego, Pso | 59 | D3 |
| Fámjin | 96 | A4 |
| Fanad Head | 13 | D1 |
| Fanári (Pelopónissos) | 87 | E2 |
| Fanári (Pelopónissos) | 86 | C2 |
| Fanári (Thessalía) | 83 | D2 |
| Fanári (Thráki) | 81 | D2 |
| Fanári, Akr | 89 | D2 |
| Fanefjord | 108 | C4 |
| Fani i Madh | 76 | C3 |
| Fani i Vogël | 76 | C3 |
| Fanjeaux | 32 | A1 |
| Fannich, L | 2 | C3 |
| Fano | 61 | E3 |
| Fanø | 108 | A3 |
| Fanø Bugt | 108 | A3 |
| Fanós | 79 | F2 |
| Faouët, le | 22 | B3 |
| Faou, le | 22 | B3 |
| Farángi Samariás | 90 | B4 |
| Farángi Víkou | 78 | C4 |
| Fara Novarese | 58 | A4 |
| Fardes, R | 44 | A3 |
| Fareham | 9 | E3 |
| Fåreveile | 108 | B3 |
| Färgelanda | 105 | D4 |
| Färila | 101 | F3 |
| Farindola | 63 | F1 |
| Faringdon | 9 | E2 |
| Farini d'Olmo | 60 | B2 |
| Färjestaden | 109 | E2 |
| Farkadóna | 83 | E1 |
| Farkaždin | 72 | C2 |
| Farlete | 37 | D3 |
| Farmakoníssi | 89 | F2 |
| Farnborough | 9 | F3 |
| Farnese | 63 | D2 |
| Farnham | 9 | F3 |
| Faro | 42 | B3 |
| Fårö | 109 | F3 |
| Fårösund | 109 | F3 |
| Farra d'Alpago | 59 | E3 |
| Fársala | 83 | E2 |
| Farsø | 108 | A2 |
| Farsund | 104 | A4 |
| Farum | 108 | C3 |
| Fasano | 65 | E3 |
| Fašku Vaskojoki | 95 | E3 |
| Fastov | 113 | E2 |
| Fátima | 38 | B3 |
| Fatmomakke | 97 | E4 |
| Faucille, Col de la | 27 | D3 |
| Faucogney | 27 | D1 |
| Faulquemont | 21 | D3 |
| Fauquembergues | 19 | E1 |
| Fauske | 97 | F2 |
| Fauville | 19 | D3 |
| Fåvang | 100 | C3 |
| Favara | 68 | C4 |
| Favareta | 41 | E4 |
| Faverges | 27 | D4 |
| Faverney | 27 | D1 |
| Faversham | 11 | D3 |
| Favignana, I | 68 | A3 |
| Fawley | 9 | E3 |
| Faxaflói | 96 | A2 |
| Fayence | 31 | D4 |
| Fayl-Billot | 26 | C1 |
| Fayón | 37 | E4 |
| Fay-sur-Lignon | 30 | B2 |
| Fažana | 70 | A4 |
| Feale | 14 | B3 |
| Fécamp | 19 | D2 |
| Féclaz, la | 31 | D1 |
| Feda | 104 | B4 |
| Feggesund | 108 | A2 |
| Fehmarn | 48 | B1 |
| Fehmarnbelt | 48 | B1 |
| Fehmarnsund | 48 | B1 |
| Fehrbellin | 49 | D3 |
| Fehring | 57 | F4 |
| Fejø | 108 | B4 |
| Feketić | 72 | B2 |
| Felanitx | 45 | F3 |
| Felbertauern-tunnel | 59 | E2 |
| Feld | 59 | F2 |
| Feldafing | 56 | A3 |
| Feldbach | 57 | F4 |
| Feldberg (D) | 54 | C4 |
| Feldberg (DDR) | 49 | D3 |
| Feldkirch | 58 | B2 |
| Feldkirchen | 59 | F2 |
| Felgueiras | 34 | A4 |
| Felixstowe | 11 | D2 |
| Fellbach | 55 | D2 |
| Felletin | 25 | F4 |
| Fellingsbro | 105 | F3 |
| Felton | 5 | E3 |
| Feltre | 59 | D3 |
| Femer Bælt | 108 | B4 |
| Femundsmarka | 101 | D3 |
| Fene | 34 | B1 |
| Fener | 59 | D3 |
| Fenestrelle | 31 | E1 |
| Fénétrange | 21 | E3 |
| Feolin Ferry | 4 | B2 |
| Fer à Cheval, Cirque du | 27 | E4 |
| Feraklós | 93 | F2 |
| Ferbane | 12 | C4 |
| Ferdinandovac | 71 | D1 |
| Ferdinandshof | 49 | E2 |
| Fère-Champenoise | 20 | B4 |
| Fère-en-Tardenois | 20 | A3 |
| Fère, la | 20 | A2 |
| Ferentino | 63 | F3 |
| Féres | 81 | F2 |
| Feria | 43 | D1 |
| Feričanci | 71 | E2 |
| Ferlach | 70 | A1 |
| Fermanagh | 12 | C2 |
| Fermo | 61 | F4 |
| Fermoselle | 34 | C4 |
| Fermoy | 14 | C4 |
| Fernancaballero | 40 | A4 |
| Fernán Núñez | 43 | F2 |
| Ferney-Voltaire | 27 | D4 |
| Fernpaß | 58 | C1 |
| Ferrandina | 65 | D4 |
| Ferrara | 61 | D2 |
| Ferreira | 34 | C1 |
| Ferreira do Alentejo | 42 | B1 |
| Ferreira do Zêzere | 38 | B3 |
| Ferreiras | 42 | A3 |
| Ferreras de Abajo | 35 | D3 |
| Ferreries | 45 | F2 |
| Ferreruela de Huerva | 41 | D1 |
| Ferret, Cap | 28 | A2 |
| Ferrette | 27 | E2 |
| Ferriere | 60 | B2 |
| Ferrières | 25 | F1 |
| Ferrol | 34 | B1 |
| Ferru, M | 66 | B3 |
| Ferté-Alais, la | 19 | f4 |
| Ferté-Bernard, la | 23 | F3 |
| Ferté-Frênel, la | 19 | D4 |
| Ferté-Gaucher, la | 20 | A4 |
| Ferté-Macé, la | 18 | C4 |
| Ferté-Milon, la | 20 | A3 |
| Ferté-St-Aubin, la | 25 | E2 |
| Ferté-sous-Jouarre, la | 20 | A3 |
| Ferté-Vidame, la | 19 | D4 |
| Fervenza, Emb de | 34 | A1 |
| Festós | 91 | D4 |
| Festre, Col du | 30 | C2 |
| Festvåg | 97 | E1 |
| Fethard | 14 | C3 |
| Fetlar | 3 | F1 |
| Fetsund | 105 | D3 |
| Feucht | 55 | F1 |
| Feuchtwangen | 55 | E2 |
| Feunte Dé | 35 | E2 |
| Feurs | 26 | B4 |
| Feyzin | 30 | B1 |
| Ffestiniog | 6 | A3 |
| Fflint | 6 | B2 |
| Fiano R. | 63 | E3 |
| Fiastra | 61 | F4 |
| Ficarolo | 60 | C2 |
| Fichtel-gebirge | 53 | D4 |
| Fidenza | 60 | B2 |
| Fieberbrunn | 59 | E1 |
| Fier | 114 | B3 |
| Fiera di Primiero | 59 | D3 |
| Fierzës, Liq i | 76 | C3 |
| Fiesole | 61 | D3 |
| Fife | 5 | D2 |
| Fife Ness | 5 | D1 |
| Figália | 86 | C2 |
| Figeac | 29 | E2 |
| Figline Valdarno | 61 | D4 |
| Figueira da Foz | 38 | B2 |
| Figueira de Castelo Rodrigo | 39 | D1 |
| Figueiró dos Vinhos | 38 | B2 |
| Figueras | 32 | B3 |
| Figueres | 32 | B3 |
| Figueruela de Arriba | 34 | C3 |
| Fíhtio | 87 | D2 |
| Filabres, Sa de los | 44 | B3 |
| Filadélfi | 80 | B3 |
| Filadelfia | 67 | F3 |
| Filáki | 83 | E2 |
| Filákio | 81 | F1 |
| Filakopi | 88 | A4 |
| Filérimos | 93 | F1 |
| Filey | 7 | E1 |
| Filfola | 68 | B4 |
| Fili | 87 | F1 |
| Fília (Lésvos) | 85 | F2 |
| Fília (Pelopónissos) | 86 | C1 |
| Filiátes | 82 | B1 |
| Filiatrá | 86 | B3 |
| Filicudi, I | 68 | C2 |
| Filiourí | 81 | E2 |
| Filipi | 80 | C2 |
| Filipiáda | 82 | C2 |
| Filipjakov | 74 | C1 |
| Filipos, Akr | 88 | B3 |
| Filipstad | 105 | E3 |
| Filira | 81 | E2 |
| Fillan | 100 | C1 |
| Fille-fjell | 104 | B1 |
| Fílo | 83 | E2 |
| Filótas | 79 | D3 |
| Filottrano | 61 | F4 |
| Finale Emilia | 60 | C2 |
| Finale Ligure | 31 | F3 |
| Fiñana | 44 | B3 |
| Finca de la Concepción | 43 | F3 |
| Finchingfield | 11 | D2 |
| Findhorn | 3 | D3 |
| Fínikas | 88 | B2 |
| Finikoúndas | 86 | C4 |

Finistère 22 B3
Finisterre, Emb de 40 A3
Finja 109 D3
Finn 13 D1
Finneidfjord 97 E3
Finnentrop 17 F4
Finnmark 95 D2
Finnmarksvidda 95 D3
Finnøy 104 A3
Finnsnes 94 B3
Finow 49 E3
Finowfurt 49 E3
Finskij Zaliv 110 C1
Finspång 105 F4
Finsteraarhorn 27 F3
Finsterau 56 C2
Finsterwalde 53 E1
Finström 106 C3
Fintona 13 D2
Fintown 12 C1
Fionnphort 4 A1
Fiorenzuola
  d'Arda 60 B2
Firenze 60 C3
Firenzuola 61 D3
Firminy 30 B1
Firmo 67 E2
Fischamend
  Markt 57 F2
Fischbach 55 F1
Fischbeck 48 C4
Fischen 55 E4
Fishbourne 9 E3
Fishguard 8 B1
Fiskárdo 82 B4
Fiskebøl 94 A3
Fismes 20 A4
Fissíni 85 D1
Fisterra 34 A2
Fitero 36 C3
Fities 82 C3
Fitjar 104 A2
Fiuggi 63 F3
Fiumicino 63 E3
Fivemiletown 13 D2
Fivizzano 60 B3
Fjällåsen 94 C4
Fjällbacka 105 D4
Fjällnäs 101 D2
Fjärdhundra 106 B3
Fjærland 100 A3
Fjätervålen 101 D3
Fjelie 108 C3
Fjellerup 108 B2
Fjerritslev 108 A2
Fjerze 76 C3
Flå 104 C2
Fladså 108 A3
Fladungen 52 B3
Flaine 27 E4
Flakk 100 C2
Flåm 104 B2
Flamborough
  Head 7 E1
Flambourári 82 C1
Flámbouro
  (Makedonía) 79 D3
Flámbouro
  (Makedonía) 80 B2
Flamignano 63 F2
Flamouriá 79 E3
Flannan I 2 A2
Flåsjön 101 F1
Flåten 94 C2
Flatey 96 A1
Flatråker 104 A2
Flattnitz 59 F2
Flatval 100 C1
Flèche, la 23 E4
Fleetwood 6 B1
Flekkefjord 104 A4
Flen 106 A4
Flensborg Fjord 108 A4
Flensburg 48 A1
Flers 18 C4
Flesberg 104 C3
Flesnes 94 A3
Fleurance 28 C4
Fleurier 27 D3
Fleurus 50 C4
Fleury 19 F4
Fleury-sur-Andelle 19 E3
Fléves, N 87 F2

Flevoland 16 C2
Flexenpaß 58 B2
Flims Waldhaus 58 B2
Flint 6 B2
Flisa 105 D2
Flix 37 E4
Flixecourt 19 F2
Flize 20 C2
Floda 105 F2
Flogny 26 B1
Flöha 53 E3
Flomohóri 87 D4
Flora 77 F3
Florac 29 F3
Flor da Rosa 38 C3
Florennes 50 C4
Florensac 30 A4
Florenville 20 C2
Florešty 113 E3
Floriáda 82 C2
Floridia 69 D4
Flórina 79 D2
Flórina (Nomos) 79 D3
Florø 104 A1
Flörsheim-
  Dalsheim 54 C1
Flötningen 101 D3
Floúda, Akr 92 C1
Floúnda 91 E3
Flüelapass 58 B2
Flüelen 58 A2
Flühli 27 F3
Flumendosa 66 C3
Flumen, R 37 D3
Flumet 27 D4
Fluminimaggiore 66 A4
Flums 58 B2
Fluvià, R 32 B3
Foča 76 A1
Foça 115 E4
Foce Verde 63 F3
Fochabers 3 D3
Fockbek 48 A2
Focşani 113 E4
Fódele 91 D3
Foggia 64 C3
Föglö 106 C3
Fohnsdorf 57 D4
Föhr 47 F1
Foiano della
  Chiana 61 D4
Foinaven 2 C2
Foix 32 A2
Fojnica (Bosna i
  Hercegovina) 75 F1
Fojnica (Bosna i
  Hercegovina) 75 F2
Fokí 83 E4
Fokstuhø 100 C3
Folda 97 E1
Foldereid 97 D4
Foldfjorden 97 D4
Foleá 80 C2
Folégandros 91 D1
Folégandros, N 91 D1
Følen 104 A3
Folgaria 59 D4
Folgefonna 104 B2
Folgoët, le 22 A2
Folgoso de la
  Ribera 35 D2
Foligno 63 E1
Folkestad 100 A3
Folkestone 11 D3
Follafoss 101 D1
Folldal 100 C3
Follebu 104 C1
Follina 59 E3
Föllinge 101 E1
Follonica 62 C1
Folmava 56 B1
Folói 86 C2
Fombellida 35 F4
Fond-de-France,
  le 31 D1
Fondevila 34 B3
Fondi 63 F3
Fondo 59 D3
Fonfría (Aragón) 37 D4
Fonfría (Castilla-
  León) 35 D4
Fongen 101 D2
Fonn 100 A3
Fonni 66 B3

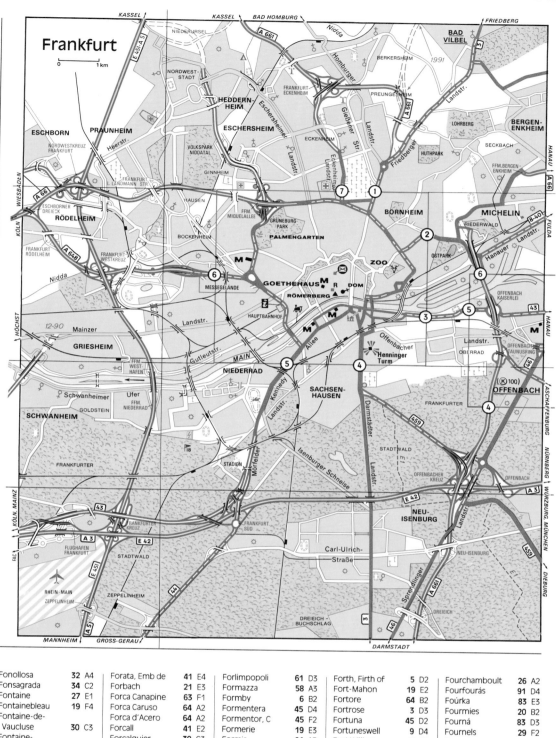

Frankfurt

Fonollosa 32 A4
Fonsagrada 34 C2
Fontaine 27 E1
Fontainebleau 19 F4
Fontaine-de-
  Vaucluse 30 C3
Fontaine-
  Française 26 C2
Fontaine-Henry 18 C3
Fontaine-le-Dun 19 D2
Fontanigorda 60 A3
Fonte Longa 34 B4
Fontenay 26 B2
Fontenay-le-
  Comte 24 C3
Fontenay-
  Trésigny 19 F4
Fontevraud-
  l'Abbaye 25 D2
Fontfroide,
  Abbaye de 32 B2
Fontgombault 25 D3
Fontibre 35 F2
Fontiveros 39 F1
Fontoy 21 D3
Font-Romeu 32 A2
Fontvieille 30 B4
Fonz 37 E3
Fonzaso 59 D3
Foppolo 58 B3

Forata, Emb de 41 E4
Forbach 21 E3
Forca Canapine 63 F1
Forca Caruso 64 A2
Forca d'Acero 64 A2
Forcall 41 E2
Forcalquier 30 C3
Forcarei 34 A2
Forchheim 55 F1
Forclaz, Col de la 27 E4
Forcola di Mte
  Rest 59 E3
Førde 100 A3
Førdefjorden 104 A1
Förderstedt 52 C1
Fordingbridge 9 E3
Fordongianus 66 B3
Foreland 9 F3
Forenza 64 C3
Foresta di Burgos 66 B2
Føresvik 104 A3
Forêt d'Orient, Lac
  de la 26 B1
Forez, Monts du 29 F1
Forfar 5 D1
Forges-les-Eaux 19 E3
Forggensee 55 F4
Forio 64 A4
Forli 61 D3
Forli del Sannio 64 A2

Forlimpopoli 61 D3
Formazza 58 A3
Formby 6 B2
Formentera 45 D4
Formentor, C 45 F2
Formerie 19 E3
Formia 64 A3
Formigine 60 C2
Fornaci di Barga 60 C3
Fornells 45 F1
Forni Avoltri 59 E2
Forni di Sopra 59 E3
Forno di Zoldo 59 E3
Fornos de
  Algodres 38 C1
Fornovo di Taro 60 B2
Forøy 97 E2
Forøyar 96 A3
Forres 3 D3
Forsa 101 F3
Forserum 109 D1
Forshaga 105 E3
Forsnes 100 B1
Forssa 107 E2
Forst 53 F1
Forte dei Marmi 60 B3
Forth 55 F1
Forth R 4 C2
Forth Bridges 5 D2

Forth, Firth of 5 D2
Fort-Mahon 19 E2
Fortore 64 B2
Fortrose 3 D3
Fortuna 45 D2
Fortuneswell 9 D4
Fort William 2 C4
Forvik 97 D3
Fos (Ariège) 37 F2
Fos (Bouches-du-
  Rhône) 30 C4
Foscagno, Pso di 58 C3
Fosnavåg 100 A2
Fossacesia 64 B2
Fossano 31 E2
Fossat, le 37 F1
Fossbakken 94 B3
Fosses 50 C4
Fossli 104 B2
Fossombrone 61 E3
Fotiná 79 D4
Fotolívos 80 B2

Fouesnant 22 B3
Foug 21 D4
Fougères 23 D3
Fougerolles 27 D1
Foula 3 E2
Foulness Pt 11 D2
Fountains Abbey 6 C1
Fouras 24 B4

Fourchamboult 26 A2
Fourfourás 91 D4
Foúrka 83 E3
Fourmies 20 B2
Fourná 83 D3
Fournels 29 F2
Fournés 90 B3
Foúrni
  (Dodekánissa) 89 E2
Fourni (Kriti) 91 E3
Foúrni
  (Pelopónissos) 87 E2
Fourniá, Akr 85 E2
Foúrni, N 89 E2
Fours 26 B3
Fousseret, le 37 F1
Foústani 79 E2
Fowey 8 B4
Foxford 12 B2
Foyers 2 C4
Foyle, L 13 D1
Foyle, R 13 D1
Foz 34 C1
Foz do Arelho 38 A3
Foz do Douro 34 A4
Foz Giraldo 38 C2
Frabosa Soprana 31 F3
Fraddon 8 B4
Fraga 37 E4
Frailes 44 A3

| | | | | | | | | | | |
|---|---|---|---|---|---|---|---|---|---|---|
| Fraize | 27 E1 | Fratta Polesine | 61 D2 | Frêne, Col du | 31 D1 | Friesack | 49 D4 | Froússa | 82 C2 | Fuente el Fresno | 40 A4 | Furci | 64 B2 |
| Fram | 70 C1 | Frauenfeld | 58 A1 | Freren | 17 E2 | Friesland | 16 C1 | Frövi | 105 F3 | Fuenteguinaldo | 39 D2 | Furkapass | 58 A3 |
| Frammersbach | 52 B4 | Frauenkirchen | 57 F3 | Freshford | 12 C4 | Friesoythe | 17 E1 | Frøya | 100 B1 | Fuente la Higuera | 45 D1 | Furnace | 4 B2 |
| Fræna | 100 B2 | Frauenstein | 53 E3 | Freshwater | 9 E3 | Frigiliana | 44 A4 | Frøyfjorden | 100 B1 | Fuentelapeña | 39 E1 | Furnás | 45 D3 |
| Francavilla al Mare | 64 A1 | Frechen | 17 E4 | Fresnay-sur- | | Frihetsli | 94 c3 | Frøysjøen | 100 A3 | Fuente Obéjuna | 43 E1 | Fürstenau | 17 E2 |
| Francavilla di Sicilia | 69 D3 | Frechilla | 35 E4 | Sarthe | 23 F3 | Friis veien | 100 C3 | Fruges | 19 F1 | Fuente Palmera | 43 E2 | Fürstenberg | 49 D3 |
| Francavilla | | Freckenhorst | 17 F3 | Fresne-St-Mamès | 27 D2 | Frikes | 82 B4 | Fruška | 72 b2 | Fuentepinilla | 36 B3 | Fürstenfeld | 57 F4 |
| Fontana | 65 E4 | Fredensborg | 108 C3 | Fresnes-en- | | Frilingiánika | 90 A1 | Frutigen | 27 E3 | Fuentesaúco | 39 E1 | Fürstenfeldbruck | 55 F3 |
| Francavilla in Sinni | 65 D4 | Fredericia | 108 B3 | Woëvre | 20 C3 | Frinton-on-Sea | 11 D2 | Frýdek-Mistek | 112 B3 | Fuentes de | | Fürstenlager | 54 C1 |
| Francker | 16 C1 | Frederikshavn | 108 B1 | Fresno Alhándiga | 39 E1 | Friol | 34 B2 | Fteliá | 80 C2 | Andalucía | 43 E2 | Fürstenwalde | 49 E4 |
| Francofonte | 69 D4 | Frederikssund | 108 C3 | Fresvikbreen | 104 B1 | Fristad | 109 D1 | Ftéri (Makedonía) | 79 E4 | Fuentes de | | Fürstenwerder | 49 E3 |
| Francoli, R | 37 F4 | Frederiksværk | 108 C3 | Freudenberg (Baden- | | Fritsla | 108 C1 | Ftéri | | Ayódar | 41 E3 | Fürstenzell | 56 C2 |
| Francorchamps | 51 D4 | Fredrika | 102 A1 | Württemberg) | 55 D1 | Fritzlar | 52 A3 | (Pelopónissos) | 86 C1 | Fuentes de Ebro | 37 D4 | Furtei | 66 B3 |
| Frändefors | 105 D4 | Fredriksberg | 105 E3 | Freudenberg (Nordrhein- | | Friuli-Venezia | | Fthiótida | 83 E3 | Fuentes de León | 43 D1 | Fürth | 55 E1 |
| Frangádes | 82 C1 | Fredrikstad | 105 D3 | Westfalen) | 17 F4 | Giulia | 59 E3 | Fucecchio | 60 C4 | Fuentes de Nava | 35 E3 | Furth | 56 B1 |
| Frangísta | 83 D3 | Fregenal de la | | Freudenstadt | 54 C3 | Frizington | 5 D4 | Fuencaliente (Castilla- | | Fuentes de Oñoro | 39 D1 | Furtwangen | 54 C3 |
| Frangokástelo | 90 B4 | Sierra | 42 C1 | Frévent | 19 F2 | Frodsham | 6 B2 | la-Mancha) | 43 F1 | Fuentes de Ropel | 35 D3 | Furudal | 101 E4 |
| Frangy | 27 D4 | Fregene | 63 E3 | Freyburg | 52 C2 | Frogner | 105 D3 | Fuencaliente (Is | | Fuentes de | | Furuflaten | 94 C2 |
| Frankenberg (D) | 52 A3 | Fréhel, Cap | 22 C2 | Freyenstein | 48 C3 | Frohavet | 100 C1 | Canarias) | 42 A4 | Valdepero | 35 F3 | Fuscaldo | 67 E2 |
| Frankenberg | | Frei | 100 B2 | Freyung | 56 C2 | Frohburg | 53 D2 | Fuendejalón | 36 C3 | Fuentidueña | 35 F4 | Fusch | 59 E1 |
| (DDR) | 53 E3 | Freiberg | 53 E3 | Fri | 93 D3 | Frohnleiten | 57 E4 | Fuendetodos | 37 D4 | Fuentidueña de | | Fuschl | 56 C3 |
| Frankenburg | 56 C3 | Freiberger Mulde | 53 D2 | Frias | 36 A2 | Froissy | 19 F3 | Fuengirola | 43 F4 | Tajo | 40 B3 | Fuseta | 42 B3 |
| Frankenmarkt | 56 C3 | Freiburg (Baden- | | Frias de Albarracin | 41 D2 | Froitzheim | 51 D3 | Fuenlabrada | 40 A2 | Fuerte del Rey | 44 A2 | Fushë Arrez | 76 C3 |
| Frankenstein | 54 C1 | Württemberg) | 54 C4 | Fribourg | 27 E3 | Frome | 9 D3 | Fuenlabrada de | | Fuerteventura | 42 C4 | Fushë Muhur | 76 C3 |
| Frankenthal | 54 C1 | Freiburg | | Fridingen | 55 D3 | Fromentine | 24 A3 | los Montes | 39 F4 | Fügen | 59 D1 | Fusignano | 61 D2 |
| Frankfurt am Main | 52 A4 | (Niedersachsen) | 48 A2 | Friedberg (A) | 57 F3 | Frómista | 35 F3 | Fuenmayor | 36 B2 | Fuglebjerg | 108 B4 | Füssen | 55 E4 |
| Frankfurt an der | | Freienhufen | 53 E1 | Friedberg (Bayern) | 55 F3 | Fronteira | 38 C2 | Fuensalida | 40 A3 | Fugløysundet | 94 C2 | Fustiñana | 36 C3 |
| Oder | 49 F4 | Freilassing | 56 C3 | Friedberg | | Frontenay-Rohan- | | Fuensanta de | | Fulda | 52 B3 | Futa, Pso della | 60 C3 |
| Fränk Rezat | 55 E2 | Freilingen | 51 F4 | (Hessen) | 52 A4 | Rohan | 24 C4 | Martos | 43 F2 | Fulda R | 52 B3 | Futog | 72 C2 |
| Fränk Saale | 52 B4 | Freising | 55 F3 | Friedeburg | 47 E3 | Frontenhausen | 56 B2 | Fuensanta, Emb | | Fulgatore | 68 A3 | Futrikelv | 94 B2 |
| Františkovy Lázně | 53 D4 | Freistadt | 57 D2 | Friedersdorf | 49 E4 | Frontera | 42 A4 | de la | 44 C1 | Fulpmes | 59 D2 | Fuzine | 70 B3 |
| Franzburg | 49 D1 | Freital | 53 E2 | Friedland (D) | 52 B2 | Frontignan | 30 A4 | Fuente-Alamo | 45 D1 | Fulufjället | 101 D4 | Fyn | 108 B4 |
| Franz-Josephs- | | Freiwalde | 53 E1 | Friedland (DDR) | 49 D2 | Fronton | 29 D3 | Fuente Alamo | 45 D2 | Fumay | 20 B2 | Fyne, L | 4 B2 |
| Höhe | 59 E2 | Freixedas | 38 C1 | Friedrichroda | 52 B3 | Frosinone | 63 F3 | Fuentecén | 35 F4 | Fumel | 28 C3 | Fynshav | 108 B4 |
| Frascati | 63 E3 | Freixido | 34 C3 | Friedrichshafen | 55 D4 | Frosolone | 64 B3 | Fuente de Cantos | 43 D1 | Funäsdalen | 101 D2 | Fyresdal | 104 B3 |
| Frascineto | 67 E2 | Freixo de Espada à | | Friedrichskoog | 47 F2 | Frösön | 101 E2 | Fuente del | | Funchal | 42 A3 | Fyresvatn | 104 B3 |
| Frasdorf | 56 B3 | Cinta | 39 D1 | Friedrichsort | 48 A1 | Frosta | 100 C1 | Maestre | 43 D1 | Fundão | 38 C2 | Fyrkat | 108 B2 |
| Fraserburgh | 3 E3 | Fréjus | 31 D4 | Friedrichstadt | 47 F1 | Frostavallen | 109 D3 | Fuente de Pedro | | Funes | 59 D2 | | |
| Frasno, Pto del | 36 C4 | Fréjus, Tunnel du | 31 D1 | Friedrichsthal | 54 B2 | Frøstrup | 108 A2 | Naharro | 40 B3 | Fuorn, Pso dal | 58 C3 | | |
| Fratel | 38 C3 | Frenchpark | 12 C3 | Friesach | 57 D4 | Frouard | 21 D4 | Fuente de Piedra | 43 E3 | Furadouro | 38 B1 | | |

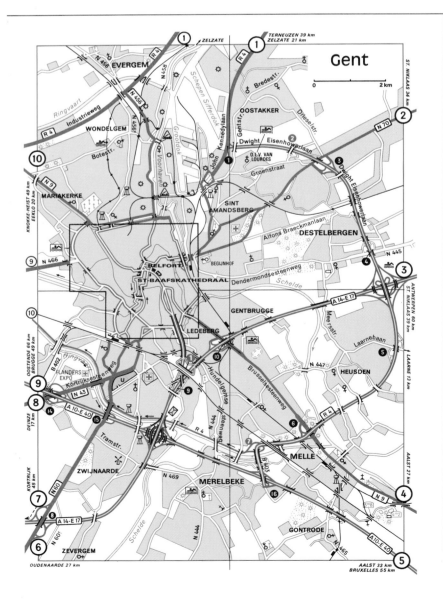

## G

| | | | | | | |
|---|---|---|---|---|---|---|
| Gaaldorf | 57 D4 | Galapagar | 40 A2 | Gallur | 36 C3 |
| Gabarret | 28 B3 | Galarinós | 80 A3 | Gälöfjärden | 106 B4 |
| Gabela | 75 F2 | Galaroza | 42 C2 | Galston | 4 C2 |
| Gaberl-Sattel | 57 E4 | Galashiels | 5 D2 | Galten | 108 B3 |
| Gabia la Grande | 44 A3 | Galatádes | 79 E3 | Galtür | 58 C2 |
| Gabicce Mare | 61 E3 | Galatáki | 84 A3 | Galty Mts | 14 C3 |
| Gabriel y Galán, | | Galatás (Argolída) | 87 E2 | Galveias | 38 B3 |
| Emb de | 39 E2 | Galatás (Korinthía) | 87 D1 | Gálvez | 40 A3 |
| Gabrovka | 70 B2 | Galati | 113 E4 | Galway | 12 B3 |
| Gabrovo | 115 D2 | Galatina | 65 F4 | Galway (Co) | 12 B3 |
| Gacé | 19 D4 | Galatini | 79 D3 | Galway B | 12 B4 |
| Gacilly, la | 23 D4 | Galátista | 80 A3 | Gamaches | 19 E2 |
| Gacko | 76 A2 | Galatone | 65 F4 | Gambarie | |
| Gad'ač | 113 F1 | Galaxidi | 83 E4 | d'Aspromonte | 67 E4 |
| Gäddede | 97 E4 | Galdakao | 36 B1 | Gaming | 57 D3 |
| Gadebusch | 48 B2 | Galdhøpiggen | 100 B3 | Gamleby | 109 E1 |
| Gádor | 44 B3 | Galeata | 61 D3 | Gammelstaden | 98 C3 |
| Gádor, Sa de | 44 B3 | Galegos | 38 C3 | Gammertingen | 55 D3 |
| Gadžin Han | 77 E1 | Galende | 34 C3 | Campenjoch | 58 C3 |
| Găeşti | 115 D1 | Galera | 44 B2 | Gams | 58 B2 |
| Gaeta | 64 A3 | Galiano del Capo | 65 F4 | Gamvik | 95 E1 |
| Gaeta, Golfo di | 64 A3 | Galibier, Col du | 31 D1 | Gamzigrad | 73 E4 |
| Gagarin | 111 F2 | Galicia | 34 B2 | Ganacker | 56 B2 |
| Gaggenau | 54 C2 | Galičica | 77 D4 | Gand | 50 B3 |
| Gagnef | 105 F2 | Galičnik | 77 D3 | Gándara | 34 B1 |
| Gail | 59 E2 | Galikós | 79 F3 | Ganderkesee | 17 F1 |
| Gailbergsattel | 59 E2 | Galipsós | 80 B2 | Gandesa | 41 F1 |
| Gaildorf | 55 D2 | Galisteo | 39 D2 | Gandía | 41 E4 |
| Gailey | 9 E1 | Galiz, Pto de | 43 D4 | Gandino | 58 B4 |
| Gaillac | 29 D3 | Gallarate | 60 A1 | Gandria | 58 A4 |
| Gaillimh | 12 B3 | Gallardon | 19 E4 | Gangáles | 91 D4 |
| Gaillon | 19 E3 | Gallargues | 30 B3 | Ganges | 29 F3 |
| Gainsborough | 7 D2 | Gállego, R | 37 D3 | Gangi | 68 C3 |
| Gairloch | 2 B3 | Galley Head | 14 B4 | Gangkofen | 56 B2 |
| Gaj | 73 D2 | Galliate | 60 A1 | Gannat | 26 A4 |
| Gajdobra | 72 B2 | Gallipoli | 65 F4 | Gänserndorf | 57 F2 |
| Gajsin | 113 E2 | Gällivare | 98 B2 | Gañuelas | 45 D2 |
| Gajvoron | 113 E3 | Gallneukirchen | 57 D2 | Gap | 31 D2 |
| Gakovo | 72 B1 | Gällö | 101 E2 | Garabit, Viaduc de | 29 F2 |
| Galan | 37 E1 | Gallo, C | 68 B2 | Garajonay | 42 A4 |
| Galanádo | 88 C3 | Gallocanta, L de | 41 D1 | Garajonay (Parque | |
| Galanianá | 90 A2 | Gallo, R | 41 D2 | Nac) | 42 A4 |
| Galanta | 112 A3 | Galloway Forest | | Gara, L | 12 C3 |
| | | Park | 4 C3 | Garching | 56 B3 |
| | | Gallspach | 56 C3 | Garcia | 37 E4 |

| | | | | | | |
|---|---|---|---|---|---|---|
| Garcia de Sola, Emb de | 39 F4 | Garpenberg | 105 F3 | | | |
| Garciaz | 39 E3 | Garphyttan | 105 F4 | | | |
| Gard (Dépt) | 30 B3 | Garraf | 32 A4 | | | |
| Gard R | 30 B3 | Garrafe de Torio | 35 D2 | | | |
| Garda | 60 C1 | Garray | 36 B3 | | | |
| Garda, L di | 58 C4 | Garrel | 17 E1 | | | |
| Gardanne | 30 C4 | Garrovillas | 39 D3 | | | |
| Gårdby | 109 E2 | Garrucha | 44 C3 | | | |
| Garde | 109 F4 | Gars | 57 E2 | | | |
| Garde-Freinet, la | 31 D4 | Gartempe | 25 E4 | | | |
| Gardelegen | 48 C4 | Gartow | 48 C3 | | | |
| Gardermoen | 105 D3 | Gartz | 49 E3 | | | |
| Gardiken | 97 F3 | Garvagh | 13 D1 | | | |
| Gardiki | 83 D3 | Garvão | 42 A2 | | | |
| Garding | 47 F2 | Garve | 2 C3 | | | |
| Gardjönäs | 97 F3 | Garynahine | 2 B2 | | | |
| Gärdnäs | 101 E1 | Garz | 49 D1 | | | |
| Gardone Riviera | 60 C1 | Gaschurn | 58 B2 | | | |
| Gardone Val Trompia | 60 B1 | Gassino Torinese | 31 E1 | | | |
| Gärdslösa | 109 E2 | Gastoúni | 86 B1 | | | |
| Gardunha, Sa da | 38 C2 | Gata (Extremadura) | 39 D2 | | | |
| Garður | 96 A2 | Gata (Valencia) | 45 E1 | | | |
| Garešnica | 71 D2 | Gata, C de | 44 C4 | | | |
| Garessio | 31 F3 | Gata, Sa de | 39 D2 | | | |
| Garforth | 7 D2 | Gatčina | 111 D1 | | | |
| Gargaliáni | 86 B3 | Gatehouse of Fleet | 4 C3 | | | |
| Gargano, Promontorio del | 64 C2 | Gateshead | 5 E3 | | | |
| Garganta | 44 B2 | Gattinara | 31 F1 | | | |
| Garganta del Chorro | 43 E3 | Gattorna | 60 A3 | | | |
| Garganta del Escalar | 37 E2 | Gatwick Airport | 10 C3 | | | |
| Garganta la Olla | 39 E2 | Gaucín | 43 E4 | | | |
| Gargantas | 40 C2 | Gauja | 110 C2 | | | |
| Gargantas del Sil | 34 B2 | Gaula | 100 C2 | | | |
| Gargellen | 58 B2 | Gauldalen | 100 C2 | | | |
| Gargilesse | 25 E3 | Gaulstad | 101 D1 | | | |
| Gargnano | 58 C4 | Gausta | 104 C3 | | | |
| Gargnäs | 98 A3 | Gauting | 56 A3 | | | |
| Garigliano | 64 A3 | Gavà | 32 A4 | | | |
| Gariglione, Mte | 67 F3 | Gavardo | 60 B1 | | | |
| Garípa | 91 E4 | Gavarnie | 37 E2 | | | |
| Garlasco | 60 A2 | Gavarnie, Cirque de | 37 E2 | | | |
| Garlin | 28 B4 | Gavdopoúla, N | 90 B4 | | | |
| Garlstorf | 48 B3 | Gávdos, N | 90 C4 | | | |
| Garmisch-Parten-kirchen | 55 F4 | Gave d'Oloron | 28 A4 | | | |
| Garona, R | 37 F2 | Gavi | 60 A2 | | | |
| Garonne | 28 B2 | Gavião | 38 B3 | | | |
| | | Gavia, Pso di | 58 C3 | | | |
| | | Gavirate | 58 A4 | | | |
| | | Gävle | 106 B2 | | | |

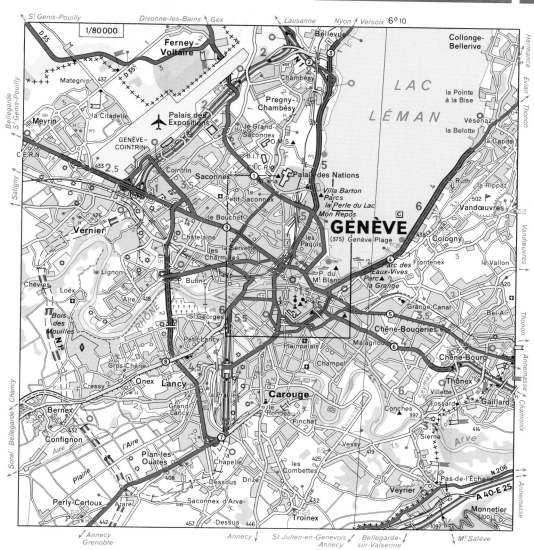

1/80 000

| | | | | | | |
|---|---|---|---|---|---|---|
| Gävleborgs Län | 101 E3 | Gdynia | 110 A4 | Geesthacht | 48 B3 |
| Gävlebukten | 106 B2 | Geaune | 28 B4 | Gefell | 53 D3 |
| Gavoi | 66 B2 | Gebesee | 52 C2 | Géfira (Makedonía) | 79 F3 |
| Gavray | 18 B4 | Gebze | 115 F3 | Géfira (Pelopónissos) | 87 E4 |
| Gávrio | 88 B1 | Gedern | 52 A4 | Gefíria | 83 E2 |
| Gåvsta | 106 B3 | Gediz | 115 F4 | Gefrees | 53 D4 |
| Gåxsjö | 101 E1 | Gediz R | 115 E4 | Gehren | 52 C3 |
| Gazzuolo | 60 C2 | Gedser | 108 C4 | Geilenkirchen | 17 D4 |
| Gdańsk | 110 A4 | Geel | 50 C3 | | |
| Gdov | 111 D1 | Geertruidenberg | 16 C3 | | |

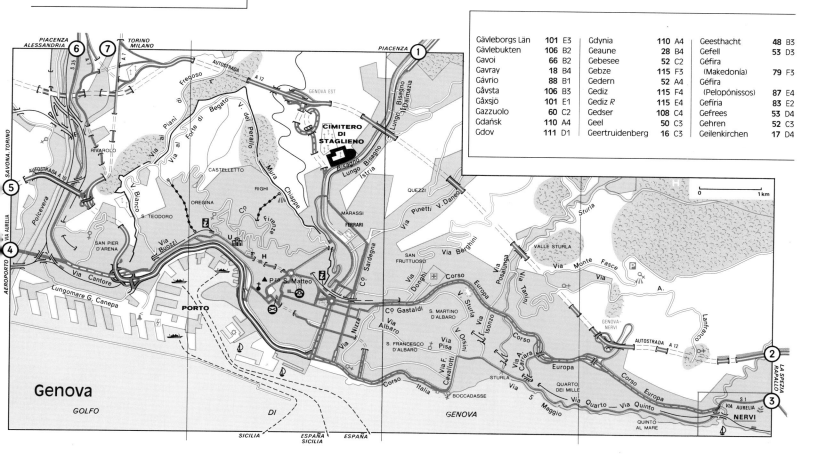

Genova

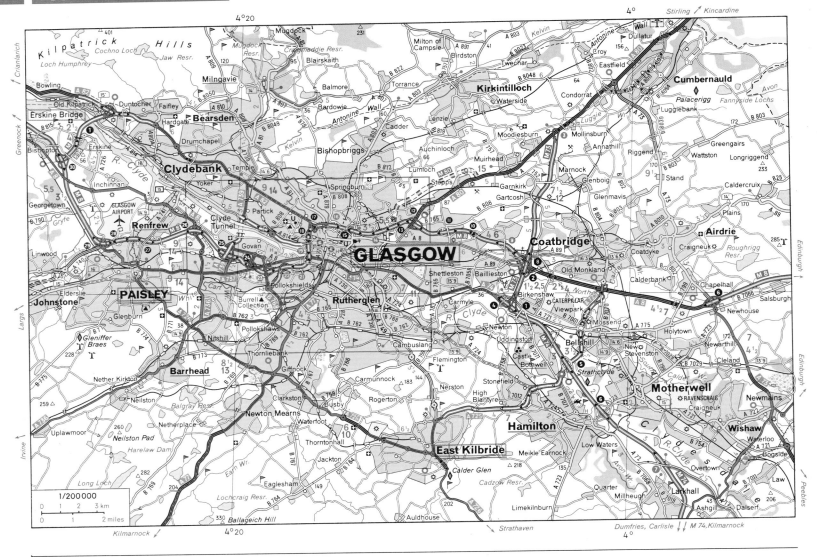

| | | | | | | | | | | | | | |
|---|---|---|---|---|---|---|---|---|---|---|---|---|---|
| Geilo | 104 C2 | Generalisimo, Emb | | Geráki | 87 D3 | Gerswalde | 49 E3 | Gibostad | 94 B2 | Giovinazzo | 65 D3 | Gláma | 96 A1 |
| Geiranger | 100 B3 | del | 41 D3 | Gerakiní | 80 B4 | Gesäuse | 57 D3 | Gibraleón | 42 C2 | Giovi, Pso dei | 60 A3 | Glamis | 5 D1 |
| Geirangerfjorden | 100 B3 | Generalski Stol | 70 C3 | Gerakovoúni | 83 F3 | Gescher | 17 E3 | Gibraltar | 43 E4 | Girifalco | 67 F3 | Glamis Castle | 5 D1 |
| Geisa | 52 B3 | General-Toševo | 115 E2 | Geránia | 87 E1 | Geseke | 17 F3 | Gideå | 102 A2 | Giromagny | 27 E1 | Glamoč | 71 E4 |
| Geiselhöring | 56 B2 | Generoso, Mte | 58 A4 | Gérardmer | 27 D4 | Gesualdo | 64 B3 | Gideälven | 102 A2 | Girona | 32 B3 | Glamorgan | 8 C2 |
| Geisenfeld | 55 F2 | Genève | 27 D4 | Geras | 57 E2 | Geta | 106 C2 | Gieboldehausen | 52 B2 | Gironde | 28 B3 | Glamsbjerg | 108 B3 |
| Geisenhausen | 56 B2 | Genil, R | 43 E2 | Gerbeviller | 21 D4 | Getafe | 40 A2 | Gien | 26 A2 | Gironde (Dépt) | 28 B2 | Glan | 54 B1 |
| Geising | 53 E3 | Genisséa | 81 D2 | Gerbier de Jonc | 30 B2 | Gets, les | 27 E4 | Giengen | 55 E2 | Gironella | 32 A3 | Glandon, |  |
| Geisingen | 54 C4 | Génissiat, Barrage | | Gerbini | 69 D3 | Gettorf | 48 A1 | Giens | 31 D4 | Girvan | 4 C3 | Col du | 31 D1 |
| Geislingen | 55 E2 | de | 27 D4 | Gerbstedt | 52 C2 | Gevelsberg | 17 E4 | Gießen | 51 F3 | Gisburn | 6 C2 | Glandorf | 17 F2 |
| Geismar | 52 B2 | Genk | 50 C3 | Gerena | 43 D2 | Gevgelija | 77 F4 | Giethoorn | 17 D2 | Gislaved | 109 D2 | Glan-Münchweiler | 54 B1 |
| Geisnes | 97 D4 | Genlis | 26 C2 | Gerês | 34 B3 | Gévora, R | 38 C4 | Gifhorn | 48 B4 | Gisors | 19 E3 | Glanshammar | 105 F4 |
| Geithain | 53 D2 | Genna Cruxi | 66 C3 | Gerês, Sa do | 34 B3 | Gevrey- | | Gigha I | 4 B2 | Gissi | 64 B2 | Glarus | 58 A2 |
| Gela | 68 C4 | Gennargentu, Mti | | Geretsried | 56 A3 | Chambertin | 26 C2 | Giglio, I del | 62 C2 | Gistel | 50 A3 | Glasgow | 4 C2 |
| Gelderland | 17 D2 | del | 66 B3 | Gérgal | 44 B3 | Gex | 27 D3 | Giglio Porto | 62 C2 | Githio | 87 D4 | Glas Maol | 3 D4 |
| Geldern | 17 D3 | Gennep | 17 D3 | Geringswalde | 53 E2 | Geysir | 96 B2 | Gignac | 30 A4 | Gittun | 98 A2 | Glastonbury | 9 D3 |
| Geldrop | 16 C4 | Gennes | 24 C2 | Gerlitzen | 59 F2 | Geyve | 115 F3 | Gijón | 35 D1 | Giugliano in | | Glauchau | 53 D3 |
| Geleen | 17 D4 | Génolhac | 29 F3 | Gerlos | 59 D2 | Gföhl | 57 E2 | Gilching | 56 A3 | Campo | 64 B4 | Glava | 105 D3 |
| Gelibolu | 115 E3 | Genova | 60 A3 | Gerlospaß | 59 D1 | Ghedi | 60 B1 | Gilford | 13 E2 | Giulianova | 64 A1 | Glavatičevo | 75 F1 |
| Gelnhausen | 52 A4 | Genova, Golfo di | 60 A4 | Gérmas | 79 D3 | Gheorghe | | Giljevo | 76 C1 | Giurgiu | 115 D2 | Glavičice | 72 B3 |
| Gelsa | 37 D4 | Genova, Val di | 58 C3 | Germering | 55 F3 | Gheorghiu-Dej | 113 D4 | Gilleleje | 108 C3 | Give | 108 A3 | Glavnik | 77 D1 |
| Gelsdorf | 51 E4 | Gent | 50 B3 | Germersheim | 54 C2 | Gheorgheni | 113 D4 | Gillhov | 101 E2 | Givors | 30 B1 | Gledić | 73 D4 |
| Gelsenkirchen | 17 E3 | Genthin | 49 D4 | Gernika-Lumo | 36 B1 | Ghilarza | 66 B3 | Gillingham | | Givry | 26 C3 | Gledićske pl | 73 D4 |
| Gelting | 48 A1 | Gentioux | 29 D1 | Gernrode | 52 C2 | Ghisonaccia | 33 F3 | (Dorset) | 9 D3 | Givry-en-Argonne | 20 C3 | Gleinalmtunnel | 57 E4 |
| Gembloux | 50 C4 | Genzano di | | Gernsbach | 54 C2 | Ghisoni | 33 F3 | Gillingham (Kent) | 11 D2 | Gizéla | 81 D2 | Gleisdorf | 57 E4 |
| Gemeaux | 26 C2 | Lucania | 64 C3 | Gernsheim | 54 C1 | Giali, N | 89 F4 | Gill, L | 12 C2 | Giżycko | 110 B4 | Glen Albyn | 2 C4 |
| Gémenos | 30 C4 | Genzano di Roma | 63 E3 | Gerola Alta | 58 B3 | Giáltra | 83 F3 | Gilze | 16 C3 | Gjalicë, M | 77 D3 | Glenamoy | 12 B2 |
| Gemert | 17 D3 | Georgiani | 79 E3 | Geroliménas | 87 D4 | Gianitsá | 79 E3 | Gimenells | 37 E3 | Gjendesheim | 100 B3 | Glénan, I de | 22 B4 |
| Gemlik | 115 F3 | Georgioúpoli | 90 C3 | Gerolstein | 51 D4 | Gianitsi | 84 C4 | Gimnó | 84 B4 | Gjermundshavn | 104 A2 | Glenariff | 13 E1 |
| Gemona del Friuli | 59 F3 | Georgitsi | 87 D3 | Gerolzhofen | 52 B4 | Giannádes | 82 A1 | Gimo | 106 B3 | Gjesvær | 95 D1 | Glenarm | 13 E1 |
| Gémozac | 28 B1 | Gera | 53 D3 | Gerona | 32 B3 | Giannutri, I di | 63 D2 | Gimont | 28 C4 | Gjirokastër | 114 C4 | Glenbeigh | 14 A4 |
| Gemünd | 51 D4 | Geraardsbergen | 50 B3 | Geroplátanos | 80 B3 | Gianoúli | 81 F2 | Gingst | 49 D1 | Gjøra | 100 C2 | Glen Carron | 2 C3 |
| Gemünden | | Gerabronn | 55 E2 | Gerovo | 70 B3 | Giant's Causeway | 13 E1 | Ginosa | 65 D4 | Gjøv | 96 A3 | Glen Coe | 4 C1 |
| (Bayern) | 52 B4 | Gerace | 67 F4 | Gerri de la Sal | 37 F3 | Giardini | 69 D3 | Ginzling | 59 D2 | Gjøvik | 105 D2 | Glencolumbkille | 12 C1 |
| Gemünden | | Gerakári (Kriti) | 90 C4 | Gers | 28 C3 | Giáros, N | 88 B2 | Giogo di Scarperia | 61 D3 | Gjuhëzës, Kepi i | 114 B4 | Glendalough | 13 D4 |
| (Hessen) | 52 A3 | Gerakári | | Gers (Dépt) | 28 C4 | Giarratana | 69 D4 | Gioia del Colle | 65 E3 | Gla | 83 F4 | Glenelg | 2 B4 |
| Gemünden | | (Makedonia) | 79 F2 | Gersau | 58 A2 | Giarre | 69 D3 | Gioia Tauro | 67 E4 | Gladbeck | 17 E3 | Glenfinnan | 2 B4 |
| (Rheinland-Pfalz) | 54 B1 | Gerakaroú | 80 A3 | Gersfeld | 52 B4 | Giat | 29 E1 | Gióna, Óros | 83 E3 | Gladenbach | 17 F4 | Glengarriff | 14 A4 |
| Genádio | 93 E2 | Gerakás | 87 E4 | Gerstetten | 55 E2 | Giaveno | 31 E1 | Gioúhtas | 91 D4 | Gladstad | 97 D3 | Glenluce | 4 C3 |
| Gençay | 25 D4 | Gérakas, Akr | 84 B2 | Gersthofen | 55 E3 | Giba | 66 B4 | Gioúra, N | 84 B2 | Glafsfjorden | 105 E3 | Glen More | 2 C4 |

| | | |
|---|---|---|
| Glen More Forest Park | 3 | D4 |
| Glennamaddy | 12 | C3 |
| Glenrothes | 5 | D2 |
| Glenties | 12 | C1 |
| Glifa | 83 | F3 |
| Glifáda (Atiki-Piréas) | 87 | F1 |
| Glifáda (Fokida) | 83 | D4 |
| Gliki | 82 | B2 |
| Glikóvrissi | 87 | D4 |
| Glina | 70 | C3 |
| Glittertind | 100 | B3 |
| Gliwice | 112 | A2 |
| Globino | 113 | F2 |
| Globočica | 77 | D2 |
| Gloggnitz | 57 | E3 |
| Głogów | 112 | A2 |
| Glomfjord | 97 | E2 |
| Glomma | 105 | D3 |
| Glommersträsk | 98 | B3 |
| Gloppet | 102 | B2 |
| Glossop | 6 | C2 |
| Gloucester | 9 | D2 |
| Gloucestershire | 9 | D2 |
| Gložan | 72 | B2 |
| Głubczyce | 112 | A2 |
| Glubokoje | 111 | D3 |
| Głuchołazy | 112 | A2 |
| Gluchov | 113 | F1 |
| Glücksburg | 48 | A1 |
| Glückstadt | 48 | A2 |
| Glumsø | 108 | C4 |
| Glušci | 72 | C3 |
| Glyn Ebwy | 9 | D2 |
| Gmund (D) | 56 | A4 |
| Gmünd (Kärnten) | 59 | F2 |
| Gmünd (Niederösterreich) | 57 | D2 |
| Gmunden | 56 | C3 |
| Gnarp | 101 | F3 |
| Gnesta | 106 | B4 |
| Gniezno | 112 | A1 |
| Gnjilane | 77 | D2 |
| Gnoien | 49 | D2 |
| Gnosjö | 109 | D2 |
| Goat Fell | 4 | B2 |
| Goce Delčev | 115 | D3 |
| Goch | 17 | D3 |
| Goðafoss | 96 | B1 |
| Godalming | 9 | F3 |
| Godby | 106 | C3 |
| Godelheim | 52 | A2 |
| Goderville | 19 | D3 |
| Godmanchester | 9 | F1 |
| Gödöllő | 112 | B4 |
| Godovič | 70 | A2 |
| Goduš | 72 | B3 |
| Goeree | 16 | B3 |
| Goes | 16 | B3 |
| Göggingen | 55 | F3 |
| Göhren | 49 | D1 |
| Goirle | 16 | C3 |
| Góis | 38 | B2 |
| Goito | 60 | C1 |
| Gokčanica | 73 | D4 |
| Gökçe | 115 | E3 |
| Gol | 104 | C2 |
| Gola | 71 | D1 |
| Golada | 34 | B2 |
| Golaja Pristan | 113 | F3 |
| Golczewo | 49 | F2 |
| Goldbach | 52 | A4 |
| Goldberg | 48 | C2 |
| Goldenstedt | 17 | F1 |
| Golegã | 38 | B3 |
| Golema reka | 77 | D3 |
| Golemo Selo | 77 | E2 |
| Goleniów | 49 | F2 |
| Goleš | 77 | E2 |
| Golfe-Juan | 31 | E4 |
| Golfo Aranci | 66 | C1 |
| Goli | 70 | B4 |
| Golija (Crna Gora) | 76 | A2 |
| Golija (Srbija) | 76 | C1 |
| Goljak | 77 | D2 |
| Goljaki, M. | 70 | A2 |
| Goljam Perelik | 115 | D3 |
| Göllersdorf | 57 | E2 |
| Golling | 59 | E1 |
| Golo | 33 | F3 |
| Golpejas | 39 | E1 |
| Golspie | 3 | D3 |
| Golßen | 53 | E1 |
| Golubac | 73 | E3 |
| Golubovci | 76 | B3 |
| Golubovec | 70 | C2 |
| Golzow | 49 | D4 |
| Gómara | 36 | B3 |
| Gomáti | 80 | B3 |
| Gombrèn | 32 | A3 |
| Gomecello | 39 | E1 |
| Gomel' | 111 | E4 |
| Gomera | 42 | A4 |
| Gómfi | 83 | D2 |
| Gommern | 52 | C1 |
| Goncelin | 31 | D1 |
| Gondomar (P) | 34 | A4 |
| Gondomar (E) | 34 | A3 |
| Gondrecourt | 20 | C4 |
| Gönen | 115 | E3 |
| Góni | 83 | E1 |
| Goniá | 90 | B3 |
| Goniés | 91 | D3 |
| Gonnesa | 66 | B4 |
| Gonnosfanadiga | 66 | B4 |
| Goole | 7 | D2 |
| Goor | 17 | D2 |
| Goppenstein | 27 | F3 |
| Göppingen | 55 | D2 |
| Gora | 70 | C3 |
| Goražde | 76 | A1 |
| Gördalen | 101 | D3 |
| Gordes | 30 | C3 |
| Gorenja Vas | 70 | A2 |
| Gorey (GB) | 18 | B3 |
| Gorey (IRL) | 15 | D3 |
| Gorgona, I di | 60 | B4 |
| Gorgonzola | 60 | A1 |
| Gorgopótamos | 78 | C4 |
| Gorica (Bosna i Hercegovina) | 75 | E2 |
| Gorica (Makedonija) | 77 | D4 |
| Goričan | 71 | D1 |
| Gorice | 70 | B3 |
| Gorinchem | 16 | C3 |
| Goritsá | 87 | D3 |
| Gorizia | 59 | F3 |
| Gorjanci | 70 | C2 |
| Gorki | 111 | E3 |
| Gorleston-on-Sea | 7 | F4 |
| Görlitz | 53 | F2 |
| Gorna Orjahovica | 115 | D2 |
| Gornja Dobrinja | 72 | C4 |
| Gornja Grabovica | 75 | F1 |
| Gornja Kamenica | 73 | F4 |
| Gornja Klina | 77 | D2 |
| Gornja Ljubovidđa | 75 | F1 |
| Gornja Ljuta | 75 | F1 |
| Gornja Ploča | 70 | C4 |
| Gornja Radgona | 70 | C1 |
| Gornja Sabanta | 73 | D4 |
| Gornja Sanica | 71 | D4 |
| Gornja Slatina | 71 | F3 |
| Gornja Toplica | 72 | C4 |
| Gornja Toponica | 73 | E4 |
| Gornja Tuzla | 72 | B3 |
| Gornje Dubočke | 76 | A2 |
| Gornje Ratkovo | 71 | E4 |
| Gornje Selo | 75 | D2 |
| Gornji Grad | 70 | B2 |
| Gornji Kokoti | 76 | B3 |
| Gornji Kosinj | 70 | C4 |
| Gornji Lapac | 71 | D4 |
| Gornji Lukavac | 76 | A2 |
| Gornji Milanovac | 73 | D4 |
| Gornji Petrovci | 70 | C1 |
| Gornji Podgradci | 71 | D3 |
| Gornji Rajić | 71 | E3 |
| Gornji Stepoš | 73 | E4 |
| Gornji Vakuf | 75 | E1 |
| Gornji Zabar | 71 | F3 |
| Gorno Orizari | 77 | E3 |
| Goro | 61 | D2 |
| Gorodišče | 113 | F2 |
| Gorodn'a | 111 | E4 |
| Gorodok (Belorussija) | 111 | D3 |
| Gorodok (Ukraina) | 112 | C2 |
| Gorredijk | 17 | D1 |
| Gorron | 23 | E3 |
| Gort | 12 | B4 |
| Gorteen | 12 | C3 |
| Gortin | 13 | D2 |
| Górtis | 91 | D4 |
| Gortmore | 12 | B3 |
| Gorumna I | 12 | B3 |
| Goryn' | 113 | D2 |
| Góry Świętokrzyskie | 112 | B2 |
| Görzke | 53 | D1 |
| Gorzów Wielkopolski | 49 | F3 |
| Gosaldo | 59 | D3 |
| Gosau | 59 | F1 |
| Gosausee | 59 | F1 |
| Göschenen | 58 | A3 |
| Goścíno | 49 | F1 |
| Gosforth | 5 | D4 |
| Goslar | 52 | B1 |
| Gospić | 70 | C4 |
| Gospoddinci | 72 | C2 |
| Gosport | 9 | E3 |
| Gößl | 56 | C3 |
| Gossau | 58 | B2 |
| Gosselies | 50 | B4 |
| Gossensass | 59 | D2 |
| Gößnitz | 53 | D3 |
| Gössweinstein | 52 | C4 |
| Gostivar | 77 | D3 |
| Göstling | 57 | D3 |
| Gostyń | 112 | A2 |
| Götaälv | 108 | C1 |
| Göta Kanal | 105 | E4 |
| Göteborg | 108 | C1 |
| Göteborgs och Bohus Län | 108 | C1 |
| Götene | 105 | E4 |
| Gotha | 52 | C3 |
| Gothem | 109 | F4 |
| Gotland | 109 | F4 |
| Gotlands Län | 109 | F4 |
| Gotska Sandön | 106 | C4 |
| Göttingen | 52 | B2 |
| Gottwaldov | 112 | A3 |
| Götzis | 58 | B2 |
| Gouarec | 22 | C3 |
| Gouda | 16 | C3 |
| Gouménissa | 79 | F2 |
| Goumois | 27 | E2 |
| Goúra | 87 | D1 |
| Gourdon | 29 | D2 |
| Gourin | 22 | B3 |
| Gournay-en-Bray | 19 | E3 |
| Goúrnes | 91 | E3 |
| Gourniá | 91 | E4 |
| Gourock | 4 | C2 |
| Gouveja | 38 | C2 |
| Goúves | 91 | E3 |
| Gouviá | 82 | A1 |
| Gouzon | 25 | F4 |
| Goveddari | 75 | E2 |
| Goverla | 113 | D3 |
| Gowienica | 49 | F2 |
| Göynük | 115 | F3 |
| Gozd | 70 | A1 |
| Gozo | 68 | B4 |
| Gozzano | 58 | A4 |
| Graal-Müritz | 48 | C1 |
| Graben-Neudorf | 54 | C2 |
| Grabenstätt | 56 | B3 |
| Grabovac | 75 | E2 |
| Grabovci | 72 | C3 |
| Grabow | 48 | C3 |
| Gračac | 70 | C4 |
| Gračanica (Bosna i Hercegovina) | 71 | F3 |
| Gračanica (Crna Gora) | 76 | B2 |
| Gračanica (Kosovo) | 77 | D2 |
| Gračanica (Srbija) | 72 | C4 |
| Graçay | 25 | E2 |
| Grächen | 27 | F4 |
| Gradac (Crna Gora) | 76 | B1 |
| Gradac (Hrvatska) | 75 | E2 |
| Gradac (Srbija) | 76 | C1 |
| Gradačac | 71 | F3 |
| Gradara | 61 | E3 |
| Gradče, Ez | 77 | F2 |
| Gradec | 71 | D2 |
| Gradefes | 35 | E2 |
| Gradeška pl | 77 | F3 |
| Gradina | 77 | F1 |
| Gradisca d'Isonzo | 59 | F3 |
| Gradište (Hrvatska) | 71 | E2 |
| Gradište (Makedonija) | 77 | E2 |
| Grado (E) | 35 | D1 |
| Grado (I) | 59 | F4 |
| Gradsko | 77 | E3 |
| Gradskovo | 73 | F3 |
| Grafelfing | 56 | A3 |
| Grafenau | 56 | C2 |
| Gräfenberg | 55 | F1 |
| Gräfenhainichen | 53 | D1 |
| Grafenwöhr | 55 | F1 |
| Grafing | 56 | B3 |
| Gragnano | 64 | B4 |
| Grahovo (Bosna i Hercegovina) | 76 | A2 |
| Grahovo (Slovenija) | 70 | A2 |
| Graiguenamanagh | 15 | D3 |
| Grain | 11 | D2 |
| Grainau | 55 | F4 |
| Grajewo | 110 | C4 |
| Gram | 108 | A3 |
| Gramat | 29 | D2 |
| Gramatikó | 83 | E2 |
| Gramatikoú | 83 | D4 |
| Graméni | 80 | B2 |
| Graméno | 82 | B1 |
| Grametten | 57 | D1 |
| Grammichele | 69 | D4 |
| Grámos, Óros | 78 | C3 |
| Grampian | 3 | E4 |
| Grampian Mts | 4 | C1 |
| Gramsh | 77 | D4 |
| Gramzow | 49 | E3 |
| Gran | 105 | D2 |
| Granada | 44 | A3 |
| Granadella | 37 | E4 |
| Granadilla de Abona | 42 | B4 |
| Granard | 12 | C3 |
| Gran Canaria | 42 | B4 |
| Grancey-le-Château | 26 | C2 |
| Grandas | 34 | C1 |
| Grand Ballon | 27 | E1 |
| Grand Bois, Col du | 30 | B1 |
| Grand-Bornand, le | 27 | D4 |
| Grand-Bourg | 25 | E4 |
| Grandcamp-Maisy | 18 | C3 |
| Grand Canal d'Alsace | 27 | E1 |
| Grand Canyon du Verdon | 31 | D3 |
| Grand-Champ | 22 | C4 |
| Grand-Colombier | 27 | D4 |
| Grand-Combe, la | 30 | B3 |
| Grand Combin | 27 | E4 |
| Grand-Couronne | 19 | D3 |
| Grand-Croix | 30 | B1 |
| Grande Casse | 31 | E1 |
| Grande de Europa, Punta | 43 | E4 |
| Grande Dixence, Bge de la | 27 | E4 |
| Grande-Motte, la | 30 | B4 |
| Grande Sassière | 31 | E1 |
| Grandes Rousses | 31 | D1 |
| Grand-Fougeray | 23 | D4 |
| Grand-Lemps, le | 30 | C1 |
| Grand Lieu, L de | 24 | B3 |
| Grand-Lucé, le | 23 | F4 |
| Grand Morin | 20 | A4 |
| Grándola | 42 | A1 |
| Grandpré | 20 | C3 |
| Grand-Pressigny, le | 25 | D3 |
| Grand Rhône | 30 | B4 |
| Grandrieu | 29 | F2 |
| Grand-Serre, le | 30 | C1 |
| Grands Goulets | 30 | C2 |
| Grandval, Bge de | 29 | F2 |
| Grandvilliers | 19 | E3 |
| Grañén | 37 | D3 |
| Grangärde | 105 | F3 |
| Grangemouth | 5 | D2 |
| Grange-Over-Sands | 6 | B1 |
| Grängesberg | 105 | F3 |
| Granges-sur-Vologne | 27 | E1 |
| Granier, Col du | 30 | C1 |
| Granítis | 80 | B1 |
| Granítsa | 83 | D2 |
| Granja (Alentejo) | 42 | C1 |
| Granja (Douro) | 34 | A4 |
| Granja de Torrehermosa | 43 | E1 |
| Granja, Pto de la | 43 | D1 |
| Gränna | 109 | D1 |
| Granollers | 32 | A4 |
| Granön | 102 | A3 |
| Gran Paradiso | 31 | E1 |
| Gran San Bernardo, Colle di | 27 | E4 |
| Gran San Bernardo, Traforo del | 27 | E4 |
| Gran Sasso d'Italia | 63 | F1 |
| Gransee | 49 | D3 |
| Gran Tarajal | 42 | C4 |
| Grantham | 7 | D3 |
| Grantown-on-Spey | 3 | D3 |
| Granville | 18 | B4 |
| Granvin | 104 | B2 |
| Grappa, Mte | 59 | D3 |
| Grasleben | 52 | C1 |
| Grasmere | 5 | D4 |
| Grassano | 65 | D4 |
| Grasse | 31 | E3 |
| Gråstenn | 108 | A4 |
| Grästorp | 108 | C1 |
| Gratangen | 94 | B3 |
| Gratiní | 81 | E2 |
| Gratkorn | 57 | E4 |
| Graubünden | 58 | B2 |
| Grau-du-Roi, le | 30 | B4 |
| Graulhet | 29 | D4 |
| Graus | 37 | E3 |
| Gravalos | 36 | C3 |
| Gravdal | 97 | E1 |
| Grave | 17 | D3 |
| Grave, la | 31 | D1 |
| Gravedona | 58 | B3 |
| Gravelines | 19 | F1 |
| Gravellona-Toce | 58 | A4 |
| Grave, Pointe de | 28 | A1 |
| Gravesend | 11 | D2 |
| Graviá | 83 | E3 |
| Gravina in Puglia | 65 | D3 |
| Gravona | 33 | F3 |
| Gravoúna | 80 | C2 |
| Gray | 26 | C2 |
| Grays Thurrock | 10 | C2 |
| Graz | 57 | E4 |
| Grazalema | 43 | E3 |
| Grazzanise | 64 | A3 |
| Grdelica | 77 | E2 |
| Great Blasket I. | 14 | A3 |
| Great Driffield | 7 | D1 |
| Great Dunmow | 11 | D2 |
| Great Grimsby | 7 | E2 |
| Great Malvern | 9 | D1 |
| Great Ormes Head | 6 | A2 |
| Great Ouse | 7 | E3 |
| Great Torrington | 8 | C3 |
| Great Yarmouth | 7 | F4 |
| Grebbestad | 105 | D4 |
| Greccio | 63 | E2 |
| Greding | 55 | F2 |
| Gredos | 39 | F2 |
| Gredos, Sa de | 39 | F2 |
| Greenhead | 5 | D3 |
| Greenlaw | 5 | E2 |
| Greenock | 4 | C2 |
| Greenodd | 6 | B1 |
| Greggio | 31 | F1 |
| Gregolímano | 83 | F3 |
| Greifenburg | 59 | D2 |
| Greiffenberg | 49 | E3 |
| Greifswald | 49 | D1 |
| Greifswalder Bodden | 49 | D1 |
| Grein | 57 | D2 |
| Greiz | 53 | D3 |
| Grenå | 108 | B2 |
| Grenade (Haute-Garonne) | 29 | D4 |
| Grenade (Landes) | 28 | B4 |
| Grenchen | 27 | E2 |
| Grenoble | 30 | C1 |
| Grense Jakobselv | 95 | F2 |
| Gréoux-les-Bains | 31 | D3 |
| Gressåmoen | 101 | E1 |
| Gresse | 30 | C2 |
| Gressoney-la-Trinite | 27 | F4 |
| Gressoney-St-Jean | 27 | F4 |
| Gresten | 57 | D3 |
| Grésy | 31 | D1 |
| Greußen | 52 | C2 |
| Greve | 61 | D4 |
| Greven | 17 | E2 |
| Grevená | 79 | D4 |
| Grevená (Nomos) | 79 | D4 |
| Grevenbroich | 17 | D4 |
| Grevenbrück | 17 | F4 |
| Grevenítio | 82 | C1 |
| Grevesmühlen | 48 | B2 |
| Greve Strand | 108 | C3 |
| Greyabbey | 13 | E2 |
| Greystones | 13 | E4 |
| Grez-en-Bouère | 23 | E3 |
| Grezzana | 60 | C1 |
| Grgur | 70 | B4 |
| Griá, Akr | 88 | B1 |
| Grianan of Aileach | 13 | D1 |
| Griebenow | 49 | D2 |
| Gries | 59 | D2 |
| Gries im Sellrain | 58 | C2 |
| Grieskirchen | 56 | C3 |
| Griffen | 70 | B1 |
| Grignan | 30 | B2 |
| Grignano | 59 | D3 |
| Grignols | 28 | B3 |
| Grimaldi | 67 | E3 |
| Grimaud | 31 | D4 |
| Grimma | 53 | D2 |
| Grimmen | 49 | D2 |
| Grimone, Col de | 30 | C2 |
| Grimsby | 100 | C3 |
| Grimselpass | 27 | F3 |
| Grimsey | 96 | B1 |
| Grimstad | 104 | B4 |
| Grindaheim | 104 | C2 |
| Grindavík | 96 | A2 |
| Grindelwald | 27 | F3 |
| Grindsted | 108 | A3 |
| Griñon | 40 | A2 |
| Grintavec | 70 | B2 |
| Gripsholm | 106 | B4 |
| Grisignano | 61 | D1 |
| Gris Nez, Cap | 19 | E1 |

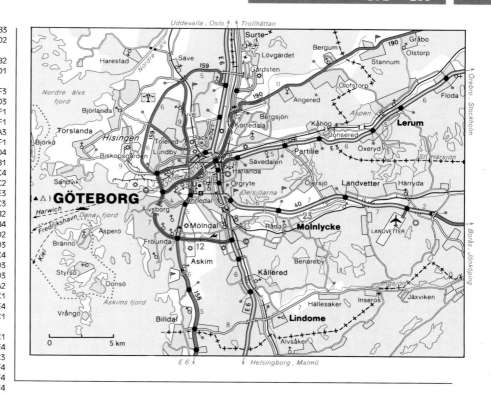

| | | |
|---|---|---|
| Grisolles | 29 | D4 |
| Grisslehamn | 106 | B3 |
| Griva | 79 | E2 |
| Grizáno | 83 | D1 |
| Grk | 71 | F3 |
| Grljan | 73 | F3 |
| Grmec | 71 | D4 |
| Grøa | 100 | B2 |
| Gröbming | 59 | F1 |
| Grocka | 73 | D3 |
| Gröditz | 53 | E2 |
| Grodno | 110 | C4 |
| Groenlo | 17 | D3 |
| Gröer Arber | 56 | B1 |
| Groitzsch | 53 | D2 |
| Groix | 22 | B4 |
| Groix, I de | 22 | B4 |
| Grömitz | 48 | B2 |
| Gronau | 17 | D3 |
| Grönenbach | 55 | E4 |
| Grong | 97 | D4 |
| Grönhögen | 109 | E3 |
| Groningen | 47 | D3 |
| Groningen (Prov) | 47 | D3 |
| Gröningen | 52 | C1 |
| Grönskåra | 109 | E2 |
| Grønsund | 108 | C4 |
| Gropello Cairoli | 60 | A2 |
| Groscavallo | 31 | E1 |
| Grosio | 58 | C3 |
| Grosne | 26 | C3 |
| Gross Beerberg | 52 | C3 |
| Gross Bösenstein | 57 | D4 |
| Großbreitenbach | 52 | C3 |
| Großburgwedel | 48 | A4 |
| Großenbrode | 48 | B1 |
| Großenhain | 53 | E2 |
| Großenzersdorf | 57 | F2 |
| Grosse Pierre | 27 | E1 |
| Grosse Röder | 53 | E2 |
| Grosser Plöner See | 48 | B2 |
| Grosseto | 62 | C1 |
| Gross Feldberg | 51 | F4 |
| Gross-Gerau | 54 | C1 |
| Groß Gerungs | 57 | D2 |
| Großglockner Hochalpenstraße | 59 | E2 |
| Großglockner | 59 | E2 |
| Großhabersdorf | 55 | E1 |
| Groß Ötscher | 57 | E3 |
| Großpetersdorf | 57 | F4 |
| Gross Priel | 57 | D3 |
| Gross Rachel | 56 | C2 |
| Großraming | 57 | D3 |
| Groß Braschen | 53 | E1 |
| Groß Reken | 17 | E3 |
| Großröhrsdorf | 53 | F2 |
| Groß Rosennock | 59 | F2 |
| Grossschönau | 53 | F2 |
| Groß-Schönebeck | 49 | E3 |
| Groß Siegharts | 57 | E2 |
| Gross-Umstadt | 55 | D1 |
| Großvenediger | 59 | E2 |
| Großweil | 56 | A4 |
| Grostenquin | 21 | D3 |
| Grosuplje | 70 | B2 |
| Grötlingbo | 109 | F4 |
| Grøtsundet | 94 | C2 |
| Grotta di Nettuno | 66 | A2 |
| Grottaglie | 65 | E4 |
| Grottaminarda | 64 | B3 |
| Grottammare | 61 | F4 |
| Grotte di Pertosa | 64 | C4 |
| Grotteria | 67 | F4 |
| Grouin, Pte du | 18 | B4 |
| Grove | 34 | A2 |
| Grövelsjön | 101 | D3 |
| Grovfjord | 94 | B3 |
| Grubišno Polje | 71 | D2 |
| Gruda | 76 | A3 |
| Grude | 75 | E2 |
| Grudziądz | 112 | B1 |
| Gruinard B | 2 | C3 |
| Gruissan | 32 | B2 |
| Grums | 105 | E3 |
| Grünau | 56 | C3 |
| Grünberg | 52 | A3 |
| Grünburg | 57 | D3 |
| Grundarfjörður | 96 | A2 |
| Grundforsen | 101 | D4 |
| Grundlsee | 56 | C3 |
| Grundlsee L | 56 | C3 |
| Grundsund | 108 | C1 |
| Grundtjärn | 101 | F2 |
| Grünstadt | 54 | C1 |
| Grünwald | 56 | A3 |
| Grupčin | 77 | D3 |
| Gruyères | 27 | E3 |
| Gruža | 73 | D4 |
| Gruža R | 73 | D4 |
| Grycksbo | 105 | F2 |
| Gryfice | 49 | F2 |
| Gryfino | 49 | E3 |
| Gryllefjord | 94 | B2 |
| Grythyttan | 105 | E3 |
| Grytøya | 94 | B3 |
| Grza | 73 | E4 |
| Gschütt, Paß | 59 | F1 |
| Gstaad | 27 | E3 |
| Gstadt | 56 | B3 |
| Guadahortuna | 44 | A2 |
| Guadaira, R | 43 | E3 |
| Guadazón, R | 40 | C3 |
| Guadajoz, R | 43 | F2 |
| Guadalajara | 40 | B2 |
| Guadalaviar | 41 | D2 |
| Guadalaviar, R | 41 | D2 |
| Guadalcacín, Emb de | 43 | D3 |
| Guadalcanal | 43 | D1 |
| Guadalén, Emb de | 44 | A1 |
| Guadalén, R | 44 | B1 |
| Guadalest | 45 | E1 |
| Guadalete, R | 43 | D4 |
| Guadalfeo, R | 44 | A4 |
| Guadalhorce, R | 43 | E4 |
| Guadalimar, R (Andalucia) | 43 | D3 |
| Guadalimar, R (Andalucia) | 44 | B2 |
| Guadalmellato, Emb de | 43 | F2 |
| Guadalmena, Emb de | 44 | B1 |
| Guadalmena, R | 44 | B1 |
| Guadalmez, R | 43 | F1 |
| Guadalope, R | 41 | E2 |
| Guadalquivir, R | 43 | D3 |
| Guadal, R | 44 | B2 |
| Guadalteba-Guadalhorce, Emb del | 43 | E3 |
| Guadalupe | 39 | E3 |
| Guadalupe, Sa de | 39 | E3 |
| Guadarrama | 40 | A2 |
| Guadarrama, Pto de | 40 | A2 |
| Guadarrama, R | 40 | A2 |
| Guadarrama, Sa de | 40 | A1 |
| Guadarranque, Emb del | 43 | E4 |
| Guadasuar | 41 | E4 |
| Guadiamar, R | 43 | D3 |
| Guadiana Menor, R | 44 | B2 |
| Guadiana, R | 39 | F4 |
| Guadiaro | 43 | E4 |
| Guadiaro, R | 43 | E4 |
| Guadiato, R | 43 | E2 |
| Guadiela, R | 40 | C2 |
| Guadix | 44 | B3 |
| Guajaraz, Emb de | 40 | A3 |
| Gualdo Tadino | 61 | E4 |
| Guara, Sa de | 37 | E3 |
| Guarda | 38 | C1 |
| Guardamar del Segura | 45 | D2 |
| Guardiagrele | 64 | A2 |
| Guardia Sanframondi | 64 | B3 |
| Guardias Viejas | 44 | B4 |
| Guardo | 35 | E2 |
| Guareña | 39 | D4 |
| Guarrizas, R | 44 | A1 |
| Guarromán | 44 | A2 |
| Guastalla | 60 | C2 |
| Gubbio | 61 | E4 |
| Guben | 53 | F1 |
| Guberevac | 73 | D4 |
| Gubin | 53 | F1 |
| Guča | 73 | D4 |
| Guca Gora | 71 | E4 |
| Gudavac | 71 | D3 |
| Gudbrandsdalen | 100 | C3 |
| Guderup | 108 | A4 |
| Gudhjem | 109 | D4 |
| Gudingen | 109 | E1 |
| Gudow | 48 | B3 |
| Gudvangen | 104 | B2 |
| Guebwiller | 27 | E1 |
| Guémené | 22 | B3 |
| Guémené-Penfao | 23 | D4 |
| Güeñes | 36 | B1 |
| Guer | 23 | D3 |
| Guérande | 22 | C4 |
| Guerche-de-Bretagne, la | 23 | D3 |
| Guerche, la | 26 | A3 |
| Guéret | 25 | E4 |
| Guérigny | 26 | A2 |
| Guerlédan, L de | 22 | C3 |
| Guernsey | 18 | A3 |
| Guéthary | 28 | A4 |
| Gueugnon | 26 | B3 |
| Güglingen | 55 | D2 |
| Guglionesi | 64 | B2 |
| Guía | 42 | B4 |
| Guía de Isora | 42 | A4 |
| Guichen | 23 | D3 |
| Guidonia | 63 | E2 |
| Guignes | 19 | E4 |
| Guijo de Granadilla | 39 | D2 |
| Guijuelo | 39 | E2 |
| Guildford | 9 | F3 |
| Guillaumes | 31 | E3 |
| Guillena | 43 | D2 |
| Guillestre | 31 | D2 |
| Guillon | 26 | B2 |
| Guilvinec | 22 | A3 |
| Güimar | 42 | B4 |
| Guimarães | 34 | A4 |
| Guimiliau | 22 | B2 |
| Guînes | 19 | E1 |
| Guingamp | 22 | C2 |
| Guipavas | 22 | A2 |
| Guisborough | 5 | F4 |
| Guiscard | 19 | F3 |
| Guise | 20 | A2 |
| Guissona | 37 | F3 |
| Guist | 7 | F3 |
| Guitiriz | 34 | B1 |
| Guîtres | 28 | B2 |
| Gujan-Mestras | 28 | A2 |
| Gulbene | 110 | C2 |
| Guldborg Sund | 108 | C4 |
| Gullesfjorden | 94 | A3 |
| Gullfoss | 96 | B2 |
| Gullkrona fjärd | 107 | D3 |
| Gullspång | 105 | E4 |
| Gumiel de Hizán | 36 | A3 |
| Gummersbach | 17 | E4 |
| Gundelfingen | 55 | E1 |
| Gundelsheim | 55 | D2 |
| Gunnarn | 97 | F4 |
| Gunnarsbyn | 98 | B3 |
| Gunnärsfjärden | 98 | C3 |
| Gunnarskog | 105 | E3 |
| Gunten | 27 | F3 |
| Günterode | 52 | B2 |
| Guntin de Pallares | 34 | B2 |
| Günzburg | 55 | E3 |
| Gunzenhausen | 55 | E2 |
| Gurk | 70 | A1 |
| Gurk R | 59 | F2 |
| Gurrea de Gállego | 37 | D3 |
| Gusev | 110 | B4 |
| Gusinje | 76 | C2 |
| Guspini | 66 | B3 |
| Güssing | 57 | F4 |
| Güsten | 52 | C1 |
| Güstrow | 48 | C2 |
| Gutcher | 3 | F1 |
| Gutenstein | 57 | E3 |
| Gütersloh | 17 | F3 |
| Gutulia | 100 | D3 |
| Gützkow | 49 | D2 |
| Guyhirn | 10 | C1 |
| Gvardejsk | 110 | B4 |
| Gvarv | 104 | C3 |
| Gvozd | 76 | B2 |
| Gweebarra B | 12 | C1 |
| Gwent | 9 | D2 |
| Gwynedd | 6 | A3 |
| Gy | 27 | D2 |
| Gyöngyös | 112 | B4 |
| Győr | 112 | A4 |
| Gysinge | 106 | A3 |
| Gyula | 112 | C4 |

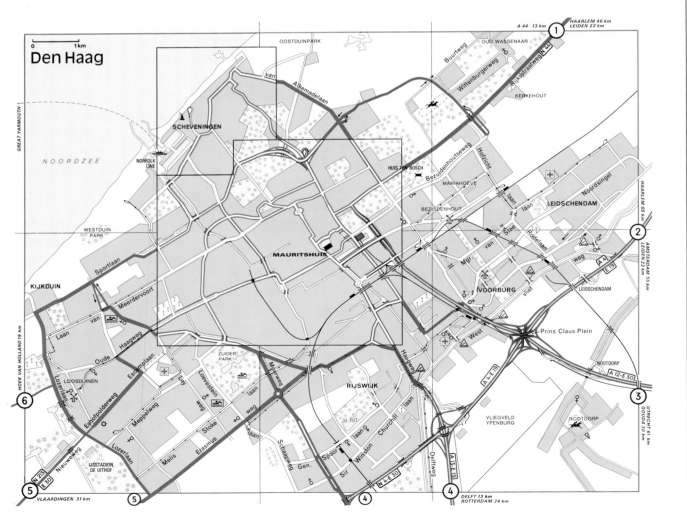

Den Haag

## H

| | | |
|---|---|---|
| Haag (A) | 57 | D3 |
| Haag (D) | 56 | B3 |
| Haag am Hausruck | 56 | C3 |
| Haaksbergen | 17 | D2 |
| Haamstede | 16 | B3 |
| Haapajärvi | 103 | D1 |
| Haapajärvi L | 103 | D1 |
| Haapakoski | 103 | E2 |
| Haapamäki (Keski-Suomen Lääni) | 102 | C3 |
| Haapamäki (Oulun Lääni) | 103 | D1 |
| Haapavesi | 103 | D1 |
| Haapsalu | 110 | B2 |
| Haar | 56 | A3 |
| Haaren | 17 | F3 |
| Haarlem | 16 | B2 |
| Habay | 20 | C2 |
| Habo | 109 | D1 |
| Habsheim | 27 | E1 |
| Hachenburg | 51 | F3 |
| Hachmühlen | 52 | A1 |
| Hackås | 101 | E2 |
| Hadamar | 51 | F4 |
| Haddington | 5 | D2 |
| Hadersdorf | 57 | E2 |
| Haderslev | 108 | A4 |
| Hadleigh | 11 | D2 |
| Hadmersleben | 52 | C1 |
| Hadrian's Wall | 5 | E3 |
| Hadselfjorden | 94 | A3 |
| Hadsten | 108 | B2 |
| Hadsund | 108 | B2 |
| Hadžići | 75 | F1 |
| Haganj | 71 | D2 |
| Hægebostad | 104 | B4 |
| Hagen (Niedersachsen) | 47 | F3 |
| Hagen (Nordrhein-Westfalen) | 17 | E4 |
| Hagenow | 48 | B3 |
| Hagetmau | 28 | B4 |
| Hagfors | 105 | E3 |

Häggdånger 101 F3
Haggenås 101 E2
Hagondange 21 D3
Hague, Cap de la 18 B2
Haguenau 21 E3
Hahn 47 F3
Hahnbach 55 F1
Haigerloch 55 D3
Hailsham 10 C3
Hailuoto 99 D4
Hainaut 50 B4
Hainburg 57 F2
Hainfeld 57 E3
Hainichen 53 E2
Hajdúböszörmény 112 C4
Hajdučica 73 D2
Hajdúszoboszló 112 C4
Hajla 76 C2
Hajnówka 112 C1
Hakarp 109 D3
Hakkas 98 B2
Häkkilä 103 D2
Halámky 57 D2
Halandritsa 86 C1
Halbe 53 E1
Halberstadt 52 C1
Halden 105 D4
Haldensleben 48 C4
Halesowen 9 E1
Halesworth 11 E1
Halhjem 104 A2
Halifax 6 C2
Halikko 107 E2
Halju 95 D4
Halkeró 80 C2
Hálki (Dodekánissa) 93 E1
Halkí (Kikládes) 88 C3
Hálki (Thessalía) 83 E1
Halkiádes 83 E2
Halkída 84 B4
Halkidikí 80 B3
Hálki, N 93 E1
Halkidóna 79 F3
Halkió 85 F4
Halkío 87 D1
Halkodóni, Óros 83 E2
Hallands Län 108 C2
Halle (B) 50 B3
Halle (D) 17 F2
Halle (DDR) 53 D2
Hällefors 105 E3
Hälleforsnäs 105 F4
Hallein 56 C3
Hällekis 105 E4
Hallenberg 17 F4
Hallencourt 19 E2
Halle-Neustadt 53 D2
Hällesjö 101 F2
Hällevadsholm 105 D4
Halligen 47 F1
Hallingdal 104 C2
Hallingskarvet 104 B2
Hall in Tirol 59 D1
Hällnäs 102 A1
Hallsberg 105 F4
Hallstadt 52 C4
Hallstahammar 105 F3
Hallstatt 59 F1
Hallstavik 106 B3
Halluin 19 F1
Halmstad 108 C2
Hals 108 B2
Halsa 100 B2
Halsafjorden 100 B2
Hälsingtuna 101 F3
Halsskov 108 B3
Halstead 11 D2
Halsteren 16 B3
Halsua 102 C2
Haltdålen 101 D2
Haltern 17 E3
Halti-Haldi 94 C3
Halver 17 E4
Ham 19 F2
Hamar 105 D2
Hamarøy 94 A4
Hamburg 48 A3
Hambye 18 B4
Hamdorf 48 A2
Hämeenkyrö 102 C3
Hämeen Lääni 102 C3
Hämeenlinna 107 E2
Hämelerwald 52 B1

Hameln 52 A1
Hamersleben 52 C1
Hamilí, N 92 C2
Hamilton 4 C2
Hamina 103 F4
Hamm 17 E3
Hammarland 106 C3
Hammarstrand 101 F2
Hammaslahti 103 F2
Hammel 108 B3
Hammelburg 52 B4
Hammerdal 101 E2
Hammerfest 95 D1
Hammershus 109 D4
Hamneidet 94 C2
Hamningberg 95 F1
Hamoir 50 C4
Hampshire 9 E3
Hamra 101 E3
Hamra (Reg) 101 E3
Hamre 104 B4
Hamzali 77 F3
Hamzići 75 F2
Hanákia 86 B2
Hanau 52 A4
Handrás 91 F4
Hanerau-Hademarschen 48 A2
Hangö 107 E3
Hangon läntinenselkä 107 D3
Hangö västra fjärd 107 D3
Haniá (Haniá) 90 B3
Hánia (Lakonía) 87 D3
Haniá (Nomos) 90 B3
Hánia (Thessalía) 83 F2
Hani i Hotit 76 B3
Hanión, Kólpos 90 B3
Haniótis 80 B4
Hankamäki 103 E1
Hankasalmen as 103 D3
Hankasalmi 103 D3
Hankensbüttel 48 B4
Hanko 107 E3
Hannover 48 A4
Hannut 50 C4
Hanöbukten 109 D3
Han Pijesak 72 B4
Hansnes 94 C2
Han-sur-Lesse 50 C4
Hanstedt 48 A3
Hanstholm 108 A2
Haparanda 98 C3
Harads 98 B3
Harafjärden 98 C3
Haraldshaugen 104 A3
Haranes 97 D4
Haravgi 79 E3
Harburg (Bayern) 55 E2
Harburg (Hamburg) 48 A3
Hårby 108 B4
Hardangerfjorden 104 A2
Hardangerjøkulen 104 B2
Hardangervidda 104 B2
Hardbakke 104 A1
Hardegg 57 E1
Hardegsen 52 B2
Hardelot 19 E1
Hardenberg 17 D2
Harderwijk 16 C2
Hardheim 55 D1
Hardwick Hall 7 D3
Hareid 100 A2
Harelbeke 50 A3
Haren (D) 17 E1
Haren (NL) 47 D3
Harewood 6 C2
Haria 42 C3
Haringvlietdam 16 B3
Haritoméni 80 B2
Härjångsfjällen 101 D2
Harjavalta 107 D2
Harjunpää 107 D1
Hårkan 101 E2
Härkmeri 102 B3
Harlech 6 A3
Harlesiel 47 E3
Harleston 11 D1
Harlingen 16 C1
Harlow 10 C2
Harmånger 101 F3
Harmanli 115 E3
Härnösand 101 F3

Haro 36 B2
Harokopió 86 C4
Haroldswick 3 F1
Haroué 21 D4
Harøyfjorden 100 A2
Harpenden 9 F2
Harplinge 108 C2
Harpstedt 17 F1
Harris 2 A2
Harrislee 47 F1
Harris, Sd of 2 A3
Harrogate 6 C1
Härryda 108 C1
Harsefeld 48 A3
Harsprånget 98 B2
Harstad 94 B3
Harsvik 96 C4
Hartberg 57 F4
Hårteigen 104 B2
Hartha 53 E2
Hartkjölen 101 E1
Hartland Pt 8 B3
Hartlepool 5 F4
Hartmannsdorf 53 E3
Hartola 103 D3
Harwich 11 D2
Harz 52 B2
Harzgerode 52 C2
Hase 17 E2
Haselünne 17 E2
Haskovo 115 D3
Haslach (A) 56 C2
Haslach (D) 54 C3
Hasle 109 D4
Haslemere 9 F3
Haslev 108 C4
Hasparren 28 A4
Hassela 101 F3
Hasselfelde 52 C2
Hasselt 50 C3
Haßfurt 52 C4
Hässleholm 109 D3
Hastière 50 C4
Hastings 11 D3
Hasvik 95 D1

Hatě 57 E1
Hateg 114 C1
Hatfield 9 F2
Hatherleigh 8 C3
Hattem 17 D2
Hattfjelldal 97 E3
Hattingen 17 E3
Hattula 107 E2
Hattuvaara (Lieksa) 103 F1
Hattuvaara (Ilomantsi) 103 F2
Hatvan 112 B4
Hatvik 104 A2
Hatzí 82 C2
Haubourdin 19 F1
Hauge 104 A4
Haugesund 104 A3
Hauho 107 E2
Haukelifjell 104 B2
Haukeligrend 104 B3
Haukipudas 99 D3
Haukivesi 103 E3
Haukivuori 103 E3
Haunstetten 55 F3
Haus 59 F1
Hausach 54 C3
Hausham 56 A4
Hausjärvi 107 E2
Hautajärvi 99 E2
Hautecombe 27 D4
Haute-Corse 33 F3
Hautefort 29 D1
Haute-Garonne 29 D4
Haute-Loire 29 F2
Haute-Marne 26 C1
Hautes-Alpes 31 D2
Haute-Saône 27 D1
Haute-Savoie 27 D4
Haute-Vienne (Dépt) 29 D1
Hauteville-Lompnes 27 D4
Hautmont 20 B2
Haut-Rhin (Dept) 27 E1
Havant 9 F3
Havári 86 B1

Havdalsfjellet 97 E4
Havdáta 82 B4
Havel 49 D4
Havelange 50 C4
Havelberg 48 C3
Haverfordwest 8 B2
Haverhill 11 D1
Haverö 101 E3
Havneby 108 A4
Havøysund 95 D1
Havraň 53 E3
Havre, Le 19 D3
Hawes 6 C1
Hawick 5 D3
Hawkhurst 11 D3
Hayange 21 D3
Haye-du-Puits, la 18 B3
Haye-Pesnel, la 18 B4
Hayle 8 A4
Hay-on-Wye 9 D1
Haywards Heath 10 C3
Hazebrouck 19 F1
Headford 12 B3
Heanor 7 D3
Héas 37 E2
Heathfield 10 C3
Heathrow Airport 9 F2
Hebrides, Outer 2 A2
Hebrides, Sea of the 2 A3
Heby 106 B3
Hechingen 55 D3
Hecho 37 D2
Hechtel 50 C3
Hecklingen 52 C1
Hedal 104 C2
Heddal 104 C3
Hédé 23 D3
Hede 101 E3
Hedemora 105 F3
Hedenäset 98 C2
Hedensted 108 B3
Hedesundafjärdarna 106 B3
Hedeviken 101 E3
Hedmark 104 C1

Hedon 7 E2
Heemstede 16 C2
Heerde 17 D2
Heerenveen 17 D1
Heerlen 51 D3
Heeze 16 C4
Hegge 104 C1
Hegra 101 D2
Heia 94 C3
Heide 47 F1
Heidelberg 54 C1
Heidenau 53 E2
Heidenheim 55 E2
Heidenreichstein 57 D1
Heikendorf 48 A1
Heikkila 99 F3
Heilbronn 55 D2
Heiligenberg 55 D4
Heiligenblut 59 E2
Heiligenhafen 48 B1
Heiligenkirchen 17 F3
Heiligenkreuz 57 F4
Heiligenstadt 52 B2
Heilsbronn 55 E1
Heimari 103 E3
Heimdal 100 C2
Heimertingen 55 E3
Heinävaara 103 F2
Heinävesi 103 E2
Heinola 107 F1
Heinolan mlk 107 F1
Heinsberg 17 D4
Heist 50 A3
Heist-op-den-Berg 50 C3
Hejde 109 F4
Hekla 96 B2
Hekuravë, Maj'e 76 C2
Helagsfjället 101 D2
Hélatros, Akr 93 D3
Heldeburg 52 C4
Heldrungen 52 C2
Helechal 43 E1
Helensburgh 4 C2
Helgåa (N) 101 D1
Helgaå (S) 109 D3

Helgasjön 109 D2
Helgoland 47 E2
Hella Is 96 B2
Hella N 104 B1
Hellemofjorden 97 F1
Hellendoorn 17 D2
Hellesylt 100 A3
Hellevoetsluis 16 B3
Hellin 44 C1
Hellvik 104 A4
Helmbrechts 53 D4
Helme 52 C2
Helmond 17 D3
Helmsdale 3 D2
Helmsley 7 D1
Helmstadt 55 D1
Helmstedt 52 C1
Helpter Berge 49 E2
Helsa 52 B2
Helsingborg 108 C3
Helsinge 108 C3
Helsingfors 107 F3
Helsingør 108 C3
Helsinki 107 F3
Helston 8 B4
Helvetinjärvi 102 C3
Helvick Head 14 C4
Hemau 55 F2
Hemavan 97 E3
Hemel Hempstead 9 F2
Hemer 17 E3
Hemme 100 C2
Hemmoor 48 A2
Hemnefjorden 100 C1
Hemnes 105 D3
Hemnesberget 97 E2
Hemsedal 104 C2
Hemsedal V 104 C2
Henares, R 40 B2
Hendaye 28 A4
Hengelo 17 D2
Hengersberg 56 B2
Hengstpaß 57 D3
Hénin-Beaumont 19 F1
Henley 9 E1
Henley-on-Thames 9 F2

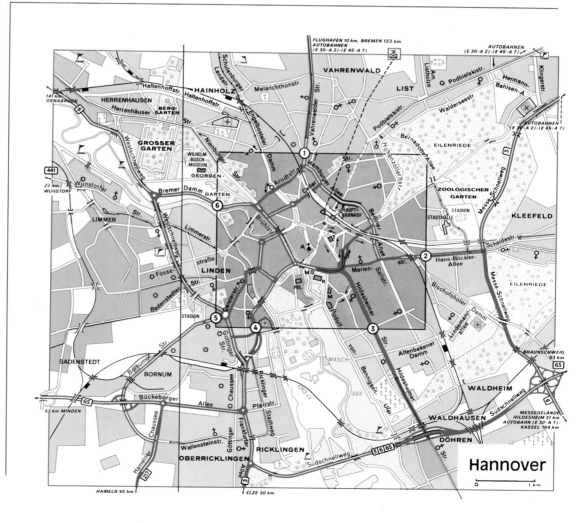

Hannover

HAMELN 45 km   ELZE 30 km

| Name | Page | Grid |
|---|---|---|
| Henneberg | 52 | B3 |
| Hennebont | 22 | B3 |
| Hennef | 51 | E3 |
| Hennigsdorf | 49 | D4 |
| Henrichemont | 25 | F2 |
| Henstedt-Ulzburg | 48 | A2 |
| Henstridge | 9 | D3 |
| Hepoköngäs | 99 | E4 |
| Heppenheim | 54 | C1 |
| Heraclea | 77 | E4 |
| Hérault | 29 | F4 |
| Hérault (Dépt) | 30 | A4 |
| Herbault | 25 | E2 |
| Herbertingen | 55 | D3 |
| Herbiers, les | 24 | B3 |
| Herbignac | 22 | C4 |
| Herbolzheim | 54 | C3 |
| Herborn | 51 | F3 |
| Herbrechtingen | 55 | E2 |
| Herbstein | 52 | A3 |
| Herceg Novi | 76 | A3 |
| Hercegovac | 71 | D2 |
| Hercegov Goleša | 76 | B1 |
| Hereford | 9 | D1 |
| Hereford and Worcester | 9 | D1 |
| Herencia | 40 | B4 |
| Herentals | 50 | C3 |
| Herford | 17 | F2 |
| Héricourt | 27 | E2 |
| Heringsdorf | 49 | E2 |
| Herisau | 58 | B2 |
| Hérisson | 26 | A3 |
| Hérisson, Cascades du | 27 | D3 |
| Herk | 50 | C3 |
| Herleshausen | 52 | B3 |
| Hermagor | 59 | F2 |
| Herma Ness | 3 | F1 |
| Hermannsburg | 48 | B4 |
| Hermansverk | 104 | B1 |
| Hermenault, l' | 24 | C3 |
| Herment | 29 | E1 |
| Hermeskeil | 54 | B1 |
| Hermigua | 42 | A4 |
| Hermsdorf | 53 | D3 |
| Hernani | 36 | C1 |
| Hernansancho | 39 | F1 |
| Herne | 17 | E3 |
| Herne Bay | 11 | D3 |
| Herning | 108 | A3 |
| Heroldsberg | 55 | F1 |
| Herónia | 83 | F4 |
| Herøy | 100 | A2 |
| Herrala | 107 | F2 |
| Herre | 104 | C3 |
| Herrenberg | 55 | D3 |
| Herrenchiemsee | 56 | B3 |
| Herrera (Andalucía) | 43 | E3 |
| Herrera (Aragón) | 37 | D4 |
| Herrera Mt | 37 | D4 |
| Herrera de Alcántara | 38 | C3 |
| Herrera del Duque | 39 | F4 |
| Herrera de Pisuerga | 35 | F3 |
| Herrera, Pto de | 36 | B2 |
| Herreruela | 39 | D3 |
| Herrestad | 108 | C1 |
| Herrieden | 55 | E2 |
| Herrljunga | 109 | D1 |
| Herrnburg | 48 | B2 |
| Herrnhut | 53 | F2 |
| Herrsching | 56 | A3 |
| Herrskog | 102 | A2 |
| Hersbruck | 55 | F1 |
| Herselt | 50 | C3 |
| Hérso | 79 | F2 |
| Hersónissos Akrotiri | 90 | C3 |
| Hersónissos Methánon | 87 | E2 |
| Hersónissos Spinalónga | 91 | E3 |
| Herstal | 51 | D3 |
| Herten | 17 | E3 |
| Hertford | 9 | F2 |
| Hertfordshire | 9 | F2 |
| Hervás | 39 | E2 |
| Herzberg (D) | 52 | B2 |
| Herzberg (DDR) | 53 | E1 |
| Herzogenaurach | 55 | E1 |
| Herzogenburg | 57 | E2 |
| Herzsprung | 49 | D3 |
| Hesdin | 19 | E2 |
| Hesel | 47 | E3 |
| Hessen | 52 | A3 |
| Hesseng | 95 | F2 |
| Hessisch-Lichtenau | 52 | B2 |
| Hessisch Oldendorf | 52 | A1 |
| Hestfjørður | 96 | A4 |
| Hetekylä | 99 | E3 |
| Hetin | 72 | C1 |
| Hettange | 21 | D3 |
| Hettstedt | 52 | C2 |
| Heubach | 55 | E2 |
| Heuchin | 19 | F1 |
| Heukuppe | 57 | E3 |
| Hevlin | 57 | F1 |
| Hexham | 5 | E3 |
| Heyrieux | 30 | C1 |
| Heysham | 6 | B1 |
| Hiddensee | 49 | D1 |
| Hieflau | 57 | D3 |
| Hiekkasarkät | 102 | C1 |
| Hierbas | 41 | E3 |
| Hierro | 42 | A4 |
| Hiersac | 28 | C1 |
| Hietaniemi | 95 | F4 |
| Higham Ferrers | 9 | F1 |
| Highland | 2 | C3 |
| High Peak | 6 | C2 |
| High Willhays | 8 | C3 |
| High Wycombe | 9 | F2 |
| Higuera de Arjona | 44 | A2 |
| Higuera de la Serena | 43 | E1 |
| Higuera de la Sierra | 43 | D2 |
| Higuera de Vargas | 42 | C1 |
| Higuera la Real | 42 | C1 |
| Higueruela | 41 | D4 |
| Hiidenportti | 103 | E1 |
| Hiiumaa | 110 | B1 |
| Hijar | 37 | D4 |
| Hódmezővásárhely | 114 | B1 |
| Hodnet | 6 | B3 |
| Hodonín | 57 | F1 |
| Hodoš | 70 | C1 |
| Hodovo | 75 | F2 |
| Hoedekenskerke | 16 | B4 |
| Hoek van Holland | 16 | B3 |
| Hoemsbu | 100 | B2 |
| Hof | 53 | D4 |
| Hofgeismar | 52 | A2 |
| Hofheim | 52 | B4 |
| Hofles | 97 | D4 |
| Höfn | 96 | C2 |
| Hofolding | 56 | A3 |
| Hofors | 105 | F2 |
| Hofsjökull | 96 | B2 |
| Höganäs | 108 | C3 |
| Høgebru | 100 | A3 |
| Höglekardalen | 101 | E2 |
| Högsäter | 105 | D4 |
| Högsby | 109 | E2 |
| Høgset | 100 | B2 |
| Hohe Acht | 51 | E4 |
| Hohenau | 57 | F2 |
| Hohenberg | 57 | E3 |
| Hohenems | 58 | B2 |
| Hohengandern | 52 | B2 |
| Hohenlimburg | 17 | E4 |
| Hohenlinden | 56 | B3 |
| Hohenlockstedt | 48 | A2 |
| Hohenmölsen | 53 | D2 |
| Hohenpeißenberg | 56 | A4 |
| Hohenseeden | 48 | C4 |
| Hohenstein | 53 | D3 |
| Hohentauern | 57 | D4 |
| Hirschau | 55 | F1 |
| Hirschberg | 53 | D3 |
| Hirschegg | 58 | B2 |
| Hirsingue | 27 | E2 |
| Hirson | 20 | B2 |
| Hirşova | 115 | E1 |
| Hirtshals | 108 | B1 |
| Hirvasvaara | 99 | E2 |
| Hirvensalmi | 103 | E3 |
| Hirvilahti | 103 | E2 |
| Hirwaun | 8 | C2 |
| Hisarja | 115 | D2 |
| Histria | 115 | E1 |
| Hitchin | 9 | F2 |
| Hitra | 100 | C1 |
| Hitzacker | 48 | B3 |
| Hjälmaren | 105 | F4 |
| Hjartdal | 104 | C3 |
| Hjellestad | 104 | A2 |
| Hjelmeland | 104 | A3 |
| Hjelmsøya | 95 | D1 |
| Hjo | 109 | D1 |
| Hjørring | 108 | B1 |
| Hjørundfjorden | 100 | A2 |
| Hlebine | 71 | D1 |
| Hlemoútsi | 86 | B1 |
| Hlomó, Óros | 83 | F3 |
| Hluboká | 57 | D1 |
| Hobro | 108 | B2 |
| Höchberg | 55 | D1 |
| Hochdorf | 27 | F2 |
| Hochfeiler | 59 | D2 |
| Hochfelden | 21 | E4 |
| Hochgolling | 59 | F1 |
| Hochgrabe | 59 | E2 |
| Hochosterwitz | 70 | B1 |
| Hochreichart | 57 | D4 |
| Hochschober | 59 | E2 |
| Hochschwab | 57 | D3 |
| Hochspeyer | 54 | C1 |
| Höchst | 55 | D1 |
| Höchstadt | 55 | E1 |
| Höchstädt | 55 | E2 |
| Hochtannbergpaß | 58 | B2 |
| Hochtor (Osttirol) | 59 | E2 |
| Hochtor (Steiermark) | 57 | D3 |
| Hockenheim | 54 | C2 |
| Hoddesdon | 9 | F2 |
| Hodenhagen | 48 | A4 |
| Hœdic | 22 | C4 |
| Hohenwestedt | 48 | A2 |
| Hohenzollern | 55 | D3 |
| Hoher Zinken | 56 | C3 |
| Hohe Tauern | 59 | E2 |
| Hohe Tauern, Nat Pk | 59 | E2 |
| Hóhlakas | 93 | E2 |
| Hohneck | 27 | E1 |
| Hohwachter Bucht | 48 | B1 |
| Hohwald, le | 21 | E4 |
| Højer | 108 | A4 |
| Hokksund | 104 | C3 |
| Hol | 104 | C2 |
| Holbæk | 108 | C3 |
| Holbeach | 7 | E3 |
| Holdorf | 17 | F2 |
| Holíč | 57 | F1 |
| Höljäkkä | 103 | E1 |
| Höljes | 101 | D4 |
| Hollabrunn | 57 | E2 |
| Høllen | 104 | B4 |
| Hollenstedt | 48 | A3 |
| Höllental | 57 | E3 |
| Holles | 97 | D4 |
| Hollfeld | 52 | C4 |
| Hollingsholm | 100 | B2 |
| Hollola | 107 | F2 |
| Hollum | 16 | C1 |
| Hollywood | 13 | D4 |
| Holm (N) | 97 | D3 |
| Holm (S) | 101 | F2 |
| Hólmavík | 96 | A1 |
| Holmec | 70 | B1 |
| Holmen | 105 | D2 |
| Holmestrand | 104 | C3 |
| Holmfirth | 6 | C2 |
| Holmön | 102 | B1 |
| Holmsjön | 101 | E3 |
| Holmslands Klit | 108 | A3 |
| Holmsund | 102 | B1 |
| Holomóndas, Óros | 80 | B3 |
| Holstebro | 108 | A2 |
| Holsted | 108 | A3 |
| Holsworthy | 8 | C3 |
| Holt | 7 | F3 |
| Holwerd | 47 | D3 |
| Holycross Abbey | 14 | C3 |
| Holyhead | 6 | A2 |
| Holy I (Anglesey) | 6 | A2 |
| Holy I (Northumberland) | 5 | E2 |
| Holywell | 6 | B2 |
| Holywood | 13 | E2 |
| Holzappel | 51 | F4 |
| Holzgau | 58 | C2 |
| Holzkirchen | 56 | A3 |
| Holzleitner Sattel | 58 | C2 |
| Holzminden | 52 | A2 |
| Homberg (Hessen) | 52 | A2 |
| Homberg (Nordrhein-Westfalen) | 17 | D3 |
| Homburg | 54 | B2 |
| Hommelstø | 97 | D3 |
| Hommelvik | 100 | C2 |
| Hommersåk | 104 | A3 |
| Homoljske planine | 73 | E3 |
| Hondarribia Fuenterrabia | 36 | C1 |
| Hondón de las Nieves | 45 | D2 |
| Hönebach | 52 | B3 |
| Hønefoss | 104 | C3 |
| Honfleur | 19 | D3 |
| Høng | 108 | B3 |
| Hónikas | 87 | D2 |
| Honiton | 9 | D3 |
| Honkajoki | 102 | B3 |
| Honningsvåg | 95 | E1 |
| Honrubia | 40 | C3 |
| Honrubia de la Cuesta | 36 | A3 |
| Hontalbilla | 40 | A1 |
| Hontoria del Pinar | 36 | A3 |
| Hooge | 47 | F1 |
| Hoogeveen | 17 | D2 |
| Hoogezand | 47 | D3 |
| Hoogstraten | 50 | C2 |
| Hook Head | 15 | D4 |
| Höör | 109 | D3 |
| Hoorn | 16 | C2 |
| Hopetoun House | 5 | D2 |
| Hopfgarten | 59 | D1 |
| Hopperstad | 104 | B1 |
| Hóra (Dodekánissa) | 89 | E2 |
| Hóra (Pelopónissos) | 86 | C3 |
| Hora Svatého Šebestiána | 53 | E3 |
| Horažd'ovice | 56 | C1 |
| Horb | 54 | C3 |
| Hörby | 109 | D3 |
| Horcajo de los Montes | 39 | F4 |
| Horcajo de Santiago | 40 | B3 |
| Horcajo de Trevélez | 44 | A3 |
| Horcajo-Medianero | 39 | E2 |
| Horche | 40 | B2 |
| Hordaland | 104 | B2 |
| Horden | 5 | E4 |
| Horeftó | 83 | F2 |
| Horezu | 115 | D1 |
| Horgen | 58 | A2 |
| Horgoš | 72 | C1 |
| Horley | 10 | C3 |
| Horn (A) | 57 | E2 |
| Horn (Baden-Württemberg) | 55 | D4 |
| Horn (N) | 97 | D3 |
| Horn (Nordrhein-Westfalen) | 52 | A2 |
| Hornachos | 43 | D1 |
| Hornachuelos | 43 | E2 |
| Hornavan | 98 | A2 |
| Hornberg | 54 | C3 |
| Hornbjarg | 96 | A1 |
| Hornburg | 52 | B1 |
| Horncastle | 7 | E3 |
| Horndal | 106 | A3 |
| Horneburg | 48 | A3 |
| Hörnefors | 102 | A2 |
| Hörnerkirchen | 48 | A2 |
| Hornet | 100 | C2 |
| Hornindal | 100 | A3 |
| Hornindalsvatn | 100 | A3 |
| Hørning | 108 | B3 |
| Horni Počernice | 53 | F3 |
| Hornisgrinde | 54 | C3 |
| Horni Slavkov | 53 | E4 |
| Hornos | 44 | B2 |
| Hornoy | 19 | E2 |
| Hornsea | 7 | E2 |
| Hörnum | 47 | F1 |
| Hořovice | 53 | F4 |
| Horsens | 108 | B3 |
| Horsham | 10 | C3 |
| Hørsholm | 108 | C3 |
| Horšovký Týn | 56 | B1 |
| Horst | 48 | B3 |
| Horstmar | 17 | E2 |
| Hortafjorden | 97 | D3 |
| Horten | 104 | C3 |
| Hortezuela | 36 | B4 |
| Hortiátis | 80 | A3 |
| Hospental | 58 | A3 |
| Hospital | 14 | C3 |
| Hospital de Orbigo | 35 | D3 |
| Hossa | 99 | F3 |
| Hossegor | 28 | A4 |
| Hostalric | 32 | B4 |
| Hotagen | 101 | E1 |
| Hotagen L | 101 | E1 |
| Hotagsfjällen | 101 | E1 |
| Hoting | 101 | F1 |
| Hotton | 50 | C4 |
| Houat | 22 | C4 |
| Houches, les | 27 | E4 |
| Hooge | 47 | F1 |
| Houdain | 19 | F1 |
| Houdan | 19 | E4 |
| Houeillès | 28 | B3 |
| Houffalize | 51 | D4 |
| Houghton-le-Spring | 5 | E4 |
| Houlgate | 18 | C3 |
| Houmnikó | 80 | B2 |
| Hoúni | 83 | D3 |
| Hourtin | 28 | A2 |
| Houtskår | 107 | D3 |
| Hov | 108 | B3 |
| Hovärken | 101 | D3 |
| Hovden | 104 | B3 |
| Hove | 10 | C3 |
| Hovet | 104 | B2 |
| Hovmantorp | 109 | E2 |
| Høvringen | 100 | C3 |
| Howden | 7 | D2 |
| Howth | 13 | E4 |
| Höxter | 52 | A2 |
| Hoy | 3 | D1 |
| Hoya | 17 | F1 |
| Høyanger | 100 | A3 |
| Hoyerswerda | 53 | F2 |
| Hoylake | 6 | B2 |
| Høylandet | 97 | D4 |
| Hoym | 52 | C1 |
| Hoyos | 39 | D2 |
| Höytiainen | 103 | F2 |
| Hoz de Beteta | 40 | C2 |
| Hozoviótissa | 89 | D3 |
| Hracholuská přehr nádrž | 53 | E4 |
| Hradec-Králove | 112 | A2 |
| Hrádek | 57 | E1 |
| Hrádek nad Nisou | 53 | F2 |
| Hranice (Severomoravský) | 112 | A3 |
| Hranice (Západočeský) | 53 | D4 |
| Hrasnica | 75 | F1 |
| Hrastnik | 70 | B2 |
| Hrastovlje | 70 | A3 |
| Hřensko | 53 | F2 |
| Hrisey | 96 | B1 |
| Hríssafa | 87 | D3 |
| Hrissi, N | 91 | E4 |
| Hrissó | 80 | B2 |
| Hrissoskalítissa | 90 | B3 |
| Hrissoúpoli | 80 | C2 |
| Hrissovitsi | 86 | C2 |
| Hristianí, N | 91 | D1 |
| Hristianó | 86 | C3 |
| Hristós | 89 | D2 |
| Hrómio | 79 | D4 |
| Hrtkovci | 72 | C3 |
| Hrušovany | 57 | F1 |
| Hrvace | 75 | D1 |
| Hrvatska | 70 | C2 |
| Hückeswagen | 17 | E4 |
| Hucknall | 7 | D3 |
| Hucqueliers | 19 | E1 |
| Huddersfield | 6 | C2 |
| Hude | 47 | F3 |
| Hudiksvall | 101 | F3 |
| Huebra, R | 39 | E1 |
| Huebra, R | 39 | E1 |
| Huédin | 112 | C4 |
| Huélago | 44 | A3 |
| Huélamo | 40 | C2 |
| Huelgoat | 22 | B3 |
| Huelma | 44 | A2 |
| Huelva | 42 | C2 |
| Huelva, Riv. de | 43 | D2 |
| Huércal-Overa | 44 | C3 |
| Huérguina | 41 | D3 |
| Huerta del Rey | 36 | A3 |
| Huerta de Valdecarábanos | 40 | A3 |
| Huertahernando | 40 | C2 |
| Huerto | 37 | E3 |
| Huerva, R | 37 | D4 |
| Huesa | 44 | B2 |
| Huesca | 37 | D3 |
| Huéscar | 44 | B2 |
| Huesna, Emb de | 43 | D2 |
| Huete | 40 | B3 |
| Huétor-Santillán | 44 | A3 |
| Huétor-Tájar | 43 | F3 |
| Hüfingen | 54 | C4 |
| Huftarøy | 104 | A2 |
| Huisne | 23 | F3 |
| Huittinen | 107 | D2 |
| Huizen | 16 | C2 |
| Hulst | 16 | B4 |
| Hultsfred | 109 | E2 |
| Humada | 35 | F3 |
| Humanes | 40 | B1 |
| Humber Bridge | 7 | D2 |
| Humber, R | 7 | E2 |
| Humberside | 7 | D2 |
| Humberside (Airport) | 7 | D2 |
| Humenné | 112 | C3 |
| Humppila | 107 | E2 |
| Hundested | 108 | C3 |
| Hundorp | 100 | C3 |
| Hunedoara | 114 | C1 |
| Hünfeld | 52 | B3 |
| Hungerford | 9 | E2 |
| Hunnebostrand | 105 | D4 |
| Húnsflói | 96 | A1 |
| Hunspach | 21 | F3 |
| Hunsrück | 54 | B1 |
| Hunstanton | 7 | E3 |
| Hunte | 17 | F1 |
| Huntingdon | 9 | F1 |
| Huntly | 3 | E3 |
| Hurdal | 105 | D2 |
| Huriel | 25 | F4 |
| Hurones, Emb de los | 43 | D3 |
| Hurskaala | 103 | E3 |
| Hürth | 17 | E4 |
| Hurum | 104 | C1 |
| Hurup | 108 | A2 |
| Husafell | 96 | B2 |
| Húsavik (N) | 96 | B1 |
| Husavik (N) | 104 | A2 |
| Husbands Bosworth | 9 | F1 |
| Hushinish | 2 | A2 |
| Huşi | 113 | E4 |
| Huskvarna | 109 | D1 |
| Husnes | 104 | A2 |
| Hustadvika | 100 | B2 |
| Hustopeče | 57 | F1 |
| Husum (D) | 47 | F1 |
| Husum (S) | 102 | A2 |
| Hutovo | 75 | F2 |
| Hutovo Blato | 75 | F2 |
| Hüttenberg | 57 | D4 |
| Hüttschlag | 59 | E1 |
| Huttula | 103 | D3 |
| Huttwil | 27 | F2 |
| Huy | 50 | C4 |
| Hvalba | 96 | A4 |
| Hvalfjörður | 96 | A2 |
| Hvalpsund | 108 | A2 |
| Hvalvik | 96 | A3 |
| Hvar | 75 | D2 |
| Hvar I | 75 | E2 |
| Hvarski kan | 75 | D2 |
| Hveragerði | 96 | A2 |
| Hveravellir | 96 | B2 |
| Hvidbjerg | 108 | A2 |
| Hvide Sande | 108 | A3 |
| Hvítá | 96 | B2 |
| Hvittingfoss | 104 | C3 |
| Hvitträsk | 107 | E3 |
| Hvolsvöllur | 96 | B3 |
| Hwlffordd | 8 | B2 |
| Hyde | 6 | C2 |
| Hyen | 100 | A3 |
| Hyères | 31 | D4 |
| Hyères, Iles d' | 31 | D4 |
| Hylsfjorden | 104 | A3 |
| Hyltebruk | 108 | C2 |
| Hyrynsalmi | 99 | E4 |
| Hythe | 11 | D3 |
| Hyvinkää | 107 | E2 |
| Hyypiö | 99 | D2 |

# I

| | | | | | | | | |
|---|---|---|---|---|---|---|---|---|
| Ía | 91 E1 | Illana | 40 B2 | Inkee | 99 E3 | | | |
| Ialomiţa | 115 E1 | Illano | 34 C1 | Inkoo | 107 E3 | | | |
| Iaşi | 113 E3 | Illar | 44 B3 | Inn (CH) | 58 B3 | | | |
| Íasmos | 81 D2 | Ille | 23 D3 | Inn (D) | 56 B3 | | | |
| Ibañeta, Pto | 36 C1 | Ille et Rance, | | Innbygda | 104 C1 | | | |
| Ibar | 73 D4 | Canal d' | 23 D3 | Inndyr | 97 E2 | | | |
| Ibbenbüren | 17 E2 | Ille-et-Vilaine | 23 D3 | Innellan | 4 B2 | | | |
| Ibestad | 94 B3 | Iller | 55 E4 | Innerleithen | 5 D2 | | | |
| Ibi | 45 E1 | Illertissen | 55 E3 | Inner Sd | 2 B3 | | | |
| Ibias, R | 34 C2 | Illescas | 40 A2 | Innfield | 13 D3 | | | |
| Ibiza | 45 D4 | Ille-sur-Têt | 32 B2 | Innhavet | 97 F1 | | | |
| Ibiza / | 45 D3 | Illhæusern | 27 E1 | Innichen | 59 E2 | | | |
| Iblei, Mti | 69 D4 | Illiers | 25 E1 | Inning | 56 A3 | | | |
| Ičn'a | 113 F1 | Illingen | 55 D2 | Innsbruck | 59 D2 | | | |
| Icod de los Vinos | 42 A4 | Illmitz | 57 F3 | Innset | 94 B3 | | | |
| Idanha a Nova | 38 C2 | Illora | 44 A3 | Innvik | 100 A3 | | | |
| Idar-Oberstein | 54 B1 | Illueca | 36 C4 | Inói (Pelopónissos) | 86 B1 | | | |
| Idéo Ándro | 91 D4 | Ilm | 52 C3 | Inói (Stereá Eláda) | 84 A4 | | | |
| Ídi, Óros | 91 D4 | Ilmajoki | 102 C2 | Inoússes | 85 F3 | | | |
| Idoméni | 79 F2 | Ilmenau R | 48 B3 | Inoússes, N | 85 F4 | | | |
| Iddoš | 72 C1 | Ilmenau | 52 C3 | Inowrocław | 112 A1 | | | |
| Ídra | 87 F2 | Il'men, Ozero | 111 D1 | Ins | 27 E2 | | | |
| Ídra, N | 87 F3 | Ilminster | 9 D3 | Iňsko | 49 F2 | | | |
| Ídras, Kólpos | 87 E2 | Ilok | 72 B2 | Interlaken | 27 F3 | | | |
| Idre | 101 D3 | Ilomantsi | 103 F2 | Întorsura Buzăuli | 113 D4 | | | |
| Idrigill Pt | 2 B3 | Ilova | 71 D2 | Inveraray | 4 B1 | | | |
| Idrija | 70 A2 | Ilovik | 70 B4 | Inverbervie | 3 E4 | | | |
| Idrijca | 70 A2 | Ilsenburg | 52 B1 | Invergarry | 2 C4 | | | |
| Idro | 58 C4 | Ilsfeld | 55 D2 | Invergordon | 3 D3 | | | |
| Idstein | 51 F4 | Imathía | 79 E3 | Inverkeithing | 5 D2 | | | |
| Ielsi | 64 B3 | Imatra | 103 F4 | Invermoriston | 2 C4 | | | |
| Ieper | 50 A3 | Ímeros | 81 E2 | Inverness | 2 C3 | | | |
| Ierápetra | 91 E4 | Imitós | 87 F1 | Inverurie | 3 E4 | | | |
| Ierissós | 80 B3 | Immenstaad | 55 D4 | Inzell | 56 B3 | | | |
| Ieropigí | 78 C3 | Immenstadt | 55 E4 | Ioánina | 82 C1 | | | |
| If, Château d' | 30 C4 | Immingham | 7 E2 | Ioánina (Nomos) | 82 B1 | | | |
| Ifestía | 85 D1 | Immingham Dock | 7 E2 | Ioaninon, L | 82 C1 | | | |
| Ifjord | 95 E1 | Imola | 61 D3 | Iona | 4 A1 | | | |
| Ifjordfjellet | 95 E1 | Imotski | 75 E1 | Ionia | 79 F3 | | | |
| Igalo | 76 A3 | Imperia | 31 F3 | Iónia Nissiá | 82 A2 | | | |
| Iga Vas | 70 B2 | Imphy | 26 A3 | Íos | 88 C4 | | | |
| Iggesund | 101 F3 | Impruneta | 61 D4 | Íos, N | 88 C4 | | | |
| Iglesias | 66 B4 | Imst | 58 C2 | Ipáti | 83 E3 | | | |
| Igls | 59 D2 | Ina | 49 F3 | Ipéria | 83 E2 | | | |
| Igoumenítsa | 82 B2 | Inari | 95 E3 | Iphofen | 55 E1 | Isar | 56 B2 |
| Igrane | 75 E2 | Inarijärvi | 95 E3 | Ípiros | 82 B2 | Isarco | 59 D2 |
| Igualada | 37 F4 | Inarijoki | 95 E3 | Ipsilí Ráhi | 80 C2 | Isbister | 3 F1 |
| Ihtiman | 115 D2 | Inca | 45 F2 | Ípsos | 82 A1 | Iscar | 35 E4 |
| Ii | 99 D3 | Inchnadamph | 2 C2 | Ipsoúnda | 86 C2 | Ischgl | 58 C2 |
| Iijarvi | 95 E2 | Inchtree | 2 C4 | Ipswich | 11 D2 | Ischia | 64 A4 |
| Iijoki | 99 D3 | Indal | 101 F3 | Iput' | 111 E4 | Ischia, I d' | 64 A4 |
| Iisalmi | 103 E1 | Indalsälven | 101 F3 | Iráklia (Makedonía) | 80 A2 | Ise | 105 D3 |
| Iisvesi | 103 E2 | Indija | 72 C2 | Iráklia (Stereá | | Isefjord | 108 C3 |
| IJmuiden | 16 B2 | Indre (Dépt) | 25 E3 | Eláda) | 83 E3 | Iselle | 58 A3 |
| IJssel | 17 D3 | Indre-et-Loire | 25 D2 | Iráklia, N | 88 C3 | Iselsberg | 59 E2 |
| IJsselmeer | 16 C2 | Infiesto | 35 E1 | Iráklio (Nomos) | 91 D4 | Iseo | 60 B1 |
| IJsselmuiden | 17 D2 | Ingå | 107 E3 | Irati, R | 36 C2 | Iseo, L d' | 58 B4 |
| IJzendijke | 16 B4 | Ingelmunster | 50 A3 | Irbes Šaurums | 110 B2 | Iseran, Col de l' | 31 E1 |
| IJzer | 50 A3 | Ingleton | 6 C1 | Irdning | 57 D4 | Isère (Dépt) | 30 C1 |
| Ikaalinen | 102 C3 | Ingolstadt | 55 F2 | Iregua, R | 36 B2 | Isère (R) | 30 C1 |
| Ikaría, N | 89 D2 | Ingrandes | 23 E4 | Iréo (Argolída) | 87 D2 | Iserlohn | 17 E3 |
| Ikast | 108 A3 | Ingul | 113 F3 | Iréo (Dodekánissa) | 89 E2 | Isernia | 64 A3 |
| Ilandža | 73 D2 | Ingulec | 113 F3 | Iréo (Korinthía) | 87 E1 | Isfjellet | 94 C2 |
| Ilanz | 58 B3 | Ingulec R | 113 F3 | Iréo, Akr | 87 E1 | Isfjorden | 100 B2 |
| Ilche | 37 E3 | Ingwiller | 21 E3 | Íria | 87 E2 | Ishavsleden | 94 C3 |
| Ilchester | 9 D3 | Iniesta | 41 D4 | Irig | 72 C2 | Ishëm | 76 C4 |
| Ile-Bouchard, I' | 25 D3 | Inió | 107 D2 | Irish Sea | 13 F3 | Ishëm R | 76 C4 |
| Ile-Rousse, I' | 33 F2 | Iniön aukko | 107 D2 | Iriški venac | 72 C2 | Isigny | 18 C3 |
| Ilfracombe | 8 C3 | Inis | 12 B4 | Irixoa | 34 B1 | Isili | 66 B3 |
| Ílhavo | 38 B1 | Inis Córthaidh | 15 D3 | Irnijärvi | 99 E3 | Iskâr | 115 D2 |
| Ília | 83 F3 | Inishbofin | 12 A3 | Iron-Bridge | 9 D1 | Is'kuras | 95 E3 |
| Ilía | 86 B1 | Inishcrone | 12 B2 | Irschenberg | 56 B3 | Isla | 3 D4 |
| Il'íčevsk | 113 F4 | Inisheer | 12 B4 | Irsina | 65 D4 | Isla | 36 A1 |
| Ílida | 86 B1 | Inishkea | 12 A2 | Irún | 36 C1 | Isla Cristina | 42 C3 |
| Ilidza | 75 F1 | Inishmaan | 12 B4 | Irurzun | 36 C1 | Isla Mayor | 43 D3 |
| Ilijas | 71 F4 | Inishmore | 12 B4 | Irvine | 4 C2 | Island Magee | 13 E2 |
| Ilíki | 84 A4 | Inishmurray | 12 C2 | Irvinestow | 12 C2 | Islay | 4 A2 |
| Ilíki, L | 84 A4 | Inishowen | 13 D1 | Irxleben | 52 C1 | Isle | 28 C2 |
| Iliókastro | 87 E2 | Inishowen Head | 13 D1 | Isaba | 37 D2 | Isle-Adam, I' | 19 F3 |
| Ilirska Bistrica | 70 B3 | Inishshark | 12 A3 | Isaccea | 113 E4 | Isle-de-Noé, I' | 28 C4 |
| Ilkeston | 7 D3 | Inishtrahull | 13 D1 | Ísafjarðardjúp | 96 A1 | Isle-en-Dodon, I' | 37 F1 |
| Ilkley | 6 C2 | Inishturk | 12 A3 | Ísafjörður | 96 A1 | Isle-Jourdain, I' | |
| | | | | Ísala | 115 E3 | (Gers) | 28 C4 |
| | | | | Isane | 100 A3 | Isle-Jourdain, I' | |
| | | | | | | (Vienne) | 25 D4 |

| | | | | | | |
|---|---|---|---|---|---|---|
| Isle of Man | 6 A1 | Istán | 43 E4 | Ivančna Gorica | 70 B2 |
| Isle of Portland | 9 D4 | İstanbul | 115 F3 | Ivanec | 70 C1 |
| Isle of Whithorn | 4 C4 | Istarske Toplice | 70 A3 | Ivangrad | 76 C2 |
| Isle of Wight | 9 E4 | Istérnia | 88 B2 | Ivanić Grad | 71 D2 |
| Isleornsay | 2 B4 | Istha | 52 A2 | Ivanjica | 73 D4 |
| Isles of Scilly | 8 A4 | Isthmía | 87 E1 | Ivanjska | 71 E3 |
| Isle-sur-la- | | Istibanja | 77 F2 | Ivankovo | 71 F2 |
| Sorgue,I' | 30 C3 | Istiéa | 83 F3 | Ivano-Frankovsk | 113 D3 |
| Isle-sur-le- | | Istindan | 94 B3 | Ivanščica | 70 C2 |
| Doubs, l' | 27 D2 | Istok | 76 C2 | Ivan Sedlo | 75 F1 |
| Isle-sur-Serein, l' | 26 B2 | Istres | 30 C4 | Ivanska | 71 D2 |
| Iseo | 60 B1 | Ístrios | 93 E2 | Iveland | 104 B4 |
| Ismaning | 55 F3 | Isturits et d'Oxocelhaya, | | Iveragh | 14 A4 |
| Isnäs | 107 F2 | Grottes d' | 28 A4 | Ívira | 80 B2 |
| Isny | 55 E4 | Itä-Aure | 102 C3 | Íviron | 80 C4 |
| Iso-Evo | 107 E2 | Itainen | | Ivrea | 31 F1 |
| Isojärvi | 103 D3 | Suomenlahti | 107 F2 | Ivry-la-Bataille | 19 E4 |
| Isojoki | 102 B3 | Itanós | 91 F3 | Ixiá | 93 F1 |
| Isokylä | 99 E2 | Itéa (Flórina) | 79 D2 | Ixworth | 11 D1 |
| Isokyrö | 102 B2 | Itéa (Grevená) | 79 D4 | Iž | 74 C1 |
| Isola | 31 E3 | Itéa (Stereá Eláda) | 83 E4 | Izeda | 34 C4 |
| Isola del Gran | | Itéa (Thessalía) | 83 E2 | Izegem | 50 A3 |
| Sasso d'Italia | 63 F1 | Itéas, Kólpos | 83 E4 | Izernore | 26 C4 |
| Isola della Scala | 60 C1 | Itháki | 82 B4 | Izlake | 70 B2 |
| Isola del Liri | 64 A3 | Itháki, N | 82 B4 | Izmail | 113 E4 |
| Isola di Capo | | Ithómi | 86 C3 | İzmir | 115 E4 |
| Rizzuto | 67 F3 | Íti | 83 E3 | İzmit | 115 F3 |
| Isona | 37 F3 | Ítilo | 87 D4 | Iznájar | 43 F3 |
| Isonzo | 59 F3 | Íti, Óros | 83 E3 | Iznájar, Emb de | 43 F3 |
| Isorella | 60 B1 | Iton | 19 E3 | Iznallos | 44 A3 |
| Iso-Syöte | 99 E3 | Itri | 64 A3 | Iznik | 115 F3 |
| Ispica | 69 D4 | Itta | 52 B3 | İznik Gölü | 115 F3 |
| Issambres, les | 31 D4 | Ittiri | 66 A2 | Izoard, Col d' | 31 D2 |
| Issel | 17 D3 | Itz | 52 C4 | Izola | 70 A3 |
| Issigeac | 28 C2 | Itzehoe | 48 A2 | Iz Veli | 74 C1 |
| Issoire | 29 F1 | Ivaceviči | 112 C1 | Izvor (Makedonija) | 77 D4 |
| Issóva, M. | 86 C2 | Ivajlovgrad | 115 E3 | Izvor (Makedonija) | 77 E3 |
| Íssoma | 86 C1 | Ivalo | 95 E3 | Izvor (Srbija) | 73 E4 |
| Issoudun | 25 E3 | Ivalojoki Ävvil | 95 E3 | | |
| Is-sur-Tille | 26 C2 | Ivančice | 57 F1 | | |
| Issy-l'Evêque | 26 B3 | Ivančići | 71 F4 | | |
| Ist | 74 B1 | | | | |

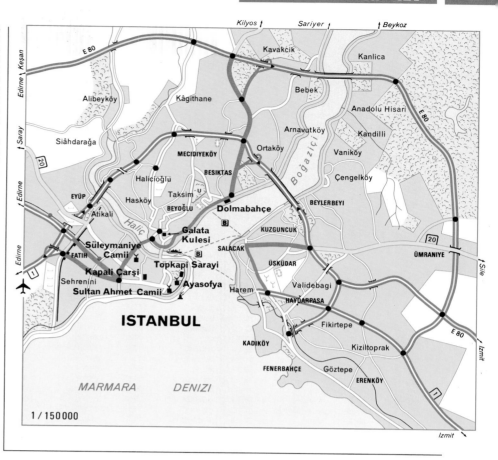

# J


Jaala 107 F2
Jääsjärvi 103 D3
Jabalón, R 44 A1
Jabbeke 50 A3
Jablanac 70 B4
Jablan Do 76 A2
Jablanica 75 F1
Jablanica (Reg) 77 D4
Jablanica *R* 77 D1
Jabličko jez 75 F1
Jablonec nad Nisou 112 A2
Jablonné v Podještědí 53 F3
Jabugo 42 C2
Jabuka (Bosna i Hercegovina) 76 A1
Jabuka (Srbija) 76 B1
Jabuka (Vojvodina) 73 D2
Jabuka, I 74 C2
Jabukovac (Hrvatska) 71 D3
Jabukovac (Srbija) 73 F3
Jabukovik 77 E1
Jaca 37 D2
Jáchymov 53 E3
Jadar (Bosna i Hercegovina) 72 C4
Jadar (Srbija) 72 B3
Jäder 106 A3
Jaderberg 47 F3
Jadovik 76 B1
Jadovnik 71 D4
Jadranska Lešnica 72 B3
Jadransko More 74 B2
Jadraque 40 B1
Jaén 44 A2
Jagodnjac 71 F2
Jagotin 113 F2
Jagst 55 E2
Jagsthausen 55 D2
Jahorina 76 A1
Jahorina (Reg) 76 A1
Jajce 71 E4
Jäkkvik 97 F2
Jakobselv 95 F2
Jakobstad 102 C1
Jakšić 71 E2
Jakupica 77 E3
Jalasjärvi 102 C3
Jaligny 26 A3
Jalón, R 36 C3
Jalovik Izvor 73 F4
Jambol 115 E2
Jamena 72 B3
Jämijärvi 102 C3
Jäminkipohja 102 C3
Jämjö 109 E3
Jammerbugten 108 A2
Jamnička Kiselica 70 C2
Jämsä 103 D3
Jämsänkoski 103 D3
Jämtlands Län 101 E2
Janakkala 107 E2
Janče 77 D3
Jandía, Pta de 42 C4
Jándula, Emb del 44 A1
Jandula, R 44 A1
Jänisselkä 103 F2
Janja 72 B3
Janjevo 77 D2
Janjina 75 E2
Jankov kamen 76 C1
Jañona 39 D2
Jantra 115 D2
Janville 25 E1
Janzé 23 D3
Japetić 70 C2
Jäppilä 103 E2
Jaraba 36 C4
Jarafuel 41 D4
Jaraicejo 39 E3
Jaráiz 39 E2
Jarak 72 C3
Jarama, R 40 B2
Jarandilla de la Vera 39 E2
Järbo 106 A2
Jarcevo 111 E3
Jard 24 B3
Jæren 104 A4
Jaren 105 D2
Jargeau 25 E1
Jarkovac 73 D2
Jarmen 49 D2
Jarmenovci 73 D3
Jarnac 28 B1
Jarnages 25 E4
Järna (Kopparbergs Län) 105 E2
Järna (Stockholms Län) 106 B4
Jarny 21 D3
Jarocin 112 A2
Jaroměřice 57 E1
Jarosław 112 C2
Järpen 101 E2
Jarrow 5 E3
Jarvelä 107 F2
Järvenpää 107 E2
Järvsö 101 F3
Jaša Tomić 73 D2
Jasenak 70 B3
Jasenica (Bosna i Hercegovina) 71 D3
Jasenica (Srbija) 73 D3
Jasenovac 71 D3
Jasenovo (Crna Gora) 76 B2
Jasenovo (Srbija) 76 B1
Jasenovo (Vojvodina) 73 D2
Jasień 53 F1
Jasika 73 E4
Jasikovo 73 E3
Jasło 112 C3
Jasmund 49 D1
Jastrebarsko 70 C2
Jastrowie 112 A1
Jászberény 112 B4
Jau, Col de 32 B2
Jaufenpass 59 D2
Jaunay-Clan 25 D3
Jaunpass 27 E3
Jausiers 31 D2
Javalambre 41 D3
Javalambre, Sa de 41 E3
Javalón 41 D2
Javea 45 E1
Jävenitz 48 C4
Javie, la 31 D3
Javor 76 C1
Javořice 57 D1
Javornjača 71 D4
Javorov 112 C2
Jävre 98 B4
Javron 23 E3
Jedburgh 5 D3
Jedincy 113 D3
Jędrzejów 112 B2
Jeesiö 95 E4
Jeetze 48 B3
Jegun 28 C4
Jegunovce 77 D3
Jekabpils 110 C3
Jektevik 104 A2
Jelah 71 E3
Jelašca 76 A1
Jelenia Góra 112 A2
Jelenje 70 B3
Jelgava 110 C3
Jelling 108 A3
Jel'n'a 111 E3
Jelsa (N) 104 A3
Jelsa (YU) 75 E2
Jemnice 57 E1
Jena 52 C3
Jenbach 59 D1
Jengejetneme 97 E4
Jennersdorf 57 F4
Jeppo 102 C2
Jerez de la Frontera 43 D3
Jerez de los Caballeros 42 C1
Jérica 41 E3
Jerichow 49 D4
Jerisjärvi 95 D4
Jerpoint Abbey 15 D3
Jersey 18 A3
Jerte 39 E2
Jerte, R 39 E2
Jerxheim 52 B1
Jerzu 66 C3
Jesenice (CS) 53 E4
Jesenice (YU) 70 A1
Jeseník 112 A2
Jesi 61 F4
Jesolo 59 E4
Jessen 53 D1
Jessheim 105 D3
Jeßnitz 53 D2
Jetzelsdorf 57 E2
Jeumont 20 B1
Jevenstedt 48 A2
Jever 47 E3
Jevišovice 57 E1
Jevnaker 105 D2
Jezerane 70 C3
Jezerce 77 D2
Jezercë, M 76 C2
Jezero 71 E4
Jezero Šćit 75 E1
Jezersko 70 B1
Ježevica 72 C4
Jičín 112 A2
Jiekkevarre 94 C2
Jihlava 57 E1
Jihlava *R* 57 E1
Jijona 45 E1
Jiloca, R 41 D2
Jílové u Prahy 53 F4
Jimbolia 114 C1
Jimena 44 A2
Jimena de la Frontera 43 E4
Jindřichovice 53 D3
Jindřichuv Hradec 57 D1
Jirkov 53 E3
Jiu 115 D2
Jizera 53 F3
Joachimsthal 49 E3
Jockfall 98 C2
Jódar 44 A2
Jodoigne 50 C3
Joensuu 103 F2
Jogeva 110 C1
Johanngeorgenstadt 53 D3
John o'Groats 3 D2
Johnstone 4 C2
Johovac 71 F3
Joigny 26 A1
Joinville 20 C4
Jokela 107 E2
Jokijärvi 99 E3
Jokikylä 99 E4
Jokioinen 107 E2
Jokkmokk 98 B2
Jökulsá-á Fjöllum 96 C1
Joloskylä 99 D3
Jølstravatnet 100 A3
Jomala 106 C3
Jönåker 106 A4
Jondal 104 B2
Jongunjärvi 99 E3
Joniškis 110 C3
Jönköping 109 D1
Jönköpings Län 109 D2
Jonzac 28 B1
Jordbro 106 B4
Jordbruksveien 95 D2
Jormlien 97 E4
Jörn 98 B4
Joroinen 103 E3
Jørpeland 104 A3
Jørstadmoen 105 D2
Jošanica 73 E4
Jošanička Banja 76 C1
Jošavka 71 E3
Josenfjorden 104 A3
Jose Toran, Emb de 43 E2
Josipdol 70 C3
Josipovac 71 F2
Josselin 22 C3
Jostedalsbreen 100 A3
Jotunheimen 100 B3
Jou, Coll de 32 A3
Joué 25 D2
Jougne 27 D3
Joutjärvi 107 F2
Joutsa 103 D3
Joutseno 103 E4
Joutsijärvi 99 E2
Joyeuse 30 B2
Juankoski 103 E2
Juan-les-Pins 31 E4
Júcar, R 41 E4
Jüchen 17 D4
Juchnov 111 F3
Judaberg 104 A3
Judenau 57 E2
Judenburg 57 D4
Judio 43 F1
Juelsminde 108 B3
Jugenheim 54 C1
Jugon 22 C3
Jugorje 70 B2
Juillac 29 D1
Juist 47 E3
Jukkasjärvi 94 C4
Jülich 17 D4
Julierpass 58 B3
Jullouville 18 B4
Jumaliskylä 99 F4
Jumeaux 29 F1
Jumièges 19 D3
Jumilhac-le-Grand 29 D1
Jumilla 45 D1
Jumilla, Pto de 45 D1
Juminen 103 E1
Jumisko 99 E2
Juneda 37 F4
Jungfrau 27 F3
Junik 76 C2
Juniville 20 B3
Junkeren 97 E2
Junosuando 95 D4
Junsele 101 F2
Juntusranta 99 F3
Juojärvi 103 E2
Juoksenki 98 C2
Juorkuna 99 E4
Jura 4 B2
Jura (Canton) 27 E2
Jura (Dépt) 27 D3
Jura, Sd of 4 B2
Jurbarkas 110 C3
Jurjevo 70 B4
Jurmala 110 C2
Jurmofjärden 107 D3
Jurmu 99 E3
Juromenha 38 C4
Jurva 102 B2
Jussey 27 D1
Justel 34 D3
Jüterbog 53 E1
Juuka 103 E2
Juupajoki 103 D3
Juurusvesi 103 E2
Juva (Mikkelin Lääni) 103 E3
Juva (Turun ja Porin Lääni) 107 D2
Juvigny-le-Tertre 18 C4
Juvigny-sous-Andaine 18 C4
Juvola 103 E3
Juzennecourt 26 C1
Južna Morava 73 E4
Južnyj Bug 113 E2
Jyderup 108 B3
Jylland 108 A3
Jyrkkä 103 E1
Jyväskylä 103 D3


# K


Kaakamo 99 D3
Kaamanen 95 E3
Kaamaskoki 95 E2
Kaaresuvanto 95 D3
Kaarina 107 D2
Kaatsheuvel 16 C3
Kaavi 103 E2
Kaavinjärvi 103 E2
Kåbdalis 98 B3
Kablart 72 C4
Kać 72 C2
Kačanik 77 D2
Kačarevo 73 D2
Kačikol 77 D2
Kadaň 53 E3
Kadi Bogaz 73 F4
Kadrifakovo 77 E3
Kafiréas, Akr 84 C4
Kafiréa, Stenó 88 B1
Kåfjord 95 E1
Kåfjorden 94 C2
Kaga 106 A4
Kagarlyk 113 E2
Kagul 113 E4
Kahla 52 C3
Kaiáfas 86 B2
Kailbach 55 D1
Kaïmaktsalán 79 E2
Kainasto 102 B3
Kaindorf 57 E4
Kaipola 103 D3
Kairala 95 F4
Kaisergebirge 59 D1
Kaiserslautern 54 B1
Kaisheim 55 E2
Kaitumälven 94 C4
Kaiudđerovo 73 E2
Kajaani 99 E4
Kakan 74 C1
Kakanj 71 F4
Kakí Thálassa 88 A1
Kakí Vígla 87 F1
Kakslauttanen 95 E3
Kalajoki 102 C1
Kalajoki *R* 102 C1
Kalak 95 E1
Kalamáki (Lárissa) 83 F2
Kalamáki (Magnissía) 84 A2
Kalamáki, Akr 85 D2
Kalamáta 86 C3
Kalambáka 83 D1
Kalambáki 80 C2
Kalámi 89 E1
Kalamiótissa 91 F1
Kalamítsi (Makedonía) 80 B4
Kalamítsi (Stereá Eláda) 82 B3
Kálamos, N 82 C3
Kalamotí 85 F4
Kalamotó 80 A3
Kalándra 80 A4
Kalá Nerá 83 F2
Kalá Nissiá 87 E1
Kalanti 107 D2
Kalapódi 83 F3
Kalaraš 113 E3
Kälarne 101 F2
Kalavárda 93 E1
Kalávrita 86 C1
Kal'azin 111 F1
Kalbe 48 C4
Kalce 70 A2
Kaldakvísl 96 B2
Kaléndzi (Ípiros) 82 C2
Kaléndzi (Pelopónissos) 86 C1
Kalenić 73 D4
Kalérgo 84 C4
Kalesija 72 B3
Kali 74 C1
Kaliakoúda 83 D3
Kaliáni 87 D1
Kalídromo, Óros 83 E3
Kalifítos 80 C2
Kalí Liménes 91 D4
Kali Limni 93 D3
Kalimassiá 85 F4
Kalimenci, Ez 77 F2
Kálimnos 89 F3
Kálimnos, N 89 E3
Kalinin 111 F2
Kaliningrad 110 B4
Kalinkoviči 113 E1
Kalinovik 75 F1
Kalipéfki 79 E4
Kalirráhi 79 D4
Kalithéa (Dodekánissa) 93 F1
Kalithéa (Ilía) 86 C2
Kalithéa (Makedonía) 80 B2
Kalithéa (Messinía) 86 C3
Kalithéa (Stereá Eláda) 83 D3
Kalithéa (Thessalía) 80 B4
Kalithiés 93 F1
Kalíthiro 83 D2
Kaliváni 88 B1
Kalíves (Kríti) 90 C3
Kalíves (Thássos) 80 C3
Kalívia (Ahaïa) 86 C1
Kalívia (Atikí-Piréas) 87 F1
Kalívia (Etolía-Akarnanía) 82 C3
Kalívia (Korinthía) 87 D1
Kalívia Varikoú 79 F4
Kalix 98 C3
Kalixälven 98 C2
Kaljord 94 A3
Kalkar 17 D3
Kalkkinen 107 F1
Kall 101 D2
Kallaktjåkkå 94 B4
Kallavesi 103 E2
Kållby 102 C1
Källby 105 E4
Kallinge 109 E3
Kallio 102 C3
Kalliojoki 99 F4
Kallislahti 103 E3
Kallmünz 55 F2
Kallsjön 101 D1
Kalmar 109 E2
Kalmar Län 109 E2
Kalmar sund 109 E2
Kalmit 54 C2
Kalna 73 F4
Kalnik 71 D2
Kalnik *Mt* 71 D2
Kalocsa 112 B4
Kalogerikoú 87 D2
Kalogriá 86 B1
Kalohóri 83 D1
Kaló Horió 91 E4
Kalókastro 80 A2
Kaló Neró 86 C3
Kaloní (Lésvos) 85 F2
Kaloní (Pelopónissos) 87 E2
Kalonís, Kólpos 85 F2
Kaloskopí 83 E3
Kalotássi, Akr 89 D4
Kalø Vig 108 B3
Kalpáki 78 C4
Kals 59 E2
Kalsdorf 57 E4
Kaltbrunn 58 A2
Kaltenkirchen 48 A2
Kaltennordheim 52 B3
Kaltern 59 D3
Kaltezés 87 D2
Kaluga 111 F3
Kalundborg 108 B3
Kaluš 112 C3
Kalvåg 104 A1
Kalvehave 108 C4
Kälviä 102 C1
Kalvola 107 E2
Kalvträsk 98 B4
Kamáres (Kríti) 91 D4
Kamáres (Páros) 88 C3
Kamáres (Pelopónissos) 83 D4
Kamáres (Sífnos) 88 B3
Kamári 91 E1
Kamariótissa 81 E3
Kambanós, Akr 88 B1
Kambiá 85 E4
Kámbos (Kríti) 90 B3
Kámbos (Pelopónissos) 86 C3
Kámbos (Stereá Eláda) 83 D4
Kamčija 115 E2
Kamen 17 E3
Kamenari 76 A3
Kaména Voúria 83 F3
Kamenec-Podol'skij 113 D3
Kamenica 77 F2
Kamenice 57 D1
Kaméni, N 91 E1
Kamenjak, Rt 70 A4
Kamenka 113 F2
Kamensko (Hrvatska) 71 E2
Kamensko (Hrvatska) 75 E1
Kamenz 53 F2
Kamień Pomorski 49 E2
Kamieński, Zalew 49 E2
Kamilári 91 D4
Kamínia 86 B1
Kámiros 93 E1
Kamnik 70 B2
Kamp 57 E2
Kamp-Bornhofen 51 E4
Kampen (D) 47 F1
Kampen (NL) 17 D2
Kamp-Lintfort 17 D3
Kanal 70 A2
Kanála 88 A2
Kanal Dunav-Tisa-Dunav 73 D2
Kanália 55 D4
Kanatádika 83 F3
Kánava 88 A4
Kándanos 90 B3
Kandel 54 C2
Kandel *Mt* 54 C3
Kandern 54 C4
Kandersteg 27 F3
Kándia 87 E2
Kandíla (Pelopónissos) 87 D2
Kandíla (Stereá Eláda) 82 C3
Kandíli 84 A3
Kandira 115 F3
Kandrše 70 B2
Kanestraum 100 B2
Kanev 113 F2
Kanfanar 70 A3
Kangádio 86 B1
Kangasala 107 E1
Kangaslampi 103 E2
Kangasniemi 103 D3
Kangosjärvi 95 D4
Kanjiža 72 C1
Kankaanpää 102 C3
Kannonkoski 103 D2
Kannus 102 C1
Kannusjärvi 103 E4
Kanturk 14 B3
Kaona 73 D4
Kaonik (Bosna i Hercegovina) 71 F4

| Name | Pg | Grid |
|---|---|---|
| Kaonik (Srbija) | 73 | E4 |
| Kapandríti | 87 | F1 |
| Kaparéli | 83 | F4 |
| Kapariá | 88 | B2 |
| Kapele, Vrh | 70 | C3 |
| Kapellskär | 106 | C3 |
| Kapélo, Akr | 90 | A2 |
| Kapfenberg | 57 | E3 |
| Kaplice | 57 | D2 |
| Kaposvár | 114 | B1 |
| Kapp | 105 | D2 |
| Kappel | 51 | E4 |
| Kappeln | 48 | A1 |
| Kappelshamnsviken | 109 | F3 |
| Kaprije | 74 | C1 |
| Kaprun | 59 | E1 |
| Kapsáli | 90 | A2 |
| Kápsas | 87 | D2 |
| Kapsoúri | 88 | B1 |
| Kapsukas | 110 | C4 |
| Kapuvár | 112 | A4 |
| Karabiga | 115 | E3 |
| Karaburun | 115 | E4 |
| Karačev | 111 | F4 |
| Karadeniz Boğazi | 115 | F3 |
| Karan | 72 | C4 |
| Karasjåkka | 95 | E2 |
| Karasjok | 95 | E2 |
| Karasu | 115 | F3 |
| Karats | 98 | A2 |
| Karavás | 90 | A1 |
| Karavómilos | 83 | F3 |
| Karavónissia | 92 | C2 |
| Karavostássis | 91 | D1 |
| Kårböle | 101 | E3 |
| Karcag | 112 | B4 |
| Kardámena | 89 | F3 |
| Kardámila | 85 | E4 |
| Kardamíli | 86 | C3 |
| Kardeljevo | 75 | E2 |
| Kärdla | 110 | B1 |
| Karditsa | 55 | D4 |
| Karditsa (Nomos) | 55 | D4 |
| Kårdžali | 115 | D3 |
| Karerpass | 59 | D3 |
| Karesuando | 95 | D3 |
| Karfás | 85 | F4 |
| Karhukangas | 99 | D3 |
| Karhula | 103 | F4 |
| Karhunkierros | 99 | F2 |
| Karhutunturi | 95 | F4 |
| Kariá (Pelopónnissos) | 87 | D2 |
| Kariá (Stereá Eláda) | 83 | F3 |
| Kariés (Makedonía) | 80 | C4 |
| Kariés (Pelopónnissos) | 87 | D3 |
| Karigasniemi | 95 | E2 |
| Karijoki | 102 | B3 |
| Karinainen | 107 | D2 |
| Kariótisa | 79 | E3 |
| Karis | 107 | E3 |
| Káristos | 88 | A1 |
| Karítena | 86 | C2 |
| Karjaa | 107 | E3 |
| Karjalohja | 107 | E3 |
| Karkaloú | 86 | C2 |
| Karkinágri | 89 | D2 |
| Karkku | 107 | D1 |
| Kärköla | 107 | E2 |
| Karleby | 102 | C1 |
| Karlevi | 109 | E3 |
| Karlino | 49 | F1 |
| Karl-Marx-Stadt | 53 | E3 |
| Karlobag | 70 | C4 |
| Karlovac | 70 | C3 |
| Karlovássi | 89 | E1 |
| Karlovo | 115 | D2 |
| Karlovy Vary | 53 | E4 |
| Karlsborg | 105 | E4 |
| Karlsburg | 49 | D2 |
| Karlsfeld | 55 | F3 |
| Karlshamn | 109 | D3 |
| Karlshuld | 55 | F2 |
| Karlskoga | 105 | E4 |
| Karlskrona | 109 | E3 |
| Karlsøy | 94 | C2 |
| Karlsruhe | 54 | C2 |
| Karlstad | 105 | E3 |
| Karlstadt | 52 | B4 |
| Karlštejn | 53 | F4 |
| Karlstift | 57 | D2 |
| Karmøy | 104 | A3 |
| Karnezéika | 87 | E2 |
| Karnobat | 115 | E2 |
| Kärnten | 59 | F2 |
| Karolinerleden | 101 | E2 |
| Karow | 48 | C2 |
| Kärpankylä | 99 | F2 |
| Kárpathos | 93 | D3 |
| Kárpathos, N | 93 | D3 |
| Karpeníssi | 83 | D3 |
| Karperí | 80 | A2 |
| Karperó | 79 | D4 |
| Kärsämäki | 103 | D1 |
| Kårsatjåkka | 94 | B4 |
| Kårsava | 111 | D2 |
| Karstädt | 48 | C3 |
| Karstula | 103 | D2 |
| Kartal | 115 | F3 |
| Kartéri (Ípiros) | 82 | B2 |
| Kartéri (Pelopónnissos) | 87 | D1 |
| Karterós | 91 | D3 |
| Kártsino, Akr | 84 | C3 |
| Karttula | 103 | E2 |
| Kartuzy | 110 | A4 |
| Karungi | 98 | C3 |
| Karunki | 98 | C3 |
| Karup | 108 | A2 |
| Karvala | 102 | C2 |
| Kärväskylä | 103 | D2 |
| Karvia | 102 | C3 |
| Karviná | 112 | B3 |
| Karvoskylä | 103 | D1 |
| Karvounári | 82 | B2 |
| Karwendelgebirge | 59 | D1 |
| Kašalj | 76 | C1 |
| Kašin | 111 | F1 |
| Kašina | 70 | C2 |
| Kaskinen | 102 | B3 |
| Kasko | 102 | B3 |
| Káspakas | 85 | D1 |
| Kašperské Hory | 56 | C1 |
| Kassándra | 80 | B4 |
| Kassándras, Kólpos | 80 | B4 |
| Kassándria | 80 | A4 |
| Kassel | 52 | A2 |
| Kassiópi | 82 | A1 |
| Kassópi | 82 | B2 |
| Kássos, N | 93 | D3 |
| Kastaniá (Makedonia) | 79 | E3 |
| Kastaniá (Pelopónnissos) | 87 | D1 |
| Kastaniá (Thessalía) | 82 | C1 |
| Kastaniá (Thessalía) | 83 | D2 |
| Kastaniés | 81 | F1 |
| Kastaniótissa | 83 | F3 |
| Kastéla | 84 | B4 |
| Kastellaun | 51 | E4 |
| Kastelhoms | 106 | C3 |
| Kastéli (Kríti) | 90 | B3 |
| Kastéli (Kríti) | 91 | E4 |
| Kastellórizo | 93 | F2 |
| Kastélou, Akr | 93 | D3 |
| Kastelruth | 59 | D3 |
| Kaštel Stari | 75 | D1 |
| Kaštel Žegarski | 75 | D1 |
| Kasterlee | 50 | C3 |
| Kastl | 55 | F1 |
| Kastorf | 48 | B2 |
| Kastóri | 87 | D2 |
| Kastoriá | 79 | D3 |
| Kastoriá (Nomos) | 78 | C3 |
| Kastoriás, L | 79 | D3 |
| Kastós, N | 82 | C4 |
| Kastráki (Kikládes) | 88 | C3 |
| Kastráki (Stereá Eláda) | 82 | C3 |
| Kastráki (Thessalía) | 83 | D1 |
| Kastrákiou, Teh L | 82 | C3 |
| Kastrí (Pelopónnissos) | 87 | D2 |
| Kastrí (Stereá Eláda) | 83 | E3 |
| Kastrí (Thessalía) | 83 | F1 |
| Kástro (Pelopónnissos) | 86 | B1 |
| Kástro (Skíathos) | 84 | A2 |
| Kástro (Stereá Eláda) | 83 | F4 |
| Kastrossikiá | 82 | B2 |
| Katafígio | 79 | E4 |
| Katáfito | 80 | B1 |
| Katáfourko | 82 | C3 |
| Katahás | 79 | F3 |
| Katákolo | 86 | B2 |
| Katálako | 85 | D1 |
| Kátano, Akr | 88 | A3 |
| Katápola | 89 | D3 |
| Katára | 82 | C1 |
| Katastári | 86 | A1 |
| Katavía | 93 | E2 |
| Katelimátsa | 91 | F1 |
| Kateliós | 86 | A1 |
| Kateríni | 79 | F4 |
| Katerloch | 57 | E4 |
| Katharó | 91 | E4 |
| Kathení | 84 | B4 |
| Katići | 76 | C1 |
| Kätkäsuvanto | 95 | D4 |
| Katlanovo | 77 | E3 |
| Katlanovska Banja | 77 | E3 |
| Katlenburg-Duhm | 52 | B2 |
| Káto Ahaía | 86 | B1 |
| Káto Alissós | 86 | B1 |
| Káto Asséa | 87 | D2 |
| Káto Dolianá | 87 | D2 |
| Káto Figália | 86 | C2 |
| Káto Gadzéa | 83 | F2 |
| Katohí | 82 | C4 |
| Káto Kamila | 80 | B2 |
| Káto Klinés | 79 | D2 |
| Káto Makrinoú | 83 | D4 |
| Katoméri, Akr | 88 | C3 |
| Káto Moussounitsa | 83 | E3 |
| Káto Nevrokópi | 80 | B1 |
| Káto Ólimbos | 83 | E1 |
| Káto Tithoréa | 83 | E4 |
| Katoúna (Lefkáda) | 82 | B3 |
| Katoúna (Stereá Eláda) | 82 | C3 |
| Káto Vassiliki | 83 | D4 |
| Káto Vérga | 86 | C3 |
| Káto Vérmio | 79 | E3 |
| Káto Vlassía | 86 | C1 |
| Katowice | 112 | B2 |
| Káto Zahloroú | 86 | C1 |
| Káto Zákros | 91 | F4 |
| Katrineholm | 106 | A4 |
| Katschberg | 59 | F2 |
| Katschberg-Tunnel | 59 | F2 |
| Kattegat | 108 | C2 |
| Katwijk aan Zee | 16 | B2 |
| Kaub | 51 | F4 |
| Kaufbeuren | 55 | E4 |
| Kauhajärvi | 102 | C2 |
| Kauhajoki | 102 | B3 |
| Kauhaneva-Pohjankangas | 102 | C3 |
| Kauhava | 102 | C2 |
| Kaukonen | 95 | E4 |
| Kaunas | 110 | C4 |
| Kaupanger | 104 | B1 |
| Kaušany | 113 | E4 |
| Kaustinen | 102 | C2 |
| Kautokeino | 95 | D3 |
| Kautokeinoelva | 95 | D3 |
| Kauttua | 107 | D2 |
| Kavadarci | 77 | E3 |
| Kavajë | 76 | C4 |
| Kavála | 80 | C2 |
| Kavála (Nomos) | 80 | C2 |
| Kaválas, Kólpos | 80 | C2 |
| Kavarna | 115 | E2 |
| Kavili | 81 | F1 |
| Kavírio-Hlói | 81 | E4 |
| Kävlinge | 108 | C3 |
| Kávos | 82 | A2 |
| Kavoússi | 91 | F4 |
| Käyla | 99 | F2 |
| Kaysersberg | 27 | E1 |
| Kazan | 73 | E2 |
| Kažani | 77 | E4 |
| Kazanlâk | 115 | D2 |
| Kazárma | 86 | C3 |
| Kazatin | 113 | E2 |
| Kazimierz Dolny | 112 | C2 |
| Kazincbarcika | 112 | B3 |
| Kdyně | 56 | B1 |
| Kéa | 88 | A2 |
| Keadew | 12 | C2 |
| Keady | 13 | D2 |
| Keähkkiljohka | 95 | D3 |
| Keal, L na | 4 | B1 |
| Kéa Meriá | 88 | A2 |
| Kéa, N | 88 | A2 |
| Kéas, Stenó | 88 | A2 |
| Kebnekaise | 94 | B4 |
| Kebnekaise Mt | 94 | B4 |
| Kebock Head | 2 | B2 |
| Kecskemét | 112 | B4 |
| Kédainiai | 110 | C3 |
| Kédros | 83 | D2 |
| Keel | 12 | A2 |
| Keerbergen | 50 | C3 |
| Kefalári | 87 | D2 |
| Kefálas, Akr | 80 | C3 |
| Kefáli, Akr | 90 | A2 |
| Kefaloniá, N | 82 | B4 |
| Kéfalos | 89 | F4 |
| Kéfalos, Akr | 88 | A2 |
| Kefalóvrisso (Ípiros) | 78 | C4 |
| Kefalóvrisso (Pelopónnissos) | 86 | C3 |
| Kefalóvrisso (Stereá Eláda) | 82 | C4 |
| Kefalóvrisso (Thessalía) | 83 | D1 |
| Keflavík | 96 | A2 |
| Kehl | 54 | C3 |
| Kehlstein | 56 | C4 |
| Kehrókambos | 80 | C2 |
| Kéhros | 81 | E2 |
| Keighley | 6 | C2 |
| Keimaneigh, Pass of | 14 | B4 |
| Keitele | 103 | D2 |
| Keitele L | 103 | D2 |
| Keith | 3 | D3 |
| Kéla | 79 | D2 |
| Kelankylä | 99 | E3 |
| Kelberg | 51 | E4 |
| Kelbra | 52 | C2 |
| Këlcyrë | 114 | C4 |
| Kelebija | 72 | B1 |
| Kelefá | 87 | D4 |
| Kelheim | 55 | F2 |
| Kellinghusen | 48 | A2 |
| Kellojärvi | 99 | F4 |
| Kellokoski | 107 | E2 |
| Kells | 13 | D3 |
| Kelso | 5 | E2 |
| Kelujärvi | 95 | E4 |
| Kemberg | 53 | D1 |
| Kembs | 27 | E1 |
| Kemi | 99 | D3 |
| Kemihaara | 95 | F4 |
| Kemijärvi | 99 | E2 |
| Kemijärvi L | 99 | E2 |
| Kemijoki | 99 | D2 |
| Keminmaa | 99 | D3 |
| Kemiö | 107 | D3 |
| Kemnath | 53 | D4 |
| Kempele | 99 | D4 |
| Kempen | 17 | D4 |
| Kempenich | 51 | E4 |
| Kempten | 55 | E4 |
| Kendal | 6 | B1 |
| Kéndras, Akr | 88 | B3 |
| Kendríko | 79 | F2 |
| Kenilworth | 9 | E1 |
| Kenmare | 14 | A4 |
| Kenmare River | 14 | A4 |
| Kennacraig | 4 | B2 |
| Kenoúrgio | 83 | D3 |
| Kent | 11 | D3 |
| Kentallen | 4 | B1 |
| Kenzingen | 54 | C3 |
| Keramía | 85 | F2 |
| Keramídi | 83 | F2 |
| Keramítsa | 82 | B1 |
| Kéramos | 85 | E4 |
| Keramotí | 81 | D2 |
| Kerassiá (Évia) | 84 | A3 |
| Kerassiá (Thessalía) | 83 | F2 |
| Kerassiés | 79 | E2 |
| Kerassohóri | 83 | D3 |
| Kerassóna | 82 | C2 |
| Kérata, Akr | 83 | F3 |
| Keratéa | 87 | F2 |
| Kerava | 107 | E2 |
| Kerdília, N | 80 | B3 |
| Kérës | 12 | C2 |
| Keri | 86 | A2 |
| Kerimäki | 103 | F3 |
| Kerken | 17 | D3 |
| Kerketéas, Óros | 89 | E1 |
| Kerkétio, Óri | 83 | D2 |
| Kerkíni, Óros | 80 | A1 |
| Kerkínis, L | 80 | A2 |
| Kérkira | 82 | A1 |
| Kérkira, N | 82 | A1 |
| Kerkonkoski | 103 | D2 |
| Kerkrade | 51 | D3 |
| Kernascléden | 22 | B3 |
| Kéros, N | 88 | C3 |
| Kerpen | 17 | D4 |
| Kerrera | 4 | B1 |
| Kerry | 14 | B3 |
| Kerry Head | 14 | A3 |
| Kerteminde | 108 | B3 |
| Kértezi | 86 | C1 |
| Kerzers | 27 | E2 |
| Kesälahti | 103 | F3 |
| Keşan | 115 | E3 |
| Kesch, Piz | 58 | B3 |
| Kesh | 12 | C2 |
| Keski-Suomen Lääni | 103 | D2 |
| Kessariani | 87 | F1 |
| Kestilä | 99 | D4 |
| Keswick | 5 | D4 |
| Keszthely | 112 | A4 |
| Kętrzyn | 110 | B4 |
| Kettering | 9 | F1 |
| Kettletoft | 3 | E1 |
| Kettwig | 17 | E4 |
| Ketzin | 49 | D4 |
| Keukenhof | 16 | B2 |
| Keurusselkä | 103 | D3 |
| Keuruu | 102 | C3 |
| Kevelaer | 17 | D3 |
| Kevo | 95 | E2 |
| Kevo (Nat Pk) | 95 | E2 |
| Key, L | 12 | C3 |
| Keynsham | 9 | D2 |
| Kežmarok | 112 | B3 |
| Kianí | 81 | F1 |
| Kiantajärvi | 99 | F3 |
| Kiáto | 87 | D1 |
| Kiberg | 95 | f1 |
| Kičevo | 77 | D3 |
| Kidderminster | 9 | D1 |
| Kidlington | 9 | E2 |
| Kidsgrove | 6 | C3 |
| Kidwelly | 8 | C2 |
| Kiefersfelden | 56 | B4 |
| Kiekinkoski | 99 | F4 |
| Kiel | 48 | A1 |
| Kielce | 112 | B2 |
| Kielder Reservoir | 5 | E3 |
| Kieler Bucht | 48 | A1 |
| Kiental | 27 | F3 |
| Kierinki | 99 | D1 |
| Kietz | 49 | F4 |
| Kifissiá | 87 | F1 |
| Kifissos | 83 | F4 |
| Kifjord | 95 | E1 |
| Kihlanki | 95 | D4 |
| Kihniö | 102 | C3 |
| Kihti Skiftet | 107 | D3 |
| Kiihtelysvaara | 103 | F2 |
| Kiikala | 107 | E2 |
| Kiikka | 107 | D2 |
| Kiikoinen | 107 | D1 |
| Kiiminen | 99 | E4 |
| Kiiminginjoki | 99 | D3 |
| Kiiminki | 99 | D3 |
| Kiiskilä | 102 | C1 |
| Kiistala | 95 | E4 |
| Kijev | 113 | E2 |
| Kijevo (Hrvatska) | 75 | D1 |
| Kijevo (Kosovo) | 77 | D1 |
| Kijevskoje Vodochranilišče | 113 | E2 |
| Kikinda | 72 | C1 |
| Kikládes | 88 | B2 |
| Kil | 105 | E3 |
| Kíla | 79 | D3 |
| Kiláda (Makedonía) | 79 | E3 |
| Kiláda (Pelopónnissos) | 87 | E2 |
| Kilafors | 101 | F4 |
| Kilbaha | 12 | A4 |
| Kilbeggan | 12 | C4 |
| Kilbirnie | 4 | C2 |
| Kilbotn | 94 | B3 |
| Kilbrannan Sd | 4 | B2 |
| Kilchoan | 2 | B4 |
| Kilcock | 13 | D4 |
| Kilcormac | 12 | C4 |
| Kilcreggan | 4 | C2 |
| Kilcullen | 13 | D4 |
| Kildare | 13 | D4 |
| Kildare (Co) | 13 | D4 |
| Kildorrery | 14 | C3 |
| Kilfenora | 12 | B4 |
| Kilgarvan | 14 | B4 |
| Kilija | 113 | E4 |
| Kilingi-Nōmme | 110 | C2 |
| Kilíni | 86 | B1 |
| Kilíni, Óros | 87 | D1 |
| Kilkee | 12 | A4 |
| Kilkeel | 13 | E3 |
| Kilkenny | 15 | D3 |
| Kilkenny (Co) | 15 | D3 |
| Kilkhampton | 8 | B3 |
| Kilkieran B | 12 | A3 |
| Kilkís | 79 | F2 |
| Kilkís (Nomos) | 79 | F2 |
| Killadysert | 12 | B4 |
| Killala B | 12 | B2 |
| Killaloe | 12 | B4 |
| Killarney | 14 | B4 |
| Killary Harbour | 12 | A3 |
| Killashandra | 12 | C3 |
| Killenaule | 14 | C3 |
| Killimer | 12 | B4 |
| Killin | 4 | C1 |
| Killinkoski | 102 | C3 |
| Killorglin | 14 | A3 |
| Killybegs | 12 | C2 |
| Killyleagh | 13 | E2 |
| Kilmaing | 12 | B3 |
| Kilmallock | 14 | B3 |
| Kilmarnock | 4 | C2 |
| Kilmartin | 4 | B2 |
| Kilmore Quay | 15 | D4 |
| Kilmurry | 12 | B4 |
| Kilninver | 4 | B1 |
| Kilnsea | 7 | E2 |
| Kilpisjärvi | 94 | C3 |
| Kilpisjärvi L | 94 | C3 |
| Kilrea | 13 | D1 |
| Kilronan | 12 | B4 |
| Kilrush | 12 | B4 |
| Kilsyth | 4 | C2 |
| Kiltamagh | 12 | B3 |
| Kiltealy | 15 | D3 |
| Kilwinning | 4 | C2 |
| Kilyos | 115 | F3 |
| Kimássi | 84 | A3 |
| Kiméria | 81 | D2 |
| Kími | 84 | B3 |
| Kimina | 79 | F3 |
| Kimis, Órmos | 84 | B4 |
| Kimito | 107 | D3 |
| Kímolos | 88 | B4 |
| Kímolos, N | 88 | B4 |
| Kimólou Sifnou, Stenó | 88 | B3 |
| Kimry | 111 | F2 |
| Kimstad | 105 | F4 |
| Kínaros, N | 89 | D3 |
| Kinbrace | 3 | D2 |
| Kincardine | 5 | D2 |
| Kindberg | 57 | E3 |
| Kindelbrück | 52 | C2 |
| Kinéta | 87 | E1 |
| Kingisepp | 111 | D1 |
| Kingissepp | 110 | B2 |
| Kingsbridge | 8 | C4 |
| Kingscourt | 13 | D3 |
| King's Lynn | 7 | E3 |
| Kingston | 9 | F2 |
| Kingston-upon-Hull | 7 | E2 |
| Kingswear | 8 | C4 |
| Kington | 9 | D1 |
| Kingussie | 3 | D4 |
| Kínira | 81 | D3 |
| Kinlochbervie | 2 | C2 |
| Kinlochewe | 2 | C3 |
| Kinloch Rannoch | 4 | C1 |
| Kinna | 108 | C1 |
| Kinnairds Head | 3 | E3 |
| Kinnasniemi | 103 | F2 |
| Kinnegad | 12 | C4 |
| Kinnitty | 12 | C4 |
| Kinnula | 103 | D2 |
| Kinross | 5 | D2 |
| Kinsale | 14 | B4 |
| Kinsarvik | 104 | B2 |
| Kintaus | 103 | D3 |
| Kintore | 3 | E4 |
| Kintyre | 4 | B2 |
| Kinvarra | 12 | B4 |
| Kinzig | 54 | C3 |
| Kióni | 82 | B4 |
| Kiparíssi | 87 | E3 |
| Kiparissía | 86 | C3 |
| Kiparissiakós Kólpos | 86 | B2 |
| Kiparissías, Óri | 86 | C3 |
| Kipárissos | 83 | E2 |
| Kípi (Ípiros) | 78 | C4 |
| Kípi (Thráki) | 81 | F2 |
| Kipinä | 99 | D3 |
| Kípos, Akr | 81 | E3 |
| Kipourío | 79 | D4 |
| Kippure | 13 | D4 |
| Kipséli | 83 | E2 |
| Kir | 76 | C3 |
| Kirá Panagiá, N | 84 | B2 |
| Kirchbach | 57 | E4 |
| Kirchberg (D) | 54 | B1 |
| Kirchberg (DDR) | 53 | D3 |
| Kirchberg (Nieder österreich) | 57 | E2 |
| Kirchberg (Tirol) | 59 | E1 |
| Kirchberg an der Pielach | 57 | E3 |
| Kirchdorf | 57 | D3 |
| Kirchenlamitz | 53 | D4 |
| Kirchenthumbach | 53 | D4 |
| Kirchhain | 52 | A3 |
| Kirchheim (Baden-Württemberg) | 55 | D2 |
| Kirchheim (Hessen) | 52 | B3 |
| Kirchheimbolanden | 54 | C1 |
| Kirchheim unter Teck | 55 | D2 |
| Kirchhundem | 17 | F4 |
| Kirchlengern | 17 | F2 |
| Kirchmöser | 49 | D4 |
| Kirchschlag | 57 | F3 |
| Kiriaki | 81 | F1 |
| Kiriáki | 83 | F4 |
| Kiriši | 111 | E1 |
| Kirkağaç | 115 | E4 |
| Kirkby Lonsdale | 6 | C1 |
| Kirkby Stephen | 5 | E4 |
| Kirkcaldy | 5 | D2 |
| Kirkcolm | 4 | B3 |
| Kirkcudbright | 4 | C3 |
| Kirkenær | 105 | D2 |
| Kirkenes | 95 | F2 |
| Kirkeøy | 105 | D4 |
| Kirkestinden | 94 | B3 |
| Kirkham | 6 | B2 |
| Kirki | 81 | E2 |
| Kirkintilloch | 4 | C2 |
| Kirkjubøur | 96 | A4 |
| Kirkkonummi | 107 | E3 |
| Kirklareli | 115 | E3 |
| Kirkonmaanselkä | 103 | F4 |
| Kirkwall | 3 | E1 |
| Kirn | 54 | B1 |
| Kirov | 111 | F3 |
| Kirovograd | 113 | F2 |
| Kirovsk | 111 | D1 |
| Kirriemuir | 5 | D1 |
| Kirtorf | 52 | A3 |
| Kiruna | 94 | C4 |
| Kisa | 109 | E1 |
| Kisac | 72 | C2 |
| Kiseljak (Loznica) | 72 | B3 |
| Kiseljak (Sarajevo) | 75 | F1 |
| Kiseljak (Tuzla) | 71 | F3 |
| Kišin'ov | 113 | E3 |
| Kisko | 107 | E3 |
| Kiskőrös | 112 | B4 |
| Kiskunfélegyháza | 112 | B4 |
| Kiskunhalas | 114 | B1 |
| Kissámou, Kólpos | 90 | B3 |
| Kißlegg | 55 | E4 |
| Kissoú Kámbos | 90 | C4 |
| Kistanje | 75 | D1 |
| Kisújszállás | 112 | B4 |
| Kisvárda | 112 | C3 |
| Kíta | 87 | D4 |
| Kíthira | 90 | A2 |
| Kíthira, N | 90 | A2 |
| Kíthnos | 88 | A2 |

| | | | | | | | | | | | | |
|---|---|---|---|---|---|---|---|---|---|---|---|---|
| Kíthnos, N | 88 A2 | Kitriés, Akr | 86 C3 | Kitzingen | 55 E1 | Kivalo | 99 D3 | Kivijärvi L | 103 D2 | Kivotós | 79 D4 | Kjerringvåg | 100 C1 |
| Kíthnou, Stenó | 88 A2 | Kittilä | 95 E4 | Kiukainen | 107 D2 | Kivéri | 87 D2 | Kivijärvi L | 103 E4 | Kizário | 81 E2 | Kjerringvik | 101 D1 |
| Kitinen | 95 E4 | Kittsee | 57 F2 | Kiuruvesi | 103 D1 | Kívi | 88 B2 | Kivilahti | 103 F2 | Kjellerup | 108 A2 | Kjølifjell | 101 D2 |
| Kitka | 99 E2 | Kitzbühel | 59 E1 | Kiutaköngäs | 99 E2 | Kivijärvi | 103 D2 | Kivitaipale | 99 D2 | Kjerringøy | 97 E1 | Kjøllefjord | 95 E1 |

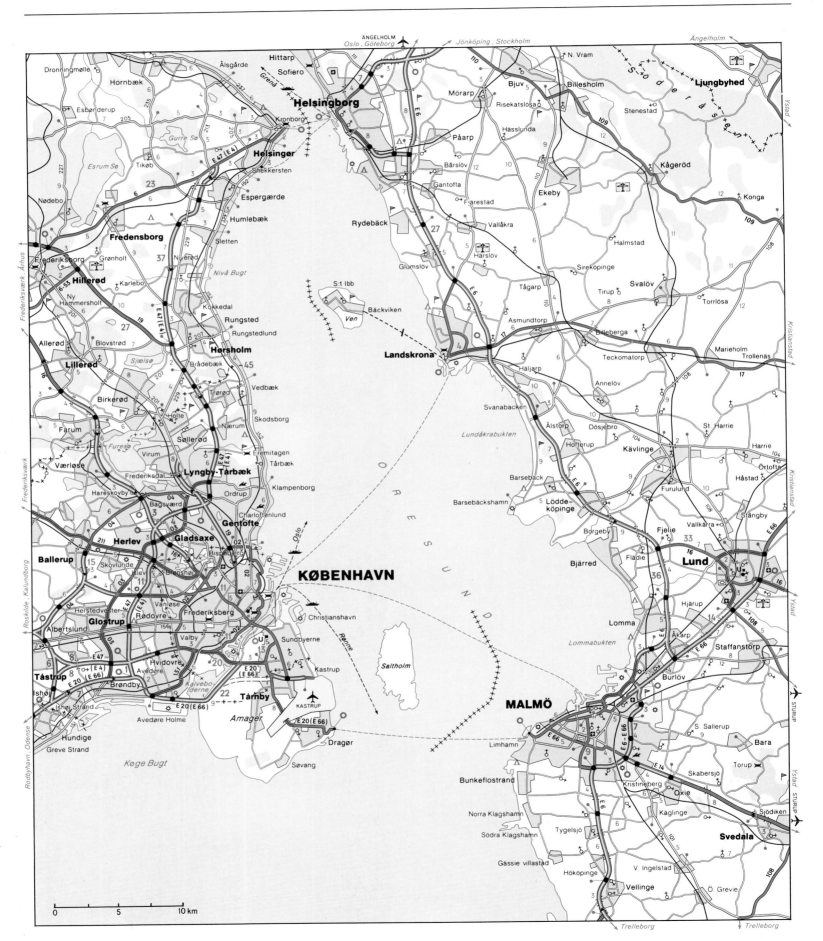

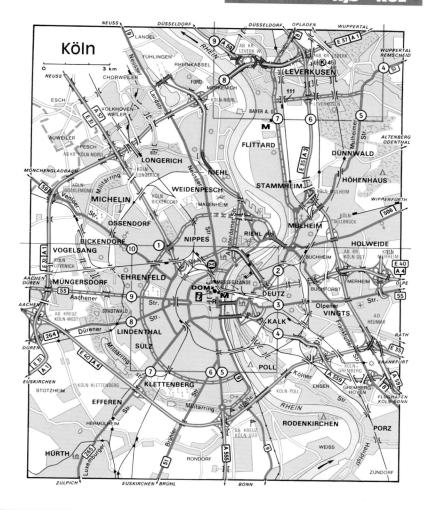

Köln

Kjøpsvik 94 B4
Kjustendil 114 C3
Klæbu 100 C2
Kladanj 72 B4
Kladnica 76 C1
Kladnice 75 D1
Kladno 53 F4
Kladovo 73 F2
Klagenfurt 70 A1
Klaipėda 110 B3
Klaksvik 96 A3
Klana 70 B3
Klanac 70 C4
Klanxbüll 47 F1
Klarälven 105 E2
Klašnice 71 E3
Klässbol 105 E3
Klášterec 53 E3
Klasvik 96 A3
Klatovy 56 C1
Klaukkala 107 E2
Klausen 59 D2
Klausenpass 58 A2
Klazienaveen 17 E2
Kleinhaugsdorf 57 E2
Kleinheubach 55 D1
Kleinwalsertal 55 E4
Klekovača 71 D4
Klenike 77 E2
Klenovica 70 B3
Kleppe 104 A3
Kleppestø 104 A2
Kleve 17 D3
Kličevac 73 D2
Klimoviči 111 E4
Klimpfjäll 97 E4
Klin 111 F2
Klina 76 C2
Klinča Selo 70 C2
Klincy 111 E4
Klingenbach 57 F3
Klingenthal 53 D3
Klinovec 53 E3
Klintehamn 109 F4
Klippan 108 C3
Klippen 97 E3
Klippitztörl 57 D4
Klis 75 D1
Klissoúra 79 D3
Klisura (Makedonija) 77 F3
Klisura (Srbija) 77 E1
Klitoria 86 C1
Klitten 53 F2
Klixbüll 47 F1
Kljajićevo 72 B2
Ključ 71 D4
Kłodzko 112 A2
Kløfta 105 D3
Klokkarvik 104 A2
Klokočevac 73 F3
Klos 76 C4
Kloštar 71 D2
Kloštar Ivanić 71 D2
Klösterle 58 B2
Klosterneuburg 57 F2
Klosters 58 B3
Kloten 58 A2
Klötze 48 C4
Klöverträsk 98 B3
Klövsjö 101 E3
Kluczbork 112 A2
Klupe 71 E3
Klütz 48 B2
Knapdale 4 B2
Knappogue Castle 12 B4
Knäred 109 D2
Knaresborough 6 C1
Knarvik 104 A2
Kneginec 71 D1
Kneža 115 D2
Knežak 70 B3
Kneževi Vinogradi 71 F2
Kneževo 71 F2
Knežica 71 D3
Knežina 72 B4
Knić 73 D4
Knídi 79 D4
Knighton 9 D1
Knight's Town 14 A4
Knin 75 D1
Knittelfeld 57 D4
Knivskjellodden 95 D1
Knivsta 106 B3

Knjaževac 73 F4
Knockmealdown Mts 14 C3
Knokke-Heist 50 A3
Knole House 10 C3
Knossós 91 D3
Knutsford 6 C2
Koarvikodds 95 E3
Kobarid 70 A2
Kobbfjorden 95 D1
Kobel'aki 113 F2
København 108 C3
Kobern-Gondorf 51 E4
Kobišnica 73 F3
Koblenz 51 E4
Kobrin 112 C1
Koca D 115 F3
Kočani 77 F2
Koceljevo 72 C3
Kočerin 75 E2
Kočevje 70 B2
Kočevski rog 70 B2
Kochel 56 A4
Kocher 55 E2
Kodiksami 107 D2
Kodisjoki 107 D2
Köflach 57 E4
Køge 108 C3
Køge Bugt 108 C3
Kohtla-Järve 110 C1
Koikkala 103 E1
Koirakoski 103 E1
Koitajoki 103 F2
Koitelainen 95 E4
Koitere 103 F2
Koivujärvi 103 D1
Koivusuo 103 F2
Kokála 87 D4
Kökar 106 C3
Kokári 89 E1
Kökarsfjärden 106 C3
Kokemäenjoki 107 D1
Kokemäki 107 D2
Kokin Brod 76 B1
Kókino Neró 83 F1
Kokkola 102 C1
Kokotí 83 F3
Koksijde-Bad 50 A3
Kola 71 E3
Koláka 83 F4
Kolari (SF) 98 C1
Kolari (YU) 73 D3
Kolåsen 101 D1
Kolašin 76 B2
Kolbäck 105 F3
Kolbacz 49 F2
Kołbaskowo 49 E2
Kolbermoor 56 B3
Kolby Kås 108 B3
Kolding 108 A3
Kolho 103 D3
Koli 103 F2
Kolima 103 D2
Kolimvári 90 B3
Kolín 112 A3
Kolindrós 79 F3
Kolínes 87 D3
Kolka 110 B2
Kolkanlahti 103 D2
Kolkasrags 110 B2
Kölleda 52 C2
Kolmården 106 A4
Köln 17 E4
Kołobrzeg 49 F1
Koločep 75 F2
Kolomyja 113 D3
Koloveč 56 B1
Kolovrat 76 B1
Kolpino 111 D1
Kolsva 105 F3
Kolubara 72 C3
Kolvereid 97 D4
Komagfjord 95 D2
Kómanos 79 D3
Komar 71 E4
Kómara 81 F1
Komarnica 76 B2
Komárno 112 B4
Kombóti 82 C2
Koméno 82 C3
Kómi (Kikládes) 88 B2
Kómi (Híos) 89 D1
Komílio 82 B3

Komin 70 C2
Kómito 88 B1
Komiža 75 D2
Komló 114 B1
Komninádes 78 C3
Komniná (Makedonía) 79 D3
Komniná (Thráki) 81 D2
Komorane 77 D2
Komotiní 81 E2
Komovi 76 B2
Komrat 113 E4
Komulanköngäs 99 E4
Konak 73 D2
Konakovo 111 F2
Končanica 71 D2
Kondiás 85 D1
Kondopoúli 85 D1
Kondós, Akr 88 B3
Kondovázena 86 C1
Kondrić 71 F2
Konečka pl 77 E3
Køng 108 C4
Köngernheim 54 C1
Konginkangas 103 D2
Kongsberg 104 C3
Kongselva 94 A3
Kongsfjord 95 F1
Kongsvinger 105 D3
Kœnigsbourg 27 E1
Königsbrück 53 E2
Königsbrunn 55 F3
Königsee 52 C3
Königsfeld 54 C3
Königslutter 52 B1
Königsschlösser 55 F4
Königssee 56 C4
Königssee L 56 C4
Königstein (D) 51 F4
Königstein (DDR) 53 F2
Königswiesen 57 D2
Königswinter 51 E3
Königs-Wusterhausen 49 E4
Konin 112 A1
Koniskós 83 D1
Konístres 84 B4
Kónitsa 78 C4
Konj 75 E1
Konjevrate 75 D1
Konjic 75 F1
Konjsko 76 A2
Konjuh 71 F4
Konkämäälven 94 C3
Könnern 52 C2
Konnevesi 103 D2
Konnevesi L 103 D2
Könönpelto 103 E3
Konopište 77 E3
Konotop 113 F1
Konsko 77 F4
Konsmo 104 B4
Konstantinovy Lázně 53 E4
Konstanz 55 D4
Kontich 50 B3
Kontiolahti 103 F2
Kontiomäki 99 E4
Konttajärvi 98 C2
Konz 54 A1
Kopaída 83 F4
Kopáni 82 C2
Kopanós 79 E3
Kopaonik 77 D1
Koparnes 100 A2
Kópasker 96 C1
Köpenick 49 E4
Koper 70 A3
Kopervik 104 A3
Köping 105 F3
Köpingsvik 109 E2
Koplik 76 B3
Köpmanholmen 102 A2
Koporiće 77 D1
Koppang 100 C3
Kopparberg 105 F3
Kopparbergs Län 105 E2
Kopparleden 101 E2
Kopperby 48 A1
Kopperveien 100 D3
Koprivna 71 F3
Koprivnica (Bosna i Hercegovina) 71 D1
Koprivnica (Srbija) 73 F3

Korab 77 D3
Kórakas, Akr 88 C3
Koralpe 70 B1
Korana 70 C3
Korbach 52 A2
Korbevac 77 E2
Korbovo 73 F2
Korçë 114 C3
Korčula 75 E2
Korčula I 75 E2
Korčulanski kan 75 E2
Korenska sedlo 70 A1
Kórfos 87 D2
Korgåsen 95 F2
Korgen 97 E3
Koria 107 F2
Korifássi 86 C3
Koríkio Ándro 83 E4
Kórimvos 81 F1
Korini 83 F4
Korinós 79 F4
Korinthía 87 D1
Korinthiakós Kólpos 87 D1
Kórinthos 87 E1
Korissía 88 A2
Korissós 79 D3
Korita (Bosna i Hercegovina) 76 A2
Korita (Crna Gora) 76 B2
Korita (Mljet) 75 F2
Korithi 86 A1
Koritnik 76 C1
Koritnik, M. 77 D3
Korkeakangas 103 F3
Korkeakoski 103 D2
Körmend 114 A4
Kornat 74 C1
Kornati 74 C1
Korneuburg 57 F2
Kornofoléa 81 F2
Kornwestheim 55 D2
Koromacno 70 B4

Koróna 79 F2
Koróni 86 C4
Korónia 83 F4
Korónia, L 80 A3
Koronida 88 C3
Koronissía 82 C3
Kóronos 88 C3
Koronoúda 80 A2
Koropí 87 F1
Körös 112 B4
Korosten' 113 E2
Korostyšev 113 E2
Korouoma 99 E2
Korpilahti 103 D3
Korpilombolo 98 C2
Korpo 107 D3
Korppoo 107 D3
Korsberga 109 E2
Korsfjorden 104 A2
Korsholm 102 B2
Korsnäs 102 B2
Korsør 108 B4
Korsun-Ševčenkovskij 113 F2
Korsvoll 100 B2
Kortesjärvi 102 C2
Korthio 88 B2
Kortrijk 50 A3
Kortteenperä 99 D2
Korvala 99 D2
Korvaluoma 102 C3
Korvatunturi 95 F3
Kos 89 F3
Kosančić 77 D1
Kosanica 76 B1
Kościan 112 A2
Kościerzyna 110 A4
Kosel 77 D4
Koserow 49 E1
Košice 112 C3
Kosjerić 72 C4
Koška 71 F2
Koskenkorva 102 B2

Koskenpää 103 D3
Koski (Hameen Lääni) 107 E2
Koski (Turun ja Porin Lääni) 107 D2
Kóskina 84 B4
Koskue 102 C3
Kosmaj 73 D3
Kosmás 87 D3
Kósmio 81 E2
Kos, N 89 F3
Kosovo 77 D2
Kosovo Polje 77 D2
Kosovska Kamenica 77 D2
Kostajnica 71 D3
Kostanjevac 70 C2
Kostanjevica 70 C2
Kostenec 115 D3
Koster 105 D4
Kostolac 73 D3
Kostonjärvi 99 E3
Kostopol' 113 D2
Kóstos 88 C3
Kosturino 77 F3
Kosula 103 E2
Koszalin 110 A4
Kőszeg 112 A4
Kotala (Keski-Suomen Lääni) 102 C3
Kotala (Lapin Lääni) 99 E1
Kótas 79 D3
Kotel 115 E2
Köthen 53 D1
Kotka 103 F4
Kotor 76 B3
Kotoriba 71 D1
Kotorsko 71 F3
Kotor Varoš 71 E4

Kotovsk (Moldavija) 113 E4
Kotovsk (Ukraina) 113 E3
Kotraža 73 D4
Kótronas 87 D4
Kotroniá 81 F2
Kötschach-Mauthen 59 E2
Köttsjön 101 F2
Kötzting 56 B1
Koufália 79 F3
Koufoníssi (Kikládes) 88 C3
Koufoníssi (Kríti) 91 F4
Koufós 80 B4
Kouklií 82 B1
Koukounariés 84 A2
Koúla 81 D1
Kouméika 89 E2
Koúndouros 88 A2
Kounoupéli 86 B1
Koúra 102 C2
Koúrenda 82 B1
Kourkoulí 84 A3
Kournás 90 C3
Kouroúta 86 B2
Koutselió 82 C1
Koutsó 81 D2
Koutsóhero 83 E1
Kouvola 107 F2
Kovačica 72 C2
Kovel' 112 C2
Kovero 103 F2
Kovin 73 D3
Köyliö 107 D2
Kozáni 79 D3
Kozáni 79 D3
Kozara 71 D3
Kozarac (Bosna i Hercegovina) 71 D3
Kozarac (Hrvatska) 71 F2
Kožel'sk 111 F3
Kozica 75 E2

| Name | Pg | Ref |
|---|---|---|
| Kozina | 70 | A3 |
| Kozjak | 77 | E4 |
| Kozluk | 72 | B3 |
| Kožuf | 77 | F4 |
| Kragenæs | 108 | B4 |
| Kragerø | 104 | C4 |
| Kragujevac | 73 | D4 |
| Krajišnik | 73 | D2 |
| Krajkovac | 77 | D1 |
| Krajn | 76 | C3 |
| Krajnik Dln | 49 | E3 |
| Krakhella | 104 | A1 |
| Krakow | 48 | C2 |
| Kraków | 112 | B2 |
| Kraljeva Sutjeska | 71 | F4 |
| Kraljevica | 70 | B3 |
| Kraljevo | 73 | D4 |
| Kralovice | 53 | E4 |
| Kralupy | 53 | F3 |
| Kramfors | 101 | F2 |
| Kranenburg | 17 | D3 |
| Krani | 77 | E4 |
| Kraniá Elassónas | 79 | E4 |
| Kraniá (Makedonía) | 79 | D4 |
| Kraniá (Thessalía) | 82 | C1 |
| Kranichfeld | 52 | C3 |
| Kranídi | 87 | E2 |
| Kranj | 70 | A2 |
| Kranjska Gora | 70 | A1 |
| Krapina | 70 | C2 |
| Krapinske Toplice | 70 | C2 |
| Krašić | 70 | C2 |
| Kráslava | 111 | D3 |
| Kraslice | 53 | D3 |
| Krasná Lipa | 53 | F2 |
| Kraśnik | 112 | C2 |
| Krasno Polje | 70 | C4 |
| Krasnyj Cholm | 111 | F1 |
| Krasnystaw | 112 | C2 |
| Kráthio | 87 | D1 |
| Krátigos | 85 | F3 |
| Kratovo | 77 | E2 |
| Kratovska-Stena | 72 | C4 |
| Krauchenwies | 55 | D3 |
| Krautheim | 55 | D1 |
| Kravarsko | 70 | C2 |
| Krefeld | 17 | D4 |
| Kremasti (Pelopónnisos) | 87 | E3 |
| Kremasti (Ródos) | 93 | F1 |
| Kremastón, Teh L | 83 | D3 |
| Kremenčug | 113 | F2 |
| Kremenčugskoje Vodochranilišče | 113 | F2 |
| Kremenec | 113 | D2 |
| Kremídi, Akr | 87 | E4 |
| Kremmen | 49 | D3 |
| Kremna | 72 | C4 |
| Kremnica | 112 | B3 |
| Krems | 57 | E2 |
| Kremsmünster | 57 | D3 |
| Krepoljin | 73 | E3 |
| Kreševo | 75 | F1 |
| Krestcy | 111 | E1 |
| Kréstena | 86 | B2 |
| Kreuth | 56 | A4 |
| Kreuzbergpass | 59 | E2 |
| Kreuzlingen | 58 | A1 |
| Kreuztal | 17 | F4 |
| Kria Vríssi (Évia) | 84 | A3 |
| Kria Vríssi (Makedonía) | 79 | E3 |
| Kričev | 111 | E4 |
| Krieglach | 57 | E3 |
| Kriens | 27 | F2 |
| Krikelo | 83 | D3 |
| Krikelos | 82 | C3 |
| Krikelos, Akr | 89 | F4 |
| Krimml | 59 | D2 |
| Krimmler Wasserfälle | 59 | D2 |
| Krimpen | 16 | C3 |
| Krinídes | 80 | C2 |
| Krionéri (Makedonía) | 80 | A2 |
| Krionéri (Pelopónnisos) | 86 | C3 |
| Krionéri (Pelopónnisos) | 87 | D1 |
| Kriopigí | 80 | B4 |
| Kriós, Akr | 90 | B4 |
| Kristalopigi | 78 | C3 |
| Kristdala | 109 | E2 |
| Kristiansand | 104 | B4 |
| Kristianstad | 109 | D3 |
| Kristianstads Län | 109 | D3 |
| Kristiansund | 100 | B2 |
| Kristiinankaupunki | 102 | B3 |
| Kristineberg | 98 | A4 |
| Kristinehamn | 105 | E4 |
| Kristinehov | 109 | D3 |
| Kristinestad | 102 | B3 |
| Krithéa | 79 | F2 |
| Krithína, Óros | 87 | E4 |
| Kritikó Pélagos | 90 | B2 |
| Kriti, N | 91 | E3 |
| Kritinía | 93 | E1 |
| Kritsá | 91 | E4 |
| Kriva Feja | 77 | E2 |
| Krivaja (Bosna i Hercegovina) | 71 | F4 |
| Krivaja (Vojvodina) | 72 | B1 |
| Kriva Palanka | 77 | E2 |
| Kriva reka | 77 | E2 |
| Krivogaštani | 77 | E4 |
| Krivoj Rog | 113 | F3 |
| Krivolak | 77 | E3 |
| Křižanov | 57 | E1 |
| Križevci | 71 | D2 |
| Krk | 70 | B3 |
| Krk I | 70 | B3 |
| Krka | 70 | B2 |
| Krka R | 75 | D1 |
| Krkonoše | 112 | A2 |
| Krmčine | 74 | C1 |
| Krn | 70 | A2 |
| Krnjača | 72 | C3 |
| Krnjak | 70 | C3 |
| Krnjeuša | 71 | D4 |
| Krnjevo | 73 | D3 |
| Krnov | 112 | A3 |
| Krnovo | 76 | B2 |
| Krøderen | 104 | C2 |
| Krokeés | 87 | D3 |
| Krokeide | 104 | A2 |
| Krokek | 106 | A4 |
| Krokilio | 83 | D4 |
| Krokom | 101 | E2 |
| Krókos | 79 | E4 |
| Kroksjö | 98 | A4 |
| Krolevec | 113 | F1 |
| Kröller Müller | 17 | D3 |
| Kroměříž | 112 | A3 |
| Kronach | 52 | C4 |
| Kronobergs Län | 109 | D2 |
| Kronoby | 102 | C1 |
| Kronshagen | 48 | A1 |
| Kronštadt | 111 | D1 |
| Kröpelin | 48 | C2 |
| Kropp | 48 | A1 |
| Kroppenstedt | 52 | C1 |
| Krosno | 112 | C3 |
| Krosno Odrzańskie | 53 | F1 |
| Krotoszyn | 112 | A2 |
| Kroussónas | 91 | D4 |
| Krovili, Pal. | 81 | E2 |
| Krrabe, M | 76 | C3 |
| Krško | 70 | C2 |
| Krstac | 76 | A2 |
| Krstača | 76 | C2 |
| Krstinja | 70 | C3 |
| Kruë i Fushës | 76 | C3 |
| Kruiningen | 16 | B4 |
| Krujë | 76 | C4 |
| Krumbach | 55 | E3 |
| Krumpendorf | 70 | A1 |
| Krün | 55 | F4 |
| Krupà | 53 | E4 |
| Krupac (Bosna i Hercegovina) | 75 | F1 |
| Krupac (Crna Gora) | 76 | B2 |
| Krupac (Srbija) | 77 | E1 |
| Krupaja | 73 | E3 |
| Krupa na Vrbasu | 71 | E4 |
| Krupanj | 72 | C3 |
| Krupište | 77 | E3 |
| Krupka | 53 | E3 |
| Kruša | 108 | A4 |
| Kruščica | 71 | E4 |
| Kruščica, Jezero | 70 | C4 |
| Krušedol Selo | 72 | C2 |
| Kruševac | 73 | E4 |
| Kruševica | 73 | D3 |
| Kruševo | 77 | E4 |
| Krute | 76 | B3 |
| Kruunupyy | 102 | C1 |
| Krvavec | 70 | B2 |
| Krynica | 112 | B3 |
| Krzeszyce | 49 | F4 |
| Kteniás, Óros | 87 | D2 |
| Ktísmata | 82 | B1 |
| Kubitzer Bodden | 49 | D1 |
| Küblis | 58 | B2 |
| Kučaj | 73 | E4 |
| Kučevište | 77 | D2 |
| Kučevo | 73 | E3 |
| Kuchl | 59 | E1 |
| Kučina Kosa | 71 | D4 |
| Kućište | 75 | E2 |
| Kućište | 76 | C2 |
| Kudowa-Zdrój | 112 | A2 |
| Kufstein | 59 | D1 |
| Kühlungsborn | 48 | C2 |
| Kuhmalahti | 103 | D3 |
| Kuhmo | 99 | F4 |
| Kuhmoinen | 103 | D3 |
| Kuivajärvi | 99 | F4 |
| Kuivajoki | 99 | D3 |
| Kuivalahti | 107 | D2 |
| Kuivaniemi | 99 | D3 |
| Kuivasjärvi | 102 | C3 |
| Kuivi | 95 | E2 |
| Kuk | 70 | C4 |
| Kukavica | 77 | E1 |
| Kukës | 76 | C3 |
| Kukkia | 107 | E1 |
| Kukko | 102 | C2 |
| Kukujevci | 72 | B2 |
| Kukulje | 71 | E3 |
| Kula (BG) | 114 | C2 |
| Kula (TR) | 115 | F4 |
| Kula (YU) | 72 | B2 |
| Kuldīga | 110 | B3 |
| Kulennoinen | 103 | F3 |
| Kulen Vakuf | 71 | D4 |
| Kulina | 73 | E4 |
| Kulju | 107 | E1 |
| Kulkjica | 74 | C1 |
| Kullaa | 107 | D1 |
| Kulm | 27 | F2 |
| Kulmbach | 52 | C4 |
| Kuloharju | 99 | E2 |
| Külsheim | 55 | D1 |
| Kultakero | 99 | E1 |
| Kultsjön | 97 | E4 |
| Kum | 70 | B2 |
| Kumane | 72 | C2 |
| Kumanovo | 77 | E2 |
| Kumla | 105 | F4 |
| Kumlinge | 106 | C3 |
| Kummavuopio | 94 | C3 |
| Kummerower See | 49 | D2 |
| Kumputunturi | 95 | E4 |
| Kumrovec | 70 | C2 |
| Kungälv | 108 | C1 |
| Kungsbacka | 108 | C1 |
| Kungshamn | 105 | D4 |
| Kungsör | 105 | F3 |
| Kunoy | 96 | A3 |
| Kunrau | 48 | B4 |
| Kunszentmárton | 112 | B4 |
| Künzelsau | 55 | D2 |
| Kuolimo | 103 | E4 |
| Kuolio | 99 | E3 |
| Kuopio | 103 | E2 |
| Kuopion Lääni | 103 | E2 |
| Kuorboaivi | 95 | E2 |
| Kuorevesi | 103 | D3 |
| Kuortane | 102 | C2 |
| Kuortovare | 94 | C4 |
| Kuortti | 103 | D3 |
| Kupa | 70 | B3 |
| Kupa | 70 | C3 |
| Kupferzell | 55 | D2 |
| Kupinova Glava | 73 | E3 |
| Kupinovo | 72 | C3 |
| Kupres | 75 | E1 |
| Kupreška vrata | 75 | E1 |
| Kurfar | 59 | D3 |
| Kurikka | 102 | B2 |
| Kuřim | 57 | F1 |
| Kuršenai | 110 | C3 |
| Kuršskij Zaliv | 110 | B3 |
| Kursu | 99 | E2 |
| Kuršumlija | 77 | D1 |
| Kuršumlijska Banja | 77 | D1 |
| Kurtakko | 95 | D4 |
| Kuru | 102 | C3 |
| Kusadak | 73 | D3 |
| Kuşadasi | 115 | E4 |
| Kusel | 54 | B1 |
| Küsnacht | 58 | A2 |
| Küssnacht | 58 | A2 |
| Kustavi | 107 | D2 |
| Küstenkanal | 17 | E1 |
| Kütahya | 115 | F3 |
| Kutina | 71 | D2 |
| Kutjevo | 71 | E2 |
| Kutná-Hora | 112 | A3 |
| Kutno | 112 | B1 |
| Kuttanen | 95 | D3 |
| Kuttura | 95 | E3 |
| Kúty | 57 | F2 |
| Kuumu | 99 | F4 |
| Kuusamo | 99 | E3 |
| Kuusamojärvi | 99 | F3 |
| Kuusankoski | 107 | F2 |
| Kuusjärvi | 103 | E2 |
| Kuusjoki | 107 | E2 |
| Kuvšinovo | 111 | E2 |
| Kuzma | 70 | C1 |
| Kuzmin | 72 | B3 |
| Kvæfjord | 94 | A3 |
| Kvaløy | 94 | B2 |
| Kvaløya | 95 | D1 |
| Kvalsund | 95 | D1 |
| Kvalvøg | 100 | B2 |
| Kvam | 100 | C3 |
| Kvænangen | 94 | C2 |
| Kvænangsbotn | 95 | D2 |
| Kvanndal | 104 | B2 |
| Kvanne | 100 | B2 |
| Kværndrup | 108 | B4 |
| Kvarner | 70 | B4 |
| Kvarnerič | 70 | B4 |
| Kvernes | 100 | B2 |
| Kvevlax | 102 | B2 |
| Kvikkjokk | 98 | A2 |
| Kvikne | 100 | C2 |
| Kvina | 104 | B4 |
| Kvinesdal | 104 | B4 |
| Kvinesdal V | 104 | B4 |
| Kvisvik | 100 | B2 |
| Kviteseid | 104 | B3 |
| Kvitnes | 100 | B2 |
| Kvitsøy | 104 | A3 |
| Kwidzyn | 110 | B4 |
| Kyjov | 57 | F1 |
| Kyläinpää | 102 | B2 |
| Kylänlahti | 103 | F1 |
| Kyleakin | 2 | B3 |
| Kyle of Lochalsh | 2 | B3 |
| Kyle of Tongue | 2 | C2 |
| Kylerhea | 2 | B3 |
| Kylestrome | 2 | C2 |
| Kyll | 51 | D4 |
| Kyllburg | 51 | D4 |
| Kylmäkoski | 107 | E2 |
| Kylmälä | 99 | D4 |
| Kymen Lääni | 103 | F4 |
| Kynsivesi | 103 | D3 |
| Kyritz | 49 | D3 |
| Kyrksæterøra | 100 | C2 |
| Kyrkslätt | 107 | E3 |
| Kyrönjoki | 102 | C2 |
| Kyrösjärvi | 102 | C2 |
| Kyselka | 53 | E3 |
| Kyšice | 53 | F4 |
| Kyyjärvi | 102 | C2 |
| Kyyvesi | 103 | E3 |

# L

| Name | Pg | Ref |
|---|---|---|
| Laa an der Thaya | 57 | F2 |
| La Adrada | 39 | F2 |
| Laage | 48 | C2 |
| Laakajärvi | 103 | E1 |
| La Alberca | 39 | E2 |
| La Alberca de Záncara | 40 | C3 |
| La Albergueria de Argañán | 39 | D2 |
| La Albuera | 38 | C4 |
| La Albufera | 41 | E4 |
| La Alcarria | 40 | C2 |
| La Algaba | 43 | D2 |
| La Almarcha | 40 | C3 |
| La Almunia de Doña Godina | 36 | C4 |
| La Antillas | 42 | C3 |
| La Azohia | 45 | D3 |
| Labacolla | 34 | A2 |
| La Baells, Emb de | 32 | A3 |
| Labajos | 40 | A1 |
| La Bañeza | 35 | D3 |
| La Barca de la Florida | 43 | D3 |
| Labasheeda | 12 | B4 |
| Labastida | 36 | B2 |
| Labastide-Clairence | 28 | A4 |
| Labastide-Murat | 29 | D2 |
| Labastide-Rouairoux | 32 | B1 |
| Labe | 53 | F3 |
| Labin | 70 | A3 |
| Labinot Fushë | 76 | C4 |
| La Bisbal de Falset | 37 | E4 |
| La Bisbal d'Empordà | 32 | B3 |
| Laboe | 48 | A1 |
| Labouheyre | 28 | A3 |
| Labouret, Col du | 31 | D3 |
| La Bóveda de Toro | 35 | D4 |
| La Brède | 28 | B2 |
| Labrit | 28 | B3 |
| Labruguière | 32 | B1 |
| Labudnjača | 72 | B2 |
| Laç | 76 | C4 |
| La Cabrera | 40 | B1 |
| Lacalahorra | 44 | B3 |
| La Campana | 43 | E2 |
| Lacanau | 28 | A2 |
| Lacanau-Océan | 28 | A2 |
| Lacapelle-Marival | 29 | D2 |
| Lacārak | 72 | B3 |
| La Carlota | 43 | E2 |
| La Carolina | 44 | A1 |
| Lacaune | 32 | B1 |
| Lacaune, Mts de | 32 | B1 |
| La Cava | 41 | F2 |
| La Cazada de Oropesa | 39 | E3 |
| Lacedonia | 64 | C3 |
| Läckö | 105 | E4 |
| Lac Léman | 27 | E3 |
| La Codosera | 38 | C3 |
| Laconi | 66 | B3 |
| La Coronada | 39 | E4 |
| La Coruña | 34 | B1 |
| Lacq | 28 | B4 |
| La Cumbre | 39 | E3 |
| La Espina | 35 | D1 |
| Ladbergen | 17 | E2 |
| Ládi | 81 | F1 |
| Ladispoli | 63 | E2 |
| Ladoeiro | 38 | C3 |
| Ladožskoje Ozero | 111 | D1 |
| Láerma | 93 | E2 |
| La Felguera | 35 | D1 |
| Laferté | 27 | D1 |
| Laffrey | 30 | C2 |
| Láfka | 87 | D1 |
| Láfkos | 83 | F2 |
| Lafnitz | 57 | F4 |
| La Franca | 35 | E1 |
| Lafrançaise | 29 | D3 |
| La Fregeneda | 39 | D1 |
| La Frontera | 40 | C2 |
| La Fuente de San Esteban | 39 | D1 |
| Lagan | 109 | D2 |
| Lagan R | 109 | D2 |
| Laganá, Kólpos | 86 | A2 |
| Laganás | 86 | A2 |
| Lagarfljót | 96 | C2 |
| La Garganta | 34 | C1 |
| La Garriga | 32 | B4 |
| Lagartera | 39 | E3 |
| Lage | 17 | F3 |
| Lagen | 100 | C3 |
| Lågen (Buskerud) | 104 | C3 |
| Lågen (Oppland) | 100 | C3 |
| Laggan | 2 | C1 |
| Laggan, L | 2 | C4 |
| Laginá (Makedonía) | 79 | F3 |
| Laginá (Thráki) | 81 | F2 |
| La Gineta | 40 | C4 |
| Lagnieu | 26 | C4 |
| Lagny | 19 | F4 |
| Lago | 67 | E3 |
| Lagoa | 42 | A2 |
| Lagoaça | 34 | C4 |
| Lagonegro | 65 | D4 |
| Lagoníssi | 87 | F2 |
| Lagos | 42 | A2 |
| Lágos | 81 | D2 |
| Lagów | 49 | F4 |
| La Granjuela | 43 | E1 |
| Lagrasse | 32 | B2 |
| Laguardia | 36 | B2 |
| La Guardia | 40 | B3 |
| La Guardia de Jaén | 44 | A2 |
| Laguarres | 37 | E3 |
| Laguarta | 37 | E2 |
| Laguiole | 29 | E2 |
| Laguna de Duero | 35 | E4 |
| Lahanás | 80 | A2 |
| La Hermida | 35 | E2 |
| La Herradura | 44 | A4 |
| Lahinch | 12 | B4 |
| Lahn | 17 | F4 |
| Lahnstein | 51 | E4 |
| Laholm | 108 | C2 |
| Laholmsbukten | 108 | C2 |
| La Horcajada | 39 | E2 |
| La Horra | 35 | F4 |
| Lahr | 54 | C3 |
| Lahti | 107 | F2 |
| Laichingen | 55 | D3 |
| Laide | 2 | B3 |
| La Iglesuela del Cid | 41 | E2 |
| Laignes | 26 | B1 |
| Laigueglia | 31 | F3 |
| Laihia | 102 | B2 |
| Lailiás | 80 | B2 |
| Laimbach | 57 | D2 |
| Laimoluokta | 94 | C3 |
| Lainate | 60 | A1 |
| Lainioälven | 95 | D4 |
| Lairg | 2 | C2 |
| Laissac | 29 | E3 |
| Laïsta | 78 | C4 |
| Laisvall | 97 | F3 |
| Laitikkala | 107 | E2 |
| Laitila | 107 | D2 |
| La Jana | 41 | F2 |
| Lajkovac | 72 | C3 |
| La Jonquera | 32 | B3 |
| Laká | 82 | A2 |
| Lakavica | 77 | E3 |
| Lake District Nat Pk | 5 | D4 |
| Lakí | 89 | E3 |
| Láki | 90 | B3 |
| Lákmos, Óri | 82 | C1 |
| Lákoma | 81 | E3 |
| Lákones | 82 | A1 |
| Lakonía | 87 | D3 |
| Lakonikós Kólpos | 87 | D4 |
| Lakópetra | 86 | B1 |
| Laksefjorden | 95 | E1 |
| Lakselv | 95 | D2 |
| Laktaši | 71 | E3 |
| La Laguna | 42 | B4 |
| La Lantejuela | 43 | E3 |
| Lálas | 86 | C2 |
| Lalbenque | 29 | D3 |
| L'Alcudia | 41 | E4 |
| L'Aldea | 41 | F2 |
| Lalín | 34 | B2 |
| Lalinac | 73 | F4 |
| Lalinde | 28 | C2 |
| La Línea de la Concepción | 43 | E4 |
| Laliótis | 87 | D1 |
| Lalm | 100 | C3 |
| Lalouvesc | 30 | B1 |
| Lalueza | 37 | E3 |
| La Luisiana | 43 | E2 |
| Lalzit, Gjiri i | 76 | C4 |
| Lam | 56 | B1 |
| Lama dei Peligni | 64 | A2 |
| La Magdalena | 35 | D2 |
| Lamalou | 30 | A4 |
| La Manche | 10 | A4 |
| La Manga del Mar Menor | 45 | D2 |
| Lamarche | 27 | D1 |
| La Marmora, P | 66 | B3 |
| Lamarque | 28 | B2 |
| Lamastre | 30 | B2 |
| Lambach | 56 | C3 |
| Lamballe | 22 | C3 |
| Lambesc | 30 | C4 |
| Lámbia | 86 | C1 |
| Lambiri | 83 | D4 |
| Lámbou Míli | 85 | F2 |
| Lambrecht | 54 | C2 |
| Lamego | 34 | B4 |
| La Mesa Roldán | 44 | C3 |
| Lamía | 83 | E3 |
| Lamlash | 4 | B2 |
| Lammermuir Hills | 5 | D2 |
| Lammhult | 109 | D2 |
| Lammi | 107 | E2 |
| La Molina | 32 | A3 |
| Lamotte-Beuvron | 25 | E2 |
| Lampaul | 22 | A2 |
| Lampedusa | 68 | A4 |
| Lampedusa, I di | 68 | A4 |
| Lampertheim | 54 | C1 |
| Lampeter | 8 | C1 |
| L'Ampolla | 41 | F2 |
| Lamstedt | 47 | F3 |
| La Mudarra | 35 | E4 |
| La Muela | 37 | D4 |
| Lamure | 26 | B4 |
| Lana | 58 | C3 |
| Lanaja | 37 | D3 |
| Lanaken | 51 | D3 |
| Lanark | 4 | C2 |
| La Nava de Ricomalillo | 39 | F3 |

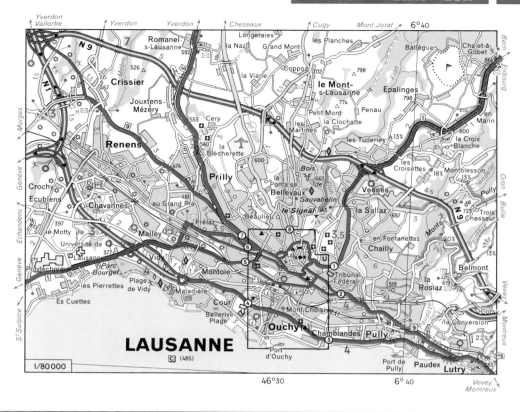

| Name | Page | Grid |
|---|---|---|
| La Nava de Santiago | 39 | D4 |
| Lancashire | 6 | B2 |
| Lancaster | 6 | B1 |
| Lanchester | 5 | E4 |
| Lanciano | 64 | A2 |
| Landaù (Bayern) | 56 | B2 |
| Landau (Rheinland-Pfalz) | 54 | C2 |
| Landeck | 58 | C2 |
| Landerneau | 22 | B2 |
| Landes | 28 | B3 |
| Landes de Lanvaux | 22 | C3 |
| Landete | 41 | D3 |
| Landévennec | 22 | A3 |
| Landivisiau | 22 | B2 |
| Landivy | 18 | C4 |
| Landmannalaugar | 96 | B2 |
| Landquart | 58 | B2 |
| Landrecies | 20 | A2 |
| Landriano | 60 | A1 |
| Landsberg | 53 | D2 |
| Landsberg | 56 | A3 |
| Land's End | 8 | A4 |
| Landshut | 56 | B2 |
| Landskapet Åland | 106 | C2 |
| Landskrona | 108 | C3 |
| Landstuhl | 54 | B2 |
| Landverk | 101 | D2 |
| Lanersbach | 59 | D2 |
| Lanesborough | 12 | C3 |
| Langåda (Híos) | 85 | F4 |
| Langáda (Pelopónissos) | 87 | D4 |
| Langadás | 79 | F3 |
| Langádas | 87 | D3 |
| Langa de Duero | 36 | A3 |
| Langádia | 86 | C2 |
| Langadíkia | 80 | A3 |
| Langangen | 104 | C4 |
| Langeac | 29 | F2 |
| Langeais | 25 | D2 |
| Langeland | 108 | B4 |
| Langelandsbælt | 108 | B4 |
| Langelmäki | 103 | D3 |
| Langelmävesi | 103 | D3 |
| Langelsheim | 52 | B1 |
| Langenargen | 55 | D4 |
| Langenau | 55 | E3 |
| Langenberg | 53 | D3 |
| Langenbruck | 55 | F2 |
| Langenburg | 55 | D2 |
| Langeneß | 47 | F1 |
| Langenfeld | 17 | E4 |
| Längenfeld | 58 | C2 |
| Langenhagen | 48 | A4 |
| Langenhahn | 51 | F3 |
| Langen (Hessen) | 52 | A4 |
| Langen (Niedersachsen) | 47 | F3 |
| Langenlois | 57 | E2 |
| Langenthal | 27 | F2 |
| Langenwang | 57 | E3 |
| Langenzenn | 55 | E1 |
| Langeoog | 47 | E3 |
| Långeserud | 105 | E3 |
| Langeskov | 108 | B3 |
| Langesund | 104 | C4 |
| Langevåg | 100 | A2 |
| Langevåg | 104 | A3 |
| Långfjället | 101 | D3 |
| Langfjord | 95 | D2 |
| Langfjorden | 95 | E1 |
| Langfjordjøkelen | 94 | C2 |
| Langforden | 100 | B2 |
| Langhirano | 60 | B2 |
| Langholm | 5 | D3 |
| Langjökull | 96 | B2 |
| Langnau | 27 | F2 |
| Langogne | 29 | F2 |
| Langon | 28 | B2 |
| Langøya | 94 | A3 |
| Langport | 9 | D3 |
| Langres | 26 | C1 |
| Langrune | 18 | C3 |
| Långsele | 101 | F2 |
| Långshyttan | 105 | F2 |
| Långträsk | 98 | B3 |
| Lanjarón | 44 | A3 |
| Lanke | 49 | E3 |
| Länkipohja | 103 | D3 |
| Lanmeur | 22 | B2 |
| Lannemezan | 37 | E1 |
| Lannilis | 22 | A2 |
| Lannion | 22 | B2 |
| Lanouaille | 29 | D1 |
| Lans-en-Vercors | 30 | C1 |
| Lanslebourg | 31 | E1 |
| Lanta | 29 | D4 |
| Lantosque | 31 | E3 |
| La Nuez de Arriba | 35 | F3 |
| Lanusei | 66 | C3 |
| Lanvollon | 22 | C2 |
| Lanzahita | 39 | F2 |
| Lanzarote | 42 | C3 |
| Lanzo Torinese | 31 | E1 |
| Laois | 12 | C4 |
| La Oliva (Is Canarias) | 42 | C4 |
| La Oliva (Navarra) | 36 | C2 |
| Laon | 20 | A3 |
| La Orotava | 42 | B4 |
| La Paca | 44 | C2 |
| Lapalisse | 26 | B4 |
| La Palma | 42 | A4 |
| La Palma del Condado | 42 | C2 |
| La Panadella | 37 | F4 |
| Lápas | 86 | B1 |
| Lapa, Sa da | 38 | C1 |
| Laperdiguera | 37 | E3 |
| La Pinilla | 36 | A4 |
| Lapinjärvi | 107 | F2 |
| Lapin Lääni | 95 | E4 |
| Lapinlahti | 103 | E2 |
| La Platja d'Aro | 32 | B4 |
| La Plaza | 35 | D2 |
| Lapleau | 29 | E1 |
| Laplume | 28 | C3 |
| La Pobla | 41 | E4 |
| La Pobla de Lillet | 32 | A3 |
| La Pobla de Massaluca | 37 | E4 |
| La Pobla de Segur | 37 | F3 |
| La Pobla de Vallbona | 41 | E3 |
| Lapoutroie | 27 | E1 |
| Lapovo | 73 | D3 |
| Lappajärvi | 102 | C2 |
| Lappajärvi L | 102 | C2 |
| Lappalaisten-Kesätuvat | 95 | D3 |
| Lappea | 98 | C2 |
| Lappeenranta | 103 | F4 |
| Lappfjärd | 102 | B3 |
| Lappfors | 102 | C2 |
| Lappi | 107 | D2 |
| Lappoo | 102 | C2 |
| Lappohja | 107 | E3 |
| Lappträsk | 98 | C3 |
| Lappträsk | 107 | F2 |
| Lappvesi | 106 | C3 |
| Lapua | 102 | C2 |
| Lapuanjoki | 102 | C2 |
| La Puebla de Almoradiel | 40 | B3 |
| La Puebla de Cazalla | 43 | E3 |
| La Puebla de Híjar | 37 | D4 |
| La Puebla de los Infantes | 43 | E2 |
| La Puebla del Río | 43 | D3 |
| La Puebla de Montalbán | 39 | F3 |
| La Puebla de Valverde | 41 | D2 |
| La Pueblanueva | 39 | F3 |
| La Puerta de Segura | 44 | B1 |
| Lapväärtti | 102 | B3 |
| L'Aquila | 63 | F2 |
| La Rábida | 42 | C3 |
| La Rábita | 44 | B4 |
| Laracha | 34 | A1 |
| Laragh | 13 | D4 |
| Laragne-Montéglin | 30 | C3 |
| La Rambla | 43 | F2 |
| Lärbro | 109 | F3 |
| Larche (Alpes-de-Haute-Provence) | 31 | E2 |
| Larche (Corrèze) | 29 | D2 |
| Larche, Col de | 31 | E2 |
| Lærdalsøyri | 104 | B1 |
| Lardarello | 60 | C4 |
| Lárdos | 93 | F2 |
| Lárdos, Akr | 93 | F2 |
| Laredo | 36 | A1 |
| Laren | 16 | C2 |
| Largentière | 30 | B2 |
| Largs | 4 | C2 |
| Lárimna | 84 | A4 |
| La Rinconada | 43 | D3 |
| Larino | 64 | B2 |
| La Rioja | 36 | B2 |
| Lárissa | 83 | E1 |
| Lárissa (Nomos) | 83 | E2 |
| Larmor | 22 | B4 |
| Larne | 13 | E2 |
| La Robla | 35 | D2 |
| La Roca | 32 | B4 |
| La Roca de la Sierra | 39 | D4 |
| Larochette | 21 | D2 |
| La Roda (Andalucía) | 43 | E3 |
| La Roda (Castilla-la-Mancha) | 40 | C4 |
| Laroles | 44 | B3 |
| Laroquebrou | 29 | E2 |
| Laroque-d'Olmes | 32 | A2 |
| Laroque-Timbaut | 28 | C3 |
| Larouco | 34 | B3 |
| Larraga | 36 | C2 |
| Larrau, Pto de | 37 | D2 |
| Larseng | 94 | B2 |
| Larsmo | 102 | C1 |
| Larv | 109 | D1 |
| Larvik | 104 | C4 |
| Lasalle | 29 | F3 |
| Las Alpujarras | 44 | A3 |
| Las Arenas | 36 | B1 |
| Lasarte | 36 | C1 |
| Las Batuecas | 39 | E2 |
| Las Cabezas de San Juan | 43 | D3 |
| Las Cabrillas, Pto de | 41 | E2 |
| Las Caldas de Besaya | 35 | F2 |
| Las Campanas | 36 | C2 |
| Lascaux, Grotte de | 29 | D2 |
| La Seca | 35 | E4 |
| La Selva del Camp | 37 | F4 |
| La Sénia | 41 | F2 |
| La Seu d'Urgell | 32 | A3 |
| Las Huelgas Reales | 35 | F3 |
| Lasinjski Sjeničak | 70 | C3 |
| Laško | 70 | B2 |
| Las Mesas | 40 | B4 |
| Las Mestas | 39 | E2 |
| Las Minas | 44 | C1 |
| Las Navas de la Concepción | 43 | E2 |
| Las Navas del Marqués | 40 | A2 |
| Las Negras | 44 | C4 |
| Læsø | 108 | B2 |
| La Solana | 40 | B4 |
| Las Pajanosas | 43 | D2 |
| Las Palmas de Gran Canaria | 42 | B4 |
| Las Pedroñeras | 40 | C4 |
| Las Pedrosas | 37 | D3 |
| La Spezia | 60 | B3 |
| Las Portas, Emb de | 34 | B3 |
| Las Rozas | 40 | A2 |
| Lassan | 49 | E2 |
| Lassay | 23 | E3 |
| Lassigny | 19 | F3 |
| Lassíthi | 91 | E4 |
| Lassíthi (Nomos) | 91 | F4 |
| Lastovo | 75 | E3 |
| Lastovo I | 75 | E3 |
| Lastovski kan | 75 | E2 |
| Lastra a Signa | 60 | C3 |
| Lastres | 35 | E1 |
| Lastrup | 17 | E1 |
| Lastva | 76 | A2 |
| Lašva | 71 | F4 |
| Las Veguillas | 39 | E1 |
| Las Ventas con Peña Aguilera | 40 | A3 |
| Las Vertientes | 44 | B3 |
| Las Viñas | 43 | F2 |
| Lätäseno | 95 | D3 |
| Laterza | 65 | D4 |
| Lathen | 17 | E1 |
| Latheron | 3 | D2 |
| Latiano | 65 | E3 |
| Latikberg | 97 | F4 |
| Latina | 63 | F2 |
| Latisana | 59 | E3 |
| Lató | 91 | E4 |
| Latour-de-France | 32 | B2 |
| Latronico | 65 | D4 |
| Latronquière | 29 | E2 |
| Latvija | 110 | C3 |
| Lauchhammer | 53 | E2 |
| Lauder | 5 | D2 |
| Lauenau | 52 | A1 |
| Lauenburg | 48 | B3 |
| Lauenstein | 53 | E3 |
| Lauf | 55 | F1 |
| Laufen (CH) | 27 | E2 |
| Laufen (D) | 56 | B3 |
| Laufenburg | 54 | C4 |
| Lauffen | 55 | D2 |
| Laugafell | 96 | B2 |
| Laugar | 96 | A2 |
| Laugarvatn | 96 | B2 |
| Lauhanvuori | 102 | B3 |
| Lauingen | 55 | E2 |
| Laujar de Andarax | 44 | B3 |
| Laukaa | 103 | D3 |
| Lauksundskaret | 94 | C2 |
| Launceston | 8 | B3 |
| La Unión | 45 | D3 |
| Laupheim | 55 | E3 |
| Lauragh | 14 | A4 |
| Laureana di Borrello | 67 | E4 |
| Laurencekirk | 3 | E4 |
| Laurenzana | 65 | D4 |
| Lauria | 67 | E1 |
| Laurière | 25 | E4 |
| Lausanne | 27 | D3 |
| Lauta | 53 | E2 |
| Lautaret, Col du | 31 | D2 |
| Lautenthal | 52 | B1 |
| Lauter | 54 | C2 |
| Lauterbach | 52 | A3 |
| Lauterbourg | 21 | F3 |
| Lauterbrunnen | 27 | F3 |
| Lauterecken | 54 | B1 |
| Lautrec | 32 | A1 |
| Lauttakylä | 107 | D2 |
| Lauvstad | 100 | A2 |
| Lauvvik | 104 | A3 |
| Lauzet-Ubaye, le | 31 | D2 |
| Lauzun | 28 | C2 |
| Lavagna | 60 | A3 |
| Laval | 23 | E3 |
| Lavamünd | 70 | B1 |
| Lavandou, le | 31 | D4 |
| Lavangen | 94 | B3 |
| Lavant | 70 | B1 |
| Lávara | 81 | F2 |
| Lavardac | 28 | C3 |
| Lavelanet | 32 | A2 |
| Lavello | 64 | C3 |
| Lavelsloh | 17 | F2 |
| Lavenham | 11 | D1 |
| Laveno | 58 | A4 |
| Lavéra | 30 | C4 |
| La Verna | 61 | D3 |
| Lavia | 102 | C3 |
| Laviano | 64 | C4 |
| Lavik | 104 | A1 |
| La Villa de Don Fadrique | 40 | B3 |
| Lavinio Lido di Enea | 63 | E3 |
| La Virgen del Camino | 35 | D2 |
| Lavis | 59 | D3 |
| Lavit | 28 | C3 |
| Lavour | 29 | D4 |
| Låvong | 97 | E3 |
| Lavoûte-Chilhac | 29 | F2 |
| Lavre | 38 | B4 |
| Lávrio | 88 | A2 |
| Lavvuoai'vi | 95 | D3 |
| Laxå | 105 | E4 |
| Laxe | 34 | A1 |
| Laxford Bridge | 2 | C2 |
| Laxo | 3 | F1 |
| Lay | 24 | C3 |
| La Yesa | 41 | D3 |
| Layos | 40 | A3 |
| Laza | 34 | B3 |
| Lazarevac | 72 | C3 |
| Lazarev Krst | 76 | B2 |
| Lazaropole | 77 | D3 |
| Lazio | 63 | E2 |
| Lazise | 60 | C1 |
| Lázně Kynžvart | 53 | D4 |
| Laznica | 73 | D3 |
| Leadenham | 7 | D3 |
| Leamington Spa, Royal | 9 | E1 |
| Leane, L | 14 | B4 |
| Łeba | 110 | A4 |
| Lebach | 54 | B2 |
| Lebane | 77 | D1 |
| Lebedin | 113 | F1 |
| Lebesby | 95 | E1 |
| Lebork | 110 | A4 |
| Lebrija | 43 | D3 |
| Lebus | 49 | F4 |
| Lecce | 65 | F4 |
| Lecco | 58 | B4 |
| Lécera | 37 | D4 |
| Lečevica | 75 | D1 |
| Lech (D) | 55 | E2 |
| Léchère, la | 31 | D1 |
| Lechlade | 9 | E2 |
| Leciñena | 37 | D3 |
| Leck | 47 | F1 |
| Lecques, les | 30 | C4 |
| Lectoure | 28 | C3 |
| Lecumberri | 36 | C1 |
| Ledaña | 41 | D4 |
| Ledanca | 40 | B1 |
| Ledbury | 9 | D1 |
| Ledesma | 39 | E1 |
| Lédignan | 30 | B3 |
| Ledmore | 2 | C2 |
| Lee | 14 | B4 |
| Leeds | 6 | C2 |
| Leek | 6 | C3 |
| Leenane | 12 | B3 |
| Leer | 47 | E3 |
| Leerdam | 16 | C3 |
| Leese | 48 | A1 |
| Leeuwarden | 16 | C1 |
| Lefkáda | 82 | B3 |
| Lefkáda, N | 82 | B3 |
| Lefkádia | 79 | E3 |
| Lefkadíti | 83 | E3 |
| Lefkandí | 84 | B4 |
| Lefká Óri | 90 | B3 |
| Léfkara | 79 | E4 |
| Léfkes | 88 | C3 |
| Lefkími | 81 | F2 |
| Lefkími, Akr | 82 | A2 |
| Lefkógia | 80 | B1 |
| Lefkopigí | 79 | D4 |
| Léfktra | 83 | F4 |
| Legan | 48 | A2 |
| Leganés | 40 | A2 |
| Legé | 24 | B3 |
| Legnago | 60 | C1 |
| Legnano | 60 | A1 |
| Legnica | 112 | A2 |
| Legrad | 71 | D1 |
| Legrená | 87 | F2 |
| Léguevin | 29 | D4 |
| Legutiano | 36 | B1 |
| Le Havre | 19 | D3 |
| Lehená | 86 | B1 |
| Lehnin | 49 | D4 |
| Léhovo | 79 | D3 |
| Lehrberg | 55 | E1 |
| Lehre | 52 | B1 |
| Lehrte | 52 | B1 |
| Lehtimäki | 102 | C2 |
| Lehtovaara (Lapin Lääni) | 99 | D1 |
| Lehtovaara (Oulun Lääni) | 103 | E1 |

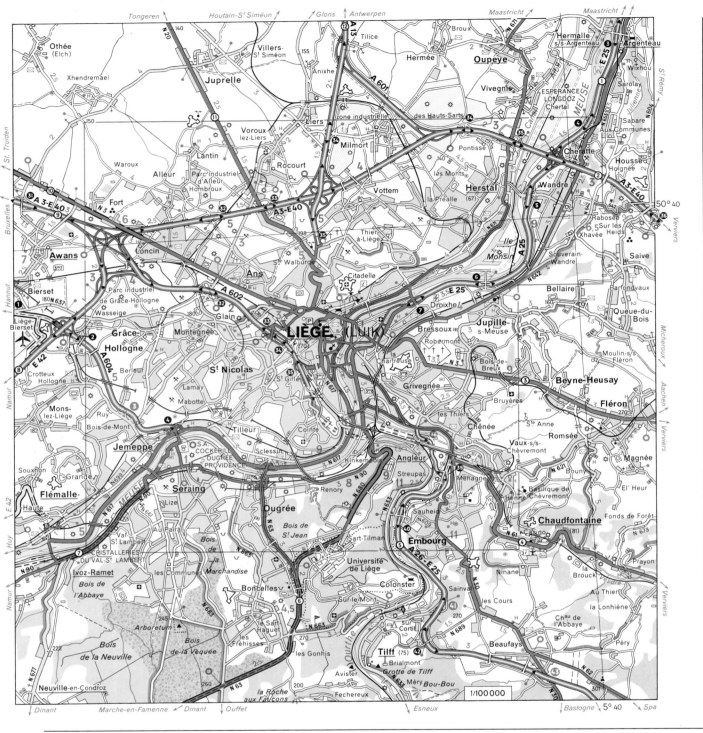

| | | |
|---|---|---|
| Leptokariá (Makedonía) | 79 | F4 |
| Leptokariá (Thráki) | 81 | E2 |
| Lercara Friddi | 68 | B3 |
| Léré | 26 | A2 |
| Lerici | 60 | B3 |
| Lérida | 37 | E4 |
| Lerín | 36 | C2 |
| Lérins | 31 | E4 |
| Lerma | 35 | F3 |
| Lermoos | 58 | C1 |
| Lérni | 87 | D2 |
| Léros, N | 89 | E3 |
| Lerum | 108 | C1 |
| Lerwick | 3 | F2 |
| Les | 37 | F2 |
| Lešak | 76 | C1 |
| Lešani | 77 | D4 |
| Les Borges Blanques | 37 | F4 |
| L'Escala | 32 | C3 |
| Lescar | 28 | B4 |
| Lesce | 70 | A2 |
| Lešće | 70 | C3 |
| Lescun | 37 | D2 |
| Leshnicë | 77 | D4 |
| Lesima, Mte | 60 | B2 |
| Lesina | 64 | C2 |
| Lesina, L di | 64 | C2 |
| Lesja | 100 | B3 |
| Lesjöfors | 105 | E3 |
| Leskovac | 77 | E1 |
| Les Llosses | 32 | A3 |
| Lesneven | 22 | B2 |
| Lešnica | 72 | B3 |
| Lesparre-Médoc | 28 | A1 |
| L'Espina | 41 | F2 |
| L'Espluga de Francoli | 37 | F4 |
| Les Portes de Fer | 73 | E3 |
| L'Espunyola | 32 | A3 |
| Lessay | 18 | B3 |
| Lessebo | 109 | E2 |
| Lessines | 50 | B3 |
| Lessini | 82 | C4 |
| L'Estartit | 32 | C3 |
| Lestelle-Bétharram | 37 | E1 |
| Lestijärvi | 102 | C2 |
| Lestijoki | 102 | C1 |
| Lestkov | 53 | E4 |
| Lésvos, N | 85 | F2 |
| Leszno | 112 | A2 |
| Letchworth | 9 | F2 |
| Letenye | 114 | A1 |
| Letino | 64 | C3 |
| Letmathe | 17 | E4 |
| Letterfrack | 12 | A3 |
| Letterkenny | 12 | C1 |
| Lettermullan | 12 | A3 |
| Letur | 44 | C1 |
| Letuš | 70 | B1 |
| Letzlingen | 48 | C4 |
| Leuca | 65 | F4 |
| Leuchars | 5 | D1 |
| Leuk | 27 | F3 |
| Leukerbad | 27 | E3 |
| Leuna | 53 | D2 |
| Leutenberg | 52 | C3 |
| Leutershausen | 55 | E1 |
| Leutkirch | 55 | E4 |
| Leutschach | 70 | B1 |
| Leuven | 50 | C3 |
| Leuze | 50 | B4 |
| Levajok | 95 | E2 |
| Levanger | 101 | D1 |
| Levanjska Varoš | 71 | F2 |
| Levant, I du | 31 | E4 |
| Levanto | 60 | B3 |
| Levanzo, I di | 68 | A3 |
| Levásjoki | 102 | B3 |
| Levene | 108 | C1 |
| Leven (England) | 7 | F2 |
| Leven (Scotland) | 5 | D2 |
| Levens | 31 | E3 |
| Leverano | 65 | F4 |
| Leverburgh | 2 | A3 |
| Leverkusen | 17 | E4 |
| Levet | 25 | F3 |
| Levi | 95 | E4 |
| Levice | 112 | B3 |
| Levico Terme | 59 | D3 |
| Levídi | 87 | D2 |
| Levie | 33 | F4 |

| | | | | | | | | | | | | |
|---|---|---|---|---|---|---|---|---|---|---|---|---|
| Leibnitz | 70 | B1 | Leirvik (Hordaland) | 104 | A3 | Leknes (Nordland) | 97 | E1 | Lemmer | 16 | C1 | |
| Leicester | 9 | F1 | Leirvik (Sogn og | | | Łeknica | 53 | F1 | Lemonodássos | 87 | F2 | |
| Leicestershire | 9 | E1 | Fjordane) | 104 | A1 | Leksand | 101 | E4 | Lempäälä | 107 | E1 | |
| Leiden | 16 | B3 | Leisnig | 53 | E2 | Leksvik | 100 | C1 | Lempdes | 29 | F1 | |
| Leie | 50 | B4 | Leiston | 11 | E1 | Leland | 97 | D3 | Lemvig | 108 | A2 | |
| Leighton Buzzard | 9 | F2 | Leitáriegos, Pto de | 34 | C2 | Lelång | 105 | D4 | Lemart | 70 | C1 | |
| Leikanger | 100 | A3 | Leith | 5 | D2 | Lelija | 76 | A1 | Lencloître | 25 | D3 | |
| Leiknes | 97 | F1 | Leitha | 57 | F2 | Lelystad | 16 | C2 | Lend | 59 | E1 | |
| Leine | 48 | A4 | Leitir Ceanainn | 12 | C1 | Lelystad-Haven | 16 | C2 | Léndas | 91 | D4 | |
| Leinefelde | 52 | B2 | Leitrim | 12 | C1 | Léman, Lac | 27 | E3 | Lendava | 71 | D1 | |
| Leini | 31 | E1 | Leitzkau | 52 | C1 | Le Mans | 23 | F3 | Lendava R | 70 | C1 | |
| Leipheim | 55 | E3 | Leivonmäki | 103 | D3 | Lembach | 21 | E3 | Lendinara | 61 | D2 | |
| Leipzig | 53 | D2 | Leiza | 36 | C1 | Lembeye | 28 | B4 | Lengefeld | 53 | E3 | |
| Leira (Møre og | | | Lek | 16 | C3 | Lemförde | 17 | F2 | Lengenfeld | 53 | D3 | |
| Romsdal) | 100 | B2 | Léka | 89 | E1 | Lemgo | 17 | F2 | Lengerich | 17 | E2 | |
| Leira (Oppland) | 104 | C2 | Leka | 97 | D3 | Lemgow | 48 | C3 | Lenggries | 56 | A4 | |
| Leirbotn | 95 | D2 | Lekáni | 80 | C2 | Lemi | 103 | E4 | Lenhovda | 109 | E2 | |
| Leiria | 38 | B2 | Lekeitio | 36 | B1 | Lemland | 106 | C3 | Leningrad | 111 | D1 | |
| Leiro | 34 | B2 | Lekenik | 71 | D2 | Lemmenjoki | 95 | E3 | Lenk | 27 | E3 | |
| Leirpollskogen | 95 | F1 | Leknes (Møre og | | | Lemmenjoki (Nat Pk) | 95 | E3 | Lenne | 17 | F4 | |
| Leirvåg | 104 | A1 | Romsdal) | 100 | A2 | Lemmenjoki R | 95 | E3 | Lennestadt | 17 | F4 | |
| Leirvik (Færøerne) | 96 | A3 | | | | | | | Lens | 19 | F2 | |

| | | | | | |
|---|---|---|---|---|---|
| Lemmer | 16 | C1 | Lensahn | 48 | B2 |
| Lemonodássos | 87 | F2 | Lentföhrden | 48 | A2 |
| Lempäälä | 107 | E1 | Lenti | 114 | A1 |
| Lempdes | 29 | F1 | Lentiira | 99 | F4 |
| Lemvig | 108 | A2 | Lenting | 55 | F2 |
| Lemart | 70 | C1 | Lentini | 69 | D4 |
| Lencloître | 25 | D3 | Lentua | 99 | F4 |
| Lend | 59 | E1 | Lenvik | 94 | B3 |
| Léndas | 91 | D4 | Lenzburg | 27 | F2 |
| Lendava | 71 | D1 | Lenzen | 48 | C3 |
| Lendava R | 70 | C1 | Lenzerheide Valbella | 58 | B3 |
| Lendinara | 61 | D2 | Lenzkirch | 54 | C4 |
| Lengefeld | 53 | E3 | Leoben | 57 | E4 |
| Lengenfeld | 53 | D3 | Leobersdorf | 57 | F3 |
| Lengerich | 17 | E2 | Leogang | 59 | E1 |
| Lenggries | 56 | A4 | Leominster | 9 | D1 |
| Lenhovda | 109 | E2 | Léon | 28 | A3 |
| Leningrad | 111 | D1 | León | 35 | D2 |
| Lenk | 27 | E3 | León, Mtes de | 35 | D2 |
| Lenne | 17 | F4 | Leonberg | 55 | D2 |
| Lennestadt | 17 | F4 | Léoncel | 30 | C2 |
| Lens | 19 | F2 | | | |

| | | | | | |
|---|---|---|---|---|---|
| Leondári (Pelopónissos) | 86 | C2 | Levajok | 95 | E2 |
| Leondári (Thessalía) | 83 | E2 | | | |
| Leóndio | 87 | D2 | | | |
| Leonessa | 63 | E1 | | | |
| Leonforte | 68 | C3 | | | |
| Leonídio | 87 | E3 | | | |
| León, Pto del | 43 | F3 | | | |
| Leopoldsburg | 50 | C3 | | | |
| Leopoldsdorf | 57 | F2 | | | |
| Leopoldsteinersee | 57 | D3 | | | |
| Leovo | 113 | E4 | | | |
| Lepel' | 111 | D3 | | | |
| Lepenoú | 80 | C3 | | | |
| Lepenski vir | 73 | E3 | | | |
| Lepetane | 76 | B3 | | | |
| Lepoglava | 70 | C1 | | | |
| Leposavić | 77 | D1 | | | |
| Lépoura | 84 | B4 | | | |
| Leppäjärvi | 95 | D3 | | | |
| Leppävirta | 103 | E2 | | | |

Levier 27 D3
Levítha, N 89 E3
Levoča 112 B3
Levroux 25 E3
Lévy, Cap 18 B2
Lewes 10 C3
Lewis 2 B2
Leyburn 6 C1
Leyland 6 B2
Leyre 37 D2
Leysdown-on-Sea 11 D2
Leysin 27 E3
Lézardrieux 22 C2
Lézat 37 F1
Lezay 24 C4
Lezhë 76 C3
Lézignan-Corbières 32 B2
Ležimir 72 C2
Lezoux 29 F1
Lezuza 40 C4
L'gov 111 F4
L'Hospitalet de l'Infant 37 F4
Liabygda 100 B2
Liákoura 83 E4
Lianokládi 83 E3
Liathach 2 C3
Liberec 112 A2
Libochovice 53 F3
Libourne 28 B2
Librazhd 77 D4
Librilla 45 D2
Licata 68 C4
Licciana Nardi 60 B3
Lich 52 A4
Lichfield 9 E1
Lichoslavl' 111 F2
Lichtenberg 53 D3
Lichtenfels 52 C4
Lichtenstein 53 D3
Lichtenvoorde 17 D3
Lička Jesenica 70 C3
Lički Osik 70 C4
Ličko Lešće 70 C4
Lida 110 C4
Liddel Water 5 D3
Liden 101 F2
Lidhult 109 D2
Lidingö 106 B4
Lidköping 105 E4
Lido degli Estensi 61 D2
Lido delle Nazioni 61 D2
Lido di Camaiore 60 B3
Lido di Classe 61 E3
Lido di Jesolo 59 E4
Lido di Metaponto 65 E4
Lido di Ostia 63 E3
Lido di Savio 61 E3
Lido di Spina 61 D2
Lido di Venezia 61 D1
Lidoríki 83 E4
Lido Silvana 65 E4
Lidzbark Warmiński 110 B4
Liebenwalde 49 D3
Lieberose 53 F1
Liège 51 D4
Liège (Prov) 51 D4
Lieksa 103 F1
Lienz 59 E2
Liepāja 110 B3
Lier 50 C3
Liérganes 35 F2
Liernais 26 B2
Lieser 59 F2
Liesjärvi 107 E2
Liestal 27 E2
Lieto 107 D2
Liétor 44 C1
Lieurey 19 D3
Lievestuore 103 D3
Liévin 19 F1
Liezen 57 D3
Liffey 13 D4
Liffol-le-Grand 20 C4
Lifford 13 D1
Liffré 23 D3
Lifjell 104 C3
Ligiá 86 B1
Lignano Sabbiadoro 59 F4
Ligné 23 D4
Lignières 25 F3

Ligny-en-Barrois 20 C4
Ligny-le-Châtel 26 B1
Ligourió 87 E2
Ligueil 25 D3
Liguria 60 A3
Liháda 83 F3
Liikasenvaara 99 E2
Lijeva Rijeka 76 B2
Lijevi Dubravčak 71 D2

Lima 101 D4
Limáni Hersoníssou 91 E3
Limáni Litohórou 79 F4
Lima, R 34 A3
Limavady 13 D1
Limbach 53 D3
Limbara, M 66 B2
Limburg (B) 50 C3

Linariá 84 C3
Linas, M 66 B4
Lincoln 7 D3
Lincolnshire 7 D3
Lindås 104 A2
Lindau 55 D4
Linden 52 C4
Lindenberg 55 E4
Linderhof 55 F4

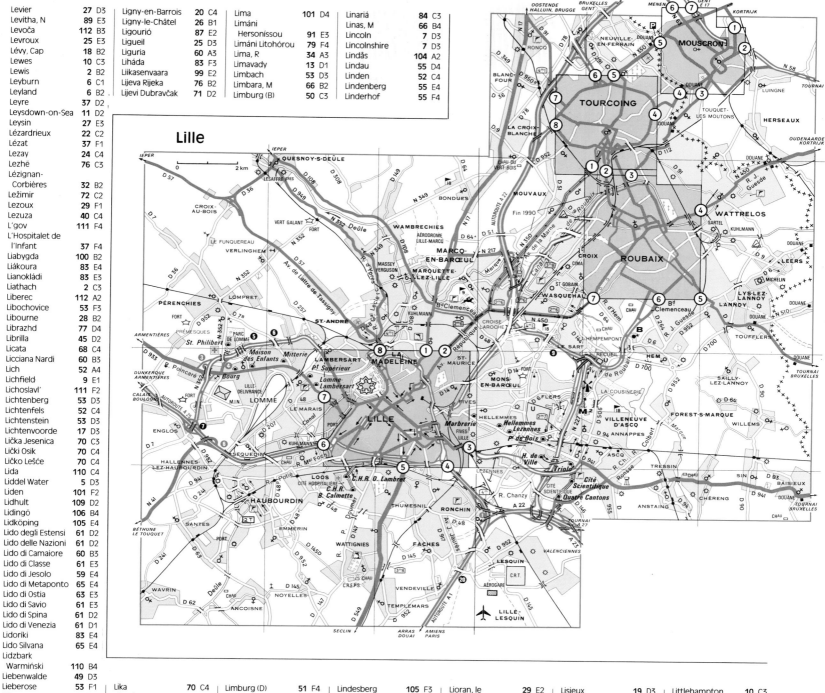

Lille

Lika 70 C4
Likenäs 105 E2
Likeo, Óri 86 C2
Likódimo, Óros 86 C3
Likófos 81 F2
Likoporiá 87 D1
Likórahi 78 C4
Likóstomo 80 C2
Likouría 86 C1
Liland 94 B3
Lilea 83 E3
Lilienfeld 57 E3
Liljendal 107 F2
Lilla Edet 108 C1
Lillby 102 C2
Lille 19 F1
Lille Bælt 108 A3
Lillebonne 19 D3
Lillehammer 105 D2
Lillerød 108 C3
Lillers 19 F1
Lillesand 104 B4
Lillestrøm 105 D3
Lillhärdal 101 E3
Lillo 40 B3
Lillögda 102 A1
Lillsholmsjön 101 E1
Lim 76 B1

Limburg (D) 51 F4
Limburg (NL) 17 D4
Limenária 80 C3
Limerick 14 B3
Limerick (Co) 14 B3
Limfjorden 108 A2
Limia, R 34 B3
Limingen 97 E4
Liminka 99 D4
Liminpuro 99 E4
Limljani 76 B3
Límnes 87 E2
Limni 84 A3
Limniá 80 C2
Limnitsa 83 D4
Límnos, N 85 D1
Limoges 29 D1
Limogne 29 D3
Limone Piemonte 31 E3
Limonest 26 C4
Limours 19 E4
Limoux 32 B2
Lin 77 D4
Linares 44 A2
Linares del Arroyo, Emb de 36 A3
Linares de Mora 41 E2
Linares de Riofrio 39 E2

Lindesberg 105 F3
Lindesnes 104 B4
Lindhem 106 A4
Lindö 106 A4
Lindos 93 F2
Lindoso 34 B3
Lindow 49 D3
Lindsdal 109 E2
Lingbo 106 A2
Linge 100 B2
Lingen 17 E2
Linguaglossa 69 D3
Linken 49 E2
Linköping 106 A4
Linlithgow 5 D2
Linnansaari 103 E3
Linnhe, L 4 B1
Linosa, I di 68 A4
Linsell 101 E3
Linslade 9 F2
Linthal 58 A2
Linyola 37 F3
Linz 77 D4
Linz 51 E4
Linz 57 D2
Lion 18 C3
Lion-d'Angers, le 23 E4
Lioni 64 C4
Lióprasso 83 D1

Lioran, le 29 E2
Lipar 72 B2
Lipari 69 D2
Lipari, I 69 D2
Lipenská přehr nádrž 56 C2
Liperi 103 F2
Lipiany 49 F3
Lipica 70 A3
Lipik 71 D2
Lipkovo 77 E2
Lipljan 77 D2
Lipno 57 D2
Lipova 112 C4
Lipovac 72 B3
Lippe 17 E3
Lippstadt 17 E3
Lipsí 89 E2
Lipsí, N 89 E2
Liptovský Mikuláš 112 B3
Liqenas 77 D4
Lírkia 87 D2
Lis 76 C3
Lisac 71 E4
Lisboa 38 A4
Lisburn 13 E2
Liscia 66 B1
Lisdoonvarna 12 B4

Lisieux 19 D3
Lisina 71 E4
Liskeard 8 B4
Lisková 56 B1
Lisle 29 D3
Lismore (GB) 4 B1
Lismore (IRL) 14 C4
Lisnaskea 13 D2
Lišnja 71 E3
Lisovići 71 F3
Lisse 16 C2
List 47 F1
Listafjorden 104 A4
Lištica 75 E2
Listowel 14 B3
Lit 101 E2
Lit-et-Mixe 28 A3
Lithakiá 86 A2
Lithári, Akr 84 C3
Lithínes 91 F3
Lithino, Akr 91 D4
Lithío 85 E4
Lití 79 F3
Litija 70 B2
Litóhoro 79 F4
Litoměřice 53 F3
Litomyšl 112 A3
Litschau 57 D1

Littlehampton 10 C3
Little Minch, The 2 A3
Little Moreton Hall 6 C3
Littleport 10 C1
Litva 110 C3
Litvínov 53 E3
Livaara 99 F3
Livádi, Akr 88 C2
Livade 70 A3
Livaderó (Dráma) 80 C2
Livaderó (Kozáni) 79 E4
Livádi (Makedonía) 80 A3
Livádi (Sérifos) 88 A3
Livádi (Thessalía) 79 E4
Livadiá (Makedonía) 80 A2
Livadiá (Stereá Eláda) 83 F4
Livádia (Tílos) 89 F4
Livadítis 80 C1
Livadohóri 85 D1
Livanátes 83 F3
Livári 76 B3
Livarot 19 D4
Livenza 59 E4
Liverá 79 D3
Liverdun 21 D4

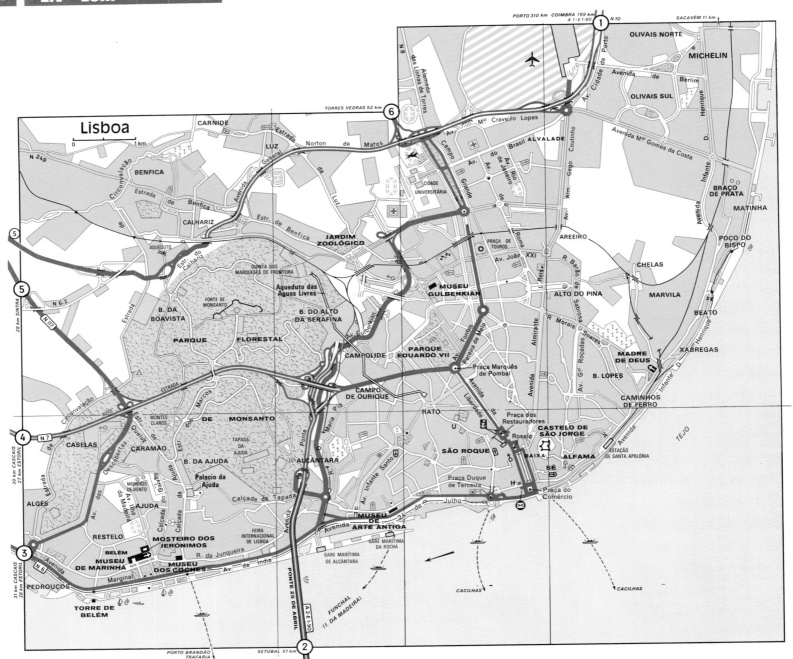

Lisboa

| | | | | | | | | | | | | | | | |
|---|---|---|---|---|---|---|---|---|---|---|---|---|---|---|---|
| Livernon | 29 D2 | Ljubljana | 70 B2 | Llandysul | 8 C1 | Llodio | 36 B1 | Lochmaddy | 2 A3 | Löffingen | 54 C4 | Loing | 26 A2 |
| Liverpool | 6 B2 | Ljubno | 70 B1 | Llanelli | 8 C2 | Lloret de Mar | 32 B4 | Loch Ness | 2 C3 | Lofoten | 97 E1 | Loir | 25 E1 |
| Liverpool B | 6 B2 | Ljubojno | 77 E4 | Llanerchymedd | 6 A2 | Llucmajor | 45 F3 | Lochranza | 4 B2 | Lofsdalen | 101 D3 | Loire | 23 E4 |
| Livigno | 58 C3 | Ljubostinja | 73 D4 | Llanes | 35 E1 | Llynclys | 6 B3 | Lochvica | 113 F2 | Lofthus | 104 B2 | Loire (Dépt) | 29 F1 |
| Livingston | 5 D2 | Ljuboten | 77 D2 | Llanfairfechan | 6 A2 | Lnáre | 56 C1 | Lochy, L | 2 C4 | Loftus | 5 F4 | Loire-Atlantique | 23 D4 |
| Livno | 75 E1 | Ljubovija | 72 C4 | Llanfair-ym-Muallt | 9 D1 | Loanhead | 5 D2 | Lockenhaus | 57 F3 | Log | 70 A2 | Loire-et-Cher | 25 E2 |
| Livo | 99 E3 | Ljubuša | 75 E1 | Llanfyllin | 6 B3 | Loano | 31 F3 | Lockerbie | 5 D3 | Logarska dolina | 70 B1 | Loiret | 25 E1 |
| Livojärvi | 99 E2 | Ljubuški | 75 E2 | Llangadog | 8 C2 | Löbau | 53 F2 | Löcknitz | 49 E2 | Logatec, D. | 70 A2 | Loiri | 66 B1 |
| Livojoki | 99 E3 | Ljugarn | 109 F4 | Llangefni | 6 A2 | Löbejün | 53 D2 | Locle, le | 27 E2 | Logroño | 36 B2 | Loiron | 23 E3 |
| Livold | 70 B3 | Ljungan | 101 F3 | Llangollen | 6 B3 | Lobenstein | 52 C3 | Locmariaquer | 22 C4 | Logrosán | 39 E3 | Loitz | 49 D2 |
| Livorno | 60 C4 | Ljungby | 109 D2 | Llangurig | 8 C1 | Łobez | 49 F2 | Locminé | 22 C3 | Løgstør | 108 A2 | Loja | 43 F3 |
| Livorno Ferraris | 31 F1 | Ljungbyhed | 109 D3 | Llanidloes | 8 C1 | Löbnitz | 49 D1 | Locorotondo | 65 E3 | Løgten | 108 B3 | Lojsta | 109 F4 |
| Livron | 30 B2 | Ljungdalen | 101 D2 | Llano, Pto | 39 E3 | Lobo | 36 A4 | Locquirec | 22 B2 | Løgumkloster | 108 A4 | Lokalahti | 107 D2 |
| Lixoúri | 82 B4 | Ljungsbro | 105 F4 | Llanrhystud | 8 C1 | Lobón | 39 D4 | Locri | 67 F4 | Lohals | 108 B4 | Lokan Tekojärvi | 95 F4 |
| Lizard | 8 B4 | Ljungskile | 108 C1 | Llanrwst | 6 A3 | Loburg | 53 D1 | Locronan | 22 B3 | Lohberg | 56 B1 | Løken | 105 D3 |
| Lizard Pt | 8 B4 | Ljusdal | 101 F3 | Llanwrtyd-Wells | 8 C1 | Locana | 31 E1 | Loctudy | 22 B3 | Lohilahti | 103 E3 | Lokeren | 50 B3 |
| Lizy | 19 F3 | Ljusnan | 101 E3 | Llanymyddfri | 8 C1 | Locarno | 58 A3 | Lodè | 66 C2 | Lohiniva | 99 D1 | Loket | 53 E4 |
| Lizzano in | | Ljusne | 101 F4 | Llarga | 41 E4 | Lochaline | 4 B1 | Lodève | 30 A4 | Lohja | 107 E3 | Lokka | 95 F4 |
| Belvedere | 60 C3 | Ljutiči | 76 B1 | Llavorsi | 37 F2 | Lochboisdale | 2 A3 | Lodi | 60 B1 | Lohjanjärvi | 107 E2 | Løkken (N) | 100 C3 |
| Ljeskove Vode | 71 E3 | Ljutoglav | 77 D2 | Lleida | 37 E4 | Lochcarron | 2 B3 | Løding | 97 E1 | Lohne | 17 F2 | Løkken (S) | 108 B1 |
| Ljig | 72 C3 | Ljutomer | 70 C1 | Llera | 43 D1 | Lochearnhead | 4 C1 | Lødingen | 94 A3 | Löhne | 17 F2 | Lokn'a | 111 D2 |
| Ljubaništá | 77 D4 | Llagostera | 32 B3 | Llerena | 43 D1 | Lochem | 17 D2 | Lodosa | 36 C2 | Lohr | 52 B4 | Lokrum | 76 A2 |
| Ljubata, D | 77 E2 | Llanberis | 6 A3 | Lles | 32 A3 | Loches | 25 D3 | Łódź | 112 B2 | Lohtaja | 102 C1 | Lokve (Hrvatska) | 70 B3 |
| Ljubelj | 70 A1 | Llanca | 32 C3 | Llessui | 37 F2 | Loch Garman | 15 D3 | Loeches | 40 B2 | Loiano Rioveggio | 60 C3 | Lokve (Slovenija) | 70 A2 |
| Ljubija | 71 D3 | Llandeilo | 8 C2 | Lleyn Pen | 6 A3 | Lochgelly | 5 D2 | Loen | 100 A3 | Loibltunnel | 70 A1 | Lokve (Vojvodina) | 73 D2 |
| Ljubinje | 75 F2 | Llandovery | 8 C1 | Liria | 41 E3 | Lochgilphead | 4 B2 | Løfallstrand | 104 A2 | Loimaa | 107 D2 | Lolland | 108 B4 |
| Ljubiš | 72 C4 | Llandrindod Wells | 9 D1 | Llívia | 32 A2 | Lochinver | 2 C2 | Lofário | 81 E2 | Loimaan kunta | 107 D2 | L'Ollería | 45 E1 |
| Ljubišnja | 76 B1 | Llandudno | 6 A2 | Llobregat, R | 32 A3 | Lochmaben | 5 D3 | Lofer | 59 E1 | Loimijoki | 107 D2 | Lom (BG) | 115 D2 |

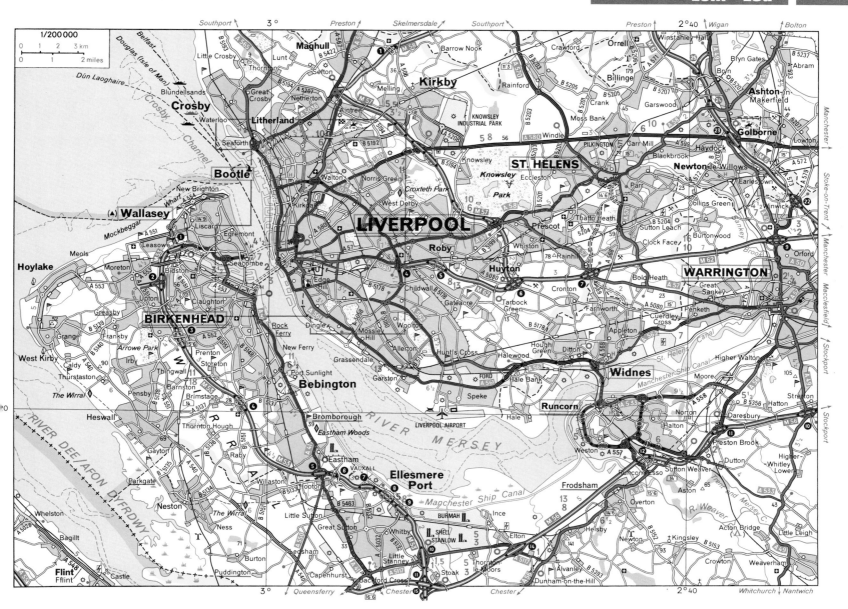

| | | | | | | | | | | | |
|---|---|---|---|---|---|---|---|---|---|---|---|
| Lom (CS) | 53 E3 | Longford (Co) | 12 C3 | Lora del Río | 43 E2 | Los Cortijos | 40 A4 | Lötschbergtunnel | 27 F3 | Lousã, Sa da | 38 B2 | Louviers | 19 E3 |
| Lom (N) | 100 B3 | Longleat House | 9 D3 | Lorca | 44 C2 | Los Cristianos | 42 B4 | Löttorp | 109 E2 | Louth | 7 E2 | Louvigné-du- | |
| Loma Negra | 36 C3 | Longny | 19 D4 | Lorcé | 51 D4 | Los Dolores | 45 D2 | Loučná | 53 E3 | Louth | 13 D3 | Désert | 18 B4 |
| Lomazzo | 60 A1 | Longobucco | 67 F2 | Lorch (Baden- | | Los Gallardos | 44 C3 | Loudéac | 22 C3 | Loutrá Aridéas | 79 E2 | Lovag | 76 B1 |
| Lombarda, Colle | | Longós | 82 A2 | Württemberg) | 55 D2 | Losheim | 54 B1 | Loudias | 79 F3 | Loutrá Edipsoú | 83 F3 | Lövånger | 102 B1 |
| della | 31 E3 | Long Preston | 6 C1 | Lorch (Hessen) | 51 F4 | Los Hinojosos | 40 B3 | Loudias R | 79 F3 | Loutrá Eleftherón | 80 C3 | Lövberga | 101 F1 |
| Lombardia | 60 A1 | Long Sutton | 7 E3 | Loreley | 51 F4 | Losinj | 70 B4 | Loudun | 25 D3 | Loutrá Ipátis | 83 E3 | Lovćen | 76 B3 |
| Lombez | 28 C4 | Longué | 23 E4 | Loreo | 61 D1 | Los Llanos de | | Loué | 23 E3 | Loutrá Kaïtsas | 83 E3 | Loveč | 115 D2 |
| Lomello | 60 A2 | Longueville-sur- | | Loreto | 61 F4 | Aridane | 42 A4 | Loue | 26 C2 | Loutrá (Kikládes) | 88 A2 | Lovere | 58 B4 |
| Lomen | 104 C1 | Scie | 19 E2 | Loreto Aprutino | 64 A1 | Los Lobos | 44 C3 | Loughborough | 7 D3 | Loutráki | | Loviisa | 107 F2 |
| Lomma | 108 C3 | Longuyon | 20 C3 | Lorgues | 31 D4 | Los | | Loughrea | 12 B4 | (Pelopónissos) | 87 E1 | Lovisa | 107 F2 |
| Lommatzsch | 53 E2 | Longwy | 20 C3 | Lorica | 67 F3 | Navalmorales | 39 F3 | Louhans | 26 C3 | Loutráki (Skópelos) | 84 B2 | Lovosice | 53 F3 |
| Lommel | 50 C3 | Lonigo | 60 C1 | Lorient | 22 B4 | Los Navalucillos | 39 F3 | Louhisaari | 107 D2 | Loutráki (Stereá | | Lovran | 70 B3 |
| Lomond, L | 4 C2 | Löningen | 17 E2 | Loriga | 38 C2 | Los Palacios y | | Louisburgh | 12 B3 | Eláda) | 82 C3 | Lovrenc na |
| Lomonosov | 111 D1 | Lonja | 71 D3 | Loriguilla, Emb de | 41 D3 | Villafranca | 43 D3 | Loukinen | 95 E4 | Loutrá Kilínis | 86 B1 | Pohorju | 70 B1 |
| Lomont, Mts du | 27 E2 | Lonja R | 71 D2 | Loriol | 30 B2 | Los Santos | 39 E2 | Loukíssa | 84 A4 | Loutrá Langadá | 80 A3 | Lövstabruk | 106 B2 |
| Lompolo | 95 E4 | Lons-le-Saunier | 26 C3 | Lormes | 26 B2 | Los Santos de | | Loulay | 24 C4 | Loutrá (Lésvos) | 85 F3 | Lövstabukten | 106 B2 |
| Łomża | 112 B1 | Lönsboda | 109 D3 | Lorn, Firth of | 4 B1 | Maimona | 43 D1 | Loulé | 42 B3 | Loutrá | | Lovund | 97 D2 |
| Lonato | 60 B1 | Lønsdal | 97 E2 | Loro Ciuffenna | 61 D4 | Los Sauces | 42 A4 | Louny | 53 E3 | (Makedonia) | 80 B4 | Löwenberg | 49 D3 |
| Lončari | 71 F3 | Lønset | 100 B2 | Loroux-Botteraeu, | | Loßburg | 54 C3 | Loupe, la | 19 E4 | Loutrá | | Lower L Erne | 12 C2 |
| Lončarica | 71 E2 | Looe | 8 B4 | le | 24 B2 | Lossiemouth | 3 D3 | Loup, Gorge du (L) | 21 D2 | (Pelopónissos) | 86 C2 | Lowestoft | 11 E1 |
| Londinières | 19 E2 | Loop Head | 12 A4 | Lorquin | 21 E4 | Lossnen | 101 D3 | Loup, Gorges du | | Loutrá Smokóvou | 83 D2 | Lowicz | 112 B1 |
| London | 9 F2 | Loosdorf | 57 E2 | Lörrach | 54 C4 | Loßnitz | 53 D3 | (F) | 31 E3 | Loutrá Vólvis | 80 A3 | Low Street | 7 F3 |
| Londonderry | 13 D1 | Lopar | 70 B4 | Lorrez-le-Bocage | 25 F1 | Lostwithiel | 8 B4 | Lourdes | 37 E1 | Loutró Elénis | 87 E1 | Lož | 70 B2 |
| Londonderry (Co) | 13 D1 | Lopare | 72 B3 | Lorris | 25 F1 | Los Villares | 44 A2 | Loures | 38 A4 | Loutropigí | 83 D2 | Lozère | 29 F2 |
| Longa | 86 C3 | Los | 101 E3 | Los | 101 E3 | Los Yébenes | 40 A3 | Louriçal | 38 B2 | Loutrópirgos | 87 E1 | Lozère, Mt | 29 F3 |
| Longádes | 82 C1 | Lopcombe Corner | 9 E3 | Los Alcázares | 45 D2 | Lot | 29 E2 | Lourinhã | 38 A3 | Loutrós | 81 F2 | Lozna | 73 D4 |
| Longanikos | 87 D3 | Lopera | 43 F2 | Losar | 39 E2 | Lot (Dépt) | 29 D3 | Loúros | 82 B2 | Loutsá (Ípiros) | 82 B2 | Loznica | 72 B3 |
| Longares | 36 C4 | Lopes, Mal i | 76 C4 | Los Arcos | 36 B2 | Lote | 100 A3 | Loúros R | 82 B2 | Loútsa (Stereá | | Lozovac | 75 D1 |
| Longarone | 59 E3 | Loppa | 94 C2 | Los Barreros | 40 C4 | Løten | 105 D2 | Louroux, le | 23 E4 | Eláda) | 88 A1 | Lozovik | 73 D3 |
| Long Eaton | 7 D3 | Loppi | 107 E2 | Los Barrios | 43 D4 | Lothian | 5 D2 | Lousa | 38 A4 | Louvain | 50 C3 | Lozoyuela | 40 B1 |
| Longeau | 26 C1 | Lopud | 75 F2 | Los Corrales de | | Lot-et-Garonne | 28 C3 | Lousã | 38 B2 | Louvain-la-Neuve | 50 C4 | Luanco | 35 D1 |
| Longford | 12 C3 | Lopud I | 75 F2 | Buelna | 35 F2 | Lothian | 5 D2 | Lousada | 34 A4 | Louvière, La | 50 B4 | Luarca | 35 D1 |

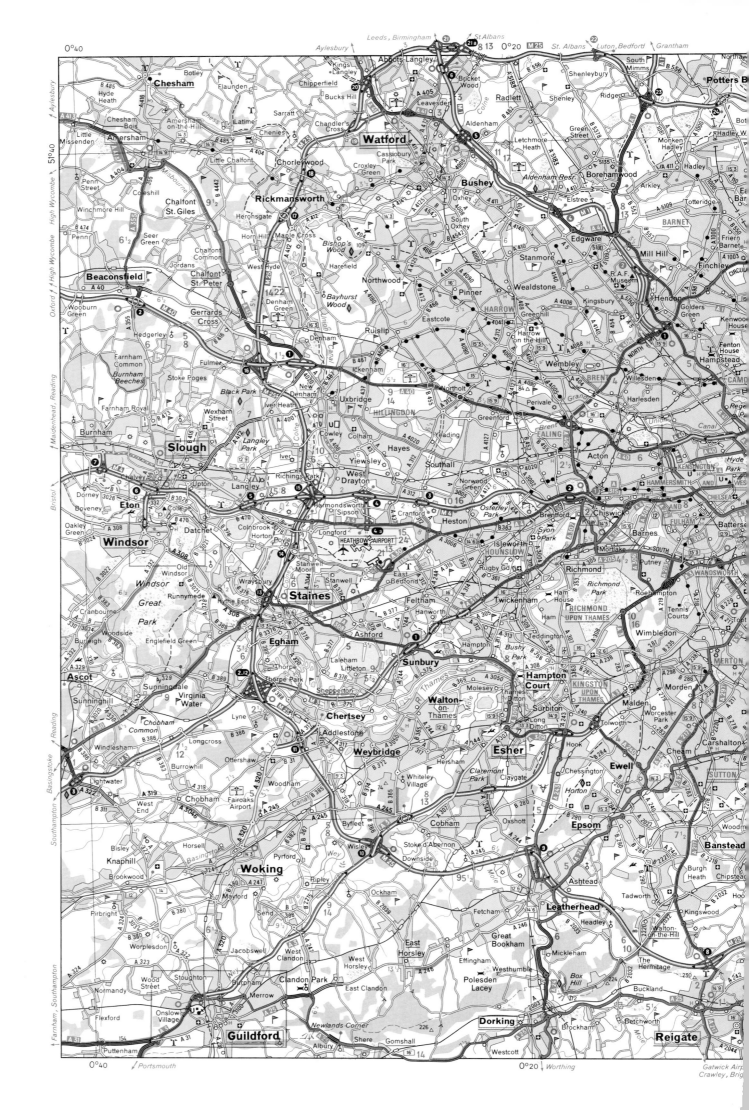

London

1/200 000

0 1 2 3 4 5 6 km
0 1 2 3 4 miles

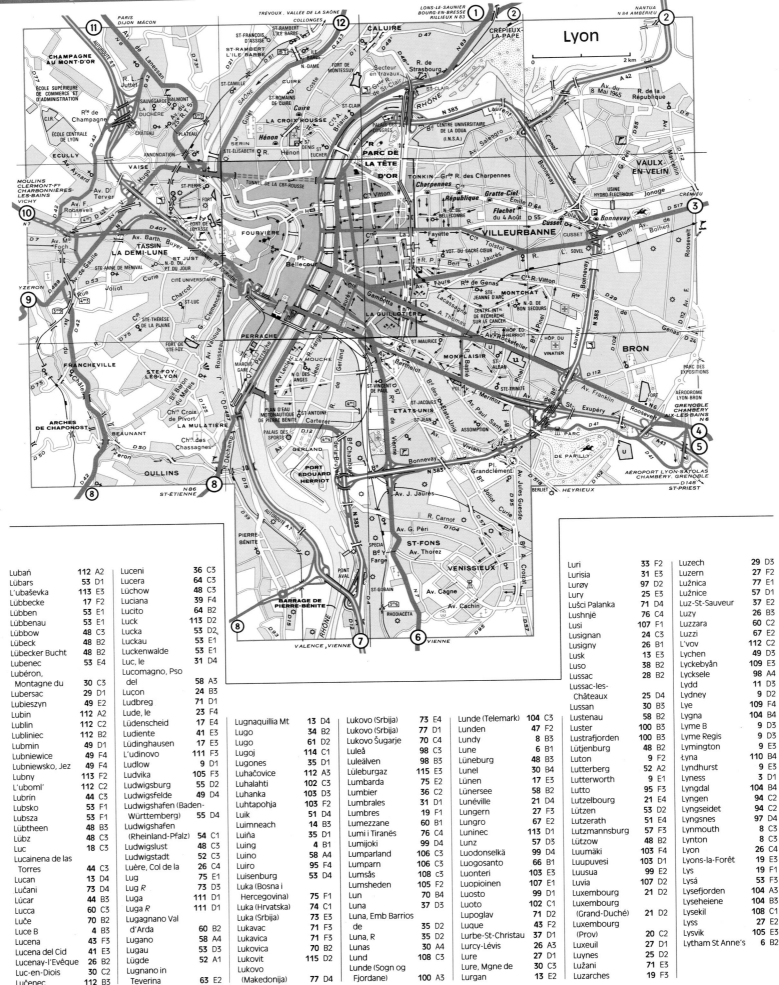

Lyon

| | | | | | | |
|---|---|---|---|---|---|---|
| Lubań | 112 A2 | Luceni | 36 C3 | Luri | 33 F2 | Luzech | 29 D3 |
| Lübars | 53 D1 | Lucera | 64 C3 | Lurisia | 31 E3 | Luzern | 27 F2 |
| L'ubaševka | 113 E3 | Lüchow | 48 C3 | Lurøy | 97 D2 | Lužnica | 77 E1 |
| Lübbecke | 17 F2 | Luciana | 39 F4 | Lury | 25 E3 | Lužnice | 57 D1 |
| Lübben | 53 E1 | Lucito | 64 B2 | Lušci Palanka | 71 D4 | Luz-St-Sauveur | 37 E2 |
| Lübbenau | 53 E1 | Luck | 113 D2 | Lushnjë | 76 C4 | Luzy | 26 B3 |
| Lübbow | 48 C3 | Lucka | 53 D2 | Lusi | 107 F1 | Luzzara | 60 C2 |
| Lübeck | 48 B2 | Luckau | 53 E1 | Lusignan | 24 C3 | Luzzi | 67 E2 |
| Lübecker Bucht | 48 B2 | Luckenwalde | 53 E1 | Lusigny | 26 B1 | L'vov | 112 C2 |
| Lubenec | 53 E4 | Luc, le | 31 D4 | Lusk | 13 E3 | Lychen | 49 D3 |
| Lubéron, | | Lucomagno, Pso | | Luso | 38 B2 | Lyckebyån | 109 E3 |
| Montagne du | 30 C3 | del | 58 A3 | Lussac | 28 B2 | Lycksele | 98 A4 |
| Lubersac | 29 D1 | Lucon | 24 B3 | Lussac-les- | | Lydd | 11 D3 |
| Lubieszyn | 49 E2 | Ludbreg | 71 D1 | Châteaux | 25 D4 | Lydney | 9 D2 |
| Lubin | 112 A2 | Lude, le | 23 F4 | Lussan | 30 B3 | Lye | 109 F4 |
| Lublin | 112 C2 | Lüdenscheid | 17 E4 | Lustenau | 58 B2 | Lygna | 104 B4 |
| Lubliniec | 112 B2 | Ludiente | 41 E3 | Luster | 100 B3 | Lyme B | 9 D3 |
| Lubmin | 49 D1 | Lüdinghausen | 17 E3 | Lustrafjorden | 100 B3 | Lyme Regis | 9 D3 |
| Lubniewice | 49 F4 | L'udinovo | 111 F3 | Lune | 6 B1 | Lymington | 9 E3 |
| Lubniewsko, Jez | 49 F4 | Ludlow | 9 D1 | Lüneburg | 48 B3 | Luton | 9 F2 |
| Lubny | 113 F2 | Ludvika | 105 F3 | Lünen | 17 E3 | Lutterberg | 52 A2 | Lyndhurst | 9 E3 |
| L'uboml' | 112 C2 | Ludwigsburg | 55 D2 | Lünersee | 58 B2 | Lutterworth | 9 E1 | Lyness | 3 D1 |
| Lubrin | 44 C3 | Ludwigsfelde | 49 D4 | Lutto | 95 F3 | Lyngdal | 104 B4 |
| Lubsko | 53 F1 | Ludwigshafen (Baden- | | Lune | 30 B4 | Lutzelbourg | 21 E4 | Lyngen | 94 C2 |
| Lubsza | 53 E1 | Württemberg) | 55 D4 | Lunel | 30 B4 | Lützen | 53 D2 | Lyngseidet | 94 C2 |
| Lübtheen | 48 B3 | Ludwigshafen | | Lunéville | 21 D4 | Lutzerath | 51 E4 | Lyngsnes | 97 D3 |
| Lübz | 48 C3 | (Rheinland-Pfalz) | 54 C1 | Lumbarda | 75 E2 | Lungern | 27 F3 | Lynmouth | 8 C3 |
| Luc | 18 C3 | Ludwigslust | 48 C3 | Lumbier | 36 C2 | Lungro | 67 E2 | Lynton | 8 C3 |
| Lucainena de las | | Ludwigstadt | 52 C3 | Lumbrales | 31 D1 | Luninec | 113 D1 | Lyon | 26 C4 |
| Torres | 44 C3 | Luère, Col de la | 26 C4 | Lumbres | 19 F1 | Lunz | 57 D3 | Lyons-la-Forêt | 19 E3 |
| Lucan | 13 D4 | Lug | 75 E1 | Lumezzane | 60 B1 | Luodonselkä | 99 D4 | Lys | 19 F1 |
| Lučani | 73 D4 | Lug R | 73 D3 | Lumijoki | 99 D4 | Luogosanto | 66 B1 | Lysá | 53 F3 |
| Lúcar | 44 B3 | Luga | 111 D1 | Lumparland | 106 C3 | Luonteri | 103 E3 | Lysefjorden | 104 A3 |
| Lucca | 60 C3 | Luga R | 111 D1 | Lumparn | 106 C3 | Luopioinen | 107 E1 | Lyseheiene | 104 B3 |
| Luče | 70 B2 | Lugagnano Val | | Lumsås | 108 c3 | Luosto | 99 D1 | Lysekil | 108 C1 |
| Luce B | 4 B3 | d'Arda | 60 B2 | Lumsheden | 105 F2 | Luoto | 102 C1 | Lyss | 27 E2 |
| Lucena | 43 F3 | Lugano | 58 A4 | Lun | 70 B4 | Lupoglav | 71 D2 | Lysvik | 105 E3 |
| Lucena del Cid | 41 E3 | Lugau | 53 D3 | Luna, Emb Barrios | | Luque | 43 F2 | Lytham St Anne's | 6 B2 |
| Lucenay-l'Evêque | 26 B2 | Lukavac | 71 F3 | de | 35 D2 | Lurbe-St-Christau | 37 D2 | |
| Luc-en-Diois | 30 C2 | Lukavica | 71 F3 | Luna, R | 35 D2 | Lurcy-Lévis | 26 A3 | |
| Lučenec | 112 B3 | Lukovica | 70 B2 | Lunas | 30 A4 | Lure | 27 D1 | |
| | | Lukovit | 115 D2 | Lund | 108 C3 | Lure, Mgne de | 30 C3 | |
| Lugnaquillia Mt | 13 D4 | Lukovo | | Lunde (Sogn og | | Lurgan | 13 E2 | |
| Lugo | 34 B2 | (Makedonija) | 77 D4 | Fjordane) | 100 A3 | | | |
| Lugo | 61 D2 | Lukovo (Srbija) | 73 E4 | Lunde (Telemark) | 104 C3 | | | |
| Lugoj | 114 C1 | Lukovo (Srbija) | 77 D1 | Lunden | 47 F2 | | | |
| Lugones | 35 D1 | Lukovo Šugarje | 70 C4 | Lundy | 8 B3 | | | |
| Luhačovice | 112 A3 | Luleå | 98 C3 | | | | | |
| Luhalahti | 102 C3 | Luleälven | 98 B3 | | | | | |
| Luhanka | 103 D3 | Lüleburgaz | 115 E3 | | | | | |
| Luhtapohja | 103 F2 | Lumbarda | 75 E2 | | | | | |
| Luik | 51 D4 | | | | | | | |
| Luimneach | 14 B3 | | | | | | | |
| Luiña | 35 D1 | | | | | | | |
| Luing | 4 B1 | | | | | | | |
| Luino | 58 A4 | | | | | | | |
| Luiro | 95 F4 | | | | | | | |
| Luisenburg | 53 D4 | | | | | | | |
| Luka (Bosna i | | | | | | | | |
| Hercegovina) | 75 F1 | | | | | | | |
| Luka (Hrvatska) | 74 C1 | | | | | | | |
| Luka (Srbija) | 73 E3 | | | | | | | |

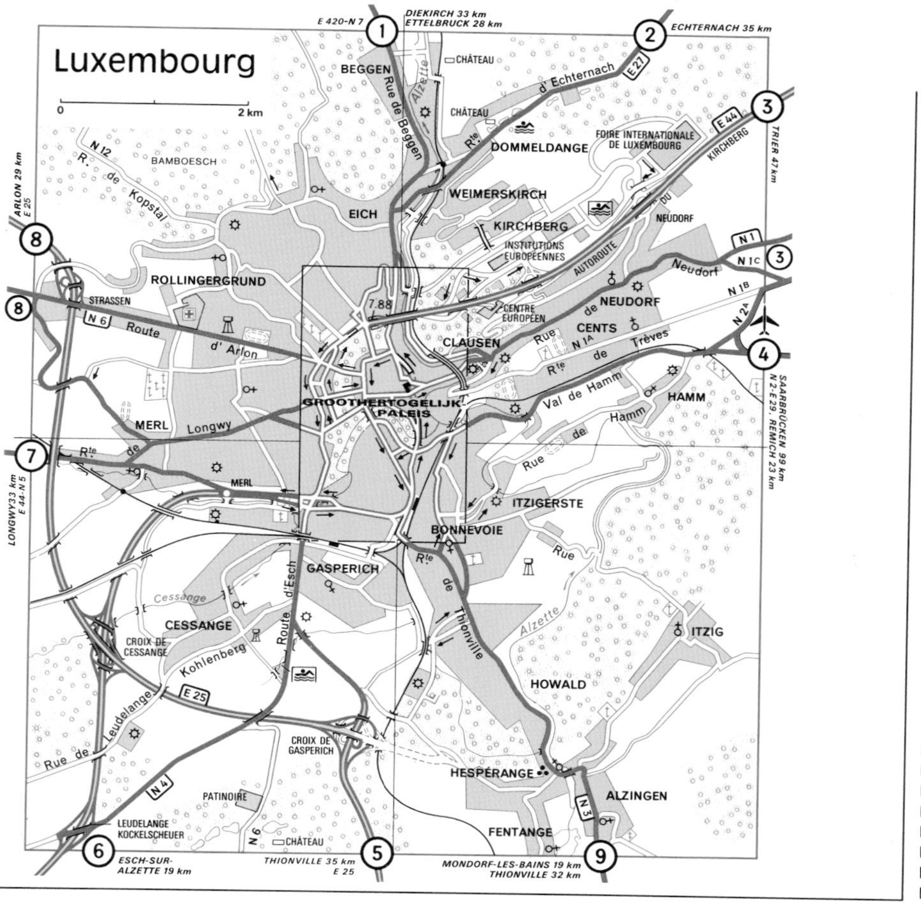
Luxembourg
0
2 km
E 420-N 7
DIEKIRCH 33 km
ETTELBRUCK 28 km
ECHTERNACH 35 km
TRIER 47 km
ARLON 29 km E 25
LONGWY 33 km E 44-N 5
SAARBRÜCKEN 99 km N 2-E 29: REMICH 23 km
ESCH-SUR-ALZETTE 19 km
THIONVILLE 35 km E 25
MONDORF-LES-BAINS 19 km THIONVILLE 32 km
BEGGEN
CHÂTEAU
Rue de Beggen
Rte d'Echternach
DOMMELDANGE
FOIRE INTERNATIONALE DE LUXEMBOURG
KIRCHBERG
BAMBOESCH
R. de Kopstal
WEIMERSKIRCH
EICH
NEUDORF
INSTITUTIONS EUROPÉENNES
AUTOROUTE
ROLLINGERGRUND
STRASSEN
Route d'Arlon
CENTRE EUROPÉEN
NEUDORF
CLAUSEN
CENTS
Rue de Trèves
GROOTHERTOGELIJK PALEIS
Val de Hamm
HAMM
MERL
Longwy
Rue de Hamm
ITZIGERSTE
BONNEVOIE
GASPERICH
Rte de Thionville
Cessange
CESSANGE
CROIX DE CESSANGE
Kohlenberg
Route d'Esch
ITZIG
Alzette
HOWALD
Rue de Leudelange
CROIX DE GASPERICH
HESPÉRANGE
PATINOIRE
ALZINGEN
LEUDELANGE KOCKELSCHEUER
CHÂTEAU
FENTANGE

# M


Maakalla 102 C1
Maalanti 102 B2
Maam Cross 12 B3
Maaninka 103 E2
Maaninkavaara 99 E2
Maanselkä 103 E1
Maarestatunturit 95 E3
Maarianhamina 106 C3
Maarianvaara 103 E2
Maas 16 C3
Maaseik 51 D3
Maasmechelen 51 D3
Maassluis 16 B3
Maastricht 51 D3
Määttälänvaara 99 F2
Mablethorpe 7 E2
Macael 44 C3
Mação 38 B3
Macclesfield 6 C3
Macduff 3 E3
Maceda 34 B3
Macedo de Cavaleiros 34 C4
Macelj 70 C1
Macerata 61 F4
Macerata Feltria 61 E3
Macgillycuddy's Reeks 14 A4
Machault 20 B3
Machecoul 24 B3
Machero 39 F4
Machichaco, C 36 B1
Machine, la 26 A3
Máchovo jez 53 F3
Machrihanish 4 B3
Machynlleth 6 A3
Mackendorf 52 C1
Mackenrode 52 B2
Mačkovci 70 C1
Macocha 57 F1
Macomer 66 B2
Mâcon 26 C4
Macotera 39 F1
Macroom 14 B4
Macugnaga 27 F4
Mačvanska Mitrovica 72 C3
Mačvanski Pričinović 72 C3
Madara 115 E2
Maddalena, Arc della 66 B1
Maddalena, Colle della 31 E2
Maddalena, I 66 B1
Maddalena La 66 B1
Maddaloni 64 B3
Madeira, Arquipélago da 42 A3
Madeira, I da 42 A3
M'adel' 111 D3
Madeleine, Col de la 31 D1
Madero, Pto del 36 C3
Maderuelo 36 A3
Madesimo 58 B3
Madine, Lac de 20 C3
Madon 21 D4
Madona 110 C2
Madonie Nebrodi 68 C3
Madonna di Campiglio 58 C3
Madrid 40 A2
Madrid (Prov) 40 A2
Madridejos 40 B3
Madrigal de las Altas Torres 39 F1
Madrigal de la Vera 39 E2
Madrigalejo 39 E4
Madrona 40 A1
Madrona, Sa 44 A1
Madroñera 39 E3
Maël-Carhaix 22 B3
Maella 37 E4
Maesteg 8 C2
Mafra 38 A3
Magacela 39 E4
Magallón 36 C3
Magaña 36 B3
Magaz 35 F3
Magdalena, Pto de la 35 D2
Magdeburg 52 C1
Magenta 60 A1
Magerøya 95 E1
Maggia 58 A3
Maggiore, L 58 A4
Maghera 13 D1
Magherafelt 13 D2
Mágina 44 A2
Magione 61 E4
Maglaj 71 F3
Magliano di Marsi 63 F2
Magliano in Toscana 63 D2
Magliano Sabina 63 E2
Maglić 73 D4
Maglić *Mt* 76 A1
Maglie 65 F4
Magnac-Laval 25 E4
Magnissía 83 E2
Magnor 105 D3
Magny-en-Vexin 19 E3
Magoúla 86 B2
Magro, R 41 D4
Magura 77 D2
Maherádo 86 A1
Mahlu 103 D2
Mahón 45 F2
Mahora 41 D4
Mahovo 71 D2
Mähring 53 D4
Maia 34 A4
Maials 37 E4
Maîche 27 E2
Maida 67 F3
Maidenhead 9 F2
Maidstone 11 D3
Maiella, la 64 A2
Maienfeld 58 B2
Maignelay 19 F3
Maigue 14 B3
Maillezais 24 C4
Mailly-le-Camp 20 B4
Main 55 D1
Mainar 36 C4
Mainburg 55 F2
Maine-et-Loire 23 E4
Mainistir na Búille 12 C3
Mainland (Orkney) 3 D1
Mainland (Shetland) 3 F2
Maintenon 19 E4
Mainz 51 F4
Maira 31 E2
Mairena del Alcor 43 D2
Maisach 55 F3
Maison-Neuve 26 B1
Maisons-Blanches, les 25 D4
Maissau 57 E2
Maizières 21 D3
Maja 70 C3
Majales, Pto de los 40 A4
Majdanpek 73 E3
Majevica 72 B3
Majšperk 70 C1
Makarska 75 E2
Makce 73 E3
Makedonía 79 F2
Makedonija 77 E3
Makedonija 77 F3
Makedonski Brod 77 D3
Makljen 75 E1
Makó 114 B1
Makovo 77 E4
Makrakómi 83 E3
Mákri 81 E2
Makríamos 80 C3
Makrígialos 79 F3
Makrigialós 91 F4
Makrihóri (Makedonía) 80 C2
Makrihóri (Thessalía) 83 E1
Makrinítsa 83 F2
Makrinóros 82 C3
Makriplágio 80 C2
Makriráhi 83 E3
Makrívrahos, Akr 81 E3
Makrohóri 79 E3
Makroníssi 88 A2
Maksniemi 99 D3
Mala 14 B4
Malå 98 A4
Mala Bosna 72 B1
Malacky 57 F2
Maladeta 37 E2
Malaga 43 F4
Malagón 40 A4
Malahide 13 E4
Malaja Višera 111 E1
Malaja Viska 113 F2
Mala Kapela 70 C3
Mala Krsna 73 D3
Malalbergo 61 D2
Malámata 83 D4
Malandrino 83 E4
Malangen 94 B2
Mälaren 106 B3
Mala Subotica 71 D1
Malaucène 30 C3
Malax 102 B2
Malbork 110 B4
Malbuisson 27 D3
Malcata, Sa de 39 D2
Malcesine 58 C4
Malchin 49 D2
Malchiner See 49 D2
Malchow 49 D2
Maldegem 50 B3
Maldon 11 D2
Malé 58 C3
Maléas, Akr 87 E4
Máleme 90 B3
Malène, la 29 F3
Malente Gremsmühlen 48 B2
Male Pijace 72 C1
Máles 91 E4
Malesherbes 25 F1
Malessína 83 F3
Malestroit 22 C3
Malgomaj 97 F4
Malgrat de Mar 32 B4
Mália 91 E3
Malicorne 23 E4
Mali Haian 70 C4
Mali Iđđos 72 B2
Mali kanal 72 B2
Mali Lošinj 70 B4
Malin 113 E2
Malines 50 B3
Malin Head 13 D1
Malinska 70 B3
Mali Požerevac 73 D3
Mališevo 77 D2
Maliskylä 103 D1
Malit, Maj'e 76 C3
Mali Zvornik 72 B4
Maljen 72 C4
Malko Târnovo 115 E2
Mallaig 2 B4
Mållejus 95 D2
Mallén 36 C3
Mallersdorf-Pfaffenberg 56 B2
Malles Venosta 58 C2
Mallnitz 59 E2
Mallorca 45 E2
Mallow 14 B4
Mallwyd 6 A3
Malm 101 D1
Malmberget 98 B2
Malmédy 51 D4
Malmesbury 9 E2
Malmköping 106 A4
Malmö 108 C3
Malmöhus Län 109 D3
Malmslätt 106 A4
Malo 59 D4
Maloja 58 B3
Malojaroslavec 111 F3
Malo Konjari 77 E4
Malo-les-Bains 19 F1
Malónas 93 F1
Malori 64 B4
Måløy 100 A3
Malpartida de Cáceres 39 D3
Malpartida de Plasencia 39 E2
Malpica (E) 34 A1
Malpica (P) 38 C3
Mals 58 C2
Målselv 94 B3
Målselva 94 B3
Målsnes 94 B3
Malsta 101 F3
Malta 59 F2
Malta / 68 B4
Maltby 7 D2
Maltiotunturi 95 F4
Malton 7 D1
Maluenda 36 C4
Malung 105 E2
Malungsfors 101 D4
Malveira 38 A4
Malvik 100 C2
Malzieu-Ville, le 29 F2
Mamaia 115 E1
Mamarrosa 38 B1
Mamers 23 F3
Mammola 67 F4
Mamonovo 110 B4
Mampodre 35 E2
Mamry, Jez 110 B4
Manacor 45 F3
Manacore 64 C2
Manamansalo 99 E4
Manasija 73 E3
Mancha Real 44 A2
Manche 18 B3
Manchester 6 C2
Manching 55 F2
Manciano 63 D2
Mandal 104 B4
Mandal selva 104 B4
Mandamádos 85 F2
Mandas 66 B3
Mandela 63 F2
Mandelieu 31 E4
Manderscheid 51 E4
Mandínia 87 D2
Mandoúdi 84 A3
Mandráki 89 F4
Mándra (Stereá Eláda) 87 F1
Mándra (Thráki) 81 F2
Mandre 70 B4
Mandrikó 93 E1
Mandrioli, Pso dei 61 D3
Manduria 65 E4
Måne 104 C3
Manerbio 60 B1
Manětín 53 E4
Manfredonia 64 C2
Manfredonia, G di 64 C2
Mangalia 115 E2
Mángana 81 D2
Manganári 88 C4
Manger 104 A2
Mangerton Mt 14 B4
Mangrt, Planica 59 F2
Mangualde 38 C1
Maniago 59 E3
Manilva 43 E4
Man, I of 6 A1
Máni (Pelopónissos) 87 D4
Máni (Thráki) 81 F1
Manisa 115 E4
Mánises 41 E4
Manjača 71 E4
Mank 57 E3
Månkarbo 106 B3
Manlleu 32 B3
Mannersdorf 57 F3
Mannheim 54 C1
Mannu 66 B4
Manojlovac slap 75 D1
Manojlovce 77 E1
Manoppello 64 A2
Manorhamilton 12 C2
Manosque 30 C3
Manresa 32 A4
Manschnow 49 F4
Mansfeld 52 C2
Mansfield 7 D3
Mansilla de las Mulas 35 E3
Mansilla, Emb de 36 B3
Mansle 25 D4
Manteigas 38 C2
Mantes 19 E4
Mantiel 40 C2
Mäntlahti 103 F4
Mantorp 109 E1
Mantova 60 C2
Mäntsälä 107 F2
Mänttä 103 D3
Mäntyharju 103 E3
Mäntyjärvi 99 E2
Mäntyluoto 102 B3
Manzanal, Pto del 35 D2
Manzanares 40 B4
Manzanares el Real 40 A2
Manzaneda 34 C3
Manzanera 41 E3
Manzat 26 A4
Manziana 63 E2
Maó 45 F2
Maqellarë 77 D3
Maqueda 40 A2
Maramureș 112 C3
Maranchón 40 C1
Maranchón, Pto de 40 C1
Maranello 60 C2
Maranhão, Bgem do 38 B4
Marano 59 F3
Marano di Napoli 64 B4
Marano, L di 59 F4
Marans 24 B4
Marão, Sa do 34 B4
Marássia 81 F1
Maratea 67 E2
Marateca 38 A4
Marathéa 83 D2
Marathiá, Akr 86 A2
Marathiás 83 D4
Marathókambos 89 E1
Marathónas 87 F1
Marathópoli 86 B3
Márathos 83 F2
Marbach 55 D2
Mårbacka 105 E3
Marbella 43 E4
Marburg 17 F4
Marby 101 E2
Marčana 70 A4
March (A) 57 F2
March (GB) 10 C1
Marchamalo 40 B2
Marchaux 27 D2
Marche 61 E4
Marche-en-Famenne 50 C4
Marchegg 57 F2
Marchena 43 E3
Marchenoir 25 E1
Marchiennes 20 A1
Marciac 28 C4
Marciana Marina 62 C1
Marcianise 64 B3
Marcigny 26 B4
Marcilla 36 C2
Marcillac-Vallon 29 E3
Marcillat-en-Combraille 25 F4
Marcilly-le-Hayer 20 B4
Marckolsheim 27 E1
Marco de Canaveses 34 A4
Marcoule 30 B3
Mære 101 D1
Maree, L 2 C3
Mare Ligure 60 A4
Marene 31 E2
Marennes 28 A1
Marentes 34 C2
Marèttimo, I- 68 A3
Mareuil (Dordogne) 28 C1
Mareuil (Vendée) 24 B3
Margarites 91 D3
Margariti 82 B2
Margate 11 D2
Margherita di Savoia 65 D3
Marguerittes 30 B3
María 44 C2
María Cristina, Emb de 41 E3
Mariannelund 109 E1
Mariánské Lázně 53 E4
Maria Saal 70 A1
Maria Taferl 57 E2
Mariazell 57 E3
Maribo 108 B4
Maribor 70 C1
Mariborsko Pohorje 70 C1
Marica 115 D3
Mariefred 106 B4
Mariehamn 106 C3
Marienberg 53 E3
Marienborn 52 C1
Marienburg 51 E4
Marienstedt 48 B3
Mariestad 105 E4
Marignane 30 C4
Marigny 18 B3
Marigny-le-Châtel 20 B4
Marija Bistrica 70 C2
Marikirk 3 E4
Marín 34 A2
Marina 75 D2
Marina di Camerota 67 D2
Marina di Campo 62 C2
Marina di Carrara 60 B3

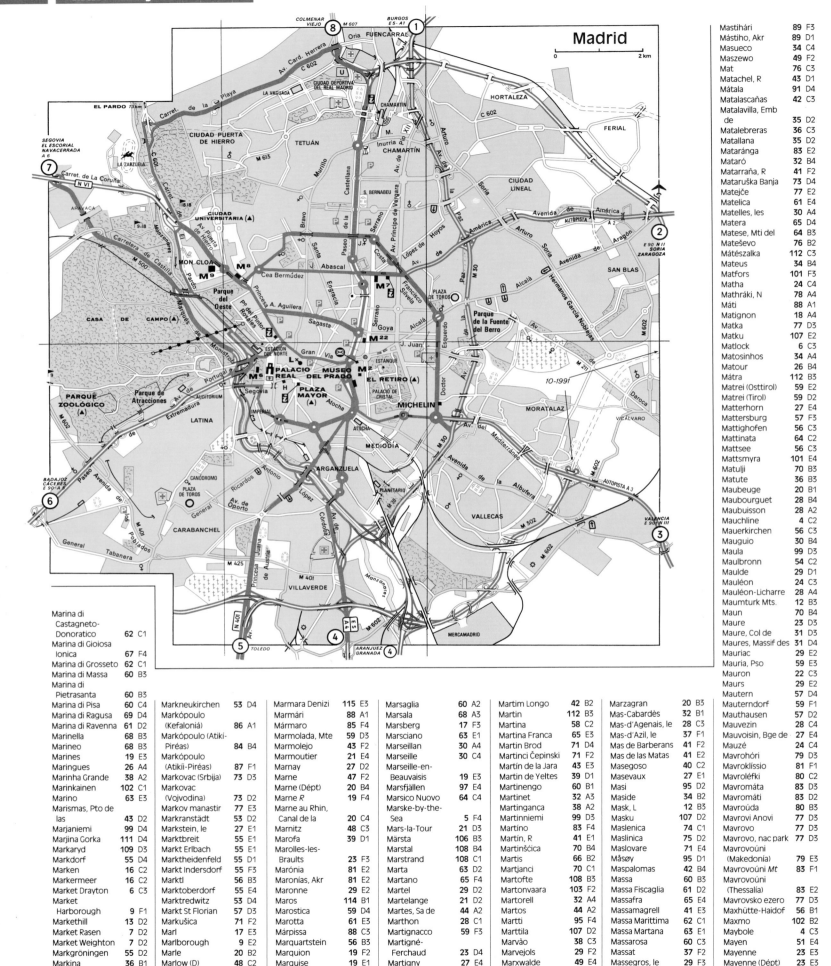

Madrid

0      2 km

| | | |
|---|---|---|
| Mastihári | 89 | F3 |
| Mástiho, Akr | 89 | D1 |
| Masueco | 34 | C4 |
| Maszewo | 49 | F2 |
| Mat | 76 | C3 |
| Matachel, R | 43 | D1 |
| Mátala | 91 | D4 |
| Matalascañas | 42 | C3 |
| Matalavilla, Emb de | 35 | D2 |
| Matalebreras | 36 | C3 |
| Matallana | 35 | D2 |
| Mataránga | 83 | E2 |
| Mataró | 32 | B4 |
| Matarraña, R | 41 | F2 |
| Mataruška Banja | 73 | D4 |
| Matejče | 77 | E2 |
| Matelica | 61 | E4 |
| Matelles, les | 30 | A4 |
| Matera | 65 | D4 |
| Matese, Mti del | 64 | B3 |
| Mateševo | 76 | B2 |
| Mátészalka | 112 | C3 |
| Mateus | 34 | B4 |
| Matfors | 101 | F3 |
| Matha | 24 | C4 |
| Mathráki, N | 78 | A4 |
| Máti | 88 | A1 |
| Matignon | 18 | A4 |
| Matka | 77 | D3 |
| Matku | 107 | E2 |
| Matlock | 6 | C3 |
| Matosinhos | 34 | A4 |
| Matour | 26 | B4 |
| Mátra | 112 | B3 |
| Matrei (Osttirol) | 59 | E2 |
| Matrei (Tirol) | 59 | D2 |
| Matterhorn | 27 | E4 |
| Mattersburg | 57 | F3 |
| Mattighofen | 56 | C3 |
| Mattinata | 64 | C2 |
| Mattsee | 56 | C3 |
| Mattsmyra | 101 | E4 |
| Matulji | 70 | B3 |
| Matute | 36 | B3 |
| Maubeuge | 20 | B1 |
| Maubourguet | 28 | B4 |
| Maubuisson | 28 | A2 |
| Mauchline | 4 | C2 |
| Mauerkirchen | 56 | C3 |
| Mauguio | 30 | B4 |
| Maula | 99 | D3 |
| Maulbronn | 54 | C2 |
| Maulde | 29 | D1 |
| Mauléon | 24 | C3 |
| Mauléon-Licharre | 28 | A4 |
| Maumturk Mts. | 12 | B3 |
| Maun | 70 | B4 |
| Maure | 23 | D3 |
| Maure, Col de | 31 | D3 |
| Maures, Massif des | 31 | D4 |
| Mauriac | 29 | E2 |
| Mauria, Pso | 59 | E3 |
| Mauron | 22 | C3 |
| Maurs | 29 | E2 |
| Mautern | 57 | D4 |
| Mauterndorf | 59 | F1 |
| Mauthausen | 57 | D2 |
| Mauvezin | 28 | C4 |
| Mauvoisin, Bge de | 27 | E4 |
| Mauzé | 24 | C4 |
| Mavrohóri | 79 | D3 |
| Mavroklíssio | 81 | F1 |
| Mavroléfki | 80 | C2 |
| Mavromáta | 83 | D3 |
| Mavromáti | 83 | D2 |
| Mavroúda | 80 | B3 |
| Mavrovi Anovi | 77 | D3 |
| Mavrovo | 77 | D3 |
| Mavrovo, nac park | 77 | D3 |
| Mavrovoúni (Makedonía) | 79 | E3 |
| Mavrovoúni Mt | 83 | F1 |
| Mavrovoúni (Thessalía) | 83 | E2 |
| Mavrovsko ezero | 77 | D3 |
| Maxhütte-Haidof | 56 | B1 |
| Maxmo | 102 | B2 |
| Maybole | 4 | C3 |
| Mayen | 51 | E4 |
| Mayenne | 23 | E3 |
| Mayenne (Dépt) | 23 | E3 |
| Mayenne R | 23 | E3 |
| Mayerling | 57 | E3 |

| | | |
|---|---|---|
| Marina di Castagneto-Donoratico | 62 | C1 |
| Marina di Gioiosa Ionica | 67 | F4 |
| Marina di Grosseto | 62 | C1 |
| Marina di Massa | 60 | B3 |
| Marina di Pietrasanta | 60 | B3 |
| Marina di Pisa | 60 | C4 |
| Marina di Ragusa | 69 | D4 |
| Marina di Ravenna | 61 | D2 |
| Marinella | 68 | B3 |
| Marineo | 68 | B3 |
| Marines | 19 | E3 |
| Maringues | 26 | A4 |
| Marinha Grande | 38 | A2 |
| Marinkainen | 102 | C1 |
| Marino | 63 | E3 |
| Marismas, Pto de las | 43 | D2 |
| Marjaniemi | 99 | D4 |
| Marjina Gorka | 111 | D4 |
| Markaryd | 109 | D3 |
| Markdorf | 55 | D4 |
| Marken | 16 | C2 |
| Markermeer | 16 | C2 |
| Market Drayton | 6 | C3 |
| Market Harborough | 9 | F1 |
| Markethill | 13 | D2 |
| Market Rasen | 7 | D2 |
| Market Weighton | 7 | D2 |
| Markgröningen | 55 | D2 |
| Markina | 36 | B1 |
| Märkisch Buchholz | 53 | E1 |
| Markkleeberg | 53 | D2 |

| | | |
|---|---|---|
| Markneukirchen | 53 | D4 |
| Markópoulo (Kefaloniá) | 86 | A1 |
| Markópoulo (Atiki-Piréas) | 84 | B4 |
| Markópoulo (Atiki-Piréas) | 87 | F1 |
| Markovac (Srbija) | 73 | D3 |
| Markovac (Vojvodina) | 73 | D2 |
| Markov manastir | 77 | E3 |
| Markranstädt | 53 | D2 |
| Markstein, le | 27 | E1 |
| Marktbreit | 55 | E1 |
| Markt Erlbach | 55 | E1 |
| Markt Indersdorf | 55 | F3 |
| Marktl | 56 | B3 |
| Marktoberdorf | 55 | E4 |
| Marktredwitz | 53 | D4 |
| Markt St Florian | 57 | D3 |
| Markušica | 71 | F2 |
| Marl | 17 | E3 |
| Marlborough | 9 | E2 |
| Marle | 20 | B2 |
| Marlow (D) | 48 | C2 |
| Marlow (GB) | 9 | F2 |
| Marmande | 28 | C3 |

| | | |
|---|---|---|
| Marmara Denizi | 115 | E3 |
| Marmári | 88 | A1 |
| Mármaro | 85 | F4 |
| Marmolada, Mte | 59 | D3 |
| Marmolejo | 43 | F2 |
| Marmoutier | 21 | E4 |
| Marnay | 27 | D2 |
| Marne | 47 | F2 |
| Marne (Dépt) | 20 | B4 |
| Marne R | 19 | F4 |
| Marne au Rhin, Canal de la | 20 | C4 |
| Marnitz | 48 | C3 |
| Marofa | 39 | D1 |
| Marolles-les-Braults | 23 | F3 |
| Marónia | 81 | E2 |
| Maronías, Akr | 81 | E2 |
| Maronne | 29 | E2 |
| Maros | 114 | B1 |
| Marostica | 59 | D4 |
| Marotta | 61 | E3 |
| Márpissa | 88 | C3 |
| Marquartstein | 56 | B3 |
| Marquion | 19 | F2 |
| Marquise | 19 | E1 |
| Marradi | 61 | D3 |
| Marraskoski | 99 | D2 |

| | | |
|---|---|---|
| Marsaglia | 60 | A2 |
| Marsala | 68 | A3 |
| Marsberg | 17 | F3 |
| Marsciano | 63 | E1 |
| Marseillan | 30 | A4 |
| Marseille | 30 | C4 |
| Marseille-en-Beauvaisis | 19 | E3 |
| Marsfjället | 97 | E4 |
| Marsico Nuovo | 64 | C4 |
| Marske-by-the-Sea | 5 | F4 |
| Mars-la-Tour | 21 | D3 |
| Märsta | 106 | B3 |
| Marstal | 108 | B4 |
| Marstrand | 108 | C1 |
| Marta | 63 | D2 |
| Martano | 65 | F4 |
| Martel | 29 | D2 |
| Martelange | 21 | D2 |
| Martes, Sa de | 44 | A2 |
| Marthon | 28 | C1 |
| Martigné-Ferchaud | 23 | D4 |
| Martigny | 27 | E4 |
| Martigny-les-Bains | 27 | D1 |
| Martigues | 30 | C4 |

| | | |
|---|---|---|
| Martim Longo | 42 | B2 |
| Martin | 112 | B3 |
| Martina | 58 | C2 |
| Martina Franca | 65 | E3 |
| Martín Brod | 71 | D4 |
| Martinci Čepinski | 71 | F2 |
| Martín de la Jara | 43 | E3 |
| Martin de Yeltes | 39 | D1 |
| Martinengo | 60 | B1 |
| Martinet | 32 | A3 |
| Martinniemi | 99 | D3 |
| Martíno | 83 | F4 |
| Martín, R | 41 | E1 |
| Martinščica | 70 | B4 |
| Martis | 66 | B2 |
| Martjanci | 70 | C1 |
| Martofte | 108 | B3 |
| Martonvaara | 103 | F2 |
| Martorell | 32 | A4 |
| Martos | 44 | A2 |
| Martti | 95 | F4 |
| Marttila | 107 | D2 |
| Marvão | 38 | C3 |
| Marvejols | 29 | F2 |
| Marxwalde | 49 | E4 |
| Maryport | 5 | D4 |
| Mary, Puy | 29 | E2 |

| | | |
|---|---|---|
| Marzagran | 20 | B3 |
| Mas-Cabardès | 32 | B1 |
| Mas-d'Agenais, le | 28 | C3 |
| Mas-d'Azil, le | 37 | F1 |
| Mas de Barberans | 41 | F2 |
| Mas de las Matas | 41 | E2 |
| Masegoso | 40 | C2 |
| Masevaux | 27 | E1 |
| Masi | 95 | D2 |
| Maside | 34 | B2 |
| Mask, L | 12 | B3 |
| Masku | 107 | D2 |
| Maslenica | 74 | C1 |
| Maslinica | 75 | D2 |
| Maslovare | 71 | E4 |
| Måsøy | 95 | D1 |
| Maspalomas | 42 | B4 |
| Massa | 60 | B3 |
| Massa Fiscaglia | 61 | D2 |
| Massafra | 65 | E4 |
| Massamagrell | 41 | E3 |
| Massa Marittima | 62 | C1 |
| Massa Martana | 63 | E1 |
| Massarosa | 60 | C3 |
| Massat | 37 | F2 |
| Massegros, le | 29 | F2 |
| Masseube | 28 | C4 |
| Massiac | 29 | F1 |

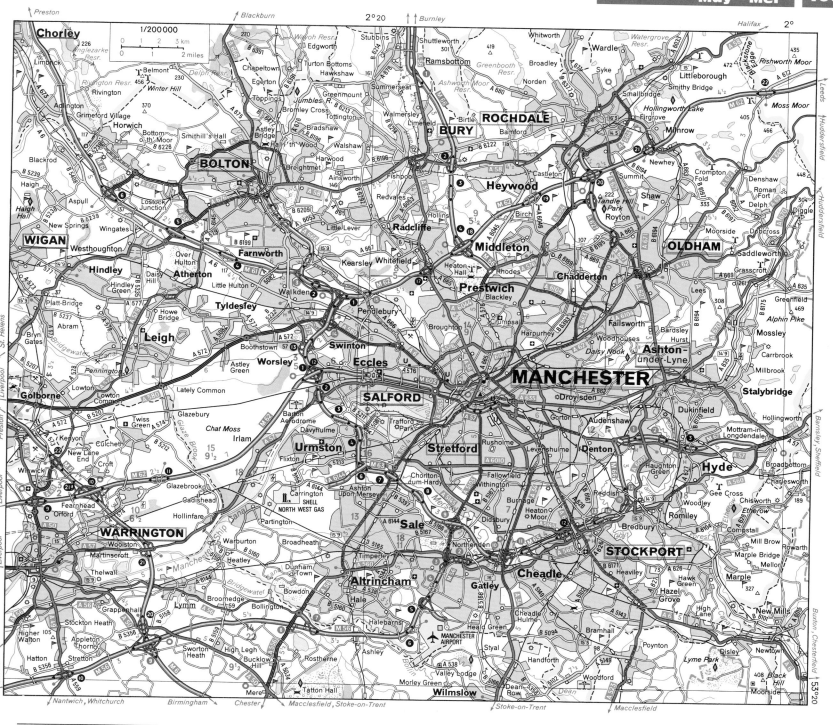

| | | | | | | | | | | | | | |
|---|---|---|---|---|---|---|---|---|---|---|---|---|---|
| Mayet | 23 F4 | Mazorra, Pto de la | 36 A2 | Mediaş | 113 D4 | Medyn' | 111 F3 | Megísti | 93 F2 | Meisenheim | 54 B1 | Melgar de |  |
| Mayet-de- | | Mazury | 110 B4 | Medicina | 61 D2 | Medžitlija | 77 E4 | Megísti, N | 93 F2 | Meißen | 53 E2 | Fernamental | 35 F3 |
| Montagne, le | 26 B4 | Mazzarino | 68 C4 | Medina Azahara | 43 E2 | Meerane | 53 D3 | Megístis Lávras | 80 C4 | Meitingen | 55 E3 | Melhus | 100 C2 |
| Maynooth | 13 D4 | Mazzarò | 69 D3 | Medinaceli | 36 B4 | Meersburg | 55 D4 | Meg. Livádi | 88 A3 | Mel | 59 E3 | Melía | 83 E2 |
| Mayo | 12 B2 | Mealhada | 38 B2 | Medina del Campo | 35 E4 | Mées, les | 31 D3 | Meg. Panagía | 80 B3 | Melalahti | 99 E4 | Melide | 34 B2 |
| Mayor, C | 35 F1 | Meath | 13 D3 | Medina de Pomar | 36 A1 | Mefjordbotn | 94 B2 | Meg. Vólvi | 80 B3 | Mélambes | 91 D4 | Melides | 42 A1 |
| Mayorga | 35 E3 | Meaux | 19 F4 | Medina de Ríoseco | 35 E4 | Mefjordvær | 94 B2 | Méga Dério | 81 F2 | Melaniós | 85 E4 | Melidóni | 91 D3 |
| Mayrhofen | 59 D2 | Mechelen | 50 B3 | Medina-Sidonia | 43 D4 | Mehamn | 95 E1 | Mega Horió | | Melánthio | 78 C3 | Meligalás | 86 C3 |
| Maza, Barrié Emb | | Meckenbeuren | 55 D4 | Médous, | | Mehedeby | 106 B2 | (Stereá Eláda) | 83 D3 | Melátes | 82 C2 | Melíki | 79 E3 |
| de la | 34 A2 | Mecklenburger B | 48 C1 | Grotte de | 37 E1 | Mehov Krš | 76 C2 | Megalohóri | 83 D1 | Melbeck | 48 B3 | Melilli | 69 D4 |
| Mazagón | 42 C3 | Meda | 38 C1 | Médoussa | 81 D1 | Mehun | 25 F2 | Megalópoli | 86 C2 | Melbu | 94 A3 | Mélisey | 27 D1 |
| Mazamet | 32 B1 | Medda | 73 D2 | Medugorje | 75 F2 | Meigle | 5 D1 | Meganíssi | 82 B3 | Meldal | 100 C2 | Mélissa | 81 D2 |
| Mazara d. Vallo | 68 A3 | Medak | 70 C4 | Medulin | 70 A4 | Meijel | 17 D4 | Megaplátanos | 83 F3 | Meldola | 61 D3 | Mélissa, Akr | 82 B4 |
| Mazarakiá | 82 B4 | Mede | 60 A2 | Medđumajdan | 71 D3 | Meije, la | 31 D3 | Mégara | 87 E1 | Meldorf | 47 F2 | Melissáni | 82 B4 |
| Mazarete | 40 C1 | Medebach | 17 F4 | Meduna | 59 E3 | Meilen | 58 A2 | Megárhi | 83 D1 | Melegnano | 60 A1 | Melíssi | 87 D1 |
| Mazarrón | 45 D3 | Medđedđa | 76 B1 | Meduno | 59 E3 | Meillant | 25 F3 | Mégève | 27 E4 | Melendugno | 65 F4 | Melissohóri | 84 A4 |
| Mazarrón, G de | 45 D3 | Medelim | 38 C2 | Medđurečje | 76 C1 | Meina | 58 A4 | Megaló Horió | | Melenci | 72 C2 | Melissópetra | 78 C4 |
| Mažeikiai | 110 B3 | Medellín | 39 E4 | Medvedđa | 77 D1 | Meinerzhagen | 17 E4 | (Agathoníssi) | 89 F2 | Melendugno | | Melissourgós | 80 B3 |
| Mazères | 32 A1 | Medel, Piz | 58 A3 | Medvednica | 70 C2 | Meiningen | 52 B3 | Megaló Horió | | Melfi | 64 C3 | Melíti | 279 D2 |
| Mázi | 78 C4 | Medemblik | 16 C2 | Medveja | 70 B3 | Meira | 34 C1 | (Tílos) | 89 F4 | Melfjorden | 97 E2 | Melito di Porto |  |
| Mazières-en- | | Medena Selišta | 71 E4 | Medvida | 74 C1 | Meira, Sa de | 34 C1 | | | Melgaço | 34 B3 | Salvo | 67 E4 |
| Gâtine | 24 C3 | Mediano, Emb de | 37 E2 | Medvode | 70 B2 | Meiringen | 27 F3 | Melgar de Abajo | 35 E3 | | | Melívia (Thessalía) | 83 F1 |

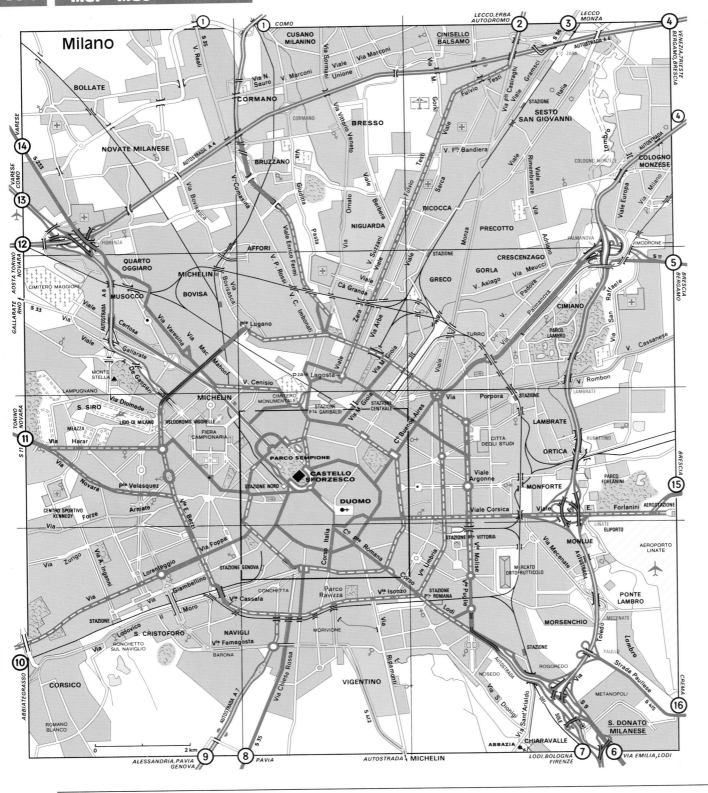

Milano

| | | |
|---|---|---|
| Mer Égée | 85 | D4 |
| Méréville | 25 | F1 |
| Mergozzo | 58 | A4 |
| Méribel | 31 | D1 |
| Mérida | 39 | D4 |
| Mérignac | 28 | B2 |
| Mérihas | 88 | A2 |
| Merijärvi | 99 | D4 |
| Merikarvia | 102 | B3 |
| Mering | 55 | F3 |
| Merkendorf | 55 | E2 |
| Merklingen | 55 | D3 |
| Merlerault, le | 19 | D4 |
| Mer Noir | 115 | F1 |
| Merošina | 77 | D1 |
| Merrenkurkku | 102 | B2 |
| Merrick | 4 | C3 |
| Mers | 19 | E2 |
| Mersch | 21 | D2 |
| Merseburg | 53 | D2 |
| Merthyr Tydfil | 8 | C2 |
| Mértola | 42 | B2 |
| Méru | 19 | F3 |
| Méry | 20 | B4 |
| Merville (Calvados) | 18 | C3 |
| Merville (Pas-de-Calais) | 19 | F1 |
| Merzig | 54 | A2 |
| Mesagne | 65 | F3 |
| Mesão Frio | 34 | B4 |
| Meschede | 17 | F3 |
| Mescherin | 49 | E3 |
| Meschers | 28 | A1 |
| Mešeišta | 77 | D4 |
| Mesići | 76 | A1 |
| Mesihovina | 75 | E1 |
| Meslay | 23 | E3 |
| Mesocco | 58 | B3 |
| Mesola | 61 | D2 |
| Mesón do Vento | 34 | B1 |
| Mesoraca | 67 | F3 |
| Mespelbrunn | 52 | A4 |
| Messanagrós | 93 | E2 |
| Messarás, Órmos | 91 | D4 |
| Messariá | 88 | B1 |
| Meßdorf | 48 | C4 |
| Messei | 18 | C4 |
| Méssi | 81 | D2 |
| Messiméri | 79 | F3 |
| Messimvría | 81 | E2 |
| Messina | 69 | D2 |
| Messíni | 86 | C3 |
| Messinía | 86 | C3 |
| Messiniakós Kólpos | 86 | C4 |
| Meßkirch | 55 | B3 |
| Messlingen | 101 | D2 |
| Messohóra | 82 | C2 |
| Messohóri (Kárpathos) | 93 | D3 |
| Messohóri (Thessalía) | 83 | E1 |
| Messolóngi | 82 | C4 |
| Messongi | 82 | A2 |
| Messopótamo | 82 | B2 |
| Messótopos | 85 | E2 |
| Meßstetten | 55 | D3 |
| Mestá | 85 | E4 |
| Mesta | 115 | D3 |
| Mestanza | 44 | A1 |
| Mésti | 81 | E2 |
| Mestlin | 48 | C2 |
| Mestre | 61 | D1 |
| Mesvres | 26 | B3 |
| Metajna | 70 | C4 |
| Meta, la | 64 | A2 |
| Metalika | 76 | B1 |
| Metalikó | 79 | F2 |
| Metalio | 83 | E3 |
| Metamórfossi (Halkidiki) | 80 | B4 |
| Metamórfossi (Kilkis) | 79 | F2 |
| Metangítsi | 80 | B4 |
| Metanopoli | 60 | A1 |
| Metauro | 61 | E3 |
| Metaxádes | 81 | F1 |
| Metéora | 83 | D1 |
| Méthana | 87 | E2 |
| Methil | 5 | D2 |
| Methóni (Makedonía) | 79 | F3 |
| Methóni (Pelopónnissos) | 86 | C3 |

| | | | | | | | | | | | | | | | | | | | | |
|---|---|---|---|---|---|---|---|---|---|---|---|---|---|---|---|---|---|---|---|---|
| Melívia (Thráki) | 81 | D1 | Melnice | 70 | B3 | Memmingen | 55 | E3 | Menen | 50 | A3 | Mens | 30 | C2 | Mercante, Pso di | 67 | E4 | | | |
| Melk | 57 | E2 | Mělnik | 53 | F3 | Mena | 113 | F1 | Menesjärvi | 95 | E3 | Mentana | 63 | E2 | Mercantour, Parc Nat du | 31 | E3 | Metalikó | 79 | F2 |
| Melksham | 9 | E2 | Mělník | 53 | F4 | Menaggio | 58 | B4 | Menetés | 93 | D3 | Menthon | 27 | D4 | Mercatale (Marche) | 61 | E3 | Metalio | 83 | E3 |
| Mellan Fryken | 105 | E3 | Melogno, Colle di | 31 | F3 | Menai Bridge | 6 | A2 | Ménez-Hom | 22 | B3 | Menton | 31 | E3 | Mercatale (Toscana) | 61 | D4 | Metamórfossi (Halkidiki) | 80 | B4 |
| Mellansel | 102 | A2 | Meløy | 97 | E2 | Ménalo, Óros | 86 | C2 | Menfi | 68 | B3 | Méntrida | 40 | A2 | Mercatino Conca | 61 | E3 | Metamórfossi (Kilkis) | 79 | F2 |
| Melle (D) | 17 | F2 | Meløyfjorden | 97 | E2 | Menasalbas | 40 | A3 | Mengamuñoz | 39 | F2 | Menuires, les | 31 | D1 | Mercato San Severino | 64 | B4 | Metangítsi | 80 | B4 |
| Melle (F) | 24 | C4 | Melpers | 52 | B3 | Menat | 26 | A4 | Menga, Pto de | 39 | F2 | Meppel | 17 | D2 | Mercator | | | Metanopoli | 60 | A1 |
| Mellerstair | 5 | D2 | Melrose | 5 | D2 | Mencal | 44 | B3 | Mengara | 61 | E4 | Meppen | 17 | E2 | Mercato Saraceno | 61 | D3 | Metauro | 61 | E3 |
| Mellerud | 105 | D4 | Melsungen | 52 | A3 | Mendavia | 36 | B2 | Mengen | 55 | D3 | Mequinenza | 37 | E4 | Mercato Saraceno | 61 | D3 | Metaxádes | 81 | F1 |
| Mellieha | 68 | B4 | Meltaus | 99 | D2 | Mende | 29 | F3 | Mengeš | 70 | B2 | Mequinenza, Emb de | 37 | E4 | Mercez | 77 | D1 | Metéora | 83 | D1 |
| Mellifont Abbey | 13 | D3 | Melton Mowbray | 7 | D3 | Mendelpass | 59 | D3 | Mengíbar | 44 | A2 | Mer Adriatique | 74 | A2 | Mercœur | 29 | D2 | Méthana | 87 | E2 |
| Mellilä | 107 | D2 | Meltosjärvi | 99 | D2 | Menden | 17 | E3 | Mengíbar | 44 | A2 | Meråker | 101 | D2 | Mercœur | 29 | D2 | Methil | 5 | D2 |
| Mellin | 48 | B4 | Melun | 19 | F4 | Mendenítsa | 83 | E3 | Ménigoute | 24 | C3 | Meran | 59 | D2 | Mer de Crète | 90 | C2 | Methóni (Makedonía) | 79 | F3 |
| Mellingen | 52 | C3 | Melvich | 3 | D1 | Menderes, B | 115 | F4 | Meníkio, Óros | 80 | B2 | Merano | 59 | D2 | Merdrignac | 22 | C3 | Methóni | | |
| Mellrichstadt | 52 | B4 | Melvin, L | 12 | C2 | Mendola, Pso della | 59 | D3 | Mennetou | 25 | E2 | Merate | 60 | A1 | Mer du Nord | 16 | A2 | (Pelopónnissos) | 86 | C3 |
| Mellum | 47 | F3 | Membrilla | 40 | B4 | Mendrisio | 58 | A4 | Menorca | 45 | F1 | Mercadal | 45 | F1 | Mere | 9 | D3 | | | |
| Melnica | 73 | E3 | Membrio | 38 | C3 | Menée, Col de | 30 | C2 | Menor, Mar | 45 | D2 | | | | | | | | | |

Metković 75 F2
Metlika 70 C2
Metnitz 57 D4
Metóhi (Ahaïa) 86 B1
Metóhi (Argolída) 87 E2
Metóhi (Évia) 84 B3
Metóhi (Thessalía) 83 F2
Metsäkylä 99 E3
Metsäkylä 103 F4
Metsämaa 107 E2
Métsovo 82 C1
Mettingen 17 E2
Mettlach 54 A1
Mettmann 17 E4
Metz 21 D3
Metzervisse 21 D3
Metzingen 55 D3
Meulan 19 E3
Meung 25 E2
Meursault 26 C3
Meurthe-et-Moselle 21 D4
Meuse 20 C3
Meuse (Dépt) 20 C3
Meuselwitz 53 D2
Mevagissey 8 B4
Meximieux 26 C4
Meyenburg 48 C3
Meymac 29 E1
Meyrand, Col de 30 B2
Meyrueis 29 F3
Meyzieu 26 C4
Mezas 39 D2
Mezdra 115 D2
Mèze 30 A4
Mézel 31 D3
Mézenc, Mt 30 B2
Mežgorje 112 C3
Mežica 70 B1
Mézidon 18 C3
Mézières 25 D4
Mezières-en-Brenne 25 E3
Mézin 28 C3
Mezőberény 112 C4
Mezőkövesd 112 B4
Mezőtúr 112 B4
Mezquita de Jarque 41 E2
Mezzano 59 D3
Mezzolombardo 58 C3
Mgarr 68 B4
Miajadas 39 E4
Miastko 110 A4
Michalovce 112 C3
Micheldorf 57 D3
Michelstadt 55 D1
Michendorf 49 D4
Mičurin 115 E2
Middelburg 16 B3
Middelfart 108 B3
Middelharnis 16 B3
Middelkerke-Bad 50 A3
Middlesbrough 5 F4
Middleton-in-Teesdale 5 E4
Middlewich 6 C3
Midhurst 9 F3
Midi, Canal du 32 B1
Midi de Bigorre, Pic du 37 E2
Midi d'Ossau, Pic du 37 D2
Midleton 14 C4
Midouze 28 B3
Midsund 100 B2
Mid Yell 3 F1
Miedes 36 C4
Miedwie, Jez 49 F3
Międzychód 112 A1
Międzylesie 112 A2
Międzyrzec Podlaski 112 C1
Międzyzdroje 49 E2
Miehikkälä 103 F4
Miekojärvi 98 C2
Miélan 28 C4
Mielec 112 B2
Mielno 49 F1
Mieluskylä 103 D1
Miera, R 35 F2
Miercurea-Ciuc 113 D4
Mieres 35 D2
Miesbach 56 B3
Mieszkowice 49 E3
Mietoinen 107 D2
Miettila 103 F3
Migennes 26 A1
Migliarino 61 D2
Miglionico 65 D4
Miguel Esteban 40 B3
Miguelturra 40 A4
Mihajlovac (Srbija) 73 D3
Mihajlovac (Srbija) 73 F3
Mihajlovgrad 115 D2
Mihas 86 C1
Mihói 86 B1
Mijas 43 E4
Mijoux 27 D3
Míki 81 D2
Mikines 87 D2
Mikkeli 103 E3
Mikkelin Lääni 103 E3
Mikkelvik 94 B2
Mikleuš 71 E2
Míkonos 88 C2
Míkonos, N 88 C2
Mikrí Mandínia 86 C3
Mikrí Préspa, L 78 C3
Mikró Horió 83 D3
Mikrókambos 79 F2
Mikroklissoúra 80 B1
Mikrolímni 78 C3
Mikromiliá 80 C1
Mikrón Dério 81 F1
Mikron Eleftherohóri 79 E4
Mikrópoli 80 B2
Mikulov 57 F1
Milagro 36 C2
Milano 60 A1
Milano Marittimo 61 E3
Mílatos 91 E3
Milazzo 69 D2
Mileševo (Srbija) 76 B1
Mileševo (Vojvodina) 72 C1
Milestone 14 C3
Miletići 70 C4
Mileto 67 E3
Miletto, Mte 64 B3
Milevsko 57 D1
Milford (GB) 9 F3
Milford (IRL) 13 D1
Milford Haven 8 B2
Milhão 34 C3
Míli 87 D2
Miliá (Makedonía) 79 D4
Miliá (Pelopónissos) 87 D2
Miliá (Thráki) 81 F1
Milići 72 B4
Miliés 83 F2
Milin 53 F4
Milína 83 F2
Milis 66 B3
Militello in Val di C. 69 D3
Miljevina 76 A1
Millas 32 B2
Millau 29 F3
Millesimo 31 F2
Millevaches, Plateau de 29 D1
Millom 6 B1
Millport 4 C2
Millstatt 59 F2
Millstreet 14 B4
Milltown Malbay 12 B4
Milly 19 F4
Milmarcos 36 C4
Milmersdorf 49 E3
Milna 75 D2
Miločer 76 B3
Milohnić 70 B3
Milopótamos 90 A1
Mílos 88 A4
Miloševa Kula 73 E3
Mílos, N 88 A4
Miltach 56 B1
Miltenberg 55 D1
Milton Keynes 9 F2
Milutinovac 73 F2
Mimizan 28 A3
Mimizan-Plage 28 A3
Mimoň 53 F3
Mína 87 D4
Mina de São Domingos 42 B2
Minas de Riotinto 42 C2
Minaya 40 C4
Minch, The 2 B2
Mincio 60 C1
Mindelheim 55 E3
Minden 17 F2
Mindin 24 A2
Minehead 8 C3
Minerbe 60 C1
Minerbio 61 D2
Minervino Murge 65 D3
Minglanilla 41 D3
Mingorria 39 F1
Minguez, Pto 41 D2
Mingulay 2 A4
Minho 34 A3
Minićevo 73 F4
Minilla, Emb de la 43 D2
Ministra, Sierra 36 B4
Minkiö 107 E2
Miño, R 34 B2
Minsk 111 D4
Mińsk Mazowiecki 112 B1
Minsterley 9 D1
Mínthi, Óros 86 C2
Mintlaw 3 E3
Miokovićevo 71 E2
Mionica 72 C3
Mionnay 26 C4
Mira (E) 41 D3
Mira (I) 61 D1
Mira (P) 38 B1
Mirabella Imbaccari 68 C4
Mira de Aire 38 B3
Mirador de Coto Rondo 34 A2
Mirador del Fito 35 E1
Miraflores 35 F3
Miraflores de la Sierra 40 A1
Miramar (F) 31 E4
Miramar (P) 34 A4
Miramare 61 E3
Miramas 30 C4
Mirambeau 28 B1
Mirambélou, Kólpos 91 F3
Miramont-de-Guyenne 28 C2
Miranda de Ebro 36 B2
Miranda del Castañar 39 E2
Miranda do Corvo 38 B2
Miranda do Douro 34 C4
Mirande 28 C4
Mirandela 34 C4
Mirandola 60 C2
Mirano 61 D1
Mira, R 42 A2
Mirador de Llesba 35 E2
Miravalles 34 C2
Miravci 77 F3
Miravete, Pto de 39 E3
Mirditë 76 C3
Mirebeau (Côte-d'Or) 26 C2
Mirebeau (Vienne) 25 D3
Mirecourt 27 D1
Mirepoix 32 A2
Mires 91 D4
Mirgorod 113 F2
Miribel 26 C4
Mírina 85 D1
Mirna 70 B2
Mirna *R* 70 A3
Miroč 73 E3
Mironovka 113 E2
Miroševce 77 E1
Mirotice 56 C1
Mirovice 56 C1
Mirow 49 D3
Mirsíni 87 D4
Mirtiés 89 E3
Mirtóo Pélagos 87 E3
Mírtos 91 E4
Mírtos, Akr 93 E2
Mirtou, Kólpos 82 B4
Mirueña 39 F1
Mišar 72 C3
Misi 99 D2
Misilmeri 68 B3
Miskolc 112 B3
Mislinja 70 B1
Mistelbach 57 F2
Misterbianco 69 D3
Mistrás 87 D3
Mistretta 68 C3
Místros 84 B4
Misurina 59 E2
Mitchelstown 14 C3
Mittelland-Kanal 17 F2
Míthimna 85 F2
Mítikas 82 C3
Mítikas *Mt* 79 E4
Mitilini 85 F2
Mitilinií 89 E1
Mitrašinci 77 F3
Mitrópoli 83 D2
Mitsikéli, Óros 82 B2
Mittelberg (Tirol) 58 C2
Mittelberg (Vorarlberg) 58 B2
Mittenwald 55 F4
Mittenwalde 49 E4
Mittersill 59 E1
Mitterteich 53 D4
Mittweida 53 E2
Mizen Head 14 A4
Mjällån 101 F2
Mjällom 102 A2
Mjöbäck 108 C2
Mjölby 109 E1
Mjøndalen 104 C3
Mjøsa 105 D2
Mladá Boleslav 112 A2
Mladá Vožice 57 D1
Mladenovac 73 D3
Mlado Nagoričane 77 E2
Mladost, Ez 77 E3
Mlava 73 E3
Mława 112 B1
Mlini 76 A2
Mlinište 71 D4
Mljet 75 E2
Mljetski Kanal 75 F2
Mnichovo Hradiště 53 F3
Moälven 102 A2
Moaña 34 A3
Moate 12 C3
Mocejón 40 A3
Möckern 52 C1
Möckmühl 55 D2
Moclin 44 A3
Modane 31 D1
Modbury 8 C4
Modena 60 C2
Módi 83 E3
Modica 69 D4
Modigliana 61 D3
Mödling 57 F2
Modračko jez 71 F3
Modran 71 E3
Modřany 53 F4
Modrava 56 C1
Modriča 71 F3
Modrište 77 D3
Modugno 65 D3
Moëlan 22 B3
Moelv 105 D2
Moen 94 B3
Moena 59 D3
Moers 17 D3
Moesa 58 B3
Moffat 5 D3
Mogadouro 34 C4
Mogadouro, Sa do 34 C4
Mogente 45 D1
Mogila 77 E4
Mogil'ov 111 E4
Mogil'ov-Podol'skij 113 E3
Moglia 60 C2
Mogliano Veneto 59 E4
Mogón 44 B2
Mogorrit 41 D2
Moguer 42 C2
Mohács 114 B1
Moher, Cliffs of 12 B4
Mohill 12 C3
Möhkö 103 F2
Mohlos 91 F4
Möhne 17 F3
Moholm 105 E4
Moi 104 A4
Moià 32 A4
Moie 61 E4
Moimenta 34 C3


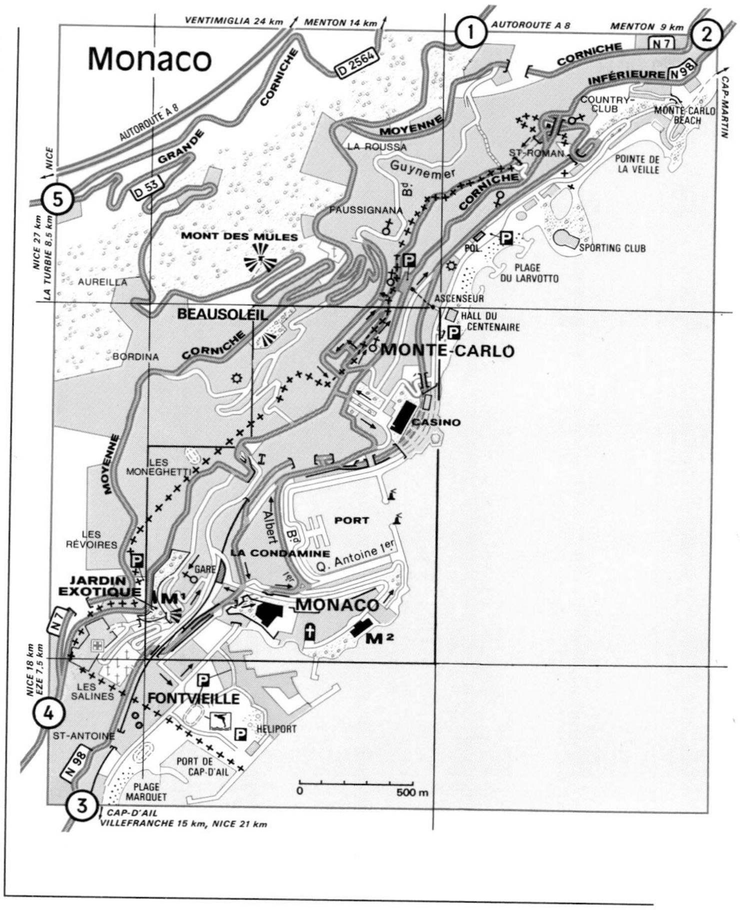

Monaco
VENTIMIGLIA 24 km
MENTON 14 km
AUTOROUTE A 8
MENTON 9 km
N7
CORNICHE
INFÉRIEURE
N98
CAP-MARTIN
COUNTRY-CLUB
MONTE-CARLO BEACH
POINTE DE LA VEILLE
MOYENNE
LA ROUSSA
ST-ROMAN
GRANDE
D 2564
D 53
Bd Guynemer
PAUSSIGNANA
MONT DES MULES
SPORTING CLUB
PLAGE DU LARVOTTO
AUREILLA
ASCENSEUR
BEAUSOLEIL
HALL DU CENTENAIRE
MONTE-CARLO
BORDINA
CASINO
LES MONEGHETTI
PORT
LES RÉVOIRES
LA CONDAMINE
Q. Antoine Ier
Bd Albert Ier
JARDIN EXOTIQUE
GARE
MONACO
LES SALINES
FONTVIEILLE
HELIPORT
ST-ANTOINE
PORT DE CAP-D'AIL
PLAGE MARQUET
CAP-D'AIL
VILLEFRANCHE 15 km, NICE 21 km
NICE 27 km
LA TURBIE 6,5 km
NICE 18 km
EZE 7,5 km
0
500 m



Moimenta da Beira 38 C1
Mo i Rana 97 E2
Moirans 30 C1
Moirans-en-Montagne 27 D3
Moisdon 23 D4
Moisiovaara 99 F4
Moisling 48 B2
Moissac 29 D3
Moita 38 A4
Mojácar 44 C3
Mojados 35 E4
Mojkovac 76 B2
Mojón Pardo, Pto de 36 B3
Mojstrana 70 A1
Mokra Gora 72 C4
Mokra Gora *Mts* 76 C2
Mokrin 72 C1
Mokronog 70 B2
Mokro Polje 75 D1
Mol (B) 50 C3
Mol (YU) 72 C1
Mola di Bari 65 E3
Molái 87 D4
Molat 74 B1
Molat *I* 74 B1
Molatón 41 D4
Mold 6 B3
Moldavija 113 E3
Molde 100 B2
Moldefjorden 100 B2
Moldova Nouă 114 C1
Moldoveanu 113 D4
Møldrup 108 B2
Moledo do Minho 34 A3
Molène 22 A2
Molfetta 65 D3
Molières 29 D3
Molina de Aragón 40 C2
Molina de Segura 45 D2
Molinella 61 D2
Molinicos 44 C1
Molins de Rei 32 A4
Molise 64 B2
Moliterno 65 D4
Molitg-les-Bains 32 B2
Mólivos, Akr 85 F2
Molkom 105 E3
Möllbrücke 59 F2
Mollerussa 37 F3
Molliens-Vidame 19 E2
Mollina 43 F3
Mölln 48 B2
Möllösund 108 C1
Mölnlycke 108 C1
Molodečno 111 D4
Mologa 111 F1
Mólos 83 E3
Molpe 102 B2
Mols 108 B3
Molsheim 21 E4
Molve 71 D1
Molveno 58 C3
Mombeltrán 39 F2
Mombuey 35 D3
Mommark 108 B4
Momo 60 A1
Møn 108 C4
Monach, Sd of 2 A3
Monadhliath Mts 2 C4
Monå fjärd 102 B2
Monaghan 13 D2
Monaghan (Co) 13 D2
Monasterace Marina 67 F4
Monasterboice 13 D3
Monasterevin 13 D4
Monasterio de Rodilla 36 A2
Monastier, le 30 B2
Monastir 66 B4
Monastiráki (Stereá Eláda) 82 C3
Monastiráki (Thráki) 81 F2
Monastíri Doukáto 81 E2
Monastíri, N 83 E2
Monbazillac 28 C2
Moncalieri 31 E2
Moncalvo 31 F1
Monção 34 A3
Moncarapacho 42 B3
Moncayo, Sa de 36 C3
Mönchdorf 57 D2
Mönchengladbach 17 D4
Monchique 42 A2
Monchique, Sa de 42 A2
Monclar-de-Quercy 29 D3
Moncófar 41 E3
Moncontour (Côtes-du-Nord) 22 C3
Moncontour (Vienne) 24 C3
Moncoutant 24 C3
Monda 43 E4
Mondariz 34 A3
Mondavio 61 E3
Mondego, Cabo 38 A2
Mondego, R 38 B2
Mondéjar 40 B2
Mondello 68 B2
Mondim 34 B4
Mondolfo 61 E3
Mondoñedo 34 C1
Mondorf 21 D3
Mondoubleau 23 F3
Mondovì 31 F2
Mondragon 30 B3
Mondragone 64 A3
Mondsee 56 C3
Monein 28 B4
Monemvassía 87 E4
Monesi 31 E3
Monesterio 43 D1
Monestier-de-Clermont 30 C2
Monestiés 29 E3
Monêtier, le 31 D2
Moneygall 12 C4
Moneymore 13 D2
Monfalcone 59 F3
Monflanquin 28 C2
Monforte 38 C4
Monforte de Lemos 34 B2
Mongie, la 37 E2
Mongó 45 E1
Monguelfo 59 D2
Monheim 55 E2
Mönichkirchen 57 F3
Mon-Idée 20 B2
Monifieth 5 D1
Moní, N 87 E2
Monistrol 32 A4
Monistrol-d'Allier 29 F2

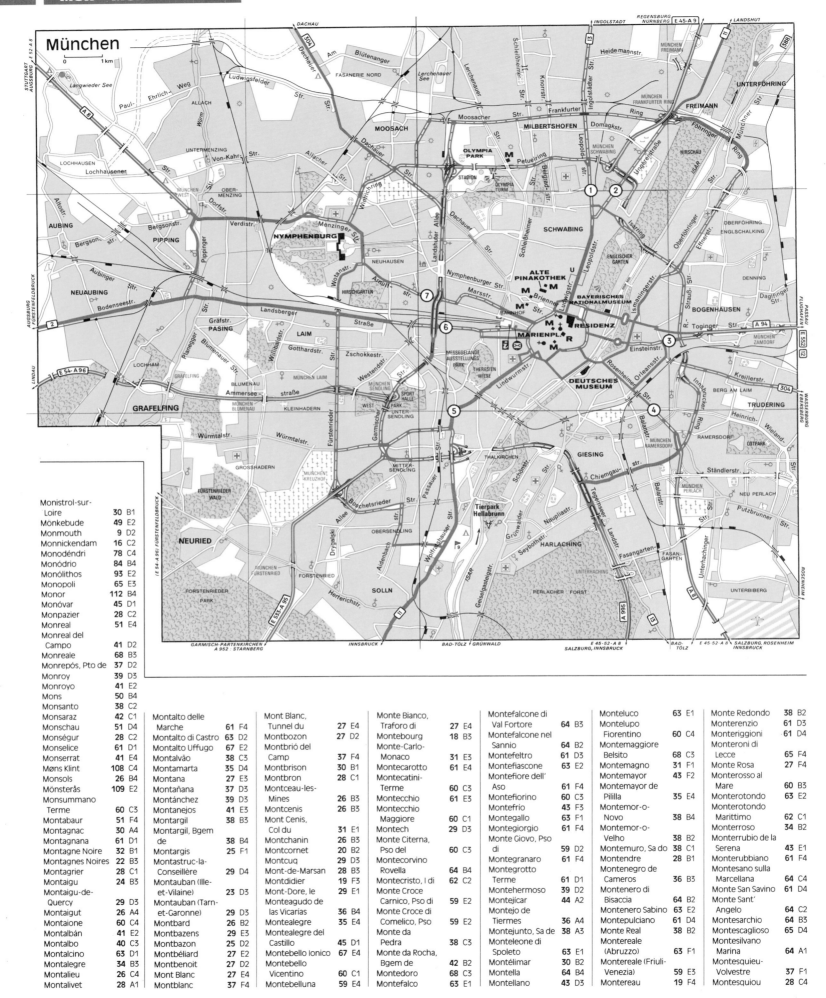

München

| | | |
|---|---|---|
| Monistrol-sur- Loire | 30 | B1 |
| Mönkebude | 49 | E2 |
| Monmouth | 9 | D2 |
| Monnickendam | 16 | C2 |
| Monodéndri | 78 | A4 |
| Monódrio | 84 | B4 |
| Monólithos | 93 | E2 |
| Monopoli | 65 | E3 |
| Monor | 112 | B4 |
| Monóvar | 45 | D1 |
| Monpazier | 28 | C2 |
| Monreal | 51 | E4 |
| Monreal del Campo | 41 | D2 |
| Monreale | 68 | B3 |
| Monrepós, Pto de | 37 | D2 |
| Monroy | 39 | D3 |
| Monroyo | 41 | E2 |
| Mons | 50 | B4 |
| Monsanto | 38 | C2 |
| Monsaraz | 42 | C1 |
| Monschau | 51 | D4 |
| Monségur | 28 | C2 |
| Monselice | 61 | D1 |
| Monserrat | 41 | E4 |
| Møns Klint | 108 | C4 |
| Monsols | 26 | B4 |
| Mönsterås | 109 | E2 |
| Monsummano Terme | 60 | C3 |
| Montabaur | 51 | F4 |
| Montagnac | 30 | A4 |
| Montagnana | 61 | D1 |
| Montagne Noire | 32 | B1 |
| Montagnes Noires | 22 | B3 |
| Montagrier | 28 | C1 |
| Montaigu | 24 | B3 |
| Montaigu-de-Quercy | 29 | D3 |
| Montaigut | 26 | A4 |
| Montaione | 60 | C4 |
| Montalbán | 41 | E2 |
| Montalbo | 40 | C3 |
| Montalcino | 63 | D1 |
| Montalegre | 34 | B3 |
| Montalieu | 26 | C4 |
| Montalivet | 28 | A1 |

| | | |
|---|---|---|
| Montalto delle Marche | 61 | F4 |
| Montalto di Castro | 63 | D2 |
| Montalto Uffugo | 67 | E2 |
| Montalvão | 38 | C3 |
| Montamarta | 35 | D4 |
| Montana | 27 | E3 |
| Montañana | 37 | D3 |
| Montánchez | 39 | D3 |
| Montanejos | 41 | E3 |
| Montargil | 38 | B3 |
| Montargil, Bgem de | 38 | B4 |
| Montargis | 25 | F1 |
| Montastruc-la-Conseillère | 29 | D4 |
| Montauban (Ille-et-Vilaine) | 23 | D3 |
| Montauban (Tarn-et-Garonne) | 29 | D3 |
| Montbard | 26 | B2 |
| Montbazens | 29 | E3 |
| Montbazon | 25 | D2 |
| Montbéliard | 27 | E2 |
| Montbenoit | 27 | D2 |
| Mont Blanc | 27 | E4 |
| Montblanc | 37 | F4 |

| | | |
|---|---|---|
| Mont Blanc, Tunnel du | 27 | E4 |
| Montbozon | 27 | D2 |
| Montbrió del Camp | 37 | F4 |
| Montbrison | 30 | B1 |
| Montbron | 28 | C1 |
| Montceau-les-Mines | 26 | B3 |
| Montcenis | 26 | B3 |
| Mont Cenis, Col du | 31 | E1 |
| Montchanin | 26 | B3 |
| Montcornet | 20 | B2 |
| Montcuq | 29 | D3 |
| Mont-de-Marsan | 28 | B3 |
| Montdidier | 19 | F3 |
| Mont-Dore, le | 29 | E1 |
| Monteagudo de las Vicarias | 36 | B4 |
| Montealegre | 35 | E4 |
| Montealegre del Castillo | 45 | D1 |
| Montebello Ionico | 67 | E4 |
| Montebello Vicentino | 60 | C1 |
| Montebelluna | 59 | E4 |

| | | |
|---|---|---|
| Monte Bianco, Traforo di | 27 | E4 |
| Montebourg | 18 | B3 |
| Monte-Carlo-Monaco | 31 | E3 |
| Montecarotto | 61 | E4 |
| Montecatini-Terme | 60 | C3 |
| Montecchio | 61 | E3 |
| Montecchio Maggiore | 60 | C1 |
| Montech | 29 | D3 |
| Monte Citerna, Pso del | 60 | C3 |
| Montecorvino Rovella | 64 | B4 |
| Montecristo, I di | 62 | C2 |
| Monte Croce Carnico, Pso di | 59 | E2 |
| Monte Croce di Comelico, Pso | 59 | E2 |
| Monte da Pedra | 38 | C3 |
| Monte da Rocha, Bgem de | 42 | B2 |
| Montedoro | 68 | C3 |
| Montefalco | 63 | E1 |

| | | |
|---|---|---|
| Montefalcone di Val Fortore | 64 | B3 |
| Montefalcone nel Sannio | 64 | B2 |
| Montefeltro | 61 | D3 |
| Montefiascone | 63 | E2 |
| Montefiore dell' Aso | 61 | F4 |
| Montefiorino | 60 | C3 |
| Montefrio | 43 | F3 |
| Montegallo | 63 | F1 |
| Montegiorgio | 61 | F4 |
| Monte Giovo, Pso di | 59 | D2 |
| Montegranaro | 61 | F4 |
| Montegrotto Terme | 61 | D1 |
| Montehermoso | 39 | D2 |
| Montejicar | 44 | A2 |
| Montejo de Tiermes | 36 | A4 |
| Montejunto, Sa de | 38 | A3 |
| Monteleone di Spoleto | 63 | E1 |
| Montélimar | 30 | B2 |
| Montella | 64 | B4 |
| Montellano | 43 | D3 |

| | | |
|---|---|---|
| Monteluco | 63 | E1 |
| Montelupo Fiorentino | 60 | C4 |
| Montemaggiore Belsito | 68 | C3 |
| Montemagno | 31 | F1 |
| Montemayor | 43 | F2 |
| Montemayor de Pililla | 35 | E4 |
| Montemor-o-Novo | 38 | B4 |
| Montemor-o-Velho | 38 | B2 |
| Montemuro, Sa do | 38 | C1 |
| Montendre | 28 | B1 |
| Montenegro de Cameros | 36 | B3 |
| Montenero di Bisaccia | 64 | B2 |
| Montenero Sabino | 63 | E2 |
| Montepulciano | 61 | D4 |
| Monte Real | 38 | B2 |
| Montereale (Abruzzo) | 63 | F1 |
| Montereale (Friuli-Venezia) | 59 | E3 |
| Montereau | 19 | F4 |

| | | |
|---|---|---|
| Monte Redondo | 38 | B2 |
| Monterenzio | 61 | D3 |
| Monteriggioni | 61 | D4 |
| Monteroni di Lecce | 65 | F4 |
| Monte Rosa | 27 | F4 |
| Monterosso al Mare | 60 | B3 |
| Monterotondo | 63 | E2 |
| Monterotondo Marittimo | 62 | C1 |
| Monterroso | 34 | B2 |
| Monterrubio de la Serena | 43 | E1 |
| Monterubbiano | 61 | F4 |
| Montesano sulla Marcellana | 64 | C4 |
| Monte San Savino | 61 | D4 |
| Monte Sant' Angelo | 64 | C2 |
| Montesarchio | 64 | B3 |
| Montescaglioso | 65 | D4 |
| Montesilvano Marina | 64 | A1 |
| Montesquieu-Volvestre | 37 | F1 |
| Montesquiou | 28 | C4 |

| Name | Page | Grid |
|---|---|---|
| Montet, le | 26 | A3 |
| Montets, Col des | 27 | E4 |
| Montevarchi | 61 | D4 |
| Monteviejo, Pto de | 35 | E2 |
| Montfaucon-en-Velay | 30 | B1 |
| Montfaucon (Maine-et-Loire) | 24 | B2 |
| Montfaucon (Meuse) | 20 | C3 |
| Montfort | 23 | D3 |
| Montfort-en-Chalosse | 28 | B4 |
| Montfort-l'Amaury | 19 | E4 |
| Montfort-sur-Risle | 19 | D3 |
| Montgaillard | 32 | A2 |
| Montgenèvre | 31 | D2 |
| Montgenèvre, Col de | 31 | D2 |
| Montgiscard | 29 | D4 |
| Montgomery | 9 | D1 |
| Montguyon | 28 | B1 |
| Monthermé | 20 | C2 |
| Monthey | 27 | E4 |
| Monthois | 20 | C3 |
| Monthureux | 27 | D1 |
| Monti | 66 | B2 |
| Montichiari | 60 | B1 |
| Monticiano | 61 | D4 |
| Montiel | 44 | B1 |
| Montier-en-Der | 20 | C4 |
| Montignac | 29 | D2 |
| Montigny-le-Roi | 26 | C1 |
| Montigny-sur-Aube | 26 | C1 |
| Montijo (E) | 39 | D4 |
| Montijo (P) | 38 | A4 |
| Montilla | 43 | F2 |
| Montioni | 62 | C1 |
| Montivilliers | 19 | D3 |
| Montjean | 23 | E4 |
| Montlhéry | 19 | f4 |
| Montlieu | 28 | B1 |
| Montlouis | 25 | D2 |
| Mont-Louis | 32 | A3 |
| Montluçon | 25 | F4 |
| Montluel | 26 | C4 |
| Montmarault | 26 | A4 |
| Montmartin | 18 | B3 |
| Montmédy | 20 | C3 |
| Montmélian | 31 | D1 |
| Montmirail (Marne) | 20 | A4 |
| Montmirail (Sarthe) | 23 | F3 |
| Montmirey-le-Château | 26 | C2 |
| Montmoreau | 28 | C1 |
| Montmorillon | 25 | D4 |
| Montmort | 20 | B3 |
| Montoggio | 60 | A3 |
| Montoire | 23 | F4 |
| Montoito | 38 | C4 |
| Montone | 61 | D3 |
| Montorio al Vomano | 63 | F1 |
| Montoro | 43 | F2 |
| Montòro, Emb de | 43 | F1 |
| Montpellier | 30 | A4 |
| Montpellier-le-Vieux, Chaos de | 29 | F3 |
| Montpezat-de-Quercy | 29 | D3 |
| Montpezat-sous-Bauzon | 30 | B2 |
| Montpon-Ménestérol | 28 | C2 |
| Montpont | 26 | C3 |
| Montréal (Aude) | 32 | A2 |
| Montréal (Gers) | 28 | C3 |
| Montréal-la-Cluse | 26 | C4 |
| Montredon-Labessonnie | 32 | B1 |
| Montréjeau | 37 | E1 |
| Montrésor | 25 | E2 |
| Montresta | 66 | A2 |
| Montreuil | 19 | E1 |
| Montreuil-Bellay | 24 | C2 |
| Montreux | 27 | E3 |
| Montrevault | 24 | B2 |
| Montrevel | 26 | C3 |
| Montrichard | 25 | E2 |
| Mont-roig del Camp | 37 | F4 |
| Montrond-les-Bains | 30 | B1 |
| Montrose | 5 | E1 |
| Mont-St-Michel, le | 18 | B4 |
| Mont-St-Vincent | 26 | B3 |
| Montsalvy | 29 | E2 |
| Montsant, Sa del | 37 | F4 |
| Montsauche | 26 | B2 |
| Montsec, Serra de | 37 | F3 |
| Montseny | 32 | B4 |
| Montseny, Sa de | 32 | B4 |
| Montserrat | 32 | A4 |
| Mont-sous-Vaudrey | 26 | C3 |
| Monts-sur-Guesnes | 25 | D3 |
| Montsûrs | 23 | E3 |
| Montuenga | 39 | F1 |
| Montuiri | 45 | F3 |
| Monviso | 31 | E2 |
| Monza | 60 | A1 |
| Monzón | 37 | E3 |
| Monzón de Campos | 35 | F3 |
| Moordorf | 47 | E3 |
| Moorfoot Hills | 5 | D2 |
| Moosburg | 56 | B2 |
| Mór | 112 | B4 |
| Mora (E) | 40 | A3 |
| Mora (P) | 38 | B4 |
| Mora (S) | 101 | E4 |
| Morača | 76 | B2 |
| Morača R | 76 | B2 |
| Morača klisura | 76 | B2 |
| Móra d'Ebre | 37 | E4 |
| Mora de Rubielos | 41 | E2 |
| Moraira | 45 | E1 |
| Moraira, Pta de | 45 | E1 |
| Morais | 34 | C4 |
| Moraïtika | 82 | A2 |
| Morakovo, G. | 76 | B2 |
| Móra la Nova | 41 | F1 |
| Moral de Calatrava | 40 | A4 |
| Moraleda de Zafayona | 44 | A3 |
| Moraleja | 39 | D2 |
| Moraleja de Sayago | 39 | E1 |
| Morales de Rey | 35 | D3 |
| Morales de Toro | 35 | E4 |
| Morano Calabro | 67 | E2 |
| Mora, Pto de la | 44 | A3 |
| Morar, L | 2 | B4 |
| Mórarp | 108 | C3 |
| Morasverdes | 39 | D2 |
| Morata de Jalón | 36 | C4 |
| Morata de Tajuña | 40 | B2 |
| Moratalla | 44 | C2 |
| Morata, Pto de | 36 | C4 |
| Morava | 57 | E1 |
| Morava R | 112 | A3 |
| Moravče | 70 | B2 |
| Moravci | 70 | C1 |
| Moravica | 73 | D4 |
| Moravské Budějovice | 57 | E1 |
| Moravske Toplice | 70 | C1 |
| Moravský Krumlov | 57 | E1 |
| Moray Firth | 3 | D3 |
| Morbach | 54 | B1 |
| Morbegno | 58 | B3 |
| Morbihan | 22 | C3 |
| Mörbisch | 57 | F3 |
| Mörbylånga | 109 | E3 |
| Morcenx | 28 | A3 |
| Morciano di Romagna | 61 | E3 |
| Morcone | 64 | B3 |
| Morcote | 58 | A4 |
| Morcuera, Pto de la | 40 | A1 |
| Mordelles | 23 | D3 |
| Morecambe | 6 | B1 |
| Morecambe Bay | 6 | B1 |
| Moreda | 44 | A3 |
| Morée | 25 | E1 |
| Moreleja del Vino | 35 | D4 |
| Morella | 41 | E2 |
| Møre og Romsdal | 100 | B2 |
| Mores | 66 | B2 |
| Morestel | 30 | C1 |
| Moret | 19 | F4 |
| Moreton | 9 | E2 |
| Moretonhampstead | 8 | C3 |
| Moreuil | 19 | F2 |
| Morez | 27 | D3 |
| Morfasso | 60 | B2 |
| Mórfio | 82 | B2 |
| Morgat | 22 | A3 |
| Morges | 27 | D3 |
| Morgex | 27 | E4 |
| Morgins, Pas de | 27 | E4 |
| Morhange | 21 | D3 |
| Mori | 58 | C4 |
| Morina | 76 | C2 |
| Moritzurg | 53 | E2 |
| Morjärv | 98 | C3 |
| Morlaàs | 37 | E1 |
| Morlaix | 22 | B2 |
| Mormanno | 67 | E2 |
| Mormant | 19 | F4 |
| Mormoiron | 30 | C3 |
| Mornant | 30 | B1 |
| Mórnou, Teh L | 83 | E4 |
| Morón de Almazán | 36 | B4 |
| Morón de la Frontera | 43 | E3 |
| Morosaglia | 33 | F3 |
| Morović | 72 | B3 |
| Morpeth | 5 | E3 |
| Morrón | 44 | B3 |
| Mörrum | 109 | D3 |
| Mors | 108 | A2 |
| Morsbach | 17 | E4 |
| Mörsil | 101 | E2 |
| Morsleben | 52 | C1 |
| Mortagne | 28 | B1 |
| Mortagne-au-Perche | 19 | D4 |
| Mortagne-sur-Sèvre | 24 | C3 |
| Mortágua | 38 | B2 |
| Mortain | 18 | C4 |
| Mortara | 60 | A2 |
| Morteau | 27 | D2 |
| Mortrée | 19 | D4 |
| Morven | 3 | D2 |
| Moryń | 49 | E3 |
| Morzine | 27 | E4 |
| Morzyczyn | 49 | F2 |
| Mosbach | 55 | D2 |
| Mosby | 104 | B4 |
| Mošćenice | 70 | B3 |
| Mošćenička Draga | 70 | B3 |
| Moschendorf | 57 | F4 |
| Mosel | 51 | E4 |
| Moselle (Dépt) | 21 | D3 |
| Moselle R | 27 | D4 |
| Moshokariá | 83 | E3 |
| Moshopótamos | 79 | E3 |
| Mosjøen | 97 | E3 |
| Moskenesøya | 97 | E1 |
| Moskenstraumen | 97 | E1 |
| Mosko | 76 | A2 |
| Moskosel | 98 | B3 |
| Moskva | 111 | F2 |
| Moskva R | 111 | F2 |
| Moslavačka gora | 71 | D2 |
| Mosonmagyaróvár | 112 | A4 |
| Mosor | 75 | E2 |
| Mosqueruela | 41 | E2 |
| Moss | 105 | D3 |
| Mossala | 107 | D3 |
| Mossat | 3 | D4 |
| Mosses, Col des | 27 | E3 |
| Mössingen | 55 | D3 |
| Most (CS) | 53 | E3 |
| Most (YU) | 70 | A2 |
| Mosta | 68 | B4 |
| Mostar | 75 | F2 |
| Mosteiro | 34 | A2 |
| Mosterhamn | 104 | A3 |
| Mostiska | 112 | C1 |
| Móstoles | 40 | A2 |
| Mostonga | 72 | B2 |
| Mostrim | 12 | C3 |
| Mosty | 110 | C4 |
| Møsvatn | 104 | B3 |
| Mosvik | 101 | D1 |
| Mota del Cuervo | 40 | B3 |
| Mota del Marqués | 35 | E4 |
| Motajica | 71 | E3 |
| Motala | 105 | F4 |
| Motala S | 106 | A4 |
| Mothe-Achard, la | 24 | B3 |
| Motherwell | 4 | C2 |
| Mothe-St-Héray, la | 24 | C4 |
| Motilla del Palancar | 40 | C3 |
| Motovun | 70 | A3 |
| Motril | 44 | A4 |
| Motta di Livenza | 59 | E4 |
| Motta S.A. | 69 | D3 |
| Motta Visconti | 60 | A1 |
| Motte-Chalancon, la | 30 | C2 |
| Motte, la | 31 | D3 |
| Mottola | 65 | E4 |
| Mouchard | 27 | D3 |
| Moudon | 27 | E3 |
| Moúdros | 85 | D1 |
| Mougins | 31 | E4 |
| Mouhijärvi | 107 | D1 |
| Mouilleron-en-Pareds | 24 | C3 |
| Moulins | 26 | A3 |
| Moulins-Engilbert | 26 | B3 |
| Moulins-la-Marche | 19 | D4 |
| Moult | 18 | C3 |
| Moúnda, Akr | 86 | A1 |
| Mountain Ash | 8 | C2 |
| Mount Bellew | 12 | C3 |
| Mountmellick | 13 | D4 |
| Mountrath | 13 | D4 |
| Mount's B | 8 | B4 |
| Mountsoúna | 88 | C3 |
| Moura | 42 | B1 |
| Mourão | 42 | C1 |
| Moúrdzeflos, Akr | 85 | D1 |
| Mourenx | 28 | B4 |
| Mouríki | 84 | A4 |
| Mourmelon-le-Grand | 20 | B3 |
| Mourne | 13 | D2 |
| Mourne Mts | 13 | E3 |
| Mourniés | 90 | B3 |
| Mourujärvi | 99 | E2 |
| Mouscron | 50 | A3 |
| Moustiers-Ste-Marie | 31 | D3 |
| Mouthe | 27 | D3 |
| Mouthier | 27 | D2 |
| Mouthoumet | 32 | B2 |
| Moutier | 27 | E2 |
| Moûtiers | 31 | D1 |
| Moutiers-les-Mauxfaits | 24 | B3 |
| Mouy | 19 | F3 |
| Mouzáki | 82 | C1 |
| Mouzon | 20 | C2 |
| Moville | 13 | D1 |
| Moy | 12 | B2 |
| Moyenneville | 19 | E2 |
| Moyeuvre | 21 | D3 |
| Moyuela | 37 | D4 |
| Možajsk | 111 | F2 |
| Mozirje | 70 | B1 |
| Mozyr' | 113 | E1 |
| Mrągowo | 110 | B4 |
| Mrakovica | 71 | D3 |
| Mramorak | 73 | D2 |
| Mratinje | 76 | A1 |
| Mrazovac | 70 | C3 |
| Mrčajevci | 73 | D4 |
| Mrežičko | 77 | E4 |
| Mrkonjić Grad | 71 | E4 |
| Mrkopalj | 70 | B3 |
| Mrzežyno | 49 | F1 |
| Mšeno | 53 | F3 |
| Msta | 111 | E1 |
| Mstislavl' | 111 | E3 |
| Mú | 42 | B2 |
| Muć | 75 | D1 |
| Muccia | 61 | E4 |
| Much | 17 | E4 |
| Mücheln | 52 | C2 |
| Much Wenlock | 9 | D1 |
| Mucientes | 35 | E4 |
| Muck | 2 | B4 |
| Muckle Roe | 3 | F1 |
| Muckross House | 14 | B4 |
| Mudanya | 115 | F3 |
| Mudau | 55 | D1 |
| Muddus | 98 | B2 |
| Muel | 37 | D4 |
| Muelas del Pan | 35 | D4 |
| Muff | 13 | D1 |
| Muge | 38 | B3 |
| Mügeln | 53 | E2 |
| Muggia | 59 | F4 |
| Mugron | 28 | B4 |
| Mugueimes | 34 | B3 |
| Mühlbach | 59 | E1 |
| Mühlberg | 53 | E2 |
| Mühldorf | 56 | B3 |
| Mühlen-Eichsen | 48 | B2 |
| Mühlhausen | 52 | B2 |
| Mühltroff | 53 | D3 |
| Muhniemi | 107 | F2 |
| Muhos | 99 | D4 |
| Muhu | 110 | B2 |
| Muine Bheag | 15 | D3 |
| Muineachán | 13 | D2 |
| Muirkirk | 4 | C3 |
| Muir of Ord | 2 | C3 |
| Mukačevo | 112 | C3 |
| Mukos | 77 | E3 |
| Mula | 45 | D2 |
| Mülacker | 54 | C2 |
| Mula, R | 45 | D2 |
| Mulargia, L | 66 | B3 |
| Mulhacén | 44 | A3 |
| Mülheim | 17 | E3 |
| Mulhouse | 27 | E1 |
| Mull | 4 | B1 |
| Müllheim | 54 | C4 |
| Mullingar | 13 | D3 |
| Mull of Galloway | 4 | B4 |
| Mull of Kintyre | 4 | B3 |
| Mull of Oa | 4 | A2 |
| Müllrose | 49 | F4 |
| Mull, Sd of | 4 | B1 |
| Mullsjö | 109 | D1 |
| Mulrany | 12 | B2 |
| Multia | 103 | D3 |
| Mumbles, The | 8 | C2 |
| Muñana | 39 | F2 |
| Münchberg | 53 | D4 |
| Müncheberg | 49 | E4 |
| München | 56 | A3 |
| Münchhausen | 17 | F4 |
| Münden | 52 | B2 |
| Mundesley | 7 | F3 |
| Mundford | 11 | D1 |
| Mundo, R | 44 | C1 |
| Munera | 40 | C4 |
| Mungia | 36 | B1 |
| Muñico | 39 | F2 |
| Muniesa | 37 | D4 |
| Munkebo | 108 | B3 |
| Munkedal | 105 | D4 |
| Munkfors | 105 | E3 |
| Münnerstadt | 52 | B4 |
| Muñogalindo | 39 | F2 |
| Munsala | 102 | B2 |
| Munsfjället | 101 | E1 |
| Münsingen (CH) | 27 | E3 |
| Münsingen (D) | 55 | D3 |
| Munster (F) | 27 | E1 |
| Münster (CH) | 27 | F3 |
| Münster (Niedersachsen) | 48 | B3 |
| Münster (Nordrhein-Westfalen) | 17 | E3 |
| Münstertal | 54 | C4 |
| Münzenberg | 52 | A4 |
| Münzkirchen | 56 | C2 |
| Muodoslompolo | 95 | D4 |
| Muojärvi | 99 | F2 |
| Muonio | 95 | D4 |
| Muonioälven | 95 | D4 |
| Muotkatonturit | 95 | E2 |
| Mur | 57 | E4 |
| Mura | 70 | C1 |
| Muraglione, Pso del | 61 | D3 |
| Murano | 61 | D1 |
| Murat | 29 | E2 |
| Murato | 33 | F3 |
| Murat-sur-Vèbre | 32 | B1 |
| Murau | 57 | D4 |
| Muravera | 66 | C4 |
| Murça | 34 | B4 |
| Murchante | 36 | C3 |
| Murcia | 45 | D2 |
| Murcia (Reg) | 44 | C2 |
| Mur-de-Barrez | 29 | E2 |
| Mur-de-Bretagne | 22 | C3 |
| Mureck | 57 | E4 |
| Mure, la | 30 | C2 |
| Mureş | 112 | C4 |
| Muret | 29 | D4 |
| Murg | 54 | C2 |
| Murguía | 36 | B1 |
| Muri | 27 | F2 |
| Murias de Paredes | 35 | D2 |
| Murino | 76 | C2 |
| Muriqan | 76 | B3 |
| Müritz See | 49 | D3 |
| Murjek | 98 | B2 |
| Murnau | 56 | A4 |
| Muro | 33 | F3 |
| Muro de Alcoy | 45 | E1 |
| Murol | 29 | E1 |
| Murole | 102 | C3 |
| Muro Lucano | 64 | C4 |
| Muros | 34 | A2 |
| Mürren | 27 | F3 |
| Murrhardt | 55 | D2 |
| Murska Sobota | 70 | C1 |
| Mursko Središče | 70 | C1 |
| Murten | 27 | E3 |
| Murter | 74 | C1 |
| Murter I | 74 | C1 |
| Murtosa | 38 | B1 |
| Murtovaara | 99 | F3 |
| Murvica | 74 | C1 |
| Murviel | 30 | A4 |
| Mürz | 57 | E3 |
| Mürzsteg | 57 | E3 |
| Mürzzuschlag | 57 | E3 |
| Musala | 115 | D3 |
| Mussalo | 103 | F4 |
| Musselburgh | 5 | D2 |
| Musselkanaal | 17 | E1 |
| Mussidan | 28 | C2 |
| Mussomeli | 68 | C3 |
| Mussy | 26 | B1 |
| Mustair | 58 | C3 |
| Mustasaari | 102 | B2 |
| Mustèr | 58 | A3 |
| Mustion as | 107 | E3 |
| Mustvee | 110 | C1 |
| Muta | 70 | B1 |
| Mutala | 102 | C3 |
| Mutterstadt | 54 | C1 |
| Mutzschen | 53 | E2 |
| Muurame | 103 | D3 |
| Muurasjärvi | 103 | D1 |
| Muuratjärvi | 103 | D3 |
| Muurla | 107 | E2 |
| Muurola | 99 | D2 |
| Muuruvesi | 103 | E2 |
| Muxía | 34 | A1 |
| Muy, le | 31 | D4 |
| Muzillac | 22 | C4 |
| Muzzana del Turgnano | 59 | F3 |
| Mweelrea Mts. | 12 | B3 |
| Myckegensjö | 101 | F2 |
| Mykines | 96 | A3 |
| Myllykoski | 107 | F2 |
| Myllykylä | 102 | C3 |
| Myllymäki | 102 | C2 |
| Mynämäki | 107 | D2 |
| Mýrdalsjökull | 96 | B3 |
| Myre | 94 | A3 |
| Myrlandshaugen | 94 | B3 |
| Myrskylä | 107 | F2 |
| Myrviken | 101 | E2 |
| Mysen | 105 | D3 |
| Mysingen | 106 | B4 |
| Mýsla | 49 | F3 |
| Myślibórskie, Jez | 49 | F3 |
| Myślibórz | 49 | F3 |
| Mývatn | 96 | B1 |
| Mže | 53 | E4 |

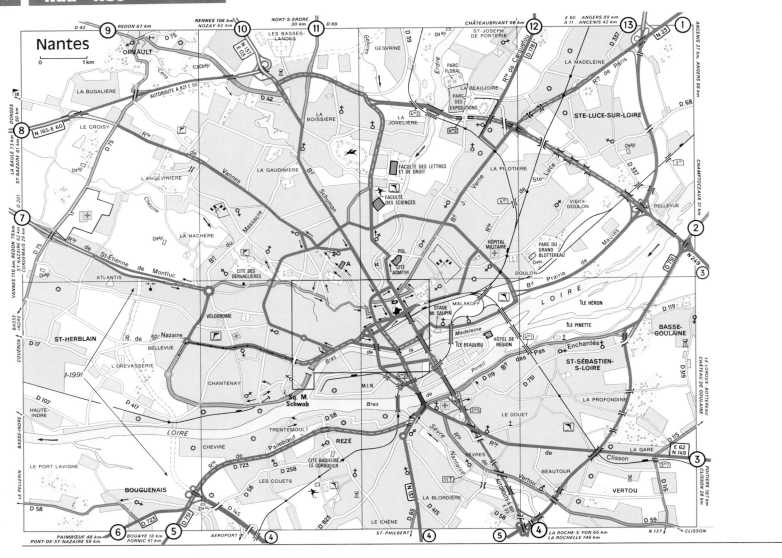

# N

| | | | | | | | | | | | | | | |
|---|---|---|---|---|---|---|---|---|---|---|---|---|---|---|
| | | | Nakskov | 108 B4 | Nardò | 65 F4 | Nauvo | 107 D3 | Navatalgordo | 39 F2 | Néa Moudaniá | 80 A4 | Neede | 17 D2 |
| | | | Näljänkä | 99 E3 | Narew | 112 C1 | Nava | 35 E1 | Nave | 60 B1 | Néa Péla | 79 F3 | Needles, The | 9 E3 |
| Naab | 55 F1 | Na Logu | 70 A2 | Narila | 103 E3 | Nava, Colle di | 31 F3 | Návekvarn | 106 A4 | Néa Péramos | | Neermoor | 47 E3 |
| Naamijoki | 98 C2 | Nalón, R | 35 E2 | Narkaus | 99 D2 | Navacelles, Cirque | | Navelli | 63 F2 | (Stereá-Eláda) | 87 E1 | Nefyn | 6 A3 |
| Naantali | 107 D2 | Naltijärvi | 95 D3 | Narni | 63 E2 | de | 29 F3 | Naver, L | 2 C2 | Néa Péramos | | Negoiu | 113 D4 |
| Naarajärvi | 103 E3 | Namdalseid | 97 D4 | Naro | 68 C4 | Navacepeda | 39 E2 | Naveros | 43 D4 | (Makedonía) | 80 C2 | Negorci | 77 F3 |
| Naarva | 103 F2 | Nämdöfjärden | 106 B4 | Naro-Fominsk | 111 F2 | Navacerrada | 40 A2 | Navia | 34 C1 | Neápoli (Kríti) | 91 E4 | Negotin | 73 F3 |
| Naas | 13 D4 | Náměšť | 57 E1 | Nærøy | 97 D4 | Navacerrada, Pto | | Navia de Suarna | 34 C2 | Neápoli | | Negotino | 77 E3 |
| Näätämöjoki | 95 F2 | Namsen | 97 D4 | Närpes | 102 B3 | de | 40 A1 | Navia, R | 34 C1 | (Makedonía) | 79 D3 | Negra de Urbión, L | 36 B3 |
| Nabburg | 56 B1 | Namsos | 97 D4 | Närpiö | 102 B3 | Navachica | 44 A3 | Navl'a | 111 F4 | Neápoli | | Negrar | 60 C1 |
| Načeradec | 57 D1 | Namsskogan | 97 D4 | Narta | 71 D2 | Navaconcejo | 39 E2 | Náxos | 88 C3 | (Pelopónnissos) | 87 E4 | Negratín, Emb del | 44 B2 |
| Náchod | 112 A2 | Namur | 50 C4 | NarthÁki | 83 E2 | Nava de la | | Náxos Días | 88 C3 | Néa Róda | 80 B3 | Negreira | 34 A2 |
| Naddvik | 104 B1 | Namur (Prov) | 50 C4 | NarthÁki, Óros | 83 E2 | Asunción | 40 A1 | Náxos, N | 88 C3 | Néa Sánda | | Nègrepelisse | 29 D3 |
| Nadela | 34 B2 | Nancy | 21 D4 | Narva | 111 D1 | Nava del Rey | 35 E4 | Nay | 37 E1 | (Makedonía) | 79 F2 | Negru Vodă | 115 E2 |
| Nádlac | 114 C1 | Nangis | 19 F4 | Narvik | 94 B3 | Navafria, Pto de | 40 A1 | Nazaré | 38 A3 | Néa Sánda (Thráki) | 81 E2 | Neheim-Hüsten | 17 F3 |
| Nadur | 68 B4 | Nannestad | 105 D2 | Nås | 105 E2 | Navahermosa | 39 F3 | Naze, The | 11 D2 | Néa Silata | 80 A3 | Neiden | 95 F2 |
| Nadvornaja | 113 D3 | Nant | 29 F3 | Näsåker | 101 F2 | Navalcán | 39 F2 | Nazilli | 115 F4 | Néa Skióni | 80 B4 | Neige, Crêt de la | 27 D3 |
| Näfels | 58 A2 | Nanterre | 19 F4 | Năsăud | 113 D4 | Navalcarnero | 40 A2 | Ndrejaj | 76 C2 | Néa Stíra | 84 B4 | Neila | 36 B3 |
| Nafpaktías, Óri | 83 D4 | Nanteuil-le- | | Nasbinals | 29 F2 | Navaleno | 36 B3 | Ndroq | 76 C4 | Néa Tríglia | 80 A4 | Neiße | 53 F1 |
| Náfpaktos | 83 D4 | Haudouin | 19 F3 | Našice | 71 E2 | Navalmanzano | 40 A1 | Nea | 101 D2 | Neath | 8 C2 | Nejdek | 53 E3 |
| Náfplio | 87 D2 | Nantiat | 25 E4 | Näsijärvi | 102 C3 | Navalmoral de la | | Néa Agathoúpoli | 79 F3 | Néa Víssa | 81 F1 | Nekromandío | |
| Naggen | 101 F3 | Nantua | 26 C4 | Naso | 69 D2 | Mata | 39 E3 | Néa Alikarnassés | 91 E3 | Néa Zoí | 79 E2 | Efíras | 82 B2 |
| Nagold | 54 C3 | Nantwich | 6 C3 | Nassau | 51 F4 | Navalperal de | | Néa Anhíalos | 83 F2 | Néa Zíhni | 80 B2 | Neksø | 109 D4 |
| Nagu | 107 D3 | Nao, C de la | 45 F1 | Nassereith | 58 C2 | Pinares | 40 A2 | Néa Artáki | 84 B4 | Nebel | 47 F1 | Nela, R | 36 A1 |
| Nagyatád | 114 A1 | Náoussa (Kikládes) | 88 C3 | Naßfeld-Paß | 59 F2 | Navaluenga | 39 F2 | Néa Éfessos | 79 F4 | Nebelhorn | 55 E4 | Nelas | 38 C1 |
| Nagykálló | 112 C3 | Náoussa | | Nässjö | 109 D1 | Navalvillar de Pela | 39 E4 | Néa Epidavros | 87 E2 | Nebljusi | 70 C4 | Nelidovo | 111 E2 |
| Nagykanizsa | 114 A1 | (Makedonía) | 79 D3 | Nastola | 107 F2 | Navamorcuende | 39 F2 | Néa Fókeada | 80 A4 | Nebra | 52 C2 | Nellim | 95 F3 |
| Nagykőrös | 112 B4 | Nahe | 48 A2 | Næstved | 108 C4 | Navan | 13 D3 | Neagh, L | 13 E2 | Nechranická přehr | | Nelson | 6 C2 |
| Nahe | 48 A2 | Nahe R | 54 B1 | Natalinci | 73 D3 | Navarra | 36 C2 | Néa Hilí | 81 E2 | nádrž | 53 E3 | Neman | 110 B3 |
| Nahe R | 54 B1 | Napapiiri | 99 D2 | Nattaset | 95 F3 | Navarredonda de | | Néa Iraklítsa | 80 C2 | Neckar | 55 D1 | Neméa | 87 D1 |
| Naila | 53 D4 | Napoli | 64 B4 | Nattavaara | 98 B2 | la Sierra | 39 F2 | Néa Kalikrátia | 79 F4 | Neckarelz | 55 D2 | Nemirov | 113 E3 |
| Nailloux | 32 A1 | Napoli, G di | 64 A4 | Nättraby | 109 E3 | Navarrenx | 28 B4 | Néa Kariá | 81 D2 | Neckargemünd | 54 C1 | Nemours | 25 F1 |
| Nailsworth | 9 D2 | Napoule, la | 31 E4 | Naucelle | 29 E3 | Navarrés | 41 E4 | Néa Karváli | 80 C2 | Neckarsteinach | 54 C1 | Nemunas | 110 C3 |
| Nairn | 3 D3 | Narberth | 8 B2 | Nauders | 58 C2 | Navarrete | 36 B2 | Néa Kerassoús | 82 C2 | Neckarsulm | 55 D2 | Nenagh | 12 C4 |
| Najac | 29 D3 | Nærbø | 104 A4 | Nauen | 49 D4 | Navascués | 37 D2 | Néa Kíos | 87 D2 | Nečujam | 75 D2 | Nene | 10 C1 |
| Nájera | 36 B2 | Narbolia | 66 B3 | Naul | 13 D3 | Navas del | | Néa Koróni | 86 C3 | Neda | 34 B1 | Nénita | 85 F4 |
| Najerilla, R | 36 B2 | Narbonne | 32 A1 | Naumburg | 52 C2 | Madroño | 39 D3 | Néa Mákri | 88 A1 | Nédas | 86 C2 | Nenzing | 58 B2 |
| Nakkila | 107 D1 | Narbonne-Plage | 30 A4 | Naunhof | 53 D2 | Navas de Oro | 40 A1 | Néa Messángala | 83 F1 | Nedelišće | 70 C1 | Neohoráki | 84 A4 |
| Nakło | 112 A1 | Narcao | 66 B4 | Naussac, Bge de | 29 F2 | Navas de San Juan | 44 B2 | Néa Mihanióna | 79 F3 | Nedervetil | 102 C1 | Neohóri (Etolía- | |
| Nakovo | 72 C1 | Narcea, R | 35 D1 | Naustdal | 100 A3 | Navasfrías | 39 D2 | Néa Moní | 85 E4 | Nedstrand | 104 A3 | Akarnanía) | 82 C4 |

| | | |
|---|---|---|
| Neohóri (Évia) | 84 | B4 |
| Neohóri (Fthiótida) | 83 | E3 |
| Neohóri (Ípiros) | 82 | C2 |
| Neohóri (Kardítsa) | 83 | D2 |
| Neohóri (Magnissía) | 84 | A2 |
| Neohóri (Pelopónissos) | 86 | C2 |
| Neohóri (Thráki) | 81 | F1 |
| Neohóri (Trikala) | 83 | D1 |
| Néo Monastíri | 83 | E2 |
| Néon Petrítsi | 80 | A2 |
| Néos Marmarás | 80 | B4 |
| Néos Skopós | 80 | B2 |
| Néouvielle, Pic de | 37 | E2 |
| Nephin | 12 | B2 |
| Nephin Beg Range | 12 | B2 |
| Nepomuk | 56 | C1 |
| Nera | 63 | E1 |
| Nérac | 28 | C3 |
| Neráida (Amárandoos) | 83 | D2 |
| Neráida (Neohóri) | 83 | D2 |
| Neratovice | 53 | F3 |
| Nerdvika | 100 | B1 |
| Neresheim | 55 | E2 |
| Nereto | 63 | F1 |
| Neretva | 76 | A1 |
| Neretva klisura | 75 | F1 |
| Neretvanski kan | 75 | E2 |
| Nestáni | 87 | D2 |
| Nesterov | 112 | C2 |
| Nestório | 78 | C3 |
| Néstos | 81 | D2 |
| Nesvik | 104 | A3 |
| Nesviž | 111 | D4 |
| Neto | 67 | F3 |
| Netolice | 56 | C1 |
| Netretić | 70 | C3 |
| Nettetal | 17 | D4 |
| Nettuno | 63 | E3 |
| Neuastenberg | 17 | F4 |
| Neubeckum | 17 | F3 |
| Neubourg, le | 19 | D3 |
| Neubrandenburg | 49 | D2 |
| Neubukow | 48 | C2 |
| Neuburg | 55 | F2 |
| Neuchâtel | 27 | E2 |
| Neu Darchau | 48 | B3 |
| Neuenburg | 47 | E3 |
| Neuenbürg | 54 | C2 |
| Neuendorf | 49 | D1 |
| Neuenhaus | 17 | E2 |
| Neuenkirchen | 48 | A3 |
| Neuenstadt | 55 | D2 |
| Neuerburg | 54 | A1 |
| Neufahrn | 56 | B2 |
| Neuf-Brisach | 27 | E1 |
| Neufchâteau | 20 | C2 |
| Neufchâteau | 20 | C4 |
| Neufchâtel | 20 | B3 |

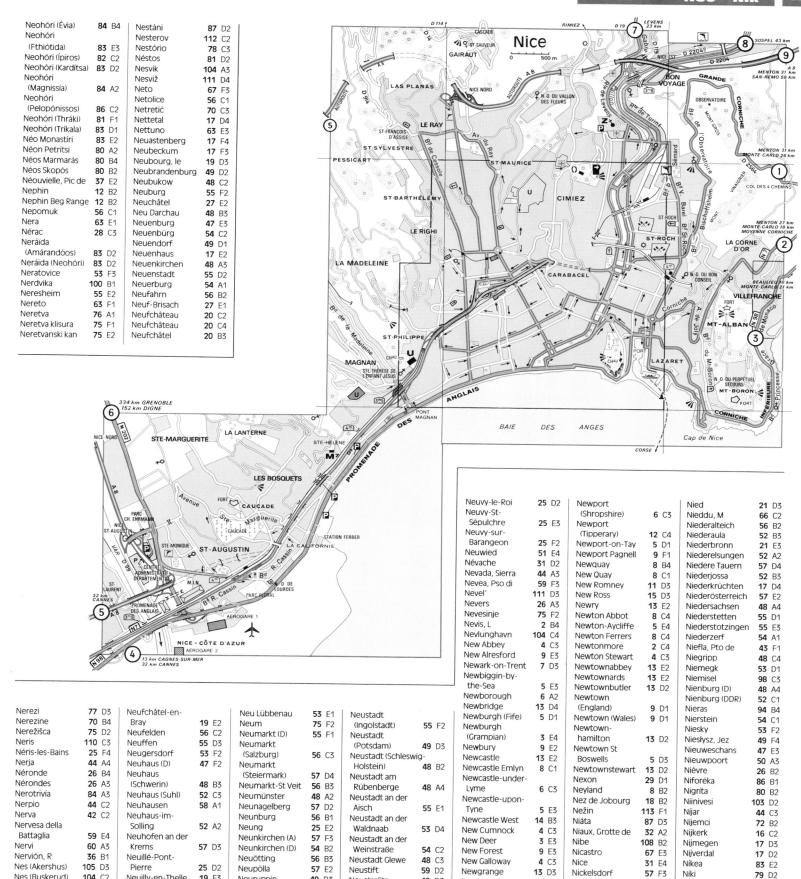

| | | |
|---|---|---|
| Nerezi | 77 | D3 |
| Nerezine | 70 | B4 |
| Nerežišča | 75 | D2 |
| Neris | 110 | C5 |
| Néris-les-Bains | 25 | F4 |
| Nerja | 44 | A4 |
| Néronde | 26 | B4 |
| Nérondes | 26 | A3 |
| Nerotrivía | 84 | A3 |
| Nerpio | 44 | C2 |
| Nerva | 42 | C2 |
| Nervesa della Battaglia | 59 | E4 |
| Nervi | 60 | A3 |
| Nervión, R | 36 | B1 |
| Nes (Akershus) | 105 | D3 |
| Nes (Buskerud) | 104 | C2 |
| Nes (NL) | 16 | C1 |
| Nesbyen | 104 | C2 |
| Nesebâr | 115 | E2 |
| Nesjøen | 101 | D2 |
| Neskaupstaður | 96 | C2 |
| Nesle | 19 | F2 |
| Nesoddtangen | 105 | D3 |
| Nesseby | 95 | F1 |
| Nesselwang | 55 | E4 |
| Ness, L | 2 | C3 |
| Neufchâtel-en-Bray | 19 | E2 |
| Neufelden | 56 | C2 |
| Neuffen | 55 | D3 |
| Neugersdorf | 53 | F2 |
| Neuhaus (D) | 47 | F2 |
| Neuhaus (Schwerin) | 48 | B3 |
| Neuhaus (Steiermark) | 57 | D4 |
| Neuhaus (Suhl) | 52 | C3 |
| Neuhausen | 58 | A1 |
| Neuhaus-im-Solling | 52 | A2 |
| Neuhofen an der Krems | 57 | D3 |
| Neuillé-Pont-Pierre | 25 | D2 |
| Neuilly-en-Thelle | 19 | F3 |
| Neuilly-le-Réal | 26 | A3 |
| Neuilly-l'Evêque | 26 | C1 |
| Neuilly-St-Front | 20 | A3 |
| Neu-Isenburg | 52 | A4 |
| Neukalen | 49 | D2 |
| Neukirch | 53 | F2 |
| Neukirchen (A) | 59 | D1 |
| Neukirchen (D) | 47 | F1 |
| Neukloster | 48 | C2 |
| Neulengbach | 57 | E2 |
| Neu Lübbenau | 53 | E1 |
| Neum | 75 | F2 |
| Neumarkt (D) | 55 | F1 |
| Neumarkt (Salzburg) | 56 | C3 |
| Neumarkt (Steiermark) | 57 | D4 |
| Neumarkt-St Veit | 56 | B3 |
| Neumünster | 48 | A2 |
| Neunagelberg | 57 | D2 |
| Neunburg | 56 | B1 |
| Neung | 55 | E3 |
| Neunkirchen (A) | 57 | F3 |
| Neunkirchen (D) | 54 | B2 |
| Neuötting | 56 | B3 |
| Neupölla | 57 | E2 |
| Neuruppin | 49 | D3 |
| Neusiedl | 57 | F3 |
| Neusiedler See | 57 | F3 |
| Neuss | 17 | D4 |
| Neustadt (Baden-Württemberg) | 54 | C4 |
| Neustadt (Coburg) | 52 | C4 |
| Neustadt (Dresden) | 53 | F2 |
| Neustadt (Gera) | 53 | D3 |
| Neustadt (Hessen) | 52 | A3 |
| Neustadt (Ingolstadt) | 55 | F2 |
| Neustadt (Potsdam) | 49 | D3 |
| Neustadt (Schleswig-Holstein) | 48 | B2 |
| Neustadt am Rübenberge | 48 | A4 |
| Neustadt an der Aisch | 55 | E1 |
| Neustadt an der Waldnaab | 53 | D4 |
| Neustadt an der Weinstraße | 54 | C2 |
| Neustadt Glewe | 48 | C3 |
| Neustift | 59 | D2 |
| Neustrelitz | 49 | D3 |
| Neu-Ulm | 55 | E3 |
| Neuve-Lyre, la | 19 | D4 |
| Neuves-Maisons | 21 | D4 |
| Neuvic (Corrèze) | 29 | E1 |
| Neuvic (Dordogne) | 28 | C2 |
| Neuville | 26 | C4 |
| Neuville-aux-Bois | 25 | E1 |
| Neuville-de-Poitou | 25 | D3 |
| Neuvy-le-Roi | 25 | D2 |
| Neuvy-St-Sépulchre | 25 | E3 |
| Neuvy-sur-Barangeon | 25 | F2 |
| Neuwied | 51 | E4 |
| Névache | 31 | D2 |
| Nevada, Sierra | 44 | A3 |
| Nevea, Pso di | 59 | F3 |
| Nevel' | 111 | D3 |
| Nevers | 26 | A3 |
| Nevesinje | 75 | F2 |
| Nevis, L | 2 | B4 |
| Nevlunghavn | 104 | C4 |
| New Abbey | 4 | C3 |
| New Alresford | 9 | E3 |
| Newark-on-Trent | 7 | D3 |
| Newbiggin-by-the-Sea | 5 | E3 |
| Newborough | 6 | A2 |
| Newbridge | 13 | D4 |
| Newburgh (Fife) | 5 | D1 |
| Newburgh (Grampian) | 3 | E4 |
| Newbury | 9 | E2 |
| Newcastle | 13 | E2 |
| Newcastle Emlyn | 8 | C1 |
| Newcastle-under-Lyme | 6 | C3 |
| Newcastle-upon-Tyne | 5 | E3 |
| Newcastle West | 14 | B3 |
| New Cumnock | 4 | C3 |
| New Deer | 3 | E3 |
| New Forest | 9 | E3 |
| New Galloway | 4 | C3 |
| Newgrange | 13 | D3 |
| Newhaven | 10 | C3 |
| Newmarket (GB) | 11 | D1 |
| Newmarket (IRL) | 14 | B3 |
| Newmarket on Fergus | 12 | B4 |
| Newnham | 9 | D2 |
| Newport (Dyfed) | 8 | B1 |
| Newport (Gwent) | 9 | D2 |
| Newport (I of Wight) | 9 | E3 |
| Newport (Mayo) | 12 | B3 |
| Newport (Shropshire) | 6 | C3 |
| Newport (Tipperary) | 12 | C4 |
| Newport-on-Tay | 5 | D1 |
| Newport Pagnell | 9 | F1 |
| Newquay | 8 | B4 |
| New Quay | 8 | C1 |
| New Romney | 11 | D3 |
| New Ross | 15 | D3 |
| Newry | 13 | E2 |
| Newton Abbot | 8 | C4 |
| Newton-Aycliffe | 5 | E4 |
| Newton Ferrers | 8 | C4 |
| Newtonmore | 2 | C4 |
| Newton Stewart | 4 | C3 |
| Newtownabbey | 13 | E2 |
| Newtownards | 13 | E2 |
| Newtownbutler | 13 | D2 |
| Newtown (England) | 9 | D1 |
| Newtown (Wales) | 9 | D1 |
| Newtown-hamilton | 13 | D2 |
| Newtown St Boswells | 5 | D3 |
| Newtownstewart | 13 | D2 |
| Nexon | 29 | D1 |
| Neyland | 8 | B2 |
| Nez de Jobourg | 18 | B2 |
| Nežin | 113 | F1 |
| Niáta | 87 | D3 |
| Niaux, Grotte de | 32 | A2 |
| Nibe | 108 | B2 |
| Nicastro | 67 | E3 |
| Nice | 31 | E4 |
| Nickelsdorf | 57 | F3 |
| Nicolosi | 69 | D3 |
| Nicosia | 68 | C3 |
| Nicotera | 67 | E4 |
| Nidda | 52 | A4 |
| Nidderau | 52 | A4 |
| Nideggen | 51 | D3 |
| Nidelva | 104 | B4 |
| Nidri | 82 | B3 |
| Niebla | 42 | C2 |
| Niebüll | 47 | F1 |
| Niechorze | 49 | F1 |
| Nied | 21 | D3 |
| Nieddu, M | 66 | C2 |
| Niederalteich | 56 | B2 |
| Niederaula | 52 | B3 |
| Niederbronn | 21 | E3 |
| Niederelsungen | 52 | A2 |
| Niedere Tauern | 57 | D4 |
| Niederjossa | 52 | B3 |
| Niederkrüchten | 17 | D4 |
| Niederösterreich | 57 | E2 |
| Niedersachsen | 48 | A4 |
| Niederstetten | 55 | E1 |
| Niederstotzingen | 55 | E3 |
| Niederzerf | 54 | A1 |
| Niefla, Pto de | 43 | F1 |
| Niegripp | 48 | C4 |
| Niemegk | 53 | D1 |
| Niemisel | 98 | C3 |
| Nienburg (D) | 48 | A4 |
| Nienburg (DDR) | 52 | C1 |
| Nieras | 94 | B4 |
| Nierstein | 54 | C1 |
| Niesky | 53 | F2 |
| Niesłysz, Jez | 49 | F4 |
| Nieuweschans | 47 | E3 |
| Nieuwpoort | 50 | A3 |
| Nièvre | 26 | B2 |
| Niforéka | 86 | B1 |
| Nigríta | 80 | B2 |
| Niinivesi | 103 | D2 |
| Nijar | 44 | C3 |
| Nijemci | 72 | B2 |
| Nijkerk | 16 | C2 |
| Nijmegen | 17 | D3 |
| Nijverdal | 17 | D2 |
| Níkea | 83 | E2 |
| Níki | 79 | D2 |
| Nikiá | 89 | F4 |
| Nikifóros | 80 | C2 |
| Nikíssiani | 80 | C2 |
| Níkitas | 80 | B3 |
| Nikkaluokta | 94 | C4 |
| Nikolajev (L'vov) | 112 | C3 |
| Nikolajev (Odessa) | 113 | F3 |
| Nikopol | 115 | D2 |
| Nikópoli | 82 | B3 |
| Nikopólis, Órmos | 82 | B2 |

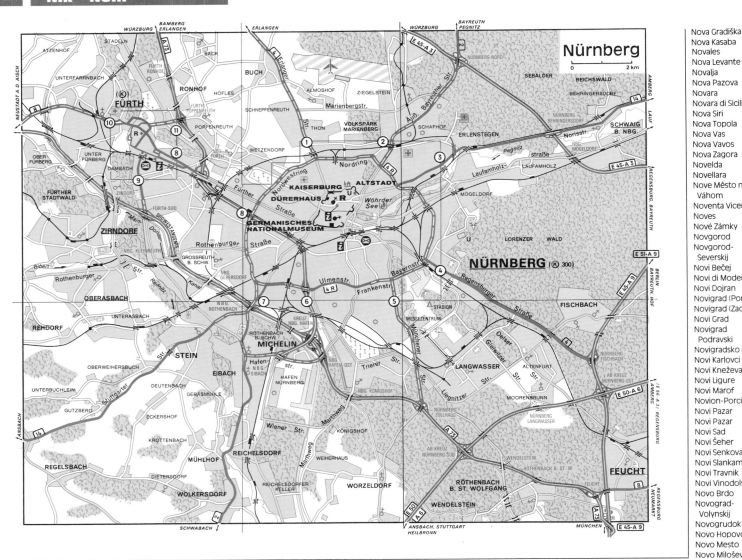

Nürnberg

0        2 km

| | | |
|---|---|---|
| Nova Gradiška | 71 | E3 |
| Nova Kasaba | 72 | B4 |
| Novales | 37 | D3 |
| Nova Levante | 59 | D3 |
| Novalja | 70 | B4 |
| Nova Pazova | 72 | C2 |
| Novara | 60 | A1 |
| Novara di Sicilia | 69 | D2 |
| Nova Siri | 65 | D4 |
| Nova Topola | 71 | E3 |
| Nova Vas | 70 | B2 |
| Nova Vavos | 76 | B1 |
| Nova Zagora | 115 | E2 |
| Novelda | 45 | D1 |
| Novellara | 60 | C2 |
| Nove Mêsto nad | | |
| Váhom | 112 | A3 |
| Noventa Vicentino | 61 | D1 |
| Noves | 30 | C3 |
| Nové Zámky | 112 | B4 |
| Novgorod | 111 | D1 |
| Novgorod- | | |
| Severskij | 111 | F4 |
| Novi Bečej | 72 | C2 |
| Novi di Modena | 60 | C2 |
| Novi Dojran | 77 | F3 |
| Novigrad (Poreč) | 70 | A3 |
| Novigrad (Zadar) | 74 | C1 |
| Novi Grad | 71 | F3 |
| Novigrad | | |
| Podravski | 71 | D2 |
| Novigradsko more | 74 | C1 |
| Novi Karlovci | 72 | C2 |
| Novi Kneževac | 72 | C1 |
| Novi Ligure | 60 | A2 |
| Novi Marof | 70 | C1 |
| Novion-Porcien | 20 | B2 |
| Novi Pazar | 76 | C1 |
| Novi Pazar | 115 | E2 |
| Novi Sad | 72 | C2 |
| Novi Šeher | 71 | F4 |
| Novi Senkovac | 71 | E2 |
| Novi Slankamen | 72 | C2 |
| Novi Travnik | 71 | E4 |
| Novi Vinodolski | 70 | B3 |
| Novo Brdo | 77 | D2 |
| Novograd- | | |
| Volynskij | 113 | D2 |
| Novogrudok | 111 | D4 |
| Novo Hopovo | 72 | C2 |
| Novo Mesto | 70 | B2 |
| Novo Miloševo | 72 | C1 |
| Novomirgorod | 113 | F2 |
| Novoržev | 111 | D2 |
| Novoselica | 113 | D3 |
| Novo Selo (Bosna i | | |
| Hercegovina) | 71 | E3 |
| Novo Selo | | |
| (Makedonija) | 77 | F3 |
| Novoukrainka | 113 | F3 |
| Novovolynsk | 112 | C2 |
| Novo Zvečevo | 71 | E2 |
| Novozybkov | 111 | E4 |
| Novska | 71 | D3 |
| Nový Bor | 53 | F3 |
| Novyj Bug | 113 | F3 |
| Nový Jičín | 112 | B3 |
| Nowa Sól | 112 | A2 |
| Nowe Warpno | 49 | E2 |
| Nowogard | 49 | F2 |
| Nowy Sącz | 112 | B3 |
| Nowy Targ | 112 | B3 |
| Noyant | 23 | F4 |
| Noyers | 26 | B1 |
| Noyers-sur- | | |
| Jabron | 30 | C3 |
| Noyon | 19 | F3 |
| Nozay | 23 | D4 |
| Nuasjärvi | 99 | E4 |
| Nueva | 35 | E1 |
| Nueva Carteya | 43 | F2 |
| Nuévalos Monasterio | | |
| de Piedra | 36 | C4 |
| Nuevo Baztán | 40 | B2 |
| Nufenenpass | 58 | A3 |
| Nuhppir | 95 | E2 |
| Nuijamaa | 103 | F4 |
| Nuits-St-Georges | 26 | C2 |
| Nules | 41 | E3 |
| Nulvi | 66 | B2 |
| Numana | 61 | F4 |
| Numancia | 36 | B3 |
| Numedal | 104 | C2 |
| Nummela | 107 | E2 |

| | | | | | | | | | | | | | | |
|---|---|---|---|---|---|---|---|---|---|---|---|---|---|---|
| Nikšić | 76 | B2 | Nizza Monferrato | 31 | F2 | Nomexy | 21 | D4 | Nordingrå | 102 | A2 | Norrby | 98 | A4 | Northwich | 6 | C2 |

| | | | | | | | | | | | |
|---|---|---|---|---|---|---|---|---|---|---|---|
| Nikšić | 76 B2 | Nizza Monferrato | 31 F2 | Nomexy | 21 D4 | Nordingrå | 102 A2 | Norrby | 98 A4 | Northwich | 6 C2 |
| Nilakka | 103 D2 | Njegoš | 76 A2 | Nómia | 87 E4 | Nordkapp | 95 E1 | Nørre Åby | 108 B3 | North York Moors | |
| Nilivaara | 98 B2 | Njivice | 70 B3 | Nonancourt | 19 E4 | Nordkinnhalvøya | 95 E1 | Nørre Alslev | 108 C4 | Nat Pk | 7 D1 |
| Nilsiä | 103 E2 | Njunis | 94 C3 | Nonant-le-Pin | 19 D4 | Nordkjosbotn | 94 C3 | Nørre Nebel | 108 A3 | North Yorkshire | 6 C1 |
| Nîmes | 30 B3 | Njupeskär | 101 D3 | Nonaspe | 37 E4 | Nordkvaløy | 94 B2 | Nørre Snede | 108 A3 | Norton | 7 D1 |
| Nimféa | 81 E2 | Noailles | 19 F3 | None | 31 E2 | Nordland | 97 E2 | Nørre Vorupør | 108 A2 | Nortort | 48 A2 |
| Nimféo | 79 D3 | Noáin | 36 A4 | Nonio | 58 A4 | Nord-Lenangen | 94 C2 | Norrfjärden | 101 F3 | Norwich | 11 D1 |
| Nimos, N | 93 E1 | Noarvaš | 95 D3 | Nontron | 28 C1 | Nordli | 97 E4 | Norrköping | 106 A4 | Nosovka | 113 E1 |
| Nin | 74 C1 | Noblejas | 40 B3 | Nónza | 33 F2 | Nördlingen | 55 E2 | Norrnäs | 102 B3 | Nossebro | 108 C1 |
| Ninove | 50 B3 | Nocera | 64 B4 | Noord-Brabant | 16 C3 | Nordmaling | 102 A2 | Norrsunda | 106 B3 | Nossen | 53 E2 |
| Niort | 24 C4 | Nocera Tirinese | 67 E3 | Noord-Holland | 16 C2 | Nordmark | 105 E3 | Norrsundet | 106 B2 | Noss Head | 3 D2 |
| Nipfjället | 101 D3 | Nocera Umbra | 61 E4 | Noord-Oost- | | Nord-Ostsee- | | Norrtälje | 106 B3 | Noteć | 112 A1 |
| Nípsa | 81 F2 | Noceto | 60 B2 | Polder | 16 C2 | Kanal | 47 F2 | Nordøyane | 100 A2 | Nótia | 79 E2 |
| Niš | 77 E1 | Noci | 65 E3 | Noordwijk aan Zee | 16 B2 | Nordøyar | 96 A3 | Norrviken | 108 C1 | Nótia Píndos | 82 C1 |
| Nisa | 38 C3 | Nodeland | 104 B4 | Noordzee | 46 B3 | Nordrana | 97 E2 | Norsjö | 98 B4 | Nótios Evoikós | |
| Nisa, Rib de | 38 C3 | Nogara | 60 C1 | Noormarkku | 102 B3 | Nordreisa | 94 C2 | Norsjø | 104 C3 | Kólpos | 84 B4 |
| Nišava | 73 F4 | Nogaro | 28 B4 | Nora | 105 F3 | Nordrhein- | | Norskehavet | 96 B4 | Nótio Stenó | |
| Niscemi | 68 C4 | Nogent | 26 C1 | Norberg | 105 F3 | Westfalen | 17 E3 | Nort | 23 D4 | Kerkíras | 82 B2 |
| Niška Banja | 77 E1 | Nogent-le-Roi | 19 E4 | Norcia | 63 F1 | Nordsee | 47 B2 | Nörten- | | Noto | 69 D4 |
| Nissáki | 82 A1 | Nogent-le-Rotrou | 23 F3 | Nord | 20 A1 | Nordseter | 105 D2 | Hardenberg | 52 B2 | Notodden | 104 C3 |
| Nissan | 109 D2 | Nogent-sur-Seine | 20 A4 | Nord Beveland | 16 B3 | Nordstrand | 47 F1 | Northallerton | 7 D1 | Notre-Dame-de- | |
| Nisser | 104 B3 | Nogueira de | | Nordborg | 108 A4 | Nord Trøndelag | 101 D1 | Northam | 8 C3 | Bellecombe | 27 E4 |
| Nissilä | 103 D1 | Ramuin | 34 B2 | Nordby (Fanø) | 108 A3 | Norðurfjörður | 96 A1 | Northampton | 9 F1 | Nottingham | 7 D3 |
| Nissiros, N | 89 F4 | Nogueira, Sa de | 34 C4 | Nordby (Samsø) | 108 B3 | Nore (IRL) | 12 C4 | Northamptonshire | 9 F1 | Nottinghamshire | 7 D3 |
| Nissum Bredning | 108 A2 | Noguera | 41 D2 | Norddeich | 47 E3 | Nore (N) | 104 C2 | North Berwick | 5 D2 | Nouan-le-Fuzelier | 25 E2 |
| Nissum Fjord | 108 A2 | Noguera | | Nordeide | 100 A3 | Norefjell | 104 C2 | North Chan | 13 E1 | Nousiainen | 107 D2 |
| Nith | 4 C3 | Pallaresa, R | 37 F2 | Norden | 47 E3 | Nore, R | 15 D3 | North Downs | 10 C3 | Nouvion | 19 E2 |
| Niton | 9 E4 | Noguera | | Nordenau | 17 F4 | Noresund | 104 C2 | Northeim | 52 B2 | Nouvion-en- | |
| Nitra | 112 B3 | Ribagorçana, R | 37 F3 | Nordenham | 47 F3 | Norfolk | 7 F3 | Northern Ireland | 13 D2 | Thiérache, le | 20 B2 |
| Nitry | 26 B2 | Nohfelden | 54 B1 | Norderney | 47 E3 | Norg | 17 D1 | North Esk | 3 D4 | Nœux | 19 F1 |
| Nittedal | 105 D3 | Noia | 34 A2 | Norderstedt | 48 A2 | Norheimsund | 104 A2 | North Foreland | 11 D2 | Nouzonville | 20 C2 |
| Nittenau | 56 B1 | Noirétable | 26 B4 | Nordfjord | 100 A2 | Norra Bergnäs | 98 A2 | Northleach | 9 E2 | Nova Breznica | 77 D3 |
| Nittendorf | 55 F2 | Noirmoutier | 24 A3 | Nordfjordeid | 100 A3 | Norra Gloppet | 102 B2 | North Ronaldsay | 3 E1 | Nová Bystřice | 57 D1 |
| Nivala | 102 C1 | Noirmoutier, I de | 24 A3 | Nordfold | 97 E1 | Norra Kvarken | 102 B2 | North Sound, The | 3 E1 | Novaci | |
| Nive | 28 A4 | Noja | 36 A1 | Nordfolda | 97 E1 | Norra Kvill | 109 E1 | North Tyne | 5 E3 | (Makedonija) | 77 E4 |
| Nivelles | 50 B4 | Nokia | 107 E1 | Nordfriesische | | Norra Råda | 105 E3 | North Uist | 2 A3 | Novaci (Srbija) | 72 C3 |
| Nivernais | 26 B3 | Nola | 64 B4 | Inseln | 47 E1 | Norra Storfjället | 97 E3 | Northumberland | 5 E3 | Nova Crnja | 72 C1 |
| Nivolet, Colle del | 31 E1 | Nolay | 26 B3 | Nordhalben | 52 C3 | Norrbottens Län | 98 B1 | Northumberland | | Novafeltria | 61 E3 |
| Niwica | 53 F1 | Noli | 60 A3 | Nordhausen | 52 C2 | | | Nat Pk | 5 E3 | Nova Gorica (I) | 59 F3 |
| Nizke Beskydy | 112 C3 | Nomeny | 21 D3 | Nordhorn | 17 E2 | Norrby | 98 A4 | North Walsham | 7 F3 | Nova Gorica (YU) | 70 A2 |

Nummi 107 E2
Nuneaton 9 E1
Nunnanen 95 D3
Nuñomoral 39 D2
Nunspeet 17 D2
Nuorajärvi 103 F2
Nuorgam 95 E2
Nuoro 66 B2
Nurallao 66 B3
Nürburg 51 E4
Núria 32 B3
Nurmes 103 E1
Nurmijärvi (Pohjois-Karjalan Lääni) 103 F1
Nurmijärvi (Uudenmaan Lääni) 107 E2
Nurmo 102 C2
Nürnberg 55 F1
Nürtingen 55 D3
Nus 27 E4
Nusse 48 B2
Nuštar 71 F2
Nuthe 49 D4
Nuttlar 17 F3
Nuttupera 103 D1
Nuutajärvi 107 E2
Nuvvos-Ailigas 95 E2
Nyåker 102 A1
Nybergsund 105 E2
Nyborg 108 B4
Nybro 109 E2
Nyírbátor 112 C3
Nyíregyháza 112 C3
Nykarleby 102 B2
Nykøbing F (Storstrøm) 108 C4
Nykøbing M (Viborg) 108 A2
Nykøbing S (Vestsjælland) 108 C3
Nyköping 106 B4
Nykvarn 106 B4
Nynäshamn 106 B4
Nyon 27 D3
Nyons 30 C3
Nýřany 53 E4
Nyrdalur 96 B2
Nýrsko 56 B1
Nyrud 95 F2
Nysa 112 A2
Nysa Łużycka 53 F1
Nysäter 105 E3
Nyseter 100 B3
Nysted 108 C4
Nyvoll 95 D2

# O

Oadby 9 F1
Oakham 9 F1
Oanes 104 A3
Óassi 87 D1
Oban 4 B1
O Barco 34 C3
Obbola 102 B1
Obdach 57 D4
Obdacher Sattel 57 D4
Obedska bara 72 C3
Obejo 43 F2
Oberalppass 58 A3
Oberammergau 55 F4
Oberau 56 A4
Oberaudorf 56 B4
Oberdrauburg 59 E2
Oberessfeld 52 C4
Obergeis 52 B3
Obergrafendorf 57 E2
Obergrünzburg 55 E4
Obergurgl 58 C2
Oberhaslach 21 E4
Oberhausen 17 E3
Oberhof 52 C3
Oberjoch-Paß 58 C1
Oberkirch 54 C3
Oberkirchen 17 F4
Oberkochen 55 E2
Obermarchtal 55 D3
Obernai 21 E4
Obernberg 56 C3
Obernburg 55 D1
Oberndorf (A) 56 C3
Oberndorf (D) 54 C3
Obernzell 56 C2
Oberölsbach 55 F1
Oberösterreich 56 C2
Oberprechtal 54 C3
Oberpullendorf 57 F3
Oberseebach 21 F3
Obersontheim 55 E2
Oberstaufen 55 E4
Oberstdorf 55 E4
Oberstein 54 B1
Obertauern 59 F1
Obertraun 59 F1
Oberursel 51 F4
Obervellach 59 E2
Oberviechtach 56 B1
Oberwart 57 F4
Oberwesel 51 E4
Oberwiesenthal 53 E3
Oberwölz 57 D4
Oberzeiring 57 D4
Óbidos 38 A3
Obilić 77 D2
Obing 56 B3
Obiou, l' 30 C2
Objat 29 D1
Obninsk 111 F3
O Bolo 34 C3
Obón 41 E1
Oborniki 112 A1
Obornjača 72 C1
Oborovo 70 C2
Obrenovac 72 C3
Obrež 72 C3
Obrov 70 A3
Obrovac (Split) 75 D1
Obrovac (Zadar) 74 C1
Obršani 77 E4
Obsteig 58 C2
Obudovac 71 F3
Obzor 115 E2
Obzova 70 B3
Očakov 113 F3
Oca, Mtes de 36 A2
Ocaña 40 B3
Oca, R 36 A2
Očauš 71 E4
Occhiobello 61 D2
Occhito, L di 64 B3
Očevlje 71 F4
Ochagavia 37 D2
Ochil Hills 5 D1
Ochsenfurt 55 E1
Ochsenhausen 55 E3
Ochtrup 17 E2
Ockelbo 106 A2
Öckerö 108 C1
Ocreza, R 38 C3
Ocrkavlje 76 A1
Ödåkra 108 C3
Odda 104 B2
Odden Færgehavn 108 B3
Odder 108 B3
Oddesund 108 A2
Odeceixe 42 A2
Odeleite 42 B2
Odelzhausen 55 F3
Odemira 42 A2
Ödemiş 115 F4
Odense 108 B3
Odenthal 17 E4
Oder 49 E3
Oderberg 49 E3
Oderbruch 49 E3
Oderbucht 49 E1
Oderhaff 49 E2
Oderzo 59 E4
Ödeshög 109 D1
Odessa 113 F4
Odet 22 B3
Odiel, R 42 C2
Odivelas 42 B1
Odivelas, Bgem de 42 B1
Odolo 60 B1
Odorheiu Secuiesc 113 D4
Odra 112 A2
Odžaci 72 B2
Odžak (Bosna i Hercegovina) 71 F3
Odžak (Crna Gora) 76 B1
Oebisfelde 48 B4
Oebro 105 F4
Oederan 53 E3
Oeiras 38 A4
Oelde 17 F3
Oelsnitz (Plauen) 53 D3
Oelsnitz (Zwickau) 53 D3
Oettingen 55 E2
Oetz 58 C2
Ofanto 64 C3
Ofenpass 58 C3
Offaly 12 C4
Offenbach 52 A4
Offenburg 54 C3
Offida 63 F1
Offranville 19 E2
Ofir 34 A4
Ofotfjorden 94 B3
Oggiono 60 A1
Ogliastro Cilento 67 D1
Oglio 58 C4
Ognon 27 D2
Ogošte 77 E2
Ogražden 77 F3
Ogre 110 C2
Ogulin 70 C3
Ohanes 44 B3
Óhi, Óros 88 A1
Ohiró 80 B1
Ohlstadt 56 A4
Ohorn 53 F2
Ohrdruf 52 C3
Ohre 48 B4
Ohře 53 E3
Ohrid 77 D4
Ohridsko Ez 77 D4
Ohringen 55 D2
Ohrit, Liq i 77 D4
Óhthia 82 C3
Ohthoniá 84 B4
Oijärvi 99 D3
Oijärvi *L* 99 D3
Oikarainen 99 D2
Oirschot 16 C3
Oise 20 B2
Oise (Dépt) 19 F3
Oisemont 19 E2
Oisterwijk 16 C3
Oitti 107 E2
Oituz 113 D4
Ojakylä 99 D4
Öje 101 E4
Öjebyn 98 B3
Ojén 43 E4
Ojos Negros 41 D2
Ojuelos Altos 43 E1
Öjung 101 E4
Okehampton 8 C3
Oker 48 B4
Oklaj 75 D1
Oknö 109 E2
Okol 76 C2
Oksbøl 108 A3
Oksby 108 A3
Øksfjord 95 D2
Øksfjorden 94 A3
Øksfjordjøkelen 94 C2
Øksnes 94 A3
Okstindan 97 E3
Okučani 71 E3
Okulovka 111 E1
Olafsfjörður 96 B1
Olafsvík 96 A2
Öland 109 E2
Olan, Pic d' 31 D2
Olargues 32 B1
Olazagutia 36 B2
Olbernhau 53 E3
Olbia 66 B1
Oldcastle 13 D3
Oldebroek 17 D2
Oldeide 100 A3
Olden 100 A3
Oldenburg (Niedersachsen) 47 F3
Oldenburg (Schleswig Holstein) 48 B1
Oldenzaal 17 E2
Olderdalen 94 C2
Oldervik 94 C2
Oldfjällen 101 E1
Oldham 6 C2
Old Head of Kinsale 14 B4
Oldmeldrum 3 E4
Oldsum 47 F1
Oleggio 60 A1
Oleiros 34 B1
Oleiros 38 C2
Ølen 104 A3
Oléron, Ile d' 24 B4
Olesa 32 A4
Oleśnica 112 A2
Oletta 33 F2
Olette 32 B2
Olevsk 113 D2
Ølgod 108 A3
Olhão 42 B3
Olhava 99 D3
Oliana 32 A3
Oliana, Emb d' 32 A3
Olib 70 B4
Olib *I* 70 B4
Oliena 66 B2
Oliete 37 D4
Olimbía 86 C2
Olimbiáda (Makedonía) 80 B3
Olimbiáda (Thessalía) 79 E4
Ólimbos 93 D2
Ólimbos, Óros (Évia) 84 B4
Ólimbos, Óros (Pieriá) 79 E4
Ólinthos 80 A4
Olite 36 C2
Oliva 45 E1
Oliva de la Frontera 42 C1
Oliva de Mérida 39 D4
Olivares 40 C3
Oliveira de Azeméis 38 B1
Oliveira de Frades 38 B1
Oliveira do Bairro 38 B1
Oliveira do Douro 34 B4
Oliveira do Hospital 38 C2
Olivenza 38 C4
Olivenza, R de 38 C4
Olivet 25 E1
Olivone 58 A3
Olleria, Pto de l' 41 E4
Ollerton 7 D3
Ollières, les 30 B2
Olliergues 29 F1
Ollioules 31 D4
Olòla 103 F2
Olmedillo de Roa 35 F4
Olmedo (E) 35 E4
Olmedo (I) 66 A2
Olmeto 33 F4
Olocau del Rey 41 E2
Olofström 109 D3
Olombrada 35 F4
Olomouc 112 A3
Olonzac 32 B1
Oloron Ste Marie 37 D1
Olost 32 A3
Olot 32 B3
Olovo 71 F4
Olpe 17 F4
Olsberg 17 F3
Olshammar 105 F4
Olst 17 D2
Ølstykke 108 C3
Olsztyn 110 B4
Olszyna 53 F1
Olt 115 D2
Oltedal 104 A3
Olten 27 F2
Oltenia 115 D1
Oltenița 115 E1
Olula del Río 44 C3
Olvega 36 C3
Olvera 43 E3
Omagh 13 D2
Omalí 79 D4
Omalós 90 B3
Omarska 71 D3
Ombrone 63 D1
Omegna 58 A4
Omiš 75 E2
Omišalj 70 B3
Omme Å 108 A3
Ommen 17 D2
Omodeo, L 66 B3
Omoljica 73 D3
Omorfohóri 83 E1
Ömossa 102 B3
Oña 36 A2
Oñati 36 B1
Oncala, Pto de 36 B3
Onda 41 E3
Ondara 45 E1
Ondárroa 36 B1
Oneglia 31 F3
Onesse-et-Laharie 28 A3
Onich 2 C4
Onkamo (Lapin Lääni) 99 E2
Onkamo (Pohjois Karjalan Lääni) 103 F2
Onkivesi 103 E2
Ons, I de 34 A2
Ontaneda 35 F2
Ontiñena 37 E3
Ontinyent 45 E1
Ontojärvi 99 F4
Ontur 45 D1
Onzain 25 E2
Oostburg 16 B4
Oostelijk-Flevoland 16 C2
Oostende 50 A3
Oosterbeek 17 D3
Oosterend 16 C1
Oosterhout 16 C3
Oostkamp 50 A3
Oostmalle 50 C3
Oost-Vlaanderen 50 B3
Oost-Vlieland 16 C1
Ootmarsum 17 E2
Opatija 70 B3
Opatovac 72 B2
Opava 112 A3
Opladen 17 E4
Oplenac 73 D3
Opočka 111 D2
Opole 112 A2
Opovo 72 C2
Oppach 53 F2
Oppdal 100 C2
Oppenau 54 C3
Oppenheim 54 C1
Opphaug 100 C1
Oppido Lucano 64 C4
Oppido Mamertina 67 E4
Oppland 104 C1
Oputten 16 C2
Opuzen 75 F2
Ora 59 D3
Oradea 112 C4
Oradour-sur-Glane 25 D4
Oradour-sur-Vayres 28 C1
Orahova 71 D3
Orahovac 77 D2
Orahovica 71 E2
Oraison 31 D3
Orajärvi 98 C2
Orange 30 B3
Orani 66 B2
Oranienbaum 53 D1
Oranienburg 49 D3
Oranmore 12 B3
Orašac (Hrvatska) 75 F2
Orašac (Srbija) 73 D3
Orasi 76 B3
Orašje 71 F3
Orăştie 114 C1
Oravainen 102 B2
Oravais 102 B2
Oravikoski 103 E2
Oravița 114 C1
Orb 30 A4
Orba 45 E1
Ørbæk 108 B4
Orbassano 31 E2
Orbe 27 D3
Orbec 19 D3
Orbetello 63 D2
Orbey 27 E1
Órbigo, R 35 D2
Orce 44 B2
Orce, R 44 B2
Orcera 44 B1
Orchies 20 A1
Orcières 31 D2
Orcival 29 E1
Orco 31 E1
Ordes 34 A1
Ordesa, Parque Nac. de 37 E2
Ordino 32 A2
Ordizia 36 C1
Orduña 36 B1
Orduña, Pto de 36 B1
Ore 101 E4
Orea 41 D2
Oreälven 102 A1
Orebić 75 E2
Örebro Län 105 F3
Öregrund 106 B3
Öregrundsgrepen 106 B2
Orei 83 F3
Orellana de la Sierra 39 E4
Orellana, Emb de 39 E4
Orellana la Vieja 39 E4
Orense 34 B3
Oréo 81 D2
Oreókastro 79 F3
Orestiáda 81 F1
Oresund 108 C3
Orfós, Akr 89 F4
Orgáni 81 E2
Organyà 32 A3
Orgañyà 37 F3
Orgaz 40 A3
Orgejev 113 E3
Orgelet 26 C3
Orgères-en-Beauce 25 E1
Orgon 30 C3
Orgosolo 66 B2
Orhi, Pic d' 37 D1
Orhomenós 83 F4
Oria 44 C3
Oria 65 E4
Oria, R 36 C1
Origny-Sainte-Benoîte 20 A2
Orihuela 45 D2
Orihuela del Tremedal 41 D2
Orimattila 107 F2
Oriní 80 B2
Oriolo 65 D4
Oripää 187 D2
Orissaare 110 B2
Oristano 66 B3
Oristano, G di 66 A3
Orivesi 102 C3
Orivesi *L* 103 F2
Orjahovo 115 D2
Ørjavik 100 B2
Ørje 105 D3
Orjen 76 A2
Orjiva 44 A3
Orkanger 100 C2
Örkelljunga 109 D3
Orkla 100 C2
Orkney Is 3 E1
Ørlandet 100 C1
Orlando, C d' 69 D2
Orlane 77 D1
Orlate 77 D2
Orléans 25 E1
Orlická přehr nádrž 56 C1
Orlovat 72 C2
Orly 19 F4
Orménio 81 F1
Ormília 80 B4
Órmos 79 F3
Órmos Korthíou 88 B1
Órmos Panagías 80 B4
Órmos Prínou 80 C3
Ormož 70 C1
Ormsjö 97 F4
Ormsjön 101 F1
Ormskirk 6 B2
Ormtjernkampen 104 C1
Ornain 20 C4
Ornans 27 D2
Orne (Calvados) 18 C4
Orne (Dépt) 20 B3
Orne (Meuse) 21 D3
Ørnes 97 E2
Ornós 88 C2
Örnsköldsvik 102 A2
Or'ol 111 F4
Orolik 72 B2
Orom 72 B1
Oron-la-Ville 27 E3
Oropesa (Castilla la Mancha) 39 F3
Oropesa (Valencia) 41 F3
Orosei 66 C2
Orosei, G di 66 C2
Orosháza 112 B4
Orpierre 30 C3
Orpington 10 C2
Orra 100 C3
Orsa 101 E4
Orša 111 E3
Orsajön 101 E4
Orsay 19 F4
Orsières 27 E4
Orsogna 64 A2
Orşova 114 C1
Ørsta 100 A2
Örsundsbro 106 B3
Orta Nova 64 C3
Orta San Giulio 58 A4
Orte 63 E2
Ortegal, C 34 B1
Orth 57 F2
Orthez 28 B4
Ortigueira 34 B1
Ortisei 59 D3
Ortles 58 C3
Ortnevik 104 B1
Orton 5 D4
Ortona 64 A2
Ortrand 53 E2
Örträsk 102 A1
Orubica 71 E3
Orune 66 B2
Orusco 40 B2
Orvalho 38 C2
Orvieto 63 E1
Órvilos, Óros 80 B1
Orvinio 63 F2

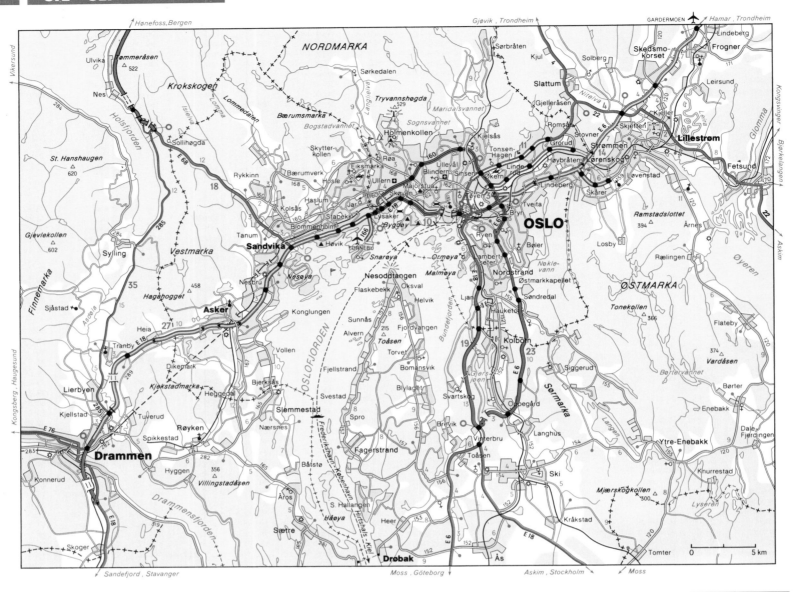

| | | | | | | | | | | | | | |
|---|---|---|---|---|---|---|---|---|---|---|---|---|---|
| Orzinuovi | 60 | B1 | Oss | 16 | C3 | Ostfriesische | | | Oświęcim | 112 | B2 | Ottobrunn | 56 | A3 | Ourique | 42 | B2 | Övre Fryken | 105 | E3 |
| Os | 100 | D3 | Össa | 80 | A2 | Inseln | 47 | D3 | Otanmäki | 103 | D1 | Ottsjö | 101 | D2 | Ourol | 34 | B1 | Øvre Pasvik | 95 | F2 |
| Osa de la Vega | 40 | B3 | Ossa de Montiel | 40 | B4 | Østhammar | 106 | B3 | Otava (CS) | 56 | C1 | Ottweiler | 54 | B2 | Ourthe | 20 | C1 | Øvre Soppero | 95 | D4 |
| Osåm | 115 | D2 | Ossa, Óros | 83 | F1 | Ostheim | 52 | B4 | Otava (SF) | 103 | E3 | Otwock | 112 | B1 | Ourville | 19 | D2 | Ovruč | 113 | E1 |
| Osby | 109 | D3 | Ossa, Sa de | 38 | C4 | Ostia Antica | 63 | E3 | Oteren | 94 | C3 | Otziás | 88 | A2 | Ouse, R | 7 | D2 | Owel, L | 13 | D3 |
| Oschatz | 53 | E2 | Ossiach | 59 | F2 | Ostiglia | 60 | C2 | Oteševo | 77 | D4 | Ötztal | 58 | C2 | Oust | 37 | F2 | Oxford | 9 | E2 |
| Oschersleben | 52 | C1 | Ossiacher See | 59 | F2 | Ostmark | 105 | E3 | Othem | 109 | F4 | Ötztaleralpen | 58 | C2 | Outes, Sa de | 34 | A2 | Oxfordshire | 9 | E2 |
| Oschiri | 66 | B2 | Óssios Loukás | 83 | F4 | Ost'or | 113 | E1 | Othery | 9 | D3 | Ouchy | 27 | D3 | Outokumpu | 103 | E2 | Oxiá, N | 82 | C4 |
| Osečina | 72 | C3 | Ossun | 37 | E1 | Ostra | 61 | E3 | Othoní, N | 78 | A4 | Oucques | 25 | E1 | Outomuro | 34 | B3 | Oxiá (Stereá Eláda) | 83 | D3 |
| Oseja de Sajambre | 35 | E2 | Ostaškov | 111 | E2 | Ostrach | 55 | D4 | Óthris, Óros | 83 | E3 | Oud Beijerland | 16 | B3 | Outwell | 10 | C1 | Oxiá (Thessalía) | 83 | D2 |
| Osen | 96 | C4 | Østbirk | 108 | B3 | Östra Gloppet | 102 | B2 | Otivar | 44 | A3 | Ouddorp | 16 | B3 | Ouvèze | 30 | C3 | Oxie | 108 | C3 |
| Osera de Ebro | 37 | D4 | Østby | 105 | D4 | Östra Silen | 105 | D4 | Otley | 6 | C2 | Oude Maas | 16 | B3 | Ouzouer | 25 | F2 | Oxilithos | 84 | B4 |
| Osijek | 71 | F2 | Oste | 47 | F3 | Ostrelj | 71 | D4 | Otnes | 100 | C3 | Oudenaarde | 50 | B3 | Ouzouer-le-Marché | 25 | E1 | Ox Mts, The | 12 | B2 |
| Osilo | 66 | B2 | Østed | 108 | C3 | Ostritz | 53 | F2 | Otočac | 70 | C4 | Oudenbosch | 16 | C3 | Ovada | 60 | A2 | Oyarzun | 36 | C1 |
| Osimo | 61 | F4 | Osterburg | 48 | C4 | Ostróda | 110 | B4 | Otočec | 70 | B3 | Oude-Pekela | 47 | E3 | Ovanåker | 101 | F4 | Oybin | 53 | F2 |
| Osinja | 71 | E3 | Osterburken | 55 | D1 | Ostrog | 113 | D2 | Otok | 72 | B2 | Ouessant, Ile d' | 22 | A2 | Ovar | 38 | B1 | Øye | 104 | C1 |
| Osipaonica | 73 | D3 | Österbybruk | 106 | B3 | Ostrołęka | 112 | B1 | Otoka | 71 | D3 | Oughterard | 12 | B3 | Ovčar Banja | 73 | D4 | Øyer | 104 | C1 |
| Osipoviči | 111 | D4 | Østerby Havn | 108 | B2 | Ostrov (CS) | 53 | E3 | Otra | 104 | B4 | Ouistreham | 18 | C3 | Ovedskloster | 109 | D3 | Øyeren | 105 | D3 |
| Osječenica | 71 | D4 | Østerbymo | 109 | E1 | Ostrov (RO) | 115 | E1 | Otranto | 65 | F4 | Oul | 51 | D4 | Overath | 17 | E4 | Oy-Mittelberg | 55 | E4 |
| Oskarshamn | 109 | E2 | Osterdalälven | 101 | D3 | Ostrov (SU) | 111 | D2 | Otsamo | 95 | E3 | Oulainen | 99 | D4 | Øverbygd | 94 | C3 | Oyntdartfjordur | 96 | A3 |
| Oskarström | 108 | C2 | Østerdalen | 100 | C3 | Ostrowiec | | | Otta | 100 | C3 | Oulanka | 99 | E2 | Overflakkee | 16 | B3 | Oyón | 36 | B2 |
| Oslava | 57 | E1 | Österfärnebo | 106 | A3 | Świętokrzyski | 112 | B2 | Ottana | 66 | B2 | Oulankajoki | 99 | E2 | Overhalla | 97 | D4 | Oyonnax | 27 | D4 |
| Oslo | 105 | D3 | Osterfeld | 53 | D2 | Ostrów | | | Ottaviano | 64 | B4 | Oulu | 99 | D3 | Överhörnäs | 102 | A2 | Øystese | 104 | B2 |
| Oslo (Fylke) | 105 | D3 | Östergötlands Län | 109 | E1 | Mazowiecki | 112 | B1 | Ottenschlag | 57 | E2 | Oulujärvi | 99 | E4 | Overijssel | 17 | D2 | Oyten | 47 | F3 |
| Oslofjorden | 104 | C3 | Osterhofen | 56 | B2 | Ostrów | | | Ottensheim | 57 | D2 | Oulujoki | 99 | D4 | Overijse | 50 | C3 | Ozalj | 70 | C2 |
| Osmo | 106 | B4 | Osterholz | | | Wielkopolski | 112 | A2 | Otterburn | 5 | E3 | Oulun Lääni | 99 | D4 | Överkalix | 98 | C2 | Ožbalt | 70 | B1 |
| Osnabrück | 17 | F2 | Scharmbeck | 47 | F3 | Ostrožac (Bosna i | | | Otter Ferry | 4 | B2 | Oulunsalo | 99 | D4 | Övermark | 102 | B2 | Ózd | 112 | B3 |
| Ośno Lubuskie | 49 | F4 | Osterode | 52 | B2 | Hercegovina) | 70 | C3 | Otterlo | 17 | D3 | Oulx | 31 | D2 | Översjuktan | 97 | F3 | Ozeblin | 70 | C4 |
| Osogovija | 77 | F2 | Osterøya | 104 | A2 | Ostrožac (Bosna i | | | Otterndorf | 47 | F2 | Ounasjoki | 99 | D2 | Övertorneå | 98 | C2 | Ozieri | 66 | B2 |
| Osogovske planine | 77 | E2 | Östersund | 101 | E2 | Hercegovina) | 75 | F1 | Otterøy | 97 | D4 | Oundle | 9 | F1 | Överum | 109 | E1 | Ozren | 71 | F3 |
| Osoppo | 59 | E3 | Östersundom | 107 | F2 | Ostsee | 48 | C1 | Ottersberg | 47 | F3 | Our | 54 | A1 | Överuman | 97 | E3 | Ozren Devica | 73 | E4 |
| Osor | 70 | B4 | Østervåla | 106 | B3 | Osttirol | 59 | E2 | Otterup | 108 | B3 | Ouranópoli | 80 | B4 | Our | 35 | D1 | | | |
| Osorno | 35 | F3 | Øster Vrå | 108 | B3 | Ostuni | 65 | E3 | Ottery St Mary | 9 | D3 | Ource | 26 | C1 | Ovindoli | 63 | F2 | | | |
| Osøyri | 104 | A2 | Osterwieck | 52 | B1 | Osuna | 43 | E3 | Ottmarsheim | 27 | E1 | Ourcq | 20 | A3 | Øvre Anarjokka | 95 | D3 | | | |
| Ospedaletti | 31 | E3 | Østfold | 105 | D3 | Oswestry | 6 | B3 | Ottnang | 56 | C3 | Ourense | 34 | B3 | Øvre Årdal | 100 | B3 | | | |
| Ospitaletto | 60 | B1 | | | | | | | | | | Ottobeuren | 55 | E3 | | | | Øvre Dividalen | 94 | C3 | | | |

# P

Paakkila 103 E2
Paalasmaa 103 E1
Páamo de Masa, Pto de 35 F3
Paar 55 F3
Paasselkä 103 F3
Paavola 99 D4
Pabianice 112 B2
Pacaudière, la 26 B4
Paceco 68 A3
Pachino 69 D4
Packsattel 57 E4
Paço de Sousa 34 A4
Paços de Ferreira 34 A4
Pacov 57 D1
Pacy 19 E4
Padasjoki 107 E1
Padej 72 C1
Padd̄ene 75 D1
Paderborn 17 F3
Paderne 42 B2
Padiham 6 C2
Padina 72 C2
Padinska Skela 72 C2
Padirac, Gouffre de 29 D2
Padjelanta 97 F1
Padornelo 34 C3
Padova 61 D1
Padrela, Sa da 34 B4
Padrón 34 A2
Padru 66 B2
Padstow 8 B3
Padul 44 A4
Paesana 31 E2
Paestum 64 B4
Pag 70 C4
Pag I 70 B4
Paganico 63 D1
Pagassés, N 83 F2
Pagassitikós Kólpos 83 F2
Paglia 63 D1
Pagny 21 D3
Pagóndas (Évia) 84 A3
Pagóndas (Sámos) 89 E2
Pagoúria 81 D2
Paguera 45 E3
Páhi 87 E1
Pahiá Ámos 91 F4
Pahís, Akr 80 C3
Paide 110 C1
Paignton 8 C4
Päijänne 103 D3
Páiko, Óros 79 E2
Paimbœuf 23 D4
Paimio 107 D2
Paimpol 22 C2
Painswick 9 E2
Paisley 4 C2
Paistunturit 95 E2
País Vasco 36 B1
Paittasjärvi 94 C4
Paiva, R 38 B1
Pajala 98 C1
Pájara 42 C4
Pajares, Pto de 35 D2
Paklenica Nac Park 70 C4
Pakoštane 74 C1
Pakrac 71 E2
Pakračka Poljana 71 D2
Paks 112 B4
Palacios de la Sierra 36 A3
Palacios del Sil 34 C3
Palacios de Sanabria 34 C3
Palade, Pso del 58 C3
Paládio 81 D2
Paladru 30 C1
Palafrugell 32 C3
Palagía 81 E2
Palagiano 65 E4
Palagonia 69 D3
Palagruža 75 D3
Palaia 60 C4
Palaiseau 19 F4
Palais, le 22 C4
Palamás 83 E2
Palamós 32 C3
Palancia, R 41 E3
Palanga 110 B3

Pala, Pto del 34 C1
Palas de Rei 34 B2
Palata 64 B2
Palatitsía 79 E3
Palatna 77 D1
Palau 66 B1
Palavas 30 B4
Palazzo del Pero 61 D4
Palazzolo Acreide 69 D4
Palazzolo sull' Oglio 60 B1
Palazzo San Gervasio 64 C3
Palazzuolo sul Senio 61 D3
Paldiski 110 C1
Pale 76 A1
Paléa Epídavros 87 E2
Palékastro 91 F4
Palena 64 A2
Palencia 35 E3
Paleohóra (Égina) 87 E2
Paleohóra (Kríti) 90 B4
Paleohóri (Grevená) 79 D4
Paleohóri (Halkidikí) 80 B3
Paleohóri (Ípiros) 82 B2
Paleohóri (Lésvos) 85 F3
Paleohóri (Pelopónissos) 87 D3
Paleohóri (Thessalía) 83 D1
Paleokastrítsa 82 A1
Paleókastro (Halkidikí) 80 A3
Paleókastro (Kozáni) 79 D4
Paleókastro (Sámos) 89 F2
Paleókastro (Séres) 80 B2
Paleókastro (Stereá Eláda) 83 D3
Paleokómi 80 B2
Paleópirgos (Stereá Eláda) 83 D4
Paleópirgos (Thessalía) 83 F1
Paleópoli (Ándros) 88 B1
Paleópoli (Samothráki) 81 E3
Paleós Kaválla 80 C2
Paleós Xánthis 81 D2
Palermo 68 B3
Páleros 82 C3
Palérou, Órm 82 B3
Palestrina 63 F2
Palež 72 B4
Páli 89 F4
Paliano 63 F3
Palić 72 B1
Palidoro 63 E2
Palinges 26 B3
Palinuro 67 D2
Palioúri 80 B4
Paliouriá 79 D4
Paliseul 20 C2
Pälkäne 107 E1
Pålkem 98 B2
Pallas Ounastunturi 95 D3
Pallastunturi 95 D4
Pallice, la 24 B4
Palluau 24 B3
Palma 45 E3
Palma del Río 43 E2
Palma di Montechiaro 68 C4
Palmadula 66 A2
Palmanova 59 F3
Palmela 38 A4
Palmi 67 E4
Palo del Colle 65 D3
Palojoensuu 95 D3
Palojoki 95 D3
Palokki 103 E2
Palomäki 103 E1
Palomares del Campo 40 C3
Palomas 39 D4
Palomas, Pto de las 44 B2

Palombara Sabina 63 E2
Palombera, Pto de 35 F2
Palomera 41 D2
Pálos, Akr 88 B2
Palos, C de 45 D3
Palos de la Frontera 42 C3
Pals 32 C3
Pålsboda 105 F4
Paltamo 99 E4
Paltaselkä 99 E4
Paluzza 59 E2
Pámfila 85 F2
Pamhagen 57 F3
Pamiers 32 A2
Pampilhosa 38 B2
Pampilhosa da Serra 38 C2
Pampliega 35 F3
Pamplona 36 C2
Pamporovo 115 D3
Pamukkale 115 F4
Panagía (Ípiros) 82 C2
Panagía (Límnos) 85 D1
Panagía (Makedonía) 79 D4
Panagía (Thássos) 81 D3
Panagía (Thessalía) 82 C1
Panagjurište 115 D2
Panahaïkó, Óros 83 D4
Panaro 60 C3
Pancalieri 31 E2
Pančevo 73 D2
Pančićev vrh 77 D1
Pancorbo 36 A2
Pandánassa 87 E4
Pandeleimónas 79 E4
Pandino 60 B1
Pandokrátor 82 A1
Pandrup 108 B2
Panes 35 F2
Panetolikó, Óros 83 D3
Panetólio 82 C4
Panév, Óros 80 B2
Pangéo, Óros 80 B2
Paniza, Pto de 36 C4
Pankajärvi 103 F1
Pankakoski 103 F1
Pankow 49 E4
Panórama (Dráma) 80 B2
Panórama (Thessaloníki) 80 A3
Panormítis 93 E1
Pánormos (Kikládes) 88 B2
Pánormos (Kriti) 91 D3
Päntäne 102 B3
Pantelleria 68 A4
Pantelleria, I di 68 A4
Paola 67 E2
Pápa 112 A4
Papádes 84 A3
Papadós 85 F3
Páparis 86 C2
Pápas, Akr 89 D2
Papasídero 67 E2
Papa Stour 3 E1
Papenburg 47 E3
Papíkio 81 D2
Pápingo 78 C4
Pappenheim 55 F2
Papuk Mt 71 E2
Papuk (Reg) 71 E2
Parabita 65 F4
Paracin 73 E2
Paracuellos de Jiloca 36 C4
Parada de Cunhos 34 B4
Paradas 43 E3
Paradela 34 B3
Paradísia 86 C2
Parádissos 81 D2
Parainen 107 D3
Parajes 34 C1
Parakálamos 78 C4
Parákila 85 F2
Paralía (Ahaïa) 86 C1
Paralía (Lakonía) 87 E3
Paralía (Makedonía) 79 F4
Paralía (Stereá Eláda) 83 F4

Paralía Akrátas 87 D1
Parália Ástros 87 D2
Paralía Kímis 84 B3
Paralía Kotsikiás 84 A3
Paralía Skotínas 79 F4
Paralía Tiroú 87 E3
Paralímni 84 A4
Paralovo 77 D2
Paramé 18 B4
Paramera, Pto de 39 F2
Paramithiá 82 B2
Páramo del Sil 34 C2
Paranésti 80 C2
Parapanda 43 F3
Parapótamos 82 B1
Paraspóri, Akr 93 D2
Paray-le-Monial 26 B3
Parchim 48 C3
Pardubice 112 A3
Paredes 34 A4
Paredes de Coura 34 A3
Paredes de Nava 35 E3
Pareja 40 C2
Pareloup, Lac de 29 E3
Parentis-en-Born 28 A3
Párga 82 B2
Pargas 107 D3
Parikkala 103 F3
Parīngului, M 114 C1
Paris 19 F4
Parkalompolo 95 D4
Parkano 102 C3
Parla 40 A2
Parlavà 32 A3
Parma 60 B2
Parnassós, Óros 83 E4
Parndorf 57 F2
Párnitha, Óros 87 F1
Párnonas, Óros 87 D3
Pärnu 110 C2
Parola 107 E2
Páros 88 C3
Páros, N 88 B3
Parrett 9 D3
Parsberg 55 F2
Parsdorf 56 A3
Parseierspitze 58 C2
Parsęta 49 F1
Parsteiner See 49 E3
Partakko 95 F2
Partanna 68 B3
Partenen 58 B2
Partenkirchen 55 F4
Parthenay 24 C3
Parthéni 89 E3
Partille 108 C1
Partinico 68 B3
Partizani 73 D3
Partizanske Vode 72 C4
Partney 7 E3
Partry Mountains 12 B3
Pasaia-Pasajes 36 C1
Pas de Calais 11 E3
Pas-de-Calais (Dépt) 19 E1
Pas de la Case 32 A2
Pas-en-Artois 19 F2
Pasewalk 49 E2
Pashalítsa 83 E2
Pasikovci 71 E2
Pašman 74 C1
Pašman I 74 C1
Passais 18 C4
Passá-Limáni 85 E4
Passás, N 85 F4
Passau 56 C2
Passavás 87 D4
Passero, C 69 D4
Passignano sul Trasimeno 61 D4
Passwang 27 E2
Pastrana 40 B2
Pastrik 76 C3
Pásztó 112 B4
Patay 25 E1
Pateley Bridge 6 C1
Patéras, Óros 87 E1
Paterna del Campo 43 D2
Paternò 69 D3
Paternopoli 64 B3
Paterna de Rivera 43 D4
Paternion 59 F2
Patersdorf 56 B2

P'atichatki 113 F2
Patiópoulo 82 C2
Patitíri 84 B2
Pátmos 89 E2
Pátmos, N 89 E2
Pátra 83 D4
Patraïkós Kólpos 82 C4
Patreksfjörður 96 A1
Patrington 7 E2
Pattada 66 B2
Patterdale 5 D4
Patti 69 D2
Pattijoki 99 D3
Patvinsuo 103 F2
Pau 37 D1
Pauillac 28 B2
Paúl 38 C2
Paularo 59 F2
Paulhaguet 29 F2
Paullo 60 A1
Pavia (I) 60 A2
Pavia (P) 38 B4
Pavilly 19 D3
Pavino Polje 76 B1
Pávliani 83 E3
Pávlos 83 F4
Pavullo nel Frignano 60 C3
Paxí 82 A2
Paxí, N 82 A2
Payerne 27 E3
Paymogo 42 C2
Payrac 29 D2
Pazardžik 115 D2
Pazin 70 A3
Pčinja 77 E2
Péage-de-Roussillon, le 30 B1
Peak District Nat Pk 6 C2
Peal de Becerro 44 B2
Peanía 87 F1
Peares, Emb de los 34 B2
Peć 76 C2
Peca 70 B1
Peccioli 60 C4
Pečenjevce 77 E1
Pech-Merle, Grotte du 29 D3
Pečigrad 70 C3
Pećinci 72 C3
Pecka 72 C4
Peckelsheim 52 A2
Pécs 114 B1
Pécsa Banja 76 C2
Pečurice 76 B3
Pedaso 61 F4
Pederker 109 D4
Pedersöre 102 C2
Pédi 93 E1
Pedrafita do Cebreiro 34 C2
Pedrafita do Cebreiro, Pto de 34 C2
Pedrajas de San Esteban 35 E4
Pedralba (Castilla-León) 34 C3
Pedralba (Valencia) 41 E3
Pedras Salgadas 34 B4
Pedraza de la Sierra 40 A1
Pedrera 43 E3
Pedrizas, Pto de las 43 F3
Pedro Abad 43 F2
Pedro Bernardo 39 F2
Pedrógão (Alentejo) 42 B1
Pedrógão (Estremadura) 38 A2
Pedrógão Grande 38 B2
Pedrola 36 C3
Pedro Muñoz 40 B4
Peebles 5 D2
Peel 6 A1
Peene 49 D1
Peenemünde 49 E1
Peer Gynt veien 100 C3
Pefkári 80 C3
Pefkí 83 F3
Péfkos 78 C3
Pega 38 C2

Pegalajar 44 A2
Pegau 53 D2
Pegli 60 A3
Pegnitz 55 F1
Pego 45 E1
Pego do Altar, Bgem de 38 B4
Pegognaga 60 C2
Pegolotte 61 D1
Pehčevo 77 F3
Peine 52 B1
Peio Terme 58 C3
Peíra-Cava 31 E3
Peißenberg 56 A4
Peiting 56 A4
Peitz 53 F1
Pek 73 D3
Péla 79 E2
Péla (Nomos) 79 F3
Pelado 41 D3
Pelagie, Is 68 A4
Pelasgía 83 F3
Pelat, Mt 31 D3
Pelčyce 49 F3
Pelekános 79 D3
Pélekas 82 A1
Peleta 87 E3
Pelhřimov 57 D1
Pelinéo 85 E4
Pelister 77 E4
Pelješac 75 E2
Pelkosenniemi 99 E1
Pellegrino, M 68 B2
Pellegrue 28 C2
Pellerin, le 24 B2
Pellesmäki 103 E2
Pello 98 C2
Pellworm 47 F1
Pelopónissos 86 C2
Peloritani, M 69 D2
Peltosalmi 103 E1
Peltovuoma 95 D3
Pélussin 30 B1
Pelvoux, Mt 31 D2
Pembroke 8 B2
Pembroke Dock 8 B2
Pembrokeshire Coast Nat Pk 8 B1
Penacova 38 B2
Peñafiel 35 F4
Penafiel 34 A4
Peñafor 43 E2
Peñagolosa 41 E3
Peña Gorbea 36 B1
Peñalara 40 A1
Penalva do Castelo 38 C1
Penamacor 38 C2
Peña Mira 34 C3
Peña Nofre 34 B3
Peña Prieta 35 E2
Peñaranda de Bracamonte 39 F1
Peñaranda de Duero 36 A3
Peñarroya 41 E2
Peñarroya, Emb de 40 B4
Peñarroya-Pueblonuevo 43 E1
Penarth 9 D2
Peña, Sa de la 37 D2
Peña Sagra 35 F2
Peñas, C de 35 D1
Peñascosa 44 C1
Peñas de Cervera 36 A3
Peñas de San Pedro 44 C1
Peña Trevinca 34 C3
Peña Ubiña 35 D2
Peñausende 35 D4
Pendáglofo 83 D4
Pendálofos 78 C4
Pendéli 87 F1
Pendéli Mt 87 F1
Pendeória 83 E4
Pénde Vrisses 80 A2
Pendine 8 B2

Peneda-Gerês, Pque Nac da 34 A3
Peneda, Sa da 34 A3
Penedono 38 C1
Penela 38 B2
Pénestin 22 C4
Penha 34 A4
Penhas da Saude 38 C2
Penhas Juntas 34 C4
Penhir, Pte de 22 A3
Penice, Pso del 60 A2
Peniche 38 A3
Penicuik 5 D2
Penig 53 D3
Peñíscola 41 F2
Penkun 49 E3
Penmaenmawr 6 A2
Penmarch, Pte de 22 A3
Pennabilli 61 E3
Penne 63 F1
Penne-d'Agenais 28 C3
Pennes, Pso di 59 D2
Pennines, The 6 C1
Peñón de Ifach 45 E1
Penrhyndeudraeth 6 A3
Penrith 5 D4
Penryn 8 B4
Penserjoch 59 D2
Pentland Firth 3 D2
Pentland Hills 5 D2
Pentrefoelas 6 B3
Pen-y-bont 8 C2
Penzance 8 A4
Penzberg 56 A4
Penzlin 49 D2
Pegin 76 C4
Perahóra 87 E1
Peraleda de Zaucejo 43 E1
Peralejos de las Truchas 40 C2
Perales del Alfambra 41 D2
Perales del Puerto 39 D2
Perales de Tajuña 40 B2
Perales, Pto de 39 D2
Peralta 36 C2
Peralta de Alcofea 37 E3
Peralva 42 B2
Pérama (Ípiros) 82 C1
Pérama (Kérkira) 82 A1
Pérama (Kríti) 91 D3
Pérama (Lésvos) 85 F3
Pérama (Stereá Eláda) 87 F1
Peraméri 98 C3
Perä-Posio 99 E2
Peräseinäjoki 102 C2
Perast 76 B3
Peratáta 86 A1
Percy 18 B4
Perdido, M 37 E2
Pérdika (Égina) 87 F2
Pérdika (Ioánina) 82 C2
Pérdika (Thesprotia) 82 B2
Perdikáki 82 C3
Perdikas 79 D3
Peréa (Péla) 79 E3
Peréa (Thessaloníki) 79 F3
Perejaslav-Chmel'nickij 113 F2
Pereruela 35 D4
Pereval Jablonickij 113 D3
Pereval Srednij Vereckij 112 C3
Pereval Užokskij 112 C3
Perg 57 D2
Pergine Valsugana 59 D3
Pergola 61 E4
Perho 102 C2
Perhonjoki 102 C1
Periana 43 F3
Périers 18 B3
Périgueux 28 C2
Períklia 79 E2
Perino 60 B2
Períssa 91 E1
Perista 83 D3
Peristerá 80 A2
Peristerá, N 84 B2
Perithório 80 B1
Perívlepto 83 F2

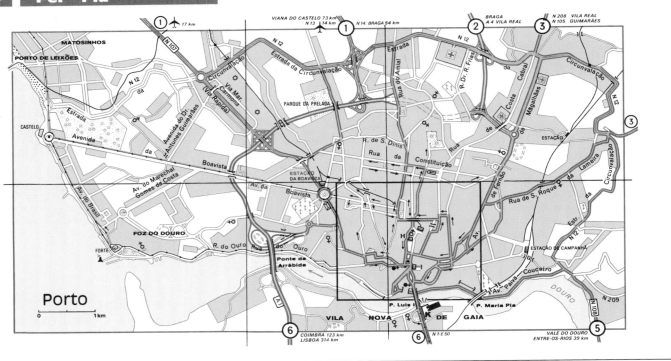

Porto

0 1km

| | | | |
|---|---|---|---|
| Perivóli | 78 C4 | Pesoz | 34 C1 |
| Perivóli, N. | 83 E2 | Pessáni | 81 F2 |
| Perivólio | 83 D3 | Peštani | 77 D4 |
| Perjasica | 70 C3 | Pešter | 76 C2 |
| Perković | 75 D1 | Pestovo | 111 F1 |
| Perleberg | 48 C3 | Pešurići | 72 B4 |
| Perlez | 72 C2 | Petačinci | 77 E1 |
| Përmet | 114 C4 | Petäjäskoski | 99 D2 |
| Pernå | 107 F2 | Petäjäves | 103 D3 |
| Pernaja | 107 F2 | Petalax | 102 B2 |
| Pernarec | 53 E4 | Petalída, Akr | 88 B3 |
| Pernes | 30 C3 | Petalidi | 86 C3 |
| Pernik | 114 C2 | Petalií, Nissí | 88 A1 |
| Perniö | 107 E3 | Petalión, Kólpos | 88 A1 |
| Pernitz | 57 E3 | Petaloúdes | 93 F1 |
| Pernštejn | 57 E1 | Pétange | 21 D3 |
| Péronne | 19 F2 | Pétas | 82 C2 |
| Perosa Argentina | 31 E2 | Petehovac | 70 B3 |
| Pérouges | 26 C4 | Peterborough | 9 F1 |
| Perpignan | 32 B2 | Peterhead | 3 E3 |
| Perrero | 31 E2 | Peterlee | 5 E4 |
| Perreux | 26 B4 | Petersfield | 9 F3 |
| Perros-Guirec | 22 B2 | Petershagen | 17 F2 |
| Persenbeug | 57 D2 | Pethelinós | 80 B2 |
| Pershore | 9 E1 | Petília Policastro | 67 F3 |
| Perstorp | 109 D3 | Petina | 64 C4 |
| Perth | 5 D1 | Petite-Pierre, la | 21 E3 |
| Perthus, le | 32 B3 | Petit Morin | 20 A4 |
| Pertisau | 59 D1 | Petit St-Bernard, | |
| Pertoča | 70 C1 | Col du | 27 E4 |
| Pertoúli | 83 D1 | Petkula | 95 E4 |
| Pertteli | 107 E2 | Petlovača | 72 C3 |
| Pertuis | 30 C3 | Petoússio | 82 B2 |
| Pertunmaa | 103 D3 | Petra (E) | 45 F3 |
| Pertusa | 37 E3 | Pétra (Lésvos) | 85 F2 |
| Perućac Vrelo | 72 C4 | Pétra (Makedonía) | 79 E4 |
| Peručko jez | 75 D1 | Petralia | 68 C3 |
| Perugia | 61 E4 | Petrálona | 80 A3 |
| Perušić | 70 C4 | Petraná | 79 E4 |
| Péruwelz | 50 B4 | Petrčane | 74 C1 |
| Pervenchères | 23 F3 | Petrel | 45 D1 |
| Pervomajsk | 113 F3 | Petrella, Mte | 64 A3 |
| Pesaro | 61 E3 | Pétres | 79 D3 |
| Pescara | 64 A1 | Petreto- | |
| Pescasseroli | 64 A2 | Bicchisano | 33 F4 |
| Peschici | 64 C2 | Petrič | 115 D3 |
| Peschiera del | | Petrijevci | 71 F2 |
| Garda | 60 C1 | Petrína | 86 C3 |
| Pescia | 60 C3 | Petrinja | 71 D3 |
| Pescina | 63 F2 | Petrodvorec | 111 D1 |
| Pescocostanzo | 64 A2 | Petrohóri | 83 D4 |
| Pescolanciano | 64 A2 | Pétrola | 45 D1 |
| Pescopagano | 64 C4 | Petróna | 82 C3 |
| Pescorocchiano | 63 F2 | Petrosani | 114 C1 |
| Peshkopi | 77 D3 | Petrotá | 81 F1 |
| Pesiökylä | 99 E3 | Petrothálassa | 87 E2 |
| Pesmes | 26 C2 | Petroússa | 80 B2 |
| Pesočani | 77 D4 | Petrovac (Bosna i | |
| Pêso da Régua | 34 B4 | Hercegovina) | 70 C3 |

| | | | |
|---|---|---|---|
| Petrovac (Crna | | Piatra-Neamţ | 113 D4 |
| Gora) | 76 B3 | Piave | 59 E4 |
| Petrovac (Srbija) | 73 E3 | Piazza al Serchio | 60 B3 |
| Petrovaradin | 72 C2 | Piazza Armerina | 68 C3 |
| Petrovčić | 72 C3 | Piazza Brembana | 58 B4 |
| Petrovec | 77 E3 | Piazzola sul Brenta | 59 D4 |
| Petrovice | 53 F4 | Piber | 57 E4 |
| Petrovići | 72 B4 | Pibeste, P de | 37 E1 |
| Pettenbach | 56 C3 | Pićan | 70 A3 |
| Pettigoe | 12 C2 | Picassent | 41 E4 |
| Petworth | 9 F3 | Piccolo San Bernardo, | |
| Peuerbach | 56 C2 | Colle del | 27 E4 |
| Peura | 99 D2 | Picerno | 64 C4 |
| Pewsey | 9 E2 | Pickering | 7 D1 |
| Peyrat-le-Château | 29 D1 | Pico | 64 A3 |
| Peyrehorade | 28 A4 | Pico, Pto del | 39 F2 |
| Peyresourde, C de | 37 E2 | Pico Ruivo | 42 A3 |
| Peyriac-Minervois | 32 B1 | Picos de Europa | 35 E2 |
| Peyrolles | 30 C4 | Picote, Bgem de | 34 C4 |
| Peyrol, Pas de | 29 E2 | Picquigny | 19 F2 |
| Peyruis | 31 D3 | Pídna | 79 F3 |
| Pézenas | 30 A4 | Piedicavallo | 27 F4 |
| Pezinok | 112 A3 | Piedicroce | 33 F3 |
| Pezoúla | 81 D2 | Piediluco | 63 E2 |
| Pfaffenhofen | 55 F2 | Piedimonte d'A. | 64 B3 |
| Pfäffikon | 58 A2 | Piedrabuena | 40 A4 |
| Pfalzgrafenweiler | 54 C3 | Piedrafita | 35 D2 |
| Pfarrkirchen | 56 B2 | Piedrahita | 39 E2 |
| Pfeffenhausen | 56 B2 | Piedralaves | 39 F2 |
| Pforzheim | 54 C2 | Piedra, R | 36 C4 |
| Pfreimd | 56 B1 | Piedras Albas | 39 D3 |
| Pfronten | 55 E4 | Piedra San Martín, | |
| Pfullendorf | 55 D4 | Collado de la | 37 D2 |
| Pfullingen | 55 D3 | Piedras, Emb de | 42 C2 |
| Pfunds | 58 C2 | Piedrasluengas, | |
| Pfungstadt | 54 C1 | Pto de | 35 F2 |
| Phalsbourg | 21 E4 | Piedratajada | 37 D3 |
| Philippeville | 50 C4 | Pieksämäki | 103 E3 |
| Philippsreut | 56 C2 | Pielavesi | 103 D2 |
| Piacenza | 60 B2 | Pielavesi L | 103 D2 |
| Piadena | 60 B2 | Pielinen | 103 F1 |
| Piana | 33 E3 | Pieljekaise | 97 F2 |
| Piana d. Albanesi | 68 B3 | Piemonte | 31 E2 |
| Piancastagnaio | 63 D1 | Piennes | 20 C3 |
| Piancavallo | 59 E3 | Pienza | 61 D4 |
| Piandelagotti | 60 C3 | Pieriá | 79 E3 |
| Pian delle | | Piéria, Óri | 79 E4 |
| Fugazze, Pso | 59 D4 | Pierowall | 3 E1 |
| Pian del Voglio | 60 C3 | Pierre-Buffière | 29 D1 |
| Pianella | 64 A1 | Pierre-de-Bresse | 26 C3 |
| Pianello | 61 E4 | Pierrefitte | 20 C3 |
| Pianoro | 61 D3 | Pierrefitte- | |
| Pianosa, I (Mare | | Nestaias | 37 E2 |
| Adriatico) | 64 C1 | Pierrefonds | 19 F3 |
| Pianosa, I (Mare | | Pierrefontaine- | |
| Tirreno) | 62 B2 | les-Varans | 27 D2 |
| Piansano | 63 D2 | Pierrefort | 29 E2 |
| Piapaxaro, P | 34 C2 | Pierrelatte | 30 B3 |
| Pias | 42 B1 | Pieskehaure | 97 F2 |

| | | | |
|---|---|---|---|
| Piešt'any | 112 A3 | Pineda de Mar | 32 B4 |
| Pietersaaren mlk | 102 C2 | Pinerolo | 31 E2 |
| Pietersaari | 102 C1 | Pineto | 64 A1 |
| Pietra Ligure | 31 F3 | Piney | 20 B4 |
| Pietralunga | 61 E4 | Pinhal de Leiria | 38 A2 |
| Pietraperzia | 68 C3 | Pinhal Novo | 38 A4 |
| Pietrasanta | 60 B3 | Pinhão | 34 B4 |
| Pietra Spada, Pso | | Pinheiro | 34 A4 |
| di | 67 F4 | Pinhel | 39 D1 |
| Pietrosu | 113 D3 | Piniós | |
| Pieux, les | 18 B3 | (Pelopónissos) | 86 C1 |
| Pieve de' Burgondi | | Piniós (Thessalía) | 83 E1 |
| del Cairo | 60 A2 | Pinkafeld | 57 F3 |
| Pieve di Bono | 58 C4 | Pinneberg | 48 A3 |
| Pieve di Cadore | 59 E3 | Pino | 33 F2 |
| Pieve di Soligo | 59 E3 | Pinofranqueado | 39 D2 |
| Pieve di Teco | 31 F3 | Pinols | 29 F2 |
| Pievepelago | 60 C3 | Pinoso | 45 D1 |
| Pieve Santo | | Pinos Puente | 44 A3 |
| Stefano | 61 D4 | Pinsk | 113 D1 |
| Pigádi | 83 F3 | Pintado, Emb de | 43 D2 |
| Pigés | 82 C2 | Pintamo | 99 E3 |
| Pigí | 83 D4 | Pinto | 40 A2 |
| Pigón, L | 82 C1 | Pinzano al | |
| Pigna | 31 E3 | Tagliamento | 59 E3 |
| Pihlajaveden as | 102 C3 | Pinzolo | 58 C3 |
| Pihlajavesi | 102 C3 | Piobbico | 61 E4 |
| Pihlajavesi L | 103 F3 | Piombino | 62 C1 |
| Pihlava | 102 B3 | Pione | 60 B2 |
| Pihtipudas | 103 D2 | Pionsat | 26 A4 |
| Piikkiö | 107 D2 | Piotrków | |
| Piippola | 103 D1 | Trybunalski | 112 B2 |
| Piispajärvi | 99 F3 | Piove di Sacco | 61 D1 |
| Pikal'ovo | 111 E1 | Piovene | |
| Pikérmi | 87 F1 | Rocchette | 59 D4 |
| Piła | 112 A1 | Pipéri, N | 84 C2 |
| Pilat-Plage | 28 A2 | Pipriac | 23 D3 |
| Pilas | 43 D3 | Piqueras, Pto de | 36 B3 |
| Pila, Sa de la | 45 D2 | Piran | 70 A3 |
| Pilat, Mt | 30 B1 | Pir'atin | 113 F2 |
| Pilatus | 27 F2 | Pireás | 87 F1 |
| Piléa | 81 F2 | Pirgadíkia | 80 B3 |
| Piles | 41 E4 | Pirgetós | 83 E1 |
| Pilés | 93 D3 | Pírgi (Dráma) | 80 B2 |
| Pili (Makedonía) | 78 C2 | Pírgi (Híos) | 85 E4 |
| Pili (Stereá Eláda) | 87 F1 | Pirgí (Kérkira) | 82 A1 |
| Pili (Thessalía) | 83 D2 | Pírgi (Kozáni) | 79 E3 |
| Pilica | 112 B2 | Pírgos (Íos) | 88 C4 |
| Pílio | 84 A3 | Pírgos (Kríti) | 91 D4 |
| Pílio | 89 F3 | Pírgos | |
| Pílio, Óros | 83 F2 | (Makedonía) | 79 F3 |
| Pillon, Col du | 27 E3 | Pírgos | |
| Pilori | 79 D4 | (Pelopónissos) | 86 B2 |
| Pilos | 86 C3 | Pírgos (Sámos) | 89 E2 |
| Pilštanj | 70 C2 | Pírgos (Stereá | |
| Piña de Campos | 35 E3 | Eláda) | 83 F4 |
| Pina | 37 D4 | Pírgos Diroú | 87 D4 |
| Piña de Campos | 35 E3 | Piriac | 22 C4 |
| Pinar | 43 E3 | Pirin | 115 D3 |
| Pineda de la Sierra | 36 A2 | | |

| | |
|---|---|
| Pirkkala | 107 E1 |
| Pirmasens | 54 B2 |
| Pirna | 53 F2 |
| Pirok | 77 D3 |
| Pirot | 77 E1 |
| Pirovac | 74 C1 |
| Pirsógiani | 78 C4 |
| Pirttikoski | 99 E2 |
| Pisa | 60 C4 |
| Pisciotta | 67 D1 |
| Pisek | 56 C1 |
| Piškorevci | 71 F2 |
| Pisogne | 58 C4 |
| Pisses | 88 A2 |
| Pissodéri | 79 D3 |
| Pissónas | 84 B4 |
| Pissos | 28 B3 |
| Pisticci | 65 D4 |
| Pistoia | 60 C3 |
| Pisuerga, R | 35 E2 |
| Piteå | 98 B3 |
| Piteälven | 98 B3 |
| Piteşti | 115 D1 |
| Pithagório | 89 E2 |
| Pithio (Thessalía) | 79 E4 |
| Pithio (Thráki) | 81 F1 |
| Pithiviers | 25 F1 |
| Pitigliano | 63 D2 |
| Pitlochry | 3 D4 |
| Pitomača | 71 D2 |
| Pittenweem | 5 D2 |
| Pivka | 70 A3 |
| Pivnica | 71 E2 |
| Pivnice | 72 B2 |
| Pivsko jezero | 76 A2 |
| Pizarra | 43 F3 |
| Piz Buin | 58 B2 |
| Pizzighettone | 60 B2 |
| Pizzo | 67 E3 |
| Pizzoli | 63 F2 |
| Pjórsá | 96 B2 |
| Plabennec | 22 A2 |
| Plaćenska pl | 77 D4 |
| Plačkovica | 77 F3 |
| Plagiá (Makedonía) | 79 F2 |
| Plagiá (Thráki) | 81 E2 |
| Plagne, la | 31 D1 |
| Plaisance | 28 B4 |
| Pláka (Límnos) | 85 D1 |
| Pláka | |
| (Pelopónissos) | 87 E3 |
| Pláka (Thráki) | 81 E2 |
| Pláka, Akr | 85 D1 |
| Pláka Litohórou | 79 F4 |
| Plakiás | 90 C4 |
| Planá | 53 E4 |
| Plana | 76 A2 |
| Planches-en- | |
| Montagne, les | 27 D3 |
| Plancoët | 22 C3 |
| Plandište | 73 D2 |
| Planica Mangrt | 70 A1 |
| Plánice | 56 C1 |
| Planina (Celje) | 70 C2 |
| Planina (Jesenice) | 70 A1 |
| Planina (Postojna) | 70 A2 |
| Planinica | 73 E4 |
| Planitz | 53 D3 |
| Plános | 86 A1 |
| Plansee | 58 C1 |
| Plasencia | 39 D2 |
| Plaški | 70 C3 |
| Plasy | 53 E4 |
| Platamona Lido | 66 A2 |
| Platamónas | |
| (Kavalá) | 80 C2 |
| Platamónas | |
| (Pieria) | 79 F4 |
| Platanákia | 79 F2 |
| Platanés | 90 C3 |
| Platani | 68 B3 |
| Plataniá | |
| (Makedonía) | 80 C2 |
| Platánia | |
| (Pelopónissos) | 86 C2 |
| Plataniá (Thessalía) | 84 A2 |
| Platanistós | 88 A1 |
| Platanítis | 83 D4 |
| Plátanos (Kríti) | 90 B3 |
| Plátanos | |
| (Pelopónissos) | 87 D3 |
| Plátanos | |
| (Thessalía) | 83 F2 |
| Plataría | 82 B2 |

Plateau-d'Assy 27 E4
Plateés 87 E1
Pláti 81 F1
Platiána 86 C2
Platičevo 72 C3
Platíkambos 83 E1
Platís Gialós (Kefaloniá) 86 A1
Platís Gialós (Míkonos) 88 C2
Platís Gialós (Sífnos) 88 B3
Platístomo 83 E3
Plattling 56 B2
Plau 48 C3
Plaue 49 D4
Plauen 53 D3
Plauer See (Potsdam) 49 D4
Plauer See (Schwerin) 48 C3
Plav 76 C2
Plavča 70 C3
Plavna 73 E3
Plavnica 76 B3
Plavnik *I* 70 B4
Plavnik *Mt* 70 B3
Playa Blanca 42 C4
Playa de Gandía 41 E4
Playa de San Juan 45 E1
Pleaux 29 E2
Pleine-Fougères 18 B4
Pleinfeld 55 F2
Pleiße 53 D2
Plélan-le-Grand 23 D3
Plélan-le-Petit 22 C3
Pléneuf 22 C2
Plentzia 36 B1
Plépi 87 E2
Plešin 76 C1
Plestin 22 B2
Pleternica 71 E2
Plettenberg 17 F4
Pletvar 77 E3
Pleumartin 25 D3
Pleumeur-Bodou 22 B2
Pleven 115 D2
Pleyben 22 B3
Pliego 44 C2
Plítra 87 D4
Plitvice 70 C3
Plitvička jezera 70 C3
Plitvički Ljeskovac 70 C4
Plješevica 70 C4
Pljevlja 76 B1
Ploaghe 66 B2
Ploče 75 E2
Plochingen 55 D2
Płock 112 B1
Plöckenpaß 59 E2
Plöckenstein 56 C2
Pločno 75 E1
Ploërmel 22 C3
Ploiești 115 D1
Plomári 85 F3
Plomb du Cantal 29 E2
Plombières 27 D1
Plomin 70 B3
Plön 48 B2
Plonéour-Lanvern 22 A3
Płoń, Jez 49 F3
Płońsk 112 B1
Płoty 49 F2
Plouagat 22 C2
Plouaret 22 B2
Plouay 22 B3
Ploubalay 18 A4
Plœuc 22 C3
Ploudalmézeau 22 A2
Plouescat 22 B2
Plougasnou 22 B2
Plougastel-Daoulas 22 A3
Plougonven 22 B2
Plouguenast 22 C3
Plouha 22 C2
Plouigneau 22 B2
Ploumanach 22 B2
Plouzévédé 22 B2
Plovdiv 115 D3
Plumbridge 13 D2
Plungė 110 B3
Pl'ussa 111 D1
Pluvigner 22 C3
Plužine 76 A1
Plympton 8 C4
Plymstock 8 C4
Plzeň 53 E4
Po 60 C2
Poarta de Fier 114 C1
Pobierowo 49 F1
Poblet 37 F4
Pobrđe 76 C1
Počep 111 F4
Pöchlarn 57 E2
Počinok 111 E3
Počitelj 75 F2
Pocking 56 C2
Poćuta 72 C4
Pódareš 77 F3
Podbořany 53 E3
Podčetrtek 70 C2
Podensac 28 B2
Podersdorf 57 F3
Podgajci Posavski 72 B3
Podgarič 71 D2
Podgora 75 E2
Podgorač (Hrvatska) 71 F2
Podgorac (Srbija) 73 E3
Podgrad 70 A3
Podhum 75 E1
Podjuchy 49 E2
Podkoren 70 A1
Podlugovi 71 F4
Podnovlje 71 F3
Podogorá 82 C3
Podohóri 80 B2
Podol'sk 111 F2
Podol'skaja Vozvyšennost' 113 D3
Podpec 70 B2
Podrašnica 71 E4
Podravska Slatina 71 E2
Podromanija 72 B4
Podsreda 70 C2
Podsused 70 C2
Podturen 71 D1
Podujevo 77 D1
Podunavci 73 D4
Poel 48 C2
Poganovo 77 E1
Poggibonsi 60 C4
Poggio Imperiale 64 C2
Poggio Mirteto 63 E2
Poggio Renatico 61 D2
Poggio Rusco 60 C2
Pöggstall 57 E2
Pogonianí 78 B4
Pogradec 77 D4
Pohja 107 E3
Pohja-Lankila 103 F3
Pohjaslahti (Keski-Suomen Lääni) 102 C3
Pohjaslahti (Lapin Lääni) 99 D2
Pohjois-Karjalan Lääni 103 F2
Pohořelice 57 F1
Pohorje 70 B1
Poiana Brașov 113 D4
Poio 34 A2
Poiré, le 24 B3
Poirino 31 F2
Poissons 20 C4
Poitiers 25 D3
Pöitsamaa 110 C2
Poix 19 E2
Poix-Terron 20 B2
Pojate 73 E4
Pojo 107 E3
Pokka 95 E3
Poklečani 75 E1
Pokljuka 70 A2
Pokupsko 70 C3
Polače 75 E2
Polacra, Pta de la 44 C4
Pola de Allande 34 C1
Pola de Gordón, la 35 D2
Pola de Laviana 35 E2
Pola de Lena 35 D2
Pola de Siero 35 D1
Polán 40 A3
Polcenigo 59 E3
Połczyn-Zdrój 110 A4
Polegate 10 C3
Poles 113 D1
Polesella 61 D2
Polessk 110 B4
Polhov Gradec 70 A2
Policastro 67 D1
Policastro, Golfo di 67 D2
Police 49 E2
Poličnik 74 C1
Policoro 65 D4
Polidéndri 84 B4
Polidrossos 83 E3
Políegos, N 88 B4
Poliégou Folegándrou, Stenó 88 B4
Polígiros 80 A3
Polignano a Mare 65 E3
Poligny 27 D3
Polihnitos 85 F3
Polikárpi 79 E2
Polikástano 78 C3
Políkastro 79 F2
Polímilos 79 E3
Polinéri (Makedonía) 79 D4
Polinéri (Thessalía) 82 C2
Polióhni 85 D1
Polipótamo 79 D3
Polipótamos 84 C4
Políraho 79 E4
Polirinía 90 B3
Polis, M 77 D4
Polissito 81 D2
Polistena 67 E4
Polithéa 82 C1
Politiká 84 A4
Poljana (Slovenija) 70 B1
Poljana (Srbija) 73 D3
Poljčane 70 C1
Polje 71 E3
Poljica 75 E2
Poljice 71 F4
Polla 64 C4
Pölläkkä 103 E2
Pöllau 57 E4
Polle 52 A1
Pollença 45 F2
Pollfoss 100 B3
Pollino, Mte 67 E2
Pollos 35 E4
Polmak 95 E2
Polock 111 D3
Polonnoje 113 D2
Polperro 8 B4
Poltava 113 F2
Polvijärvi 103 F2
Polzela 70 B2
Pomar 37 E3
Pomarance 60 C4
Pomarkku 102 B3
Pombal 38 B2
Pómbia 91 D4
Pomellen 49 E2
Pomezi 53 D4
Pomezia 63 E3
Pomigliano d'Arco 64 B4
Pommersfelden 55 E1
Pomokaira 95 E4
Pomorie 115 E2
Pomorze 110 A4
Pomovaara 95 E4
Pompei 64 B4
Pomposa 61 D2
Poncin 26 C4
Pondoiráklia 79 F2
Pondokómi 79 D3
Ponferrada 34 C2
Ponikovica 72 C4
Pons 28 B1
Ponsacco 60 C4
Pontacq 37 E1
Pontailler 26 C2
Pont-à-Marcq 19 F1
Pont-à-Mousson 21 D3
Pontão 38 B2
Pontardawe 8 C2
Pontarddulais 8 C2
Pontarion 25 E4
Pontarlier 27 D3
Pontassieve 61 D3
Pontaubault 18 B4
Pont-Audemer 19 D3
Pontaumur 26 A4
Pont-Aven 22 B3
Pont Canavese 31 E1
Pontcharra 31 D1
Pontchartrain 19 E4
Pontchâteau 23 D4
Pont-Croix 22 A3
Pont-d'Ain 26 C4
Pont-de-Beauvoisin, le 30 C1
Pont-de-Chéruy 26 C4
Pont-de-Claix, le 30 C2
Pont-de-Dore 26 A4
Pont-de-l'Arche 19 E3
Pont-de-Montvert, le 29 F3
Pont-de-Roide 27 E2
Pont-de-Salars 29 E3
Pont-d'Espagne 37 E2
Pont de Suert 37 F2
Pont-de-Vaux 26 C3
Pont-de-Veyle 26 C4
Pont-d'Oléron 28 A1
Pont-d'Ouilly 18 C4
Pont-du-Château 26 A4
Pont-du-Gard 30 B3
Ponte Arche 58 C3
Ponteareas 34 A3
Pontebba 59 F2
Pontecagnano 64 B4
Ponte Caldelas 34 A2
Ponteceno 60 B2
Ponte Ceso 34 A1
Pontecorvo 64 A3
Ponte da Barca 34 A3
Pontedecimo 60 A3
Ponte de Lima 34 A3
Pontedera 60 C4
Ponte de Sor 38 B3
Pontedeume 34 B1
Ponte di Legno 58 C3
Ponte di Piave 59 E4
Pontefract 7 D2
Pontelandolfo 64 B3
Ponte-Leccia 33 F3
Pontenelle Alpi 59 E3
Pont-en-Royans 30 C1
Ponte San Pietro 60 B1
Pontet, le 30 C3
Ponte Tresa 58 A4
Pontevico 60 B1
Pontfaverger-Moronvilliers 20 B3
Pontgibaud 29 E1
Pontigny 26 B1
Pontinia 63 F3
Pontinvrea 31 F2
Pontivy 22 C3
Pont-l'Abbé 22 A3
Pont-l'Evêque 19 D3
Pontlevoy 25 E2
Pontoise 19 E3
Pontones 44 B2
Pontón, Pto del 35 E2
Pontoon 12 B2
Pontorson 18 B4
Pontremoli 60 B3
Pontresina 58 B3
Pontrieux 22 C2
Pontrilas 9 D2
Ponts 37 F3
Pont-Ste-Maxence 19 F3
Pont-St-Esprit 30 B3
Pont St-Martin 31 E1
Pont-St-Vincent 21 D4
Pont-Scorff 22 B3
Ponts-de-Cé, les 23 E4
Pontsenni 8 C1
Pont-sur-Yonne 26 A1
Pontvallain 23 F4
Pontypool 9 D2
Pontypridd 8 C2
Ponza, I 63 F4
Ponziane, I 63 F4
Poole 9 E3
Poperinge 50 A3
Popinci 72 C3
Popoli 64 A2
Popovac 73 E4
Popovača 71 D2
Popova Šapka 77 D3
Popov Most 76 A1
Popovo 115 E2
Poppenhausen 52 B4
Poppi 61 D3
Poprad 112 B3
Porcari 60 C3
Porchov 111 D2
Porcuna 43 F2
Pordenone 59 E3
Poreč 70 A3
Pori 107 D1
Porjus 98 B2
Porkkalanselkä 107 E3
Porma, Emb del 35 E2
Porma, R 35 E2
Pornainen 107 F2
Pörnbach 55 F2
Pornic 24 A2
Pornichet 24 A2
Póros (Kefaloniá) 86 A1
Póros (Lefkáda) 82 B3
Póros (Póros) 87 F2
Póros, N 87 F2
Porozina 70 B3
Pórpi 81 D2
Porquerolles 31 D4
Porrentruy 27 E2
Porretta Terme 60 C3
Porriño 34 A3
Porsangen 95 E1
Porsangerhalvøya 95 D1
Porsgrunn 104 C3
Pórshöfn 96 C1
Portadown 13 D2
Portaferry 13 E2
Portaje, Emb de 39 D3
Porta, la 33 F3
Portalegre 38 C3
Portalé, Pto del 37 D2
Portalrubio 41 D2
Portariá 83 F2
Portarlington 13 D4
Port Askaig 4 B2
Portavogie 13 E2
Porta-Westfalica 51 F1
Port-Bacarès 32 B2
Portbail 18 B3
Portbou 32 C3
Port Charlotte 4 A2
Port, Col de 37 F2
Port-Cros 31 D4
Port-de-Bouc 30 C4
Porte, Col de 30 C1
Port-Einon 8 C2
Portella Femmina Morta 69 D3
Port Ellen 4 A2
Portelo 34 C3
Port-en-Bessin 18 C3
Port Erin 6 A1
Pórtes 87 F2
Portet-d'Aspet, Col de 37 F2
Portezuelo 39 D3
Port Glasgow 4 C2
Portglenone 13 E1
Porthcawl 8 C2
Porthmadog 6 A3
Porthmós Elafonissou 90 A1
Portici 64 B4
Portile de Fier 114 C1
Portilla de la Reina 35 E2
Portillo 35 E4
Portillo de la Canda 34 C3
Portillo de Padornelo 34 C3
Portillo, Pto del 39 E2
Portimão 42 A2
Portimo 99 D2
Portinatx, Cala de 45 D3
Portishead 9 D2
Port-Joinville 24 A3
Port Láirge 15 D4
Portland, Bill of 9 D4
Port-la-Nouvelle 32 B2
Portlaoise 13 D4
Port-Leucate 32 B2
Port-Louis 22 B4
Portman 45 D3
Port-Manech 22 B3
Portmarnock 13 E4
Portnacroish 4 B1
Portnaguran 2 B2
Portnahaven 4 A2
Port-Navalo 22 C4
Porto (F) 33 E3
Porto (P) 34 A4
Porto Azzurro 62 C1
Pórto Carrás 80 B4
Porto Ceresio 58 A4
Porto Cervo 66 B1
Porto Cesareo 65 F4
Porto Cristo 45 F3
Porto de Envalira 32 A2
Porto de Lagos 42 A2
Porto de Mós 38 A3
Portodemouros, Emb de 34 B2
Porto do Barqueiro 34 B1
Porto do Son 34 A2
Porto Empedocle 68 B4
Porto Ercole 63 D2
Portoferraio 62 C1
Portofino 60 A3
Port of Ness 2 B2
Porto Garibaldi 61 D2
Porto, G de 33 E3
Pórto Germenó 87 E1
Portogruaro 59 E4
Portohéli 87 E2
Pórto Kágio 87 D4
Pörtom 102 B2
Portomaggiore 61 D2
Portomarin 34 B2
Porto-Maurizio 31 F3
Porto Moniz 42 A3
Portomouro 34 A2
Portonovo 34 A2
Porto Petro 45 F3
Porto Pino 66 B4
Pórto Ráfti 88 A1
Porto Recanati 61 F4
Porto Rotondo 66 C1
Portorož 70 A3
Porto San Giorgio 61 F4
Porto Sant' Elpidio 61 F4
Porto Santo 42 A3
Porto Santo, I de 42 A3
Porto Santo Stefano 63 D2
Portoscuso 66 A4
Porto Tolle 61 D2
Porto Torres 66 A2
Porto-Vecchio 33 F4
Portovenere 60 B3
Portpatrick 4 B3
Portree 2 B3
Portrush 13 D1
Port-Ste-Marie 28 C3
Port-St-Louis 30 B4
Port St Mary 6 A1
Portsalon 13 D1
Pörtschach 70 A1
Portsmouth 9 F3
Portstewart 13 D1
Port-sur-Saône 27 D1
Port Talbot 8 C2
Porttipahdan tekojärvi 95 E4
Portugalete 36 B1
Portumna 12 C4
Port-Vendres 32 B2
Port William 4 C4
Porvoo 107 F2
Porvoonjoki 107 F2
Porzuna 40 A4
Posada 66 C2
Posadas 43 E2
Pöschenhöhe 56 C3
Pošechonje-Volodarsk 111 F1
Posedarje 74 C1
Posets, Pico 37 E2
Posio 99 E2
Positano 64 B4
Poßneck 52 C3
Possídi 80 A4
Possidonía 88 B2
Posta 63 F1
Postavy 111 D3
Postira 75 D2
Postojna 70 B2
Postojnska jama 70 A2
Poštorná 57 F1
Posušje 75 E1
Potamí 80 C1
Potamiá 87 D3
Potamiés 91 E4
Potamós (Andikíthira) 90 A2
Potamós (Kíthira) 90 A1
Potamoúla 82 C3
Potenza 64 C4
Potenza *R* 61 E4
Potenza Picenza 61 F4
Potes 35 E2
Potídea, N. 80 A4
Potigny 18 C3
Potoci 75 F1
Potok 71 D2
Potós 80 C3
Potpećko jez 76 B1
Potsdam 49 D4
Pottenstein 57 E3
Potters Bar 9 F2
Pöttmes 55 F2
Potton 9 F1
Pouancé 23 D4
Pougues-les-Eaux 26 A2
Pouilly (Nièvre) 26 A2
Pouilly (Rhône) 26 B4
Pouilly-en-Auxois 26 C2
Poulaphouca Reservoir 13 D4
Poúlari, Akr 92 C1
Pouldu, le 22 B3
Pouliguen, le 24 A2
Poúlithra 87 E3
Poúnda 88 C3
Poúnda, Akr 84 B4
Pournári 83 E2
Pournári, Teh L 82 C2
Pourniás, Kólpos 85 D1
Pourri, Mt 31 D1
Poussu 99 F3
Pouyastruc 37 E1
Pouzauges 24 C3
Pouzin, le 30 B2
Považská Bystrica 112 B3
Poveda 40 C2
Povlja 75 E2
Povljana 70 C4
Povljen 72 C4
Povoa de Lanhoso 34 A4
Póvoa de Varzim 34 A4
Powerscourt 13 D4
Powys 9 D1
Poysdorf 57 F2
Pöytyä 107 D2
Poza de la Sal 36 A2
Požarevac 73 D3
Požega 72 C4
Požeranje 77 D2
Poznań 112 A1
Pozo Alcón 44 B2
Pozoblanco 43 F1
Pozo Cañada 44 C1
Pozo de Guadalajara 40 B2
Pozo Higuera 44 C3
Pozohondo 44 C1
Pozondón 41 D2
Pozozal, Pto 35 F2
Pozuelo (Castilla-la-Mancha) 44 C1
Pozuelo (Extremadura) 39 D2
Pozuelo de Calatrava 40 A4
Pozzallo 69 D4
Pozzomaggiore 66 B2
Pozzuoli 64 A4
Pozzuolo 59 F3
Prábichl 57 D3
Prača 76 A1
Prachatice 56 C1
Prada, Emb de 34 C3
Pradairo 34 C2
Pradarena, Pso di 60 B3
Pradelles 29 F2
Prádena 36 A4
Prades (E) 37 F4
Prades (F) 32 B2
Prado del Rey 43 D3
Pradoluengo 36 A2
Prägraten 59 E2
Praha 53 F4
Prahecq 24 C4
Prahova 115 D1
Prahovo 73 F3
Praia a Mare 67 E2
Praia da Barra 38 B1
Praia da Rocha 42 A2
Praia da Vieira 38 A2
Praia de Mira 38 B1
Praia de Santa Cruz 38 A3

| Name | Page | Grid |
|---|---|---|
| Praia de Tocha | 38 | B2 |
| Prali | 31 | E2 |
| Pralognan | 31 | D1 |
| Pra-Loup | 31 | D2 |
| Prámanda | 82 | C2 |
| Pramollo, Pso di | 59 | F2 |
| Prangio | 81 | F1 |
| Pranjani | 72 | C4 |
| Prapatnica | 75 | D1 |
| Prassiá | 83 | D2 |
| Prassiés | 90 | C3 |
| Præstø | 108 | C4 |
| Prat de Compte | 41 | F1 |
| Pratella | 64 | A3 |
| Prati di Tivo | 63 | F1 |
| Prato (Toscana) | 60 | C3 |
| Prato (Umbria) | 63 | E1 |
| Pratola Peligna | 64 | A2 |
| Pratomagno | 61 | D4 |
| Prato-Sornico | 58 | A3 |
| Prats-de-Mollo | 32 | B3 |
| Pravdinsk | 110 | B4 |
| Pravia | 35 | D1 |
| Praz | 27 | E4 |
| Prebold | 70 | B2 |
| Précy-sous-Thil | 26 | B2 |
| Predappio | 61 | D3 |
| Predazzo | 59 | D3 |
| Preddvor | 70 | B2 |
| Predeal | 113 | D4 |
| Predejane | 77 | E1 |
| Predel | 70 | A2 |
| Predela | 115 | D3 |
| Predil, Pso di | 59 | F2 |
| Predjama | 70 | A2 |
| Predoi | 59 | D2 |
| Predošćica | 70 | B3 |
| Pré-en-Pail | 23 | E3 |
| Preetz | 48 | B2 |
| Pregarten | 57 | D2 |
| Preiner Gscheid | 57 | E3 |
| Prekaja | 71 | D4 |
| Prekestolen | 104 | A3 |
| Preko | 74 | C1 |
| Preljina | 73 | D4 |
| Prelog | 71 | D1 |
| Preloščica | 71 | D2 |
| Premantura | 70 | A4 |
| Prémery | 26 | A2 |
| Premià de Mar | 32 | B4 |
| Premilcuore | 61 | D3 |
| Premnitz | 49 | D4 |
| Premuda | 74 | B1 |
| Premuda I | 74 | B1 |
| Prenj | 75 | F1 |
| Prenjas | 77 | D4 |
| Prenzlau | 49 | E3 |
| Prepolac | 77 | D1 |
| Přerov | 112 | A3 |
| Prerow | 48 | C1 |
| Pré-St-Didier | 27 | E4 |
| Prešovo | 77 | E2 |
| Presjeka | 76 | B2 |
| Preslav | 115 | E2 |
| Presolana, Pso della | 58 | B4 |
| Prešov | 112 | B3 |
| Prespansko Ez | 77 | D4 |
| Pressath | 53 | D4 |
| Pressbaum | 57 | E2 |
| Prestatyn | 6 | B2 |
| Presteigne | 9 | D1 |
| Preste, la | 32 | B3 |
| Prestfoss | 104 | C3 |
| Přeštice | 56 | C1 |
| Preston | 6 | B2 |
| Prestonpans | 5 | D2 |
| Prestwick | 4 | C2 |
| Pretoro | 64 | A2 |
| Prettau | 59 | D2 |
| Prettin | 53 | D1 |
| Pretzsch | 53 | D1 |
| Preuilly | 25 | D3 |
| Préveli | 90 | C4 |
| Préveza | 82 | B3 |
| Préveza (Nomos) | 82 | B2 |
| Prevršac | 71 | D3 |
| Prezid | 70 | B3 |
| Pribini | 71 | E4 |
| Priboj (Bosna i Hercegovina) | 72 | B3 |
| Priboj (Srbija) | 76 | B1 |
| Příbram | 53 | F4 |
| Priego | 40 | C2 |
| Priego de Córdoba | 43 | F3 |
| Prien | 56 | B3 |
| Prienai | 110 | C4 |
| Prievidza | 112 | B3 |
| Prigradica | 75 | E2 |
| Prijeboj | 70 | C3 |
| Prijedor | 71 | D3 |
| Prijepolje | 76 | B1 |
| Prilep | 77 | E3 |
| Prilike | 73 | D4 |
| Priluka | 75 | E1 |
| Priluki | 113 | F1 |
| Primaube, la | 29 | E3 |
| Primel-Trégastel | 22 | B2 |
| Primišlje | 70 | C3 |
| Primolano | 59 | D3 |
| Primorsk | 111 | D1 |
| Primošten | 75 | D2 |
| Primstal | 54 | B1 |
| Princetown | 8 | C3 |
| Prinés | 90 | C3 |
| Prinos | 80 | C3 |
| Prior, C | 34 | B1 |
| Prip' at' | 112 | C1 |
| Prisad | 77 | E3 |
| Prislop | 113 | D3 |
| Prisoje | 75 | E1 |
| Priština | 77 | D2 |
| Pritzerbe | 49 | D4 |
| Pritzier | 48 | B3 |
| Pritzwalk | 48 | C3 |
| Privas | 30 | B2 |
| Priverno | 63 | F3 |
| Privlaka (Vincovci) | 71 | F2 |
| Privlaka (Zadar) | 70 | C4 |
| Prizren | 77 | D2 |
| Prizzi | 68 | B3 |
| Prnjavor (Bosna i Hercegovina) | 71 | E3 |
| Prnjavor (Srbija) | 72 | B3 |
| Proaza | 35 | D1 |
| Probištip | 77 | E2 |
| Probstzella | 52 | C3 |
| Procida | 64 | A4 |
| Pródromos | 83 | F4 |
| Proenca-a-Nova | 38 | B3 |
| Proevska Banja | 77 | E2 |
| Profitis Ilías | 93 | E1 |
| Profondeville | 50 | C4 |
| Próhoma | 79 | F3 |
| Prokletije | 76 | C2 |
| Prokópi | 84 | A3 |
| Prokuplje | 77 | D1 |
| Prolom | 77 | D1 |
| Prómahi | 79 | E2 |
| Promahónas | 80 | A1 |
| Promina, V. | 75 | D1 |
| Promíri | 84 | A2 |
| Pronsfeld | 51 | D4 |
| Propriano | 33 | F4 |
| Proskinás | 83 | F4 |
| Prosna | 112 | A2 |
| Prossedi | 63 | F3 |
| Prossílio | 81 | D2 |
| Prossotsáni | 80 | B2 |
| Prostějov | 112 | A3 |
| Próti | 80 | B2 |
| Próti, N | 86 | B3 |
| Protoklíssio | 81 | F1 |
| Prötzel | 49 | E4 |
| Proussós | 83 | D3 |
| Provatónas | 81 | F2 |
| Provence, Canal de | 30 | C4 |
| Provenchères | 21 | E4 |
| Provins | 20 | A4 |
| Prozor | 75 | E1 |
| Prudhoe | 5 | E3 |
| Prukljansko jezero | 75 | D1 |
| Prüm | 51 | D4 |
| Pruna | 43 | E3 |
| Prunetta | 60 | C3 |
| Prut | 113 | D3 |
| Prut | 113 | E4 |
| Pružany | 112 | C1 |
| Prvić | 70 | B4 |
| Przasnysz | 112 | B1 |
| Przełęcz Dukielska | 112 | C3 |
| Przemyśl | 112 | C2 |
| Przybiernów | 49 | F2 |
| Psača | 77 | E2 |
| Psahná | 84 | B4 |
| Psáka | 82 | B2 |
| Psális, Akr | 88 | A4 |
| Psará | 85 | E4 |
| Psarádes | 78 | C2 |
| Psará, N | 85 | E4 |
| Psári (Arkadía) | 86 | C2 |
| Psári (Korinthía) | 87 | D1 |
| Psári (Mt) | 80 | C3 |
| Psáthi | 88 | B4 |
| Psathópirgos | 83 | D4 |
| Psathotópi | 82 | C2 |
| Psérimos, N | 89 | F3 |
| Psihikó | 83 | E2 |
| Psihró | 91 | E4 |
| Psinthos | 93 | F1 |
| Pskov | 111 | D2 |
| Pskovskoje Ozero | 111 | D2 |
| Ps'ol | 113 | F2 |
| Pšov | 53 | E3 |
| Psunj | 71 | E2 |
| Ptéleá | 80 | C2 |
| Ptéri | 83 | D2 |
| Ptolemaïda | 79 | D3 |
| Ptóo | 84 | A4 |
| Ptuj | 70 | C1 |
| Puchberg | 57 | E3 |
| Pučišća | 75 | E2 |
| Puckeridge | 9 | F2 |
| Puçol | 41 | E3 |
| Pudasjärvi | 99 | E3 |
| Puebla de Alcocer | 39 | E4 |
| Puebla de Almenara | 40 | B3 |
| Puebla de Beleña | 40 | B1 |
| Puebla de Benifasar | 41 | F2 |
| Puebla de Don Fadrique | 44 | B2 |
| Puebla de D. Rodrigo | 39 | F4 |
| Puebla de Guzmán | 42 | C2 |
| Puebla de la Calzada | 39 | D4 |
| Puebla de la Reina | 39 | D4 |
| Puebla del Caramiñal | 34 | A2 |
| Puebla de Lillo | 35 | E2 |
| Puebla de Obando | 39 | D3 |
| Puebla de Sanabria | 34 | C3 |
| Puebla de Trives | 34 | C3 |
| Puebla Tornesa | 41 | F3 |
| Puebla de V. | 35 | D3 |
| Pueblica de V. | 35 | D3 |
| Puente de Domingo Flórez | 34 | C3 |
| Puente de Génave | 44 | B1 |
| Puente de los Fierros | 35 | D2 |
| Puente Genil | 43 | F3 |
| Puente la Reina | 36 | C2 |
| Puente la Reina de Jaca | 37 | D2 |
| Puentenansa | 35 | F2 |
| Puente Nuevo, Emb de | 43 | E1 |
| Puentes, Emb de | 44 | C2 |
| Puentes Viejas, Emb de | 40 | B1 |
| Puente Viesgo | 35 | F2 |
| Puerto Castilla | 39 | E2 |
| Puerto de Alcudia | 45 | F2 |
| Puerto de Andratx | 45 | E3 |
| Puerto de la Cruz | 42 | B4 |
| Puerto de la Encina | 43 | E3 |
| Puerto del Rosario | 42 | C4 |
| Puerto de Mazarrón | 45 | D3 |
| Puerto de Pollença | 45 | F2 |
| Puerto de San Vicente | 39 | F3 |
| Puerto de Sóller | 45 | E2 |
| Puerto Lápice | 40 | B4 |
| Puertollano | 44 | A1 |
| Puerto Lumbreras | 44 | C3 |
| Puerto Real | 43 | D4 |
| Puerto Serrano | 43 | E3 |
| Pugets-Théniers | 31 | E3 |
| Puglia | 65 | D3 |
| Puhos (Oulun Lääni) | 99 | E3 |
| Puhos (Pohjois-Karjalan Lääni) | 103 | F3 |
| Puhosjärvi | 99 | E3 |
| Puhovac | 271 | F4 |
| Puigcerda | 32 | A3 |
| Puig Major | 45 | E2 |
| Puignal | 32 | A2 |
| Puig-reig | 32 | A3 |
| Puigsacalm | 32 | B3 |
| Puiseaux | 25 | F1 |
| Puisserguier | 30 | A4 |
| Pujols | 28 | B2 |
| Pukë | 76 | C3 |
| Pukiš | 72 | B3 |
| Pukkila | 107 | F2 |
| Pula (I) | 66 | B4 |
| Pula (YU) | 70 | A4 |
| Pulaj | 76 | B3 |
| Puławy | 112 | C2 |
| Pulborough | 10 | C3 |
| Pulkau | 57 | E2 |
| Pulkkila | 99 | D4 |
| Pulpi | 44 | C3 |
| Pulsnitz | 53 | E2 |
| Pułtusk | 112 | B1 |
| Punat | 70 | B3 |
| Punkaharju | 103 | F3 |
| Punkalaidun | 107 | E2 |
| Punta Ala | 62 | C1 |
| Punta di Penna | 64 | B2 |
| Puntagorda | 42 | A4 |
| Punta Križa | 70 | B4 |
| Punta Raisi | 68 | B2 |
| Punta Umbría | 42 | C3 |
| Puokio | 99 | E4 |
| Puolanka | 99 | E4 |
| Purbach | 57 | F3 |
| Purchena | 44 | B3 |
| Purgstall | 57 | E3 |
| Purkersdorf | 57 | E2 |
| Purmerend | 16 | C2 |
| Purnu | 103 | D3 |
| Purullena | 44 | B3 |
| Puruvesi | 103 | F3 |
| Puškin | 111 | D1 |
| Püspökladány | 112 | C4 |
| Pustoška | 111 | D2 |
| Pusula | 107 | E2 |
| Puszcza | 112 | C1 |
| Putanges | 18 | C4 |
| Putbus | 49 | D1 |
| Putgarten | 49 | D1 |
| Putignano | 65 | E3 |
| Putinci | 72 | C2 |
| Putivl' | 113 | F1 |
| Putlitz | 48 | C3 |
| Puttelange | 21 | E3 |
| Puttgarden | 48 | B1 |
| Puula | 103 | D3 |
| Puumala | 103 | E3 |
| Puy de Dôme | 29 | E1 |
| Puy-de-Dôme (Dépt) | 29 | E1 |
| Puy de Sancy | 29 | E1 |
| Puy-en-Velay, le | 30 | A2 |
| Puy-Guillaume | 26 | A4 |
| Puylaurens | 29 | D4 |
| Puy-l'Evêque | 29 | D3 |
| Puymirol | 28 | C3 |
| Puymorens, Col de | 32 | A2 |
| Pwllheli | 6 | A3 |
| Pyhä-Häkki | 103 | D2 |
| Pyhäjärvi (Hameen Lääni) | 107 | E1 |
| Pyäjärvi (Oulun Lääni) | 103 | D1 |
| Pyhäjärvi (Pohjois-Karjalan Lääni) | 103 | F3 |
| Pyhäjärvi (Turun ja Porin Lääni) | 107 | D2 |
| Pyhäjärvi L | 103 | D1 |
| Pyhäjoki (Oulun Lääni) | 99 | D4 |
| Pyhäjoki (Turun ja Porin Lääni) | 107 | D2 |
| Pyhäjoki R | 99 | D4 |
| Pyhälto | 103 | F4 |
| Pyhäntä (Piipola) | 103 | D1 |
| Pyhäntä (Ristijärvi) | 99 | E4 |
| Pyhäranta | 107 | D2 |
| Pyhäsalmi | 103 | D1 |
| Pyhäselkä | 103 | F2 |
| Pyhäselkä L | 103 | F2 |
| Pyhätunturi | 99 | D2 |
| Pyhätunturi | 99 | E2 |
| Pyhävuori | 102 | C2 |
| Pyhitysvaara | 99 | E3 |
| Pyhrnpaß | 57 | D3 |
| Pyhtää | 107 | F2 |
| Pyla | 28 | A2 |
| Pylkönmäki | 103 | D2 |
| Pyrénées | 37 | E2 |
| Pyrénées-Atlantiques | 28 | A4 |
| Pyrénées-Orientales | 32 | B2 |
| Pyrénées, Parc Nat des | 37 | E2 |
| Pyrzyce | 49 | F3 |
| Pyttis | 107 | F2 |

# Q

| Name | Page | Grid |
|---|---|---|
| Qaf'e Shllahut | 76 | C3 |
| Qaf'e Shtamës | 76 | C4 |
| Quakenbrück | 17 | E2 |
| Quarré-les-Tombes | 26 | B2 |
| Quarteira | 42 | B3 |
| Quarto d'Altino | 61 | D1 |
| Quartu San Elena | 66 | B4 |
| Quatre Chemins | 24 | B3 |
| Quatretonda | 41 | E4 |
| Quedlinburg | 52 | C2 |
| Queenborough | 11 | D2 |
| Queen Elizabeth Forest Park | 4 | C2 |
| Queensferry | 6 | B2 |
| Quejigares, Pto de | 40 | A4 |
| Queluz | 38 | A4 |
| Queralbs | 32 | B3 |
| Querfurt | 52 | C2 |
| Quérigut | 32 | A2 |
| Quero | 40 | B3 |
| Quesada | 44 | B2 |
| Quesnoy, le | 20 | A2 |
| Questembert | 22 | C4 |
| Quettehou | 18 | B3 |
| Quiberon | 22 | C4 |
| Quickborn | 48 | A2 |
| Quiévrain | 50 | B4 |
| Quigley's Point | 13 | D1 |
| Quillan | 32 | B2 |
| Quillane, Col de la | 32 | A2 |
| Quillebeuf | 19 | D3 |
| Quimper | 22 | B3 |
| Quimperlé | 22 | B3 |
| Quincinetto | 31 | E1 |
| Quincoces de Yuso | 36 | A1 |
| Quingey | 27 | D2 |
| Quintana (Andalucía) | 43 | E2 |
| Quintana (Extremadura) | 39 | E4 |
| Quintana del Puente | 35 | F3 |
| Quintana Martín Galindez | 36 | A2 |
| Quintanar de la Orden | 40 | B3 |
| Quintanar de la Sierra | 36 | B3 |
| Quintanar del Rey | 40 | C4 |
| Quintana Redonda | 36 | B3 |
| Quintanilha | 34 | C4 |
| Quintanilla de Onésimo | 35 | F4 |
| Quintin | 22 | C3 |
| Quinto | 37 | D4 |
| Quinzano d'Oglio | 60 | B1 |
| Quipar, R | 44 | C2 |
| Quiroga | 34 | C2 |
| Quissac | 30 | B3 |
| Qukës | 77 | D4 |
| Quoich, L | 2 | C4 |

# R

| Name | Page | Grid |
|---|---|---|
| Raab | 56 | C2 |
| Raab R | 57 | E4 |
| Raabs | 57 | E1 |
| Raahe | 99 | D4 |
| Raajärvi | 99 | D2 |
| Rääkkylä | 103 | F2 |
| Raalte | 17 | D2 |
| Raanujärvi | 99 | D2 |
| Raasay | 2 | B3 |
| Raasay, Sd of | 2 | B3 |
| Raattama | 95 | D4 |
| Rab | 70 | B4 |
| Rab I | 70 | B4 |
| Rába | 112 | A4 |
| Rabac | 70 | B3 |
| Rábade | 34 | B1 |
| Rabastens | 29 | D4 |
| Rabastens-de-Bigorre | 37 | E1 |
| Rabat | 68 | B4 |
| Rabe | 72 | C1 |
| Rabka | 112 | B3 |
| Rabrovo (Makedonija) | 77 | F3 |
| Rabrovo (Srbija) | 73 | E3 |
| Rača (Kragujevac) | 73 | D3 |
| Rača (Radan) | 77 | D1 |
| Rače | 70 | C1 |
| Rachov | 112 | C3 |
| Racibórz | 112 | A2 |
| Račinovci | 72 | B3 |
| Račišće | 75 | E2 |
| Radalj | 72 | B3 |
| Radan | 77 | D1 |
| Rădăuţi | 113 | D3 |
| Radbuza | 56 | B1 |
| Rade | 48 | A3 |
| Råde | 105 | D3 |
| Radeberg | 53 | E2 |
| Radebeul | 53 | E2 |
| Radeburg | 53 | E2 |
| Radeče | 70 | B2 |
| Radechov | 112 | C2 |
| Radenci | 70 | C1 |
| Radenthein | 59 | F2 |
| Radevowald | 17 | E4 |
| Radici, Pso delle | 60 | C3 |
| Radicondoli | 60 | C4 |
| Radika | 77 | D3 |
| Radimlje | 75 | F2 |
| Radiovce | 77 | D3 |
| Radlje | 70 | B1 |
| Radljevo | 72 | C3 |
| Radnice | 53 | E4 |
| Radohinës, Maj'e | 76 | C2 |
| Radojevo | 73 | D1 |
| Radom | 112 | B2 |
| Radomsko | 112 | B2 |
| Radomyšl' | 113 | E2 |
| Radotin | 53 | F4 |
| Radovče | 76 | B2 |
| Radovići | 76 | B3 |
| Radoviš | 77 | F3 |
| Radovljica | 70 | A2 |
| Radovnica | 77 | E2 |
| Radøy | 104 | A2 |
| Radstadt | 59 | F1 |
| Radstädter Tauernpaß | 59 | F1 |
| Radstock | 9 | D2 |
| Raduša | 75 | E1 |
| Radusa | 77 | D3 |
| Radviliškis | 110 | C3 |
| Radzyn' Podlaski | 112 | C2 |

| Name | Ref |
|---|---|
| Raesfeld | 17 E3 |
| Raffadali | 68 B4 |
| Rafina | 88 A1 |
| Ragama | 39 F1 |
| Raglan | 9 D2 |
| Rago | 97 F1 |
| Ragua, Pto de la | 44 B3 |
| Raguhn | 53 D1 |
| Ragunda | 101 F2 |
| Ragusa | 69 D4 |
| Rahden | 17 F2 |
| Ráhes | 83 F3 |
| Rahlstedt | 48 B3 |
| Raia, Rib de | 38 B4 |
| Rain | 55 F2 |
| Räisäla | 99 E2 |
| Raisduoddarhal'di | 94 C2 |
| Raisio | 107 D2 |
| Raittijärvi | 94 C3 |
| Rajac | 73 F3 |
| Raja-Jooseppi | 95 F3 |
| Rajamäki | 107 E2 |
| Rajince | 77 E2 |
| Raka | 70 C2 |
| Rakalj | 70 A4 |
| Rakitna | 70 B2 |
| Rakitnica | 71 D2 |
| Rakkestad | 105 D3 |
| Rakova Bara | 73 E3 |
| Rakovac | 71 E3 |
| Rakovica | 70 C3 |
| Rakovnik | 53 E4 |
| Rakvere | 110 C1 |
| Ralja | 73 D3 |
| Ram | 73 D2 |
| Ramacca | 69 D3 |
| Ramales de la Victoria | 36 A1 |
| Ramallosa | 34 A2 |
| Ramberg | 97 E1 |
| Rambervillers | 21 D4 |
| Rambouillet | 19 E4 |
| Rambucourt | 20 C4 |
| Ramno | 77 D2 |
| Ramnoûs | 84 B4 |
| Ramor, L | 13 D3 |
| Ramsau | 56 B4 |
| Ramsau | 59 F1 |
| Ramsele | 101 F2 |
| Ramsey (Cambridge) | 9 F1 |
| Ramsey (I of Man) | 6 A1 |
| Ramsgate | 11 D3 |
| Ramsjö | 101 E3 |
| Ramstein | 54 B1 |
| Ramsund | 94 B3 |
| Ramundberget | 101 D2 |
| Ramvik | 101 F2 |
| Rana | 97 D3 |
| Ranalt | 59 D2 |
| Rance | 22 C3 |
| Randaberg | 104 A3 |
| Randak | 104 B3 |
| Randalstown | 13 E2 |
| Randan | 26 A4 |
| Randanne | 29 E1 |
| Randazzo | 69 D3 |
| Randers | 108 B2 |
| Randijaure | 98 A2 |
| Randow | 49 E2 |
| Randsfjorden | 105 D2 |
| Rånea | 98 C3 |
| Rånealven | 98 B2 |
| Rangsdorf | 49 E4 |
| Rankweil | 58 B2 |
| Rannoch, L | 4 C1 |
| Ranovac | 73 E3 |
| Rantasalmi | 103 E3 |
| Rantsila | 99 D4 |
| Ranua | 99 D3 |
| Raon-l'Etape | 21 E4 |
| Rapallo | 60 A3 |
| Rapolano Terme | 61 D4 |
| Rapolla | 64 C3 |
| Rapperswil | 58 A2 |
| Rapsáni | 83 E1 |
| Raptópoulo | 86 C3 |
| Raša | 70 A3 |
| Räsälä | 103 E2 |
| Raša R | 70 A3 |
| Rasbo | 106 B3 |
| Rascafría | 40 A1 |
| Rasdorf | 52 B3 |
| Raseiniai | 110 C3 |
| Rasimbegov Most | 77 E4 |
| Rasina | 73 E4 |
| Raška | 76 C1 |
| Rasno | 75 E2 |
| Rasquera | 41 F1 |
| Rastatt | 54 C2 |
| Rastede | 47 F3 |
| Rastegai'sa | 95 E2 |
| Rastenberg | 52 C2 |
| Rastenfeld | 57 E2 |
| Rasueros | 39 F1 |
| Rätan | 101 E3 |
| Rateče | 70 A1 |
| Ratekau | 48 B2 |
| Rates | 34 A4 |
| Rathdowney | 12 C4 |
| Rathdrum | 13 D4 |
| Rathenow | 49 D4 |
| Rathfriland | 13 E2 |
| Rathkeale | 14 B3 |
| Rathlin I | 13 E1 |
| Rath Luirc | 14 B3 |
| Rathmelton | 13 D1 |
| Rathmore | 14 B4 |
| Rathmullan | 13 D1 |
| Raticosa, Pso della | 61 D3 |
| Ratingen | 17 E4 |
| Ratkovac | 76 C2 |
| Ratkovo | 72 B2 |
| Ratten | 57 E3 |
| Rattenberg | 59 D1 |
| Rattersdorf | 57 F3 |
| Rattray | 5 D1 |
| Rattray Head | 3 E3 |
| Rättvik | 101 E4 |
| Ratzeburg | 48 B2 |
| Raubling | 56 B3 |
| Raucourt-et-Flaba | 20 C2 |
| Raudanjoki | 99 D2 |
| Raudaskylä | 102 C1 |
| Raufarhöfn | 96 C1 |
| Raufoss | 105 D2 |
| Rauha | 103 E4 |
| Rauhamäki | 103 D3 |
| Rauland | 104 B3 |
| Rauma (N) | 100 B3 |
| Rauma (SF) | 107 D2 |
| Rauris | 59 E1 |
| Rautalampi | 103 D2 |
| Rautas | 94 C4 |
| Rautavaara | 103 E1 |
| Rautio | 102 C1 |
| Rautjärvi | 103 F3 |
| Ravan | 71 F4 |
| Ravanica | 73 E4 |
| Ravanjska | 70 C4 |
| Ravanusa | 68 C4 |
| Ravello | 64 B4 |
| Raven | 71 D2 |
| Ravenna | 61 D2 |
| Ravensbrück | 49 D3 |
| Ravensburg | 55 D4 |
| Ravna Dubrava | 77 E1 |
| Ravna Gora | 70 B3 |
| Ravna Reka | 73 E3 |
| Ravne na Koroškem | 70 B1 |
| Ravnište | 77 D1 |
| Ravnje | 72 B3 |
| Ravno | 75 F2 |
| Ravno Bučje | 73 F4 |
| Ravno, G. | 75 E1 |
| Rawicz | 112 A2 |
| Rawtenstall | 6 C2 |
| Rayleigh | 11 D3 |
| Rayol | 31 D4 |
| Räyrinki | 102 C2 |
| Ražana | 72 C4 |
| Ražanac | 70 C4 |
| Razboj | 71 E3 |
| Razbojna | 77 D1 |
| Raždaginja | 76 C2 |
| Razelm | 113 E4 |
| Razgrad | 115 E2 |
| Razlog | 115 D3 |
| Razlovci | 77 F2 |
| Raz, Pte du | 22 A3 |
| Reading | 9 F2 |
| Reales | 43 E4 |
| Réalmont | 32 B1 |
| Rebais | 20 A4 |
| Rebbenesøy | 94 B2 |
| Rebordelo | 34 C4 |
| Reç | 76 C3 |
| Recanati | 61 F4 |
| Recco | 60 A3 |
| Recey | 26 C1 |
| Rechnitz | 57 C4 |
| Rečica (SU) | 111 E4 |
| Rečica (YU) | 70 C3 |
| Recke | 17 E2 |
| Recklinghausen | 17 E3 |
| Recknitz | 48 C2 |
| Recoaro Terme | 59 D4 |
| Recuerda | 36 A4 |
| Recz | 49 F2 |
| Red B | 13 E1 |
| Redange | 21 D2 |
| Redcar | 5 F4 |
| Redditch | 9 E1 |
| Redhill | 10 C3 |
| Redon | 23 D4 |
| Redondela | 34 A3 |
| Redondo | 38 C4 |
| Redruth | 8 A4 |
| Ree, L | 12 C3 |
| Rees | 17 D3 |
| Reeth | 6 C1 |
| Refsnes | 94 A3 |
| Reftele | 109 D2 |
| Rega | 49 F2 |
| Regalbuto | 69 D3 |
| Regen | 56 B2 |
| Regensburg | 56 B2 |
| Regenstauf | 56 B2 |
| Reggello | 61 D4 |
| Reggio di Calabria | 67 E4 |
| Reggiolo | 60 C2 |
| Reggio nell' Emilia | 60 C2 |
| Reghin | 113 D4 |
| Regnitz | 55 E1 |
| Reguengos de Monsaraz | 42 B1 |
| Rehau | 53 D4 |
| Rehburg-Loccum | 48 A4 |
| Rehden | 17 F2 |
| Rehna | 48 B2 |
| Reichenau (A) | 57 E3 |
| Reichenau (CH) | 58 B2 |
| Reichenbach (Dresden) | 53 F2 |
| Reichenbach (Karl-Marx-Stadt) | 53 D3 |
| Reichertshofen | 55 F2 |
| Reichshoffen | 21 E3 |
| Reigate | 10 C3 |
| Reignier | 27 D4 |
| Ré, Ile de | 24 B4 |
| Reillanne | 30 C3 |
| Reims | 20 B3 |
| Reinach | 27 F2 |
| Reinbek | 48 B3 |
| Reinberg | 49 D1 |
| Reine | 97 E1 |
| Reinfeld | 48 B2 |
| Reinheim | 54 C1 |
| Reinli | 104 C2 |
| Reinosa | 35 F2 |
| Reinøy | 94 C2 |
| Reisaelva | 94 C2 |
| Reischenhart | 56 B3 |
| Reisjärvi | 103 D1 |
| Reiss | 3 D2 |
| Reit im Winkl | 56 B4 |
| Reitzenhain | 53 E3 |
| Reka | 70 A3 |
| Rekovac | 73 E4 |
| Remagen | 51 E4 |
| Rémalard | 23 F3 |
| Remeskylä | 103 D1 |
| Remich | 21 D2 |
| Remiremont | 27 D1 |
| Remolinos | 36 C3 |
| Remouchamps | 51 D4 |
| Remoulins | 30 B3 |
| Rempstone | 7 D3 |
| Remscheid | 17 E4 |
| Rémuzat | 30 C2 |
| Rena | 105 D2 |
| Renaix | 50 B3 |
| Renazé | 23 E4 |
| Renchen | 54 C3 |
| Rende | 67 E2 |
| Rendína (Makedonía) | 80 B3 |
| Rendína (Thessalía) | 83 D3 |
| Rendsburg | 48 A2 |
| Rengínio | 83 F3 |
| Rengsdorf | 51 E4 |
| Reni | 113 E4 |
| Renish Pt | 2 A3 |
| Renko | 107 E2 |
| Renkum | 17 D3 |
| Rennebu | 100 C2 |
| Rennerod | 51 F3 |
| Rennes | 23 D3 |
| Rennes-les-Bains | 32 B2 |
| Rennesøy | 104 A3 |
| Rennweg | 59 F2 |
| Reno | 61 D2 |
| Rensjön | 94 C4 |
| Renwez | 20 B2 |
| Réole, la | 28 B2 |
| Replot | 102 B2 |
| Replotfjärden | 102 B2 |
| Repojoki | 95 E3 |
| Reposaari | 102 B3 |
| République, Col de la | 30 B1 |
| Repvåg | 95 E1 |
| Requena | 41 D4 |
| Réquista | 29 E3 |
| Rerik | 48 C2 |
| Resanovci | 71 D4 |
| Resavica | 73 E3 |
| Reschenpaß | 58 C2 |
| Resen (Makedonija) | 77 D4 |
| Resen (Srbija) | 77 E2 |
| Resende | 34 B4 |
| Resia, Pso di | 58 C2 |
| Resita | 114 C1 |
| Resko | 49 F2 |
| Resmo | 109 E3 |
| Resna | 76 B3 |
| Resnik | 73 D3 |
| Ressons | 19 F3 |
| Restafjorden | 94 C2 |
| Restelica | 77 D3 |
| Resuttano | 68 C3 |
| Retezatului, M | 114 C1 |
| Rethel | 20 B3 |
| Rethem | 48 A4 |
| Rethen | 52 B1 |
| Réthimno | 90 C3 |
| Réthimno (Nomos) | 90 C3 |
| Retiers | 23 D3 |
| Retortillo, Emb de | 43 E2 |
| Retuerta | 41 D1 |
| Retuerta del Bullaque | 39 F3 |
| Retuerta, Emb de | 36 A3 |
| Retz | 57 E2 |
| Reuilly | 25 E3 |
| Reus | 37 F4 |
| Reusel | 16 C4 |
| Reuss | 27 F2 |
| Reuterstadt-Stavenhagen | 49 D2 |
| Reutlingen | 55 D3 |
| Reutte | 58 C1 |
| Revard, Mt | 27 D4 |
| Revel | 29 D4 |
| Revesbotn | 95 D1 |
| Revigny | 20 C4 |
| Revin | 20 B2 |
| Ševníkov | 53 F3 |
| Revolcadores | 44 C2 |
| Revonlahti | 99 D4 |
| Revsnes | 104 B1 |
| Rewal | 49 F1 |
| Reyðarfjörður | 96 C2 |
| Reykholt | 96 A2 |
| Reykjavik | 96 A2 |
| Rēzekne | 111 D2 |
| Rezzato | 60 B1 |
| Rezzoaglio | 60 A3 |
| Rgotina | 73 F3 |
| Rhaeadr | 8 C1 |
| Rhayader | 8 C1 |
| Rheda-Wiedenbrück | 17 F3 |
| Rhede | 17 D3 |
| Rhein | 17 D3 |
| Rheinbach | 51 E4 |
| Rheinberg | 17 D3 |
| Rheinböllen | 54 B1 |
| Rheine | 17 E2 |
| Rheinfelden (CH) | 27 F2 |
| Rheinfelden (D) | 54 C4 |
| Rheinhausen | 17 D3 |
| Rheinland-Pfalz | 51 E4 |
| Rheinsberg | 49 D3 |
| Rheinwaldhorn | 58 B3 |
| Rhêmes N.D. | 31 E1 |
| Rhenen | 16 C3 |
| Rheydt | 17 D4 |
| Rhinau | 21 E4 |
| Rhinow | 49 D4 |
| Rho | 60 A1 |
| Rhondda | 8 C2 |
| Rhône | 26 C4 |
| Rhône (Dépt) | 26 B4 |
| Rhône à Sète, Canal du | 30 B3 |
| Rhosneigr | 6 A2 |
| Rhossili | 8 C2 |
| Rhüden | 52 B1 |
| Rhum | 2 B4 |
| Rhum, Sd of | 2 B4 |
| Rhune, la | 28 A4 |
| Rhuthun | 6 B3 |
| Rhyl | 6 B2 |
| Rhynern | 17 E3 |
| Rhynie | 3 E4 |
| Riaillé | 23 D4 |
| Riákia | 79 E3 |
| Rial | 34 A2 |
| Riaño | 35 E2 |
| Riaño, Emb de | 35 E2 |
| Rians | 30 C4 |
| Riansares R | 40 B3 |
| Rianxo | 34 A2 |
| Riaza | 36 A4 |
| Ribadavia | 34 B3 |
| Ribadelago | 34 C3 |
| Ribadeo | 34 C1 |
| Ribadesella | 35 E1 |
| Ribarci | 77 E2 |
| Ribarić | 76 C1 |
| Riba-roja, Emb de | 37 E4 |
| Ribarska Banja | 73 E4 |
| Ribas de Campos | 35 E3 |
| Ribas de Sil | 34 B2 |
| Ribatejo | 38 B3 |
| Ribble | 6 C2 |
| Ribe | 108 A3 |
| Ribeauvillé | 27 E1 |
| Ribécourt | 19 F3 |
| Ribeira de Pena | 34 B4 |
| Ribeira, Emb de la | 41 D1 |
| Ribemont | 20 A2 |
| Ribera | 68 B3 |
| Ribérac | 28 C1 |
| Ribera de Cardós | 32 A2 |
| Ribera del Fresno | 43 D1 |
| Ribera de Freser | 32 B3 |
| Ribiers | 30 C3 |
| Ribnica (Bosna i Hercegovina) | 71 F4 |
| Ribnica (Kočevje) | 70 B2 |
| Ribnica (Postojna) | 70 A3 |
| Ribnica na Pohorju | 70 B1 |
| Ribnik | 70 C2 |
| Ribnitz-Damgarten | 48 C1 |
| Ribolla | 62 C1 |
| Řičany | 53 F4 |
| Riccia | 64 B3 |
| Riccione | 61 E3 |
| Riceys, les | 26 B1 |
| Richelieu | 25 D3 |
| Richmond (London) | 9 F2 |
| Richmond (Yorks) | 6 C1 |
| Richtenberg | 49 D1 |
| Rickling | 48 A2 |
| Ricla | 36 C4 |
| Ricobayo, Emb de | 35 D4 |
| Riddica | 72 B1 |
| Riec | 22 B3 |
| Ried (Oberösterreich) | 56 C3 |
| Ried (Tirol) | 58 C2 |
| Riego de la Vega | 35 D3 |
| Riesa | 53 E2 |
| Riesi | 68 C4 |
| Riestedt | 52 C2 |
| Rietberg | 17 F3 |
| Rieti | 63 E2 |
| Rieumes | 29 D4 |
| Rieupeyroux | 29 E3 |
| Rieux | 37 F1 |
| Riez | 31 D3 |
| Riezlern | 58 B2 |
| Rīga | 110 C2 |
| Rigáni | 83 D4 |
| Rigeo | 83 E2 |
| Rigi | 58 A2 |
| Rignac | 29 E3 |
| Rignano Flaminio | 63 E2 |
| Rihéa | 87 E3 |
| Riihimäki | 107 E2 |
| Riisitunturi | 99 E2 |
| Riistavesi | 103 E2 |
| Rijeca | 72 B4 |
| Rijeka | 70 B3 |
| Rijeka Crnojevića | 76 B3 |
| Rijssen | 17 D2 |
| Riksgränsen | 94 B3 |
| Rila | 115 D3 |
| Rila Mts | 115 D3 |
| Rillo | 41 D2 |
| Rillo de Gallo | 40 C1 |
| Rimavská-Sobota | 112 B3 |
| Rimbo | 106 B3 |
| Rimini | 61 E3 |
| Rîmnicu Sărat | 113 E4 |
| Rîmnicu Vîlcea | 115 D1 |
| Rimnio | 79 E4 |
| Rimske Toplice | 70 B2 |
| Rincón de la Victoria | 43 F4 |
| Rincón de Soto | 36 C2 |
| Rindal | 100 C2 |
| Ringaskiddy | 14 C4 |
| Ringe | 108 B4 |
| Ringebu | 100 C3 |
| Ringford | 4 C3 |
| Ringkøbing | 108 A3 |
| Ringkøbing Fjord | 108 A3 |
| Ring of Kerry | 14 A4 |
| Ringsaker | 105 D2 |
| Ringstad | 104 A1 |
| Ringsted | 108 C3 |
| Ringvassøy | 94 B2 |
| Ringwood | 9 E3 |
| Rínia, N | 88 C2 |
| Rinkaby | 109 D3 |
| Rinns Pt | 4 A2 |
| Rinteln | 52 A1 |
| Rinvyle Pt | 12 A3 |
| Rio | 83 D4 |
| Riocavado de la Sierra | 36 A3 |
| Riogordo | 43 F3 |
| Riola Sardo | 66 A3 |
| Riolo Terme | 61 D3 |
| Riom | 26 A4 |
| Riomaggiore | 60 B3 |
| Rio Maior | 38 A3 |
| Rio Marina | 62 C1 |
| Riom-ès-Montagnes | 29 E1 |
| Rionero in Vulture | 64 C3 |
| Rio, Punta del | 44 B4 |
| Rioseco de Tapia | 35 D2 |
| Rioz | 27 D2 |
| Ripač | 70 C4 |
| Ripanj | 73 D3 |
| Riparbella | 60 C4 |
| Ripatransone | 61 F4 |
| Ripley | 7 D1 |
| Ripoli | 32 A3 |
| Ripollet | 32 A4 |
| Ripon | 6 C1 |
| Riquewihr | 27 E1 |
| Risan | 76 B2 |
| Risbäck | 97 E4 |
| Risca | 9 D2 |
| Riscle | 28 B4 |
| Risle | 19 D4 |
| Risnes | 104 B4 |
| Risnjak | 70 B3 |
| Risør | 104 C4 |
| Risøyhamn | 94 A3 |
| Risøysundet | 94 A3 |
| Rissa | 100 C1 |
| Ristiina | 103 E3 |
| Ristijärvi | 99 E4 |
| Ristilampi | 99 D2 |
| Ristovac | 77 E2 |
| Risum-Lindholm | 47 F1 |
| Ritini | 79 E4 |
| Ritoniemi | 103 E2 |
| Ritsóna | 84 A4 |
| Rittmannshausen | 52 B3 |
| Riudoms | 37 F4 |
| Riva | 58 C4 |
| Rivarolo Canavese | 31 E1 |
| Rive-de-Gier | 30 B1 |
| Rives | 30 C1 |
| Rivesaltes | 32 B2 |
| Rivière-Thibouville, la | 19 D3 |
| Rívio | 82 C3 |
| Rivisondoli | 64 A2 |
| Rivoli | 31 E1 |
| Rivolta d'Adda | 60 B1 |
| Riza | 83 D4 |
| Rizário | 79 E2 |
| Rízia | 81 F1 |
| Rizoma | 83 D1 |
| Rizómilos | 83 F2 |
| Rizovoúni | 83 D2 |
| Rižskij Zaliv | 110 B2 |
| Rjånes | 100 A2 |
| Rjukan | 104 C3 |
| Roa | 35 F4 |
| Roadside | 3 D2 |
| Roan | 96 C4 |
| Roanne | 26 B4 |
| Roaringwater B | 14 A4 |
| Robbio | 60 A1 |
| Röbel | 49 D3 |
| Robertsfors | 102 B1 |
| Robertville | 51 D4 |
| Robič | 70 A2 |
| Roble | 44 C1 |
| Robledillo de Gata | 39 D2 |
| Robledo | 44 C1 |
| Robledo de Chavela | 40 A2 |
| Robres | 37 D3 |
| Roca, C da | 38 A4 |
| Rocamadour | 29 D2 |
| Rocca d'Aspide | 64 C4 |
| Rocca di Mezzo | 63 F2 |
| Rocca di Papa | 63 E3 |
| Roccalbegna | 63 D1 |
| Roccalumera | 69 D2 |
| Roccamonfina | 64 A3 |
| Roccapalumba | 68 B3 |
| Roccaraso | 64 A2 |
| Rocca San Casciano | 61 D3 |
| Rocca Sinibalda | 63 F2 |
| Roccastrada | 63 D1 |
| Roccella Ionica | 67 F4 |
| Rocchetta Sant' Antonio | 64 C3 |
| Roc de Fraussa | 32 B3 |
| Rochdale | 6 C2 |
| Roche-Bernard, la | 22 C4 |
| Rochebonne | 30 B2 |
| Roche-Canillac, la | 29 D2 |
| Roche-Chalais, la | 28 B2 |
| Rochechouart | 28 C1 |
| Roche-Derrien, la | 22 C2 |
| Roche-en-Ardenne, la | 51 D4 |
| Rochefort (B) | 50 C4 |
| Rochefort (F) | 24 B4 |
| Rochefort-en-Terre | 22 C4 |
| Rochefort-Montagne | 29 E1 |
| Rochefort-sur-Nenon | 26 C2 |
| Rochefoucauld, la | 28 C1 |
| Roche-Guyon, la | 19 E3 |
| Rochehaut | 20 C2 |
| Rochelle, La | 24 B4 |
| Rochemaure | 30 B2 |
| Roche-Posay, la | 25 D3 |
| Rochepot, le | 26 C3 |
| Roches, Col des | 27 E2 |
| Rocheservière | 24 B3 |
| Rochester | 11 D2 |
| Roche-sur-Foron, la | 27 D4 |
| Roche-sur-Yon, la | 24 B3 |
| Rochette, la | 31 D1 |
| Rochlitz | 53 D2 |
| Rociana del Condado | 42 C3 |

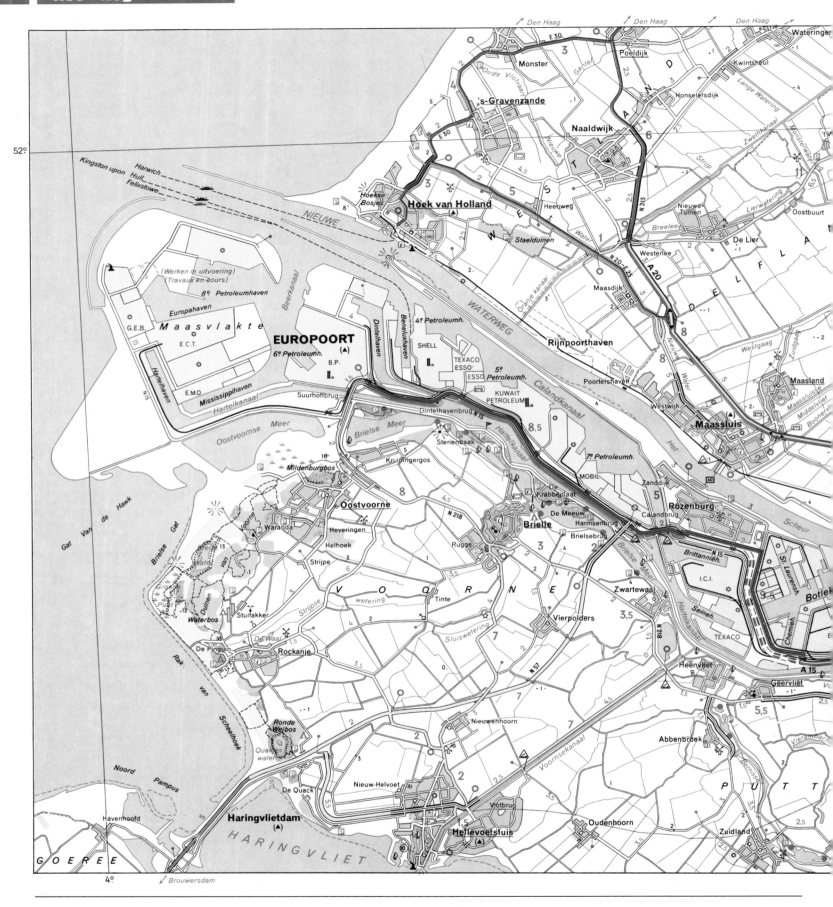

| | | | | | | | | | | | | | |
|---|---|---|---|---|---|---|---|---|---|---|---|---|---|
| Rockenhausen | **54** B1 | Rødberg | **104** C2 | Rødekro | **108** A4 | Rodez | **29** E3 | Rodohóri | **79** E3 | Rodopós | **90** B3 | Roermond | **17** D4 |
| Rocroi | **20** B2 | Rødby | **108** B4 | Rodel | **2** A3 | Rodiezmo | **35** D2 | Rodolivos | **80** B2 | Ródos | **93** F1 | Roeselare | **50** A3 |
| Róda | **82** A1 | Rødbyhavn | **108** B4 | Rodellar | **37** E3 | Rodi Garganico | **64** C2 | Rödön | **101** E2 | Ródos, N | **93** F2 | Rogač | **75** D2 |
| Rodach | **52** C4 | Rødding (Ribe) | **108** A3 | Roden | **47** D3 | Roding | **56** B1 | Rodonit, Gjiri i | **76** C4 | Rodováni | **90** B3 | Rogača | **73** D3 |
| Rodacherbrunn | **52** C3 | Rødding (Viborg) | **108** A2 | Ródenas | **41** D2 | Roditis | **81** E2 | Rodópi (Nomos) | **81** E2 | Rodvattnet | **102** A1 | Rogačica (Kosovo) | **77** D2 |
| Roda de Isábena | **37** E3 | Rödeby | **109** E3 | Rödermark | **52** A4 | Rodnei, M | **113** D3 | Rodopi *Mts* | **115** D3 | Rødven | **100** B2 | Rogačica (Srbija) | **72** C4 |
| Rodavgí | **82** C2 | Rodeiro | **34** B2 | Rodewisch | **53** D3 | Rododáfni | **83** D4 | Rodópoli | **79** F2 | Rødvig | **108** C4 | Rogačov | **111** E4 |

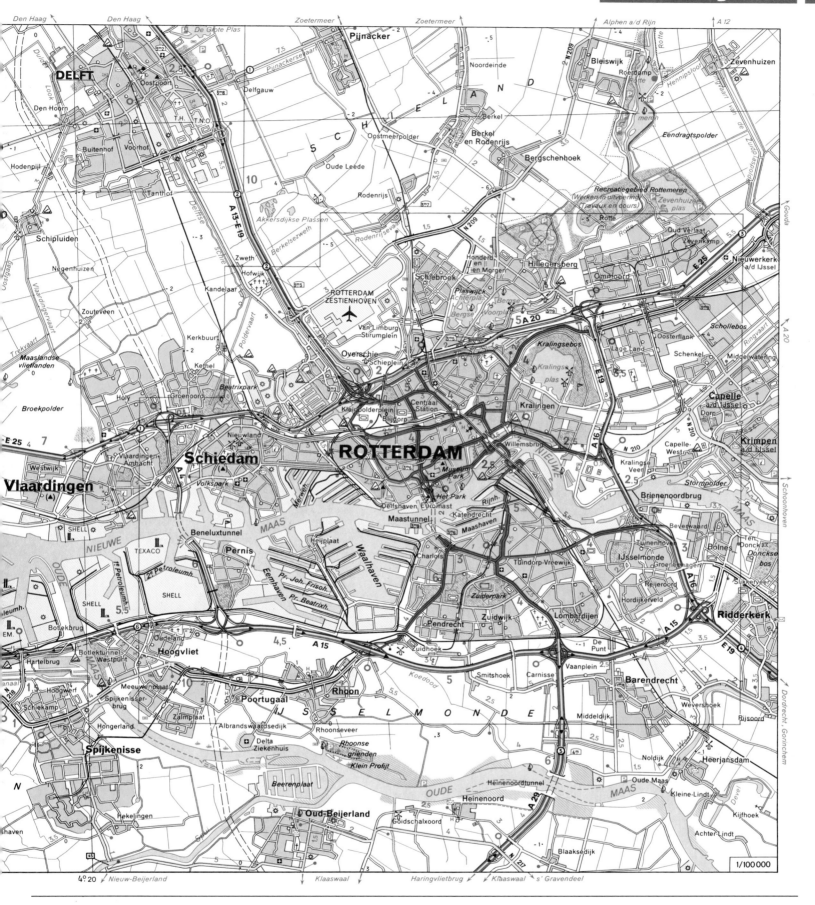

| | | | | | | | | | | | | | | |
|---|---|---|---|---|---|---|---|---|---|---|---|---|---|---|
| Rogaland | **104** A3 | Rogén *L* | **101** D3 | Rogozna | **76** C1 | Rohrer Sattel | **57** E3 | Rokiškis | **110** C3 | Rolla | **94** B3 | Roman | **113** D4 |
| Rogaška Slatina | **70** C1 | Roggendorf | **48** B2 | Rogoznica | **75** D2 | Roignais | **27** E4 | Røkland | **97** F2 | Rollag | **104** C3 | Romana | **66** B2 |
| Rogatec | **70** C2 | Roggiano Gravina | **67** E2 | Rohan | **22** C3 | Roine Mallasvesi | **107** E1 | Rokovci | **71** F2 | Rolle | **27** D3 | Romanche | **31** D1 |
| Rogatica | **76** A1 | Roggosen | **53** F1 | Rohr | **52** B3 | Roisel | **19** F2 | Rokua | **99** E4 | Rolle, Pso di | **59** D3 | Romangordo | **39** E3 |
| Rogatin | **113** D3 | Rogliano (F) | **33** F2 | Rohrbach (A) | **56** C2 | Roissy | **19** F4 | Rokycany | **53** E4 | Rolvsøya | **95** D1 | România | **73** D1 |
| Rogätz | **48** C4 | Rogliano (I) | **67** E3 | Rohrbach (F) | **21** E3 | Rojales | **45** D2 | Røldal | **104** B3 | Roma | **63** E2 | Romanija | **71** F4 |
| Rogen | **101** D3 | Rognan | **97** E2 | Rohrbrunn | **52** A4 | Rök | **109** D1 | Rolfstorp | **108** C2 | Romagnano Sesia | **31** F1 | Romans | **30** C2 |

| | | | |
|---|---|---|---|
| Romanshorn | 58 B1 | Roquefort | 28 B3 |
| Romantische straße | 55 E3 | Roquefort-sur-Soulzon | 29 F3 |
| Rombas | 21 D3 | Roque-Gageac, la | 29 D2 |
| Rombo, Pso del | 58 C2 | Roquemaure | 30 B3 |
| Römhild | 52 B4 | Roquesteron | 31 E3 |
| Romilly | 20 B4 | Roquetas de Mar | 44 B4 |
| Romny | 113 F1 | Roquevaire | 30 C4 |
| Rømø | 108 A3 | Rora Head | 3 D1 |
| Romont | 27 E3 | Rore | 71 D4 |
| Romorantin | 25 E2 | Røros | 101 D2 |
| Romsdalen | 100 B2 | Rørøy | 97 D3 |
| Romsdalsfjorden | 100 B2 | Rorschach | 58 B1 |
| Romsey | 9 E3 | Rørvig | 108 C3 |
| Rona | 2 B3 | Rørvik (Nord Trøndelag) | 97 D4 |
| Ronaldsway | 6 A1 | Rørvik (Sør Trøndelag) | 100 C1 |
| Roncade | 59 E4 | Ros' | 113 E2 |
| Roncal | 37 D2 | Rosà | 59 D4 |
| Ronce | 28 A1 | Rosal de la Frontera | 42 C1 |
| Roncegno | 59 D3 | Rosans | 30 C2 |
| Roncesvalles | 36 C1 | Rosarito, Emb de | 39 E2 |
| Ronchamp | 27 D1 | Rosarno | 67 E4 |
| Ronchi | 59 F3 | Roscoff | 22 B2 |
| Ronciglione | 63 E2 | Ros Comáin | 12 C3 |
| Roncobilaccio | 60 C3 | Roscommon | 12 C3 |
| Ronda | 43 E4 | Roscommon (Co) | 12 C3 |
| Ronda, Serr de | 43 E4 | Roscrea | 12 C4 |
| Rønde | 108 B3 | Rose (I) | 67 E2 |
| Rondane | 100 C3 | Rose (YU) | 76 A3 |
| Rondeslottet | 100 C3 | Rosegg | 70 A1 |
| Rondissone | 31 F1 | Roselend, Cormet de | 27 E4 |
| Rondvassbu | 100 C3 | Rosell | 41 F2 |
| Rönnäng | 108 C1 | Rosendal | 104 A2 |
| Rønne | 109 D4 | Rosenheim | 56 B3 |
| Ronneburg | 53 D3 | Rosenhof | 56 B2 |
| Ronneby | 109 E3 | Rosenthal | 53 F3 |
| Ronnebyån | 109 E3 | Roses | 32 C3 |
| Rønnede | 108 C4 | Roses, Golfo de | 32 C3 |
| Rönnöfors | 101 E1 | Roseto degli Abruzzi | 64 A1 |
| Ronse | 50 B3 | Rosheim | 21 E4 |
| Roosendaal | 16 B3 | Rosice | 57 F1 |
| Roperuelos del Páramo | 35 D3 | Rosières | 19 F2 |
| Ropi | 94 C3 | Rosiers, les | 24 C2 |
| Ropinsalmi | 94 C3 | Rosignano Marittimo | 60 C4 |
| Ropotovo | 77 E3 | Roşiori de Vede | 115 D2 |
| Roquebillière | 31 E3 | Roskilde | 108 C3 |
| Roquebrun | 30 A4 | Roški slap | 75 D1 |
| Roquebrune-Cap-Martin | 31 E3 | | |
| Roquebrussanne, la | 31 D4 | | |
| Roquecourbe | 32 B1 | | |

| | | | |
|---|---|---|---|
| Roslavl' | 111 E3 | Rotondo, M | 33 F3 |
| Rosmaninhal | 38 C3 | Rott (Bayern) | 56 A3 |
| Røsnæs | 108 B3 | Rott (Bayern) | 56 B3 |
| Rosolina Mare | 61 D1 | Rott R | 56 B2 |
| Rosolini | 69 D4 | Rottach-Egern | 56 A4 |
| Rosoman | 77 E3 | Rotten | 27 F3 |
| Rosova dolina | 115 D2 | Rottenbach | 52 C4 |
| Rosporden | 22 B3 | Rottenburg (Baden-Württemberg) | 55 D3 |
| Rossano | 67 F2 | Rottenburg (Bayern) | 56 B2 |
| Rossan Pt | 12 C1 | Rottenmann | 57 D4 |
| Rosscarbery | 14 B4 | Rottenmanner Tauern | 57 D4 |
| Roßdorf | 54 C1 | Rotterdam | 16 B3 |
| Rosses Point | 12 C2 | Rottne | 109 D2 |
| Roßhaupten | 55 E4 | Rottneros | 105 E3 |
| Rossija | 111 E2 | Rottweil | 54 C3 |
| Rossio | 38 B3 | Rötz | 56 B1 |
| Rosskreppfjorden | 104 B3 | Roubaix | 20 A1 |
| Rosslare | 15 D4 | Roudnice | 53 F3 |
| Rosslare Harbour | 15 D4 | Rouen | 19 E3 |
| Roßau | 55 D1 | Rouffach | 27 E1 |
| Rosslea | 13 D2 | Rougé | 23 D4 |
| Rossön | 101 F1 | Rougemont | 27 D2 |
| Ross-on-Wye | 9 D2 | Rougemont-le-Château | 27 E1 |
| Røssvatnet | 97 E3 | Rouillac | 28 B1 |
| Roßwein | 53 E2 | Roujan | 30 A4 |
| Rosthwaite | 5 D4 | Roulans | 27 D2 |
| Røstlandet | 97 D1 | Roulers | 50 A3 |
| Rostock | 48 C2 | Roundstone | 12 A3 |
| Rostrenen | 22 B3 | Rousay | 3 E1 |
| Rostrevor | 13 E3 | Roússa | 81 E1 |
| Rostujávri | 94 C3 | Rousses, les | 27 D3 |
| Røsvik | 94 A4 | Rousset, Col de | 30 C2 |
| Rosvik | 98 C3 | Rovaniemi | 99 D2 |
| Rota | 43 D3 | Rovato | 60 B1 |
| Rotenburg (Hessen) | 52 B3 | Rovereto | 59 D4 |
| Rotenburg (Niedersachsen) | 48 A3 | Roverud | 105 D3 |
| Roth | 55 F1 | Roviés | 83 F3 |
| Rötha | 53 D2 | Rovigo | 61 D2 |
| Rothbury | 5 E3 | Rovinj | 70 A3 |
| Röthenbach | 55 F1 | Roviśće | 71 D2 |
| Rothenburg | 53 F2 | Rovno | 113 D2 |
| Rothenburg ob der Tauber | 55 E1 | Roxen | 106 A4 |
| Rothéneuf | 18 B4 | Roxo, Bgem do | 42 B1 |
| Rotherham | 7 D2 | Royal Canal | 12 C3 |
| Rothes | 3 D3 | Royal Leamington Spa | 9 E1 |
| Rothesay | 4 B2 | Royal Tunbridge Wells | 10 C3 |
| Rothwell | 9 F1 | Royan | 28 A1 |
| Rotja, Pta | 45 D4 | | |
| Rotonda | 67 E2 | | |
| Rotondella | 65 D4 | | |

| | | | |
|---|---|---|---|
| Royat | 29 E1 | Ruecas, R | 39 E4 |
| Roybon | 30 C1 | Rueda | 35 E4 |
| Roye | 19 F3 | Rueda de Jalón | 36 C3 |
| Royère-de-Vassivière | 25 E4 | Ruelle | 28 C1 |
| Røyrvik | 97 E4 | Ruffec | 25 D4 |
| Royston | 9 F2 | Ruffieux | 27 D4 |
| Röyttä | 98 C3 | Rugby | 9 E1 |
| Rožaje | 76 C2 | Rugeley | 6 C3 |
| Rožanstvo | 72 C4 | Rügen | 49 D1 |
| Rozay-en-Brie | 19 F4 | Rugles | 19 D4 |
| Rozier, le | 29 F3 | Rugovska klisura | 76 C2 |
| Rožmberk | 57 D1 | Ruhla | 52 B3 |
| Rožmitál | 53 F4 | Ruhland | 53 E2 |
| Rožňava | 112 B3 | Ruhner Berge | 48 C3 |
| Rozoy | 20 B2 | Ruhpolding | 56 B3 |
| Roztocze | 112 C2 | Ruhr | 17 E3 |
| Roztoky | 53 F3 | Ruidera | 40 B4 |
| Rozvadov | 56 B1 | Rüiena | 110 C2 |
| Rrasë | 76 C3 | Ruka | 99 E2 |
| Rrëshen | 76 C3 | Rukatunturi | 99 E2 |
| Rrogozhinë | 76 C4 | Ruma | 72 C2 |
| Rtanj | 73 E4 | Rumblar, Emb del | 44 A2 |
| Rtanj (Reg) | 73 E4 | Rumboci | 75 E1 |
| Ruabon | 6 B3 | Rumburk | 53 F2 |
| Rubbestadneset | 104 A2 | Rumengol | 22 B3 |
| Rubena | 35 F3 | Rumenka | 72 C2 |
| Rubeži | 76 B2 | Rumigny | 20 B2 |
| Rubha a'Mhail | 4 B2 | Rumija | 76 B3 |
| Rubha Còigeach | 2 C2 | Rumilly | 27 D4 |
| Rubha Réidh | 2 B3 | Runcorn | 6 B2 |
| Rubi | 32 A4 | Runde | 100 A2 |
| Rubiães | 34 A3 | Rundvik | 102 A2 |
| Rubi de Bracamonte | 39 F1 | Runn | 105 F2 |
| Rubielos de Mora | 41 E3 | Runni | 103 D1 |
| Rubiera | 60 C2 | Runtuna | 106 B4 |
| Rubio | 35 F4 | Ruohtir | 95 E2 |
| Rudare | 77 D1 | Ruokojärvi | 103 F3 |
| Rüdersdorf | 49 E4 | Ruokolahti | 103 F3 |
| Rüdesheim | 51 F4 | Ruokovesi | 103 E2 |
| Rudkøbing | 108 B4 | Ruokto | 98 B1 |
| Rudn'a | 111 E3 | Ruoms | 30 B2 |
| Rudna Glava | 73 E3 | Ruotsinpyhtää | 107 F2 |
| Rudnica (Crna Gora) | 76 B1 | Ruovesi | 102 C3 |
| Rudnica (Srbija) | 76 C1 | Rupa | 70 B3 |
| Rudnik (Kosovo) | 76 C2 | Rupea | 113 D4 |
| Rudnik (Reg) | 73 D4 | Ruppiner See | 49 D3 |
| Rudnik (Srbija) | 73 D4 | Rupt | 27 D1 |
| Rudo | 76 B1 | Rur | 17 D4 |
| Rudolstadt | 52 C3 | Ruše | 70 C1 |
| Rue | 19 E2 | Ruse | 115 D2 |
| | | Ruševo | 71 E2 |
| | | Rush | 13 E3 |
| | | Rushden | 9 F1 |

| | |
|---|---|
| Ruski Krstur | 72 B2 |
| Rusko | 107 D2 |
| Rusko Selo | 72 C1 |
| Rusksele | 98 A4 |
| Rüsselsheim | 51 F4 |
| Russenes | 95 D1 |
| Russey, le | 27 E2 |
| Russi | 61 D3 |
| Rust | 57 F3 |
| Rustefjelbma | 95 E1 |
| Ruswil | 27 F2 |
| Rute | 43 F3 |
| Rüthen | 17 F3 |
| Ruthin | 6 B3 |
| Rüti | 58 A2 |
| Rutigliano | 65 E3 |
| Rutledal | 104 A1 |
| Ruukki | 99 D4 |
| Ruuhitunturi | 99 E2 |
| Ruuponsaari | 103 D2 |
| Ruurlo | 17 D3 |
| Ruvo di Puglia | 65 D3 |
| Ruwer | 54 A1 |
| Ruynes-en-Margeride | 29 F2 |
| Ružomberok | 112 B3 |
| Ry | 108 B3 |
| Rybinsk | 111 F1 |
| Rybinskoje Vodochranilišče | 111 F1 |
| Rybnica | 113 E3 |
| Rybnik | 112 B3 |
| Rychnov nad Kněžnou | 112 A3 |
| Ryd | 109 D3 |
| Ryde | 9 E3 |
| Rye | 11 D3 |
| Ryfylke | 104 A3 |
| Rygge | 105 D3 |
| Rykene | 104 B4 |
| Ryl'sk | 113 F1 |
| Rymań | 49 F1 |
| Rymättylä | 107 D2 |
| Rypefjord | 95 D1 |
| Rysjedalsvika | 104 A1 |
| Ryttylä | 107 E2 |
| Rzepin | 49 F4 |
| Rzeszów | 112 C2 |
| Ržev | 111 F2 |

## S

| | | | |
|---|---|---|---|
| Sääksjärvi | 102 C2 | Sabero | 35 E2 |
| Saal | 55 F2 | Sabiñánigo | 37 D2 |
| Saalach | 59 E1 | Sabini, Mti | 63 E3 |
| Saalbach | 59 E1 | Sabiote | 44 B2 |
| Saale | 52 C1 | Sablé | 23 E4 |
| Saaler Bodden | 48 C1 | Sables-d'Olonne, les | 24 B3 |
| Saales | 21 E4 | Sables-d'Or | 22 C2 |
| Saalfeld | 52 C3 | Sæbø | 100 A2 |
| Saalfelden | 59 E1 | Sæbo | 42 A2 |
| Saane | 27 E3 | Sabôr, R | 34 C4 |
| Saanen | 27 E3 | Sabres | 28 B3 |
| Saar | 54 A1 | Sabrosa | 34 B4 |
| Saarbrücken | 54 B2 | Sabugal | 39 D2 |
| Saarburg | 54 A1 | Sæby | 108 B2 |
| Saaremaa | 110 B2 | Sa Calobra | 45 E2 |
| Saarenkylä | 99 D2 | Sacavém | 38 A4 |
| Saari | 103 F3 | Sacedon | 40 C2 |
| Saariharju | 99 E3 | Saceruela | 39 F4 |
| Saarijärvi | 103 D2 | Sacile | 59 E3 |
| Saarikoski | 94 C3 | Sacra di San Michele | 31 E1 |
| Saariselkä | 95 F3 | Sacramenia | 35 F4 |
| Saariselkä (Reg) | 95 F3 | Sacratif, C | 44 A4 |
| Saaristomeri | 107 C2 | Sada | 34 B1 |
| Saarland | 54 A2 | Sádaba | 36 C2 |
| Saarlouis | 54 B2 | Sado, R | 38 A4 |
| Saas-Fee | 27 F4 | Sadurniño | 34 B1 |
| Šabac | 72 C3 | Saelices | 40 B3 |
| Sabadell | 32 A4 | Safara | 42 C1 |
| Sabaudia | 63 F3 | Säffle | 105 E4 |
| Sabbioneta | 60 C2 | Saffron Walden | 10 C2 |

| | | | |
|---|---|---|---|
| Safonovo | 111 E3 | St Alban | 29 F2 |
| Sagard | 49 D1 | St Albans | 9 F2 |
| S'Agaró | 32 B4 | St Alban's Head | 9 E4 |
| Sagéika | 86 B1 | St-Amand-en-Puisaye | 26 A2 |
| Sagfjorden | 94 A4 | St-Amand-les-Eaux | 20 A1 |
| Sagiáda | 82 B1 | St-Amand-Longpré | 25 D2 |
| Sagra, Sa de la | 44 B2 | St-Amand-Montrond | 25 F3 |
| Sagres | 42 A3 | St-Amans-des-Cots | 29 E2 |
| Sagres, Pta de | 42 A3 | St-Amans | 29 F2 |
| Sagunto | 41 E3 | St-Amans-Soult | 32 B1 |
| Sagvåg | 104 A3 | St-Amant | 29 F1 |
| Sahagún | 35 E3 | St-Amant-Roche-Savine | 29 F1 |
| Sahalahti | 107 E1 | St-Amarin | 27 E1 |
| Šahinoviči | 71 E3 | St-Ambroix | 30 B3 |
| Sahl | 108 A2 | St-Amé | 27 D1 |
| Sahloinen | 103 D3 | St-Amour | 26 C3 |
| Saidus | 110 B3 | St Andrä | 70 B1 |
| Saignelégier | 27 E2 | St Andreasberg | 52 B2 |
| Saija | 95 F4 | St-André-de-Cubzac | 28 B2 |
| Saillagouse | 32 A3 | St-André-de-l'Eure | 19 E4 |
| Saillans | 30 C2 | St-André-de-Vézines | 29 F3 |
| Saimaa | 103 E3 | St-André-les-Alpes | 31 D3 |
| Saimaanranta | 103 E4 | St Andrews | 5 D1 |
| Sains-du-Nord | 20 B2 | | |
| Sains-Richaumont | 20 B2 | | |
| St Abb's Head | 5 E2 | | |
| St Aegyd | 57 E3 | | |
| St-Affrique | 29 E3 | | |
| St-Agnant | 24 B4 | | |
| St-Agrève | 30 B2 | | |
| St-Aignan | 25 E2 | | |
| St-Aignan-sur-Roë | 23 E3 | | |

| | | | |
|---|---|---|---|
| St-Anthème | 30 B1 | St-Brévin | 24 A2 |
| St-Antonin-Noble-Val | 29 D3 | St-Briac | 18 A4 |
| St Anton | 58 C2 | St-Brice-en-Coglès | 18 B4 |
| St-Arnoult | 19 E4 | St Brides B | 8 B2 |
| St Asaph | 6 B2 | St-Brieuc | 22 C2 |
| St-Astier | 28 C2 | St-Calais | 23 F3 |
| St-Auban | 31 D3 | St-Cast | 18 A4 |
| St-Aubin-d'Aubigné | 23 D3 | St Catherine's Pt | 9 E4 |
| St-Aubin-du-Cormier | 23 D3 | St-Cergue | 27 D3 |
| St-Aubin | 18 C3 | St-Cernin | 29 E2 |
| St-Aulaye | 28 C2 | St-Céré | 29 D2 |
| St Austell | 8 B4 | St-Chamas | 30 C4 |
| St-Avold | 21 D3 | St-Chamond | 30 B1 |
| St-Aygulf | 31 D4 | St-Chély-d'Apcher | 29 F2 |
| St-Beauzély | 29 E3 | St-Chély-d'Aubrac | 29 E2 |
| St Bees Head | 4 C4 | St-Chinian | 32 B1 |
| St-Benoît-du-Sault | 25 E3 | St Christophen | 57 E3 |
| St-Benoît | 25 F2 | St-Ciers | 28 B1 |
| St-Bertrand-de-Comminges | 37 E1 | St-Cirq-Lapopie | 29 D3 |
| St-Béat | 37 F2 | St-Clair-sur-l'Elle | 18 C3 |
| St-Bénin-d'Azy | 26 A3 | St-Clar | 28 C3 |
| St Blasien | 54 C4 | St-Claud | 25 D4 |
| St-Blin | 26 C1 | St-Claude | 27 D3 |
| St-Bonnet | 31 D2 | St Clears | 8 C2 |
| St-Bonnet-de-Joux | 26 B3 | St-Cyprien | 29 D2 |
| St-Bonnet-le-Château | 30 B1 | St-Cyprien-Plage | 32 B2 |
| | | St David's | 8 B1 |
| | | St David's Head | 8 B1 |
| | | St-Denis (Charente-Maritime) | 24 B4 |
| | | St-Denis-d'Orques | 23 E3 |

| | |
|---|---|
| St-Denis (Seine-St-Denis) | 19 F4 |
| St-Didier-en-Velay | 30 B1 |
| St-Dié | 21 E4 |
| St-Dier-d'Auvergne | 29 F1 |
| St-Dizier | 20 C4 |
| St-Donat-sur-l'Herbasse | 30 C1 |
| St-Eloy-les-Mines | 26 A4 |
| St-Emilion | 28 B2 |
| St-Etienne (Alpes-de-Haute-Provence) | 30 C3 |
| St-Etienne-Cantalès, Bge de | 29 E2 |
| St-Etienne-de-Baigorry | 28 A4 |
| St-Etienne-de-Lugdarès | 29 F2 |
| St-Etienne-de-Montluc | 24 B2 |
| St-Etienne-de-St-Geoirs | 30 C1 |
| St-Etienne-de-Tinée | 31 E3 |
| St-Etienne-en-Dévoluy | 31 D2 |
| St-Etienne (Loire) | 30 B1 |
| St-Fargeau | 26 A2 |
| St-Félicien | 30 B2 |
| St Finan's B | 14 A4 |

St-Firmin 31 D2
St-Florent (Cher) 25 F3
St-Florent (Corse) 33 F2
St-Florentin 26 B1
St-Flour 29 F2
St-François-Longchamp 31 D1
St-Fulgent 24 B3
St Gallen (A) 57 D3
St Gallen (CH) 58 B2
St-Gallenkirch 58 B2
St-Galmier 30 B1
St-Gaudens 37 F1
St-Gaultier 25 E3
St-Genest-Malifaux 30 B1
St-Gengoux-le-National 26 C3
St-Geniez-d'Olt 29 E3
St-Genis-de-Stonge 28 B1
St-Genis-Laval 30 B1
St-Genix 30 C1
St-Geoire 30 C1
St Georgen (A) 56 C3
St Georgen am Langsee 70 B1
St Georgen (D) 54 C3
St-Georges 23 E4
St Georges Channel 8 A1
St-Georges-de-Didonne 28 A1
St-Georges-en-Couzan 29 F1
St-Germain-de-Calberte 29 F3
St-Germain-des-Fossés 26 A4
St-Germain-du-Bois 26 C3
St-Germain-du-Plain 26 C3
St-Germain-du-Teil 29 F3
St-Germain 19 F4
St-Germain-Laval 26 B4
St-Germain-Lembron 29 F1
St-Germain-les-Belles 29 D1
St-Germain-l'Herm 29 F1
St-Gertraud 58 C3
St-Gervais-d'Auvergne 26 A4
St-Gervais 27 E4
St-Gervais-sur-Mare 30 A4
St-Géry 29 D3
St-Gildas-de-Rhuys 22 C4
St-Gildas-des-Bois 23 D4
St-Gildas, Pte de 24 A2
St Gilgen 56 C3
St-Gilles-Croix-de-Vie 24 A3
St-Gilles 30 B4
St-Gingolph 27 E3
St-Girons 37 F2
St-Girons-Plage 28 A3
St Goar 51 E4
St Goarshausen 51 E4
St-Gobain 20 A3
St Govan's Head 8 B2
St-Guénolé 22 A3
St-Guilhem-le-Désert 29 F4
St-Haon-le-Châtel 26 B4
St Helens 6 B2
St-Hélier 18 B3
St-Hilaire-des-Loges 24 C3
St-Hilaire-de-Villefranche 28 B1
St-Hilaire-du-Harcouet 18 B4
St-Hilaire 32 B2
St-Hippolyte-du-Fort 29 F3
St-Hippolyte 27 E2
St-Honoré 26 B3
St-Hubert 20 C2
St-Imier 27 E2

St Ingbert 54 B2
St Ives (Cambs) 9 F1
St Ives (Cornwall) 8 A4
St-Jacques 23 D3
St-Jacut 18 A4
St Jakob 59 D2
St Jakob im Rosental 70 A1
St James 18 B4
St-Jean-Brévelay 22 C3
St-Jean-Cap-Ferrat 31 E3
St-Jean-d'Angély 24 C4
St-Jean-de-Bournay 30 C1
St-Jean-de-Daye 18 B3
St-Jean-de-Losne 26 C2
St-Jean-de-Luz 28 A4
St-Jean-de-Maurienne 31 D1
St-Jean-de-Monts 24 A3
St-Jean-du-Bruel 29 F3
St-Jean-du-Gard 30 A3
St-Jean-en-Royans 30 C2
St-Jean-Pied-de-Port 28 A4
St-Jeoire 27 D4
St Johann im Pongau 59 E1
St Johann in Tirol 59 E1
St John's Pt 13 E2
St-Jouin-de-Marnes 24 C3
St-Juéry 29 E3
St-Julien-Chapteuil 30 B2
St-Julien-de-Vouvantes 23 D4
St-Julien-du-Sault 26 A1
St-Julien-en-Genevois 27 D4
St-Julien 26 C3
St-Julien-l'Ars 25 D3
St-Junien 25 D4
St Just 8 A4
St-Just-en-Chaussée 19 F3
St-Just-en-Chevalet 26 B4
St-Justin 28 B3
St Keverne 8 B4
St Lambrecht 57 D4
St-Lary-Soulan 37 E2
St-Laurent (Calvados) 18 C3
St-Laurent-de-la-Salanque 32 B2
St-Laurent-du-Pont 30 C1
St-Laurent-en-Grandvaux 27 D3
St-Laurent-les-Bains 29 F2
St-Laurent-Médoc 28 B2
St-Laurent (Vendée) 24 C3
St-Laurent (Vienne) 28 C1
St-Léger 26 B3
St Leonhard (I) 59 D2
St Leonhard (Nieder österreich) 57 E3
St Leonhard (Tirol) 58 C2
St-Léonard-de-Noblat 25 E4
St Lorenzen 59 E2
St-Lô 18 C3
St-Louis 27 E2
St-Loup-Lamairé 24 C3
St-Loup-sur-Semouse 27 D1
St-Luc 27 F3
St-Lunaire 18 B4
St-Lys 29 D4
St-Macaire 28 B2
St Magnus B 3 F1
St-Maixent-l'Ecole 24 C3
St-Malo-de-la-Lande 18 B3
St-Malo 18 B4
St-Mamet-la-Salvetat 29 E2

St-Mandrier 31 D4
St-Marcellin 30 C1
St-Margarethen 48 A2
St Margaret's Hope 3 E1
St-Mars-la-Jaille 23 D4
St-Martin (Charente-Maritime) 24 B4
St-Martin-d'Auxigny 25 F2
St-Martin-de-Belleville 31 D1
St-Martin-de-Crau 30 B4
St-Martin-de-Londres 29 F4
St-Martin-de-Seignan 28 A4
St-Martin-de-Valamas 30 B2
St-Martin-en-Bresse 26 C3
St-Martin (Pyrénées-Orientales) 32 B2
St Martin's 8 A4
St-Martin-Vésubie 31 E3
St-Martory 37 F1
St Mary's 8 A4
St Märgen 54 C3
St-Mathieu 28 C1
St-Mathieu, Pte de 22 A3
St Maurice 27 E4
St Mawes 8 B4
St-Maximin-la-Ste Baume 31 D4
St-Médard-en-Jalles 28 B2
St-Méen 22 C3
St Michaelisdonn 48 A2
St Michael (Salzburg) 59 F2
St Michael's Mount 8 A4
St Michael (Steiermark) 57 E4
St-Michel-de-Maurienne 31 D1
St-Michel-en-Grève 22 B2
St-Michel-en-l'Herm 24 B4
St-Michel 20 B2
St-Michel-Mont-Mercure 24 C3
St-Mihiel 20 C3
St Monance 5 D2
St-Moritz 58 B3
St-Nazaire 24 A2
St-Nectaire 29 E1
St Neots 9 F1
St-Nicolas-d'Aliermont 19 E2
St-Nicolas-de-la-Grave 28 C3
St-Nicolas-de-Port 21 D4
St-Nicolas-du-Pélem 22 C3
St-Niklaas 50 B3
St Niklaus 27 F4
St-Oedenrode 16 C3
St-Omer 19 F1
St Oswald 59 F2
St-Pair 18 B4
St-Palais (Charente-Maritime) 28 A1
St-Palais (Pyrénées-Atlantiques) 28 A4
St-Pardoux-la-Rivière 28 C1
St Paul (A) 70 B1
St-Paul (Alpes-de-Haute-Provence) 31 D2
St-Paul (Alpes-Maritimes) 31 E3
St-Paul-Cap-de-Joux 29 D4
St-Paul-de-Fenouillet 32 B2
St-Paulien 29 F2
St-Paul-Trois-Châteaux 30 B3
St-Père-en-Retz 24 A2
St-Pé-de-Bigorre 37 E1
St-Pée 28 A4
St-Péray 30 B2

St Peter in der Au 57 D3
St-Peter-Ording 47 F2
St Peter Port 18 A3
St-Philbert 24 B3
St-Pierre Charente-Maritime) 24 B4
St-Pierre-d'Albigny 31 D1
St-Pierre-de-Chartreuse 30 C1
St-Pierre-de-Chignac 28 C2
St-Pierre-Eglise 18 B2
St-Pierre-le-Moûtier 26 A3
St-Pierre (Morbihan) 22 C4
St-Pierre-sur-Dives 18 C3
St-Pois 18 C4
St-Pol-de-Léon 22 B2
St-Pol-sur-Ternoise 19 F2
St-Pons-de-Thomières 32 B1
St-Porchaire 28 B1
St Pölten 57 E2
St-Pourçain 26 A4
St-Privat 29 E2
St-Quay-Portrieux 22 C2
St-Quentin 20 A2
St-Rambert 30 B1
St-Rambert-d'Albon 30 B1
St-Rambert-en-Bugey 26 C4
St-Raphaël 31 E4
St-Renan 22 A2
St-Rémy-de-Provence 30 B3
St-Rémy-sur-Durolle 26 B4
St-Riquier 19 E2
St-Romain-de-Colbosc 19 D3
St-Rome-de-Tarn 29 E3
St-Saëns 19 E3
St-Satur 26 A2
St-Saulge 26 A2
St-Sauveur-en-Puisaye 26 A2
St-Sauveur-Lendelin 18 B3
St-Sauveur-le-Vicomte 18 B3
St-Sauveur-sur-Tinée 31 E3
St-Savin (Gironde) 28 B2
St-Savinien 24 C4
St-Savin (Vienne) 25 D3
St-Seine-l'Abbaye 26 C2
St-Sernin-sur-Rance 29 E3
St-Sever (Calvados) 18 C4
St-Sever (Landes) 28 B4
St-Sulpice-les-Feuilles 25 E4
St-Symphorien-de-Lay 26 B4
St-Symphorien-d'Ozon 30 B1
St-Symphorien 28 B3
St-Symphorien-sur-Coise 30 B1
St-Trivier-de-Courtes 26 C3
St-Trivier-sur-Moignans 26 C4
St-Trojan 28 A1
St-Tropez 31 D4
St-Truiden 50 C3
St Ulrich 59 D3
St-Vaast-la-Hougue 18 B3
St Valentin an der Haide 58 C2
St Valentin 57 D3
St-Valery 19 E2
St-Valery-en-Caux 19 D2
St-Valier 30 B1
St-Vallier-de-Thiey 31 D3
St-Varent 24 C3
St-Vaury 25 E4

St Veit 70 A1
St-Véran 31 E2
St-Vincent 27 F4
St-Vincent-de-Tyrosse 28 A4
St Vith 51 D4
St-Vivien-de-Médoc 28 A1
St-Wandrille 19 D3
St Wendel 54 B1
St Wolfgang 56 C3
St-Yorre 26 A4
St-Yrieix-la-Perche 29 D1
Ste-Adresse 19 D3
Ste-Anne-d'Auray 22 C4
Ste-Baume, la 31 D4
Ste-Croix-du-Mont 28 B2
Ste-Croix 27 D3
Ste-Croix, Lac de 31 D3
Ste-Croix-Volvestre 37 F1
Ste-Enimie 29 F3
Ste-Foy-la-Grande 28 C2
Ste-Foy-l'Argentière 30 B1
Ste-Geneviève-sur-Argence 29 E2
Ste-Hélène 28 B2
Ste-Hermine 24 B3
Ste-Livrade 28 C3
Ste-Lucie-de-Tallano 33 F4
Ste-Marie-aux-Mines 21 E4
Ste-Maure-de-Touraine 25 D2
Ste-Menehould 20 C3
Ste-Mère-Eglise 18 B3
Ste-Odile, Mt 21 E4
Ste-Sévère 25 F3
Ste-Suzanne 23 E3
Ste-Tulle 30 C3
Saintes 28 B1
Stes-Maries-de-la-Mer 30 B4
Saissac 32 B1
Sakarya 115 F3
Sakskøbing 108 B4
Sakule 72 C2
Säkylä 107 D2
Sala 106 A3
Salacgrīva 110 C2
Sala Consilina 64 C4
Salada 41 E3
Salakovac 73 D3
Salamajärvi 102 C2
Salamajärvi L 103 D2
Salamanca 39 E1
Salamína 87 F1
Salamina, N 87 E1
Salándi 87 E2
Salangen 94 B3
Salar 43 F3
Salardú 37 F2
Salas 35 D1
Salaš 73 F3
Salas de los Infantes 36 A3
Salazar, R 37 D2
Salbohed 105 F3
Salbris 25 E2
Salcombe 8 C4
Saldaña 35 E3
Sale 60 A2
Sålekinna 100 D3
Salem 55 D4
Salemi 68 A3
Sälen 101 D4
Salen (Highland) 2 B4
Salen (Mull) 4 B1
Salernes 31 D4
Salerno 64 B4
Salerno, Golfo di 64 B4
Salers 29 E2
Salève, Mt 27 D4
Salgótarján 112 B3
Salgueiro do Campo 38 C2
Sali 74 C1
Salice Terme 60 A2
Salies-de-Béarn 28 A4

Salies-du-Salat 37 F1
Salignac-Eyvigues 29 D2
Salihli 115 F4
Salime, Emb de 34 C1
Salina, I 69 D2
Salinas (Andalucía) 43 F3
Salinas (Asturias) 35 D1
Salinas, C 45 F3
Salindres 30 B3
Sälinkää 107 F2
Salins 27 D3
Salisbury 9 E3
Salla 99 E2
Sallanches 27 E4
Sallent 32 A4
Sallent-de-Gállego 37 D2
Salles 32 A1
Salles-Curan 29 E3
Salling 108 A2
Salling Sund 108 A2
Salmerón 40 C2
Salmoral 39 F1
Salò 60 B1
Salo 107 E2
Salobreña 44 A4
Salona 75 D1
Salon-de-Provence 30 C4
Salonta 112 C4
Salorino 38 C3
Salor, R 39 D3
Salou 37 F4
Salou, C de 37 F4
Salpausselkä 107 F2
Salsbruket 97 D4
Salses-le-Château 32 B2
Salso 68 C3
Salsomaggiore Terme 60 B2
Salsta 106 B3
Saltash 8 C4
Saltburn-by-the-Sea 5 F4
Saltcoats 4 C2
Saltee Is 15 D4
Saltfjellet 97 E2
Saltfjorden 97 E2
Salto 34 B4
Saltoluokta 94 B4
Saltvik 106 C3
Saluggia 31 F1
Saluzzo 31 E2
Salvacañete 41 D3
Salvagnac 29 D3
Salvan 27 E4
Salvaterra de Magos 38 A3
Salvatierra-Agurain 36 B2
Salvatierra de los Barros 42 C1
Salvatierra de Miño 34 A3
Salvetat-Peyralès, la 29 E3
Salvetat-sur-Agout, la 32 B1
Salviac 29 D2
Sælvig 108 B3
Salza 57 E3
Salzach 56 B3
Salzburg 56 C3
Salzburg (Prov) 59 E1
Salzgitter-Bad 52 B1
Salzgitter-Lebenstedt 52 B1
Salzhausen 48 B3
Salzkammergut 56 C3
Salzkotten 17 F3
Salzwedel 48 C4
Šamac Slavonski 71 F3
Sama de Langreo 35 D1
Samarina 78 C2
Samatan 28 C4
Sambatikí 87 E3
Sambiase 67 E3
Samboal 40 A1
Sambor 112 C3
Sambre 50 B4
Sambuca di Sicilia 68 B3
Sameiro, Mte 34 A4
Samer 19 E1
Samedan 58 B3
Sámi 82 B4

Samikó 86 B2
Sammatti 107 E2
Sammichele 65 E3
Samnanger 104 A2
Samobor 70 C2
Samodreža 77 D2
Samoëns 27 E4
Samokov (BG) 115 D3
Samokov (YU) 77 D2
Samora Correia 38 A4
Samos 34 C2
Samoš 73 D2
Sámos 89 F1
Sámos, N 89 E1
Samothráki 81 E3
Samothráki, N 81 E3
Samper de Calanda 37 D4
Sampeyre 31 E2
Samsø 108 B3
Samsø Bælt 108 B3
Samtens 49 D1
Samugheo 66 B3
San 112 C2
San Adrián 36 C2
San Adrián, C de 34 A1
San Agata de Goti 64 B3
San Agata di Militello 69 D2
San Agustín 40 B2
San Amaro 34 B2
San Andrea Frius 66 B3
San Andrés del Rabanedo 35 D2
San Antioco, I di 66 A4
San Antioco 66 B4
San Antonio Abad 45 D3
San Antonio 66 B1
San Antonio, C de 45 F1
San Bartolomé de las Abiertas 39 F3
San Bartolomé de la Torre 42 C2
San Bartolomeo in Galdo 64 B3
San Benedetto del Tronto 61 F4
San Benedetto in Alpe 61 D3
San Benedetto Po 60 C2
San Bernardino 58 B3
San Bernardino, Psodel 58 B3
San Biagio Platani 68 B3
San Bonifacio 60 C1
San Candido 59 E2
San Carlos de la Ràpita 41 F2
San Carlos del Valle 40 B4
San Casciano in Val di Pesa 60 C4
San Cataldo (Puglia) 65 F4
San Cataldo (Sicilia) 68 C3
San Cipirello 68 B3
San Clemente, Emb de 44 B2
San Clemente 40 C4
San Colombano al Lambro 60 B2
San Cosme 34 C1
San Cristóbal 42 C1
San Cristóbal de Entreviñas 35 D3
San Cristóbal de la Polantera 35 D3
San Cristóbal de la Vega 39 F1
San Damiano d'Asti 31 F2
San Daniele del Friuli 59 E3
San Daniele Po 60 B2
San Demetrio Corone 67 E2
San Donaci 65 F4
San Donà di Piave 59 E4
San Emiliano 35 D2
San Esteban de Gormaz 36 A3
San Esteban del Molar 35 D3

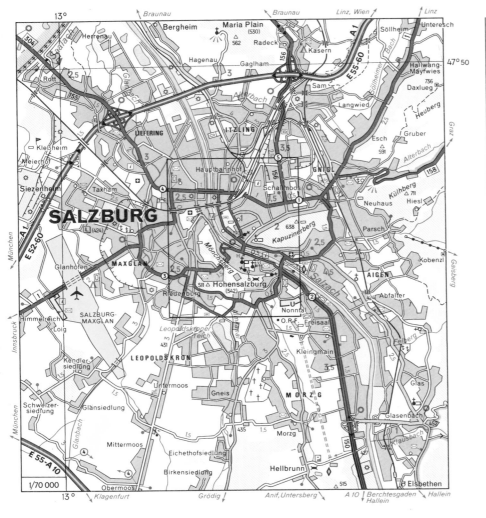

SALZBURG

1/70 000

San Esteban del
Valle 39 F2
San Esteban de
Pravia 35 D1
San Fele 64 C4
San Felice a
Cancello 64 B3
San Felice Circeo 63 F3
San Felices de Los
Gallegos 39 D1
San Felice sul
Panaro 60 C2
San Felipe 40 C2
San Feliu de
Guíxols 32 B4
San Ferdinando di
Puglia 64 C3
San Ferdinando di
Puglia 64 C3
San Fernando 43 D4
San Francisco
Javier 45 D4
San Fratello 69 D2
San Gavino
Monreale 66 B3
San Gemini 63 E1
San Giacomo 59 D2
San Gimignano 60 C4
San Ginesio 61 F4
San Giorgio del
Sannio 64 B3
San Giorgio di
Nogaro 59 F3
San Giorgio Ionico 65 E4
San Giorgio 31 E1
San Giorgio
Piacentino 60 B2
San Giovanni a Piro 67 D2
San Giovanni di
Sinis 66 A3
San Giovanni in
Fiore 67 F2

San Giovanni in
Persiceto 60 C2
San Giovanni
Lupatoto 60 C1
San Giovanni
Rotondo 64 C2
San Giovanni
Suergiu 66 B4
San Giovanni
Valdarno 61 D4
San Giuliano
Terme 60 C4
San Giustino 61 D4
San Glorio, Pto de 35 E2
San Gottardo, Pso
del 58 A3
San Ildefonso o la
Granja 40 A1
San Isidro 44 C3
San Isidro, Pto de 35 E2
San Javier 45 D2
San José
(Andalucía) 44 C4
San José (Ibiza) 45 D4
San Juan Bautista 45 D3
San Juan de
Alicante 45 E1
San Juan de
Aznalfarache 43 D2
San Juan de la
Peña 37 D2
San Juan del Olmo 39 F2
San Juan de los
Terreros 44 C3
San Juan del
Puerto 42 C2
San Juan, Emb de 40 A2
San Just Desvern 32 A4
San Just, Sa de 41 E2
San Lazzaro di
Savena 61 D2
San Leo 61 E3

San Leonardo de
Yagüe 36 A3
San Leonardo 59 D2
San Leonardo, Pso 64 A2
San Lorenzo 36 B2
San Lorenzo 63 D1
San Lorenzo de
Calatrava 44 A1
San Lorenzo de la
Parrilla 40 C3
San Lucido 67 E3
San Luis de
Sabanillas 43 E4
San Luis 45 F2
San Marcello 61 F4
San Marcello
Pistoiese 60 C3
San Marco
Argentano 67 E2
San Marco dei
Cavoti 64 B3
San Marco in
Lamis 64 C2
San Marino 61 E3
San Martino di
Castrozza 59 D3
San Martín de
Castañeda 34 C3
San Martín de la
Vega 40 B2
San Martín de
Mondoñedo 34 C1
San Martín de
Montalbán 39 F3
San Martín de
Valdeiglesias 40 A2
San Mateo 41 F2
San Mateo de
Gállego 37 D3
San Mauro Forte 65 D4
San Michele all'
Adige 59 D3

San Miguel 45 D3
San Miguel de
Escalada 35 E3
San Miguel del
Arroyo 35 E4
San Miguel de
Salinas 45 D2
San Millán 36 A2
San Millán de la
Cogolla 36 B2
San Millán de Lara 36 A3
San Miniato 60 C4
San Nicolás del
Puerto 43 E2
San Nicolás de
Tolentino 42 B4
San Nicolò
Ferrarese 61 D2
San Nicolò Gerrei 66 B3
San Ninfa 68 B3
San Pancrazio
Salentino 65 F4
San Pedro 44 C1
San Pedro de
Alcántara 43 E4
San Pedro del
Arroyo 39 F1
San Pedro de
Latarce 35 E4
San Pedro del
Pinatar 45 D2
San Pedro de
Mérida 39 D4
San Pedro
Manrique 36 B3
San Pedro, Sa de 39 D3
San Pellegrino,
Pso 59 D3
San Pellegrino
Terme 58 B4
San Piero a Sieve 61 D3
San Pietro, I di 66 A4

San Pietro in
Casale 60 C2
San Pietro
Vernotico 65 F4
San Polo d'Enza 60 C2
San Quirico d'Orcia 63 D1
San Rafael de
Navallana, Emb
de 43 F2
San Rafael 40 A2
San Remo 31 F3
San Roque
(Andalucía) 43 E4
San Roque (Galicia) 34 A1
San Rufo 64 C4
San Salvador de
Cantamuda 35 F2
San Salvador 45 F3
San Salvo 64 B2
San Sebastiano
Curone 60 A2
San Sebastián,
Emb de 34 C3
San Sebastián 42 A4
San Severino
Marche 61 F4
San Severo 64 C2
San Silvestre de
Guzmán 42 C2
San Sperate 66 B4
San Stefano di
Camastra 68 C3
San Stefano
Quisquina 68 B3
San Telmo 42 C2
San Valentino alla
Muta 58 C2
San Vicente de
Alcántara 38 C3
San Vicente de la
Barquera 35 F1
San Vicente de la
Cabeza 35 D3
San Vicente del
Raspeig 45 E1
San Vicenzo 62 C1
San Vigilio di
Marebbe 59 D2
San Vigilio, Pso di 60 C1
San Vitero 34 C4
San Vito al
Tagliamento 59 E3
San Vito Chietino 64 A2
San Vito dei
Normanni 65 E3
San Vito di C. 59 E3
San Vito 66 C4
San Vito lo Capo 68 A3
San Vito sullo Ionio 67 F3
San Vittore del
Lazio 64 A3
Sana 71 D4
Saná 80 A3
Sanabria, L de 34 C3
Sanary 30 C4
Sancergues 26 A2
Sancerre 26 A2
Sanchidrián 39 F1
Sancho, Emb de 42 C2
Sanclêr 8 C2
Sancoins 26 A3
Sancti Petri 43 D4
Sancti Spíritus 39 D1
Sand (Hedmark) 105 D2
Sand (Rogaland) 104 A3
Sandane 100 A3
Sandanski 115 D3
Sandarne 101 F4
Sandau 48 C4
Sanday 3 E1
Sandbach 6 C3
Sanddøla 97 D4
Sande (D) 47 E3
Sande (Møre og
Romsdal) 100 A2
Sande (P) 34 A4
Sande (Vestfold) 104 C3
Sandefjord 104 C3
Sandeid 104 A3
Sandfjellet 95 E1
Sandgerði 96 A2
Sand in Taufers 59 D2
Sandnes 104 A3
Sandness 3 F1

Sandnessjøen 97 D3
Sando 39 E1
Sandoméri 86 B1
Sandomierz 112 C2
Sandown 9 E3
Sandoy 96 A4
Sandøy 100 A2
Sandrigo 59 D4
Sandringham
House 7 E3
Sandstad 100 C1
Sandur 96 A4
Sandviken 106 B2
Sandvikvåg 104 A3
Sandwich 11 D3
Sandy 9 F1
Sånfjället 101 E3
Sangarcia 40 A1
Sangerhausen 52 C2
Sangis 98 C3
Sangonera, R 45 D2
Sangro 64 A2
Sangüesa 36 C2
Sanguinaires, Iles 33 E4
Sanguinet 28 A3
Saní 80 A4
Sanitz 48 C2
Sankt Olof 109 D3
Sanlúcar de
Barrameda 43 D3
Sanlúcar de
Guadiana 42 B2
Sanlúcar la Mayor 43 D2
Sanluri 66 B3
Sannainen 107 F2
Sannazzaro 60 A2
Sannicandro di
Bari 65 D3
Sannicandro
Garganico 64 C2
Sanok 112 C3
Sanquhar 4 C3
Sansepolcro 61 D4
Sanski Most 71 D3
Sant' Agata di
Puglia 64 C3
Sant Agusti de
Llucanès 32 A3
Sant Andreu de
Llavaneres 32 B4
Sant' Angelo de'
Lombardi 64 C3
Sant' Angelo in
Vado 61 E4
Sant' Angelo
Lodigiano 60 A2
Sant Antoni de C. 32 B3
Sant Antoni, Emb
de 37 F3
Sant' Apollinare in
Classe 61 D3
Sant' Arcangelo di
Romagna 61 E3
Sant Boi de
Llucanès 32 A3
Sant Celoni 32 B4
Sant Cugat 32 A4
Sant' Elia a Pianisi 64 B2
Sant' Elpidio a
Mare 61 F4
Sant Esteve d'en
Bas 32 B3
Sant'Eufemia,
Golfodi 67 E3
Sant'Eufemia
Lamezia 67 E3
Sant Gervàs 37 F3
Sant Hilari Sacalm 32 B3
Sant Hipòlit de
Voltregà 32 A3
Sant Joan de les
Abadesses 32 B3
Sant Julià de Lòria 32 A3
Sant Llorenc de
Morunys 32 A3
Sant'Onofrio 67 E3
Sant Pau de
Seguries 32 B3
Sant Pere de Roda 32 C3
Sant Pol de Mar 32 B4
Sant Ponç, Emb
de 32 A3
Sant Quirze de
Besora 32 B3

Sant Quirze Safaja 32 A4
Sant Ramon 37 F3
Sant Sadurní
d'Anoia 32 A4
Santa Amalia 39 D4
Santa Ana 40 C4
Santa Anna, Emb
de 37 E3
Santa Bàrbara
(Catalunya) 41 F2
Santa Bàrbara
(Andalucía) 42 C2
Santa Bàrbara *Mt* 44 B3
Santa Catarina 42 B3
Santa Caterina
Pittinuri 66 A3
Santa Caterina
Valfurva 58 C3
Santa Caterina
Villarmosa 68 C3
Santa Cesarea
Terme 65 F4
Santa Clara-a-
Velha 42 A2
Santa Clara, Bgem
de 42 A2
Santa Coloma de
Farners 32 B3
Santa Coloma de
Queralt 37 F4
Santa Colombo de
Somoza 35 D3
Santa Comba Dão 38 B2
Santa Comba de
Rossas 34 C4
Santa Comba 34 A1
Santa Cristina de
Lena 35 D2
Santa Croce di
Magliano 64 B2
Santa Cruz de
Campezo 36 B2
Santa Cruz de la
Palma 42 A4
Santa Cruz de la
Sierra 39 E3
Santa Cruz de la
Zarza 40 B3
Santa Cruz del
Retamar 40 A2
Santa Cruz de
Moya 41 D3
Santa Cruz de
Mudela 44 A1
Santa Cruz de
Tenerife 42 B4
Santa Cruz 36 C4
Santa Elena 44 A1
Santa Eufemia 43 E1
Santa Eugenia 34 A2
Santa Eulalia del
Río 45 D3
Santa Eulalia de
Oscos 34 C1
Santa Eulalia 41 D2
Santa Eulàlia 38 C4
Santa Fe 44 A3
Santa Fé 32 B4
Santa Fiora 63 D1
Santa Galdana,
Cala 45 F2
Santa Gertrude 58 C3
Santa Giusta 66 B3
Santa Inés, Pto de 36 B3
Santa Liestra y San
Quilez 37 E3
Santa Lucia d. Mela 69 D2
Santa Luz 34 C4
Santa Luzia 42 A2
Santa Magdalena
de Pulpis 41 F2
Santa Margarida
do Sádão 42 B1
Santa Margarida i
Els Monjos 32 A4
Santa Margarita 45 F2
Santa Margherita 66 B4
Santa Margherita
di Belice 68 B3
Santa Margherita
Ligure 60 A3
Santa Maria Capua
Vetere 64 B3
Santa Maria, C de 42 B3

Santa Maria da Feira **38** B1
Santa Maria d'Angeli **63** E1
Santa Maria del Campo Rus **40** C3
Santa Maria della Versa **60** A2
Santa Maria di Leuca,C **65** F4
Santa Maria la Real de Nieva **40** A1
Santa Maria la Real de Oseira **34** B2
Santa Maria Maggiore **58** A3
Santa Marina **35** E2
Santa Marina del Rey **35** D3
Santa Marinella **63** D2
Santa María de Huerta **36** B4
Santa María del Campo **35** F3
Santa María del Páramo **35** D3
Santa María de Nieva **44** C3
Santa María de Valverde **35** D3
Santa-Maria-Siché **33** F4
Santa Marta **39** D4
Santa Marta de Penaguião **34** B4
Santa Marta de Tormes **39** E1
Santa Olalla del Cala **43** D2
Santa Olalla **39** F3
Santa Pau **32** B3
Santa Pola **45** E2
Santa Ponsa **45** E3
Santa Sofia **61** D3
Santa Sofia d'Epiro **67** E2
Santa Susanna **32** B4
Santa Tecla **34** A3
Santa Teresa di Riva **69** D2
Santa Teresa, Emb de **39** E2
Santa Teresa Gallura **66** B1
Santaella **43** E2
Santana (Estremadura) **38** A4
Santana (Madeira) **42** A3
Santana de Serra **42** A2
Santander **35** F1
Santanyí **45** F3
Santarém **38** B3
Santas Martas **35** E3
Santeramo in Colle **65** D3
Santes Creus **37** F4
Santesteban **36** C1
Santhià **31** F1
Santiago de Alcántara **38** C3
Santiago de Compostela **34** A2
Santiago de la Espada **44** B2
Santiago de la Ribera **45** D2
Santiago do Cacém **42** A1
Santiago do Escoural **38** B4
Santibáñez de Béjar **39** E2
Santibáñez de la Peña **35** E2
Santibáñez de la Sierra **39** E2
Santibáñez de Vidriales **35** D3
Santillana del Mar **35** F1
Santiponce **43** D2
Säntis **58** B2
Santisteban del Puerto **44** B1
Santo Domingo de la Calzada **36** B2
Santo Domingo de Silos **36** A3
Santo Domingo, Ptode **43** D1
Santo Estêvão (Beira Baixa) **38** C2
Santo Estêvão (Estremadura) **38** A4
Santo Estêvão, Rib de **38** A4
Santo Pedro da Torre **34** A3
Santo Severa **63** D2
Santo Stefano di Cadore **59** E2
Santo Stefano d'Aveto **60** B2
Santo Stino di Livenza **59** E4
Santo Tirso **34** A4
Santo Tomé **44** B2
Santok **49** F3
Santolea, Emb de **41** E2
Santomera, Emb de **45** D2
Santoña **36** A1
Santo-Pietro-di-Tenda **33** F2
Santorini, N **91** E1
Santuario de San Ignacio de Loyola **36** B1
Santuario d'Oropa **27** F4
Santu Lussurgiu **66** B3
Santurtzi **36** B1
Sanxenxo **34** A2
Sanza **67** D1
São Bartolomeu de Messines **42** A2
São Brás de Alportel **42** B3
São Cristóvão **38** B4
São Domingos **42** A1
São Gregório **34** B3
São Jacinto **38** B1
São João da Pesqueira **34** B4
São João de Madeira **38** B1
São João de Tarouca **38** C1
São João dos Caldeireiros **42** B2
São José da Lamarosa **38** B3
São Leonardo **42** C1
São Mamede, Sa de **38** C3
São Manços **42** B1
São Marcos da Serra **42** A2
São Marcos do Campo **42** B1
São Martinho das Amoreiras **42** A2
São Martinho do Porto **38** A3
São Matias **42** B1
São Miguel de Machede **38** B4
São Pedro de Acor **38** C2
São Pedro de Moel **38** A2
São Pedro do Sul **38** C1
São Romão **38** C2
São Teotónio **42** A2
São Vicente, C de **42** A2
São Vicente da Beira **38** C2
Saône **26** C3
Saône-et-Loire **26** B3
Saorge **31** E3
Sapanca **115** F3
Sapataria **38** A3
Sápes **81** E2
Sapiéndza, N **86** C4
Sa Pobla **45** F2
Sappada **59** E2
Sappee **107** E2
Sapri **67** D1
Säräisniemi **99** E4
Sarajärvi **99** E3
Sarajevo **76** A1
Sarakiní **79** E2
Sarakíniko **84** B3
Saramon **28** C4
Sarandáporo **79** E4
Sarandáporos **78** C4
Sarandë **114** C4
Saraváli **86** C1
Saray **115** E3
Sarayköy **115** F4
Šarbanovac **73** E3
Sarbinowo (Gorzów Wlkp) **49** F3
Sarbinowo (Koszalin) **49** F1
Sárbogárd **112** B4
Sarca **58** C3
Sardara **66** B3
Sardegna **66** A2
Sardínia **82** C3
Sardoal **38** B3
Sardona, Piz **58** B2
Sarek **98** A1
Šarengrad **72** B2
Sarentino **59** D2
Särfjället **101** D2
Sargans **58** B2
Sariá, N **93** D2
Sari-d'Orcino **33** F3
Sarine **27** E3
Sariñena **37** E3
Sark **18** A3
Särkisalmi **103** F3
Särkisalo **107** D3
Sarlat-la-Canéda **29** D2
Sarmitunturi **95** F3
Särna **101** D3
Sarnano **61** F4
Sarnen **27** F2
Sarnico **60** B1
Sarno **64** B4
Sarnthein **59** D2
Sarny **113** D2
Sarö **108** C1
Sarón **35** F2
Sarone **59** E3
Saronída **87** F2
Saronikós Kólpos **87** F1
Saronno **60** A1
Sárospatak **112** C3
Sar Planina **77** D3
Sarpsborg **105** D3
Sarracín **35** F3
Sarral **37** F4
Sarralbe **21** E3
Sarrans, Bge de **29** E2
Sarre **21** E3
Sarrebourg **21** E4
Sarreguemines **21** E3
Sarre-Union **21** E3
Sarriá **34** B2
Sarrión **41** E3
Sarroch **66** B4
Sarsina **61** D3
Sars-Poteries **20** B2
Sarstedt **52** B1
Sarteano **63** D1
Sartène **33** F4
Sarthe **23** E4
Sarthe (Dépt) **23** F3
Sárti **80** B4
Sartilly **18** B4
Sarule **66** B2
Sárvár **112** A4
Sarvsjö **101** D2
Sarzana **60** B3
Sarzeau **22** C4
Sarzedas **38** C2
Sasa **77** F2
Sassari **66** A2
Sassello **60** A3
Sassenage **30** C1
Sassenberg **17** F3
Sassenheim **16** B2
Sassetta **62** C1
Saßnitz **49** D1
Sasso **63** E2
Sassoferrato **61** E4
Sassoleone **61** D3
Sasso Marconi **60** C3
Sassuolo **60** C2
Sástago **37** D4
Sasyk, Ozero **113** E4
Sátão **38** C1
Säter **105** F3
Satillieu **30** B1
Satolas **30** C1
Šator **75** D1
Sátoraljaújhely **112** C3
Šatorina **70** B4
Satov **57** E1
Satow **48** C2
Sátres **81** D2
Satrup **48** A1
Sattel **58** A2
Sattledt **57** D3
Satu Mare **112** C3
Saualpe **70** B1
Sauca **36** B4
Saucelle, Emb de **39** D1
Sauda **104** A3
Sauðárkrókur **96** B1
Sau, Emb de **32** B3
Sauerlach **56** A3
Sauerland **17** F4
Saugues **29** F2
Saujon **28** B1
Saukkovaara **99** E4
Sauland **104** C3
Sauldre **26** A2
Saulgau **55** D3
Saulieu **26** B2
Sault **30** C3
Saulx **27** D1
Saulxures **27** E1
Saumur **24** C2
Saundersfoot **8** B2
Sauris **59** E3
Saut du Doubs **27** E2
Sautet, Bge du **30** C2
Sautusjärvi **94** C4
Sauve **30** B3
Sauveterre-de-Béarn **28** A4
Sauveterre-de-Guyenne **28** B2
Sauveterre-de-Rouergue **29** E3
Sauvo **107** D2
Sauxillanges **29** F1
Sauze d'Oulx **31** E2
Sauze, le **31** D2
Sauze-Vaussais **24** C4
Sauzon **22** B4
Sava (I) **65** E4
Sava (YU) **71** E3
Savália **86** B1
Sävar **102** B1
Savelli **67** F2
Savenay **23** D4
Saverdun **32** A1
Saverne **21** E4
Savigliano **31** E2
Savignac-les-Eglises **28** C1
Savignano Irpino **64** C3
Savignano sul Rubicone **61** E3
Savigny-sur-Braye **23** F4
Saviñán **36** C4
Savine, Col de la **27** D3
Savines-le-Lac **31** D2
Savinja **70** B1
Savino Selo **72** B2
Savitaipale **103** E4
Sävja **106** B3
Šavnik **76** B2
Savognin **58** B3
Savona **60** A3
Savonlinna **103** E3
Savonranta **103** F3
Sævråsvåg **104** A2
Sävsjö **109** D2
Savudrija **70** A3
Savukoski **95** F4
Sawbridgeworth **10** C2
Sawel Mt **13** D1
Sax **45** D1
Saxmundham **11** E1
Saxnäs **97** E4
Sayatón **40** B2
Säynätsalo **103** D3
Säyneinen **103** E2
Sazadón, Pto de **35** D3
Sázava **112** A3
Scaër **22** B3
Scafa **64** A2
Scafati **64** B4
Scafell Pikes **5** D4
Scala di Santa Regina **33** F3
Scalasaig **4** B2
Scalby **7** D1
Scalea **67** E2
Scalloway **3** F2
Scalpay **2** B3
Scandiano **60** C2
Scanno **64** A2
Scansano **63** D1
Scanzano **65** D4
Scapa Flow **3** D1
Scarba **4** B1
Scarborough **7** D1
Scardovari **61** E2
Scarinish **2** A4
Scarpe **20** A1
Scarriff **12** B4
Šćedro **75** E2
Šćepan Polje **76** A1
Scey-sur-Saône **27** D2
Schaalsee **48** B2
Schachendorf **57** F4
Schafberg **56** C3
Schaffhausen **58** A1
Schafstädt **52** C2
Schagen **16** C2
Schaprode **49** D1
Scharbeutz **48** B2
Schärding **56** C2
Scharhörn **47** F2
Scharmützelsee **49** E4
Scharnitz **59** D1
Schauinsland Feldberg **54** C4
Scheeßel **48** A3
Scheggia **61** E4
Scheibbs **57** E3
Scheifling **57** D4
Scheinfeld **55** E1
Schelde **50** B3
Schenefeld (Hamburg) **48** A3
Schenefeld (Itzehoe) **48** A2
Scherfede **52** A2
Schermbeck **17** E3
Scheßlitz **52** C4
Scheveningen **16** B3
Schia **60** B3
Schiedam **16** B3
Schieder-Schwalenberg **52** A1
Schiehallion **4** C1
Schierling **56** B2
Schiermonnikoog **47** D3
Schiermonnikoog I **47** D3
Schiers **58** B2
Schifferstadt **54** C2
Schildau **53** D2
Schilpario **58** C4
Schiltach **54** C3
Schio **59** D4
Schirmeck **21** E4
Schirnding **53** D4
Schkeuditz **53** D2
Schkölen **53** D3
Schladming **59** F1
Schlagsdorf **48** B2
Schlanders **58** C3
Schlangenbad **51** F4
Schleching **56** B3
Schlei **48** A1
Schleiden **51** D4
Schleiz **53** D3
Schleswig **48** A1
Schleswig-Holstein **48** A1
Schleusingen **52** C3
Schlieben **53** E1
Schliersee **56** B4
Schlitz **52** B3
Schlotheim **52** B2
Schluchsee **54** C4
Schlucht, Col de la **27** E1
Schlüchtern **52** B4
Schluderbach **59** E2
Schluderns **58** C3
Schlüsselfeld **55** E1
Schlutup **48** B2
Schmalkalden **52** B3
Schmallenberg **17** F4
Schmidmühlen **55** F1
Schmilka **53** F2
Schmölln (Leipzig) **53** D3
Schmölln (Neubrandenburg) **49** E3
Schnackenburg **48** C3
Schnaittenbach **55** F1
Schneeberg (A) **57** E3
Schneeberg (D) **53** D4
Schneeberg (DDR) **53** D3
Schneverdingen **48** A3
Schoberpaß **57** D4
Schöckl **57** E4
Schönau **54** C4
Schönberg (A) **59** D2
Schönberg (Bayern) **56** C2
Schönberg (Karl-Marx-Stadt) **53** D4
Schönberg (Rostock) **48** B2
Schönberg (Schleswig-Holstein) **48** B1
Schönbrunn **57** F2
Schönebeck **52** C1
Schöneck **53** D3
Schönecken **51** D4
Schönefeld **49** E4
Schönewalde **53** E1
Schongau **55** F4
Schöningen **52** C1
Schönmünzach **54** C3
Schönsee **56** B1
Schönthal **56** B1
Schönwald **54** C3
Schönwalde **48** B2
Schoonhoven **16** C3
Schopfheim **54** C4
Schöppenstedt **52** B1
Schoppernau **58** B2
Schorndorf **55** D2
Schortens **47** E3
Schotten **52** A4
Schouwen Duiveland **16** B3
Schramberg **54** C3
Schrems **57** D2
Schrobenhausen **55** F2
Schröcken **58** B2
Schrozberg **55** E1
Schruns **58** B2
Schuls **58** C2
Schüttorf **17** E2
Schwaan **48** C2
Schwabach **55** E1
Schwäbisch Gmünd **55** D2
Schwäbisch Hall **55** D2
Schwabmünchen **55** E3
Schwaigern **55** D2
Schwalmstadt-Treysa **52** A3
Schwalmstadt-Ziegenhain **52** A3
Schwandorf **56** B1
Schwanebeck **52** C1
Schwanenstadt **56** C3
Schwanewede **47** F3
Schwarmstedt **48** A4
Schwarza (A) **57** E3
Schwarza (DDR) **52** C3
Schwarzach **59** E1
Schwarze Elster **53** E1
Schwarzenbach **53** D4
Schwarzenbek **48** B3
Schwarzenberg **53** E3
Schwarzenburg **27** E3
Schwarzenfeld **56** B1
Schwarzheide **53** E2
Schwarzsee **27** E3
Schwarzwald **54** C3
Schwaz **59** D1
Schwechat **57** F2
Schwedt **49** E3
Schweich **54** A1
Schweinfurt **52** B4
Schweinitz **53** E1
Schwelm **17** E4
Schwendi **55** E3
Schwenningen **54** C3
Schwerin **48** C2
Schweriner See **48** C2
Schwerte **17** E3
Schwetzingen **54** C1
Schwielochsee **53** F1
Schwyz **58** A2
Sciacca **68** B3
Scicli **69** D4
Scilla **67** E4
Scilly, Is of **8** A4
Scole **11** D1
Sconser **2** B3
Scopello **58** A4
Scordia **69** D3
Scorff **22** B3
Ščors **113** E1
Scorzè **59** E4
Scotch Corner **6** C1
Scotland **2** C4
Scourie **2** C2
Scrabster **3** D2
Scridain, L **4** B1
Scrivia **60** A2
Ščučin **110** C4
Scunthorpe **7** D2
Scuol **58** C2
Seaford **10** C3
Seaham **5** E4
Seaton **9** D3
Seaton Delaval **5** E3
Sebečevo **76** C1
Sebeş **114** C1
Sebež **111** D3
Sebnitz **53** F2
Sečanj **73** D2
Secchia **60** C2
Seckau **57** D4
Seclin **19** F1
Secondigny **24** C3
Sedan **20** C2
Sedano **35** F2
Seda, Rib de **38** C3
Sedbergh **6** C1
Séderon **30** C3
Sedgefield **5** E4
Sedičany **53** F4
Sedico **59** E3
Sedilo **66** B2
Sedini **66** B2
Sedlare **77** D2
Sedlec-Prčice **53** F4
Sée **18** C4
Seebenau **48** B4
Seebergsattel **70** B1
Seeboden **59** F2
Seebruck **56** B3
Seefeld **58** C1
Seehaus **56** C3
Seehausen (Magdeburg) **52** C1
Seehausen (Stendal) **48** C3
Seeheim **54** C1
Seelisberg **58** A2
Seelow **49** E4
Sées **19** D4
Seesen **52** B1
Seevetal **48** A3
Seewalchen **56** C3
Seewiesen **57** E3
Sefkerin **72** C2
Segesta **68** A3
Segl **58** B3
Segni **63** F3
Segonzac **28** B1
Segorbe **41** E3
Segovia **40** A1
Segré **23** E4
Segre **37** E3
Segre, R **32** A3
Segura **38** C3
Segura de la Sierra **44** B1
Segura de León **43** D1
Segura de los Baños **41** D1
Segura, R **45** D2
Segura, Sa de **44** B2
Sehnde **52** B1
Seia **38** C2
Seiches **23** E4
Seifhennersdorf **53** F2
Seignelay **26** B1
Seil **4** B1
Seiland **95** D1
Seilandsjøkelen **95** D1
Seilhac **29** D1
Seille (Meurthe-et-Moselle) **21** D4
Seille (Saône-et-Loire) **26** C3
Seinäjoki **102** C2
Seine **19** E3
Seine-et-Marne **19** F4
Seine-Maritime **19** D3

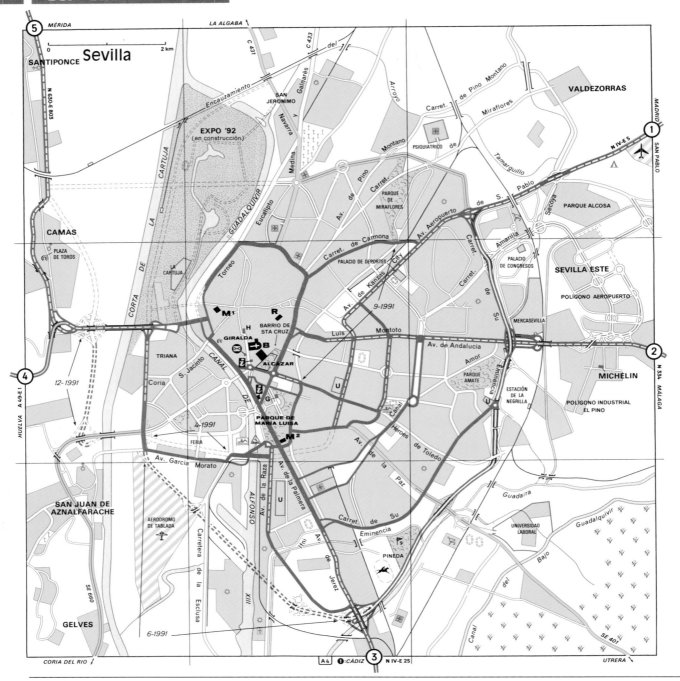

| | | |
|---|---|---|
| Sestu | 66 | B4 |
| Sesvete | 70 | C2 |
| Séta | 84 | B4 |
| Setcases | 32 | B3 |
| Sète | 30 | A4 |
| Setenil | 43 | E3 |
| Setermoen | 94 | B3 |
| Setesdalen | 104 | B3 |
| Setesdalsheiene | 104 | B3 |
| Settebagni | 63 | E2 |
| Settimo Torinese | 31 | E1 |
| Settle | 6 | C1 |
| Settons, les | 26 | B2 |
| Setúbal | 38 | A4 |
| Seudre | 28 | B1 |
| Seui | 66 | B3 |
| Seulo | 66 | B3 |
| Seurre | 26 | C2 |
| Sevastianá | 79 | E3 |
| Sevenoaks | 10 | C3 |
| Sévérac-le-Château | 29 | F3 |
| Sever do Vouga | 38 | B1 |
| Severn Bridge | 9 | D2 |
| Severn, Mouth of the | 9 | D2 |
| Severn,R | 9 | D2 |
| Sever, R | 38 | C3 |
| Seveso | 60 | A1 |
| Sevettijärvi | 95 | F2 |
| Sevilla | 43 | D2 |
| Sevilleja de la Jara | 39 | F3 |
| Sevlievo | 115 | D2 |
| Sevnica | 70 | C2 |
| Sevojno | 72 | C4 |
| Sèvre Nantaise | 24 | C3 |
| Sèvre Niortaise | 24 | C4 |
| Sévrier | 27 | D4 |
| Sevsk | 111 | F4 |
| Sexten | 59 | E2 |
| Seyches | 28 | C2 |
| Seyda | 53 | D1 |
| Seyðisfjörður | 96 | C2 |
| Seyne | 31 | D3 |
| Seyne, la | 31 | D4 |
| Seyssel | 27 | D4 |
| Sežana | 70 | A2 |
| Sézanne | 20 | B4 |
| Sezimovo-Ústí | 57 | D1 |
| Sezze | 63 | F3 |
| Sfáka | 91 | F4 |
| Sfakiá | 90 | C4 |
| Sfaktiría, N | 86 | C3 |
| Sferracavallo | 68 | B2 |
| Sfikiá, L | 79 | E3 |
| Sfîntu Gheorghe | 113 | D4 |
| Sforzacosta | 61 | F4 |
| 's Gravendeel | 16 | C3 |
| 's Gravenhage | 16 | B3 |
| Sgùrr Mór | 2 | C3 |
| Sgùrr na Ciche | 2 | B4 |
| Shaftesbury | 9 | D3 |
| Shanklin | 9 | E4 |
| Shannon | 12 | B4 |
| Shannon, Mouth of the | 12 | A4 |
| Shannon, R | 12 | B4 |
| Shap | 5 | D4 |
| Shapinsay | 3 | E1 |
| Shebenik, Mal i | 77 | D4 |
| Sheelin, L | 13 | D3 |
| Sheep Haven | 12 | C1 |
| Sheep's Head | 14 | A4 |
| 's Heerenberg | 17 | D3 |
| Sheerness | 11 | D2 |
| Sheffield | 6 | C2 |
| Shefford | 9 | F2 |
| Shëmri (Shkodër) | 76 | C3 |
| Shëmri (Tiranë) | 76 | C4 |
| Shëngjin | 76 | C3 |
| Sheppey, I of | 11 | D2 |
| Shepshed | 7 | D3 |
| Shepton Mallet | 9 | D3 |
| Sherborne | 9 | D3 |
| Shercock | 13 | D3 |
| Sheringham | 7 | F3 |
| 's Hertogenbosch | 16 | C3 |
| Shetland Is | 3 | E2 |
| Shiel Bridge | 2 | C4 |
| Shieldaig | 2 | B3 |
| Shiel, L | 2 | B4 |
| Shijak | 76 | C4 |
| Shinás | 79 | E3 |
| Shiniás | 88 | A1 |

| | | | | | | | | | | | |
|---|---|---|---|---|---|---|---|---|---|---|---|
| Sein, I de | 22 | A3 | Selianítika | 83 | D4 | Selvino | 58 | B4 | Sennestadt | 17 | F3 |
| Seitenstetten | 57 | D3 | Seligenstadt | 52 | A4 | Seman | 114 | B3 | Sennori | 66 | A2 |
| Seitsemisen | 102 | C3 | Selinia | 87 | F1 | Semeljci | 71 | F2 | Senonches | 19 | E4 |
| Seixal | 38 | A4 | Selinunte | 68 | A3 | Semič | 70 | B2 | Senones | 21 | E4 |
| Seixo | 34 | B3 | Selishtë | 76 | C3 | Seminara | 67 | E4 | Senorbi | 66 | B3 |
| Sejerø | 108 | B3 | Selište | 73 | E3 | Semizovac | 71 | F4 | Senožeče | 70 | A2 |
| Sejerø Bugt | 108 | B3 | Selje | 100 | A3 | Semmering | 57 | E3 | Sens | 26 | A1 |
| Sejm | 113 | F1 | Seljord | 104 | C3 | Semmering -Paß | 57 | E3 | Senta | 72 | C1 · |
| Sékoulas | 86 | C2 | Selkämeri | 102 | B3 | Semois | 20 | C2 | Šentilj | 70 | C1 |
| Šekovići | 72 | B4 | Selkirk | 5 | D3 | Semproniano | 63 | D1 | Šentjernej | 70 | C2 |
| Selargius | 66 | B4 | Sellajoch | 59 | D3 | Semur-en-Auxois | 26 | B2 | Šentjur | 70 | C2 |
| Selassia | 87 | D3 | Sella Nevea | 59 | F3 | Semur-en-Brionnais | 26 | B4 | Šentvid na Šlemenu | 70 | B1 |
| Selb | 53 | D4 | Sella, Pso di | 59 | D3 | Sena | 37 | E3 | Sépeaux | 26 | A1 |
| Selbekken | 100 | C1 | Selles | 25 | E2 | Sénas | 30 | C3 | Šepetovka | 113 | D2 |
| Selbu | 101 | D2 | Sellières | 26 | C3 | Sendim | 34 | C4 | Sepino | 64 | B3 |
| Selbusjøen | 100 | C2 | Sellin | 49 | D1 | Senez | 31 | D3 | Sepúlveda | 36 | A4 |
| Selby | 7 | D2 | Selm | 17 | E3 | Senftenberg | 53 | E2 | Sequeros | 39 | E2 |
| Selce | 70 | B3 | Selmsdorf | 48 | B2 | Senftenberg | 53 | E2 | Sequillo, R | 35 | E4 |
| Selçuk | 115 | E4 | Selna | 71 | F3 | Sengsengeb | 57 | D3 | Seraing | 50 | C4 |
| Sele | 64 | C4 | Selommes | 25 | E4 | Senigallia | 61 | F3 | Seravezza | 60 | B3 |
| Selečka pl | 77 | E4 | Selongey | 26 | C2 | Senise | 65 | D4 | Seregno | 60 | A1 |
| Selenter See | 48 | B1 | Seløy | 97 | D3 | Senj | 70 | B3 | Serein | 26 | B2 |
| Sélero | 81 | D2 | Selsey | 9 | F3 | Senja Ånderdalen | 94 | B3 | Serena, Emb de la | 39 | E4 |
| Sélestat | 21 | E4 | Selsey Bill | 9 | F3 | Senje | 73 | E3 | Séres | 80 | B2 |
| Selevac | 73 | D3 | Selters | 52 | A4 | Senlis | 19 | F3 | Séres (Nomos) | 80 | A2 |
| Selfoss | 96 | A2 | Seltz | 21 | F3 | Sennecey-le-Grand | 26 | C3 | Serfaus | 58 | C2 |
| Séli | 79 | E3 | Sélune | 18 | C4 | Sennen | 8 | A4 | Serfopoúla, N | 88 | B3 |
| Selía | 90 | C4 | Selva | 59 | D3 | | | | | | |

| | | | | | | | | | | | |
|---|---|---|---|---|---|---|---|---|---|---|---|
| Seriate | 60 | B1 | Serrières | 30 | B1 | | | |
| Sérifos | 88 | A3 | Serrota | 39 | F2 | | | |
| Sérifos, N | 88 | A3 | Sersale | 67 | F3 | | | |
| Serifou, Stenó | 88 | A3 | Sertã | 38 | B2 | | | |
| Sermaize-les-Bains | 20 | C4 | Servan | 18 | B4 | | | |
| Sermide | 60 | C2 | Sérvia | 79 | E4 | | | |
| Sermoneta | 63 | F3 | Servian | 30 | A4 | | | |
| Sernancelhe | 38 | C1 | Servigliano | 61 | F4 | | | |
| Serón | 44 | B3 | Servol, R | 41 | F2 | | | |
| Serón de Nágima | 36 | B4 | Sesa | 37 | D3 | | | |
| Seròs | 37 | E4 | Sesena | 40 | A2 | | | |
| Serpa | 42 | B1 | Sesia | 27 | F4 | | | |
| Serpeddì, P | 66 | B4 | Sesimbra | 38 | A4 | | | |
| Serpis, R | 45 | E1 | Sesklío, N | 93 | E1 | | | |
| Serra | 41 | E3 | Sesma | 36 | C2 | | | |
| Serracapriola | 64 | B2 | Sessa Aurunca | 64 | A3 | | | |
| Serrada | 35 | E4 | Sesta Godano | 60 | B3 | | | |
| Serradifalco | 68 | C3 | Šestanovac | 75 | E2 | | | |
| Serradilla | 39 | D3 | Sestino | 61 | E3 | | | |
| Serramanna | 66 | B4 | Sesto | 59 | E2 | | | |
| Serrana, Pto de la | 39 | E3 | Sesto Calende | 60 | A1 | | | |
| Serra San Bruno | 67 | F3 | Sesto Fiorentino | 60 | C3 | | | |
| Serravalle Scrivia | 60 | A2 | Sesto San Giovanni | 60 | A1 | | | |
| Serre Chevalier | 31 | D2 | Sestola | 60 | C3 | | | |
| Serre-Ponçon, Bge de | 31 | D2 | Sestriere | 31 | E2 | | | |
| Serres | 30 | C2 | Sestri Levante | 60 | B3 | | | |
| | | | Sestrunj | 74 | C1 | | | |
| | | | Sestrunj I | 74 | C1 | | | |

Shin, L 2 C2
Shínos 83 D3
Shinoússa, N 88 C3
Shipston-on-Stour 9 E1
Shíza, N 86 C4
Shkodër 76 B3
Shkodrës, Liq i 76 B3
Shkumbin 76 C4
Sholári 80 A3
Shoreham 10 C3
Shpat, Mal i 77 D4
Shrewsbury 6 B3
Shrewton 9 E3
Shropshire 9 D1
Shupenzë 77 D4
Sía, Pto de la 36 A1
Siátista 79 D4
Šiauliai 110 C3
Sibari 67 E2
Sibbhult 109 D3
Sibbo 107 F2
Sibbofjärden 107 F2
Šibenik 75 D1
Šibenik Mt 75 E2
Sibinj 71 E3
Sibiu 113 D4
Sićevo 73 F4
Sichar, Emb de 41 E3
Sicié, Cap 31 D4
Sicignano degli Alburni 64 C4
Sicilia 68 B2
Sicó 38 B2
Šid 72 B2
Sidári 82 A1
Sideby 102 B3
Sidensjö 102 A2
Siderno 67 F4
Síderos, Akr 91 F3
Sidiró 81 F2
Sidirókastro 80 A2
Sidirónero 80 C1
Sidlaw Hills 5 D1
Sidmouth 9 D3
Siebenlehn 53 E2
Siedlce 112 C1
Sieg 51 E3
Siegburg 51 E3
Siegen 17 F4
Siegsdorf 56 B3
Siekierki 49 E3
Siena 61 D4
Sieppijärvi 98 C1
Sieradz 112 B2
Sierck 21 D3
Sierentz 27 E1
Sierninghofen 57 D3
Sierpc 112 B1
Sierra Boyera, Emb de 43 E1
Sierra de Fuentes 39 D3
Sierra de Yeguas 43 E3
Sierre 27 E3
Sievi 102 C1
Sievin as 102 C1
Sífnos, N 88 B3
Sífnou, Stenó 88 B3
Sigean 32 B2
Sigerfjord 94 A3
Siggjarvåg 104 A3
Sighetu Marmatiei 112 C3
Sighişoara 113 D4
Siglufjörður 96 B1
Sigmaringen 55 D3
Signy-l'Abbaye 20 B2
Sigri 85 E2
Sigtuna 106 B3
Sigüenza 36 B4
Sigulda 110 C3
Siiddasjávri 94 B4
Siikainen 102 B3
Siikajoki 99 D4
Siikajoki R 99 D4
Siilinjärvi 103 E2
Sijarinska Banja 77 D1
Sikaminiá 85 F2
Sikås 101 E2
Siki 84 A2
Sikiá (Makedonía) 80 B4
Sikiá (Pelopónissos) 87 E4
Síkinos 88 C4
Síkinos, N 88 C4
Sikióna 87 D1

Sikoráhi 81 E2
Sikoúrio 83 E1
Sikovuono 95 E3
Sila, La 67 F3
Silandro 58 C3
Silba 70 B4
Silba I 70 B4
Silbaš 72 B2
Sildegapet 100 A2
Šile 115 F3
Siles 44 B1
Siliqua 66 B4
Silistra 115 E1
Silivri 115 E3
Siljan (N) 104 C3
Siljan (S) 101 E4
Siljansnäs 101 E4
Silkeborg 108 A3
Silla 41 E4
Silleda 34 B2
Silleiro, C 34 A3
Sillé-le-Guillaume 23 E3
Sillian 59 E2
Silloth 5 D4
Šilo 70 B3
Šilo 81 E2
Sil, R 34 C2
Sils 32 B4
Sils im Engadin 58 B3
Siltakylä 107 F2
Šilutė 110 B3
Silvalen 97 D3
Silvaplana 58 B3
Silvares 38 C2
Silves 42 A2
Silvi Marina 64 A1
Silvrettagruppe 58 B2
Silz 58 C2
Simancas 35 E4
Simandra 80 A3
Šimanovci 72 C3
Simav 115 F4
Simaxis 66 B3
Simbach (Inn) 56 B3
Simbach (Isar) 56 B2
Simbruini, Mti 63 F2
Simeto 69 D3
Sími 93 E1
Símići 71 E3
Sími, N 93 E1
Simlångsdalen 108 C2
Simmerath 51 D4
Simmern 54 B1
Simo 99 D3
Simojärvi 99 E2
Simojoki 99 D3
Simola 103 F4
Símonos Pétras 80 C4
Simonsbath 8 C3
Simonswald 54 C3
Simópoulo 86 B1
Simplonpass 27 F3
Simrishamn 109 D3
Sinaia 113 D4
Sinalunga 61 D4
Sinarádes 82 A1
Sinarcas 41 D3
Sindelfingen 55 D2
Sindirgi 115 F4
Síndos 79 F3
Sines 42 A1
Sines, C de 42 A1
Sinettä 99 D2
Sineu 45 F3
Singen 55 D4
Singöfjärden 106 B3
Singra, Pto de 41 D2
Siniscola 66 C2
Sinj 75 D1
Sinjajevina 76 B2
Sinni 65 D4
Sinnicolau Mare 114 C1
Sinopoli 67 E4
Sinsheim 55 D2
Sintra 38 A4
Sinzig 51 E4
Siófok 112 B4
Sion 27 E3
Sioule 26 A4
Šipan 75 F2
Šipanska Luka 75 F2
Šipka 115 D2
Sipoo 107 F2
Sipoonselkä 107 F2

Šipovo 71 E4
Sippola 107 F2
Šiprage 71 E4
Sira 104 A4
Sira R 104 B4
Siracusa 69 D4
Sirdalen 104 B4
Sirdalvatn 104 A4
Siret 113 D3
Siret R 113 E4
Sirevåg 104 A4
Sirig 72 C2
Sirino, Mte 65 D4
Širitovci 75 D1
Sirkka 95 E4
Sirma 95 E2
Sirmione 60 C1
Sírna, N 92 C1
Široko Polje 71 F2
Sirolo 61 F4
Síros, N 88 B2
Siruela 39 F4
Sisak 71 D2
Šišan 70 A4
Sisante 40 C4
Šišljavić 70 C3
Sissa 60 B2
Sissach 27 F2
Sissonne 20 B3
Sisteron 31 D3
Sistiana 59 F3
Sistranda 100 C1
Sitges 32 A4
Sithonía 80 B4
Sitia 91 F4
Sitnica 77 D2
Sittard 17 D4
Sittensen 48 A3
Sittingbourne 11 D3
Siuntio 107 E3
Siuro 107 E1
Siuro 99 D3
Siuruanjoki 99 D3
Siusi 59 D3
Sivac 72 B2
Sivasli 115 F4
Siviri 80 A4
Sivota 82 B2
Sívros 82 B3
Siziano 60 A1
Sizun 22 B3
Sjælland 108 C3
Sjællands Odde 108 B3
Sjenica 76 C1
Sjeništa 76 A1
Sjøåsen 97 D4
Sjöbo 109 D3
Sjøholt 100 B2
Sjona 97 E2
Sjötorp 105 E4
Sjoutnäset 97 E4
Sjøvegan 94 B3
Sjulsmark 102 B1
Sjundea 107 E3
Sjusjøen 104 D2
Skåbu 100 C3
Skäckerfjällen 101 D1
Skadarsko jez 76 B3
Skadovsk 113 F4
Skafidiá 86 B2
Skáfta 96 B2
Skaftafell 96 C2
Skagafjörður 96 B1
Skage 97 D4
Skagen 108 B1
Skagern 105 E4
Skagerrak 108 A1
Skaill 3 E1
Skajálfandi 96 B1
Skála (Kefaloniá) 86 A1
Skála (Lésvos) 85 F2
Skála (Pátmos) 89 E2
Skála (Pelopónissos) 87 D3
Skála (Stereá Eláda) 83 F3
Skála Eressoú 85 E2
Skála Kaliráhis 80 C3
Skaland 94 B2
Skála Oropoú 84 B4
Skála Potamiás 81 D3
Skála Rahoniou 80 C3
Skalavík 96 A4
Skála Volissoú 85 E4
Skälderviken 108 C3

Skålevik 104 B4
Skálfandafljót 96 B2
Skalka 98 A2
Skalohóri (Lésvos) 85 E2
Skalohóri (Makedonía) 79 D3
Skaloti 80 C1
Skælskør 108 B4
Skamnéli 78 C4
Skandáli 85 D1
Skandári, Akr 89 F3
Skanderborg 108 B3
Skandzoúra, N 84 B3
Skåne 109 D3
Skånevik 104 A3
Skåningsbukt 94 C2
Skånland 94 B3
Skänninge 106 A4
Skanör Falsterbo 108 C4
Skara 109 D1
Skaraborgs Län 109 D1
Skaramangás 87 F1
Skærbæk 108 A4
Skarberget 94 B4
Škarda 74 B1
Skåre 105 E3
Skárfia 83 F3
Skärgårdshavet 107 D3
Skärhamn 108 C1
Skarnes 105 D3
Skarplinge 106 B2
Skarsvåg 95 E1
Skärvången 101 E1
Skarżysko-Kamienna 112 B2
Skattungbyn 101 E4
Skatval 100 C2
Skaulo 94 C4
Skaun 100 C2
Skee 105 D4
Skegness 7 E3
Skei (Møre og Romsdal) 100 B2
Skei (Sogn og Fjordane) 100 A3
Skeiðarársandur 96 B2
Skela 72 C3
Skellefteå 98 B4
Skellefteälven 98 B4
Skelleftehamn 98 B4
Skellig 14 A4
Skelmersdale 6 B2
Skenderbeut, M i 76 C4
Skender Vakuf 71 E4
Skepastó 80 B2
Skerries 13 E3
Ski 105 D3
Skíathos 84 A2
Skiáthos, N 84 A2
Skibbereen 14 B4
Skibby 108 C3
Skibotn 94 C2
Skiddaw 5 D4
Skídra 79 E3
Skien 104 C3
Skierniewice 112 B2
Skillingaryd 109 D2
Skiloundía 86 C2
Skinári, Akr 86 A1
Skiniás 91 E4
Skinnarbu 104 B3
Skinnskatteberg 105 F3
Skipagurra 95 F1
Skipton 6 C2
Skíros 84 C3
Skíros, N 84 C3
Skíti 83 F1
Skive 108 A2
Skivjane 76 C2
Skjeberg 105 D3
Skjern 108 A3
Skjersholmane 104 A3
Skjerstad 97 E2
Skjerstadfjorden 97 E2
Skjervøy 94 C2
Skjønhaug 105 D3
Sklavopoúla 90 B3
Sklithro 83 F1
Šklov 111 E3
Skočivir 77 E4
Skocjanske jame 70 A3
Skodje 100 B2
Škofja Loka 70 A2
Skofljica 70 B2

Skog (Gävleborgs Län) 101 F4
Skog (Västernorrlands Län) 102 A2
Skógafoss 96 B3
Skogerøya 95 F2
Skoghall 105 E3
Skogstorp 105 F4
Skokloster 106 B3
Skólis 86 B1
Skópelos (Lésvos) 85 F3
Skópelos (Skópelos) 84 B2
Skópelos, N 84 B3
Skopí 91 F4
Skopiá 83 E2
Skopje 77 E3
Skopós 79 D2
Skopun 96 A4
Skorenovac 73 D3
Skorovatn 97 E4
Skorped 101 F2
Skotina 79 F4
Skotterud 105 D3
Skoulikariá 82 C2
Skoúra 87 D3
Skoúrta 87 F1
Skoútari (Makedonía) 80 B2
Skoútari (Pelopónissos) 87 D4
Skoutáros 85 E2
Skövde 109 D1
Skrá 79 E2
Skrad 70 B3
Skradin 75 D1
Skradinski buk 75 D1
Skreia 105 D2
Skrim 104 C3
Skrolsvik 94 B3
Skrydstrup 108 A4
Skudeneshavn 104 A3
Skuleskogen 102 A2
Skull 14 A4
Skultuna 106 A3
Skuodas 110 B3
Skuov'gilraš'ša 95 D2
Skurup 109 D3
Skutskär 106 B2
Skutvik 94 A4
Skvira 113 E2
Skye 2 B3
Slagelse 108 B3
Slagnäs 98 A3
Slánčev Brjag 115 E2
Slancy 111 D1
Slane 13 D3
Slaney 15 D3
Slangerup 108 C3
Slano 75 F2
Slany 53 F3
Šlapanice 57 F1
Slapská přehr nádrž 53 F4
Slapy 53 F4
Śląsk 112 A2
Slatina (Bor) 73 E3
Slatina (Bosna i Hercegovina) 71 E3
Slatina (Kraljevo) 73 D4
Slatina (Makedonija) 77 D3
Slatina (RO) 115 D1
Slatine 75 D2
Slatinski Drenovac 71 E2
Slavgorod 111 E4
Slavinja 77 F1
Slavkovica 72 C4
Slavkov u Brna 57 F1
Slavnik 70 A3
Slavonice 57 E1
Slavonska Požega 71 E2
Slavonski Brod 71 E3
Slavonski Kobaš 71 E3
Slavuta 113 D2
Sławno 110 A4
Sławoborze 49 F2
Sleaford 7 D3
Slea Head 14 A3
Sleat, Sd of 2 B4
Slettfjellet 94 C2
Sliedrecht 16 C3
Sliema 68 B4
Slieve Bloom Mts 12 C4

Slieve Donard 13 E3
Slieve Mish Mts 14 A3
Slievenamon 14 C3
Slieve Snaght 13 D1
Sligachan 2 B3
Sligeach 12 C2
Sligo 12 C2
Sligo (Co) 12 B3
Sligo B 12 C2
Slišane 77 D1
Slite 109 F4
Sliven 115 E2
Sljeme 70 C2
Šljivovica 72 C4
Slobozia 115 E1
Slonim 112 C1
Sloten 16 C1
Slough 9 F2
Slovac 72 C3
Slovenska Bistrica 70 C1
Slovenia 70 A2
Slovenj Gradec 70 B1
Slovenske Konjice 70 C1
Slovenské Rudohorie 112 B3
Slovinci 71 D3
Słubice 49 F4
Sluck 111 D4
Sluderno 58 C3
Sluis 16 A4
Sluknov 53 F2
Slunj 70 C3
Słupsk 110 A4
Slyne Head 12 A3
Småland 109 D2
Smålandsfarvandet 108 B4
Smålands-stenar 109 D2
Šmarje 70 C2
Šmarješke Toplice 70 B2
Šmartin 70 B2
Smedby 109 E2
Smederevo 73 D3
Smederevska Palanka 73 D3
Smela 113 F2
Smigáda 81 E2
Smilčić 74 C1
Smilde 17 D1
Smiltene 110 C2
Smojmirovo 77 F3
Smokovec 70 B3
Smokovljan 75 F2
Smøla 100 B1
Smolensk 111 E3
Smolevičí 111 D4
Smólikas, Óros 78 C4
Smoljan 115 D3
Smorgon 111 D4
Smørhamn 104 A1
Smygehamn 109 D4
Snaefell 6 A1
Snæfellsnes 96 A2
Snaith 7 D2
Snåsa 101 D1
Snasahögarna 101 D2
Snåsavatnet 101 D1
Sneek 16 C1
Sneem 14 A4
Snežnik 70 B3
Śniardwy, Jez 110 B4
Snigir'ovka 113 F3
Snillfjord 100 C2
Snizort, L 2 B3
Šnjegotina Velika 71 E3
Snøfjord 95 D1
Snøhefta 100 C3
Snøtinden 97 E2
Snowdon 6 A3
Snowdonia Forest and Nat Pk 6 A3
Soave 60 C1
Sobešlav 57 D1
Sobra 75 F2
Sobrado 34 B2
Sobral da Adiça 42 C1
Sobral de Monte Agraço 38 A3
Sobreira Formosa 38 C2
Sobrón, Emb de 36 B2

Soča R 70 A2
Sočanica 77 D1
Soccia 33 F3
Sochaczew 112 B1
Sochaux 27 E2
Socol 73 D2
Socovos 44 C1
Socuéllamos 40 B4
Sodankylä 95 E4
Söderåkra 109 E3
Söderbärke 105 F3
Söderfors 106 B3
Söderhamn 101 F4
Söderköping 106 A4
Södermanlands Län 106 A4
Söderskog 109 D3
Södertälje 106 B4
Sodražica 70 B2
Sodupe 36 B1
Soest (D) 17 F3
Soest (NL) 16 C2
Soestdijk 16 C2
Sofádes 83 E2
Sofia 115 D2
Sofiero 108 C3
Sofikó 87 E1
Sofó 83 E2
Sögel 17 E1
Sogliano al Rubicone 61 E3
Soglio 58 B3
Sogndal 100 B3
Søgne 104 B4
Sognefjell 100 B3
Sognefjorden 104 A1
Sognesjøen 104 A1
Sogn og Fjordane 100 A3
Soham 11 D1
Sohós 80 A2
Soignies 50 B4
Soini 102 C2
Soinlahti 103 D1
Soissons 20 A3
Söke 115 E4
Sokna 104 C2
Soko Banja 73 E4
Sokolac 72 B4
Sokolov 53 D4
Sokołow Podlaski 112 C1
Sokosti 95 F3
Sola (Rogaland) 104 A3
Sola (Sogn og Fjordane) 104 A1
Solana de los Barros 39 D4
Solana del Pino 43 F1
Solares 35 F2
Solberg 101 F1
Solbergfjorden 94 B3
Solčava 70 B1
Solda 58 C3
Sölden 58 C2
Soldeu 32 A2
Solent, The 9 E3
Solenzara 33 F4
Solesmes (Nord) 20 A2
Solesmes (Sarthe) 23 E3
Solevåg 100 A2
Solf 102 B2
Solferino 60 C1
Solholmen 100 B2
Solignac (Haute-Loire) 29 F2
Solignac (Haute-Vienne) 29 D1
Soligorsk 111 D4
Solihull 9 E1
Solin 75 D1
Soline 74 B1
Solingen 17 E4
Sölkerpaß 57 D4
Söll 59 D1
Sollana 41 E4
Sollefteå 101 F2
Sollenau 57 F3
Sollentuna 106 B3
Sóller 45 E2
Sollerön 101 E4
Søllested 108 B4
Solliès-Pont 31 D4
Solnečnogorsk 111 F2
Solofra 64 B4

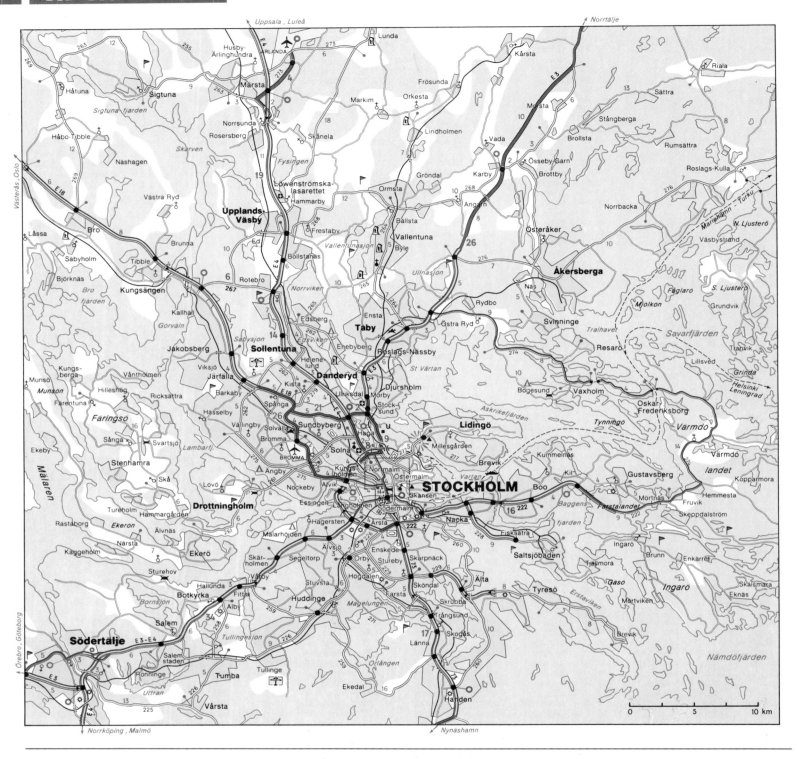

| | | | | | | | | | | | |
|---|---|---|---|---|---|---|---|---|---|---|---|
| Solosancho | 39 F2 | Somiedo, Pto de | 35 D2 | Sønder Felding | 108 A3 | Sopot (YU) | 73 D3 | Sørkjosen | 94 C2 | Sørvågen | 97 E1 | Soto de los |
| Solothurn | 27 E2 | Sommarøy | 94 B2 | Sondershausen | 52 C2 | Sopotnica | 77 D4 | Sorø | 108 B3 | Sørvágur | 96 A4 | Infantes | 35 D1 |
| Solre-le-Château | 20 B2 | Sommatino | 68 C4 | Søndersø | 108 B3 | Sopron | 112 A4 | Soroki | 113 E3 | Sørvær | 94 C1 | Soto de Luiña | 35 D1 |
| Solrød | 108 C3 | Somme | 19 E2 | Sondrio | 58 B3 | Sora | 64 A3 | Soro, M | 69 D3 | Sørværøy | 97 E1 | Soto de Sajambre | 35 E2 |
| Solsona | 32 A3 | Somme (Dépt) | 19 E2 | Songeons | 19 E3 | Soragna | 60 B2 | Soroni | 93 E1 | Sörvattnet | 101 D3 | Sotogrande | 43 E4 |
| Šolta | 75 D2 | Sommen | 109 E1 | Sonkajärvi | 103 E1 | Söråker | 101 F3 | Sørøya | 95 D1 | | | Sotopalacios | 35 F3 |
| Soltau | 48 A3 | Sömmerda | 52 C2 | Sonnblick | 59 E2 | Sørarnøy | 97 E2 | Sørøysundet | 95 D1 | Soto del Rey | | Sottomarina | 61 D1 |
| Solunska Glava | 77 E3 | Sommesous | 20 B4 | Sonneberg | 52 C4 | Sorbas | 44 C3 | Sorraia, R | 38 A4 | Católico | 37 D2 | Sottunga | 106 C3 |
| Solunto | 68 B3 | Sommières | 30 B3 | Sonnewalde | 53 E1 | Sorbe, R | 40 B1 | Sørreisa | 94 B3 | Soses | 37 E4 | Sotuélamos | 40 C4 |
| Solvay | 60 C4 | Sømna | 97 D3 | Sonogno | 58 A3 | Sore | 28 B3 | Sorrento | 64 B4 | Sosnovyj Bor | 111 D1 | Soúda | 90 C3 |
| Sölvesborg | 109 D3 | Somolinos | 36 A4 | Sonsbeck | 17 D3 | Soresina | 60 B1 | Sor, Rib de | 38 B3 | Sosnowiec | 112 B2 | Souesmes | 25 F2 |
| Solvorn | 100 B3 | Somosierra, Pto | | Sonseca | 40 A3 | Sørfjorden | 104 B2 | Sørrollnes | 94 B3 | Sospel | 31 E3 | Soufflenheim | 21 F3 |
| Solway Firth | 4 C4 | de | 36 A4 | Son Servera | 45 F3 | Sør-Flatanger | 96 C4 | Sorsakoski | 103 E2 | Šoštanj | 70 B1 | Soúfli | 81 F2 |
| Solynieve | 44 A3 | Sompio | 95 F3 | Sonta | 72 B2 | Sørfolda | 94 A4 | Sorsele | 98 A3 | Sóstis | 81 D2 | Soúgia | 90 B4 |
| Soma | 115 D4 | Somport, Pto de | 37 D2 | Sonthofen | 55 E1 | Sörfors | 102 A1 | Sorso | 66 A2 | Šostka | 111 F4 | Souillac | 29 D2 |
| Sombernon | 26 C2 | Šomrda | 73 E3 | Sontra | 52 B3 | Sorga | 52 B3 | Sort | 37 F2 | Sotaseter | 100 B3 | Souilly | 20 C3 |
| Sombor | 72 B2 | Soncillo | 35 F2 | Sopeira | 37 F3 | Sorgono | 66 B3 | Sortino | 69 D4 | Sotillo de la | | Soulac | 28 A1 |
| Someren | 17 D4 | Soncino | 60 B1 | Sopilja | 76 A1 | Sorgues | 30 B3 | Sortland | 94 A3 | Adrada | 39 F2 | Soulaines-Dhuys | 20 C4 |
| Somero | 107 E2 | Søndeled | 104 C4 | Sopište | 77 D3 | Sørgutvik | 97 D4 | Sortlandsundet | 94 A2 | Sotin | 72 B2 | Soulinári | 86 C3 |
| Somerset | 9 D3 | Sønderborg | 108 B4 | Sopoćani | 76 C1 | Soria | 36 B3 | Sør Trøndelag | 100 C2 | Sotira | 79 E2 | Soulíou, Óri | 82 B2 |
| Someş | 112 C4 | Sønderby | 108 B4 | Sopot (PL) | 110 A4 | Soriano nel Cimino | 63 E2 | Sorunda | 106 B4 | Soto del Barco | 35 D1 | Soulópoulo | 82 B1 |

Soultz (Bas-Rhin) 21 E3
Soultz (Haut-Rhin) 27 E1
Soúnio 88 A2
Soúnio, Akr 88 A2
Souppes 25 F1
Source de la Loue 27 D2
Source du Lison 27 D3
Sourdeval 18 C4
Soure 38 B2
Sournia 32 B2
Sourotí 80 A3
Soúrpi 83 F2
Sousceyrac 29 D2
Sousel 38 C4
Soustons 28 A4
Soutelo 34 B2
Souterraine, la 25 E4
Southam 9 E1
Southampton 9 E3
Southborough 10 C3
South Downs 9 F3
Southend 4 B3
Southend-on-Sea 11 D2
Southern Uplands 4 C3
South Esk 3 D4
South Foreland 11 D3
South Molten 8 C3
Southport 6 B2
South Queensferry 5 D2
South Ronaldsay 3 E1
Southsea 9 F3
South Shields 5 E3
South Tyne 5 D3
South Uist 2 A3
Southwell 7 D3
Southwold 11 E1
Souvála 87 F2
Souvigny 26 A3
Sovata 113 D4
Sövdeborg 109 D3
Soverato 67 F3
Soveria Mannelli 67 F3
Sovetsk 110 B3
Søvik 100 A2
Sož 111 E4
Sozopol 115 E2
Spa 51 D4
Spaichingen 55 D3
Spakenburg 16 C2
Spalding 7 E3
Spánda, Akr 90 B3
Spandau 49 D4
Spangenberg 52 B2
Spanish Pt 12 B4
Sparlösa 108 C1
Spárta 87 E1
Spárti 87 E3
Spartivento, C (Calabria) 67 E4
Spartivento, C (Sardegna) 66 B4
Spárto 82 C3
Spas-Demensk 111 F3
Spáta 87 F1
Spatharéi 89 E2
Spathí, Akr (Kíthira) 90 A1
Spathí, Akr (Pelopónnisos) 87 F2
Spodniji Brnik 70 B2
Spean Bridge 2 C4
Speikkogel 57 E4
Spello 63 E1
Spennymoor 5 E4
Sperhiáda 83 E3
Sperhiós 83 E3
Sperillen 104 C2
Sperlonga 63 F3
Sperrin Mts 13 D1
Spétses 87 E3
Spétses, N 87 E3
Spetsopoúla, N 87 E3
Speyer 54 C2
Spey, R 3 D3
Spezzano Albanese 67 E2
Spezzano della Sila 67 E2
Spiddle 12 B3
Spiekeroog 47 E2
Spielfeld 70 C1
Spiez 27 F3
Spijkenisse 16 B3
Spilea Diroú 87 D4
Spíli 90 C4

Spiliá 83 E1
Spilimbergo 59 E3
Spilsby 7 E3
Spinalónga 91 E3
Spinazzola 65 D3
Spincourt 20 C3
Špionica Donja 71 F3
Špišić Bukovica 71 E2
Spišská-Nová Ves 112 B3
Spital 57 D3
Spittal 59 F2
Spitz 57 E2
Spjelkavik 100 A2
Split 75 D2
Spluga, Pso dello 58 B3
Splügen 58 B3
Splügenpass 58 B3
Spodsbjerg 108 B4
Špola 113 F2
Spoleto 63 E1
Spornitz 48 C3
Spotorno 60 A3
Spreča 71 F3
Spree 49 E4
Spreewald 53 E1
Spremberg 53 F1
Spresiano 59 E4
Springe 52 A1
Sprogø 108 B4
Spurn Head 7 E3
Spuž 76 B2
Squillace, Golfo di 67 F3
Squinzano 65 F4
Srb 71 D4
Srbac 71 E3
Srbica 77 D2
Srbija 73 D4
Srbobran 72 C2
Srđđeviči 75 E1
Srebrenica 72 C4
Središče 70 C1
Sredna Gora 115 D2
Srednje 71 F4
Srednji kanal 74 C1
Srednogorie 115 D2
Sredska 77 D3
Sremska Kamenica 72 C2
Sremska Mitrovica 72 C3
Sremska Rača 72 B3
Sremski Karlovci 72 C2
Srnetica 71 D4
Srnice Donje 71 F3
Środa Wielkopolska 112 A1
Srpska Crnja 72 C1
Srpske Moravice 70 B3
Srpski Itebej 73 D1
Srpski Miletić 72 B2
Stabbursdalen 95 D2
Stade 48 A3
Stádio 87 D2
Stadskanaal 17 E1
Stadthagen 52 A1
Stadtilm 52 C3
Stadtkyll 51 D4
Stadtlohn 17 E3
Stadtoldendorf 52 A2
Stadtroda 52 C3
Stadtsteinach 52 C4
Stadt Wehlen 53 F2
Staffa 4 A1
Staffanstorp 108 C3
Staffelsee 56 A4
Staffelstein 52 C4
Staffin 2 B3
Stafford 6 C3
Staffordshire 6 C3
Stágira 80 B3
Stahle 52 A2
Stahovica 70 B2
Staines 9 F2
Stainz 57 E4
Stajovce 77 E2
Stalać 73 E4
Štalcerji 70 B3
Stalída 91 E3
Stall 59 E2
Stalle, Pso di 59 E2
Stallersattel 59 E2
Stalowa Wola 112 C2
Stamford 9 F1
Stamnes 104 A2
Stams 58 C2
Stamsund 94 A4

Stange 105 D2
Stanišić 72 B1
Stanišinci 73 D4
Štanjel 70 A2
Staňkov 56 B1
Stankovci 74 C1
Stanley 5 E4
Stanós 80 B3
Stános 82 C3
Stans 27 F2
Stansstad 27 F2
Stansted 10 C2
Stapar 72 B2
Starachowice 112 B2
Stara Gradina 71 E2
Staraja Russa 111 E2
Stara Moravica 72 B1
Stara Novalja 70 B4
Stara Pazova 72 C2
Stara Pl (BG) 115 D2
Stara Pl (YU) 73 F4
Stará Role 53 E4
Staravina 77 E4
Stara Vrata 70 C4
Stara Zagora 115 D2
Staretina 75 D1
Stargard Szczeciński 49 F2
Stårheim 100 A3
Stari 77 F3
Stari Bar 76 B3
Stari Begej 72 C2
Starica 111 F2
Starigrad (Hvar) 75 D2
Starigrad (Velebit) 70 B4
Stari Gradac 71 E2
Starigrad Paklenica 70 C4
Stari Jankovci 72 B2
Stari Log 70 B2
Stari Majdan 71 D3
Stari Mikanovci 71 F2
Starnberg 56 A3
Starnberger See 56 A3
Starodub 111 F4
Starogard Gdański 110 A4
Starokonstantinov 113 D2
Staro Nagoričane 77 E2
Staro Petrovo Selo 71 E3
Staro Slano 76 A2
Start Pt 8 C4
Starý Smokovec 112 B3
Staßfurt 52 C1
Statland 97 D4
Staußfurt 52 C2
Stavanger 104 A3
Staveley 7 D3
Stavelot 51 D4
Stavenisse 16 B3
Staveren 16 C1
Stavern 104 C4
Stavri, Akr 88 C3
Stavrodrómi 86 C1
Stavrohóri 91 F4
Stavrós (Évia) 84 B3
Stavrós (Imathía) 79 E3
Stavrós (Itháki) 82 B4
Stavrós (Kríti) 90 C3
Stavrós (Thessalía) 83 E2
Stavrós (Thessaloníki) 80 B3
Stavrós, Akr (Kríti) 91 D3
Stavrós, Akr (Thássos) 81 D3
Stavroúpoli 80 C2
Steblevë 77 D4
Štěchovice 53 F4
Steckborn 58 A1
Steeg 58 C2
Steenbergen 16 B3
Steenvoorde 19 F1
Steenwijk 17 D2
Stefáni (Ípiros) 82 B2
Stefáni (Stereá Eláda) 87 F1
Stefaniná 80 B3
Stefanovíkio 83 F2
Stege 108 C4
Stegersbach 57 F4
Steibis 55 E4
Steiermark 57 D4
Steigen 97 E1
Stein (A) 57 E2

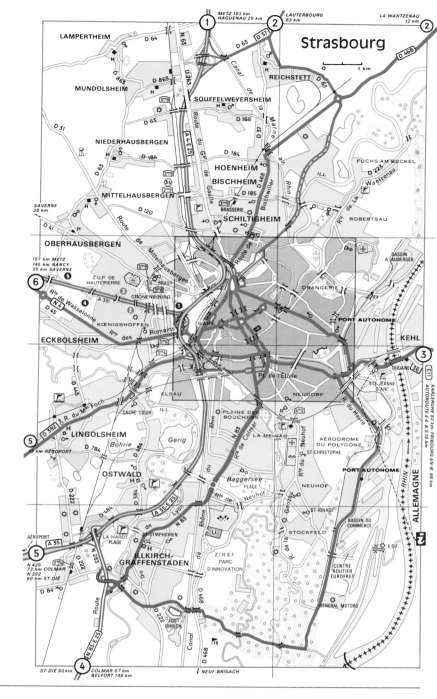

Stein (N) 105 D2
Steinach (A) 59 D2
Steinach (DDR) 52 C3
Steinau 52 A4
Steinbach-Hallenberg 52 B3
Stein (Baden-Württemberg) 55 D4
Stein (Bayern) 55 E1
Steine 104 A1
Steinestø 104 A2
Steinfeld 17 E2
Steinfeld 59 F2
Steinfurt 17 E2
Steingaden 55 F4
Steinhaus 59 D3
Steinhausen 55 D3
Steinheim (Baden-Württemberg) 55 E2
Steinheim (Bayern) 55 E3
Steinheim (Nordrhein-Westfalen) 52 A2
Steinkjer 101 D1
Steinnuder Meer 48 A4
Steinpaß 59 E1
Steinshamn 100 A2

Steinsland 104 A2
Stekene 50 B3
Stelvio, Parco Naz della 58 C3
Stelvio, Pso dello 58 C3
Stená Klissoúras 79 D3
Stenay 20 C3
Stendal 48 C4
Steni 84 B4
Stenlille 108 B3
Stenløse 108 C3
Stenness 3 D1
Stenó 87 D2
Stenó, Akr 88 B2
Stenó Ithákis 82 B4
Sténoma 83 D3
Stenudden 98 A2
Stenungsund 108 C1
Stepanci 77 E3
Stepnica 49 E2
Stepojevac 72 C3
Stereá Eláda 83 D3
Sterkrade 17 E3
Stérna (Makedonía) 80 C1
Stérna (Pelopónnisos) 87 D2

Stérna (Thráki) 81 F1
Sternberg 48 C2
Stérnes 90 C3
Sterup 48 A1
Sterza, la 60 C4
Sterzing 59 D2
Stevenage 9 F2
Stevns 108 C4
Stevns Klint 108 C4
Stewarton 4 C2
Steyr 57 D3
Steyrermühl 56 C3
Stia 61 D3
Stigliano 65 D3
Stigtomta 106 A4
Stilida 83 E3
Stilo 67 F4
Stimánga 87 D1
Stimfalía, L 87 D1
Štimlje 77 D2
Stintino 66 A1
Stípsi 85 F2
Stíra 84 C4
Stirling 4 C2

Štitar 72 C3
Štivan 70 B4
Stjärnhov 106 B4
Stjärnsund 105 F4
Stjernøya 95 D2
Stjernsund 95 D2
Stjørdal 100 C2
Stjørdalselva 101 D2
Stjørnfjorden 100 C1
Stobi 77 E3
Stockach 55 D4
Stockbridge 9 E3
Stockelsdorf 48 B2
Stockerau 57 F2
Stockholm 106 B4
Stockholms Län 106 B3
Stockport 6 C2
Stocksbridge 6 C2
Stockton-on-Tees 5 E4
Stod 53 E4
Stöde 101 F3
Stogovo 77 D4
Stoke-on-Trent 6 C3
Stokke 104 C3
Stokmarknes 94 A3
Stol 73 E3
Stolac 75 F2

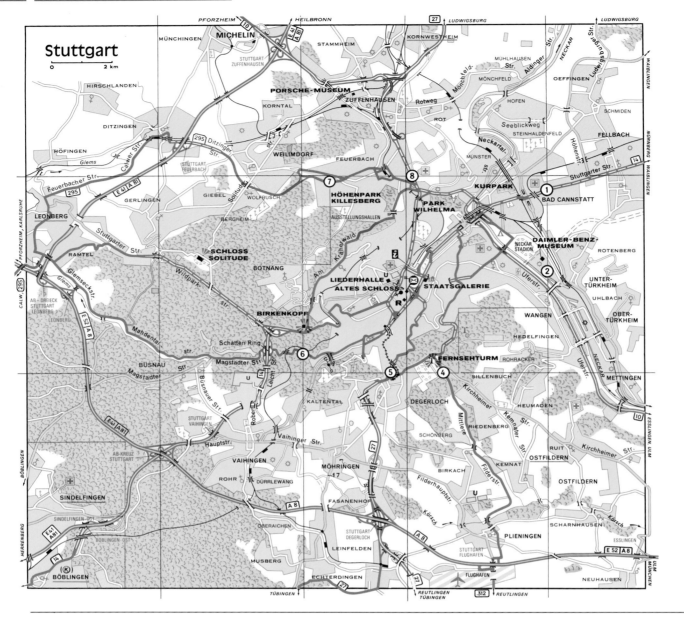

Stuttgart

0    2 km

| | | |
|---|---|---|
| Sturup | 108 | C3 |
| Stuttgart | 55 | D2 |
| Stykkishólmur | 96 | A2 |
| Styr' | 113 | D1 |
| Suances | 35 | F1 |
| Subbiano | 61 | D4 |
| Subiaco | 63 | F2 |
| Subijana | 36 | B2 |
| Subotica | 72 | B1 |
| Subotište | 72 | C3 |
| Suc-au-May | 29 | D1 |
| Suceava | 113 | D3 |
| Sučevici | 71 | D4 |
| Sucevita | 113 | D3 |
| Suchań | 49 | F2 |
| Suchiniči | 111 | F3 |
| Süchteln | 17 | D4 |
| Sucina | 45 | D2 |
| Suck | 12 | C3 |
| Sućuraj | 75 | E2 |
| Sudbury (Derbys) | 6 | C3 |
| Sudbury (Suffolk) | 11 | D2 |
| Suddesjaur | 98 | A3 |
| Sude | 48 | B3 |
| Süderbrarup | 48 | A1 |
| Suðuroy | 96 | A4 |
| Suðuroyarfjørður | 96 | A4 |
| Sueca | 41 | E4 |
| Sueros | 35 | D2 |
| Suffolk | 11 | D1 |
| Suhl | 52 | C3 |
| Suhopolje | 71 | E2 |
| Suho Polje | 72 | B3 |
| Šuica | 75 | E1 |
| Suinula | 102 | C3 |
| Suippes | 20 | B3 |
| Suir, R | 14 | C3 |
| Sukeva | 103 | E1 |
| Sukobin | 76 | B3 |
| Sukošan | 74 | C1 |
| Sukovo | 77 | E1 |
| Sukth | 76 | C4 |
| Sula | 113 | F2 |
| Suldal | 104 | B3 |
| Suldalsvatn | 104 | B3 |
| Sulden | 58 | C3 |
| Sulęcin | 49 | F4 |
| Sulina | 113 | F4 |
| Sulingen | 17 | F2 |
| Sulitjelma | 97 | F2 |
| Sulitjelma Mt | 97 | F2 |
| Sulkava | 103 | E3 |
| Sully | 25 | F2 |
| Sulmona | 64 | A2 |
| Sultanhisar | 115 | F4 |
| Sulz | 54 | C3 |
| Sulzbach (Baden-Württemberg) | 55 | D2 |
| Sulzbach (Saarland) | 54 | B2 |
| Sulzbach-Rosenberg | 55 | F1 |
| Sulzemoos | 55 | F3 |
| Sumartin | 75 | E2 |
| Sumba | 96 | A4 |
| Sumburgh | 3 | F2 |
| Sumburgh Head | 3 | F2 |
| Sümeg | 112 | A4 |
| Šumen | 115 | D3 |
| Sumiainen | 103 | D2 |
| Sumiswald | 27 | F2 |
| Šumperk | 112 | A3 |
| Sumy | 113 | F1 |
| Sunart, L | 2 | B4 |
| Sund | 106 | C3 |
| Sunde (Hordaland) | 104 | A2 |
| Sunde (Sør Trøndelag) | 100 | C1 |
| Sunderland | 5 | E4 |
| Sundern | 17 | F4 |
| Sundini | 96 | A3 |
| Sundom | 102 | B2 |
| Sundsvall | 101 | F3 |
| Sundsvallsbukten | 101 | F3 |
| Suni | 66 | B2 |
| Sunja | 71 | D3 |
| Sunnansjö | 105 | F3 |
| Sunndalen | 100 | C2 |
| Sunndalsøra | 100 | B2 |
| Sunne (Jämtlands Län) | 101 | E2 |
| Sunne (Värmlands Län) | 105 | E3 |
| Sunnemo | 105 | E3 |

| | | | | | | | | | | | | | | | |
|---|---|---|---|---|---|---|---|---|---|---|---|---|---|---|---|
| Stolac Mt | 72 | C4 | Store Bælt | 108 | B3 | Storuman | 97 | F4 | Strasbourg | 21 | E4 | Strehla | 53 | E2 | Stroud | 9 | D2 |
| Stolbcy | 111 | D4 | Storebø | 104 | A2 | Storuman L | 97 | F3 | Strasburg | 49 | E2 | Streitberg | 52 | C4 | Strovlés | 90 | B3 |
| Stolberg (D) | 51 | D3 | Storebro | 109 | E2 | Storvik (N) | 95 | D2 | Straßburg | 70 | A1 | Strengberg | 57 | D3 | Strub, Paß | 59 | E1 |
| Stolberg (DDR) | 52 | C2 | Store Heddinge | 108 | C4 | Storvik (S) | 106 | A2 | Straßwalchen | 56 | C3 | Stresa | 58 | A4 | Struer | 108 | A2 |
| Stolice | 72 | B3 | Store Molvik | 95 | F1 | Storvindeln | 97 | F3 | Stratford-upon-Avon | 9 | E1 | Streymoy | 96 | A3 | Struga | 77 | D4 |
| Stolice Mt | 73 | E4 | Store Mosse | 109 | D2 | Stotel | 47 | F3 | Strathaven | 4 | C1 | Strezimirovci | 77 | E1 | Struge | 70 | B2 |
| Stolin | 113 | D1 | Støren | 100 | C2 | Stoúpa | 86 | C3 | Strathclyde | 4 | C2 | Strezovce | 77 | D2 | Struma | 115 | D3 |
| Stollberg | 53 | E3 | Storfjellet | 97 | F2 | Stour | 11 | D2 | Strathy Pt | 3 | D2 | Stříbro | 53 | E4 | Strumble Head | 8 | B1 |
| Stöllet | 105 | E2 | Storfjorden | 100 | B2 | Stourbridge | 9 | E1 | Strathy Pt | 3 | D2 | Strimónas | 80 | B2 | Strumica | 77 | F3 |
| Stolpen | 53 | F2 | Storfors | 105 | E3 | Stournaréika | 83 | D2 | Stratóni | 80 | B3 | Strimonikó | 80 | A2 | Strumica R | 77 | F3 |
| Stølsheimen | 104 | B2 | Storforsen | 98 | B3 | Stourport | 9 | D1 | Stratoníki | 80 | B3 | Strimonikós | | | Stryj | 112 | C3 |
| Stolzenau | 48 | A4 | Storforshei | 97 | E2 | Støvring | 108 | B2 | Strátos | 82 | C3 | Kólpos | 80 | B3 | Stryn | 100 | A3 |
| Stómio | 83 | F1 | Storglomvatnet | 97 | E2 | Stowmarket | 11 | D1 | Stratton | 8 | B3 | Strmac | 71 | E2 | Strzelce Krajeńskie | 49 | F3 |
| Ston | 75 | F2 | Storkow | 49 | E4 | Stow-on-the-Wold | 9 | E2 | Straubing | 56 | B2 | Strmica | 75 | D1 | Stubalpe | 57 | D4 |
| Stone | 6 | C3 | Storlien | 101 | E2 | Strå | 61 | D1 | Straumen (Bodø) | 97 | E2 | Strobl | 56 | C3 | Stubbekøbing | 108 | C4 |
| Stonehaven | 3 | E4 | Stormi | 107 | D2 | Strabane | 13 | D1 | Straumen (Fauske) | 97 | F1 | Strofádes, N | 86 | A3 | Stubbenkammer | 49 | D1 |
| Stonéhenge | 9 | E3 | Stornoway | 2 | B2 | Stracin | 77 | E2 | Straumen (Nord Trøndelag) | 101 | D1 | Strofiliá | 84 | A3 | Štubej | 73 | E3 |
| Stonglandet | 94 | B3 | Storo | 58 | C4 | Stradella | 60 | A2 | Straumsjøen | 94 | A3 | Strojkovce | 77 | E1 | Štubik | 73 | F3 |
| Stopanja | 73 | E4 | Storožinec | 113 | D3 | Stradsett | 11 | D1 | Straumsnes (Nordland) | 97 | E1 | Strokestown | 12 | C3 | Stubličke Toplice | 70 | C2 |
| Stör | 48 | A2 | Storr, The | 2 | B3 | Straelen | 17 | D3 | Straumsnes (Troms) | 94 | B2 | Stromberg | 54 | B1 | Stubline | 72 | C3 |
| Storå | 105 | F3 | Storsjö | 101 | D2 | Stragari | 73 | D4 | Strakonice | 56 | C1 | Stromboli, I | 69 | D1 | Stučka | 110 | C3 |
| Stora Alvaret | 109 | E3 | Storsjøen | 105 | D1 | Stralsund | 49 | D1 | Stralsund | 49 | D1 | Stromeferry | 2 | B3 | Stuckenborstel | 48 | A3 |
| Stora Blåsjön | 97 | E4 | Storsjön (Gävleborgs Län) | 106 | B2 | Stranda | 100 | B2 | Straupitz | 53 | E1 | Strömfors | 107 | F2 | Studena | 77 | E1 |
| Stora Lulevatten | 98 | A2 | Storsjön (Ljungdalen) | 101 | D2 | Strandebarm | 104 | A2 | Strausberg | 49 | E4 | Stromness | 3 | D1 | Studenci | 75 | E1 |
| Stora Sjöfallet | 94 | B4 | Storsjön (Östersund) | 101 | E2 | Strandhill | 12 | C2 | Straža (Srbija) | 73 | E4 | Strömsbruk | 101 | F3 | Studenica | 76 | C1 |
| Stora Sjöfallet (National park) | 94 | B4 | Storsjouten | 97 | E4 | Strandford | 13 | E2 | Straža (Vojvodina) | 73 | D2 | Strömsnäsbruk | 109 | D2 | Stugun | 101 | F2 |
| Stora Skedvi | 105 | F2 | Storskarven | 101 | D2 | Strangford L | 13 | E2 | Straža, G. | 70 | B2 | Strömstad | 105 | D4 | Stühlingen | 54 | C4 |
| Stora Sundby | 105 | F4 | Storslett | 94 | C2 | Strängnäs | 106 | B3 | Stražbenica | 76 | B2 | Strömsund | 101 | F1 | Stuhr-Brinkum | 17 | F1 |
| Storavan | 98 | A3 | Storsteinnes | 94 | C3 | Stranice | 70 | B1 | Strážný | 56 | C2 | Ströms vattudal | 101 | E1 | Stupnik | 70 | C2 |
| Storby | 106 | C3 | Storstrømmen | 108 | C4 | Stranorlar | 12 | C1 | Strážný | 56 | C2 | Strongoli | 67 | F2 | Stura di Demonte | 31 | E3 |
| Stord | 104 | A2 | | | | Stranraer | 4 | B3 | Streatley | 9 | E2 | Stronsay | 3 | E1 | Sturehov | 106 | B4 |
| Stordal | 100 | B2 | | | | | | | Street | 9 | D3 | Stronsay Firth | 3 | E1 | Sturminster Newton | 9 | D3 |
| | | | | | | | | | Strehaia | 114 | C1 | Strontian | 2 | B4 | | | |

| Name | Pg | Grid |
|---|---|---|
| Sunnylvsfjorden | 100 | B3 |
| Suodenniemi | 107 | D1 |
| Suolahti | 103 | D2 |
| Suolijärvet | 99 | E2 |
| Suolijoki | 99 | D2 |
| Suomenlinna | 107 | E3 |
| Suomenniemi | 103 | E3 |
| Suomusjärvi | 107 | E2 |
| Suomussalmi | 99 | F3 |
| Suomutunturi | 99 | E2 |
| Suonenjoki | 103 | E2 |
| Suontee | 103 | D3 |
| Suopelto (Kuopion Lääni) | 103 | D2 |
| Suopelto (Mikkelin Lääni) | 103 | D3 |
| Super-Besse | 29 | E1 |
| Super-Molina | 32 | A3 |
| Supetar | 75 | D2 |
| Supetarska Draga | 70 | B4 |
| Supino | 63 | F3 |
| Šuplja-Stijena | 76 | B1 |
| Surahammar | 105 | F3 |
| Suraž | 111 | E4 |
| Surbo | 65 | F4 |
| Surčin | 72 | C3 |
| Surduc | 114 | C1 |
| Surdulica | 77 | E1 |
| Surdup | 76 | B2 |
| Sûre | 21 | D2 |
| Surgères | 24 | C4 |
| Súria | 32 | A3 |
| Surnadalsøra | 100 | C2 |
| Surrey | 10 | C3 |
| Sursee | 27 | F2 |
| Survilliers | 19 | F3 |
| Susa | 31 | E1 |
| Suså | 108 | C4 |
| Sušac | 75 | E3 |
| Susak | 70 | B4 |
| Susak I | 70 | B4 |
| Susch | 58 | B2 |
| Susek | 72 | B2 |
| Sušice | 56 | C1 |
| Suspiro del Moro, Ptodel | 44 | A3 |
| Susqueda, Emb de | 32 | B3 |
| Süßen | 55 | D2 |
| Sustenpass | 58 | A3 |
| Susurluk | 115 | F3 |
| Sutinjske Toplice | 70 | C2 |
| Sutivan | 75 | D2 |
| Sutjeska | 73 | D2 |
| Sutjeska nac park | 76 | A1 |
| Sutomore | 76 | B3 |
| Sutri | 63 | E2 |
| Sutterton | 7 | E3 |
| Sutton | 9 | F2 |
| Sutton Coldfield | 9 | E1 |
| Sutton-in-Ashfield | 7 | D3 |
| Sutton-on-Sea | 7 | E3 |
| Suva gora | 77 | D3 |
| Suva pl | 77 | E1 |
| Suva Reka | 77 | D2 |
| Suvasvesi | 103 | E2 |
| Suvereto | 62 | C1 |
| Suvobor | 72 | C4 |
| Suvodol | 77 | E3 |
| Suwałki | 110 | C4 |
| Suze, la | 23 | F4 |
| Suzzara | 60 | C2 |
| Sval'ava | 112 | C3 |
| Svaneke | 109 | D4 |
| Svanstein | 98 | C2 |
| Svanvik | 95 | F2 |
| Svappavaara | 94 | C4 |
| Svärdsjö | 105 | F2 |
| Svarstad | 104 | C3 |
| Svarta | 105 | E4 |
| Svartevatn | 104 | B3 |
| Svartevatn L | 104 | B3 |
| Svartisen | 97 | E2 |
| Sværvolthalvøya | 95 | E1 |
| Svattälven | 105 | F3 |
| Svedala | 108 | C3 |
| Sveg | 101 | E3 |
| Svelgen | 100 | A3 |
| Svelvik | 104 | C3 |
| Svendborg | 108 | B4 |
| Svenljunga | 108 | C2 |
| Svensby | 94 | C2 |
| Svenstavik | 101 | E2 |
| Švermov | 53 | F3 |
| Svetac | 75 | D2 |
| Sveti Andrija | 77 | D3 |
| Sveti Ilija | 75 | E3 |
| Sveti Janez | 70 | A2 |
| Sveti Jovan Bigorski | 77 | D3 |
| Sveti Naum | 77 | D4 |
| Sveti Nikita | 77 | D2 |
| Sveti Nikola | 76 | B3 |
| Sveti Nikole | 77 | E3 |
| Sveti Pantelejmon | 77 | D3 |
| Sveti Rok | 70 | C4 |
| Sveti Stefan | 76 | B3 |
| Svetlogorsk (Belorussija) | 111 | E4 |
| Svetlogorsk (Rossija) | 110 | B4 |
| Svetlovodsk | 113 | F2 |
| Svetozarevo | 73 | D4 |
| Svetozar Miletić | 72 | B1 |
| Svidnik | 112 | C3 |
| Švihov | 56 | B1 |
| Svilaja | 75 | D1 |
| Svilajnac | 73 | E3 |
| Svilengrad | 115 | E3 |
| Svingvoll | 104 | C1 |
| Svinjar | 71 | E3 |
| Svinoy | 96 | A3 |
| Svištov | 115 | D2 |
| Svitavy | 112 | A3 |
| Svodde | 77 | E1 |
| Svolvær | 94 | A4 |
| Svor | 53 | F3 |
| Svorkmo | 100 | C2 |
| Svoronáta | 86 | A1 |
| Svorónos | 79 | F4 |
| Svrljig | 73 | F4 |
| Swadlincote | 6 | C3 |
| Swaffham | 11 | D1 |
| Swale | 6 | C1 |
| Swalmen | 17 | D4 |
| Swanage | 9 | E4 |
| Swanley | 10 | C2 |
| Swanlinbar | 12 | C2 |
| Swansea | 8 | C2 |
| Świdnica | 112 | A2 |
| Świdwin | 49 | F2 |
| Świebodzin | 112 | A2 |
| Świecie | 112 | A1 |
| Świecko | 49 | F4 |
| Świerzno | 49 | F1 |
| Swilly, L | 13 | D1 |
| Swindon | 9 | E2 |
| Swinford | 12 | B3 |
| Świnoujscie | 49 | E2 |
| Swords | 13 | D3 |
| Sybil Head | 14 | A3 |
| Syčovka | 111 | F2 |
| Sykäräinen | 102 | C1 |
| Sykkylven | 100 | A2 |
| Sylene | 101 | D2 |
| Sylling | 104 | C3 |
| Sylt | 47 | F1 |
| Sylt Ost | 47 | F1 |
| Sylvenstein-Stausee | 56 | A4 |
| Synod Inn | 8 | C1 |
| Syötekylä | 99 | E3 |
| Syre | 3 | D2 |
| Sysmä | 103 | D3 |
| Sysslebäck | 101 | D4 |
| Syväjärvi | 99 | D1 |
| Syväri | 103 | E2 |
| Syvde | 100 | A3 |
| Syvdsnes | 100 | A2 |
| Syyspohja | 103 | E3 |
| Szarvas | 112 | B4 |
| Szczecin | 49 | E2 |
| Szczecinek | 110 | A4 |
| Szczeciński, Zalew | 49 | E2 |
| Szczytno | 110 | B4 |
| Szécsény | 112 | B3 |
| Szeged | 114 | B1 |
| Székesfehérvár | 112 | B4 |
| Szekszárd | 114 | B1 |
| Szentendre | 112 | B4 |
| Szentes | 112 | B4 |
| Szigetvár | 114 | B1 |
| Szolnok | 112 | B4 |
| Szombathely | 112 | A4 |

# T

| Name | Pg | Grid |
|---|---|---|
| Tabanovce | 77 | E2 |
| Tábara | 35 | D4 |
| Tabarca, I de | 45 | E2 |
| Taberg | 109 | D1 |
| Tabernas | 44 | B3 |
| Tabernes de Valldigna | 41 | E4 |
| Taboada | 34 | B2 |
| Tábor | 57 | D1 |
| Tábua | 38 | D2 |
| Tabuaço | 34 | B4 |
| Tabuenca | 36 | C3 |
| Täby | 106 | B3 |
| Tachov | 53 | E4 |
| Tadcaster | 7 | D2 |
| Tafalla | 36 | C2 |
| Tafjord | 100 | B3 |
| Taganheira | 42 | A1 |
| Taggia | 31 | F3 |
| Tagliacozzo | 63 | F2 |
| Tagliamento | 59 | E3 |
| Taglio di Po | 61 | D2 |
| Tahal | 44 | C3 |
| Tahkvuori | 103 | D2 |
| Taibilla, Sa de | 44 | C2 |
| Taígetos, Óros | 87 | D3 |
| Tain | 3 | D3 |
| Tain-l'Hermitage | 30 | B2 |
| Taipadas | 38 | A4 |
| Taipalsaari | 103 | E4 |
| Taivalkoski | 99 | E3 |
| Taivassalo | 107 | D2 |
| Tajera, Emb de la | 40 | C1 |
| Tajo, R | 40 | B2 |
| Tajuña, R | 40 | B2 |
| Takovo | 73 | D4 |
| Taktikoúpoli | 87 | E2 |
| Tálanda | 87 | E4 |
| Talarrubias | 39 | E4 |
| Talaván | 39 | D3 |
| Talave, Emb de | 44 | C1 |
| Talavera de la Reina | 39 | F3 |
| Talavera la Real | 39 | D4 |
| Talayuela | 39 | E2 |
| Talayuelas | 41 | D3 |
| Taldom | 111 | F2 |
| Talgarth | 9 | D1 |
| Talkkunapää | 95 | F3 |
| Talla | 61 | D4 |
| Taliante | 45 | D3 |
| Tallard | 31 | D2 |
| Tallberg | 101 | E4 |
| Tallinn | 110 | C1 |
| Talloires | 27 | D4 |
| Tallow | 14 | C4 |
| Talluskylä | 103 | D2 |
| Talmont | 24 | B3 |
| Tal'noje | 113 | E2 |
| Talsi | 110 | B2 |
| Talvik | 95 | D2 |
| Tamames | 39 | E1 |
| Tamar | 8 | B3 |
| Támara | 35 | F3 |
| Tamarite de Litera | 37 | E3 |
| Tamási | 112 | B4 |
| Tambre, R | 34 | A2 |
| Tâmega, R | 34 | A4 |
| Tamélos, Akr | 88 | A2 |
| Tamiš | 72 | C2 |
| Tammela | 107 | E2 |
| Tammisaari | 107 | E3 |
| Tamnava | 72 | C3 |
| Tampere | 107 | E1 |
| Tamsweg | 56 | C4 |
| Tamworth | 9 | E1 |
| Tana | 95 | E1 |
| Tana R | 95 | E1 |
| Tanafjorden | 95 | E1 |
| Tanágra | 84 | A4 |
| Tanagro | 64 | C4 |
| Tanamea, Pso di | 59 | F3 |
| Tanaro | 31 | F2 |
| Tancarville, Pont de | 19 | D3 |
| Tandådalen | 101 | D4 |
| Tandragee | 13 | D2 |
| Tandsbyn | 101 | E2 |
| Tandsjöborg | 101 | E3 |
| Tangerhütte | 48 | C4 |
| Tangermünde | 48 | C4 |
| Tanhua | 95 | F4 |
| Taninges | 27 | E4 |
| Tanlay | 26 | B1 |
| Tann | 52 | B3 |
| Tännäs | 101 | D3 |
| Tanndalen | 101 | D3 |
| Tannheim | 58 | C1 |
| Tannila | 99 | D3 |
| Tanumshede | 105 | D4 |
| Taormina | 69 | D3 |
| Tapa | 110 | C1 |
| Tapia de Casariego | 34 | C1 |
| Tar | 70 | A3 |
| Tara | 72 | C4 |
| Tara R | 76 | B1 |
| Taracena | 40 | B2 |
| Tara klisura | 76 | B2 |
| Tarancón | 40 | B3 |
| Taranto | 65 | E4 |
| Taranto, Golfo di | 65 | E4 |
| Tarare | 26 | B4 |
| Taraš | 72 | C2 |
| Tarašča | 113 | E2 |
| Tarascon (Ariège) | 32 | A2 |
| Tarascon (Vaucluse) | 30 | B3 |
| Taravo | 33 | F3 |
| Tarayuela | 41 | E2 |
| Tarazona | 36 | C3 |
| Tarazona de la Mancha | 40 | C4 |
| Tarbat Ness | 3 | D3 |
| Tarbert (IRL) | 14 | B3 |
| Tarbert (Strathclyde) | 4 | B2 |
| Tarbert (Western Is) | 2 | B2 |
| Tarbes | 37 | E1 |
| Tarbet | 4 | C1 |
| Tarcento | 59 | F3 |
| Tarčin | 75 | F1 |
| Tardets-Sorholus | 37 | D1 |
| Tardienta | 37 | D3 |
| Tärendo | 98 | C2 |
| Tärendöälven | 98 | C1 |
| Targon | 28 | B2 |
| Târgovište | 115 | E2 |
| Tarifa | 43 | D4 |
| Tarm | 108 | A3 |
| Tarmstedt | 47 | F3 |
| Tarn | 29 | D3 |
| Tarn (Dépt) | 29 | E3 |
| Tärnaby | 97 | E3 |
| Tarna, Pto de | 35 | E2 |
| Tarn-et-Garonne | 29 | D3 |
| Tarn, Gges du | 29 | F3 |
| Tarnobrzeg | 112 | C2 |
| Tarnos | 28 | A4 |
| Tarnów | 112 | B2 |
| Taro | 60 | B2 |
| Tarouca | 38 | C1 |
| Tarquinia | 63 | D2 |
| Tarporley | 6 | B3 |
| Tarragona | 37 | F4 |
| Tarrasa | 32 | A4 |
| Tàrrega | 37 | F4 |
| Tarrekaise | 98 | A2 |
| Tàrs | 108 | B4 |
| Tarsia | 67 | E2 |
| Tartas | 28 | B3 |
| Tartu | 110 | C2 |
| Tarvasjoki | 107 | D2 |
| Tarvisio | 59 | F2 |
| Täsch | 27 | F4 |
| Tåsinge | 108 | B4 |
| Tåsjo | 101 | F1 |
| Tåsjön | 101 | F1 |
| Tassin | 26 | C4 |
| Tåstrup | 108 | C3 |
| Tata | 112 | B4 |
| Tatabánya | 112 | B4 |
| Tatarbunary | 113 | E4 |
| Tatry | 112 | B3 |
| Tau | 104 | A3 |
| Tauber | 55 | D1 |
| Tauberbischofsheim | 55 | D1 |
| Taucha | 53 | D2 |
| Tauerntal | 59 | E2 |
| Tauerntunnel | 59 | E2 |
| Taufers i. M. | 58 | C3 |
| Taufkirchen | 56 | B3 |
| Taulé | 22 | B2 |
| Taunton | 9 | D3 |
| Taunus | 51 | F4 |
| Taunusstein | 51 | F4 |
| Tauplitz | 57 | D4 |
| Tauragè | 110 | B3 |
| Taurianova | 67 | E4 |
| Taurion | 25 | E4 |
| Tauste | 36 | C3 |
| Tauves | 29 | E1 |
| Tavankut | 72 | B1 |
| Tavannes | 27 | E2 |
| Tavarnelle Val di Pesa | 60 | C4 |
| Tavastila | 103 | F4 |
| Tavaux | 26 | C2 |
| Taverna | 67 | F3 |
| Tavernelle | 63 | E1 |
| Tavernes | 31 | D4 |
| Tavignano | 33 | F3 |
| Tavira | 42 | B3 |
| Tavistock | 8 | C3 |
| Tavolara, I | 66 | C1 |
| Tavropós | 83 | D2 |
| Tavropoú, Teh L | 83 | D2 |
| Tavşanli | 115 | F3 |
| Taw | 8 | C3 |
| Taxenbach | 59 | E1 |
| Taxiárhis | 80 | B3 |
| Tay | 5 | D1 |
| Tayinloan | 4 | B2 |
| Tay, L | 4 | C1 |
| Tayport | 5 | D1 |
| Tayside | 3 | D4 |
| Tazones | 35 | E1 |
| Tczew | 110 | A4 |
| Teano | 64 | A3 |
| Teba | 43 | E3 |
| Tebay | 5 | D4 |
| Tech | 32 | B3 |
| Techendorf | 59 | F2 |
| Tecklenburg | 17 | E2 |
| Tecuci | 113 | E4 |
| Tees | 5 | E4 |
| Teesside | 5 | E4 |
| Teféli | 91 | D4 |
| Tegéa | 87 | D2 |
| Tegel | 49 | E4 |
| Tegelen | 17 | D4 |
| Tegernsee | 56 | A4 |
| Teggiano | 64 | C4 |
| Teguise | 42 | C3 |
| Teide | 42 | B4 |
| Teide Mt | 42 | A4 |
| Teide, Pque Nac del | 42 | B4 |
| Teignmouth | 8 | C4 |
| Teijo | 107 | D3 |
| Teil, le | 30 | B2 |
| Teilleul, le | 18 | C4 |
| Teisendorf | 56 | B3 |
| Teisko | 102 | C3 |
| Teixeiro | 34 | B1 |
| Teixoso | 38 | C2 |
| Tejeda, Sa de | 43 | F3 |
| Tejo, R | 38 | A3 |
| Tekeriš | 72 | C3 |
| Tekija | 73 | E2 |
| Tekirdağ | 115 | E3 |
| Telč | 57 | E1 |
| Telde | 42 | B4 |
| Telemark | 104 | C3 |
| Télendos, N | 89 | E3 |
| Teleno | 34 | C3 |
| Telese | 64 | B3 |
| Telford | 6 | C3 |
| Telfs | 58 | C2 |
| Telgte | 17 | E3 |
| Telti | 66 | B1 |
| Teltow | 49 | D4 |
| Témbi | 83 | E1 |
| Tembleque | 40 | B3 |
| Temerin | 72 | C2 |
| Temmes | 99 | D4 |
| Tempelhof | 49 | E4 |
| Tempio Pausania | 66 | B1 |
| Templemore | 12 | C4 |
| Templin | 49 | D3 |
| Temse | 50 | B3 |
| Temska | 73 | F4 |
| Tenala | 107 | E3 |
| Ténaro, Akr | 87 | D4 |
| Tenbury Wells | 9 | D1 |
| Tenby | 8 | B2 |
| Tence | 30 | B2 |
| Tende | 31 | E3 |
| Tende, Col de | 31 | E3 |
| Tende, Colle di | 31 | E3 |
| Tendilla | 40 | B2 |
| Tenerife | 42 | A4 |
| Tenhola | 107 | E3 |
| Tenja | 71 | F2 |
| Tennes | 94 | B3 |
| Tenniöjoki | 95 | F4 |
| Teno | 95 | E2 |
| Tensta | 106 | B3 |
| Tenterden | 11 | D3 |
| Tentudia | 43 | D1 |
| Teolo | 61 | D1 |
| Teovo | 77 | E3 |
| Tepelenë | 114 | C4 |
| Teplá | 53 | E4 |
| Teplice | 53 | E3 |
| Tepsa | 95 | E4 |
| Teramo | 63 | F1 |
| Ter Apel | 17 | E1 |
| Tera, R | 35 | D3 |
| Terebovl'a | 113 | D3 |
| Terena | 38 | C4 |
| Terespol | 112 | C1 |
| Terezino Polje | 71 | E2 |
| Terges, Rib de | 42 | B2 |
| Tergnier | 20 | A2 |
| Terjärv | 102 | C2 |
| Terlizzi | 65 | D3 |
| Termas de Monfortinho | 39 | D2 |
| Terme Luigiane | 67 | E2 |
| Termini Imerese | 68 | B3 |
| Terminillo | 63 | F2 |
| Terminillo, Mte | 63 | F2 |
| Termoli | 64 | B2 |
| Terneuzen | 16 | B4 |
| Terni | 63 | E2 |
| Ternitz | 57 | E3 |
| Ternopol' | 113 | D2 |
| Térovo | 82 | C2 |
| Terpilos | 80 | A2 |
| Terpní | 80 | B2 |
| Terpsithéa | 83 | D4 |
| Ter, R | 32 | B3 |
| Terracina | 63 | F3 |
| Terra de Basto | 34 | B4 |
| Terradets, Emb dels | 37 | F3 |
| Terrak | 97 | D4 |
| Terralba | 66 | B3 |
| Terranova di Pollino | 67 | E2 |
| Terranuova Braccio Iini | 61 | D4 |
| Terrasini | 68 | B3 |
| Terrassa | 32 | A4 |
| Terrasson-la-Villedieu | 29 | D2 |
| Terrenoire | 30 | B1 |
| Terriente | 41 | D2 |
| Terschelling | 16 | C1 |
| Teruel | 41 | D2 |
| Tervakoski | 107 | E2 |
| Tervo | 103 | D2 |
| Tervola | 99 | D2 |
| Tervuren | 50 | C3 |
| Terzaga | 40 | C2 |
| Tešanj | 71 | F3 |
| Teslić | 71 | E3 |
| Tessin | 48 | C2 |
| Tessy | 18 | C3 |
| Teste, la | 28 | A2 |
| Tetbury | 9 | E2 |
| Teterev | 113 | E2 |
| Teterow | 49 | D2 |
| Tetica | 44 | B3 |
| Tetijev | 113 | E2 |
| Tetovo | 77 | D3 |
| Tetrákomo | 82 | C2 |
| Tettnang | 55 | D4 |
| Teuchern | 53 | D2 |
| Teufen | 58 | B2 |
| Teulada | 66 | B4 |
| Teupitz | 53 | E1 |
| Teuva | 102 | B3 |
| Tevere | 63 | E2 |
| Teviot | 5 | D3 |
| Tewkesbury | 9 | E2 |
| Texel | 16 | C1 |
| Thabor, Mt | 31 | D1 |
| Thale | 52 | C2 |
| Thalfang | 54 | B1 |
| Thalgau | 56 | C3 |
| Thalheim | 53 | E3 |
| Thalmässing | 55 | F2 |
| Thalwil | 58 | A2 |
| Thame | 9 | F2 |
| Thames, R | 11 | D2 |
| Thanes, K e | 76 | C4 |
| Thann | 27 | E1 |
| Thannhausen | 55 | E3 |
| Thaon | 27 | D1 |
| Tharandt | 53 | E2 |
| Tharsis | 42 | C2 |
| Thássos | 80 | C3 |
| Thássos, N | 81 | D3 |
| Thatë, Mal i | 77 | D4 |
| Thau, Bessin de | 30 | A4 |
| Thaya | 57 | F1 |
| Thégonnec | 22 | B2 |
| Theil, le | 23 | F3 |
| Themar | 52 | C3 |
| Thenon | 29 | D2 |
| Theológos (Stereá Eláda) | 83 | F3 |
| Theológos (Thássos) | 80 | C3 |
| Théoule | 31 | E4 |
| Thérain | 19 | F3 |
| Thérma (Ikaria) | 89 | D2 |

## Torino

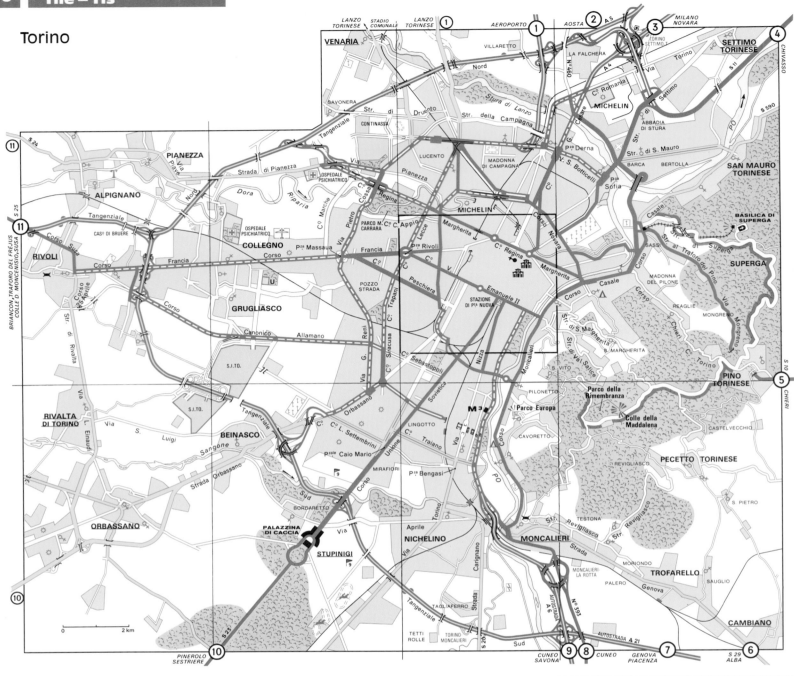

| | | | | | | | | | | | | | | |
|---|---|---|---|---|---|---|---|---|---|---|---|---|---|---|
| Thermá (Makedonía) | 80 B2 | Thiéblemont-Farémont | 20 C4 | Thomastown | 15 D3 | Thurso | 3 D2 | Tihío | 79 D3 | Timok | 73 F3 | Tipperary (Co) | 12 C4 |
| Thérma (Samothráki) | 81 E3 | Thiendorf | 53 E2 | Thônes | 27 D4 | Thury-Harcourt | 18 C3 | Tihuta | 113 D4 | Timoleague | 14 B4 | Tiranë | 76 C4 |
| Thermaikós Kólpos | 80 A4 | Thiene | 59 D4 | Thonon | 27 D3 | Thusis | 58 B3 | Tiilikkajärvi | 103 E1 | Timrå | 101 F3 | Tirano | 58 C3 |
| Thérma Lefkádas | 89 D2 | Thiers | 26 B4 | Thorens-Glières | 27 D4 | Thy | 108 A2 | Tiistenjoki | 102 C2 | Timv. Peristéria | 86 C3 | Tiraspol' | 113 E3 |
| Thérmi | 79 F3 | Thiesi | 66 B2 | Thorikó | 88 A2 | Thyborøn | 108 A2 | Tijesno | 74 C1 | Tinahely | 13 D4 | Tire | 115 F4 |
| Thermí | 85 F2 | Thiessow | 49 D1 | Thorne | 7 D2 | Tibro | 109 D1 | Tijola | 44 B3 | Tinchebray | 18 C4 | Tiree | 2 A4 |
| Thermissía | 87 E2 | Thillot, le | 27 E1 | Thornhill | 4 C3 | Tichvin | 111 E1 | Tikkakoski | 103 D3 | Tindari | 69 D2 | Tirgo-Neamt | 113 D4 |
| Thérmo | 83 D4 | Thimariá | 81 F2 | Thouarcé | 24 C3 | Ticino | 60 A1 | Tikkala | 103 F2 | Tinée | 31 E3 | Tirgoviste | 115 D1 |
| Thermopiles | 83 E3 | Thímena | 89 E2 | Thouars | 24 C3 | Ticino R | 58 A3 | Tikveš, Ez | 77 E3 | Tineo | 35 D1 | Tirgu Frumos | 113 E3 |
| Thérouanne | 19 F1 | Thimena, N | 89 E2 | Thouet | 24 C3 | Tidaholm | 109 D1 | Tilburg | 16 C3 | Tingáki | 89 F3 | Tirgu Jiu | 114 C1 |
| Thespiés | 83 F4 | Thiní, Akr | 87 E2 | Thouría | 86 C3 | Tidö | 106 A3 | Tilbury | 10 C2 | Tinglev | 108 A4 | Tirgu Mures | 113 D4 |
| Thesprotía | 82 B2 | Thionville | 21 D3 | Thoúrio | 81 F1 | Tiefenbronn | 54 C2 | Tilissos | 91 D3 | Tingsryd | 109 E2 | Tirgu Secuiesc | 113 D4 |
| Thesprotikó | 82 B2 | Thira | 91 E1 | Thráki | 81 E2 | Tiefencastel | 58 B3 | Tillberga | 106 A3 | Tingvoll | 100 B2 | Tirig | 41 F2 |
| Thessalía | 83 E2 | Thira, N | 91 E1 | Thrakikó Pélagos | 81 D3 | Tiefensee | 49 E4 | Tillières | 19 E4 | Tingvollfjorden | 100 B2 | Tirintha | 87 D2 |
| Thessaloníki | 79 F3 | Thirassía, N | 91 E1 | Thrapston | 9 F1 | Tiel | 16 C3 | Tilly-sur-Seulles | 18 C3 | Tinja | 71 F3 | Tiriolo | 67 F3 |
| Thessaloníki (Nomos) | 80 A3 | Thirsk | 7 D1 | Threshfield | 6 C1 | Tielt | 50 A3 | Tilos, N | 89 F4 | Tinn | 104 C3 | Tírnavos | 83 E1 |
| Thetford | 11 D1 | Thisted | 108 A2 | Thueyts | 30 B2 | Tienen | 50 C3 | Timanfaya, Parque Nac. de | 42 C3 | Tinnsjø | 104 C3 | Tirol | 58 C2 |
| Theux | 51 D4 | Thíva | 84 A4 | Thuin | 50 B4 | Tiengen | 54 C4 | Timbáki | 91 D4 | Tínos | 88 C2 | Tirós | 87 D3 |
| Thèze | 28 B4 | Thiviers | 28 C1 | Thuir | 32 B2 | Tierbmesvarri | 94 C3 | Tímbano | 81 D2 | Tínos, N | 88 C2 | Tirrenía | 60 C4 |
| Thézenay | 24 C3 | Thizy | 26 B4 | Thum | 53 E3 | Tiercé | 23 E4 | Tímfi, Óros | 78 C4 | Tíñoso, C | 45 D3 | Tirreno, Mare | 68 B2 |
| Thíamis | 82 B1 | Thoissey | 26 C4 | Thun | 27 E3 | Tierga | 36 C3 | Timfristós | 83 D3 | Tintagel | 8 B3 | Tirschenreuth | 53 D4 |
| Thiaucourt | 21 D3 | Tholen | 16 B3 | Thur | 58 A1 | Tierp | 106 B3 | Timfristós Mt | 83 D3 | Tinténiac | 23 D3 | Tirso | 66 B2 |
| Thiberville | 19 D3 | Tholey | 54 B1 | Thüringen | 58 B2 | Tiétar, R | 39 E2 | Timiş | 114 C1 | Tinto, R | 42 C2 | Tirstrup | 108 B3 |
| | | Thollon | 27 E3 | Thüringer Wald | 52 B3 | Tigharry | 2 A3 | Timişoara | 114 C1 | Tiobraid Árann | 14 C3 | Tirteafuera, R | 39 F4 |
| | | Tholó | 86 C2 | Thurles | 14 C3 | Tighnabruaich | 4 B2 | Timmelsjoch | 58 C2 | Tione di Trento | 58 C3 | Tisa | 72 C2 |
| | | Tholopotámi | 85 E4 | Thurn, Paß | 59 E1 | Tignes | 31 D1 | Timmendorfer Strand | 48 B2 | Tipasoja | 103 E1 | Tiscar, Pto de | 44 B2 |
| | | Tholós | 80 B2 | Thursby | 5 D4 | Tignes, Bge de | 31 E1 | Tiheró | 81 F2 | Tipperary | 14 C3 | Tišnov | 57 E1 |

| | | | |
|---|---|---|---|
| Tisvildeleje | 108 C3 | Tomiño | 34 A3 |
| Tisza | 112 B4 | Tomintoul | 3 D4 |
| Tiszafüred | 112 B4 | Tomma | 97 D2 |
| Tiszavasvári | 112 C3 | Tømmervøg | 100 B2 |
| Titaguas | 41 D3 | Tomra | 100 B2 |
| Titarissios | 83 E1 | Tomtabacken | 109 D2 |
| Titel | 72 C2 | Tona | 32 B3 |
| Titisee | 54 C4 | Tonale, Pso del | 58 C3 |
| Titlis | 58 A3 | Tonara | 66 B3 |
| Tito | 64 C4 | Tonbridge | 10 C3 |
| Titograd | 76 B3 | Tondela | 38 B1 |
| Titova Korenica | 70 C4 | Tønder | 108 A4 |
| Titova Mitrovica | 77 D1 | Tongeren | 50 C3 |
| Titov Drvar | 71 D4 | Tongue | 2 C2 |
| Titovo Užce | 72 C4 | Topla | 70 B1 |
| Titov Veles | 77 E3 | Toplica | 77 D1 |
| Titov vrh | 77 D3 | Topli Do | 73 F4 |
| Titran | 100 B1 | Toplița | 113 D4 |
| Tittmoning | 56 B3 | Toploú | 91 F4 |
| Tiumpan Head | 2 B2 | Topola | 73 D3 |
| Tivat | 76 B3 | Topolčani | 77 E4 |
| Tiveden | 105 E4 | Topol'čany | 112 B3 |
| Tivenys | 41 F2 | Topólia | 90 B3 |
| Tiverton | 8 C3 | Topolovnik | 73 E3 |
| Tivissa | 41 F1 | Topusko | 70 C3 |
| Tivoli | 63 E2 | Torà de |
| Tjaktjajaure | 98 A2 | Riubregós | 32 A3 |
| Tjällmo | 105 F4 | Torano Castello | 67 E2 |
| Tjeggelvas | 98 A2 | Torbay | 8 C4 |
| Tjeldøya | 94 B3 | Torbole | 58 C4 |
| Tjeldstø | 104 A2 | Torcello | 61 D1 |
| Tjentište | 76 A1 | Torchiarolo | 65 F3 |
| Tjøme | 104 C4 | Tordera | 32 B4 |
| Tjong | 97 E2 | Tordesillas | 35 E4 |
| Tjørnuvik | 96 A3 | Tordesilos | 41 D2 |
| Tjøtta | 97 D3 | Tore | 2 C3 |
| Tkon | 74 C1 | Töre | 98 C3 |
| Tobarra | 44 C1 | Töreboda | 105 E4 |
| Tobercurry | 12 B2 | Torella d. Sannio | 64 B3 |
| Tobermore | 13 D2 | Toreno | 34 C2 |
| Tobermory | 2 B4 | Torgau | 53 E2 |
| Toberonochy | 4 B1 | Torgelow | 49 E2 |
| Toblach | 59 E2 | Torhout | 50 A3 |
| Toce | 58 A3 | Torigni | 18 C3 |
| Tocha | 38 B2 | Torija | 40 B2 |
| Tocina | 43 D2 | Torino | 31 E1 |
| Todi | 63 E1 | Torio, R | 35 D2 |
| Todmorden | 6 C2 | Torla | 37 E2 |
| Todorići | 71 E4 | Törmänen | 95 F3 |
| Todtmoos | 54 C4 | Törmänmäki | 99 E4 |
| Todtnau | 54 C4 | Tormes, R | 39 E1 |
| Toe Head (GB) | 2 A2 | Tormos | 37 D3 |
| Toe Head (IRL) | 14 B4 | Tornavacas | 39 E2 |
| Tøfsingdalen | 101 D3 | Tornavacas, Pto |
| Toft | 3 F1 | de | 39 E2 |
| Tofte | 104 C3 | Torneälven | 94 C4 |
| Toftir | 96 A4 | Torneträsk | 94 C3 |
| Toftlund | 108 A4 | Tornik | 76 B1 |
| Tohmajärvi | 103 F2 | Tornio | 98 C3 |
| Toholampi | 102 C1 | Tornionjoki | 98 C2 |
| Toijala | 107 E2 | Tornjoš | 72 C1 |
| Toivakka | 103 D3 | Toro | 35 D4 |
| Toivala | 103 E2 | Törökszentmiklós | 112 B4 |
| Tojšići | 72 B3 | Toro, Monte | 45 F1 |
| Tok | 53 F4 | Toróni | 80 B4 |
| Tokaj | 112 C3 | Toropec | 111 E2 |
| Tolbuhin | 115 E2 | Torpo | 104 C2 |
| Toledo | 40 A3 | Torpoint | 8 C4 |
| Toledo, Mts de | 40 A3 | Torpshammar | 101 F3 |
| Tolentino | 61 F4 | Torquay | 8 C4 |
| Tolfa | 63 D2 | Torquemada | 35 F3 |
| Tolga | 100 C3 | Torralba de |
| Tollarp | 109 D3 | Calatrava | 40 A4 |
| Tollense | 49 D2 | Torrão | 42 B1 |
| Tølløse | 108 C3 | Torre | 38 C2 |
| Tolmezzo | 59 E3 | Torre Annunziata | 64 B4 |
| Tolmin | 70 A2 | Torre Baja | 41 D3 |
| Toló | 87 D2 | Torre Beretti | 60 A2 |
| Tolox | 43 E4 | Torreblanca | 41 F3 |
| Tolva | 99 E2 | Torrecaballeros | 40 A1 |
| Tolve | 65 D4 | Torrecampo | 43 F1 |
| Tomar | 38 B3 | Torre Canne | 65 E3 |
| Tomaševac | 73 D2 | Torrecilla | 43 E4 |
| Tomaševo | 76 B2 | Torrecilla en |
| Tomašica | 71 D3 | Cameros | 36 B2 |
| Tomaszów |
| Lubelski | 112 C2 |
| Tomaszów |
| Mazowiecki | 112 B2 |
| Tombebœuf | 28 C3 |
| Tomelilla | 109 D3 |
| Tomelloso | 40 B4 |

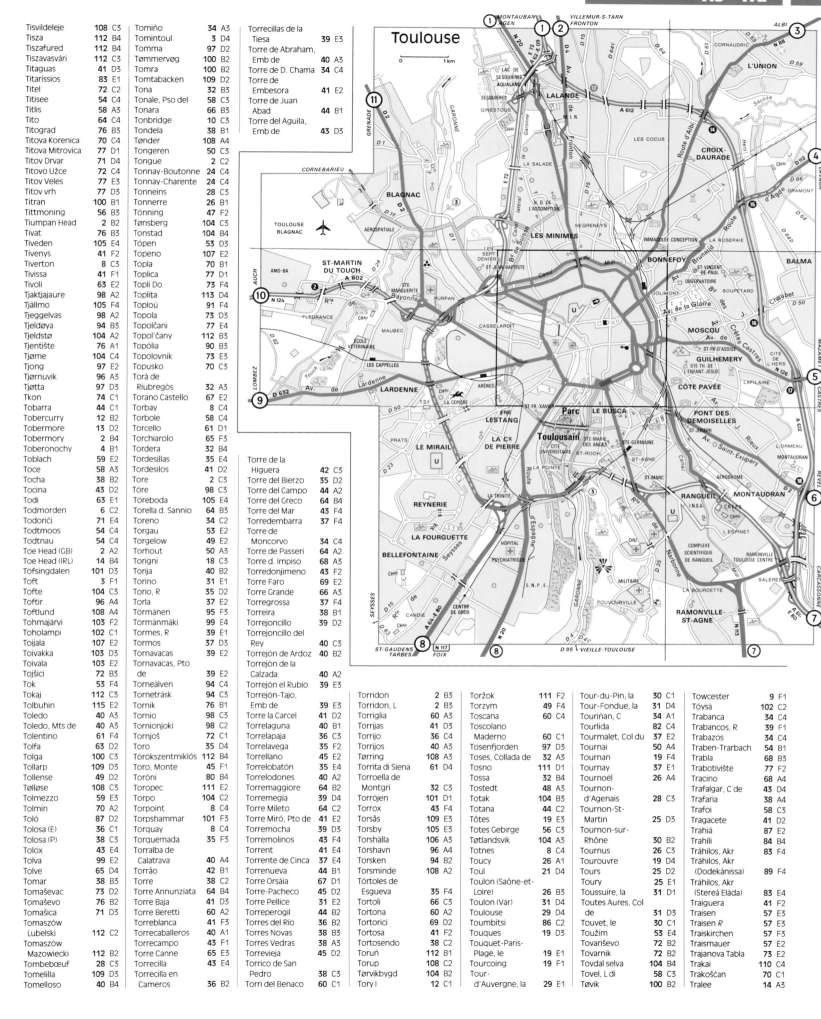

Toulouse

0    1 km

| | | | |
|---|---|---|---|
| Torrecillas de la |
| Tiesa | 39 E3 |
| Torre de Abraham, |
| Emb de | 40 A3 |
| Torre de D. Chama | 34 C4 |
| Torre de |
| Embesora | 41 E2 |
| Torre de Juan |
| Abad | 44 B1 |
| Torre del Aguila, |
| Emb de | 43 D3 |

| | | | |
|---|---|---|---|
| Torre de la |
| Higuera | 42 C3 |
| Torre del Bierzo | 35 D2 |
| Torre del Campo | 44 A2 |
| Torre del Greco | 64 B4 |
| Torre del Mar | 43 F4 |
| Torredembarra | 37 F4 |
| Torre de |
| Moncorvo | 34 C4 |
| Torre de Passeri | 64 A2 |
| Torre d. Impiso | 68 A3 |
| Torredonjimeno | 43 F2 |
| Torre Faro | 69 E2 |
| Torre Grande | 66 A3 |
| Torregrossa | 37 F3 |
| Torreira | 38 B1 |
| Torrejoncillo | 39 D2 |
| Torrejoncillo del |
| Rey | 40 C3 |
| Torrejón de Ardoz | 40 B2 |
| Torrejón de la |
| Calzada | 40 A2 |
| Torrejón el Rubio | 39 E3 |
| Torrejón-Tajo, |
| Emb de | 39 E3 |
| Torre la Carcel | 41 D2 |
| Torrelaguna | 40 B1 |
| Torrelapaja | 36 C3 |
| Torrelavega | 35 F2 |
| Torrellano | 45 E2 |
| Torrelobatón | 35 E4 |
| Torrelodones | 40 A2 |
| Torremaggiore | 64 B2 |
| Torremegía | 39 D4 |
| Torre Mileto | 64 C2 |
| Torre Miró, Pto de | 41 E2 |
| Torremocha | 39 D3 |
| Torremolinos | 43 F4 |
| Torrent | 41 E4 |
| Torrente de Cinca | 37 E4 |
| Torrenueva | 44 B1 |
| Torre Orsáia | 67 D1 |
| Torre-Pacheco | 45 D2 |
| Torre Pellice | 31 E1 |
| Torreperogil | 44 B2 |
| Torres del Río | 36 B2 |
| Torres Novas | 38 B3 |
| Torres Vedras | 38 A3 |
| Torrevieja | 45 D2 |
| Torrico de San |
| Pedro | 38 C3 |
| Torri del Benaco | 60 C1 |

| | | | | | | | |
|---|---|---|---|---|---|---|---|
| Torridon | 2 B3 | Toržok | 111 F2 | Tour-du-Pin, la | 30 C1 | Towcester | 9 F1 |
| Torridon, L | 2 B3 | Torzym | 49 F4 | Tour-Fondue, la | 31 D4 | Töysä | 102 C2 |
| Torriglia | 60 A3 | Toscana | 60 C2 | Touriñan, C | 34 A1 | Trabanca | 34 C4 |
| Torrijas | 41 D3 | Toscolano | | Tourlida | 82 C4 | Trabancos, R | 39 F1 |
| Torrijo | 36 C4 | Maderno | 60 C1 | Tourmalet, Col du | 37 E2 | Trabazos | 34 C4 |
| Torrijos | 40 C4 | Tosenfjorden | 97 D3 | Tournai | 50 A4 | Traben-Trarbach | 54 B1 |
| Torrita di Siena | 61 D4 | Toses, Collada de | 32 A3 | Tournan | 19 F4 | Trabla | 68 B3 |
| Torroella de | | Tosno | 111 D1 | Tournay | 37 E1 | Trabotivište | 77 F2 |
| Montgrí | 32 C3 | Tossa | 32 B4 | Tournoël | 26 A4 | Tracino | 68 A4 |
| Törröjen | 101 D1 | Tostedt | 48 A3 | Tournon- | | Trafalgar, C de | 43 D4 |
| Torrox | 43 F4 | Totak | 104 B3 | d'Agenais | 28 C3 | Trafaria | 38 A4 |
| Torsås | 109 E3 | Totana | 44 C2 | Tournon-St- | | Trafoi | 58 C3 |
| Torsby | 105 E3 | Totes | 19 E3 | Martin | 25 D3 | Tragacete | 41 D2 |
| Torshälla | 106 A3 | Totes Gebirge | 56 C3 | Tournon-sur- | | Trahiá | 87 E2 |
| Tórshavn | 96 A4 | Tøtlandsvik | 104 A3 | Rhône | 30 B2 | Trahili | 84 B4 |
| Torsken | 94 B2 | Totnes | 8 C4 | Tournus | 26 C3 | Tráhilos, Akr | 83 F4 |
| Torsminde | 108 A2 | Toucy | 26 A1 | Tourouvre | 19 D4 | Tráhilos, Akr |
| Tórtoles de | | Toul | 21 D4 | Tours | 25 D2 | (Dodekánissa) | 89 F4 |
| Esgueva | 35 F4 | Toulon (Saône-et- | | Toury | 25 E1 | Tráhilos, Akr |
| Tortoli | 66 C3 | Loire) | 26 B3 | Toussuire, la | 31 D1 | (Stereá Eláda) | 83 E4 |
| Tortona | 60 A2 | Toulon (Var) | 31 D4 | Toutes Aures, Col | | Traiguera | 41 F2 |
| Tortorici | 69 D2 | Toulouse | 29 D4 | de | 31 D3 | Traisen | 57 E3 |
| Tortosa | 41 F3 | Toumbitsi | 86 C2 | Touvet, le | 30 C1 | Traisen R | 57 E3 |
| Tortosendo | 38 C2 | Touques | 19 D3 | Toužim | 53 E4 | Traiskirchen | 57 F3 |
| Toruń | 112 B1 | Tovariševo | 72 B2 | Traismauer | 57 E2 |
| Torup | 108 C2 | Tovarnik | 72 B2 | Trajanova Tabla | 73 E2 |
| Tory I | 12 C1 | Tovdal selva | 104 B4 | Trakai | 110 C4 |
| | | | Tovel, L di | 58 C3 | Trakošćan | 70 C1 |
| | | | Tøvik | 100 B2 | Tralee | 14 A3 |

| Name | Pg | Grid |
|---|---|---|
| Tralee B | 14 | A3 |
| Trá Lí | 14 | A3 |
| Tramagal | 38 | B3 |
| Tramariglio | 66 | A2 |
| Tramatza | 66 | B3 |
| Tramonti di Sopra | 59 | E3 |
| Tramore | 15 | D4 |
| Tranås | 109 | D1 |
| Tranche, la | 24 | B4 |
| Tranco, Emb del | 44 | B2 |
| Trancoso | 38 | C1 |
| Trandrandsfjällen | 101 | D4 |
| Tranebjerg | 108 | B3 |
| Tranemo | 109 | D2 |
| Tranent | 5 | D2 |
| Trænfjorden | 97 | D2 |
| Trani | 65 | D3 |
| Tranóvalto | 79 | E4 |
| Tranøy | 94 | B3 |
| Tranquera, Emb de la | 36 | C4 |
| Transilvania | 113 | D4 |
| Transtrand | 101 | D4 |
| Trapani | 68 | A3 |
| Trápeza | 86 | C1 |
| Trappstadt | 52 | C2 |
| Trasacco | 63 | F2 |
| Trasimeno, L | 61 | D4 |
| Trás os Montes | 34 | B4 |
| Trassem | 54 | A1 |
| Trasvase Tajo Segura, Canal de | 40 | C4 |
| Traun | 57 | D3 |
| Traun R | 56 | C3 |
| Traunkirchen | 56 | C3 |
| Traunreut | 56 | B3 |
| Traunsee | 56 | C3 |
| Traunstein | 56 | B3 |
| Travemünde | 48 | B2 |
| Travnik | 71 | E4 |
| Trayas, le | 31 | E4 |
| Trbovlje | 70 | B2 |
| Trbuk | 71 | F3 |
| Trbušani | 73 | D4 |
| Trdinov Vrh | 70 | C2 |
| Trebbia | 60 | B2 |
| Trebbin | 49 | D4 |
| Trébeurden | 22 | B2 |
| Trebević nac park | 76 | A1 |
| Třebíč | 57 | E1 |
| Trebinje | 76 | A2 |
| Trebisacce | 67 | F2 |
| Trebišnjica | 75 | F2 |
| Trebišov | 112 | C3 |
| Trebnje | 70 | B2 |
| Třeboň | 57 | D1 |
| Tréboul | 22 | A3 |
| Trebsen | 53 | D2 |
| Trebujena | 43 | D3 |
| Trecastagni | 69 | D3 |
| Trecate | 60 | A1 |
| Tre Croci, Pso | 59 | D2 |
| Tredegar | 9 | D2 |
| Tredozio | 61 | D3 |
| Treene | 48 | A1 |
| Treffort | 26 | C4 |
| Treffurt | 52 | B3 |
| Trefynwy | 9 | D2 |
| Tregaron | 8 | C1 |
| Trégastel | 22 | B2 |
| Tregnago | 60 | C1 |
| Tregony | 8 | B4 |
| Tréguier | 22 | C2 |
| Trehörningsjö | 102 | A1 |
| Treia (D) | 47 | F1 |
| Treia (I) | 61 | F4 |
| Treignac | 29 | D1 |
| Trelleborg (S) | 108 | C4 |
| Trelleborg (SF) | 108 | B3 |
| Trélon | 20 | B2 |
| Tremblade, la | 28 | A1 |
| Tremestieri | 69 | D2 |
| Tremezzo | 58 | B4 |
| Tremiti, I | 64 | C2 |
| Tremp | 37 | F3 |
| Trenčín | 112 | B3 |
| Trendelburg | 52 | A2 |
| Trentino-Alto Adige | 58 | C3 |
| Trento | 59 | D3 |
| Trent, R | 7 | D2 |
| Trepča (Crna Gora) | 76 | C2 |
| Trepča (Kosovo) | 77 | D1 |
| Tréport, le | 19 | E2 |
| Trepuzzi | 65 | F4 |
| Tresco | 8 | A4 |
| Trescore Balneario | 60 | B1 |
| Tresenda | 58 | B3 |
| Tresfjord | 100 | B2 |
| Tresjuncos | 40 | B3 |
| Treska | 77 | D3 |
| Treskavica | 75 | F1 |
| Tres Mares, Pico de | 35 | F2 |
| Trešnjevica | 73 | E4 |
| Trešnjevik | 76 | B2 |
| Trespaderne | 36 | A2 |
| Třešť | 57 | E1 |
| Trets | 30 | C4 |
| Tretten | 104 | C1 |
| Treuchtlingen | 55 | E2 |
| Treuen | 53 | D3 |
| Treuenbrietzen | 53 | D1 |
| Treungen | 104 | B4 |
| Trevélez | 44 | A3 |
| Trèves | 29 | F3 |
| Trevi | 63 | E1 |
| Trévières | 18 | C3 |
| Treviglio | 60 | B1 |
| Trevignano Romano | 63 | E2 |
| Treviño | 36 | B2 |
| Treviso | 59 | E4 |
| Trévoux | 26 | C4 |
| Trezzo sull' Adda | 60 | A1 |
| Trgovište | 77 | E2 |
| Trhové Sviny | 57 | D2 |
| Triánda | 93 | F1 |
| Tría Nissiá | 92 | C1 |
| Triaucourt | 20 | C3 |
| Tribanj Krušćica | 70 | C4 |
| Triberg | 54 | C3 |
| Tribsees | 49 | D2 |
| Tricarico | 65 | D4 |
| Tricase | 65 | F4 |
| Tricesimo | 59 | F3 |
| Trichiana | 59 | E3 |
| Trie | 37 | E1 |
| Trieben | 57 | D4 |
| Trier | 54 | A1 |
| Trieste | 59 | F4 |
| Trieste, G di | 59 | F4 |
| Trifels | 54 | C2 |
| Trifili | 81 | F2 |
| Triglav | 70 | A2 |
| Trigóna | 82 | C1 |
| Trigueros | 42 | C2 |
| Trihonída, L | 83 | D4 |
| Trijueque | 40 | B2 |
| Tríkala (Makedonía) | 79 | F3 |
| Tríkala (Nomos) | 82 | C1 |
| Tríkala (Pelopónissos) | 87 | D1 |
| Trikala (Thessalía) | 83 | D1 |
| Tríkeri | 83 | F2 |
| Trilj | 75 | E1 |
| Trillevallen | 101 | D2 |
| Trillo | 40 | C2 |
| Trílofo | 83 | E3 |
| Trim | 13 | D3 |
| Trimouille, la | 25 | D3 |
| Trindade | 34 | C4 |
| Třinec | 112 | B3 |
| Tring | 9 | F2 |
| Tringía | 82 | C1 |
| Trinità d'Agultu e V. | 66 | B1 |
| Trinitapoli | 64 | C3 |
| Trinité, la | 22 | C4 |
| Trinité-Porhoët, la | 22 | C3 |
| Trino | 31 | F1 |
| Triora | 31 | F3 |
| Trípi | 87 | D3 |
| Tripití | 80 | B3 |
| Tripití, Akr | 85 | D2 |
| Tripoli | 87 | D2 |
| Triponzo | 63 | E1 |
| Tripótama | 86 | C1 |
| Triptis | 53 | D3 |
| Trisanna | 58 | C2 |
| Trischen | 47 | F2 |
| Trittau | 48 | B3 |
| Trittenheim | 54 | B1 |
| Trivento | 64 | B2 |
| Trizína | 87 | E2 |
| Trlica | 76 | B1 |
| Trnava | 112 | A3 |
| Trnovo (Bosna i Hercegovina) | 75 | F1 |
| Trnovo (Slovenija) | 70 | A2 |
| Trnova Poljana | 75 | D1 |
| Troarn | 18 | C3 |
| Trofa | 34 | A4 |
| Trofaiach | 57 | E4 |
| Trofors | 97 | E3 |
| Trogir | 75 | D2 |
| Troglav, V. | 75 | D1 |
| Tróhalos | 83 | E1 |
| Troia | 64 | C3 |
| Tróia, Pen de | 38 | A4 |
| Troina | 68 | C3 |
| Troisdorf | 51 | E3 |
| Trois Epis, les | 27 | E1 |
| Trois-Moutiers, les | 24 | C3 |
| Trois-Ponts | 51 | D4 |
| Trojan | 115 | D2 |
| Trojane | 70 | B2 |
| Trollhättan | 108 | C1 |
| Trollheimen | 100 | C2 |
| Troms | 94 | C3 |
| Tromsdalen | 94 | B3 |
| Tromsø | 94 | B3 |
| Trondheim | 100 | C2 |
| Trondheimsfjorden | 100 | C1 |
| Trondsheimsleia | 100 | B1 |
| Tronö | 101 | F4 |
| Tronto | 63 | F1 |
| Troo | 23 | F4 |
| Troon | 4 | C2 |
| Tropea | 67 | E3 |
| Trópea | 86 | C2 |
| Tropojë | 76 | C2 |
| Trosa | 106 | B4 |
| Trossachs, The | 4 | C1 |
| Trostan | 13 | E1 |
| Trostberg | 56 | B3 |
| Trouville | 19 | D3 |
| Trowbridge | 9 | D2 |
| Troyes | 26 | B1 |
| Trpanj | 75 | E2 |
| Trpezi | 76 | C2 |
| Trpinja | 71 | F2 |
| Trsa | 76 | B2 |
| Tršić | 72 | B3 |
| Trstenik (Kosovo) | 77 | D2 |
| Trstenik (Pelješac) | 75 | E2 |
| Trstenik (Srbija) | 73 | D4 |
| Trsteno | 75 | F2 |
| Trubčevsk | 111 | F4 |
| Trubia | 35 | D1 |
| Trubia, R | 35 | D1 |
| Trubjela | 76 | B2 |
| Truchas | 34 | C3 |
| Truchtersheim | 21 | E4 |
| Trujillo | 39 | E3 |
| Trun | 19 | D4 |
| Truro | 8 | B4 |
| Trutnov | 112 | A2 |
| Truyère, Gorges de la | 29 | E2 |
| Tryde | 109 | D3 |
| Trysilelva | 100 | D3 |
| Tržac | 70 | C3 |
| Trzcińsko-Zdrój | 49 | E3 |
| Trzebiatów | 49 | F1 |
| Trzebież | 49 | E2 |
| Tržič Golnik | 70 | A2 |
| Tsamandás | 82 | B1 |
| Tsambíka | 93 | F1 |
| Tsangaráda | 83 | F2 |
| Tsangário | 82 | B2 |
| Tsaritsani | 83 | E1 |
| Tsarkassiános | 82 | B4 |
| Tsotili | 79 | D4 |
| Tsoukaládes | 82 | B3 |
| Tuaim | 12 | B3 |
| Tuam | 12 | B3 |
| Tua, R | 34 | B4 |
| Tuath, L | 4 | B1 |
| Tubilla del Agua | 35 | F2 |
| Tübingen | 55 | D3 |
| Tubre | 58 | C3 |
| Tučepi | 75 | E2 |
| Tuchan | 32 | B2 |
| Tudela | 36 | C3 |
| Tudela de Duero | 35 | E4 |
| Tuella, R | 34 | C3 |
| Tuerto, R | 35 | D2 |
| Tuffé | 23 | F3 |
| Tuheljske Toplice | 70 | C2 |
| Tuhkakylä | 103 | E1 |
| Tui | 34 | A3 |
| Tuineje | 42 | C4 |
| Tukums | 110 | B2 |
| Tulach Mhór | 12 | C4 |
| Tulare | 77 | D1 |
| Tulcea | 113 | E4 |
| Tul'čin | 113 | E3 |
| Tulla | 12 | B4 |
| Tullamore | 12 | C4 |
| Tulle | 29 | D1 |
| Tullgarn | 106 | B4 |
| Tullins | 30 | C1 |
| Tulln | 57 | E2 |
| Tullow | 13 | D4 |
| Tulppio | 95 | F4 |
| Tulsk | 12 | C3 |
| Tumba | 106 | B4 |
| Tunbridge Wells, Royal | 10 | C3 |
| Tundža | 115 | E3 |
| Tunnhovdfjorden | 104 | C2 |
| Tunnsjøen | 97 | E4 |
| Tuohikotti | 107 | F2 |
| Tuoro sul Trasimeno | 61 | D4 |
| Tupalaki | 95 | E3 |
| Turalići | 72 | B4 |
| Turballe, la | 22 | C4 |
| Turbe | 71 | E4 |
| Turbie, la | 31 | E3 |
| Turckheim | 27 | E1 |
| Turégano | 40 | A1 |
| Turenki | 107 | E2 |
| Turgutlu | 115 | F4 |
| Turi | 65 | E3 |
| Túri | 110 | C1 |
| Túria, R | 41 | E3 |
| Turija (Bosna i Hercegovina) | 71 | F3 |
| Turija (Srbija) | 73 | E3 |
| Turija (Vojvodina) | 72 | C2 |
| Turinge | 106 | B4 |
| Turís | 41 | E4 |
| Turjak | 70 | B2 |
| Türkheim | 55 | E3 |
| Turku | 107 | D2 |
| Turmiel | 40 | C1 |
| Turnberry | 4 | C3 |
| Turnhout | 50 | C3 |
| Türnitz | 57 | E3 |
| Turnov | 112 | A2 |
| Turnu Măgurele | 115 | D2 |
| Turnu Roşu | 113 | D4 |
| Turracherhöhe | 59 | F2 |
| Turre | 44 | C3 |
| Turriff | 3 | E3 |
| Tursi | 65 | D4 |
| Turtola | 98 | C2 |
| Tuscania | 63 | D2 |
| Tuse | 108 | C3 |
| Tušilović | 70 | C3 |
| Tustna | 100 | B2 |
| Tutin | 76 | C1 |
| Tutrakan | 115 | E2 |
| Tuttlingen | 55 | D3 |
| Turun ja Porin Lääni | 107 | D2 |
| Tuturano | 65 | F3 |
| Tutzing | 56 | A3 |
| Tuulos | 107 | E2 |
| Tuupovaara | 103 | F2 |
| Tuusniemi | 103 | E2 |
| Tuusula | 107 | E2 |
| Tuxford | 7 | D3 |
| Tuzi | 76 | B3 |
| Tuzla | 71 | F3 |
| Tvedestrand | 104 | C4 |
| Tverrfjellet | 100 | B3 |
| Tvøroyri | 96 | A4 |
| Tweed, R | 5 | E2 |
| Twelve Pins, The | 12 | A3 |
| Twimberg | 70 | B1 |
| Twist | 17 | E2 |
| Twistringen | 17 | F1 |
| Tydal | 101 | D2 |
| Tyin | 104 | C1 |
| Tyin L | 100 | B3 |
| Týn | 57 | D1 |
| Tyndrum | 4 | C1 |
| Tynemouth | 5 | E3 |
| Tynkä | 102 | C1 |
| Tynset | 100 | C3 |
| Tyräjärvi | 99 | E3 |
| Tyresö | 106 | B4 |
| Tyrifjorden | 104 | C3 |
| Tyringe | 109 | D3 |
| Tyristrand | 104 | C3 |
| Tyrnävä | 99 | D4 |
| Tyrone | 13 | D1 |
| Tysfjorden | 97 | F1 |
| Tysnesøy | 104 | A2 |
| Tysse | 104 | A2 |
| Tyssebotn | 104 | A2 |
| Tyssedal | 104 | B2 |
| Tysvær | 104 | A3 |
| Tywi | 8 | C2 |
| Tywyn | 6 | A3 |

# U

| Name | Pg | Grid |
|---|---|---|
| Ub | 72 | C3 |
| Ubaye | 31 | D2 |
| Úbeda | 44 | A2 |
| Überlingen | 55 | D4 |
| Ubl'a | 112 | C3 |
| Ubli (Crna Gora) | 76 | B2 |
| Ubli (Lastovo) | 75 | E3 |
| Ubrique | 43 | E4 |
| Uchte | 17 | F2 |
| Učka | 70 | B3 |
| Uckange | 21 | D3 |
| Uckfield | 10 | C3 |
| Uclés | 40 | B3 |
| Udbina | 70 | C4 |
| Udbyhøj | 108 | B2 |
| Uddevalla | 108 | C1 |
| Uddheden | 105 | E3 |
| Uddjaure | 98 | A3 |
| Uden | 16 | C3 |
| Udine | 59 | F3 |
| Udovo | 77 | E3 |
| Udvar | 72 | A1 |
| Uebigau | 53 | E2 |
| Uecker | 49 | E2 |
| Ueckermünde | 49 | E2 |
| Uelzen | 48 | B3 |
| Uetersen | 48 | A2 |
| Uetze | 48 | B4 |
| Uffenheim | 55 | E1 |
| Ugao | 76 | C1 |
| Ugento | 65 | F4 |
| Ugijar | 44 | B3 |
| Ugine | 27 | D4 |
| Uglič | 111 | F1 |
| Ugljan | 74 | C1 |
| Ugljan I | 74 | C1 |
| Ugljane | 75 | E1 |
| Ugljevik | 72 | B3 |
| Ugra | 111 | F3 |
| Ugrinovci | 73 | D3 |
| Uherské Hradiště | 112 | A3 |
| Uhingen | 55 | D2 |
| Úhlava | 56 | C1 |
| Uhrsleben | 52 | C1 |
| Uig | 2 | B3 |
| Uimaharju | 103 | F2 |
| Uithoorn | 16 | C2 |
| Uithuizen | 47 | D3 |
| Ukkola | 103 | F2 |
| Ukmergė | 110 | C3 |
| Ukonselkä | 95 | E3 |
| Ukraina | 113 | E2 |
| Ukrina | 71 | E3 |
| Ulcinj | 76 | B3 |
| Uleåborg | 99 | D3 |
| Ulefoss | 104 | C3 |
| Uleila del Campo | 44 | C3 |
| Ulëzë | 76 | C3 |
| Ulfborg | 108 | A2 |
| Uljanik | 71 | D2 |
| Uljanovka | 113 | E3 |
| Uljma | 73 | D2 |
| Ullånger | 102 | A2 |
| Ullapool | 2 | C3 |
| Ulla, R | 34 | B2 |
| Ullared | 108 | C2 |
| Ullava | 102 | C1 |
| Ulldecona | 41 | F2 |
| Ullsfjorden | 94 | C2 |
| Ullswater | 5 | D4 |
| Ulm | 55 | E3 |
| Ulmen | 51 | E4 |
| Ulog | 75 | F1 |
| Ulricehamn | 109 | D1 |
| Ulrichsberg | 56 | C2 |
| Ulsberg | 100 | C2 |
| Ulsta | 3 | F1 |
| Ulsteinvik | 100 | A2 |
| Uludağ | 115 | F3 |
| Ul'ugai'sa | 95 | E2 |
| Ulva | 4 | B1 |
| Ulverston | 6 | B1 |
| Ulvik | 104 | B2 |
| Ulvila | 107 | D1 |
| Ulvsjö | 101 | E3 |
| Ulzës, Liq i | 76 | C3 |
| Umag | 70 | A3 |
| Uman' | 113 | E3 |
| Umbertide | 61 | E4 |
| Umbrail, Pass | 58 | C3 |
| Umbria | 63 | E1 |
| Umbukta | 97 | E3 |
| Umčari | 73 | D3 |
| Umeå | 102 | B1 |
| Umeälven | 98 | A4 |
| Umhausen | 58 | C2 |
| Umin Dol | 77 | E2 |
| Umka | 72 | C3 |
| Umljanović | 75 | D1 |
| Una | 71 | D3 |
| Unac | 71 | D4 |
| Unari | 99 | D1 |
| Unari L | 99 | D1 |
| Uncastillo | 37 | D2 |
| Unden | 105 | E4 |
| Undersåker | 101 | D2 |
| Undredal | 104 | B2 |
| Uneča | 111 | F4 |
| Unešić | 75 | D1 |
| Úněšov | 53 | E4 |
| Ungeny | 113 | E3 |
| Ungilde | 34 | C3 |
| Unhais da Serra | 38 | C2 |
| Unhošt | 53 | F4 |
| Unije | 70 | B4 |
| Universales, Mts | 41 | D2 |
| Unna | 17 | E3 |
| Unnaryd | 109 | D2 |
| Unnukka | 103 | E2 |
| Unquera | 35 | F1 |
| Unst | 3 | F1 |
| Unstrut | 52 | C2 |
| Unterach | 56 | C3 |
| Unterhaching | 56 | A3 |
| Unter-Schleissheim | 55 | F3 |
| Unterwalden | 27 | F3 |
| Unterwasser | 58 | B2 |
| Unterweißenbach | 57 | D2 |
| Upavon | 9 | E3 |
| Upinniemi | 107 | E3 |
| Upper L Erne | 13 | D2 |
| Uppingham | 9 | F1 |
| Upplands-Väsby | 106 | B3 |
| Uppsala | 106 | B3 |
| Uppsala Län | 106 | B3 |
| Upton | 9 | E1 |
| Uras | 66 | B3 |
| Urbania | 61 | E3 |
| Urbasa, Pto de | 36 | C2 |
| Urbasa, Sa de | 36 | C2 |
| Urbe | 60 | A3 |
| Urbino | 61 | E3 |
| Urbión, Sa de | 36 | B3 |
| Urdos | 37 | D2 |
| Ure | 6 | C1 |
| Uredakke | 97 | E4 |
| Urepel | 36 | C1 |
| Urfahr | 57 | D2 |
| Urfeld | 56 | A4 |
| Urho Kekkonens kansallispuisto | 95 | F3 |
| Uri (CH) | 58 | A3 |
| Uri (I) | 66 | A2 |
| Uriage | 30 | C1 |
| Urjala | 107 | E2 |
| Urk | 16 | C2 |
| Urla | 115 | E4 |
| Urlingford | 14 | C3 |
| Urnäsch | 58 | B2 |
| Urnes | 100 | B3 |
| Uroševac | 77 | D2 |
| Urovica | 73 | F3 |
| Urquiola, Pto | 36 | B1 |
| Urshult | 109 | D3 |
| Ursprungpaß | 59 | D1 |

| | | | | | | | | | | | | |
|---|---|---|---|---|---|---|---|---|---|---|---|---|
| Urtivaara | 95 D3 | Usk | 9 D2 | Ustaritz | 28 A4 | Utajärvi | 99 D4 | Utrillas | 41 E2 | Uurainen | 103 D2 | Uzin | 113 E2 |
| Ururi | 64 B2 | Usk R | 9 D2 | Uster | 58 A2 | Utåker | 104 A3 | Utsjoki | 95 E2 | Uusikaarlepyy | 102 B2 | Uzunköprü | 115 E3 |
| Ury | 25 F1 | Uskoplje | 76 A2 | Ustevatn | 104 B2 | Utbjoa | 104 A3 | Utsjoki R | 95 E2 | Uusikaupunki | 107 D2 | | |
| Urziceni | 115 E1 | Üsküdar | 115 F3 | Ustibar | 76 B1 | Utebo | 37 D3 | Uttendorf | | Uvac | 76 B1 | | |
| Usagre | 43 D1 | Uslar | 52 B2 | Ustica, I di | 68 B2 | Utelle | 31 E3 | (Oberösterreich) | 56 C3 | Uvac R | 76 B1 | | |
| Uşak | 115 F4 | Ussat-les-Bains | 32 A2 | Ustikolina | 76 A1 | Utena | 110 C3 | Uttendorf | | Uvdal | 104 C2 | | |
| Ušće | 73 D4 | Ussé | 25 D2 | Ústí nad Labem | 53 F3 | Utiel | 41 D3 | (Salzburg) | 59 E1 | Uzdin | 72 C2 | | |
| Usedom | 49 E2 | Usseglio | 31 E1 | Ustiprača | 76 B1 | Utne | 104 B2 | Utting | 56 A3 | Uzel | 22 C3 | | |
| Usedom I | 49 E1 | Ussel | 29 E1 | Ustka | 110 A4 | Utrecht | 16 C3 | Uttoxeter | 6 C3 | Uzerche | 29 D1 | | |
| Useras | 41 E3 | Usseln | 17 F4 | Ustronie Morskie | 49 F1 | Utrecht (Prov) | 16 C2 | Uudenmaan Lääni | 107 F2 | Uzès | 30 B3 | | |
| Usingen | 51 F4 | Ustaoset | 104 B2 | Usť užna | 111 F1 | Utrera | 43 D3 | Uukuniemi | 103 F3 | Užgorod | 112 C3 | | |

# V

| | | | | | | | | | | | | |
|---|---|---|---|---|---|---|---|---|---|---|---|---|
| | | Vålberg | 105 E3 | Valdelacasa de | | Valdihuela | 39 F2 | Valencia de las | | Valjevo | 72 C3 | Valle-Mosso | 31 F1 |
| Vä | 109 D3 | Valbiska | 70 B3 | Tajo | 39 E3 | Val-d'Isère | 31 D1 | Torres | 43 D1 | Valjok | 95 E2 | Vallentuna | 106 B3 |
| Vaajakoski | 103 D3 | Valbo | 106 B2 | Valdelinares | 41 E2 | Valdobbiadene | 59 D3 | Valencia del | | Valjunquera | 41 F1 | Valleraugue | 29 F3 |
| Vääkiö | 99 E3 | Valbondione | 58 B3 | Valdemarsvik | 109 E1 | Valdosa | 36 A3 | Ventoso | 43 D1 | Valkeakoski | 107 E2 | Vallet | 24 B2 |
| Vaala | 99 E4 | Valbonë | 76 C2 | Valdemeca | 41 D2 | Valdres | 104 C2 | Valencia I | 14 A4 | Valkeala | 107 F2 | Valletta | 68 B4 |
| Vaalajärvi | 95 E4 | Valbonnais | 31 D2 | Valdemorillo | 40 A2 | Valdres Flya | 100 B3 | Valenciennes | 20 A1 | Valkenburg | 51 D3 | Vallgrund | 102 B2 |
| Vaalimaa | 103 F4 | Val Camonica | 58 C4 | Valdemoro | 40 A2 | Vale de Açor | 42 B2 | Valensole | 31 D3 | Valkenswaard | 16 C4 | Valli di Comacchio | 61 D2 |
| Vaals | 51 D3 | Valcarlos | 36 C1 | Valdenoceda | 36 A2 | Vale de Cambra | 38 B1 | Valentano | 63 D2 | Valko | 107 F2 | Vallø | 108 C3 |
| Vaaraslahti | 103 D3 | Valdagno | 59 D4 | Valdeobispo, Emb | | Vale de Estrela | 38 C2 | Valentigney | 27 E2 | Valladolid | 35 E4 | Vallo della Lucania | 67 D1 |
| Vaasa | 102 B2 | Valdahon | 27 D2 | de | 39 D2 | Vale de Prazeres | 38 C2 | Valenza | 60 A2 | Vallata | 64 C3 | Valloire | 31 D1 |
| Vaasan Lääni | 102 C2 | Valdaj | 111 E1 | Valdepeñas | 44 A1 | Vale, Emb de | 37 F2 | Våler (Hedmark) | 105 D2 | Vallbo | 101 D2 | Vallombrosa | 61 D3 |
| Vaassen | 17 D2 | Val-d'Ajol, le | 27 D1 | Valdepeñas da | | Valeggio sul | | Våler (Østfold) | 105 D3 | Valldal | 100 B2 | Valldal | 100 B2 |
| Vabre | 32 B1 | Valdajskaja | | Jaén | 44 A2 | Mincio | 60 C1 | Valeria | 40 C3 | Valldemossa | 45 E2 | Vallon-en-Sully | 25 F3 |
| Vác | 112 B4 | Vozvyšennost' | 111 E2 | Valderaduey, R | 35 D4 | Valenca do | | Valevåg | 104 A3 | Vall de Uxó | 41 E3 | Vallon-Pont-d'arc | 30 B3 |
| Vaccarès, Etang | | Valdavia, R | 35 E3 | Valderas | 35 E3 | Minho | 34 A3 | Valfabbrica | 61 E4 | Valle | 104 B3 | Vallorbe | 27 D3 |
| de | 30 B3 | Valdeazogues, R | 43 F1 | Val de Reuil | 19 E3 | Valençay | 25 E2 | Valga | 110 C2 | Valleberga | 109 D4 | Vallorcine | 27 E4 |
| Vacha | 52 B3 | Valdecaballeros | 39 E4 | Valderiès | 29 E3 | Valence- | | Val Gardena | 59 D3 | Valle Castellana | 63 F1 | Valls | 37 F4 |
| Väddö | 106 B3 | Valdecabras | 40 C3 | Valderøy | 100 A2 | d'Albigeois | 29 E3 | Valgorge | 30 B2 | Valle d'Aosta | 27 E4 | Vallsta | 101 F4 |
| Vadehavet | 108 A4 | Valdecañas, Emb | | Valderrepisa, Pto | | Valence (Drôme) | 30 C2 | Valgrisenche | 31 E1 | Valle de Abdalajís | 43 E3 | Valmiera | 110 C2 |
| Vadheim | 100 A3 | de | 39 E3 | de | 43 F1 | Valence (Gers) | 28 C3 | Valguarnera | | Valle de la Serena | 39 E4 | Valmojado | 40 A2 |
| Vado Ligure | 60 A3 | Valdecarros | 39 E1 | Valderrobres | 41 F2 | Valencia | 41 E4 | Caropepe | 68 C3 | Valle de los Caidos | 40 A2 | Valmont | 19 D2 |
| Vadsø | 95 F1 | Valdecebollas | 35 F2 | Valdestillas | 35 E4 | Valencia (Prov) | 41 D4 | Valhelhas | 38 C2 | Valle de | | Valmontone | 63 F3 |
| Vadstena | 109 D1 | Valdediós | 35 E1 | Valdeverdeja | 39 E3 | Valencia de | | Valico della | | Matamoros | 42 C1 | Valogne | 18 B3 |
| Vaduz | 58 B2 | Valdeganga | 41 D4 | Valdevimbre | 35 D3 | Alcántara | 38 C3 | Forchetta | 64 A2 | Vallehermoso | 42 A4 | Valongo | 34 A4 |
| Vadvetjåkka | 94 B3 | Valdeinfierno, | | Valdezcaray | 36 B2 | Valencia de Don | | Valimitika | 83 E4 | Vallejera, Pto de | 39 E2 | Valoria la Buena | 35 E4 |
| Vaféika | 81 D2 | Emb de | 44 C2 | Valdieri | 31 E3 | Juan | 35 D3 | Valíra | 86 C3 | | | Valpaços | 34 B4 |
| Vafiohóri | 79 F2 | | | | | | | | | | | Valpalmas | 37 D3 |
| Vågaholmen | 97 E2 | | | | | | | | | | | | |
| Vågåmo | 100 B3 | | | | | | | | | | | | |
| Vågan | 97 E1 | | | | | | | | | | | | |
| Vaganj | 75 E1 | | | | | | | | | | | | |
| Vaganski vrh | 70 C4 | | | | | | | | | | | | |
| Vágar | 96 A3 | | | | | | | | | | | | |
| Våge | 104 A2 | | | | | | | | | | | | |
| Væggerløse | 108 C4 | | | | | | | | | | | | |
| Vaggeryd | 109 D2 | | | | | | | | | | | | |
| Vágia | 83 F4 | | | | | | | | | | | | |
| Vagioniá | 91 D4 | | | | | | | | | | | | |
| Vagnhärad | 106 B4 | | | | | | | | | | | | |
| Vagos | 38 B1 | | | | | | | | | | | | |
| Vågsfjorden | 94 B3 | | | | | | | | | | | | |
| Vågsøy | 100 A3 | | | | | | | | | | | | |
| Vágur | 96 A4 | | | | | | | | | | | | |
| Váh | 112 B3 | | | | | | | | | | | | |
| Vähäkyrö | 102 B2 | | | | | | | | | | | | |
| Vahto | 107 D2 | | | | | | | | | | | | |
| Vái | 91 F3 | | | | | | | | | | | | |
| Vaiano | 60 C3 | | | | | | | | | | | | |
| Vaiges | 23 E3 | | | | | | | | | | | | |
| Vaihingen | 55 D2 | | | | | | | | | | | | |
| Vailly (Aisne) | 20 A3 | | | | | | | | | | | | |
| Vailly (Cher) | 26 A2 | | | | | | | | | | | | |
| Vainikkala | 103 F4 | | | | | | | | | | | | |
| Vaisaluokta | 94 B4 | | | | | | | | | | | | |
| Vaison-la- | | | | | | | | | | | | | |
| Romaine | 30 C3 | | | | | | | | | | | | |
| Vaksdal | 104 A2 | | | | | | | | | | | | |
| Vålådalen | 101 D2 | | | | | | | | | | | | |
| Valadares | 34 A4 | | | | | | | | | | | | |
| Valais | 27 E4 | | | | | | | | | | | | |
| Valalta | 70 A3 | | | | | | | | | | | | |
| Valamen | 103 E2 | | | | | | | | | | | | |
| Valandovo | 77 D3 | | | | | | | | | | | | |
| Val-André, le | 22 C2 | | | | | | | | | | | | |
| Valareña | 36 C3 | | | | | | | | | | | | |
| Valašské Meziříčí | 112 B3 | | | | | | | | | | | | |
| Valax | 107 F2 | | | | | | | | | | | | |
| Valberg | 31 E3 | | | | | | | | | | | | |

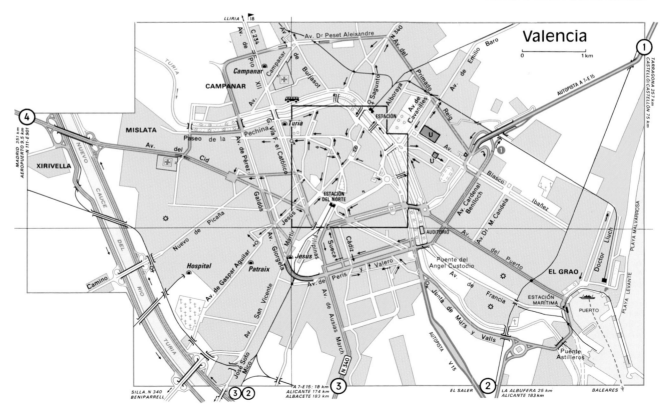

Valencia

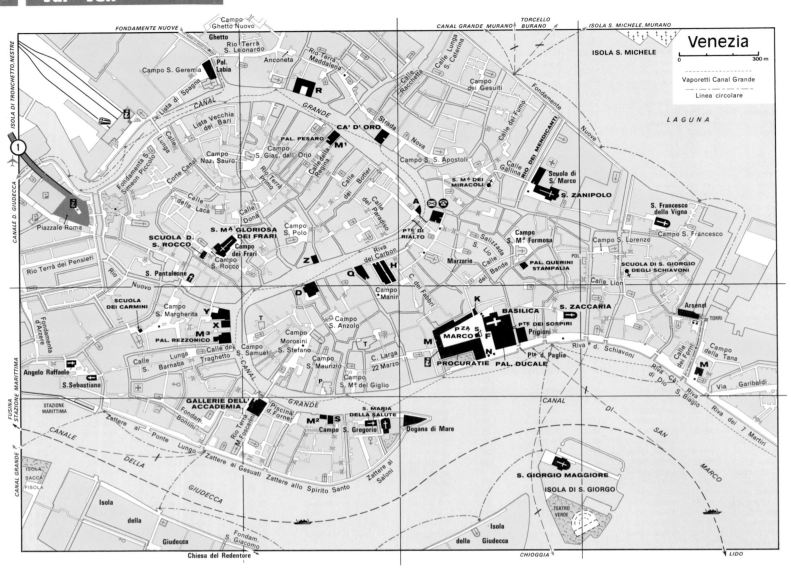

Venezia

| Name | Ref |
|---|---|
| Valparaiso, Emb de | 35 D3 |
| Val Passiria | 59 D2 |
| Valpovo | 71 F2 |
| Valprato Soana | 31 E1 |
| Valras-Plage | 30 A4 |
| Valréas | 30 C3 |
| Valsamónero | 91 D4 |
| Valsavarenche | 31 E1 |
| Valserine | 27 D4 |
| Valset | 100 C1 |
| Valsjöbyn | 101 E1 |
| Vals-les-Bains | 30 B2 |
| Valtellina | 58 B3 |
| Valtessiniko | 86 C2 |
| Val-Thorens | 31 D1 |
| Valtierra | 36 C3 |
| Valtimo | 103 E1 |
| Váltos | 81 F1 |
| Valtotópi | 80 B2 |
| Váltou, Óri | 82 C2 |
| Valtournenche | 27 F4 |
| Valun | 70 B4 |
| Valvasone | 59 E3 |
| Valverde (Is Canarias) | 42 A4 |
| Valverde (La Rioja) | 36 C3 |
| Valverde del Camino | 42 C2 |
| Valverde de Leganés | 38 C4 |
| Valverde del Fresno | 39 D2 |
| Valverde del Júcar | 40 C3 |
| Valøya | 97 D4 |
| Våmb | 109 D1 |
| Våmhus | 101 E4 |
| Vamlingbo | 109 F4 |
| Vammala | 107 D1 |
| Vampula | 107 D1 |
| Vamvakás, Akr | 85 F4 |
| Vamvakoú (Pelopónissos) | 87 D3 |
| Vamvakoú (Thessalía) | 83 E2 |
| Vanajavesi | 107 E2 |
| Vanån | 101 D4 |
| Vanda | 107 E2 |
| Vandellòs | 41 F1 |
| Vänern | 105 E4 |
| Vangshylla | 101 D1 |
| Vangsnes | 104 B1 |
| Vangsvik | 94 B3 |
| Vanha Vaasa | 102 B2 |
| Vanna | 94 C2 |
| Vännäs | 102 A1 |
| Vannavålen | 94 C2 |
| Vannes | 22 C4 |
| Vannsjø | 105 D3 |
| Vannsundet | 94 C2 |
| Vanoise, Massif de la | 31 D1 |
| Vanoise, Parc Nat de la | 31 D1 |
| Vansbro | 105 E2 |
| Vans, les | 30 B3 |
| Vanttaa | 107 E2 |
| Vanttauskoski | 99 D2 |
| Vaour | 29 D3 |
| Vaqueira | 37 F2 |
| Var | 31 D4 |
| Vara | 108 C1 |
| Varades | 23 E4 |
| Varallo | 58 A4 |
| Varangerbotn | 95 F1 |
| Varangerfjorden | 95 F1 |
| Varangerhalvøya | 95 F1 |
| Varano de' Melegari | 60 B2 |
| Varano, L di | 64 C2 |
| Varaždin | 70 C1 |
| Varaždinske Toplice | 71 D1 |
| Varazze | 60 A3 |
| Varberg | 108 C2 |
| Vârbica | 115 E2 |
| Varda | 72 C4 |
| Várda | 86 B1 |
| Vardar | 77 E3 |
| Varde | 108 A3 |
| Vardenik | 77 E2 |
| Vardø | 95 F1 |
| Vårdö | 106 C3 |
| Vardoússia, Óri | 83 D3 |
| Varel | 47 F3 |
| Vareleí | 84 C4 |
| Varengeville | 19 D2 |
| Varenna | 58 B4 |
| Varennes-en-Argonne | 20 C3 |
| Varennes-sur-Allier | 26 A4 |
| Varennes-sur-Amance | 26 C1 |
| Vareš | 71 F4 |
| Varese | 58 A4 |
| Varese Ligure | 60 B3 |
| Vårgårda | 108 C1 |
| Vargas | 35 F2 |
| Vargsund | 95 D1 |
| Varhaug | 104 A4 |
| Vári (Kikládes) | 88 B2 |
| Vári (Stereá Eláda) | 87 F1 |
| Varilhes | 32 A2 |
| Varimbómbi | 87 F1 |
| Váris | 79 D4 |
| Varkaus | 103 E3 |
| Várkiza | 87 F2 |
| Varmahlíð | 96 B1 |
| Värmlands Län | 105 E3 |
| Varmo | 59 E3 |
| Varna (BG) | 115 E2 |
| Varna (YU) | 72 C3 |
| Várnamo | 109 D2 |
| Varnhem | 109 D1 |
| Varnsdorf | 53 F2 |
| Värö | 108 C2 |
| Varoš Selo | 77 D2 |
| Varpaisjärvi | 103 E1 |
| Várpalota | 112 B4 |
| Vars | 31 D2 |
| Vars, Col de | 31 D2 |
| Vartdalsfjorden | 100 A2 |
| Vartholomió | 86 B1 |
| Vartius | 99 F4 |
| Värtsilä | 103 F2 |
| Varvára | 80 B3 |
| Varvarin | 73 E4 |
| Varzi | 60 A2 |
| Varzy | 26 A2 |
| Vasa | 102 B2 |
| Vasarapera | 99 E2 |
| Vásárosnamény | 112 C3 |
| Vascão, Rib do | 42 B2 |
| Vasikkaselkä | 95 F2 |
| Vasil'kov | 113 E2 |
| Vaskijärvi | 107 D2 |
| Vaskio | 107 E2 |
| Vaskivesi | 102 C3 |
| Vaslui | 113 E4 |
| Vassarás | 87 D3 |
| Vassés | 86 C2 |
| Vassieux | 30 C2 |
| Vassiliká (Évia) | 84 A3 |
| Vassiliká (Lésvos) | 85 F2 |
| Vassiliká (Makedonía) | 80 A3 |
| Vassiliki (Lefkáda) | 82 B3 |
| Vassiliki (Thessalía) | 83 D1 |
| Vassilikó | 84 B4 |
| Vassilikós | 86 A2 |
| Vassilis | 83 E2 |
| Vassilitsa | 78 C4 |
| Vassy | 18 C4 |
| Västanbäck | 101 F2 |
| Västanfjärd | 107 D3 |
| Vastenjaure | 97 F1 |
| Västerås | 106 A3 |
| Västerbottens Län | 98 A4 |
| Västerdalälven | 101 D4 |
| Väster Haninge | 106 B4 |
| Västernorrlands Län | 101 F2 |
| Västervik | 109 E1 |
| Västmanlands Län | 105 F3 |
| Vasto | 64 B2 |
| Vatan | 25 E3 |
| Väte | 109 F4 |
| Vaterá | 85 F3 |
| Vateró | 79 D4 |
| Váthia | 87 D4 |
| Vathí (Dodekánissa) | 84 B4 |
| Váthi (Lefkáda) | 79 F2 |
| Vathí (Makedonía) | 92 C1 |
| Vathí (Stereá Eláda) | 82 B3 |
| Vathílakos (Dráma) | 80 C2 |
| Vathílakos (Kozáni) | 79 E4 |
| Vathílakos (Thessaloníki) | 79 F3 |
| Vathípetro | 91 D4 |
| Vathís | 89 F3 |
| Vatin | 73 D2 |
| Vatnajökull | 96 B2 |
| Vatne | 100 B2 |
| Vatólakos | 79 D4 |
| Vatopediou | 80 C4 |
| Vatra Dornei | 113 D4 |
| Vättern | 109 D1 |
| Vattholma | 106 B3 |
| Vaucluse | 30 C3 |
| Vaucouleurs | 20 C4 |
| Vaud | 27 D3 |
| Vauvert | 30 B4 |
| Vauvillers | 27 D1 |
| Vaux-le-Vicomte | 19 F4 |
| Vávdos | 80 A3 |
| Växjö | 109 D2 |
| Våxtorp | 108 C3 |
| Vayrac | 29 D2 |
| V'az'ma | 111 F3 |
| Veberöd | 109 D3 |
| Vecht | 17 C2 |
| Vechta | 17 F1 |
| Vechte | 17 E2 |
| Vecinos | 39 E1 |
| Vedelago | 59 E4 |
| Vedrá, I | 45 D4 |
| Vedungfjället | 101 D3 |
| Veendam | 47 D3 |
| Veenendaal | 16 C3 |
| Veere | 16 B3 |
| Vefsna | 97 E3 |
| Vefsnfjorden | 97 D3 |
| Vega | 97 D3 |
| Vega de Espinareda | 34 C2 |
| Vegadeo | 34 C1 |
| Vega de Valcarce | 34 C2 |
| Vegafjorden | 97 D3 |
| Vegarienza | 35 D2 |
| Vegårshei | 104 C4 |
| Vegas | 35 E2 |
| Vegas del Condado | 35 E2 |
| Vegesack | 47 F3 |
| Veghel | 16 C3 |
| Vegoritída, L | 79 E3 |
| Vehkalahti | 103 F4 |
| Vehmaa | 101 D2 |

Vehmersalmi 103 E2
Veidnesklubben 95 E1
Veikkola 107 E2
Veines 95 F1
Veinge 108 C2
Veiros 38 C4
Vejen 108 A3
Vejer de la Frontera 43 D4
Vejle 108 A3
Velada 39 F3
Velagići 71 D4
Vela Luka 75 E2
Velanídia 87 E4
Velate, Pto de 36 C1
Velayos 39 F1
Velbert 17 E4
Velburg 55 F1
Velde 101 D1
Velden (A) 70 A1
Velden (Nüberg) 55 F1
Velden (München) 56 B3
Veldhoven 16 C4
Velebit 70 C4
Velebitski kanal 70 B4
Velenje 70 B1
Velešta 77 D4
Velestíno 83 F2
Veleta, Pico 44 A3
Velež 75 F2
Vélez Blanco 44 C2
Vélez de Benaudalla 44 A3
Vélez-Málaga 43 F3
Vélez Rubio 44 C2
Velfjorden 97 D3
Veličani 75 F2
Veliés 87 E4
Velika 71 E2
Velika Drenova 73 E4
Velika Gorica 70 C2
Velikaja 111 D2
Velika Jablanica 76 C2
Velika Jamnička 70 C2
Velika Kapela 70 B3
Velika Kladuša 70 C3
Velika Kopanica 71 F3
Velika Kruša 77 D2
Velika Morava 73 D3
Velika Mučna 71 D1
Velika Plana (Morava) 73 D3
Velika Plana (Prokuplje) 77 D1
Velika Tresta 73 E3
Veliki Alan 70 B4
Veliki Bastaji 71 E2
Veliki Gaj 73 D2
Veliki Grđevac 71 D2
Veliki Izvor 73 F3
Veliki Jastrebac 77 D1
Velikije Luki 111 E2
Veliki kanal 72 B2
Veliki Krš 73 E3
Veliki Popović 73 E3
Veliki Prolog 75 E2
Veliki Radinci 72 C2
Veliki Trnovac 77 E2
Veliki Vitao 76 A2
Veliki Zdenci 71 D2
Veliko Gradište 73 D2
Veliko Lašče 70 B2
Veliko Orašje 73 D3
Veliko Tărnovo 115 D2
Velilla del R Carrion 35 E2
Veli Lošinj 70 B4
Velimlje 76 A2
Vélines 28 C2
Velingrad 115 D3
Velino 63 F2
Velino, Mte 63 F2
Velíž 111 E3
Veljun 70 C3
Velká Bíteš 57 E1
Velké Meziříčí 57 E1
Velkua 107 D2
Vellahn 48 B3
Velletri 63 E3
Vellinge 108 C3
Velopoúla 87 F3
Vélos 84 B4
Velpke 48 B4
Velten 49 D4
Velvendós 79 E4
Vemdalen 101 E3
Vemdalsskalet 101 E3
Vemhån 101 E3
Véna 81 E2
Venaco 33 F3
Venafro 64 A3
Venarey-les-Laumes 26 B2
Venaria 31 E1
Venčani 73 D3
Vence 31 E3
Venda Nova 34 B4
Vendas Novas 38 B4
Vendée 24 B3
Vendel 106 B3
Vendeuvre 26 B1
Vendôme 25 E2
Vendsyssel 108 B2
Veneheitto 99 D4
Veneta, Laguna 61 D1
Veneto 61 D1
Venezia 61 D1
Vengjaneset 104 A2
Venialbo 35 D4
Venjan 101 E4
Venjansjön 101 E4
Venlo 17 D4
Vennesla 104 B4
Vennesund 97 D3
Venosa 64 C3
Venosta 58 C3
Venray 17 D3
Venta 110 B3
Venta de Cruce 43 D3
Venta de Don Quijote 40 B3
Ventana, Pto de 35 D2
Venta Nueva 34 C2
Ventas de Huelma 44 A3
Ventimiglia 31 E3
Ventnor 9 E4
Ventotene, I 63 F4
Ventoux, Mt 30 C3
Ventspils 110 B2
Venturina 62 C1
Vera (E) 44 C3
Vera (N) 101 D1
Vera de Bidasoa 36 C1
Verbania-Pallanza 58 A4
Verberie 19 F3
Verbicaro 67 E2
Verbier 27 E4
Vercelli 31 F1
Vercel-Villedieu 27 D2
Verchnedvinsk 111 D3
Verdalsøra 101 D1
Verde, Col de 33 F3
Verden 48 A4
Verdikoússa 83 D1
Verdon 31 D3
Verdon, le 28 A1
Verdun (Meuse) 20 C3
Verdun (Saône-et-Loire) 26 C3
Verdun (Tarn-et-Garonne) 29 D3
Verfeil 29 D4
Vergato 60 C3
Vérgi 80 A2
Vergiate 60 A1
Vergina 79 E3
Vergio, Col de 33 F3
Vergt 28 C2
Véria 79 E3
Verin 34 B3
Verl 17 F3
Vermand 20 A2
Vermenton 26 B2
Vérmio, Óros 79 E3
Verna, Pzo di 69 D2
Vernet-les-Bains 32 B2
Verneuil 19 D4
Vernon 19 E3
Vérno, Óros 79 D3
Vernoux-en-Vivarais 30 B2
Verny 21 D3
Veroli 63 F3
Verona 60 C1
Verpillière 30 C1
Verran 101 D1
Verrès 27 F4
Versailles 19 F4
Versmold 17 F2
Verteillac 28 C1
Vertiskos, Óros 80 A2
Vertus 20 B4
Verucchio 61 E3
Veruela 36 C3
Verviers 51 D4
Vervins 20 B2
Verzuolo 31 E2
Verzy 20 B3
Vesanto 103 D2
Vescovato 33 F3
Veselí 57 D1
Vesijärvi 107 F2
Vesilahti 107 E1
Vesivehmaa 107 F2
Vesjegonsk 111 F1
Veskoniemi 95 F3
Vesle 20 B3
Vesoul 27 D2
Véssa 85 E4
Vest-Agder 104 B4
Vestby 105 D3
Vestbygda 104 A4
Vesterålen 94 A3
Vesterø Havn 108 B2
Vestertana 95 E1
Vestfjorden 97 E1
Vestfold 104 C3
Vestmanna 96 A3
Vestmannaeyjar 96 B3
Vestnes 100 B2
Vestone 58 C4
Vestre Jakobselv 95 F1
Vestvågøy 94 A4
Vésubie, Gorges de la 31 E3
Vesuvio 64 B4
Veszprém 112 B4
Veteli 102 C2
Veternica 77 E1
Vetlanda 109 E2
Vetralla 63 E2
Vetriolo Terme 59 D3
Vetschau 53 E1
Vettore, M 63 F1
Veules-les-Roses 19 D2
Veulettes 19 D2
Veurne 50 A3
Vevey 27 E3
Vévi 79 D3
Veynes 30 C2
Veyre 29 F1
Veyrier 27 D4
Vezdemarbán 35 D4
Vézelay 26 B2
Vézelise 21 D4
Vézénobres 30 B3
Vézère 29 D2
Vézins-de-Lévézou 29 E3
Vezzani 33 F3
Vezzano 58 C3
Via Appia 63 F3
Via Aurelia 60 C4
Via Casilina 63 E2
Via Cassia 63 D1
Viadana 60 C2
Via Emilia 61 D3
Via Flaminia 61 E3
Viana 36 B2
Viana do Bolo 34 C3
Viana do Castelo 34 A3
Vianden 21 D2
Viano do Alentejo 42 B1
Viareggio 60 B3
Viar, R 43 D2
Vias 30 A4
Via Salaria 63 E2
Via Tiburtina Valeria 63 F2
Viaur 29 E3
Viborg 108 A2
Vibo Valentia 67 E3
Vibraye 23 F3
Vič 70 B1
Vic (E) 32 A3
Vic (F) 19 F3
Vicálvaro 40 B2
Vicdessos 37 F2
Vic-en-Bigorre 28 B4
Vicenza 59 D4
Vic-Fézensac 28 C4
Vich 32 A3
Vichy 26 A4
Vic-le-Comte 29 F1
Vico 33 E3
Vico del Gargano 64 C2
Vico Equense 64 B4
Vico, Lago di 63 E2
Vic-sur-Cère 29 E2
Victoria 68 B4
Vidå 108 A4
Vidago 34 B4
Viðareidi 96 A3
Vidauban 31 D4
Viddal 100 A3
Videbæk 108 A3
Vidiáki 86 C1
Vidigueira 42 B1
Vidin 114 C2
Vidio, C 35 D1
Viðoy 96 A3
Vidreres 32 B4
Vidrovan 76 B2
Vidsel 98 B3
Viduša 76 A2
Viechtach 56 B2
Viechtwang 56 C3
Vieira 38 A2
Vieira do Minho 34 B4
Viejo, Pto 39 D2
Viekinjärvi 103 F1
Vielha 37 F2
Vielle-Aure 37 E2
Vielmur 32 A1
Vielsalm 51 D4
Vienenburg 52 B1
Vienne 30 B1
Vienne (Dépt) 25 D3
Vienne *R* 25 D4
Vieremä 103 D1
Viernheim 54 C1
Vierraden 49 E3
Viersen 17 D4
Vierumäki 107 F2
Vierzehnheiligen 52 C4
Vierzon 25 F2
Vieste 64 C2
Vietas 94 B4
Vietri di Potenza 64 C4
Vietri sul Mare 64 B4
Vieux-Boucau 28 A3
Vieux Chaillol 31 D2
Vif 30 C2
Vig 108 C3
Vigan, le 29 F3
Vigeland 104 B4
Vigeois 29 D1
Vigevano 60 A1
Viggiano 65 D4
Vigla 82 C2
Vigla, Akr 91 D1
Vignale 31 F1
Vignanello 63 E2
Vignemale 37 E2
Vignes, les 29 F3
Vigneulles 20 C3
Vignola 60 C2
Vignole Borbera 60 A2
Vignory 26 C1
Vigo 34 A3
Vigo di Fassa 59 D3
Vigone 31 E2
Vigonza 61 D1
Vigrestad 104 A4
Vihanti 99 D4
Vihiers 24 C2
Vihtavuori 103 D3
Vihteljärvi 102 C3
Vihti 107 E2
Viiala 107 E2
Viinijärvi 103 F2
Viipustunturit 95 E3
Viitasaari 103 D2
Vik (Aust-Agder) 104 B4
Vik (IS) 96 B3
Vik (Nordland) 97 D3
Vik (Sogn og Fjordane) 104 B1
Vika 105 F2
Vikajärvi 99 D2
Vikanes 104 A2
Vikebukt 100 B2
Vikedal 104 A3
Vikersund 104 C3
Vikeså 104 A4
Vikevåg 104 A3
Vikingstad 106 A4
Vikna 97 D4
Vikoč 76 A1
Vikran 94 B2
Viksdalen 100 A3
Viksjö 101 F2
Viksjøfjell 95 F2
Viksta 106 B3
Vila Boim 38 C4
Vilada 32 A3
Viladamat 32 B3
Vila de Cruces 34 B2
Vila de Rei 38 B3
Vila do Bispo 42 A2
Vila do Conde 34 A4
Viladrau 32 B3
Vila Fernando 38 C4
Vila Flor 34 C4
Vila Franca das Naves 38 C1
Vilafranca del Penedès 32 A4
Vila Franca de Xira 38 A4
Vila Fresca de Azeitão 38 A4
Vilagarcia de Arosa 34 A2
Vilaine 22 C4
Vilaller 37 F2
Vilán, C 34 A1
Vilanova 34 C1
Vila Nova da Barquinha 38 B3
Vilanova de Arousa 34 A2
Vila Nova de Cerveira 34 A3
Vila Nova de Famalicão 34 A4
Vila Nova de Foz Côa 39 D1
Vila Nova de Gaia 34 A4
Vila Nova de Milfontes 42 A2
Vila Nova de Ourém 38 B3
Vila Nova de Paiva 38 C1
Vila Nova de Poiares 38 B2
Vilanova de Sau 32 B3
Vilanova i la Geltrú 32 A4
Vila Pouca de Aguiar 34 B4
Vila Praia de Âncora 34 A3
Vilar de Barrio 34 B3
Vila Real 34 B4
Vila-réal 41 E3
Vila Real de Santo António 42 B3
Vila-rodona 37 F4
Vila-seca 37 F4
Vila Velha de Ródão 38 C3
Vila Verde 34 A3
Vila Verde de Ficalho 42 C1
Vila Verde de Raia 34 B3
Vila Viçosa 38 C4
Vilches 44 A2
Vilejka 111 D4
Vilhelmina 97 F4
Vilia 87 E1
Viljakkala 102 C3
Viljandi 110 C2
Vilkaviškis 110 C4
Vilkovo 113 E4
Villa Adriana 63 E2
Villa Bartolomea 60 C1
Villablanca 42 C2
Villablino 35 D2
Villabona 36 C1
Villabrágima 35 E4
Villabuena del Puente 35 D4
Villacâas 40 B3
Villacarriedo 35 F2
Villacarrillo 44 B2
Villacastín 40 A1
Villach 59 F2
Villacidro 66 B4
Villada 35 E3
Villa del Prado 40 A2
Villa del Río 43 F2
Villadiego 35 F3
Villadossola 27 F4
Villaescusa de Haro 40 C3
Villafáfila 35 D4
Villafamés 41 E3
Villaflores 39 F1
Villafranca 36 C2
Villafranca del Bierzo 34 C2
Villafranca del Cid 41 E2
Villafranca de los Barros 43 D1
Villafranca de los Caballeros 40 B3
Villafranca di Verona 60 C1
Villafranca in Lunigiana 60 B3
Villafranca-Montes de Oca 36 A2
Villafranca Piemonte 31 E2
Villafranca Tirrena 69 D2
Villafranco del Guadalquivir 43 D3
Villafrati 68 B3
Villafrechos 35 E3
Villafruela 35 F4
Villafuerte 35 F4
Villagarcía del Llano 40 C4
Villager 35 D2
Villaggio Mancuso 67 F3
Villagonzalo 39 D4
Villaharta 43 E1
Villahermosa 44 B1
Villahoz 35 F3
Villaines-la-Juhel 23 E3
Villajoyosa 45 E1
Villa, la 59 D2
Villala 103 F3
Villalba 34 B1
Villalba de Guardo 35 E2
Villalba de la Sierra 40 C2
Villalba de los Barros 43 D1
Villalba del Rey 40 C2
Villalcampo, Emb de 35 D4
Villalcázar de Sirga 35 E3
Villalenga 36 C4
Villa Literno 64 A4
Villalón de Campos 35 E3
Villalonga 45 E1
Villalpando 35 E4
Villalpardo 41 D4
Villamañán 35 D3
Villamanrique 44 B1
Villamarchante 41 E3
Villamartín (Andalucía) 43 D3
Villamartín (Castilla-León) 35 E3
Villamassargia 66 B4
Villamayor 37 D3
Villamayor de Campos 35 E3
Villamayor de Santiago 40 B3
Villameca, Emb de 35 D2
Villa Minozzo 60 C3
Villandraut 28 B3
Villandry 25 D2
Villanova Monteleone 66 A2
Villanubla 35 E4
Villanueva de Alcardete 40 B3
Villanueva de Alcolea 41 F3
Villanueva de Alcorón 40 C2
Villanueva de Algaidas 43 F3
Villanueva de Argaño 35 F3
Villanueva de Arzobispo 44 B2
Villanueva de Bogas 40 A3
Villanueva de Cameros 36 B3
Villanueva de Córdoba 43 F1
Villanueva de Franco 40 B4
Villanueva de Gállego 37 D3
Villanueva de la Concepción 43 F3
Villanueva de la Fuente 44 B1
Villanueva de la Jara 40 C4
Villanueva de la Reina 44 A2
Villanueva de la Serena 39 E4
Villanueva de la Sierra 39 D2
Villanueva de las Torres 44 B2
Villanueva de la Vera 39 E2
Villanueva del Campo 35 D3
Villanueva del Duque 43 E1
Villanueva del Fresno 42 C1
Villanueva del Huerva 37 D4
Villanueva de los Castillejos 42 C2
Villanueva de los Infantes 44 B1
Villanueva del Rey 43 E1
Villanueva del Río y Minas 43 D2
Villanueva del Trabuco 43 F3
Villanueva de San Carlos 44 A1
Villa Opicina 59 F3
Villa Potenza 61 F4
Villaquejida 35 D3
Villaquilambre 35 D2
Villarcayo 36 A1
Villard-de-Lans 30 C2
Villar de Cañas 40 C3
Villardeciervos 35 D3
Villar de Domingo García 40 C2
Villardefrades 35 E4
Villar del Arzobispo 41 E3
Villar del Rey 39 D4
Villar de Peralonso 39 E1
Villarejo de Fuentes 40 C3
Villarejo de Orbigo 35 D3
Villarejo de Salvanés 40 B2
Villarente 35 E3
Villares de la Reina 39 E1
Villares del Saz 40 C3
Villargordo de Cabriel 41 D4
Villaricos 44 C3
Villarin de Campos 35 D4
Villarino 34 C4
Villarquemado 41 D2
Villarramiel 35 E3
Villarrobledo 40 C4
Villarroya 36 C3
Villarroya de la Sierra 36 C4
Villarroya de los Pinares 41 E2
Villarroya, Pto de 41 E2
Villarrubia de Santiago 40 B3
Villars 27 E3
Villars-les-Dombes 26 C4
Villarta de San Juan 40 B4
Villarubia de los Ojos 40 A4
Villasalto 66 C3
Villasana de Mena 36 A1
Villasandino 35 F3
Villa San Giovanni 67 E4
Villa Santa Maria 64 A2
Villasante 36 A1
Villa Santina 59 E3
Villasarracino 35 E3

| Name | Page | Grid |
|---|---|---|
| Villasayas, Pto de | 36 | B4 |
| Villaseco de los Reyes | 39 | E1 |
| Villasequilla de Yepes | 40 | A3 |
| Villasimius | 66 | C4 |
| Villasor | 66 | B4 |
| Villatobas | 40 | B3 |
| Villatoro, Pto de | 39 | F2 |
| Villatoya | 41 | D4 |
| Villava | 36 | C2 |
| Villavaara | 95 | F2 |
| Villaverde del Río | 43 | D2 |
| Villaviciosa | 35 | E1 |
| Villaviciosa de Córdoba | 43 | E2 |
| Villaviciosa de Odón | 40 | A2 |
| Villavieja de Yeltes | 39 | D1 |
| Villa Vomano | 63 | F1 |
| Villé | 21 | E4 |
| Villebois-Lavalette | 28 | C1 |
| Villedieu, la | 25 | D3 |
| Villedieu-les-Poêles | 18 | B4 |
| Ville-en-Tardenois | 20 | B3 |
| Villefagnan | 24 | C4 |
| Villefort | 29 | F3 |
| Villefranche-d'Albigeois | 29 | E3 |
| Villefranche-de-Lauragais | 29 | D4 |
| Villefranche-de-Lonchat | 28 | C2 |
| Villefranche-de-Rouergue | 29 | E3 |
| Villefranche-du-Périgord | 29 | D2 |
| Villefranche-sur-Cher | 25 | E2 |
| Villefranche-sur-Mer | 31 | E3 |
| Villefranche-sur-Saône | 26 | C4 |
| Villel | 41 | D2 |
| Villemur | 29 | D3 |
| Villena | 45 | D1 |
| Villenauxe-la-Grande | 20 | A4 |
| Villeneuve | 30 | B3 |
| Villeneuve-de-Berg | 30 | B2 |
| Villeneuve-de-Marsan | 28 | B3 |
| Villeneuve-l'Archevêque | 26 | A1 |
| Villeneuve-sur-Lot | 28 | C3 |
| Villeneuve-sur-Yonne | 26 | A1 |
| Villeréal | 28 | C2 |
| Villers | 19 | D3 |
| Villers-Bocage (Calvados) | 18 | C3 |
| Villers-Bocage (Somme) | 19 | F2 |
| Villers-Bretonneux | 19 | F2 |
| Villers-Cotterêts | 19 | F3 |
| Villers-devant-Orval | 20 | C2 |
| Villersexel | 27 | D2 |
| Villers-Farlay | 27 | D2 |
| Villers la Ville | 50 | C4 |
| Villers-le-Lac | 27 | E2 |
| Villerupt | 21 | D3 |
| Villerville | 19 | D3 |
| Ville-sur-Tourbe | 20 | C3 |
| Villeta Barrea | 64 | A2 |
| Villiers-St-Georges | 20 | A4 |
| Villingen-Schwenningen | 54 | C3 |
| Villoldo | 35 | E3 |
| Villoria | 39 | E1 |
| Villotta | 59 | E3 |
| Villuercas | 39 | E3 |
| Vilnius | 110 | C3 |
| Vilppula | 102 | C3 |
| Vils (Bayern) | 55 | F1 |
| Vils (Bayern) | 56 | B2 |
| Vilsbiburg | 56 | B2 |
| Vilseck | 55 | F1 |
| Vilshofen | 56 | C2 |
| Vilusi | 76 | A2 |
| Vilvoorde | 50 | B3 |
| Vimercate | 60 | A1 |
| Vimianzo | 34 | A1 |
| Vimieiro | 38 | B4 |
| Vimioso | 34 | C4 |
| Vimmerby | 109 | E1 |
| Vimoutiers | 19 | D4 |
| Vimpeli | 102 | C2 |
| Vimperk | 56 | C1 |
| Vinac | 71 | E4 |
| Vinadio | 31 | E3 |
| Vinaixa | 37 | F4 |
| Vinalapó, R | 45 | D2 |
| Vinaròs | 41 | F2 |
| Vinay | 30 | C1 |
| Vinça | 32 | B2 |
| Vinča | 73 | D3 |
| Vinchiaturo | 64 | B3 |
| Vinci | 60 | C3 |
| Vindafjorden | 104 | A3 |
| Vindelälven | 102 | A1 |
| Vindelfjällens N.R. | 97 | E3 |
| Vindeln | 102 | A1 |
| Vinderup | 108 | A2 |
| Vindsvik | 104 | A3 |
| Vingåker | 105 | F4 |
| Vingelen | 100 | C3 |
| Vingeveien | 100 | C3 |
| Vinhais | 34 | C3 |
| Vinica (Makedonija) | 77 | F3 |
| Vinica (Slovenija) | 70 | C3 |
| Viničani | 77 | E3 |
| Vinje | 104 | B3 |
| Vinkovci | 71 | F2 |
| Vinnica | 113 | E2 |
| Vinsternes | 100 | B3 |
| Vinstra | 100 | C3 |
| Vinstri | 104 | C1 |
| Vintilänkaira | 95 | F4 |
| Viñuelas | 40 | B2 |
| Vinuesa | 36 | B3 |
| Viotía | 83 | F4 |
| Vipava | 70 | A2 |
| Vipava R | 70 | A2 |
| Vipiteno | 59 | D2 |
| Vir (Bosna i Hercegovina) | 75 | E1 |
| Vir (Hrvatska) | 70 | C4 |
| Vir I | 70 | C4 |
| Vira | 75 | D2 |
| Vire | 18 | C4 |
| Virgen | 59 | E2 |
| Virgen de la Cabeza | 43 | F2 |
| Virginia | 13 | D3 |
| Virieu | 30 | C1 |
| Virieu-le-Grand | 27 | D4 |
| Virihaure | 97 | F1 |
| Virkby | 107 | E3 |
| Virkkala | 107 | E3 |
| Virkkula | 99 | E2 |
| Virksund | 108 | A2 |
| Virmasvesi | 103 | D2 |
| Virmutjoki | 103 | F3 |
| Virolahti | 103 | F4 |
| Virónia | 80 | A2 |
| Virovitica | 71 | E2 |
| Virpazar | 76 | B3 |
| Virrat | 102 | C3 |
| Virsbo | 105 | F3 |
| Virserum | 109 | E2 |
| Virsko more | 70 | C4 |
| Virtasalmi | 103 | E3 |
| Virton | 20 | C3 |
| Virtsu | 110 | B2 |
| Vis | 75 | D2 |
| Vis I | 75 | D2 |
| Visaurin | 37 | D2 |
| Visby | 109 | F4 |
| Visé | 51 | D3 |
| Višegrad | 72 | C4 |
| Višegradska Banja | 72 | C4 |
| Viserba | 61 | E3 |
| Viseu | 38 | C1 |
| Viševica | 70 | B3 |
| Viskan | 108 | C2 |
| Viški kan | 75 | D2 |
| Višnja Gora | 70 | B2 |
| Višnjica | 73 | D3 |
| Visočica | 75 | F1 |
| Visočica R | 73 | F4 |
| Viso del Marqués | 44 | A1 |
| Visoki Dečani | 76 | C2 |
| Visoko | 71 | F4 |
| Visovac | 75 | D1 |
| Visp | 27 | F3 |
| Víssaní | 78 | B4 |
| Visselhövede | 48 | A3 |
| Vissenbjerg | 108 | B3 |
| Vissiniá | 79 | D3 |
| Visso | 63 | F1 |
| Vistabella del Maestrazgo | 41 | E2 |
| Vistasväggi | 94 | B4 |
| Vistheden | 98 | B3 |
| Vistonída, L | 81 | D2 |
| Visuvesi | 102 | C3 |
| Vitaby | 109 | D3 |
| Vítala | 84 | B4 |
| Vitanovac | 73 | D4 |
| Vitebsk | 111 | E3 |
| Viterbo | 63 | E2 |
| Vitez | 71 | E4 |
| Vitigudino | 39 | D1 |
| Vitina | 86 | C2 |
| Vitina (Bosna i Hercegovina) | 75 | E2 |
| Vitina (Kosovo) | 77 | D2 |
| Vitlycke | 105 | D4 |
| Vito d'Asio | 59 | E3 |
| Vítoli | 83 | D3 |
| Vitolište | 77 | E4 |
| Vitomirica | 76 | C2 |
| Vitoria-Gasteiz | 36 | B2 |
| Vitorog | 71 | E4 |
| Vitoša | 115 | D2 |
| Vitovlje | 71 | E4 |
| Vitré | 23 | D3 |
| Vitrey | 27 | D1 |
| Vitry-en-Artois | 19 | F2 |
| Vitry-le-François | 20 | B4 |
| Vitsa | 78 | C4 |
| Vitsand | 105 | E2 |
| Vittangi | 94 | C4 |
| Vittangiälven | 94 | C4 |
| Vitteaux | 26 | B2 |
| Vittel | 27 | D1 |
| Vittoria | 69 | D4 |
| Vittoriosa | 68 | B4 |
| Vittorio Veneto | 59 | E3 |
| Vittsjö | 109 | D3 |
| Vitznau | 58 | A2 |
| Viù | 31 | E1 |
| Vivaro | 59 | E3 |
| Vivel del R Martín | 41 | E2 |
| Viver | 41 | E3 |
| Viverio | 34 | B1 |
| Viverols | 29 | F1 |
| Viveros | 44 | B1 |
| Vivier, le | 18 | B4 |
| Viviers | 30 | B2 |
| Vivonne | 25 | D4 |
| Vizille | 30 | C2 |
| Vižinada | 70 | A3 |
| Vizítsa | 83 | F2 |
| Vižnica | 113 | D3 |
| Vizzavona | 33 | F3 |
| Vizzavona, Col de | 33 | F3 |
| Vizzini | 69 | D4 |
| Vlaardingen | 16 | B3 |
| Vladičin Han | 77 | E1 |
| Vladievci | 77 | F3 |
| Vladimirci | 72 | C3 |
| Vladimirovac | 73 | D2 |
| Vladimirovo | 77 | F3 |
| Vladimir-Volynskij | 112 | C2 |
| Vlagtwedde | 17 | E1 |
| Vlaháva | 83 | D1 |
| Vlahérna (Ípiros) | 82 | C2 |
| Vlahérna (Pelopónissos) | 86 | C2 |
| Vlahiótis | 87 | D3 |
| Vlahokerassiá | 87 | D2 |
| Vlahomándra | 83 | D4 |
| Vlahópoulo | 86 | C3 |
| Vlanen | 16 | C3 |
| Vlasenica | 72 | B4 |
| Vlašić (Bosna i Hercegovina) | 71 | E4 |
| Vlašić (Srbija) | 72 | C3 |
| Vlasina Okruglica | 77 | E1 |
| Vlasinsko jez | 77 | E1 |
| Vlasotince | 77 | E1 |
| Vlássio | 83 | D2 |
| Vlásti | 79 | D3 |
| Vlieland | 16 | C1 |
| Vlihó | 82 | B3 |
| Vlissingen | 16 | B4 |
| Vlorë | 114 | B4 |
| Vlotho | 17 | F2 |
| Vltava | 53 | F3 |
| Vobbia | 60 | A2 |
| Voćin | 71 | E2 |
| Vöcklabruck | 56 | C3 |
| Vodice (Rijeka) | 70 | A3 |
| Vodice (Šibenik) | 74 | C1 |
| Vodna | 73 | E3 |
| Vodňany | 56 | C1 |
| Vodnjan | 70 | A4 |
| Voe | 3 | F1 |
| Vogatsikó | 79 | D3 |
| Vogel | 70 | A2 |
| Vogelsberg | 52 | A4 |
| Vogelsdorf | 49 | E4 |
| Voghera | 60 | A2 |
| Vogošća | 72 | B4 |
| Vohenstrauß | 56 | B1 |
| Vöhringen | 55 | E3 |
| Void | 20 | C4 |
| Voikoski | 107 | F1 |
| Vóio, Óros | 78 | C3 |
| Voiron | 30 | C1 |
| Voiteur | 26 | C3 |
| Voitsberg | 57 | E4 |
| Vojens | 108 | A3 |
| Vojka | 72 | C3 |
| Vojmsjön | 97 | F4 |
| Vojnić | 70 | C3 |
| Vojnik | 70 | B1 |
| Vojska | 73 | D3 |
| Vojtanov | 53 | D4 |
| Vojvodina | 72 | C2 |
| Vólakas | 80 | B1 |
| Volary | 56 | C2 |
| Volchov | 111 | E1 |
| Volchov R | 111 | E1 |
| Volda | 100 | A3 |
| Voldafjorden | 100 | A2 |
| Volders | 59 | D2 |
| Volendam | 16 | C2 |
| Volga | 111 | F1 |
| Volímes | 86 | A1 |
| Volissós | 85 | E4 |
| Volkach | 52 | B4 |
| Völkermarkt | 70 | B1 |
| Völklingen | 54 | B2 |
| Volkmarsen | 52 | A2 |
| Volkovija | 77 | D3 |
| Volkovysk | 110 | C4 |
| Volmunster | 21 | E3 |
| Voločisk | 113 | D2 |
| Volokolamsk | 111 | F2 |
| Volonne | 31 | D3 |
| Vólos | 83 | F2 |
| Voložin | 111 | D4 |
| Volpiano | 31 | E1 |
| Volta | 60 | C1 |
| Volterra | 60 | C4 |
| Voltri | 60 | A3 |
| Volturara Appula | 64 | B3 |
| Volturino, Mte | 64 | C4 |
| Volturno, R | 64 | A3 |
| Vólvi, L | 80 | B3 |
| Volyn' | 113 | D2 |
| Volyně | 56 | C1 |
| Vónitsa | 82 | C3 |
| Vonnas | 26 | C4 |
| Voors | 17 | D2 |
| Voorschoten | 16 | B3 |
| Voorthuizen | 16 | C2 |
| Vopnafjörður | 96 | C1 |
| Vörå | 102 | B2 |
| Vorarlberg | 58 | B2 |
| Vóras, Óros | 79 | E2 |
| Vorau | 57 | E3 |
| Vorchdorf | 56 | C3 |
| Vordernberg | 57 | E4 |
| Vorderrhein | 58 | A3 |
| Vorderriß | 56 | A4 |
| Vordingborg | 108 | C4 |
| Vorë | 76 | C4 |
| Voreppe | 30 | C1 |
| Vorey | 30 | A1 |
| Vóri | 91 | D4 |
| Vória Píndos | 79 | D3 |
| Vóries Sporádes | 84 | C2 |
| Vøringfossen | 104 | B2 |
| Vórios Evoïkós Kólpos | 83 | F3 |
| Vório Stenó Kerkíras | 82 | A1 |
| Vorma | 105 | D3 |
| Vormsi | 110 | B1 |
| Vorna | 99 | D4 |
| Voronet | 113 | D3 |
| Vorsfelde | 48 | B4 |
| Vorskla | 113 | F2 |
| Võrtsjärv | 110 | C2 |
| Võru | 110 | C2 |
| Vosges (Dépt) | 27 | D1 |
| Voss | 104 | B2 |
| Votice | 53 | F4 |
| Votonóssi | 82 | C1 |
| Voúdia | 88 | B4 |
| Vouga, R | 38 | C1 |
| Vouglans, Lac de | 27 | D3 |
| Vouhorína | 79 | D4 |
| Vouillé | 25 | D3 |
| Voukoliés | 90 | B3 |
| Voúla | 87 | F1 |
| Voulgára | 83 | D2 |
| Vouliagméni | 87 | F1 |
| Voulkariá, L | 82 | B3 |
| Voúlpi | 83 | D3 |
| Voulte, la | 30 | B2 |
| Vouná Goúras | 83 | E2 |
| Vouraïkós | 86 | C1 |
| Voúrinos, Óros | 79 | D4 |
| Vourkári | 88 | A2 |
| Vourliótes | 89 | E1 |
| Voúrvoura | 87 | D2 |
| Vourvouroú | 80 | B4 |
| Vouvant | 24 | C3 |
| Vouvray | 25 | D2 |
| Voúxa, Akr | 90 | B3 |
| Vouziers | 20 | B3 |
| Voves | 25 | E1 |
| Vovoússa | 78 | C4 |
| Voxnan | 101 | E4 |
| Vöyri | 102 | B2 |
| Voz | 70 | B3 |
| Vozarci | 77 | E3 |
| Voznesensk | 113 | F3 |
| Vrå | 108 | B2 |
| Vraca | 115 | D2 |
| Vraca pl | 77 | D3 |
| Vračev Gaj | 73 | D2 |
| Vračevšnica | 73 | D4 |
| Vrådal | 104 | B3 |
| Vraháti | 87 | D1 |
| Vrahiónas, Óros | 86 | A2 |
| Vrahnéika | 86 | C1 |
| Vrams-Gunnarstorp | 108 | C3 |
| Vrana | 70 | B4 |
| Vrancei, M | 113 | D4 |
| Vranduk | 71 | F4 |
| Vranica | 71 | E4 |
| Vranja | 70 | A3 |
| Vranjak | 75 | F2 |
| Vranje | 77 | E2 |
| Vranjska Banja | 77 | E2 |
| Vranovská přehr nádrž | 57 | E1 |
| Vran pl | 75 | E1 |
| Vransko | 70 | B2 |
| Vransko jezero | 74 | C1 |
| Vrástama | 80 | B3 |
| Vratarnica | 73 | F4 |
| Vratnica | 77 | D3 |
| Vratnik | 70 | B3 |
| Vratno | 70 | C1 |
| Vravróna | 88 | A1 |
| Vražogrnac | 73 | F3 |
| Vrbanja | 72 | B3 |
| Vrbanja R | 71 | E3 |
| Vrbas | 72 | B2 |
| Vrbas R | 71 | E3 |
| Vrbaška | 71 | E3 |
| Vrbas klisura | 71 | E4 |
| Vrbljani | 71 | D4 |
| Vrbnica | 77 | D3 |
| Vrbnik | 70 | B3 |
| Vrboska | 75 | E2 |
| Vrbovec | 71 | D2 |
| Vrbovsko | 70 | B3 |
| Vrčin | 73 | D3 |
| Vrdnik | 72 | C2 |
| Vreden | 17 | E3 |
| Vrela | 76 | C2 |
| Vrelo (Hrvatska) | 70 | C4 |
| Vrelo (Srbija) | 73 | E4 |
| Vreoci | 72 | C3 |
| Vresse | 20 | C2 |
| Vrésthena | 87 | D3 |
| Vreta Kloster | 106 | A4 |
| Vrginmost | 70 | C3 |
| Vrgorac | 75 | E2 |
| Vrh Kapele | 70 | C3 |
| Vrhnika | 70 | A2 |
| Vrhpolje | 71 | D4 |
| Vría | 79 | E4 |
| Vrínena | 83 | F3 |
| Vríssa | 85 | F3 |
| Vrísses | 90 | C3 |
| Vrissiá | 83 | E2 |
| Vrissoúla | 82 | B2 |
| Vrlika | 75 | D1 |
| Vrnjačka Banja | 73 | D4 |
| Vrnograč | 70 | C3 |
| Vrondádos | 85 | F4 |
| Vrondamás | 87 | D3 |
| Vronderó | 78 | C3 |
| Vrondissi | 91 | D4 |
| Vrondoú | 79 | E4 |
| Vrondoús, Óri | 80 | B2 |
| Vrossína | 82 | B1 |
| Vrouhás | 91 | E3 |
| Vrpolje (Osijek) | 71 | F2 |
| Vrpolje (Šibenik) | 75 | D1 |
| Vršac | 73 | D2 |
| Vršani | 72 | B3 |
| Vrsar | 70 | A3 |
| Vrsi | 70 | C4 |
| Vrška Čuka | 73 | F4 |
| Vrtac | 76 | B2 |
| Vrtoče | 71 | D4 |
| Vrutok | 77 | D3 |
| Vučitrn | 77 | D2 |
| Vučjak | 77 | F3 |
| Vučje | 77 | E1 |
| Vučkovica | 73 | D4 |
| Vue des Alpes | 27 | E2 |
| Vuka | 71 | F2 |
| Vukovar | 72 | B2 |
| Vulcano, I | 69 | D2 |
| Vulture, Mte | 64 | C3 |
| Vuohijärvi | 107 | F2 |
| Vuohijärvi L | 107 | F1 |
| Vuokatti | 99 | E4 |
| Vuokkijärvi | 99 | F3 |
| Vuokojaure | 94 | C3 |
| Vuoksenniska | 103 | F3 |
| Vuolijoki | 99 | E4 |
| Vuollerim | 98 | B2 |
| Vuolvojaure | 98 | A2 |
| Vuonislahti | 103 | F2 |
| Vuorji | 95 | D2 |
| Vuosjärvi | 103 | D2 |
| Vuoskuvarri | 95 | D3 |
| Vuostimo | 99 | E2 |
| Vuotso | 95 | E3 |
| Vyškov | 57 | F1 |
| Vyšnij Voloček | 111 | E2 |

# W

| | | | | | | | | | | |
|---|---|---|---|---|---|---|---|---|---|---|
| Waal | 16 C3 | Wädenswil | 58 A2 | Waidring | 59 E1 | Waldeck | 52 A2 | Waldmünchen | 56 B1 | Wallerstein | 55 E2 | Wandlitz | 49 E3 |
| Waalwijk | 16 C3 | Wagenfeld | 17 F2 | Waischenfeld | 52 C4 | Waldenbuch | 55 D3 | Waldsassen | 53 D4 | Wallingford | 9 E2 | Wanfried | 52 B2 |
| Waasmunster | 50 B3 | Wageningen | 17 D3 | Waizenkirchen | 56 C2 | Waldenburg | 53 D3 | Waldshut | 54 C4 | Walls | 3 F2 | Wangen | 55 E4 |
| Wabern | 52 A3 | Waging | 56 B3 | Wakefield | 7 D2 | Waldfischbach- | | Walensee | 58 B2 | Walsall | 9 E1 | Wangenbourg | 21 E4 |
| Wachau | 57 E2 | Wagrain | 59 E1 | Wałbrzych | 112 A2 | Burgalben | 54 B2 | Walenstadt | 58 B2 | Walsrode | 48 A4 | Wangerland- | |
| Wachow | 49 D4 | Wągrowiec | 112 A1 | Walchensee | 56 A4 | Waldheim | 53 E2 | Wales | 8 C1 | Walsum | 17 D3 | Hooksiel | 47 E3 |
| Wächtersbach | 52 A4 | Wahlstedt | 48 A2 | Walcheren | 16 B3 | Waldkappel | 52 B3 | Wallasey | 6 B2 | Waltershausen | 52 B3 | Wangerooge | 47 E2 |
| Waddeneilanden | 16 C1 | Waiblingen | 55 D2 | Walchsee | 59 D1 | Waldkirch | 54 C3 | Walldorf | 54 C2 | Walton-on-the- | | Wängi | 58 A1 |
| Wadebridge | 8 B3 | Waidhaus | 56 B1 | Wałcz | 112 A1 | Waldkirchen | 56 C2 | Walldürn | 55 D1 | Naze | 11 D2 | Wanna | 47 F2 |
| | | Waidhofen (Ybbs) | 57 D3 | Wald | 58 A2 | Waldkraiburg | 56 B3 | Wallenfels | 52 C4 | Waltrop | 17 E3 | Wanne-Eickel | 17 E3 |
| | | Waidhofen (Thaya) | 57 E2 | Waldbröl | 17 E4 | Wald-Michelbach | 54 C1 | Wallersdorf | 56 B2 | Wanderup | 48 A1 | Wantage | 9 E2 |

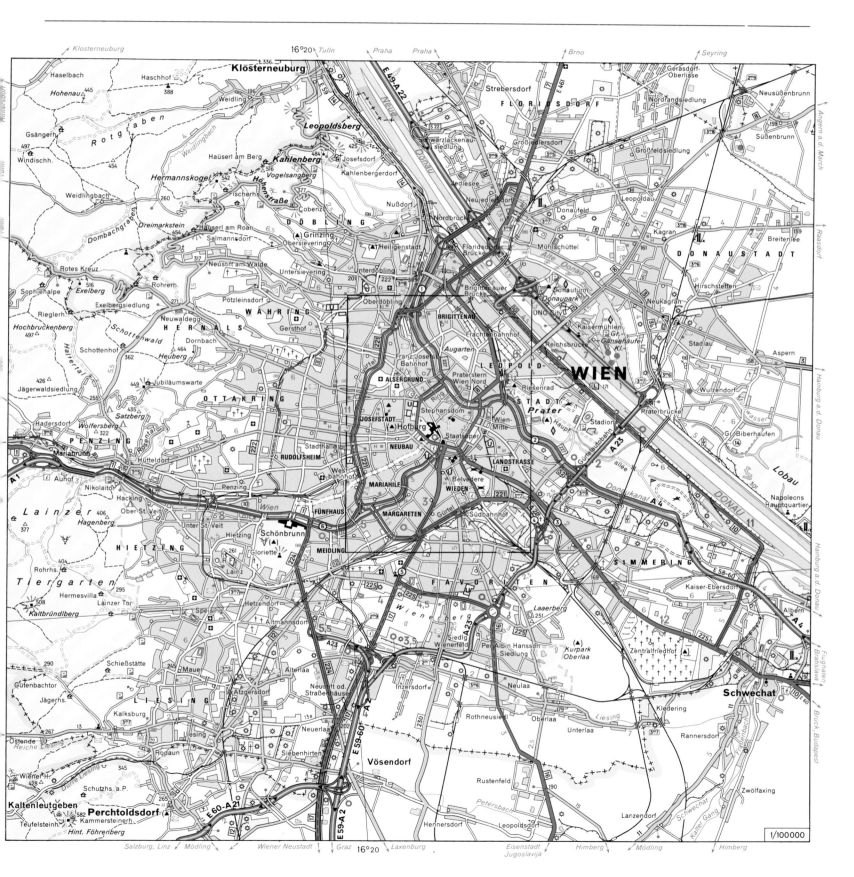

Wantzenau, la 21 F4
Wanzleben 52 C1
Warburg 52 A2
Wardenburg 47 F3
Ware 9 F2
Waregem 50 B3
Wareham 9 D3
Waremme 50 C3
Waren 49 D2
Warendorf 17 F3
Warin 48 C2
Warkworth 5 E3
Warmensteinach 53 D4
Warminster 9 E3
Warnemunde 48 C2
Warnow 48 C2
Warrenpoint 13 E3
Warrington 6 B2
Warstein 17 F3
Warszawa 112 B1
Warszów 49 E2
Warta 49 F3
Warth 58 B2
Wartha 52 B3
Warwick 9 E1
Washington 5 E4
Wash, The 7 E3
Wasselonne 21 E4
Wassen 58 A3
Wassenaar 16 B3
Wassenberg 17 D4
Wasseralfingen 55 E2
Wasserbillig 21 D2
Wasserburg 56 B3
Wasser-Kuppe 52 B3
Wassertrüdingen 55 E2
Wassigny 20 A2
Wassy 20 C4
Wasungen 52 B3
Watchet 8 C3
Waterfoot 13 E1
Waterford 15 D4
Waterford (Co) 14 C4
Waterford Harbour 15 D4
Waterloo 50 B3
Waternish Pt 2 B3
Waterville 14 A4
Watford 9 F2
Wattens 59 D2
Watton 11 D1
Wattwil 58 A2
Watzmann 56 C4
Waulsort 50 C4
Waveney 11 D1
Wavre 50 C3
Waxweiler 51 D4
Wear 5 E4
Wechsel 57 E3
Wedel 48 A3
Wedemark-Mellendorf 48 A4

Weener 47 E3
Weert 17 D4
Weferlingen 48 C4
Wegberg 17 D4
Wegeleben 52 C1
Weggis 27 F2
Węgorzewo 110 B4
Węgorzyno 49 F2
Wegscheid 56 C2
Wehr 54 C4
Weichshofen 56 B2
Weida 53 D3
Weiden 56 A1
Weikersheim 55 D1
Weilburg 51 F4
Weil der Stadt 55 D2
Weilheim (Baden-Württemberg) 55 D3
Weilheim (Bayern) 56 A3
Weimar 52 C3
Weinfelden 58 A1
Weingarten 55 D4
Weinheim 54 C1
Weinsberg 55 D2
Weismain 52 C4
Weißbriach 59 F2
Weiße Elster 53 D3
Weißenbach 58 C1
Weißenberg 53 F2
Weißenburg 55 F2
Weißenfels 53 D2
Weißenhorn 55 E3
Weissenstadt 53 D4
Weissenstein 27 E2
Weissfluhgipfel 58 B2
Weißenkirchen 57 E2
Weißensee 52 C2
Weißensee (L) 59 F2
Weißkirchen 57 D4
Weißkugel 58 C2
Weißwasser 53 F1
Weitra 57 D2
Weiz 57 E4
Wejherowo 110 A4
Weldon 9 F1
Welgetschlag 57 D2
Welland 9 F1
Wellin 20 C2
Wellingborough 9 F1
Wellington 9 D3
Wellington Bridge 15 D4
Wells 9 D3
Wells-next-the-Sea 7 E3
Wels 56 C3
Welsberg 59 D2
Welschnofen 59 D3
Welshpool 9 D1
Weltenburg 55 F2
Welwyn Garden City 9 F2

Welzheim 55 D2
Wem 6 B3
Wemding 55 E2
Wemyss Bay 4 C2
Wendelstein 56 B4
Wenden 52 B1
Wengen 27 F3
Wenns 58 C2
Werbellinsee 49 E3
Werben 48 C3
Werdau 53 D3
Werder 49 D4
Werdohl 17 E4
Werfen 59 E1
Werl 17 F3
Werlte 17 E1
Wermelskirchen 17 E4
Wermsdorf 53 E2
Wernberg 56 B1
Werne 17 E3
Werneck 52 B4
Werneuchen 49 E4
Wernigerode 52 C1
Werra 52 B3
Wertach 55 E4
Wertach (R) 55 E3
Wertheim 55 D1
Werther 17 F2
Wertingen 55 E3
Wervik 50 A3
Wesel 17 D3
Wesenbeerg 49 D3
Wesendorf 48 B4
Weser 47 F3
Weser-Elbe-Kanal 47 F4
Wesselburen 47 F2
Wessobrunn 56 A3
West Auckland 5 E4
West Bridgford 7 D3
Westbury 9 D3
Westendorf 59 D1
Westenholz 48 A4
Westerburg 51 F4
Westerholt 47 E3
Westerland 47 F1
Westerlo 50 C3
Westernbödefeld 17 F4
Western Isles 2 B2
Wester Ross 2 C3
Westerstede 47 E3
Westerwald 51 E3
Westhofen 54 C1
West Kilbride 4 C2
West Linton 5 D2
West Loch Tarbert 2 A2
Westmeath 12 C3
West Mersea 11 D2
Weston-Super-Mare 9 D2
Westport 12 B3
Westray 3 E1
Westray Firth 3 E1

West Sussex 9 F3
West-Terschelling 16 C1
West-Vlaanderen 50 A3
Wetherby 7 D2
Wetter 17 E3
Wetteren 50 B3
Wettin 52 C2
Wettringen 17 E2
Wetwang 7 D1
Wetzikon 58 A2
Wetzlar 51 F3
Wexford 15 D3
Wexford (Co) 15 D3
Weyer-Markt 57 D3
Weyhausen 48 B4
Weyhill 9 E3
Weymouth 9 D3
Weyregg 56 C3
Whaley Bridge 6 C2
Whalsay 3 F1
Wharfe 6 C1
Whernside 6 C1
Whitburn 5 D2
Whitby 5 F4
Whitchurch 6 B3
White Bridge 2 C4
Whitehaven 5 D4
Whitehead 13 E2
Whiteness 3 F2
Whiten Head 2 C2
Whithorn 4 C4
Whitland 8 B2
Whitley Bay 5 E3
Whitstable 11 D3
Whittlesey 9 F1
Wick 3 D2
Wickford 11 D2
Wicklow 13 E4
Wicklow (Co) 13 D4
Wicklow Head 13 E4
Wicklow Mts 13 D4
Widnes 6 B2
Wiehe 52 C2
Wiek 49 D1
Wieliczka 112 B3
Wieluń 112 B2
Wien 57 F2
Wiener-Neudorf 57 F2
Wiener Neustadt 57 F3
Wienerwald 57 E3
Wies (A) 70 B1
Wies (D) 56 A4
Wiesau 53 D4
Wiesbaden 51 F4
Wieselburg 57 E3
Wiesenburg 53 D1
Wiesensteig 55 D3
Wiesentheid 55 E1
Wiesenttal 52 C4
Wiesing 59 D1
Wiesloch 54 C2
Wiesmath 57 F3

Wiesmoor 47 E3
Wigan 6 C2
Wight, I of 9 E4
Wigton 5 D4
Wigtown 4 C3
Wigtown B 4 C4
Wijhe 17 D2
Wil 58 A2
Wildalpen 57 D3
Wildbad 54 C2
Wildeck 52 B3
Wildeshausen 17 F1
Wildon 57 E4
Wildspitze 58 C2
Wildstrubel 27 E3
Wilfersdorf 57 F2
Wilhelmina kan 16 C3
Wilhelm Pieck-Stadt 53 F1
Wilhelmsburg (A) 57 E3
Wilhelmsburg (D) 48 A3
Wilhelmshaven 47 F3
Wilhering 57 D2
Wilkau-Haßlau 53 D3
Willebroek 50 B3
Willemstad 16 B3
Willingen 17 F4
Williton 8 C3
Wilmslow 6 C2
Wilnsdorf 17 F4
Wilsdruff 53 E2
Wilseder Berg 48 A3
Wilster 48 A2
Wilton 9 E3
Wiltshire 9 E3
Wiltz 21 D2
Wimborne Minster 9 E3
Wimereux 19 E1
Wincanton 9 D3
Winchcombe 9 E2
Winchelsea 11 D3
Winchester 9 E3
Windeck 51 E3
Windermere 5 D4
Windischeschenbach 53 D4
Windischgarsten 57 D3
Windsbach 55 E1
Windsor 9 F2
Winkleigh 8 C3
Winklern 59 E2
Winnenden 55 D2
Winnigstedt 52 B1
Winnweiler 54 B1
Winschoten 47 E3
Winsen (Celle) 48 A4
Winsen (Lüneburg) 48 B3
Winsford 6 C3
Winsum 47 D3
Winterberg 17 F4
Winterswijk 17 D3

Winterthur 58 A2
Wintzenheim 27 E1
Wipper 52 C2
Wipperfürth 17 E4
Wisbech 10 C1
Wischhafen 48 A2
Wiselka 49 E2
Wishaw 4 C1
Wisła 110 B4
Wismar 48 C2
Wissant 19 E1
Wissembourg 21 F3
Wissen 51 E3
Witham 7 D3
Witham 11 D2
Withernsea 7 E2
Witney 9 E2
Witnica 49 F3
Wittdün 47 F1
Witte 49 D1
Witten 17 E3
Wittenberg 53 D1
Wittenberge 48 C3
Wittenburg 48 B3
Wittichenau 53 F2
Wittingen 48 B4
Wittlich 51 E4
Wittmund 47 E3
Wittow 49 D1
Wittstock 49 D3
Witzenhausen 52 B2
Władysławowo 110 A4
Włocławek 112 B1
Włodawa 112 C2
Wöbbelin 48 C3
Woburn 9 F2
Woburn Abbey 9 F2
Woensdrecht 16 B4
Woerden 16 C3
Wohlen 27 F2
Woippy 21 D3
Woking 9 F3
Wokingham 9 F3
Wołczenica 49 F2
Woldegk 49 E2
Wolfach 54 C3
Wolfegg 55 E4
Wolfen 53 D2
Wolfenbüttel 52 B1
Wolfhagen 52 A2
Wolfratshausen 56 A3
Wolfsberg 70 B1
Wolfsburg 48 B4
Wolgast 49 E2
Wolin 49 E2
Wolin (Reg) 49 E2
Woliński Park Narodowy 49 E2
Wolkenstein 59 D3
Wolkersdorf 57 F2
Wöllersdorf 57 F3
Wollersheim 51 D3

Wollin 49 D4
Wolmirstedt 48 C4
Wolsingham 5 E4
Wolsztyn 112 A2
Wolvega 17 D1
Wolverhampton 9 E1
Wolverton 9 F1
Wolznach 55 F2
Woodbridge 11 D1
Woodhall Spa 7 E3
Woodstock 9 E2
Wooler 5 E3
Worb 27 E2
Worbis 52 B2
Worcester 9 D1
Wörgl 59 D1
Workington 5 D4
Worksop 7 D2
Workum 16 C1
Wörlitz 53 D1
Wormerveer 16 C2
Wormhout 19 F1
Worms 54 C1
Worms Head 8 C2
Wörnitz 55 E2
Wörrstadt 54 C1
Wœrth 21 E3
Wörth (Donau) 56 B2
Wörth (Main) 55 D1
Wörth (Rheinland-Pfalz) 54 C2
Worther See 70 A1
Worthing 10 C3
Woświn, Jez 49 F2
Wragby 7 D3
Wrath, Cape 2 C2
Wrecsam 6 B3
Wrexham 6 B3
Wriezen 49 E4
Wrocław 112 A2
Wroughton 9 E2
Września 112 A1
Wulfen 17 E3
Wullowitz 57 D2
Wümme 48 A3
Wümme R 48 A3
Wünnenberg 17 F3
Wünsdorf 49 E4
Wunsiedel 53 D4
Wunstorf 48 A4
Wuppertal 17 E4
Würzburg 55 D1
Wurzen 53 D2
Wurzen-Paß 59 F2
Wusterhausen 49 D3
Wustrow (Rostock) 48 C1
Wustrow (Wismar) 48 C2
Wuustwezel 50 C2
Wye, R 9 D2
Wyk 47 F1
Wymondham 11 D1

# X

Xallas, R 34 A2
Xanten 17 D3
Xánthi 81 D2

Xánthi (Nomos) 81 D2
Xarrama, R 42 B1
Xàtiva 41 E4
Xeresa 41 E4
Xerovoúni 82 C2

Xerta 41 F2
Xertigny 27 D1
Xesta, Pto de la 34 C1
Xifianí 79 E2
Xilaganí 81 E2

Xiliki 83 E3
Xilis, Akr 87 D4
Xilókastro 87 D1
Xilopáriko 83 D2
Xilópoli 80 A2

Xilóskalo 90 B3
Xiniáda 83 E3
Xinó Neró 79 D3
Xinzo de Limia 34 B3
Xiró 83 F3

Xirokámbi 87 D3
Xirókambos 89 E3
Xirolimni 79 D3
Xistral 34 B1
Xódoto, Akr 89 D3

Xubia 34 B1
Xunqueira de Ambía 34 B3

# Y

Yaiza 42 C4
Yalova 115 F3
Yanguas 36 B3
Yare 7 F4
Yarmouth 9 E3
Yarmouth, Great 7 F4
Ybbs 57 D2
Ybbs R 57 D3
Yebra 40 B2

Yecla 45 D1
Yeguas, Emb de 43 F2
Yeguas, R de las 43 F1
Yell 3 F1
Yell Sd 3 F1
Yelmo 44 B2
Yeltes, R 39 D1
Yenne 27 D4
Yeovil 9 D3
Yepes 40 B3
Yerville 19 D3

Yesa 36 C2
Yesa, Emb de 37 D2
Yeşilova 115 F4
Yeste 44 C1
Yeu, I d' 24 A3
Yèvre 26 A2
Y-Fenni 9 D2
Yildiz Dağlari 115 E3
Ylämaa 103 F4
Ylämylly 103 F2
Yläne 107 D2

Ylihärmä 102 C2
Yli-Kärppä 99 D3
Ylikiiminki 99 D3
Yli-Kitka 99 E2
Yli-Ii 99 D3
Yli-Muonio 95 D4
Yli-Nampa 99 D2
Yli-Olhava 99 D3
Ylistaro 102 B2
Ylitornio 98 C2
Ylivieska 102 C1

Ylläs 95 D4
Ylläsjärvi 95 D4
Ylöjärvi 102 C3
Yngaren 106 A4
Yonne 20 A4
Yonne (Dépt) 26 A1
York 7 D2
Yorkshire Dales Nat Pk 6 C1
Youghal 14 C4
Youghal B 14 C4

Yoxford 11 E1
Ypäjä 107 E2
Yport 19 D2
Yppäri 99 D4
Ypres 50 A3
Yr Wyddgrug 6 B3
Yser 19 F1
Yssingeaux 30 B1
Ystad 109 D4
Y Trallwng 9 D1
Ytterhogdal 101 E3

Yttermalung 105 E2
Yuncos 40 A2
Yunquera 43 E4
Yunquera de Henares 40 B2
Yuste 39 E2
Yverdon 27 E3
Yvetot 19 D3
Yvoir 50 C4
Yvoire 27 D3

# Z

| | | | | | | | | |
|---|---|---|---|---|---|---|---|---|
| Zaandam | 16 C2 | Zárkos | 83 E1 | Zeven | 48 A3 | | | |
| Žabali | 72 C2 | Zarós | 91 D4 | Zevenaar | 17 D3 | | | |
| Žabari | 73 D3 | Zaroúhla | 87 D1 | Zevgaráki | 82 C4 | | | |
| Zablaće | 75 D1 | Zarrentin | 48 B3 | Zevgolatió | 86 C3 | | | |
| Žabljak (Durmitor) | 76 B1 | Žary | 112 A2 | Zevio | 60 C1 | | | |
| Žabljak (Titograd) | 76 B3 | Zarza la Mayor | 39 D2 | Zézere, R | 38 C2 | | | |
| Žabno | 71 D2 | Zasieki | 53 F1 | Žiča | 73 D4 | | | |
| Zabok | 70 C2 | Žaškov | 113 E2 | Zicavo | 33 F4 | | | |
| Zabrddđe | 72 B3 | Žatec | 53 E3 | Židlochovice | 57 F1 | | | |
| Zadar | 74 C1 | Zatoka Gdańska | 110 B4 | Ziefsdorf | 57 E2 | | | |
| Zadarski kanal | 70 B4 | Zaton | 75 F2 | Ziegenrück | 52 C3 | | | |
| Zadvarje | 75 E2 | Zavala | 75 F2 | Zielona Góra | 112 A2 | | | |
| Zafarraya | 43 F3 | Zavattarello | 60 A2 | Zierikzee | 16 B3 | | | |
| Zafóra, Ni | 92 C2 | Zavidovići | 71 F4 | Zierzow | 48 C3 | | | |
| Zafra | 43 D1 | Zavlaka | 72 C3 | Ziesar | 49 D4 | | | |
| Žaga | 70 A2 | Zavratnica | 70 B4 | Zi, Guri i | 77 D4 | | | |
| Žagań | 112 A2 | Zawiercie | 112 B2 | Zijemlje | 75 F1 | | | |
| Zaglavak | 72 C4 | Žažina | 71 D2 | Žilina | 112 B3 | | | |
| Zagorá | 83 F2 | Zbaraž | 113 D2 | Žilindar | 76 C1 | | | |
| Zagória | 82 C1 | Zbraslav | 53 F4 | Ziller | 59 D2 | | | |
| Zagorje | 70 B2 | Žďár nad Sázavou | 112 A3 | Zillertal | 59 D1 | | | |
| Zagreb | 70 C2 | Zdenac | 70 C3 | Zimnicea | 115 D2 | | | |
| Žagubica | 73 E3 | Zdice | 53 F4 | Zinal | 27 F4 | | | |
| Zagvozd | 75 E2 | Žďrelac | 74 C1 | Zingst | 49 D1 | | | |
| Zahara de los Atunes | 43 D4 | Žďrelo | 73 E3 | Zinnowitz | 49 E1 | | | |
| Zahara, Emb de | 43 E3 | Zdunje | 77 D3 | Zinnwald | 53 E3 | | | |
| Zaháro | 86 B2 | Zduńska Wola | 112 B2 | Zirbitzkogel | 57 D4 | | | |
| Zahinos | 42 C1 | Zebě, Maj'e | 76 C3 | Zirchow | 49 E2 | | | |
| Zahna | 53 D1 | Zebreira | 38 C2 | Žiri | 70 A2 | | | |
| Záhony | 112 C3 | Žednik | 72 B1 | Žirje | 74 C1 | | | |
| Zaidín | 37 E4 | Zeebrugge | 50 A3 | Zirl | 58 C2 | | | |
| Zajas | 77 D3 | Zeeland | 16 B3 | Zirndorf | 55 D4 | | | |
| Zaječar | 73 F3 | Zefiría | 88 A4 | Zirndorf | 55 E1 | | | |
| Zákinthos | 86 A1 | Žegovac | 77 D2 | Ziros | 91 F4 | | | |
| Zákinthos, N | 86 A1 | Žegra | 77 D2 | Zistersdorf | 57 F2 | | | |
| Zakopane | 112 B3 | Žegulja | 75 F2 | Žitište | 72 C2 | | | |
| Zákros | 91 F4 | Zehdenick | 49 D3 | Žitkovac | 73 E4 | | | |
| Zala | 112 A4 | Zeist | 16 C3 | Žitkovići | 113 D1 | | | |
| Zalaegerszeg | 112 A4 | Zeitz | 53 D2 | Žitomir | 113 E1 | | | |
| Zalamea de la Serena | 43 E1 | Zejtun | 68 B4 | Žitomisliči | 75 F2 | | | |
| Zalamea la Real | 42 C2 | Žekovec | 70 B1 | Žitoradđa | 77 D1 | | | |
| Zalău | 112 C4 | Zele | 50 B3 | Zittau | 53 F2 | | | |
| Žalec | 70 B2 | Zelengora | 76 A1 | Živinice | 71 F3 | | | |
| Zaleščiki | 113 D3 | Zelengora (Reg) | 76 A1 | Živogošće | 75 E2 | | | |
| Zalew Wiślany | 110 B4 | Zelenika | 76 A3 | Žizdra | 111 F3 | | | |
| Zalla | 36 A1 | Zelenogorsk | 111 D1 | Zjum | 77 D2 | | | |
| Zálongo | 82 B2 | Železná Ruda | 56 C1 | Zlarin | 75 D1 | | | |
| Zaltbommel | 16 C3 | Železnik | 72 C3 | Zlarin I | 75 D1 | | | |
| Zalužnica | 70 C4 | Železniki | 70 A2 | Zlata | 77 D1 | | | |
| Zambrana | 36 B2 | Železnogorsk | 111 F4 | Zlatar | 76 B1 | | | |
| Zamora | 35 D4 | Zelina | 70 C2 | Zlatar Bistrica | 70 C2 | | | |
| Zamość | 112 C2 | Zélio | 83 E3 | Zlatarevo | 77 F3 | | | |
| Záncara, R | 40 B4 | Željezno Polje | 71 F4 | Zlatari | 77 D1 | | | |
| Zandvoort | 16 B2 | Željin | 73 D4 | Zlatarsko jez | 76 B1 | | | |
| Zángano, Pto del | 39 D4 | Zell (D) | 54 B1 | Zlatibor | 72 C4 | | | |
| Zanglivéri | 80 A3 | Zell (Oberösterreich) | 56 C2 | Zlatica | 72 C4 | | | |
| Zannone, I | 63 F4 | Zell (Tirol) | 59 D2 | Zlatni Pjasăci | 115 E2 | | | |
| Zaorejas | 40 C2 | Zella-Mehlis | 52 C3 | Zlatokop | 77 E2 | | | |
| Zaostrog | 75 E2 | Zell am See | 59 E1 | Zletovo | 77 E2 | | | |
| Zaovine Vežanja | 72 C4 | Zellerrain | 57 E3 | Žljebovi | 72 B4 | | | |
| Zapadnaja Dvina | 111 E2 | Zeltweg | 57 D4 | Žlobin | 111 E4 | | | |
| Zapadnaja Dvina R | 111 E2 | Zelzate | 50 B3 | Zlot | 73 E3 | | | |
| Zapadna Morava | 73 D4 | Zemun | 72 C3 | Žlutice | 53 E4 | | | |
| Zapardiel, R | 39 F1 | Zenica | 71 F4 | Zmajevo | 72 C2 | | | |
| Zapatón, R | 39 D3 | Zen'kov | 113 F2 | Žman | 74 C1 | | | |
| Zápio | 83 E2 | Žep | 72 B4 | Žmerinka | 113 E3 | | | |
| Zapponeta | 64 C3 | Žepče | 71 F4 | Žminj | 70 A3 | | | |
| Zaprešić | 70 C2 | Zerbst | 53 D1 | Znamenka | 113 F2 | | | |
| Zaragoza | 37 D3 | Zeri | 60 B3 | Znojmo | 57 E1 | | | |
| Zárakes | 84 B4 | Zermatt | 27 F4 | Zoetermeer | 16 B3 | | | |
| Zaratán | 35 E4 | Zernez | 58 B3 | Zöblitz | 53 E3 | | | |
| Zarautz | 36 C1 | Zerqan | 77 D4 | Zogaj | 76 C2 | | | |
| Zarcilla de Ramos | 44 C2 | Zestoa | 36 B1 | Zollikofen | 27 E2 | | | |
| | | Zeta | 76 B2 | Zoločev | 113 D2 | | | |
| | | Zetel | 47 E3 | Zolotonoša | 113 F2 | | | |
| | | Zeulenroda | 53 D3 | Žoltyje Vody | 113 F2 | | | |
| | | | | Zonári, Akr | 93 F1 | | | |

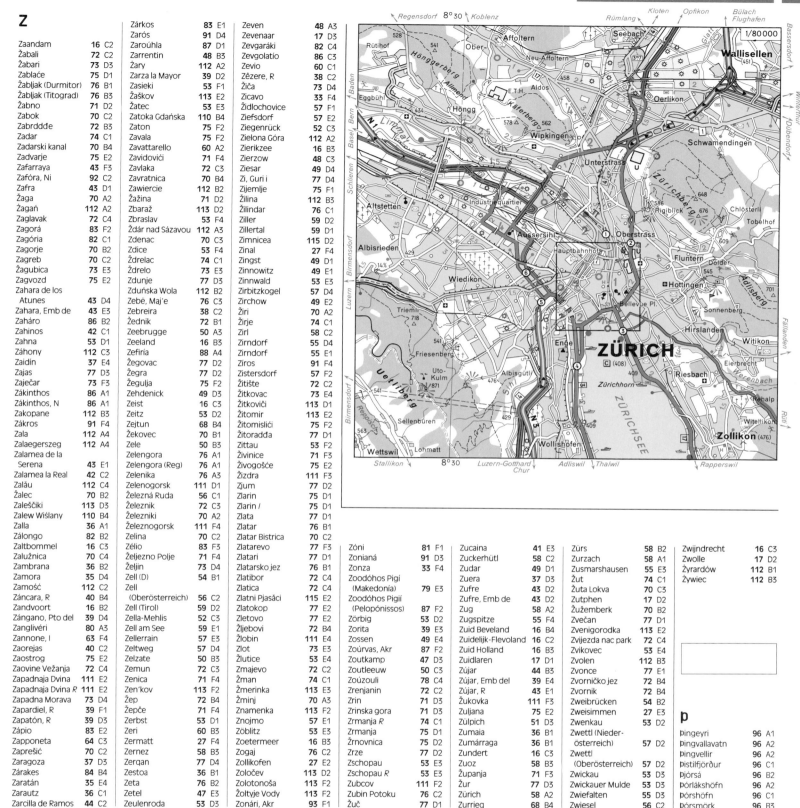

| | | | | | | | | |
|---|---|---|---|---|---|---|---|---|
| Zóni | 81 F1 | Zucaina | 41 E3 | Zürs | 58 B2 | Zwijndrecht | 16 C3 |
| Zoniáná | 91 D3 | Zuckerhütl | 58 C2 | Zurzach | 58 A1 | Zwolle | 17 D2 |
| Zonza | 33 F4 | Zudar | 49 D1 | Zusmarshausen | 55 E3 | Žyrardów | 112 B1 |
| Zoodóhos Pigí (Makedonía) | 79 E3 | Zuera | 37 D3 | Žut | 74 C1 | Żywiec | 112 B3 |
| Zoodóhos Pigí (Pelopónissos) | 87 F2 | Zufre | 43 D2 | Žuta Lokva | 70 C3 | | |
| | | Zufre, Emb de | 43 D2 | Zutphen | 17 D2 | | |
| Zórbig | 53 D2 | Zug | 58 A2 | Žužemberk | 70 B2 | | |
| Zorita | 39 E3 | Zugspitze | 55 F4 | Zvečan | 77 D1 | | |
| Zossen | 49 E4 | Zuid Beveland | 16 B4 | Zvenigorodka | 113 E3 | | |
| Zoúrvas, Akr | 87 F2 | Zuidelijk-Flevoland | 16 C2 | Zvijezda nac park | 72 C4 | | |
| Zoutkamp | 47 D3 | Zuid Holland | 16 B3 | Zvikovec | 53 E4 | | |
| Zoutleeuw | 50 C3 | Zuidlaren | 17 D1 | Zvolen | 112 B3 | | |
| Zoúzouli | 78 C4 | Zújar | 44 A3 | Zvonce | 77 E1 | | |
| Zrenjanin | 72 C2 | Zújar, Emb del | 39 E4 | Zvornicko jez | 72 B4 | | |
| Zrin | 71 D3 | Zújar, R | 43 E1 | Zvornik | 72 B4 | | |
| Zrinska gora | 71 D3 | Zuljana | 75 E2 | Zweibrücken | 54 B2 | | |
| Zrmanja R | 74 C1 | Zülpich | 51 D3 | Zweisimmen | 27 E3 | **þ** | |
| Zrmanja | 75 D1 | Zumaia | 36 B1 | Zwenkau | 53 D2 | | |
| Žrnovnica | 75 D2 | Zumárraga | 36 B1 | Zwettl (Niederösterreich) | 57 D2 | Þingeyri | 96 A1 |
| Zrze | 77 D2 | Zundert | 16 C3 | | | Þingvallavatn | 96 A2 |
| Zschopau | 53 E3 | Zuoz | 58 B3 | Zwettl (Oberösterreich) | 57 D2 | Þingvellir | 96 A2 |
| Zschopau R | 53 E3 | Žur | 77 D3 | Zwickau | 53 D3 | Þistilfjörður | 96 C1 |
| Zubcov | 111 F2 | Zürich | 58 A2 | Zwickauer Mulde | 53 D3 | Þjórsá | 96 B2 |
| Zubin Potoku | 76 C2 | Zürrieq | 68 B4 | Zwiefalten | 55 D3 | Þórlákshöfn | 96 A2 |
| Žuč | 77 D1 | | | Zwiesel | 56 C2 | Þórshöfn | 96 C1 |
| | | | | | | Þórsmörk | 96 B3 |

# Notes

# Climates in Europe